ASHEVILLE

Relocation, Retirement and Visitor Guide to Asheville and the North Carolina Mountains

By Lan Sluder

ASHEVILLE
Relocation, Retirement and Visitor Guide to Asheville
and the North Carolina Mountains

Published by Equator

This is a substantially revised, updated and expanded version of material that appeared in *Moving to the Mountains* by Lan Sluder, published and copyright © 2014.

The opinions in this book are those of the author. The author made all reasonable attempts to assure that the information in this book was correct at time of publication, but it is subject to change. Please notify us of any errors or out-of-date information, and we will attempt to correct those in future editions. Further, the author does not claim to be an expert in or hold any professional or other licenses in matters of law, taxes, finances, medicine or other matters related to relocation and retirement. The reader should consult with his or her tax, legal, financial, medical, real estate and other counsellors before acting on any advice in this book.

The Last Fire of the Season

It's not that cold here today, in the 60s,
but there was a chill in the house.
So I laid a fire and lit it.
Poured myself a couple of
fingers of Old Overholt,
with a Sierra Nevada Pale Ale back.
Turned on a early episode of "Lewis"
and picked up *Hotel Florida,*
about writers who covered the Spanish Civil War.
Just me and the old cat.
Applewood and oak.
The last fire of the season.

--Lan Sluder

TABLE OF CONTENTS

WHY CHOOSE ASHEVILLE?

Mural by Alexander Irvine and Kathy Triplett at Odyssey ClayWorks in the River Arts District – photo by Sheila M. Lambert

There are a lot of great places to live and visit in the United States, not to mention around the world. Why consider Asheville and the North Carolina mountains? Here are a few reasons:

1. **Diversity:** An eclectic mix of people creates the Asheville and Western North Carolina vibe – old hippies, young hipsters, retirees, tourists, students, artists, eccentrics, New Agers, gays and lesbians, plus locals and good ol' boys from the mountains. My daughter told me that when she was in Downtown Asheville one day someone said "Look, there's a giant gingerbread man with dreadlocks walking across the street!" The reaction was, "So what?"

2. **Setting:** Asheville is in a valley at around 2200-2400 feet, but it's surrounded by the highest mountains in the East, including **Mt. Mitchell,** highest peak east of the Rockies. You can be having a cappuccino Downtown and in 30 minutes be somewhere in nearly 2 million acres of wilderness. Two of the most visited National Park Service units in the country are here – the **Blue Ridge Parkway,** which gets 14 to 22 million visitors a year, runs through Asheville, and the **Great Smoky Mountains National Park,** which gets 9 to 10 million visitors, about an hour away. Plus, there are two huge national forests, **Pisgah** (513,000 acres) and **Nantahala** (531,000 acres) and many state and local forests and parks.

You can do just about anything outdoors. There are more than 50 golf courses around Asheville, 4,000 miles of trout streams, 1000s of miles of hiking trails, rock climbing, white water rafting on the Nantahala or other rivers, seven snow ski resorts, about 400 waterfalls (250 in the Pisgah National Forest alone), at least seven ziplines, mountain biking, gem mining and more.

Plus, right in Asheville is the amazing **Biltmore Estate** – 8,000 acres of gorgeous parkland and gardens, with the largest private home in America and the country's most-visited winery. With a relatively inexpensive annual pass, you can visit and enjoy the estate any day of the year.

3. **Amazingly Vibrant Downtown Asheville:** Downtown Asheville is active day and night, packed with visitors and locals. On a summer weekend around Pack Square you can hardly walk. Parking lots are full.

I grew up here, and until the 1980s Downtown was a dead zone, but in the last 30 or 35 years it's been transformed into one of the most vibrant small cities in the U.S. with hundreds of restaurants, clubs and bars. And it's virtually all local and independent – for instance you can walk through Downtown and find a dozen coffee shops but not a single Starbucks. There is only one big chain store Downtown, Urban Outfitters.

Downtown has several dozen condominiums developments, with hundreds of condos priced from the low $100s to well over a million. In and around Downtown, many within walking distance of the heart of Downtown, are vibrant neighborhoods with houses and apartments in all price ranges.

There are also plenty of interesting places for visitors to stay – for example, TripAdvisor lists more than 40 bed and breakfasts in Asheville and just 29 in Atlanta, a metropolitan area of more than 6 million people. By our own count there are actually more than 50 B&Bs in and around Asheville, plus many more across Western North Carolina.

Downtown Asheville is finally getting much-needed new lodging choices. It started with Hotel Indigo on Haywood Street. Aloft opened in 2013 on Biltmore Avenue, and then there was the renovation of Haywood Park Hotel and the Marriott Renaissance Asheville. Now there's going to be a new Cambria Suites near the Grove Arcade, a new Hyatt Place on Haywood Street, a Hilton Garden Inn and two hotels near Pack Square, conversions from the 17-story BB&T Building and its separate parking garage.

4. **National Art and Crafts Center:** Art and especially craft art have been keys to what Asheville has become. Nobody knows exactly how many working artists there are in and around Asheville, but it's estimated that there are several thousand potters, painters, sculptors, glass blowers, fiber artists and others. They're concentrated in the River Arts District, in West Asheville and in areas around Asheville such as Penland School near Burnsville, which is perhaps the best crafts school in the country.

There are around 50 art and crafts galleries in Asheville alone, about the same number as in Atlanta. Asheville was named the #1 and #2 (different years) small arts city in American by *AmericanStyle* magazine -- along with places like Santa Fe and Sarasota.

Big Crafty in July and December, RAD Studio Stroll in July and November and the Southern Highland Craft Guild show in July and October, plus many gallery walks in summer, are good places to see and buy crafts and art.

One of the unusual little museums here is the Black Mountain College Museum + Art Center, which is dedicated to keeping alive the history and spirit of Black Mountain College, the radical experimental college.

From 1933 to 1957 Black Mountain College was a home for artists, writers and thinkers like Robert Motherwell, Willem and Elaine de Kooning, Robert Rauschenberg, M.C. Richards, Josef Albers, John Cage, Merce Cunningham, Buckminster Fuller and Charles Olson. There are other creative workers here, too: *MovieMaker* magazine named Asheville the #1 town to live and work in as an independent moviemaker.

5. **Architecture:** In the South, Asheville rivals Savannah and Charleston for architecture and arguably has a wider variety of building styles than those cities. It was a resort area for wealthy Low Country South Carolina and Georgia planters in the 19th century.

Then came the building of Biltmore House in the 1890s with great architects, artisans and many hundreds of skilled workers, who moved on to the construction of thousands of new homes and commercial buildings in the booms of the early 20th century. Then there was the bust of the Great Depression that stopped building and reconstruction until the 1950s, leaving most of the Art Deco and other masterpieces untouched.

Thus, Asheville has a unique inventory of interesting historical buildings. Asheville has more Art Deco buildings than any city in the Southeast except Miami Beach. Prime examples are Asheville City Building, First Baptist Church, Asheville High School and the S&W Cafeteria Building.

But there also are many other styles such as All Souls Episcopal Cathedral in Biltmore (Romanesque Revival) and Basilica of St. Lawrence on Haywood St. (Spanish Baroque Revival), plus beautiful old homes the late 19th and early 20th century, with hundreds of examples each of Craftsman style (Arts and Crafts), Queen Anne, Colonial Revival, Tudor Revival and the pebbledash stucco English style of Richard Sharp Smith.

Outside Asheville, in the countryside and small towns, you'll find a surprising selection of fine old houses and log cabins, along with plenty of trailers.

6. **Unusual Things to Do:** Interesting things to do abound. Such as: sip coffee in a double decker London bus (parked on Biltmore Avenue) ... float down the French Broad River on an inner tube and stop at Bywater bar and restaurant for a drink or food ... drink wine and read a book in the Battery Park Champagne Bar and Book Exchange in the Grove Arcade.

Or, go to the Drumming Circle at Pritchard Park Friday nights from spring to early fall ... take a LaZoom tour of Asheville -- it's like a comedy club on wheels ... take an old-fashioned staffed elevator up to the Sky Bar in the 1920s-vintage Flat Iron Building for a great view of the city from the fire escapes.

Or, listen to mountain music at Shindig on the Green or the Mountain Dance & Folk Festival (oldest in U.S.) ... watch the chimney swifts migrate through Downtown each year in mid-September ... see the synchronous fireflies put on a flashing show in the Smokies in late May/early June ... come to the MoogFest electronic music festival (electronic synthesizer inventor Robert Moog lived the last three decades of his life in Asheville).

Or, buy a high heel shoe made of chocolate at Chocolate Fetish ... go to the more-than-a-century-old Grove Park Inn (now owned by Omni Hotels and Resorts) and see the room where F. Scott Fitzgerald spent a couple of summers in the 1930s, trying to work and kick his booze habit (he switched to beer, which he didn't consider alcohol, and often drank a 24-botttle case a day) and whose wife Zelda was in a mental hospital here, Highland Hospital, and died in a fire at the hospital in the 1940s.

7. **Get Your Liberal Fix:** If you tire of living with right-wing conservatives, get your liberal on in Asheville. Asheville rivals Chapel Hill-Carrboro as the most progressive city in the state and for its size is arguably the most liberal small city in the South. It went heavily for President Obama in 2008 and 2012. The local register of deeds, Drew Reisinger, was the first public official in the South to hand out applications for same-sex marriage.

PETA once named Asheville the most vegetarian-friendly city in the country. *Yoga Journal* called it one of 10 "fantastically yoga-friendly destinations."

The local NPR station, WCQS, gave away "Cesspool of Sin" tee shirts, proudly celebrating the comment of a Charlotte-area politician about Asheville. Battle Cat coffee shop in West Asheville has a bucket full of free condoms. There's an annual Erotic Poetry Slam at the Odditorium, a dive bar and event space in West Asheville, and an annual topless day Downtown.

On the other hand, if you're more on the conservative or libertarian side, you'll find plenty of like-minded souls in the mountains around Asheville, along with back-to-the-earth organic types. Much of Western North Carolina was settled by the Scots-Irish, who are notoriously independent-minded.

Whether you're left, right or just don't care, you can find your place in Asheville and Western North Carolina. Fact is, most local residents don't give a hoot what your politics are, as long as you don't try to impose your views on them.

8. Eat and Drink Like You're in a Big City: For a small city, Asheville has amazing selection of restaurants, bars and nightlife. A new restaurant opens just about every week. With more than 600 restaurants in the Asheville area, you can eat at a different spot every night for two years, and then you have the food scene at all the quaint mountain towns around Asheville to explore – Hendersonville, Black Mountain, Waynesville, Weaverville, Highlands, Bryson City, Brevard and more.

Food is happening in Asheville's River Arts District, at The Junction and elsewhere, not to mention other parts of Asheville. Just south of Pack Square along and near Biltmore Avenue has become a hot dining area, in part due to the opening of the Aloft Hotel with a big city parking lot under it. Seven Sows Bourbon and Larder, Rhubarb, Nightbell, Blackbird, Wicked Weed and Chestnut are among newer restaurants there, adding to all the popular places that have been there awhile, like Cúrate, Limones, Posana.

The so-called South Slope south of Patton has Ben's Tune-Up, Storm Rhum Bar and Bistro and a growing number of brewpubs. Elsewhere in Downtown there's Zambra, Table, Bouchon, Strada, Chorizo, Mayfel's, Salsa's, Isa's Bistro, Cucina 24, Lex 18, The Market Place ... the list goes on and on.

West Asheville is still the hipster district, and lots of restaurants and bars, such as Buffalo Nickel, Isis, WALK, The Mothlight at Mr. Fred's, King Daddy's Chicken and Waffles, plus old standbys like The Admiral, Universal Joint, Sunny Point, Rocky's Hot Chicken Shack, Westville Pub, Tastee Diner and many others. North is seeing a bunch of new spots, from Gan Shan Station to Ambrozia to King James Public House, along with well-established favorites like Nine Mile, Vinnie's, Plant and others.

Other top restaurants: Dining Room at Inn on Biltmore Estate and Fig Bistro, Corner Kitchen, Red Stag Grill and Rezza in Biltmore Village. For steak, the local outpost of Ruth's Chris Steak House is red meat leader, but dozens of other restaurants serve up great beef. Speaking of beef, try the big, inexpensive cheeseburgers at King James Public House, Storm Rhum, Farm Burger, Avenue M, Tupelo Honey, Early Girl, Buffalo Nickel and Pack's Tavern to name a few.

The prevailing food ethos in Asheville is farm-to-table, natural, organic, Southern with a twist, but of course you can also enjoy Korean, Thai, Indian, Cuban, Brazilian, French, German, Italian, Greek, Japanese, Chinese, Vietnamese, Mexican (there are around 50 Mexican places here, of all varieties and hyphenations), Lebanese, Ethiopian, Nepalese, Mediterranean or whatever your heart and stomach desire.

9. **Welcoming People:** Everybody says that about just about every place. But in the case of Asheville and Western North Carolina, it's actually true. Be forewarned, though: At first, you may think that's not true, because the original mountain people here sometimes tend to be standoffish to newcomers. But, take our word for it, they'll warm up to you. And the diversity of people from all over the country and the world who have moved here, especially over the past 20 or 30 years, adds an extra layer of welcome. Among your neighbors, you're almost certain to find someone from "back home," whether home is New York, California, Florida, Ohio, Michigan, Georgia or Mexico, Germany, the Ukraine or the U.K.

10. **Beer City USA and Bee City USA:** Asheville was voted #1 Beer City for four straight years in an online poll by *Imbibe* magazine and named one of five top beer cities by *Forbes*.

The Asheville area now has about 40 craft breweries and brewpubs (around 20 in Downtown alone), more than Atlanta and other large cities in the South, and more are coming. Nearly every serious restaurant has a long list of local beers on tap, and increasingly you'll also find artisan hard cider, sake and even upscale moonshine.

South Slope is becoming the "beer district" of Asheville, with six or eight breweries here alone. National craft brewer Sierra Nevada has opened its Eastern brewing center near Asheville (Mills River), and New Belgium is soon to open its second national brewery in the River Arts District. There are several Brews Cruises, plus a Pubcycle – 13 people pedal around to various breweries. Asheville is also America's first BEE City USA, giving a thumbs-up to the organic and natural side of Asheville and the mountains.

AMAZING ASHEVILLE

If you can't find a way to enjoy yourself in Asheville and Western North Carolina, you better make an appointment for a check-up!

• Explore the highly walkable Downtown Asheville Historic District, home to 170 architectural jewels including the largest collection of Art Deco buildings in the Southeast outside of Miami Beach.

• Express your creative side, as the Asheville area is a nationally known center for art and crafts, with more than 50 art and craft galleries.

• Asheville is often called the Santa Fe of the South (or perhaps Santa Fe is the Asheville of the West?)

• Experience the booming River Arts District, which went from being the region's riverside industrial and warehouse district to a collection of more than 160 crafts and art studios and working artists, with hip restaurants, bars and entertainment spots in lofts and old warehouses.

• Get hopping in "Beer City USA" with some 40 microbrewers and brewpubs in the area. Asheville also is the new East Coast home of two major national craft brewers, New Belgium and Sierra Nevada.

• Join the buzz about Asheville being the first Bee City USA.

• Enjoy eating the way you like it, from cheap breakfast joints and pizza spots to gourmet fine dining. Asheville has hundreds of restaurants, some drawing national attention, with food of every sort. In 2015, Asheville has three chef semifinalists for James Beard Awards, Best Chef Southeast: Katie Button of Cúrate, John Fleer of Rhubarb and Meherwan Irani of Chai Pani.

• Get caffeinated at one of more than a dozen local coffeehouses, plus Starbucks and other chain coffee places, if you must.

• Imagine life in America's largest private home, the 250-room Biltmore House with its 8,000-acre estate and the country's most-visited winery.

• Let yourself go -- with its boutiques, funky shops, galleries, eateries and drinking spots, offices and many residential apartments and condos, Downtown Asheville is alive day and night, with hard-rocking clubs, brewpubs, dance clubs for straights and gays, dive bars, street performers, more than two dozen major festivals a year and even a weekly drumming circle.

• Get high on one of the more than 125 mountain peaks here over a mile high.

• The Blue Ridge Parkway, rated as one of the most beautiful drives in America, passes through Asheville on its way north past Mt. Mitchell, the highest mountain peak east of the Rockies and on its way south to the North Carolina side of the Great Smoky Mountains National Park.

• You and your friends could stay in a different Asheville B&B just about every week of the year, or rent a mountain cabin, stay in a mile-high lodge, relax at a historic mountain resort or go camping on 2 million acres of protected national park and forest lands, or just get comfortable in one of more than a hundred leading chain motels and hotels.

• Get outside and go trout and bass fishing, boating, whitewater rafting, canoeing, ziplining, golfing, river tubing, hiking, road and mountain biking, camping, hunting, climbing, birding, rock hounding, snow skiing and more.

• Explore Asheville's 19th and 20th century neighborhoods, from tony Biltmore Forest, Lakeshore and Grove Park to edgy West Asheville and historic Montford and Biltmore Village.

• If you're not opposed to a little sin, drink some (legal or illegal) moonshine or try your luck at Harrah's Cherokee, one of the largest and busiest casinos in the East.

• Get down and cultural, as Asheville and environs has around 100 museums, a nationally known classical musical center and a tradition of authentic Appalachian mountain music.

• If you've ever wanted to express your creative side, Asheville could be the place to do it – the area seems to attract writers, painters and other creative types. Thomas Wolfe was born here, Carl Sandburg lived on a farm here for many years, F. Scott Fitzgerald drank here (his wife Zelda died in a fire in Asheville), experimental Black Mountain College attracted some of the most radical artists, writers and thinkers of the time including Robert Motherwell, Willem and Elaine de Kooning, Robert Rauschenberg, M.C. Richards, Josef and Anni Albers, John Cage and Buckminster Fuller. Today, the area is home or a second home to scores of nationally known authors.

• It's true what they say – "Asheville and the Western North Carolina mountains are amazing!"

GETTING TO AND AROUND ASHEVILLE

The Blue Ridge Parkway – photo courtesy of National Park Service

GETTING TO ASHEVILLE
BY ROAD

The vast majority of visitors to Asheville – around 95% – arrive by car. Two interstates go through Asheville: **I-40** (a major east-west highway, 2,559 miles long, that connects Wilmington, N.C., with Barstow, Calif., running through Tennessee, Arkansas, Oklahoma, Texas, New Mexico and Arizona) and **I-26** (a newer interstate connecting Kingsport, Tenn., and Charleston, S.C.)

As it crosses the country I-40 connects with eight of the 10 major north-south interstates. I-26 to the northwest connects with I-75 and U.S. Highway 23 through Ohio to the Great Lakes, and to the southeast connects with interstates 20, 77, 85 and 95.

The most scenic route to Asheville is the 469-mile **Blue Ridge Parkway,** which connects Shenandoah National Park in Virginia with the **Great Smoky Mountains National Park** in Western North Carolina. The parkway has seven entrance/exits in the Asheville area. *(See the Blue Ridge Parkway chapter.)*

You can also reach Asheville via **U.S. Highways U.S. 19/23, 25, 25A, 70 and 74** as well as on a number of secondary North Carolina roads.

Distance to Asheville by Car

These are distances in miles and time (assuming you drove the speed limit and didn't stop) from selected cities, via the shortest routes by time, using primarily interstate highways. Your time and mileage may vary.

Anchorage, 4297 miles, 3 hours
Atlanta, 208 miles, 3¾ hours
Boston, 917 miles, 15 hours
Charleston, S.C., 267 miles, 4¼ hours
Charlotte, 127 miles, 2¼ hours
Chicago, 659 miles, 10½ hours
Cincinnati, 365 miles, 6 hours
Dallas, 958, 15 hours
Denver, 1452 miles, 22 hours
Greenville, S.C., 63 miles, 1¼ hours
Houston, 1001 miles, 16 hours
Kansas City, 851 miles, 13½ hours
Knoxville, 116 miles, 2 hours
Los Angeles, 2300 miles, 34 hours
Louisville, 360 miles, 6 hours
Myrtle Beach, S.C., 302 miles, 5 hours
Nags Head, N.C., 444 miles, 7½ hours
Nashville, 294 miles, 5 hours
New Orleans, 677 miles, 11 hours
New York City, 690 miles, 11 hours
Orlando, 586 miles, 9 hours
Philadelphia, 628 miles, 10 hours
Portland, Ore., 2647 miles, 40 hours
Raleigh, 246 miles, 4 hours
Savannah, 311 miles, 5 hours
Tampa, 642 miles, 10 hours
Toronto, 788 miles, 13 hours
Washington, D.C., 470 miles, 7½ hours
Winston-Salem, 145 miles, 2½ hours

BY AIR

Asheville Regional Airport is the primary airport serving Asheville and most of Western North Carolina. Travelers to the southern mountains near the South Carolina line might also consider the **Greenville-Spartanburg International Airport**. Another option is the **Charlotte Douglas International Airport,** a little over two hours from Asheville, which has flights from most major U.S. cities and a number of international destinations in Europe, the Caribbean, Central America and Canada.

Asheville Regional Airport *(AVL, 61 Terminal Dr., Fletcher, 828-684-2226; www.flyavl.com)* near Exit 40 of I-26 is about 16 miles or 20-25 minutes from Downtown Asheville, depending on traffic. The airport originally opened in 1961 and has expanded several times since, including a major expansion in 2009. In 2014-2015, the airport is expanding its taxiway on a 45-acre tract. Currently the airport's runway is 8,001 feet long, enough to handle most aircraft except heavily loaded wide body equipment such as 747s. AVL operates 24 hours a day, and the Transportation Security Administration (TSA) checkpoint opens at 4 am.

AVL is a pleasant, modern, easy-to-deal-with small airport. The airport handles about 800,000 passengers a year, or an average of nearly 2,000 a day. Airlines serving the airport include **Allegiant, American** (which in 2015 merged with **US Airways**), **Delta** and **United** (which recently merged with **Continental**). Most flights are on regional jets, and most flights now have both first and economy class service.

Currently there are nonstop flights from AVL to Atlanta (ATL), Charlotte (CTL), Chicago (ORD), Fort Lauderdale (FLL), Fort Meyers (PGD), Newark (EWR), New York LaGuardia (LGA), Orlando Sanford (SFB) and Tampa/St. Petersburg (PIE).

Most flights from AVL are short hops to Atlanta (hub for Delta and a "focus city" for Southwest, and the world's busiest airport with more than 95 million passengers annually) and Charlotte (hub for American/US Airways). From Atlanta and Charlotte, passengers originating in Asheville have access to some 300 total non-stop and direct destinations.

In 2014, an MIT International Center for Transportation study named Asheville Regional Airport the best connected non-hub airport in the United States.

The airport has five on-site rental car agencies including **Budget, Hertz, Avis, National/Alamo** and **Enterprise,** a restaurant and tavern, newsstand and gift shop, plus free wi-fi throughout the terminal.

There are short- and long-term **parking** lots directly across from the terminal, with an overflow lot nearby. Short-term rates are $1 for the first half hour and $1 for each additional half hour, up to a maximum of $12.50 a day; long-term rates are $1.50 for the first hour, $1.50 for each additional hour, $8 a day up to a maximum of $48 per week. A cell phone waiting lot is available for those who are picking up arriving passengers.

Besides rental cars, the Asheville Regional Airport has taxi, limo, shuttle and bus service to Downtown Asheville and elsewhere. Bus service is cheap but slow. Trips on the **Asheville Redefines Transit** or ART system *(828-253-5691, www.ashevillenc.gov/)* are $1 (50 cents for students 6-19 and seniors 65 and over). Service to Downtown Asheville, Route S3, is about every 90 minutes from 6:08 am to 7:38 pm, with no service on Sunday. It takes about 80 minutes from the airport to Downtown and about 85 minutes from ART's Coxe Avenue central station in Downtown Asheville to the airport. Henderson County's **Apple County Transit** also serves the airport, connecting the airport with the towns of Fletcher and Hendersonville. The service operates Monday through Friday from 7 am until 6 pm, arriving and leaving the airport on the hour. No weekend service. Fare is 75 cents.

Taxi rates are $2.50 per mile plus a $2.50 drop charge, with a 40-cent charge for each 2 minutes of wait time, so a taxi to Downtown Asheville runs about $45 plus tip.

Shuttle flat rates to different destinations in Western North Carolina vary, but figure about $40 to Downtown Asheville, $55 to Black Mountain, $75 to Waynesville and $125 to the Great Smokies entrance at Cherokee.

Also, more than a half dozen area motels and hotels have a free shuttle service from the airport.

These include **Hampton Inn & Suites** *(18 Rockwood Rd., Fletcher, 828-687-0806, www.hamptoninn.com)* and **Fairfield Inn** *(31 Airport Rd., Fletcher, 828-684-1144, www.marriott.com)*, both near the airport, and **Hilton Biltmore Park** *(43 Town Square Blvd., Asheville, 828-209-2700, www.hilton.com)*, about midway to Downtown. The airport's guest services center *(828-209-3660, email gs@flyavl.com)* can offer assistance on transportation options.

The general aviation facility at the airport includes fixed-base operations through **Landmark Aviation,** aircraft maintenance and repairs through Belle Aircraft Maintenance and flight training through WNC Aviation.

Greenville-Spartanburg International Airport *(GSP, 200 GSP Dr., Greer, S.C., 864-877-7426; www.gspairport.com)*, about 1¼ hours by car south of Asheville, has service by Allegiant, American/US Airways, Delta, Southwest and United.

Charlotte Douglas International Airport (CLT, 5501 R C Josh Birmingham Pkwy., Charlotte, 704-359-4000, www.charlotteairport.com), about 2-¼ hours southeast of Asheville, has long been a major hub for US Airways, with more than 41 million passengers served in 2012. How the 2015 American-US Air merger will impact that is as yet unclear, but CLT is expected to remain a hub for the combined airline for years to come. CLT also has service by Air Canada, Delta, Frontier, JetBlue, Lufthansa, Southwest and United. The airport has nonstop service to about 125 destinations in the U.S. and internationally.

BY TRAIN

The nearest **Amtrak** (www.amtrak.com) stations to Asheville are in Greenville and Spartanburg, S.C., both about 1¼ hours away, and in Gastonia and Charlotte, about 2 to 2¼ hours from Asheville.

You can travel from Charlotte to Raleigh on Amtrak's Piedmont and Carolinian trains; the Carolinian continues up the East Coast to New York City. In Greenville and Spartanburg, or in Gastonia and Charlotte, you can connect with Amtrak's Crescent, which travels daily between New Orleans and New York City.

Long-considered train service from Asheville to Charlotte and then on to Raleigh was delayed first by the state of North Carolina's budget woes and then by the anti-public transport bias of the state legislature, newly Republican-dominated.

At present, the only passenger train service in Western North Carolina is on the tourist excursion train, **Great Smoky Mountain Railroad** *(226 Everett St., Bryson City, 828-586-8811, www.gsmr.com)*, which offers several trips on its 54 miles of track from its main depot in Bryson City.

BY BUS

Greyhound/Trailways *(Greyhound Bus Station, 2 Tunnel Rd., Asheville, 828-253-8451, www.trailways.com)* has daily service between Asheville and a number of other cities in the region including Charlotte, Winston-Salem, Durham, Spartanburg, S.C. and Lynchburg, Va.

GETTING AROUND

Due to limited public transportation, the best way to get around Asheville and Western North Carolina is by car, or by shank's mare or bicycle. Call 511 or visit www.tims.ncdot.gov/tims/ to get information from the NC DOT regarding highway and travel conditions in the Asheville area.

Asheville does have a bus system *(see below)* that tries hard but often fails to meet the transportation needs of both locals and tourists. Visitors to Downtown Asheville also may want to use one of the hop-on, hop-off sightseeing trollies *(see Tours section.)*

BUS SERVICE

Asheville Redefines Transportation *(Asheville Transit Center, 49 Coxe Avenue, Asheville, 828-253-5691, www.ashevillenc.gov/Departments/Transit.aspx),* operated by the City of Asheville, provides bus service to some areas in Asheville, to Asheville Regional Airport and to the town of Black Mountain.

Ridership averages around 5,500 persons per day. Asheville has a fleet of more than two dozen buses painted dark blue and light green, with the ART logo prominently displayed; the newer buses are 30-foot, low-floor diesel-electric hybrids. There are about 16 bus routes on five major corridors (Tunnel Road, Biltmore Avenue, Haywood Road, Patton Avenue and Merrimon Avenue) running from 5:30 am to 10:30 pm, Monday through Saturday (no service on Sunday.)

Routes originate from the ART Station, located at 49 Coxe Avenue Downtown Asheville (next to the U.S. Post Office). The ART Station has restrooms and indoor and outdoor seating. A staff person is on duty until 10 pm and can provide maps and schedules. Fares are $1 (50 cents for seniors 65 and over and students 6-19). Eating, drinking and smoking are prohibited on ART buses. Bicycles may be carried on buses, on front racks, at no extra charge. All ART buses have wheelchair lifts and other features to accommodate riders with disabilities.

TAXIS

Several of the Asheville cab companies, including Yellow Cab and New Blue Bird, are switching to Prius hybrid fleets. There's also a pedal-powered bike taxi in the Downtown area. You'll usually have to call to get a cab, or have your hotel or restaurant do it, as taxis in Asheville usually don't drive around looking for fares.

Asheville Bike Taxi *(828-777-5115, www.ashevillebiketaxi.com).* New rickshaw-type cab charges $5 for two persons in the Downtown area.

New Blue Bird Taxi Company *(194 Haywood Rd., West Asheville, 828-258-8331).*

Yellow Cab Company *(393 Haywood Rd., West Asheville, 828-253-3311).*

Your Cab *(445 North Louisiana Ave., Asheville, 828-259-9904).*

Uber (www.uber.com/cities/asheville-nc) also has service in Asheville.

CAR RENTALS

The **Asheville Regional Airport** has five car rental agencies in the airport terminal, plus at least one at a nearby site. Some companies also have locations in or near Downtown Asheville. Car rental companies in Asheville typically have a decent inventory of vehicles, although there can be shortages at peak tourism times such as weekends in October or on holiday weekends in summer. To be safer, reserve ahead. Use the websites to compare rental rates and discounts, which can vary widely. Many new car dealerships also rent cars, mainly for those who are having car repairs done at the dealership.

Avis *(Asheville Regional Airport, 828-684-7144 and Sears, Asheville Mall, 1 S. Tunnel Rd., Asheville, 828-299-3644, www.avis.com).*

Budget *(Asheville Regional Airport, 828-684-2273, www.budget.com).*

Enterprise *(Asheville Regional Airport, 828-684-3607; 579 Tunnel Rd., Asheville, 828-298-6914; 770 Patton Ave., Asheville, 828-255-0236; www.enterprise.com).*

Hertz *(Asheville Regional Airport, 828-684-6455; 31 Woodfin St., Asheville, 828-225-1776; 891 Patton Ave., Asheville, 828-225-1776; www.hertz.com).*

National/Alamo *(Asheville Regional Airport, 828-684-8572, www.nationalcar.com or www.alamo.com)*

U-Save *(876 Patton Ave., Asheville, 828-285-7000; Holiday Inn, 550 Airport Rd., Asheville, 828-654-7070; www.usaveash.com)* also rents trucks and Harley-Davidson motorcycles.

BRIEF HISTORY OF ASHEVILLE AND WESTERN NORTH CAROLINA

The Vance Birthplace just north of Asheville, settled in the early 19th century

For those with an interest in history, this is a brief and necessarily incomplete history of Asheville and Western North Carolina. Note the timeline at the end of this section, which puts major events in historic perspective.

Western North Carolina is part of the **Blue Ridge Mountains,** which themselves are a part of the Appalachians. The **Appalachians are among the oldest mountains on earth, formed around 480 million years ago** in the Ordovician Period, a part of the Paleozoic Era.

At one time, before tens of millions of years of erosion took their toll, the Appalachians were as tall as the European Alps or the Rocky Mountains in North America. Today, although the mountains around Asheville are the highest in the East, with at least 39 peaks over 6,000 feet and 125 over 5,000 feet, they are mere stubs compared with their original height.

The first humans in Western North Carolina were Paleoindians. The evidence is not exactly clear as to when they arrived, but historians and archeologists think it was **at least 11,000 to 12,000 years ago,** around the time of the end of the **last Ice Age.** Their ancestors had crossed the frozen Bering Straight into North America from Asia 15,000 to 40,000 years ago and gradually migrated across North America. The Cherokees today still tell tales of their ancestors hunting mastodons in the mountains.

Europeans first came to the North Carolina mountains in the 1500s. Searching for gold, Spanish explorer and conquistador **Hernando de Soto briefly visited what is now Western North Carolina in 1540.** By this time, the Cherokee Indians were settled in small villages of 30 to 60 families, primarily living by agriculture and hunting. Cherokee women did most of the farm work, tending beans, squash, corn and sunflowers, while the men hunted deer, turkey and small game with blowguns and bows and arrows. Bison and wolves still roamed the mountains in those days.

White settlers didn't arrive in the mountains until the mid- to late 1700s. Most were **Scots-Irish from what is now Northern Ireland,** along with some immigrants from **England and Germany.**

In 1763, England's King George proclaimed that land west of the Blue Ridge Mountains in North Carolina belonged to the Cherokee and prohibited the entry of white settlers, but some whites broke that law. The Cherokee sided with the British in the Revolutionary War and made raids against white settlers.

To punish the Native Americans, General Griffith Rutherford and a large group of North Carolina State Militia raided Cherokee villages in 1776, burning homes and fields along a route known as the Rutherford Trace. After the British lost the Revolutionary War, North Carolina offered land grants as payment to soldiers, including some lands in Western North Carolina.

The first settlers to the Asheville-Buncombe area in any numbers came in the 1780s. Colonel **Samuel Davidson of Pennsylvania reputedly was the first to bring his family to settle in Buncombe County.** In 1784, Davidson built a log cabin at Christian Creek in the Swannanoa Valley. Davidson was scalped and killed by the Cherokee, but other members of his family came to the area and settled in Swannanoa. Other former Revolutionary War soldiers also settled in the Asheville area. Colonel David Vance settled on a land grant in Reems Creek. Captain William Moore, brother-in-law of General Griffith Rutherford, received a land grant in the Hominy Valley, now Enka-Candler.

Buncombe County was officially created in 1792. It was named after Revolutionary War hero **Colonel Edward Buncombe of Tyrell County** in eastern North Carolina, who had never visited the mountains. Called the **"State of Buncombe,"** the county originally included a large area, including present day Buncombe, Clay, Graham, Haywood, Henderson, Jackson, Macon, Madison, Swain, Transylvania and parts of Polk and Yancey counties.

The Buncombe County seat was originally called Morristown, but in 1797 it was incorporated and renamed after **Samuel Ashe,** a North Carolina governor.

For most of the 19th century, Asheville remained hardly more than a small village. The **Buncombe Turnpike,** a toll road for hogs and other livestock from East Tennessee to market cities in South Carolina, was completed in 1828. Part of the road, from Asheville to Greenville, S.C., was made of thick oak planks. By 1860, Asheville had a population of only around 1,100, with 2,500 in the "metropolitan area."

The Civil War had relatively little impact on Asheville, although it did destroy the drovers' markets in South Carolina. Farmers in Western North Carolina mostly had small landholdings and few if any slaves. James Smith, who owned what is now known as the Smith-McDowell House, the oldest brick house in Buncombe County, was possibly the largest slaveholder in the mountains, with 44 slaves. Among the subsistence farmers in the mountains, there was considerable pro-Union sentiment.

The major change that took place after the Civil War was the creation of the **Western North Carolina Railroad, which reached Asheville in 1880.** Later called the Richmond and Danville Railroad, it eventually ran from Salisbury near Charlotte to Murphy in the far western tip of the state. The Asheville area, for decades a summer resort for wealthy Lowcountry South Carolinians escaping the heat and disease of the coast, was opened to visitors from other areas who arrived by train.

Suddenly, Asheville became a mountain resort destination for the wealthy and hangers on who had been spending time in Newport, R.I., Bar Harbor, Me., and Saratoga, N.Y. The swank Battery Park Hotel opened in 1886, and the Kenilworth Inn in 1891.

George Vanderbilt, grandson and son, respectively, of the fabulous wealthy Commodore and William Henry Vanderbilt, first visited Asheville in 1888. He took a liking to the climate and atmosphere of Asheville, and in 1890 began construction of what would become the grandest symbol of America's Gilded Age, the **250-room Biltmore House**.

Vanderbilt accumulated an estate around the French Renaissance chateaux of some 125,000 acres. Biltmore House was completed, more or less, by Christmas 1895. Biltmore put Asheville on the map, at least among the rich and *nouveau riche.*

The 1890s saw Asheville's first housing boom, and tourism continued with the opening of **The Manor** and the **Grove Park Inn,** and a new edition of the Kenilworth Inn, but the real boom didn't take place until after World War I.

The 1920s were, to this day, the decade of Asheville's greatest growth. Everyone who could put a few dollars together started speculating in real estate. The population of Asheville increased by 76% from 1920 to 1930, growing from around 28,500 to more than 50,000. Asheville became the fourth largest city in the state. Many of Asheville's best-known **Art Deco** and other buildings were constructed during this decade, including the Flat Iron Building (1926), Kress Building (1927), First Baptist Church (1927), Asheville City Hall (1928), Asheville High School (1929), S&W Cafeteria (1929), Grove Arcade (1929) and U.S. Post Office and Courthouse (1930).

By 1929, the City of Asheville had borrowed so much money in the bond market that its bonded indebtedness was the highest in the country, on a per-capita basis.

Then came the stock market crash. Most of the local banks failed. Asheville business leaders lost their fortunes. The Great Depression put an end to real estate speculation and much of the mountain tourism industry. The city defaulted on its huge debt and didn't retire the last of the debt until 1976 (but at least it did repay the debt).

Asheville stagnated for decades. However, the **Biltmore House opened its doors to the public in 1930,** construction of the **Blue Ridge Parkway began in 1935, and was mostly completed by the 1950s** and the **Great Smoky Mountains National Park was dedicated in 1940,** but Asheville remained pretty much a backwater.

When it opened in 1933, **Black Mountain College** was one of the biggest things ever to happen to the Asheville area, but at the time few people paid any attention. It is only in retrospect that it became clear that the little radical, experimental college was a major force in the arts and culture of the 20th century.

In the 1930s and 40s, many refugees from Nazi Europe and from America's Babbittvilles came to Black Mountain College, attracted by its free spirit and experimental environment.

The faculty and student body included some who would become the great abstract artists of the century such as Robert Motherwell, Willem and Elaine de Kooning, and Robert Rauschenberg and Josef Albers.

Avant garde composer and musician John Cage and dancer Merce Cunningham collaborated on one of the first "happenings," the beginning of performance art. Buckminster Fuller, who taught engineering at Black Mountain, created his first geodesic dome at the college. Albert Einstein was on the school's board and lectured at the college. Due to a dwindling enrollment and lack of funds, Black Mountain College closed in 1957.

Things deteriorated in Downtown Asheville in the 1970s, when suburban strip shopping centers and the Asheville Mall sucked department stores and retail businesses from Downtown. The population of the city of Asheville declined to about the level of 1930. Downtown was full of boarded up stores and vacant buildings.

Then, in the 1980s, the city started turning around. With dedicated work by local civic leaders and boosters, independent businesses started opening in Downtown. Arts and crafts businesses found cheap real estate and started locating in what would become River Arts District. William A. V. Cecil, grandson of the founder of Biltmore Estate, turned around Biltmore and made it a successful business. He opened what would become the most-visited winery in the country. Tourism in the Smokies and mountains around Asheville boomed. Retirees and relocatees discovered Asheville, and soon Asheville was showing up at the top of "best" lists nationwide.

It didn't happen overnight, but **before long Downtown Asheville was thriving again.** It was cited by many as an example of what could happen in urban revitalization. The metro area grew, reaching mid-size city status with a population of more than 400,000.

Even the Great Recession of 2007-2012 didn't completely slow down progress. While real estate values fell and sales slowed, Asheville weathered the recession better than many cities.

New restaurants, clubs and shops opened Downtown. For its craft beer scene, Asheville was voted "Beer City USA," and major national companies started looking at Asheville for regional and national headquarters. Asheville received recognition for its diversity, dining, outdoor sports and general livability.

HISTORY OF ASHEVILLE & WNC: A TIMELINE

10000 BC: Cherokee Indians settle Western North Carolina

1540: Spanish explorer Hernando de Soto treks through Western North Carolina

1776: General Griffith Rutherford and 25,000 state militia troops burn Cherokee villages in Western North Carolina along what became known as the Rutherford Trace; William Bartram travels through the region

1780s: First white settlers (including Davidson, Alexander, Weaver, Gudger, Vance, Patton and Moore families) arrive in Buncombe and Western North Carolina

1790: Census shows area population 1,000 (Indians and slaves not counted)

1792: Buncombe County officially formed

1793: County seat of Buncombe, Morristown, established

1797: Morristown renamed Asheville after North Carolina Governor Samuel Ashe

1821: Sequoyah invents written Cherokee language

1828: Buncombe Turnpike, used for hog and cattle drives, completed

1835: Elisha Mitchell determines the height of the highest mountain in the East, 6,684 ft.

1838: U.S. government forces 16,000 Cherokee Indians to relocate to Oklahoma, and 5,000 or more die along "Trail of Tears"

1860: Census shows Asheville population of 2,500

1865: Battle of Asheville, a minor skirmish in the Civil War, fought April 3-6

1879: Original Bank of Asheville established

1880: First rail line reaches Asheville, Western North Carolina Railroad (later Richmond and Danville Railroad) from Salisbury

1886: Swank Battery Park Hotel opens on the highest hill in Downtown Asheville (it was razed in 1921 and the hill upon which it sat was cut down)

1887: Asheville Cotton Mill, one of the first industrial concerns in area, opens on Riverside Drive in what eventually would become the River Arts District

1889: Electric street car line established in Asheville, first in state; construction begins on Biltmore House

1890s: Asheville experiences its first real estate boom; Montford, Chestnut-Liberty and Biltmore areas developed; Richmond Hill mansion (destroyed by fire in 2009) built

1890-1910 : Biltmore Village developed by architects Richard Morris Hunt and Richard Sharp Smith

1892: Young Men's Institute (YMI) for African-Americans established and YMI Building completed

1895: All Souls Episcopal Cathedral built, designed by Richard Morris Hunt

1894: Southern Railway takes over railroad operations in area

1895: Biltmore House, designed by Richard Morris Hunt and built for George Washington Vanderbilt, completed

1898: he Manor resort completed

1900: Thomas Wolfe born in Asheville

1906: Champion Paper Company opens in Canton, contributing good-paying jobs but also contributing to the deforestation of large tracts of land

1909: Basilica of St. Lawrence by Rafael Guastavino completed

1913: Grove Park Inn completed

1916: Worst flood in Asheville history hits Riverside area (now River Arts District) and Biltmore Village July 15-16, with 29 deaths and major property damage

1916: Pisgah National Forest established, with a large tract of 85,000 acres sold by Edith Vanderbilt to the U.S. government; Mt. Mitchell State Park, first state park in North Carolina, opens

1920: Lillian Exum Clement, a Democrat, elected to North Carolina General Assembly, first woman in South to serve in a state legislature

1920-30: Asheville's decade of greatest growth, with population increasing by 76% from 28,504 in 1920 to 50,193 in 1930

1920s: Asheville experiences a great real estate boom; many of the city's Art Deco and other buildings constructed during this decade, designed by architect Douglas Ellington and others, including West Asheville Fire Station (1922), Flat Iron Building (1926), Kress Building (1927), First Baptist Church (1927), Asheville City Hall (1928), Asheville High School (1929), S&W Cafeteria (1929), Grove Arcade (1929) and U.S. Post Office and Courthouse (1930); Biltmore Forest section developed

1924: Jackson Building, Asheville's first skyscraper (13 stories) opens; new 14-story Battery Park Hotel opens; McCormick Field debuts as home of the Asheville Tourists

1928: Beaucatcher Tunnel opens

1929: Asheville's bonded debt highest in country on a per capita basis; Grove Arcade opens;

Thomas Wolfe's *Look Homeward, Angel* published; S&W Cafeteria opens; American

Enka plant, owned by a Dutch company, opens in the Candler area, bringing much-needed jobs during the Great Depression (by World War II Enka has the largest payroll in the area)

1930: Central Bank & Trust and seven other local banks fail – only Wachovia (now Wells Fargo) stays open; Asheville is fourth largest city in state in population, behind Charlotte, Winston-Salem and Greensboro (now Asheville is 11th largest in state); Biltmore House opens to public for first time

1933: Black Mountain College opens in leased space at Blue Ridge Assembly

1934: Great Smoky Mountains National Park chartered; Asheville street cars replaced by buses; F. Scott Fitzgerald spends part of this year and next two years in Asheville area

1935: Construction of Blue Ridge Parkway begins September 11

1938: Thomas Wolfe dies in Baltimore at age 37

1940: Great Smoky Mountains National Park dedicated in ceremony by President Franklin D. Roosevelt; Asheville Municipal Auditorium opens

1945: Carl Sandburg moves to Connemara farm in Flat Rock

1946: Buck's Restaurant on Tunnel Road, which was to become a landmark in Asheville, opens (opening in the same area later were Wink's and Babe Maloy's)

1948: Zelda Fitzgerald dies in fire at Highland Hospital

1954: WLOS-TV, Asheville's first television station, begins broadcasting

1956: Westgate Shopping Center, Asheville's first strip mall, opens

1957: Black Mountain College at Lake Eden closes

1959: First McDonald's restaurant opens in Asheville

1960: William A.V. Cecil, George Vanderbilt's grandson, takes over operation of Biltmore House, over the years turning it into a major success in historic preservation and tourism, and then turning management over to his son, Bill Cecil, in 1995

1961: Asheville Airport opens, with service by Delta, Piedmont and Capital airlines

1962: Asheville's Maria Beale Fletcher crowned Miss America

1965: Northwestern Bank Building (now BB&T Building) at 17 stories the region's tallest building opens on West Pack Square

1966: Innsbruck Mall, area's first enclosed mall, opens on Tunnel Road, with Brendle's as original anchor

1969: Integration of Asheville city schools completed

1970s: Exodus of department stores including Sears, Ivey's, JC Penney and Bon Marché from Downtown to the Asheville Mall; as much as 75% of Downtown retail space vacant

1971: Asheville Mall, region's largest shopping center, opens on Tunnel Road, with the original major anchor being Sears and, soon, Belk; Ivey's, Woolworth and Bon Marché open soon as junior anchors

1974: Asheville Civic Center (including a renovation of the 1940 Auditorium) opens

1975: Regular train service to Asheville ends; Elvis Pressley plays three nights at Civic Center

1976: The City of Asheville finally pays off last of the bonded debt it accumulated in the 1920s; Buck's sold to Mom and Pops restaurant chain and ceases operation as the landmark local restaurant

1977: Asheville Revitalization Commission established

1979: Bele Chere street festival begins (promoters claim the name is from a Scottish dialect, a claim that has never been satisfactorily substantiated; first wines from Biltmore offered for sale (they were not very good)

1980: The City of Asheville's population declines to 54,000 from 65,000 in 1966; flight to suburbs in full swing

1980s: Independent stores, restaurants and bars begin opening Downtown

1981: Plan by a national developer, Strouse Greenberg Company, to tear down historic buildings in 11 city blocks in Downtown and build a mall defeated in referendum – proving to be a catalyst for Asheville's historic preservation movement; Akzona Building (later Biltmore Building) designed by I.M. Pei's firm opens

1984: First arts and crafts businesses locate in what would become River Arts District, and in the late 1980s and 1990s artists and craftspeople discover RAD and open studios and galleries there

1985: Original winery at Biltmore Estate opens – later expanded it would eventually become the most-visited winery in the country

1986: Asheville Downtown Association formed

1987: Final section of Blue Ridge Parkway completed

1995: Centennial of Biltmore House; George Vanderbilt's great-grandson Bill Cecil given charge of operating the now hugely successful house and estate

1996: Prince Charles visits Asheville and Biltmore Estate

2004: Severe flooding damages many buildings in Biltmore Village September 8, due to remnants of hurricanes Frances and Ivan

2005: Terry Bellamy, 33, elected Asheville's first African-American mayor, and youngest mayor in North Carolina

2007-11: Asheville weathers Great Recession better than many cities, with mostly moderate declines in real estate values; by late 2012 Asheville has second-lowest unemployment rate of any major city in North Carolina

2008: Barack Obama wins Asheville with 70% of vote and wins Buncombe with 56%

2009: Asheville voted "Beer City USA" in internet poll, outdistancing Portland, Ore. and other cities, and winning again in 2010, 2011 and 2012 (the last vote a tie with Grand Rapids); the area has more than 20 craft breweries and brewpubs

2012: Two major national craft beer companies, Sierra Nevada and New Belgium, announce plans to open their East Coast breweries and distribution centers in the Asheville area

2013: Asheville Downtown, River Arts District and West Asheville revitalizations viewed as major successes, with large numbers of art and craft galleries, restaurants, clubs, bars, boutique shops and residential condos open and streets often packed with visitors and locals; Esther Manheimer, a Democrat, elected mayor of Asheville

2015: Local tourism booms, with many lodging places seeing record occupancies; Asheville recognized as a foodie destination and a national leader in the locavore, farm-to-table movement; a half-dozen new hotels under construction or planned in the Downtown area

NATIONAL KUDOS FOR ASHEVILLE

Asheville has won national acclaim as a visitor, arts and crafts, retirement and relocation destination:

#1 Most Popular City for Retirement TopRetirements.com, 2015 (Asheville has won every year since list was first compiled in 2007, based on number of visits to TopRetirements.com website)

"Most Beautiful Place in America to Live and More" *Real Estate Scorecard,* 2015

"Hippest City in the South" *Fodor's The Carolinas & Georgia,* 2015

#3 of "Coziest Cities in America" *Elle Decor* 2015

One of "America's Best Beer Cities" *Condé Nast Traveler,* 2015

"#12 of Top 100 Best Places to Live in America" Livability.com, 2014

America's #1 "Quirkiest Town," TravelandLeisure.com, 2014

One of the top "Southern Literary Destinations" *USA Today,* 2014

One of this year's "Best Towns Ever" *Outside Magazine,* 2014

#10 among the "Friendliest Cities in the U.S." *Condé Nast Traveler,* 2014

One of "Best Places to Go in 2015" *Frommer's,* 2014

One of "America's Smartest Cities" *Forbes,* 2014

#4 of "Top 10 Foodie Cities" Livability.com, 2014

"The Biggest Little Culinary Capital in America" *Departures,* 2014

"A perfect dog-friendly city" Purina, 2014

"Best city in America for locavores" *The Daily Meal,* 2014

"The hippie capital of the South" *Huffington Post,* 2014

#1 town to live and work in as a moviemaker *MovieMaker* magazine, 2014

Scenic drive on the Blue Ridge Parkway #1 on list of "Seven Things You Absolutely Must Try in a National Park", Orbitz blog 2014

One of 6 top "Alternative Travel Destinations for 2014" *Men's Journal* and *Business Insider,* 2014

One of "10 College Towns with the Best Music Scenes in America" MusicSchoolCentral.com, 2014

One of "Five Secret Foodie Cities" *Forbes* blog, 2014

One of "Best Cities for a Spring Trip" *National Geographic,* 2014

"#1 of 12 Dreamy Towns for Vegan Living" *VegNews,* 2013

"One of Top 5 Beer Cities" *Forbes,* 2013

"One of 10 Tastiest Towns in the South" *Southern Living,* 2013

"One of America's Best River Towns" *Outside,* 2012

"#1 Beer City USA" *Imbibe* magazine online poll, 2009, 2010, 2011, 2012

"Most Romantic Place in USA and Canada" About.com Readers Choice Poll, 2012

"America's first Green Dining Destination" Green Restaurant Association, 2012

"#2 Small City Art Destination" *AmericanStyle,* 2012

"Top 10 Great Sunny Places to Retire" *AARP Magazine,* 2012

"Top 10 Food & Wine Destinations in U.S." TripAdvisor, 2011

"Best Place to Start a Fall Color Tour" Livability.com, 2011

"10 Fantastically Yoga-Friendly Destinations" *Yoga Journal,* 2011

"#2 Best Resort Area to Visit with Your Dog" DogFriendly.com

"#1 Small City Art Destination" *AmericanStyle,* 2011, 2010

"One of 15 Destinations on the Rise" TripAdvisor, 2011

"21 Places We're Going in 2011" *Fodor's,* 2011

"#6 Among American Cities as Place to Do Business" Forbes.com, 2010

"One of America's Best Affordable Places to Retire" *U.S. News & World Report,* 2009

"#1 Place to View Fall Foliage" TripAdvisor, 2010

"Top 10 Undiscovered Food Locations" Huffington Post, 2009

"One of Happiest Places in America" *Geography of Bliss,* 2008

"One of Top 7 Places to Live in U.S." *Frommer's Cities Ranked and Rated,* 2007

"One of 12 Must-See Places in World" *Frommer's,* 2007

"#1 of America's Best Vegetarian-Friendly Small Cities" PETA, 2006

"#1 Best Whitewater Town" *Outside,* 2006

"New Freak Capital of the U.S." *Rolling Stone,* 2005

"Happiest City in the U.S. for Women" *Self,* 2002

"Top 10 Literary Destinations" *USA Today,* 2002

"Top 5 Best Places to Retire" *Money Magazine,* 2000

"#1 Small Town for Retirement" *Modern Maturity,* 2000

"One of Top 5 Places to Retire" *Places Rated Almanac,* 2000

MOUNTAIN CLIMATE AND WEATHER

"The storm starts, when the drops start dropping
When the drops stop dropping then the storm starts stopping."
-- Dr. Seuss

Fall in the mountains – photo courtesy of National Park Service

The Asheville area has a **mild, temperate climate with four distinct seasons.** In general, Asheville is significantly cooler in summer than other cities in the Southeast and somewhat colder and snowier in winter than other Southeastern cities.

There are many different microclimates, however, not only in Western North Carolina but even in the immediate Asheville area. That's one reason why you'll see so many different numbers used on rain, snowfall and average and high and low temperatures.

The main difference, of course, has to do with **elevation.** Asheville itself, in a large valley, has an average elevation of about 2,160 feet above sea level, but the mountains around Asheville range up to almost 6,700 feet.

That extra 4,500 feet or makes a tremendous difference in temperature and snowfall. In the Western North Carolina mountains, average temperatures decline about 4 to 5 degrees F. with each 1,000-foot increase in elevation above sea level.

On top of that, the side of the mountain you're on has a great deal to do with the amount of precipitation. Moist winds from the southwest drop an average of 80 inches of precipitation on the western side of some mountains in Western North Carolina, while the northeast-facing slopes average less than one-half that amount.

Recognizing that averages will vary from site to site, here are some statistics on weather in Asheville:

Average annual temperature: 55

Average rainfall: 38 to 47 inches

Average snowfall: 13 to 14 inches

Average relative humidity: 74% (average 57% at 1 pm)

Average high and low temperature:

January	47 hi	25 lo
April	68 hi	43 lo
July	83 hi	63 lo
October	68 hi	48 lo

Record high: 99 degrees (August 1983)

Record low: -16 degrees (January 1985)

Average number of days a year with maximum temperatures over 90 degrees: 9 (with range of 0 in many years to 32 days in 1952)

Number of days a year with minimum temperatures below freezing (32 degrees): 98

Number of clear or partly cloudy days per year: 212

Days of year with measurable precipitation (0.01 inch or more): 126

Average wind speed: 7.5 mph

Spring sees variable weather conditions in the Western North Carolina mountains, with mild temperatures in the lower elevation areas but snow possible at higher elevations. Later in the spring, in April and May, the mountains warm up, with temps frequently in the 70s or low 80s except at the highest elevations.

Summer tends to be humid and fairly warm in the mountains, especially at the lower elevations, where temps can reach the high 80s or low 90s, with rain showers or thunderstorms common in the afternoons. With global climate change, the summers are warmer than they used to be. Still, on average in July, the hottest month, only five days see temps above 90. Evenings generally are much cooler, and at higher elevations it's always chillier.

Fall is glorious in the mountains, typically with brisk, clear days and cool to chilly nights, depending on elevation. Peak fall leaf color around Asheville is usually from mid to late October. Sometimes, the color at lower elevations lasts almost until Thanksgiving. The first frosts in the Asheville area usually occur in late October. By November, you'll have some below freezing temperatures at night, though what used to be called Indian summer usually brings a few warm days.

The author's home in the snow, winter of 2013-2014

In **winter,** snow is light and infrequent at lower elevations around Asheville, though the mountains around the city are frequently capped with snow or rime frost. The highest peaks around Asheville get an average of five feet of snow a year. Snowfall in Asheville varies considerably from year to year. Some years there will be several sizeable snowfalls, and others, such as the winter of 2012-2013, almost none. January usually sees more snow than any other month, but some of the heaviest snowfalls in Asheville have been late, in March.

For example, in March 1993 about 14 inches of snow fell in Asheville in a single day. The National Weather Service says the heaviest single snowstorm in Asheville's recorded history, 26 inches, fell in December 1886.

Best Times to Experience the Mountains

If you are scouting out the mountains for a place to live or for a second home, it is a good idea to visit at different times of year, preferably during all four seasons.

For many local residents and visitors, **spring and fall are the best times of year in the mountains.** Spring, especially the period from late March to early May, is when the mountains come back to green life and the wildflowers bloom. Weather is mild, with none of the hot, sticky days of mid-summer. Fall, particularly late September to early November, almost guarantees brisk, invigorating weather, and beautiful fall leaf color. The color season extends for six weeks or longer. Be aware, however, that hotel rates tend to peak on October weekends, restaurants are often full and traffic on busy mountain roads can be heavy.

In **summer,** although you may hit a string of hot and humid days, the evenings cool off. If you want to escape the heat all you have to do is to head up to the high mountain peaks, where it's rarely over 80 degrees even in July and August. The warm sunny days of June through early September are also great for water sports like rafting, river tubing, fishing and boating.

If you like snow skiing, boarding and tubing, or sitting by a crackling fire, naturally you'll want come in the **winter.** As noted, don't expect a lot of snow in Asheville itself, but the surrounding mountains get a good bit of snow, and all the ski resorts have snow-making equipment.

To experience the best and worst of the seasons in the mountains, we suggest visits in January (usually the coldest month), April (the height of spring), July or August (the hottest months) and October (the glorious fall).

BUGS, BEASTS AND BAD WEATHER

Asheville and Western North Carolina are lucky.

Thanks to the mountain terrain and inland location, we're protected from hurricanes and tornados. Oh, once in a blue moon maybe the tail end of a tropical storm will bring heavy rain for a day or two, or a little funnel cloud will pop up for a few minutes, but these events are rare, and rarely is there much damage. This is not Kansas, nor the Gulf or Atlantic coast. Earthquakes, although they can occur here, have always been mild. This is not California. There are no tsunamis. Occasionally, rivers in the mountains flood, but the flood plains are narrow.

Bugs and creepy-crawlies? Sure, if you go hiking you may pick up a tick or chiggers. There are two poisonous snakes native to this region, a rattlesnake and the copperhead, but the North Carolina mounts aren't the tropics or semi-tropics, where you are constantly face-to-face with scorpions, tarantulas, all kinds of venomous reptiles and amphibians, sharks, killer bees, fire ants and trees that drip stuff that turns your skin red and raw.

Here you won't even be much bothered by no-see-ums, sandflies or swarms of black flies and mosquitoes. Sure, global climate change has brought a few mozzies to a few areas – when I was growing up here I didn't even know what a mosquito was -- but this is no Alaska, Canadian outback or even Boston, where the mosquitoes are big enough to carry off Harvard undergrads.

Let's look at the risks you might face living in the mountains.

NATURAL DISASTERS
Hurricanes

The bad news: In recorded history more than 400 hurricanes have hit the state of North Carolina, the fourth-most of any state after Florida, Texas and Louisiana.

The good news: Because Asheville is some 400 miles from the coast, and the far western part of the region close to 500 miles from the ocean, these hurricanes, and others that come up from Gulf Coast or other parts of the Atlantic Coast, normally peter out before they get to the mountains. Occasionally, heavy rains from hurricanes have disturbed us here in WNC, but even that is relatively rare.

Two hurricanes that struck the Southeast in mid-July 1916 caused the worst flood in Asheville's history. It has been called the "Epic Flood of 1916." The French Broad and Swannanoa rivers, among other rivers and creeks, overflowed their banks. The high water killed a number of people and did tremendous damage in Biltmore and in what is now the River Arts District, then a manufacturing and warehousing area. It also damaged areas south of Asheville including Hendersonville. The damage to property exceeded $22 million, or more than $450 million in today's dollars. The July 17, 1916 issue of the *Asheville Citizen* newspaper said, "Asheville today staggers under the greatest catastrophe it has ever known, and its true magnitude will not be realized until the flood waters have subsided and have revealed the toll taken in human life and property."

Three hurricanes in September 2004, Frances, Ivan and Jeanne, caused heavy rains and river flooding in the mountains. In the aftermath of Frances, almost 24 inches of rain fell at the high elevations of Mt. Mitchell. The tail ends of two tropical depressions in 2005 also created heavy rains in the mountains.

Floods

Floods in Asheville and Western North Carolina generally are caused by the remnants of summer or early fall hurricanes that hit the North Carolina coast or other parts of the coastal Southeast. The Great Flood of 1916 was one of these, causing loss of life and significant property damage in Asheville and elsewhere in the region.

Serious flooding in Asheville in 2004 also was mostly the result of Hurricanes Ivan and Frances. However, occasionally flooding occurs due to other weather patterns. For instance, in 1940 heavy summer rains caused devastating floods across Western North Carolina, from Boone to Bryson City. In late January 2013, parts of Asheville including Biltmore Village flooded due to a series of severe thunderstorms.

Most flooding in Asheville and Western North Carolina occurs in the flood plains of the French Broad, Swannanoa and other rivers and large creeks. However, steep slopes anywhere in the mountains can be hit by heavy rains that cause flash floods and landslides. Many WNC counties and municipalities have passed regulations that limit building on steep slopes.

Tornedo?

"Tornado Alley" in the United States includes the Midwest and part of the Southeast, mainly from Nebraska, Kansas, Oklahoma and Texas in the west to Ohio, Kentucky, Tennessee and Alabama in the east.

Western North Carolina is outside this tornado zone. Tornadoes love plains and other wide, flat land. The hilly and mountainous terrain works here against their formation, and on the few occasions where funnel clouds form they almost always are of low intensity and of very small size.

While tornadoes can occur in Western North Carolina, they are rare here due to the terrain, and even more rarely do they cause fatal injury or damage beyond a few trees knocked down. Nearly all tornadoes reported in Western North Carolina are of mild intensity, typically just 0 or 1 on the Fujita scale (5 is the highest intensity.)

Between 1950 and 2003, only about 45 minor tornedoes occurred in Western North Carolina, according to the State Climate Office of North Carolina at North Carolina State University, and of these only two resulted in a fatality.

In the last quarter of the 20th century, six low-intensity tornadoes touched down in Asheville and Buncombe County, with a total of only six injuries and no deaths.

Earthquakes

Western North Carolina has experienced earthquakes throughout its history, with fault zones dating back as much as 500 million years. However, large and damaging earthquakes are rare, with most earthquakes in the region having a magnitude of less than 3.0. This level of seismic activity is due to the state being on a passive, not active, continental margin such as exists in California.

Western North Carolina has not seen a major earthquake in recorded history.

The most significant fault in the region is called the Brevard fault zone, which extends from Alabama to Virginia across Western North Carolina. Another fault in the region is the Linville Falls fault. However, even when minor earthquakes occur these faults don't break the ground, due to their great age, depth and relative passive state.

The largest known earthquakes in WNC were:

Wilkes County Earthquake – August 31, 1861. Magnitude 5.1. The epicenter of this earthquake was near Wilkesboro, in northwestern North Carolina. Some damage to chimneys occurred. The shock was felt from Washington, D.C., to Charleston, S.C., and Cincinnati.

Skyland Earthquake – February 21, 1916. Magnitude 5.5. Damage occurred in Skyland, Waynesville, Tryon and Forest City. Chimney tops were dislodged, and windowpanes were broken. The quake was felt over 200,000 square miles, including in the Carolinas, Alabama, Kentucky and West Virginia. It is considered the largest quake in Western North Carolina in modern times.

Mitchell County Earthquake – July 8, 1926. Magnitude 5.2. Centered in southern Mitchell County, this minor local earthquake toppled one chimney and cracked several others.

BUGS

We live in an area that is highly bio-diverse – in fact, one of the most biologically diverse areas in the world – so there are quite a few crawling, buzzing and biting creatures.

But, hey, this is nothing like New Orleans or South Florida with its giant flying cockroaches. Or Savannah and coastal Georgia and South Carolina with their incredibly irritating sand gnats or no-see-ums. Or the hot weather South where fire ants take over fields and yards. Or the blood-sucking black flies that ruin the outdoors from spring to mid-summer in Ohio, Pennsylvania, New Jersey, New York and New England, the Upper Peninsula of Michigan and Southern Canada. Or places like Minnesota, Maine and Wisconsin where mosquitoes take over every other picnic. Or Arizona and other Western states where black widow spiders seem to hide under every rock.

Here in Western North Carolina, you can enjoy a backyard cookout or a mountainside picnic without much concern about annoying insects or spiders.

Mosquitoes

It would be misleading to say that you'll never see a mosquito in the mountains. When I was growing up here, I don't remember ever seeing a single mosquito. However, with global climate change, the range of mosquitoes has grown, including to Asheville and Western North Carolina. There are thought to be about 60 different species of mosquitoes in the state, most located in the eastern part of the state along the coast. Buncombe County has just a small mosquito control department, whose function is mainly to educate citizens about getting rid of standing water around their home.

Because it is such a minor issue, the county spends only about 2 cents per resident per year on mosquito control. Most WNC counties have no formal mosquito control programs. Mosquitoes are almost totally absent in the higher elevations, but at lower elevations, especially after periods of rain in the summer and near streams and low-laying swampy areas, you may see some mosquitoes. Still, compared with most of the rest of the East and South, mosquitoes are at most a minor and occasional nuisance in Western North Carolina.

Chiggers

Trombiculidae are a family of mites that includes chiggers, also known as berry mugs, harvest mites or redbugs.

They are present throughout the world. Here in Western North Carolina, they are mainly a problem for hikers and others walking in weeds or grass in the early summer, when vegetation is at its most lush. The enzymes in their digestive systems can cause intense itching. Chiggers here don't carry any diseases, so at worst they are an annoyance. Some people are more bothered by chiggers than others. If you're in a chigger-infested area and start itching, take a shower and wash your clothes in hot, soapy water. For temporary relief of itching, apply ointments of benzocaine, hydrocortisone, calamine lotion or similar over-the-counter meds.

Bees and Wasps

I love honeybees, but I hate wasps and yellow jackets. Logically, I know that all these insects have a place in the ecosystem, but that doesn't make me any happier to stumble upon a yellow jacket nest or accidentally stick my head near a paper wasp nest.

Yellow jackets, a kind of wasp, unfortunately are common in Western North Carolina. They typically build nests in the ground and by late summer the colonies can be as large as 4,000 to 5,000. Yellow jackets are highly defensive, and can sting repeatedly, so if you happen to walk over a nest when mowing the lawn or on a hike, you can be stung many times.

A relative of the yellow jacket is the **bald-faced** or **black hornet,** *Dolichovespula maculata.* These hornets, fairly common in WNC, build beautiful conical paper nests. You may see these hanging on a branch in a tree, or on the side of a building. At their peak in late summer, the colony can consist of as many as 600 or 700 hornets. By late autumn, the colony dies (a fertilized queen lives over the winter, usually underground, to start a new colony the next year.) After the first frosts, you can "harvest" the nest and display it.

Paper wasps (yellow and black) and **black wasps** also are common in WNC. They build paper nests, umbrella shaped, often under the eaves of houses. **Bumblebees,** genus *Bombus,* which indeed are bees and not wasps, are often seen in the mountains, even at high elevations. Like honeybees, and unlike yellow jackets, they are useful pollinators as they go about their work of collecting pollen and nectar. Most species are not aggressive, except in defense of their nests.

Wild honeybees (*Apis mellifera*) used to be common in the mountains, but it is estimated that 90% or more of feral bee colonies have died due to varroa and tracheal mites, viral and bacterial disease, climate change, widespread pesticide use and the still mysterious Colony Collapse Disorder. Fortunately, commercial and hobbyist beekeepers have stepped up. There are an estimated 10,000 commercial and hobbyist beekeepers in North Carolina, and the official state insect is the honeybee. A strong colony can have 50,000 or more individual bees. In 2012, Asheville became America's first "Bee City USA." *(See www.beecityusa.org.)*

The European honeybee, which was brought to the United States in the 1600s, is the country's most important bee for crop pollination and honey production. As much as 80% of crop pollination comes from honeybees. In WNC, honeybees are especially important in pollinating the apples of Henderson County and also in pollinating domestic blackberries, but they also play a key role for other farmers and backyard gardeners. Africanized bees, or "killer bees" with their hyper-defensive character, are not yet present in Western North Carolina. It is unclear whether they will be able to adapt to the colder winters of this region and farther north.

Spiders

Most spiders have venom, but only a few are potentially harmful to humans. The **black widow** (genus *Latrodectus)* and **brown recluse** *(Loxosceles reclusa)* arachnids, close relatives of ticks, mites and scorpions, are present in Western North Carolina. Both the northern and southern black widow species are in WNC. Females (whose venom is much more powerful than that of males) are easily identified due to the red hourglass pattern on the underside of their abdomens. Black widows are relatively common in North Carolina but are rarely seen because they live under rocks, boards or hidden in crawl spaces. Brown recluse spiders are relatively *uncommon* in Western North Carolina. Often other species of spiders are misidentified as brown recluses. Neither the black widow nor the brown recluse is aggressive, and bites are relatively rare, usually the result of accidentally touching the spider.

Other Pests

The **brown marmorated stink bug** invaded the mid-Atlantic region in the early part of the 21st century, and the bug is now found in 41 states, including the mountains of Western North Carolina. They come out in warm weather. The stink bugs are a minor, smelly annoyance for homeowners, but they have caused considerable damage to agricultural crops.

Another annoying pest is the **Asian lady beetle.** Swarms of these little orange ladybugs congregate on the sunny side of your house in the spring and especially in the fall, and some of them find ways of getting inside. As autumn approaches, adult beetles leave their summer feeding sites in yards, fields and forests for protected places to spend the winter. Unfortunately, this may include your living room or attic. Though not generally harmful, the beetles emit an acrid odor and can stain surfaces with their yellowish secretions. The beetle is native to China, Russia, Korea and Japan, where it dwells in trees and fields, preying on aphids and scale insects. The first field populations in the United States were found in Louisiana in 1988. Since then the beetle has expanded its range to include much of the U.S. and parts of Canada, including Western North Carolina.

Both these alien pests have few natural predators here, and so their numbers increase unceasingly. Stink bugs can be controlled in the home using a simple, inexpensive trap (see the internet for instructions on homemade stink bug traps.) Sealing entry points such as cracks with caulk is the most effective way to stop lady beetles from entering your house. Insecticides may work on these pests, but they have negative impacts on other insect species, including many beneficial ones.

DANGEROUS CRITTERS

Western North Carolina has only a few dangerous creatures such as poisonous snakes or large predators. Many people live in the region for years without even seeing one of these up close, and only very, very infrequently are there injuries or deaths caused by them.

American black bear: The black bear is the most intelligent alpha predator in the Americas. Its intelligence level is similar to that of the Great Apes in Africa. Black bears weigh 250 to 600 pounds or more when fully mature. Bears have a shaggy black coat and a long snout, with an excellent sense of smell. They can stand and walk on their hindquarters but usually walk on all fours.

Fast runners and excellent tree climbers, if a bear wants to catch you, it can. However, serious incidents between humans and bears are rare. The only known fatal attack by a bear on a human in the region in modern times was in 2000 in the Elkmont area of the Great Smoky Mountains National Park, on the Tennessee side.

Black bears are omnivorous with their diet including insects, nuts, berries, fish, birds and small mammals. With the increase of people and the diminishing of natural habitat, bears have migrated to more populated areas, and while the danger to humans is practically nil, bears have become a nuisance to farmers and homeowners in many areas. (The author lost a hive of honeybees and several chickens to black bears in 2013.)

North Carolina now has an estimated 20,000 black bears, up from a low of as few as 2,000 in the 1960s. About 6,000 of the bears are in Western North Carolina. Bears are fairly frequently spotted in Asheville neighborhoods and occasionally even in the heart of Downtown Asheville. Contrary to popular belief, in the bears in WNC do not fully hibernate in winter, although they become less active and may sleep for long periods. Black bears in the wild normally live 8 to 12 years, though some live 20 years or longer.

Northern copperhead: This pit viper is, with the timber rattlesnake, one of only two venomous snakes in the region. Copperheads have a pale tan to pinkish tan ground color overlaid with a series of tan or light brown bands. They rarely grow to more than 3 feet in length. Many people confuse the northern water snake or other harmless snakes for a copperhead.

Timber rattlesnake: This rattlesnake is variable in color, ranging from yellow and brown to nearly black, with W-shaped lateral markings across its back. The rattles at the end of the tail distinguish it, but individual snakes sometimes lose their rattles. These rattlesnakes typically reach about 3 feet in length but can be longer. While not commonly seen, they are present in most parts of the Western North Carolina mountains.

Although many people wrongly believe otherwise, the **cottonmouth** pit viper is not present in Western North Carolina. Its range in North Carolina is limited to about the eastern half of the state. Neither is the **Eastern coral snake** or the **Eastern diamondback rattlesnake** -- the largest and arguably the most dangerous rattlesnake in America -- present in the mountains. The range of these snakes in the state is limited to a few counties in Southeastern North Carolina mostly along the South Carolina border.

Coyotes have spread into Western North Carolina, as they have in much of the East. Although occasional attacks on humans by coyote packs have been recorded in other areas, they are mainly a problem for farmers or homeowners who may lose chickens, cats or other small pets to them. Their howling at night can be blood chilling.

AIR QUALITY AND POLLEN

According to Allergy Partners of WNC, a large allergy medical practice here, the geography of Western North Carolina makes it a particularly allergy-prone area. First, this bio-diverse and bio-rich area has more species of plants here at a higher density than in most other areas of North America. Second, elevations vary from a few hundred feet above sea level to more than 6,500 feet. Willow and maple trees, for example, pollinate early in low, warm river valleys, and several weeks later at high elevations. Since pollen grains can travel up to 50 miles, those who have allergies to tree, grass and weed pollens may suffer from them throughout this span of weeks. So, the allergy seasons are longer and often more intense here.

Having said that, if you look at a national pollen map, while Asheville and Western North Carolina tend to have relatively high levels over many weeks, other regions such as agricultural areas of the Midwest and upper Midwest are "hot spots" for pollen, with pollen levels much higher than in Asheville.

Also, Asheville generally enjoys good air quality, better than many other cities in the Southeast. According to the EPA, Asheville's air quality is better than that in a number of other Southeastern cities including Knoxville, Charlotte, Raleigh, Atlanta, Savannah, Colombia, S.C., Macon, Ga., Nashville, New Orleans, Tampa-St. Petersburg and Miami. Air quality here is also rated higher by the EPA than in popular cities for relocation such as Albuquerque, Austin, Boston, Prescott and Phoenix, Ogden and Salt Lake City, San Antonio, Seattle, San Francisco and Portland, Ore.

On average in 2013, air quality in Asheville was rated "Good" 83% of the time; it was rated "Moderate" about 17% of the time. At no day in the year was air quality rated "Unhealthy for Sensitive Groups" or the lowest rating, "Unhealthy." Recent Supreme Court rulings that eventually will reduce cross-state border pollution – much of the air pollution in Western North Carolina comes from coal-burning power plants and other factories in Tennessee and the Ohio Valley – should further improve our air quality in the mountains.

PRACTICALITIES IN ESTABLISHING RESIDENCY IN NORTH CAROLINA

This section is devoted to the "mechanics" of setting up residence in North Carolina. It covers things such as vehicle registration, getting a driver's license, registering to vote and setting up utilities. Subjects such as obtaining business or professional licenses, paying state taxes or obtaining health care are covered in other sections. For those who live in North Carolina only part-time, and are permanent residents of another state or country, much of this section may not apply.

Driving and Owning Motor Vehicles in North Carolina

North Carolina highway system has the largest state-maintained road system in the nation. The state also has a lot of rules and regulations regarding driving a motor vehicle. Here are some of them. Remember, regulations and laws change frequently, so check before acting on information presented here.

Driver's License

If you plan to operate a motor vehicle as a new resident of North Carolina, you must obtain a North Carolina driver's license within 60 days of establishing a permanent residence in NC. You have to go in person to a state driver's license office. There are offices in all cities and in many small towns. Call the NC Department of Transportation at 919-715-7000 or visit www.ncdot.gov for the location of the driver's license office nearest you. DMV also has several mobile driver's license service centers where you can get a license.

As a new resident, you must take and pass a written test on North Carolina motor vehicle regulations. Also, you must pass a vision test and a sign recognition test. In most cases, if you have a driver's license from another state, you do not have to take the road test to get a NC driver's license. A copy of the latest *North Carolina Driver's Handbook* in pdf format is downloadable from www.ncdot.gov. The test isn't too difficult, and to pass the written test you only need to get 20 of 25 questions, or 80%, correct, but you should go over the *Handbook* before the test.

For the first-time issuance of an NC driver's license or, alternatively an identity card if you don't drive, you will be required to provide proof of age, identify documents and proof of residence. The *Driver's Handbook* lists the various acceptable documents, but an unexpired driver's license from another state, passport or birth certificate are among the documents that prove your age; a utility bill, property tax record, mortgage statement, apartment lease or bank statement are among documents sufficient to prove residence in the state. Applicants for an original license who are U.S. citizens must show a Social Security card or other proof of Social Security such as W-2 form or payment record. Those who are not U.S. citizens must show proof of Social Security plus documents from the U.S. government showing they have legal residency.

Individuals who are moving to North Carolina and seeking a driver's license must also show proof of liability insurance. Certification of liability insurance coverage must be submitted on DMV Form DL-123, or an original liability insurance policy, binder or an insurance card that must come from an insurance company licensed to do business in North Carolina.

The NC Department of Motor Vehicles will not issue a driver's license or identification card to an applicant who has resided in the state for less than 12 months until the division has completed a search of the National Sex Offender Public Registry and, if the person is found to be a sex offender the person has registered with the local sheriff's office.

Different licensing rules apply for young people getting their learner's permit or first driver's license. See the *Driver's Handbook* for detailed information.

Driver's licenses expire on your birthday and are valid for different periods according to your age:

Age 16: 4 years
Age 17: 5 years
Age 18-65: 8 years
Age 66 and older: 5 years

Most people moving to North Carolina will be applying for what is called a Class C non-commercial license to drive a regular car or light truck.

Motorcycle drivers also require a motorcycle endorsement on the Class C license. All operators and passengers on motorcycles and mopeds must wear a **safety helmet** of a type that complies with Federal Motor Vehicle Safety Standard (FMVSS) 218. Bicycle riders and passengers under age 16 must also wear an approved helmet.

For those 16 and over a driver's license is NOT required to operate a moped on roads. A moped is defined as a vehicle with two or three wheels, an engine displacement of no more than 50 cubic centimeters and a top speed of no more than 30 mph. Some interstates or other high-speed roads may ban the use of mopeds and scooters.

The cost of a **Class C non-commercial license (for a regular car or light truck) is $4 a year,** payable in full at the time you get the license. Thus, someone 18-65 would pay $32 for the 8-year license. A motorcycle endorsement is an additional $1.75 a year.

Fee for an identification card in lieu of a driver's license is $10 (fee is waived if you are 70 or older.) **ID cards for voter registration are free.** Unless the NC voter registration law requiring voters to present a government-issued ID in order to vote is overturned in the courts, it will be implemented beginning in 2016.

If you change addresses in North Carolina, you are supposed to file for a license with the new address within 60 days of change address. This can be done on-line without visiting a driver's license office. Cost is $10.

Payments for transactions at DMV offices, including driver's license offices, are limited to **cash**, **money order** or **personal checks**. No other forms of payment are accepted, including debit and credit cards.

Auto Liability Insurance

North Carolina law requires the registered owner of a motor vehicle maintain continuous liability insurance coverage from a company authorized to do business in the state as long as there is a valid license plate for the vehicle. Liability insurance is also required to get an NC driver's license for the first time. The minimum requirements for liability for private passenger vehicles are $30,000 for bodily injury for one person, $60,000 bodily injury for two or more people and $25,000 property damage. Most vehicle owners and drivers will want to have higher limits.

If you're moving to North Carolina, before you can register your vehicle in the state and get a NC driver's license, you need to provide proof that you have at least the minimum liability insurance. Form DL-123, available from your insurance company, is one way to provide that proof of liability insurance. Note that it is valid only for 30 days from the date of issuance and must be from an insurance company licensed to do business in North Carolina.

State Farm is the largest auto liability insurance underwriter in North Carolina, with a 14% market share, followed by **NC Farm Bureau** with a 10% share, according to figures from the North Carolina Department of Insurance. These two are followed by **Nationwide, Integon, GEICO** and **Allstate.** However, if all the various **Nationwide Insurance** companies are lumped together, their total market share approaches 16%.

Vehicle Registration

Prior to titling and registering your vehicle in the state, you must:
- Have a North Carolina driver's license;
- Have proof of state minimum liability insurance;
- Pay any due vehicle property taxes.

Normal one-time registration fee is $40. The annual license plate fee for a car is $28, motorcycle $18 and camping trailer $11. Truck plate fees range from $43.50 to $51.60. Personalized plates cost an extra $30 a year.

Vehicle Inspection

All motor vehicles except antique vehicles registered in the state must be inspected annually at a licensed inspection station. Many car dealerships, service stations, garages and quick oil change businesses serve as inspection stations. There are a total of about 7,500 inspection stations in the state. Inspections can be performed up to 90 days from the vehicle's registration date. Inspection certifications are now handled electronically, and no sticker is affixed to the window. Currently 48 counties in the state, including Buncombe, Henderson and Haywood and a few other counties in Western North Carolina, require emission inspections along with safety inspections; the other 52 counties require only a safety inspection. Combined emission/safety inspections in the 48 counties cost $30. Safety inspections in the 52 other counties cost $13.60. There is an additional fee of $10 to test tinted glass. Vehicles 35 years old and older do not require a safety inspection.

If you are moving to North Carolina, you do not have to have your vehicle inspected in NC until the time that the annual registration is required.

In cases where a vehicle is registered in North Carolina but is out of state when annual inspection and registration is due – for example, students or retirees living outside North Carolina for part of the year -- in most cases the owner can have the vehicle inspected in another state where vehicle inspection stations meet federal requirements and have that information faxed or mailed to the NC DMV.

Vehicle Property Taxes

North Carolina's property tax system requires counties and cities to assess the values of motor vehicles registered with DMV and to prepare tax bills. Property taxes vary by city and county, depending on the local property tax rate. You can estimate your annual vehicle property tax bill using an online estimator at https://edmv.ncdot.gov/TaxEstimator.

Beginning in 2013, the state began including local vehicle tax bills with the annual registration renewal. Both have to be paid before you can get your vehicle inspected.

Special or Unusual Rules for North Carolina Drivers

• All operators and occupants of motor vehicles must wear seat belts, unless there is medical condition or other special situation that prevents it.

• All operators and passengers of motorcycles must wear an approved helmet.

• Right turns at red lights are allowed, after a stop, unless a posted sign states that turns are not permitted.

• NC motorists are required to use headlights whenever they are using windshield wipers due to inclement weather.

• Texting or emailing is not allowed while operating a motor vehicle on a public roadway.

• Those under 18 may not use a mobile/cell phone while operating a motor vehicle on a public roadway.

• Tinted vehicle windows must allow at least 35% of light transmission.

• Moped or scooter (engine size 50 cc or less) operators at least 16 years old don't require a driver's license.

• Drivers must stop for stopped school buses with flashing read lights or a mechanical stop sign; vehicles in both directions must stop, even on four lane highways if the highways are not divided by a median.

• Children under 16 cannot ride in the bed of a pickup truck.

• Children under age 8 and weighing less than 80 pounds must be properly secured in a weight-appropriate child passenger restraint system. If the vehicle is equipped with a passenger-side front air bag and the vehicle has a rear seat, then a child under age 5 and weighing less than 40 pounds must be properly secured in the rear seat unless the child restraint system is designed for use with a front air bag system.

• So-called "good Samaritan" laws in NC protect persons who stop and render aid at the scene of an accident from civil liability except in the case of intentional wrongdoing or unruly conduct.

• Your driver's license will be suspended for 30 days if you are convicted of driving more than 15 mph faster than the posted limit; your license will be suspected for 60 days if you are convicted of a second offense of driving more than 15 mph over the posted limit within a year, or if you are also convicted of reckless driving on the same occasion. These are the case even if the infractions and convictions occurred in another state.

• DWI: If you are stopped and your blood alcohol level is 0.08 or higher, or if your mental or driving ability is impaired by drugs, your driving privileges are immediately suspended for 30 days. If you refuse to take a breath or blood test, your driver's license will be immediately suspended for 30 days, and the DMV will revoke your license for an additional 12 months. Additional convictions for DWI may result in license revocations of from one to four years, and, after third or fourth convictions, suspension may be permanent. If you are convicted of DWI while under a previous DWI revocation, the state may seize and sell your vehicle.

Voting and Voter Registration

Each of the 100 counties in North Carolina has a board of elections that oversees elections in that county. The **North Carolina State Board of Elections** *(441 North Harrington St., Raleigh, NC 27603, 919-733-7173, www.ncsbe.gov)* supervises the county election boards.

The **Buncombe County Board of Elections**, which oversees elections in Asheville and Buncombe County, is located at 35 Woodfin Street in Downtown Asheville. The mailing address is P.O. Box 7468, Asheville, NC 28802-7468, and the telephone number is 828-250-4200.

To register to vote in a North Carolina county, a person must meet the following qualifications:
- Must be a U.S. citizen.
- Must be a resident of North Carolina.
- Must be a resident of the county for at least 30 days prior to election day.
- Must be at least 18 years old or will be 18 by the date of the next general election.
- Must rescind any previous registration in another county or state.
- If previously convicted of a felony, the person's citizenship rights must be restored (must not be serving an active sentence, including probation or parole).

Voting Procedures

To vote, you must complete a voter registration application.

The application is available online in pdf format on the state board of elections website at www.ncsbe.gov. It is also available county board of elections offices, public libraries, high schools, college admission offices, NC Department of Motor Vehicles offices including driver's license offices and some other state government offices such as the Employment Security Commission. Forms also are available from individuals and groups that are conducting voter registration drives. Registration forms are available in English and Spanish.

You can deliver your voter registration form to the county board of elections in person or by mail, or you may fax or email your form, but if the application is for new registration or change of party affiliation, the county board of elections must receive your original signature within 20 days of the voter registration deadline for an election.

Generally, you must register at least 25 days in advance of the date of the election. Applicants who have met the voter registration deadline should expect to receive their voter card by mail within one to two weeks. The card will tell you the location of your voting place.

Currently, you are not required to bring the voter card with you to vote. However, beginning in 2016, thanks to the Republican-dominated *good!* legislature in Raleigh, North Carolina will require voters show a photo identification, such as a passport, driver's license or identification card issued by a driver's license office (the voter ID card is free) when they go to vote in person. As of this writing, the constitutionality of the voter ID law is being challenged in court.

Polling places are usually at schools, churches, libraries and other well-known places. The number of polling locations varies by county. Asheville and Buncombe County, for example, have around 75 voting locations.

Absentee and Early Voting

Any registered North Carolina voter can request a mail-in absentee ballot. This type of absentee voting allows a voter or a near relative or legal guardian to request that an absentee ballot be sent to the voter by mail. The voter may vote the ballot and return it to the county board of elections by mail or otherwise by the ballot return deadline.

Absent uniformed armed services members (and their eligible dependents) and U.S. citizens living outside of the United States may request an absentee ballot under the Uniformed and Overseas Citizens Absentee Voting Act.

Early voting allows registered voters to go in person to their county board of elections office (or to an alternative location, such as a public library or a designated polling place, to vote an absentee ballot. One-stop absentee voting is conducted starting on the second Thursday before an election and ends at 1 pm on the last Saturday before the election. Most elections in North Carolina are held on a Tuesday, The time allowed for early voting, which was reduced by the Republican-dominated legislature, which also enacted the voter ID law, also is being challenged in court.

Party Registration

There are only three recognized political parties in North Carolina for voter registration purposes: Democratic, Republican and Libertarian. Voter registration applicants may choose one of these political parties when completing a voter registration application, or they may choose to register as Unaffiliated. North Carolina has a semi-closed primary system. In a partisan primary, voters who are affiliated with a political party may only vote the partisan ballot for the party for which they are affiliated; they are closed to voting in another party's primary. Unaffiliated voters may vote in any recognized party's primary, but they may only vote in one party's primary.

Utilities

Utilities such as electricity, gas, telephone, garbage and sewerage services and their providers vary by location. Here are the major utilities and related suppliers in Asheville and Western North Carolina.

Electrical

Duke Energy *(800-452-2777, www.duke-energy.com)* is North Carolina's – and indeed the country's -- largest electrical utility company. Based in Charlotte, it is publicly held. It also produces electricity for millions of customers in Florida, South Carolina, Kentucky, Indiana and Ohio. The company also generates power in Canada and Latin America.

Duke Energy and its wholly owned subsidiary **Duke Energy Progress** *(800-452-2777, www.progress-energy.com)*, formerly Progress Energy, serve about 4 million households across North Carolina, including in the Asheville area and much of Western North Carolina.

The company has coal-fired, oil and gas-fired, nuclear, hydroelectric and some solar electrical generation plants. WNC also has a number of small electrical co-ops and municipally owned public utilities, mostly in rural areas. Coal-fired power plants typically provide about one-half of the electricity generation in North Carolina.

Duke has a 376-megawatt coal-fired plant in Skyland just south of Asheville, the largest generating plant in Western North Carolina. The site also includes two combustion turbines capable of producing 324 megawatts. This plant began commercial operation in 1964, with additions in 1971, 1999 and 2000. It has a **90-acre coal ash unlined storage site at Skyland**, but it is moving at least some of the coal ash to the Asheville Regional Airport to be used, after proper preparation, as fill. Environmentalists point to the potential risk of toxic ash spills when ash is stored in unlined chambers. Coal ash can contain such toxic chemicals as lead, arsenic, mercury and radioactive uranium, and these chemicals can contaminate local water supplies. Environmentalists point to the 2014 leakage of 39,000 tons of ash from a 27-acre pond at Duke's Dan River plant in north central North Carolina. Duke has agreed to pay $102 million in fines to settle criminal charges stemming from the Dan River plant coal ash spill.

Although no final decision has yet made, Duke officials have stated that they are considering closing the coal-fired Skyland plant.

At present, **there are no nuclear power plants in Western North Carolina.** The nearest nuclear plants to Asheville are Oconee 1, 2 and 3 in South Carolina, about 60 miles southwest of Asheville. There also are two nuclear plant complexes near Charlotte, about 90 miles southeast of Asheville. All are operated by Duke Energy.

In many cases, electrical service can be started and stopped on-line. Visit the website of the company that serves your home or business for information on how to start or change electrical service. Duke Energy charges a $15 connect fee for new customers, or a $15 move fee for existing customers. In some cases, depending on your credit history, it may also require a security deposit for new service. The company says you should allow three days to start service. Charges and start times for smaller utilities vary.

The average cost of residential electrical power in North Carolina is 11.8 cents per kilowatt-hour, slightly under the national average of 12.31 cents.

Current rate Meridian: 11.09¢ /KWh

Telephone

The telecommunications industry is changing rapidly, but currently **AT&T** *(888-757-6500 or 855-350-6010, www.att.com)* remains the primary regulated carrier for landlines in the Asheville area and Western North Carolina. No-frills plans start around $25 to $30 a month, but bundled plans with landline, long distance, internet, television, taxes, fees and other add-ons can run $100 to $200 depending on the plan you choose.

Cell Phone

Verizon *(www.verizonwireless.com)*, **AT&T** *(www.att.com)*, **T-Mobile** *(www.t-mobile.com)*, **U.S. Cellular** *(www.uscellular.com)* and **Sprint** *(www.sprint.com)* are the main mobile providers in Asheville and WNC, with Verizon having the largest share of market. Due to the mountain terrain and tower locations, reception varies greatly, often over even short distances. Sometimes, one house on a specific carrier will have good service while the house next door on the same carrier will have little or no reception. Although most wireless carriers have coverage maps on their websites, there is simply no way to predict cell service quality without checking your reception in a specific location.

Anecdotally, Verizon and U.S. Cellular provide the best reception in the Asheville area, but again service is very location-specific. T-Mobile arguably has the lowest rates.

Customer service at most cell providers ranges from awful to virtually non-existent. It recently took us nearly four hours talking with reps to activate a new phone on our Verizon family plan, after online activation failed.

Service plans are complex, change frequently and costs vary widely. Increasingly, wireless carriers offer prepaid or monthly plans with no contracts, but these plans usually do not offer any discounts on smartphones or other cell phones. T-Mobile is a leader in no-contract plans.

Natural Gas

PSNC Energy *(877-776-2427, www.psncenergy.com)* is a regulated utility that provides natural gas service via underground pipelines to about three dozens subdivisions and areas in Asheville, along with a few areas in Brevard, Waynesville and elsewhere in Western North Carolina.

Rates vary according to natural gas prices, but as of early 2014 PSNC residential rates were around $0.92 per therm in the summer and $1.01 per therm in winter, plus a $10 per month facilities charge, tax and other miscellaneous charges. A therm is approximately the energy equivalent of burning 100 cubic feet (often referred to as 1 CCF) of natural gas. How much natural gas you use depends on the size and energy efficiency of your home, what type of gas furnace, water heater and kitchen appliances you have, and of course on the current cost of natural gas. A guess is that a 2,000 sq. ft. home with gas furnace, gas water heater and gas stove, with average insulation, in Western North Carolina might use 1,500 to 2,000 therms per year.

∴ ~$1500 - 2000/yr

Propane

Some homes in Asheville and Western North Carolina use propane for heating, water heating and cooking. Propane is a by-product of the production of natural gas processing and petroleum refining. The liquefied propane is delivered to homes by truck and typically stored in 500-gallon tanks.

There are a number of propane companies in Asheville and WNC. Among the largest are **Suburban Propane** *(800-776-7263, www.suburbanpropane.com)* and **Blossman Gas** *(888-256-7762, www.blossmangas.com)*. Blossman, a regional supplier with locations in Virginia, the Carolinas, Georgia, Alabama and Mississippi, is headquartered in Asheville. As elsewhere, propane is also sold in small, portable tanks for use in gas barbecue grills. Butane is not used in this area because it is subject to freezing in winter.

Fuel Oil

Many homes in Western North Carolina use fuel oil (called #2 oil) for heating. Most oil companies are small and privately owned. They typically serve a single county area. Some also deliver kerosene (#1 oil) for heaters. Fuel oil for heating is usually stored in buried containers holding 500 gallons or more. Check the internet or the Yellow Pages for companies in your area. Fuel oil is basically just diesel fuel, usually without the additives in diesel for road use. Road diesel may also be blended differently depending on the weather and temperature. In a pinch, if you run out of oil you can go to a service station and buy five or ten gallons of diesel, and use that until you get a delivery of #2. The price of #2 fuel oil, which is dyed red to prevent its use on the road, is slightly lower than the price of diesel at service stations, but state and local sales taxes and perhaps a delivery charge are added.

Biodiesel, usually made from used cooking oil blended with diesel fuel, is available in Asheville, both for diesel vehicles and for home heating. It is manufactured by **Blue Ridge Biodiesel** *(109 Roberts St. River Arts District, Asheville, 828-253-1034, www.blueridgebiofuels.com)*. This heating oil works in all #2 oil furnaces without any modifications needed. Blue Ridge also supplies biodiesel to around a half dozen service stations in the Asheville area, along with distributors in several other states.

Water

Asheville has a municipal water system with three water treatment plants, 32 storage reservoirs, 40 pumping stations and around 1,700 miles of water lines.

Asheville's Water Resources Administration *(Asheville City Building, 828-251-1122, www.ashevillenc.gov/Departments/Water.aspx)* gets its water from a 22,000-acre watershed area around Asheville. Water rates include a $6 monthly base fee, plus a meter fee starting at $3.86 a month depending on the size of the meter, plus $3.81 per 100 cubic feet, about 748 gallons, of water used. A $55 service fee and a $100 deposit are required when establishing a new account. The $100 deposit may be waived if you are able to show you have good credit. The Asheville water system extends into parts of Buncombe County not in the Asheville city limits. A major issue with the Asheville-Buncombe water system is that many of its water lines are old, dating back to the early part of the 20th century, and line breaks occur fairly frequently.

Other towns and municipalities in Western North Carolina also have municipal water systems.

In rural areas, homeowners get their water either from mountain springs or wells. Spring water is preferred by most, because if the spring is strong, once you've prepared the spring, installed a reservoir (usually a concrete box) and laid the underground pipe, you have free water forever, even if the power is off, because most springs are situated higher than the house and use gravity to get water to the home. Wells require an electric pump, which typically must be replaced every 10 to 15 years, and electricity to run the pump.

It's also expensive to dig a well, since typically in this area you'll have to go down 200 to 800 feet or more to find water. Until you drill and find potable water, there's no guarantee that your well won't turn out to be a dry hole.

Some well drilling companies drill a second well at one-half the standard rate, if the first effort results in finding no drinking water. Drilling costs vary by location, but figure on paying $12 to $20 a foot in Western North Carolina, sometimes more. Thus, a 500-foot well may cost $6,000 to $10,000 to drill. In addition, set-up, pump and electrical costs will add another $2,500 or $3,000.

Many mountain people wouldn't think of drilling a well without hiring a local dowser to locate ground water, or doing the dowsing themselves.

Dowers use a Y-shape twig or twin metal rods. When the dowsing rods or stick move in a certain way, bending down or pulling together, that is supposed to indicate that this is a good place to drill. While some studies have found that dowsers have success rates in locating water no greater than chance, our view is that it doesn't hurt to try it.

The author borrowed a neighbor's copper dowsing rods, used them to locate a drilling spot and had the well drilled. At 250 feet, the driller hit a gusher, with more than 20 gallons a minute.

Sewerage

The **Metropolitan Sewerage District (MSD)** was created in 1962 for the purpose of constructing and operating facilities for the treatment and disposal of the sewage in the Asheville area. MSD *(2028 Riverside Dr., Asheville, 828-254-9646, www.msdbc.org)* provides sewerage services to Asheville city residents along with some areas in Buncombe County outside the Asheville city limits, including Biltmore Forest, Black Mountain, Swannanoa, Woodfin, Weaverville and parts of Enka-Candler and Fairview.

Rates for sewerage services in Asheville-Buncombe depend on usage but average around $28 a month. For a new home, a one-time set-up and facilities fee of $2,500 is charged. For hooking up to the system, there is a $750 tap fee and a charge of $2,200 if pavement is disturbed. Plan review, inspection and other fees can total as much as $1,000 or more. City residents are billed for water and sewerage services together in one bill.

Other towns and municipalities in Western North Carolina have their own sewerage systems.

However, nearly three-fourths of homes in WNC depend on individual sewage treatment and disposal systems. Much of the mountain land isn't suitable for conventional septic systems, due to steep slopes, proximity to streams or poor ground percolation. As a prospective property owner, you need to have an adequate septic system approved by the environmental health section of the county health department before a new home is allowed to be occupied or connected to electricity.

The septic tank and drainfield must be at least 100 feet from the drinking water supply; it should never be located upslope of your water supply. Septic systems are difficult to construct on slopes greater than 30% and may not function well on steep slopes.

Installation of a concrete septic tank, lines and drainfield typically costs around $6,000 to $10,000 in WNC, though costs vary considerably depending on location and type of system.

Garbage Service

Trash, garbage and recycling systems are a mish-mash in Western North Carolina. In some rural areas, there may be no trash pick-up, and you'll have to take it to a landfill yourself.

More urban areas have organized trash pick-up and recycling operations. Asheville has an automated collection system with curbside pick-up once a week. The day of the week varies depending on the area of the city where you live. Residents put their bagged garbage (no recycling items, brush, yard waste or construction debris) in 95-gallon rolling carts, which are picked up by a truck with a special lifting mechanism. One 95-gallon cart is provided for a monthly fee of $7, and additional carts can be obtained at $7 per cart per month. You are billed for garbage pick-up on your water bill. For more information, contact the City of Asheville Customer Service Division at 828-251-1122 or online visits www.ashevillenc.gov/Departments/Sanitation/GarbageCollection.aspx.

Curbside recycling in Asheville is also in effect. Recyclable items include household plastic, metal, cardboard and glass. Your recycling is placed in 95-gallon blue carts that are also picked up by trucks using automatic equipment. A few items, including light bulbs, styrofoam, plastic bags and pots and pans, are not accepted for recycling. Recycling is collected the same day of the week as garbage collection, except it is collected every other week. You can find out which week your recycling is collected by calling Curbside Management at 828-252-2532 or visit the website www.ashevillenc.gov/Departments/Sanitation/Recycling.aspx. There also are four drop-off recycling centers in Asheville and Buncombe County.

Buncombe County contracts with private garbage haulers for garbage pick-up and recycling. Currently the contract company for the county is **WastePro** *(828-684-7790, www.wasteprousa.com)*. Waste Pro does not use automated trucks, so county residents can put their bagged garbage in any kind of garbage can and put recyclable materials in blue plastic bags.

A 95-gallon garbage cart can be rented for $3.50 per month. Most areas of the county have weekly pick-up for both garbage and recycling. The cost currently is $14.77 per month, plus cart rental if desired, billed quarterly.

The Buncombe County Solid Waste Management Facility, or landfill, is located at 81 Panther Branch Road in Alexander in the north end of the county. A transfer station, which accepts residential waste only, is located at 190 Hominy Creek Road near West Asheville. There is a charge for some kinds of garbage, yard waste and hazardous materials, while other materials, such as recycling, are accepted without charge. For information, call the landfill at 828-250-5462 or visit the Buncombe County website at www.buncombecounty.org/governing/depts/solidwaste/Default.aspx.

Some towns in Western North Carolina have their own municipal trash and recycling services, while some rural areas have contracted private services.

Internet, Cable and Satellite

AT&T *(www.att.com)* is the largest internet service provider (ISP) in Western North Carolina. DSL and U-Verse services are offered, depending on where you live. AT&T's U-Verse may not be available at your home, if your area doesn't have fiber optic cable. Download speeds range from under 3 to a maximum of 18 Mbps, and upload speeds are a maximum of 1.5 Mbps. Usually there's a one-year contract required, and prices range from around $30 to $50 per month, plus taxes and fees. AT&T offers bundled internet, TV and telephone services in some parts of WNC, starting at around $85 per month plus taxes and fees. With extra channels, fastest internet speeds and all those taxes and fees, you can pay much more, as much as $200 a month or more.

Charter Communications *(888-438-2427, www.charter.com)* offers cable, internet and phone services in Asheville and in much of the rest of Western North Carolina. Cable TV with around 125 channels starts at around $60 a month plus taxes and fees, and less if bundled with other services. Internet alone starts at $30 a month plus taxes and fees. Charter's internet is faster than AT&T's, with download speeds of up to 30 Mbps and uploads up to 4 Mbps. Bundled cable TV, internet and voice start at around $110 a month, plus taxes and fees. With extra channels, all the bells and whistles and those taxes and fees, you can pay much more, as much as $200 a month or more.

With both AT&T and Charter you may need modems and routers and other equipment to take full advantage of all the services including wi-fi. These may be included in the package or may cost extra. For some services, you'll need an installer to visit your home, and that's often a ton of fun.

Many residents of WNC, especially in rural areas, prefer satellite TV to cable. Both **DirecTV** *(855-641-5895, www.directv.com)* and **Dish Network** *(888-656-2461, www.dish.com)* are available in the region. As elsewhere, prices for a basic package start at around $25 to $30 a month, plus taxes and fees, but can go much, much, much higher for premium packages with multiple TVs and recorders. Contracts are required, usually 24 months. Both satellite providers also offer voice and internet bundles. However, satellite internet typically is much slower than other types, and there may be a latency problem (signals may take a few seconds to go back and forth). In 2014 AT&T reached an agreement to purchase DirecTV; as of this writing, the final merger of the companies is pending regulatory approval.

Due to the mountainous terrain of Western North Carolina, not all homes will be able to receive satellite reception. For example, the author's home near Asheville cannot receive DirecTV or Dish, due to a mountain that rises to the south behind the home; however, another home we use as guesthouse and office less than a quarter mile away can get both Dish and DirecTV. Typically, you have to have line of sight to satellites fairly low in the west or southwest sky. The satellite installer will test your reception before installing your system.

Snail Mail

As you'd expect, most residential addresses in cities and towns in Western North Carolina have home delivery of mail. However, in rural areas your mail may be delivered by a contract mail carrier, and you may have to erect a mailbox. (Caution: Rural mailboxes are favorite targets of youths on joy rides with a baseball bat!) In a few cases, there may be no home delivery at all in your area, and you'll have to get a post office box.

You can now change your snail mailing address online. Go to the United States Postal Service's site at https://moversguide.usps.comc. It's a good idea to send in the USPS form at least a week before your move. You may want to also directly notify your banks, credit card companies, and other important personal business and personal connections of your new address well in advance of your move.

Newspapers

You may decide to subscribe to home delivery of your new hometown newspaper, pay for online access or in a few cases get it free online or, in the case of giveaways, get a free paper copy. Here is contact information for the major newspapers in Western North Carolina. Not all weekly or monthly newspapers are listed here.

Asheville Citizen-Times *(14 O. Henry Ave., Asheville, NC 28801, 800-672-2472, www.citizen-times.com),* owned by Gannett ("with the emphasis on the net"), is the largest daily newspaper in the region. The Scene, a tabloid section devoted to local entertainment, is published on Friday. Daily circulation is around 58,000 and Sunday about 68,000. The on-line edition has a pay wall. Subscription rate for home delivery start at around $12 a month, and the on-line edition is $10 a month. Check with the newspaper on mail subscription rates.

Mountain Xpress *(2 Wall St., Asheville, NC, 28801, 828-251-1333,* *www.mountainx.com*) is a popular free alternative tabloid with extensive coverage of local politics, entertainment, restaurants, clubs and music. It is published weekly on Wednesday. Print circulation is around 25,000 at about 800 locations in Asheville and the region. The paper claims a total readership of 75,000. The on-line edition also is free. If you want to subscribe to the print edition by mail, send a check to Subscription Department, P.O. Box 144, Asheville, NC 28802. An annual subscription is $115, and a six-month subscription is $60.

Hendersonville Times-News *(106 Henderson Crossing, Hendersonville, NC 28792, 828-692-5763,* *www.blueridgenow.com*), is a daily formerly owned by the New York Times Company and now a part of the Halifax Media Group. It has a circulation of around 15,000. Subscription rate for both print home delivery and online access is about $18 a month.

Other Newspapers

Asheville Blade *(www.ashevilleblade.com)* is a progressive, labor-oriented online news publication that grew out of an effort to unionize *Mountain Xpress.*

Black Mountain News *(14 O. Henry Ave., Asheville, 800-672-2472,* *www.blackmountainnews.com)* is a weekly owned by the *Asheville Citizen-Times*. It primarily runs legal ads. Subscription rates to the *Asheville Citizen-Times* start at $12 a month for home delivery (including the Black Mountain News once a week) or $10 a month for online access.

Cherokee Scout *(89 Sycamore St., Murphy, NC 28906, 828-837-5832,* *www.cherokeescout.com)* is a weekly published on Tuesdays with news of Murphy and Cherokee County.

Graham Star *(774 Tallulah Rd., Robbinsville, NC 28771, 828-479-3383,* *www.grahamstar.com)* is a weekly published on Thursdays serving Robbinsville and Graham County. It has a circulation of around 3,500. The online edition is $20 a year, and print edition subscription rates vary.

High Country Press *(www.hcpress.com),* formerly a weekly print newspaper serving Boone and the surrounding area, is now a free web-only daily. The company also produces the print magazine, *High Country Magazine,* seven times a year and a seasonal *High Country Visitor Guide* three times a year.

Smoky Mountain News *(34 Church St. Waynesville, NC 28786, 828-452-4251, www.smokymountainnews.com)* is a free weekly paper published on Wednesday covering news in Waynesville, Sylva and surrounding areas. It distributes about 16,000 copies a week at 600 locations in Haywood, Jackson, Macon and Swain counties and on the Cherokee reservation. If you want to receive the paper by mail, an annual subscription is $65.

Tryon Daily Bulletin *(16 North Trade St., Tryon, NC 28782, 828-859-9151, www.tryondailybulletin.com)*, established in 1928, bills itself as the "world's smallest daily newspaper." It covers the town of Tryon and Polk County. The newspaper has reporters on staff, but many articles are contributed by readers. Annual subscription is $84.

Magazines

From all the magazines that are published here, you wouldn't know that people say print is dead. Here are a few of the local pubs:

The Laurel of Asheville *(46 Haywood St. #210, Asheville, NC 28801, 828-670-7503, www.thelaurelofasheville.com)* bills itself as a magazine of lifestyle and the arts. It is published monthly, and an annual subscription by mail is $36.

Plough to Pantry *(46 Haywood St., #210, Asheville, NC 28801, 828-670-7503, www.ploughtopantry.com)* is another quarterly magazine from *The Laurel* folks, this one about farm-to-table living in the NC mountains and foothills. It debuted in early 2015.

Rapid River Magazine *(85 N. Main St., Canton, NC 28716, 828-646-0071, www.rapidrivermagazine.com)* says it is Asheville's oldest arts and culture magazine. It was established in 1997. Annual subscriptions to the monthly magazine are $38.95.

Sophie Magazine *(www.sophiemagazine.com)*, focused on local women, is distributed free at various locations around the Asheville area.

Verve Magazine *(828-697-1414, www.vervemag.com)*, established in 2008, claims to cover "Asheville's most fascinating women." It is published monthly and is distributed free at some 400 area locations.

WNC Magazine *(33 Patton Ave., Suite 201, Asheville, NC 28801, 828-210-5030, www.wncmagazine.com)*, published every other month, covers local people, history, travel, dining, the arts and other subjects. Six issues by mail are $11.95.

WNC Woman *(P.O. Box 951, Marshall, NC 28753, 828-649-9555, www.wncwoman.com)* is a monthly magazine about women. It is distributed free at numerous locations throughout the region.

Medical and Other Records

If possible, before you move arrange to have your medical records, or copies of them, transferred from your from your former physicians and medical centers, to your new medical providers in Western North Carolina. Should a sudden medical emergency arise, you don't want any delay in getting access to your records. Many physician groups and hospitals in WNC, including the largest medical center in the region, Asheville's Mission Health Systems, which also owns many area physician practices, now have patient records in digital form, so transfers may, or at least should, be easy.

Don't forget to transfer your prescription drug records to a pharmacy in your new hometown. Remember that some drugs, such as opiates, are controlled, and it may not be possible to transfer the prescription; you may have to get a new prescription from your new physician, and in some cases, as with oxycodone (Percocet), your physician will have to give you a prescription on paper, and you will have to deliver the prescription in person to your pharmacist. *For more information on medical subjects, see the Health section.*

You may also want to transfer legal, accounting, tax and other records if you don't have them in your personal possession.

Banking and Finance

In Asheville and WNC you have a wide choice of options for your banking and other financial services, from large national and international banks to small local banks, savings and loans and credit unions. A number of these banking companies also own brokerage or investment advisory companies. Here's a sampling, not a comprehensive list:

National Financial Institutions

Bank of America *(www.bankofamerica.com),* the second largest bank holding company in the U.S. by assets, is headquartered in nearby Charlotte. It has more than $2 trillion in assets. Its Merrill Lynch division offers brokerage and investment banking services. Bank of America has 10 offices in the Asheville area and more than 50 within a 50-mile radius of Asheville.

Wells Fargo *(www.wellsfargo.com),* based in San Francisco, is the fourth largest banking firm in the U.S. with more than $1.5 trillion in assets. It expanded into North Carolina and the Southeast with its 2008 purchase of Charlotte-based Wachovia. Wells Fargo also acquired A.G. Edwards & Sons brokerage and financial advisors services.

Wells Fargo has 12 locations in the Asheville area and many others across Western North Carolina. The author has been banking with Wachovia since the 1960s, although in our opinion service has been in a decline since Wells Fargo took over. It is known for paying very low rates on savings and CDs.

Regional Financial Institutions

BB&T Bank *(www.bbt.com)* is a regional bank with around $200 billion in assets based in Winston-Salem, N.C. It has about 1,800 locations in a dozen states. Ten locations are in Western North Carolina including six in the Asheville area.

Capital Bank *(www.capitalbank-us.com)* is a Florida-based bank holding company with around $7 billion in assets with offices in five Southeastern states. It has three offices in the Asheville area.

Fifth Third Bank *(www.53.com)* is a Cincinnati-based regional bank with more than $110 billion in assets and five locations in Western North Carolina.

First Citizens Bank *(www.firstcitizens.com)* is a regional bank holding company headquartered in Raleigh with 13 locations in the Asheville area and other locations around Western North Carolina. First Citizens is among the 50 largest banks in the U.S. with $22 billion in assets. It operates in 17 states, mostly in the Southeast.

PNC Bank *(www.pnc.com)*, a large regional bank operating in 20 states, has six offices in the Asheville area. With around $300 billion in assets, it is the sixth largest bank in the U.S.

SunTrust Bank *(www.suntrust.com)* is an Atlanta-based regional bank with around $175 billion in assets. It operates in about a dozen states in the Southeast and Middle Atlantic states. SunTrust has eight locations in the Asheville area and around 13 total in Western North Carolina. The bank also owns Robinson-Humphrey, investment advisors.

TD Bank *(www.tdbank.com)*, a part of Toronto-Dominion Bank based in Toronto, Canada, operates in about 15 Eastern U.S. states. It has 15 locations in Western North Carolina, including six in the Asheville area.

Local Financial Institutions

Asheville Savings Bank *(www.ashevillesavingsbank.com)* has 13 banking centers in Buncombe, Henderson, McDowell, Madison and Transylvania counties. The local bank, now a public company, has assets of around $800 million.

A personal note: The author has a soft spot for Asheville Savings Bank, as it was one of the first clients of an advertising agency I co-owned in the 1970s. At that time it was a mutual S&L known as Asheville Federal, run by James Westall and family, who were, to their probable regret, related to Asheville author Thomas Wolfe.

Home Trust Bank *(www.hometrustbanking.com)*, formerly Clyde Savings and Loan, has 16 locations in Western North Carolina, including five in the Asheville area. It has about $2 billion in assets.

Mountain Credit Union *(www.mountaincu.com)* is a small local credit union with seven locations in Western North Carolina, including three in the Asheville area. It tends to pay slightly higher interest rates on deposits than most local banks. Full disclosure: My family has some retirement and other accounts with this credit union.

Churches and Other Religious Organizations

There are more than 300 churches, synagogues, temples and other religious houses of worship in Asheville and Buncombe County alone, with many more around Western North Carolina. Whether your inclination is **Protestant, Catholic, Islamic, Jewish, Buddhist, Hindu, Wiccan** or other, you'll find many choices in the region. Baptists, with more than 100 churches, and Methodists, with more than 60, are the two largest denominations. It's believed that **Biltmore Baptist Church** *(35 Clayton Rd., Arden, 828) 687-1111, www.biltmorebaptist.org)*, based in Arden, with more than 6,000 attendees weekly, is the largest church in the area. There also are MeetUp and other groups for atheists, agnostics, skeptics and others who don't believe.

TAXES IN NORTH CAROLINA

Here's an overview of the taxes you'll pay in North Carolina, and specifically in Asheville and Western North Carolina. Keep in mind that taxation is a complex matter and that the author is not a tax expert. Consult with a tax or estate attorney, accountant or other professional for assistance on your own tax situation in North Carolina.

Since personal and business tax situations vary so much, it's difficult to draw a general conclusion. However, many analysts put the state and local tax burden in North Carolina as somewhere in the middle of all states, neither in the lowest nor the highest tier.

For example, in its latest available ranking of the total state and local tax burden in each state by the Tax Foundation, North Carolina was ranked #28, pretty much in the middle of all states, with a total per capita tax burden of $3,535. That compares to $6,984 in #1 Connecticut and $2,625 in #50 Mississippi. The Tax Foundation is an independent but conservative-leaning tax policy research organization and think-tank based in Washington, D.C.

In 2012 *Kiplinger* magazine also put North Carolina in the middle "mixed" level for retirees in terms of taxation, not in the 10 most tax-friendly states for retires (in order from most-friendly: Alaska, Wyoming, Georgia, Arizona, Mississippi, Delaware, Nevada, Louisiana, South Carolina and Florida) nor among the 10 least tax-friendly states (in order from least-friendly: Rhode Island, Vermont, Connecticut, Minnesota, Montana, Oregon, Nebraska, California, New Jersey and New York).

State Income Taxes

All but seven states –Alaska, Florida, Nevada, South Dakota, Texas, Washington and Wyoming -- have state income taxes. Two other states, Tennessee and New Hampshire, tax only dividends and interest, not wages and other earned income.

North Carolina's new Republican-dominated state government had as one of its **key goals the reduction of the state's income tax,** especially for corporations and wealthy individuals. In 2013, the legislature succeeded in passing a sweeping revision in state income tax law, changing from a progressive rate system where higher income individuals paid more to a flat rate system where everyone, from a poor fast-food worker to a highly paid corporate executive, pay the same flat rate.

The biggest change was to drop the state's top income tax rate of 6% to 7.75%, depending on income, to a **flat rate for everyone of 5.8% in 2014 and 5.75% in 2015.** The corporate flat tax rate is 6%, down from 6.9%.

In addition, the **new state tax law raises the standard deduction starting in 2014 from $6,000 to $15,000 for (heterosexual) married persons filing jointly,** $12,000 for head of household, $7,500 for singles and $7,500 for married persons filing separately. However, itemized deductions are limited. Charitable contributions deduction may not exceed the federal limit, and combined mortgage interest and real estate property taxes may not exceed $20,000.

North Carolina GOP leaders say tax changes that took effect in 2014 will simplify returns, create jobs and keep more money in people's wallets. Critics say the new rules will reduce funds for schools and widen the gap between haves and have-nots.

It certainly is true that North Carolina's tax structure, especially as it pertains to businesses, was due for some reform. In 2013, the conservative-leaning Tax Foundation rated North Carolina's business climate as the 7th worst in the U.S., mainly due to the state's tax structure. However, the Tax Foundation concluded that when the changes enacted in 2013 are put in effect, the state could move way up in the ratings, to as high as 17th best for business climate.

Of course, the Tax Foundation's ratings are only one of many ways to evaluate the state's business climate. For example, in 2013 *Forbes* ranked North Carolina as the #4 best state in which to do business. In recent years the magazine also ranked Raleigh and Durham in the top 10 cities in the country to do business, and ranked Charlotte and Asheville in the top 30.

CNBC in 2013 rated North Carolina as the 12th best state for business, while *Area Development* magazine rated North Carolina as #5 and Chief Executive website rated the state #3.

A comprehensive study by the N.C. Justice Center's Budget and Tax Center of North Carolina's sweeping income tax changes that went into effect in 2014 concluded that 80% of North Carolinians will pay more in state income taxes than they did previously, despite the lower top tax rate. The tax reform package eliminates an earned income tax credit that benefited lower income workers. It also eliminates several exemptions and deductions that benefited middle class taxpayers, including a popular program that allowed families a deduction on pre-tax income put into a college savings account.

One of the most surprising changes, given the Republican regime's claimed pro-business stance, was the **elimination of a tax deduction of up to $50,000 on profits of small businesses, or up to $100,000 for married persons filing jointly, if both were small business owners or professionals.** This deduction saved many small business owners and professionals such as attorneys, dentists and physicians who file Schedule Cs on their federal taxes thousands of dollars in state income taxes. The deduction had been in effect for tax years 2012 and 2013.

According to an analysis by the legislature's own Fiscal Research Division, a married couple with two children making $20,000 a year will go from receiving a $222 tax refund in 2013 to owing $40 in 2014, a net swing of $262. On the other hand, a married couple with two children making $250,000 will get a $2,318 tax cut in 2014.

No city in North Carolina has a city income tax.

For more information on North Carolina income and other related taxes: *North Carolina Department of Revenue, P.O. Box 25000, Raleigh, NC 27640-0640, 877-252-3052 or 252-467-9000, www.dornc.com.*

Estate and Inheritance Taxes

To attract and keep more extremely wealthy residents, **North Carolina's estate tax was repealed in mid-2013,** retroactive to January 1, 2013. Formerly, the state's estate tax applied to estates of more than $5.25 million and imposed taxes of up to 16% on the excess over that figure. Federal estate taxes (with an exemption for estates of under $5.25 million) still apply. North Carolina also has **no inheritance tax.**

Social Security and Pension Taxes

Like most states, North Carolina **does not tax income received by individuals from Social Security**. However, the federal government does tax up to 85% of income from Social Security, depending on the taxpayer's total income. North Carolina formerly had an exclusion of $4,000 on out-of-state government pensions and a $2,000 exclusion on private pensions, but these tax breaks were eliminated beginning in 2014.

Sales Taxes

All but five states – Alaska, Delaware, Montana, New Hampshire and Oregon -- have state sales taxes. North Carolina's **statewide sales tax is 4.75%,** and in addition counties and municipalities charge **local sales taxes** and in some cases special transportation taxes.

These local sales taxes are added to the state sales tax rate. Sales taxes apply to a wide range of products and services. In 2014, the reach of sales taxes was increased by the Republican-dominated legislature to include admission to movie theaters, museums, live performances and college and professional sports events.

In the city of **Asheville and in Buncombe County, which levy a 2.25% local tax, the total state and local sales tax is 7%.** It is slightly lower in neighboring Henderson and Madison counties, as well as in most other counties in Western North Carolina, at 6.75%. Statewide, total sales tax rates range from a low of 6.75% to a high of 7.50%.

Most **grocery food items** are subject only to a 2% state sales tax. Items such as candy and soft drinks are charged the regular state and local sales tax. **Prescription drugs** are exempt from all sales taxes.

When you buy **a new or used car or truck,** whether from a dealer or from an individual, you pay a 3% state tax on the sales price, called a **highway use tax** or car tax.

If you buy a new or used car in another state, bring it to North Carolina and register it here, you must pay the 3% NC tax. Most of this tax is used to maintain and improve roads in the state. **Aircraft and boats** are also taxed at a 3% rate, up to a maximum of $1,500 tax. **Modular or mobile homes** are taxed at a rate of 4.75%. Local taxes are not added to these tax rates.

For more information on North Carolina sales taxes: *North Carolina Department of Revenue, P.O. Box 25000, Raleigh, NC 27640-0640, 877-252-3052 or 252-467-9000, www.dornc.com.*

Real Estate Property Taxes

Real property taxes vary from county to county, with additional rates for certain cities or school districts within each county, so it is impossible to cover the rates that apply all over Western North Carolina.

In general, however, **residential property is assessed based on 100% of the appraised market value.** The appraised value is supposed to reflect market value, but often the market value as proven by an actual sale and the appraised value differ. By law, revaluations must be done at least every eight years but may be done more frequently. Median property tax on the state's median home value of $155,500 is $1,209, according to the Tax Foundation.

Here is a list of the basic annual property tax rate in WNC counties in 2013. It does not include additional rates imposed by certain municipalities, fire districts, school districts or others. The rate is per $100 of value.

Thus, if the tax rate is 0.5690, the base rate in Buncombe County, is 56.9 cents per $100. For property with a market value of $100,000 the tax would be $569 per year, a $200,000 property would be taxed at $1,138 and a $500,000 property at $2,845. Fire and school district taxes could increase the total tax amount in some areas of the county.

Buncombe:	.5690
Cherokee:	.5200
Graham:	4600
Haywood:	.5413
Henderson:	.5136
Jackson:	.2800
Macon:	.2790
Madison:	.5200
McDowell:	.5500
Polk:	.5175
Swain:	.3600
Transylvania:	.4369
Watauga:	.3130
Yancey:	.5000

The city of Asheville imposes an annual city property tax rate of an additional .460 per $100 of appraised market value, on top of the basic Buncombe County rate of .5690. In addition, there is an Asheville schools tax of .150 per $100 and a culture and recreation tax of .035. **The total for an Asheville homeowner is 1.214 per $100.** Thus, a house within the city limits of Asheville appraised at $100,000 would be taxed at $1,214, a $200,000 home taxed at $2,228 and a $500,000 home taxed at $6,070.

Property taxes in Asheville and Buncombe County are due January 6. After that, interest on the past due amount is charged. The interest rate varies year to year.

There are **exemptions** on property taxes for churches and charitable 501c(3) organizations.

Property tax deferments are available for property used for **farming, horticulture and forestry.** Such property is taxed at its "present-use value," what the property is appraised for as farmland, land for growing fruits, vegetables or flowers, or timberland. This present-use value is usually significantly less than true market value.

To quality, horticultural land must be a minimum of 5 acres, agricultural land a minimum of 10 acres and forestland a minimum of 20 acres, and there are other requirements, such as in the case of timberland a forest management plan prepared by a registered forester. There also is a 50% deferment for designated historical properties. If property in one of these deferred programs is sold or loses its deferment for any reason, deferred taxes become due for the current year plus three previous years, plus interest for all prior years.

Low-income seniors and the disabled are eligible for reductions or limitations in property taxes, regardless of where in the state they live. To qualify for the elderly or disabled property tax break, a homeowner must be at least 65 years old or totally and permanently disabled, with income of no more than $27,100 for the previous tax year. The program excludes the first $25,000 or 50% of the assessed value of the home, whichever is greater, from taxation. North Carolina also limits property taxes to 4% of an owner's income for those 65 years and older who make less than $27,100 a year, and to 5% for those making between $27,100 and $40,650.

Motor vehicles, certain personal property such as boats and campers and business personal property such as computer equipment is also taxed by the counties, using different rates than real estate property.

For more information on local property taxes, contact the property tax office in the county in which the property is located. For Asheville and Buncombe County: *Buncombe County Tax Department, 35 Woodfin St., Asheville, NC 28801, 828-250-4910, www.buncombecounty.org.*

Motor Vehicles Personal Property Tax

Motor vehicles registered in North Carolina are valued by year, make and model in accordance with the "NC Vehicle Valuation Manual" used by all 100 counties in North Carolina. They are then taxed as personal property. Motor vehicle property taxes and annual registration renewals are now billed by the Division of Motor vehicles and must be paid together by the due date. The due date depends on when your vehicle registration expires.

Taxes and registration fees can be paid by check or online. Your motor vehicle must pass inspection before you can pay the fees and register your vehicle for the new year. The inspection must be within 90 days of the registration due date.

For information on motor vehicle taxes and registration, contact your county's property tax department, or: *N. C. Division of Motor Vehicles, 3148 Mail Service Center, Raleigh, NC 27699, 919-715-7000, www.ncdot.gov.*

Intangibles Tax

North Carolina once was one of only a few states that had an "intangibles tax," a tax on the value of stocks, bonds, savings accounts and mutual funds. However, the **intangibles tax was repealed** in 1995.

Gasoline Taxes

North Carolina's **gasoline tax is the highest in the Southeast but about average for the country** as a whole. The NC state gasoline tax is 37.6 cents per gallon, not including federal gas taxes. Federal taxes currently are 18.4 cents per gallon for gasoline and 24.4 cents per gallon for diesel. Diesel fuel gets the same NC state tax rate as gasoline. The state's fuel tax rate changes from year to year, in response to the wholesale price of fuel. The state's tax rate has dropped slightly from 38.9 cents per gallon in 2012, the highest rate ever. In 2015, legislative initiatives and the formula used to compute state gas tax rates suggest the tax will be reduced at least temporarily.

Hotel Taxes

Lodging properties in North Carolina charge the state and local sales tax and, in addition, many local areas levy a special **room occupancy tax.** Hotel or room taxes in Asheville and Buncombe County are the 7% total sales tax plus 4% local room occupancy tax, for a total of 11% tax on the hotel room rate. The 4% local occupancy tax mostly goes to fund tourism promotion.

Restaurant Taxes

Prepared food sold in restaurants or for take-out is charged the combined state and local sales tax. In a few areas, there's an extra meals tax. For example, in Charlotte diners are hit with regular sales tax plus a 1% meals tax. At present, there are no additional meal taxes in Asheville or Western North Carolina.

"Sin" Taxes

North Carolina, with its history as a top tobacco growing and cigarette making state has **one of lowest tax rates on cigarettes in the country, at 45 cents a pack**.

Missouri has the lowest tax, 17 cents a pack. Compare that to taxes of $6.16 a pack in Chicago and $5.85 a pack in New York City (these are combined state and city taxes.)

The state has a less lenient approach to alcohol taxes. In North Carolina, liquor is sold only in state-operated ABC stores, and prices are the same across the state. There is a 30% state excise tax on liquor sold in ABC stores – the excise tax is figured into the retail price of the booze. In addition, a state sales tax of 7% applies to the retail sales price. Liquor sold by ABC outlets to bars and restaurants that offer liquor by the drink has an extra tax of $3.75 per 750 ml bottle.

For wine, North Carolina imposes a $1 per gallon excise tax, and $1.11 if the alcohol level is 17% or more. Again, the excise tax is figured into the price of the bottle on the shelf. This compares with a median excise tax per gallon in the U.S. of 72 cents. Standard state and local sales taxes also are charged on retail wine sales.

For beer, the state imposes a 62 cents per gallon excise tax. This compares with a median excise tax per gallon in the U.S. of 20 cents. Standard state and local sales taxes also are charged on retail beer sales.

State excise taxes on spirits, wine and beer are in addition to federal excise taxes.

North Carolina's Share of Federal Government Payments

A 2014 study by WalletHub, a personal finance social networking site, found that North Carolina citizens received $1.34 in federal benefits for every $1 they paid to the federal government in taxes. Thus, North Carolinians got a positive "return on investment" of 34%. By contrast, New Yorkers got only 79 cents in federal benefits for every dollar paid in federal taxes, and Californians received just 94 cents. However, neighboring South Carolina citizens received a whopping $7.89 in federal benefits for every dollar they paid, and Floridians received $4.57.

Generally, the WalletHub study concluded that Red States (those that tend to vote Republican) get a bigger share of federal funds that do Blue States (those that tend to vote Democratic).

This usually correlates to lower state taxes. "The more dependent a state is on the federal government, the less likely it is to charge high tax rates," WalletHub said.

CRIME AND SAFETY IN ASHEVILLE AND WNC

Crime rates are low in most small towns and rural areas in Western North Carolina – shown here is Biltmore Lake (formerly Enka Lake) in the western part of Buncombe County

Crime is everywhere. The good news is that crime rates in the four-county Asheville Metro area and throughout most of Western North Carolina are lower than the average for the United States as a whole and for the state of North Carolina.

Statewide, according to the NC State Bureau of Investigation, the crime rate per 100,000 people of Crime Index offenses reported to law enforcement agencies throughout North Carolina decreased 7.0% during 2013, the last full year for which there are reported statistics, when compared to the figures reported in 2012.

The rate of violent crime (which includes murder, rape, robbery, and aggravated assault) decreased 5.4% statewide. Individually, the murder rate decreased 3.8%, the rape rate decreased 10.2%, the robbery rate decreased 1.9%, and the aggravated assault rate decreased 6.4%.

In Buncombe County, however, the overall crime rate increased by Txn MS
1% in 2013 from 2012 and 7% in Asheville.   421

According to the Federal Bureau of Investigation for 2012, the last
year for which comprehensive data are available, the rate of violent crimes   MS
(homicides, robbery, rape and assault) was 225 per 100,000 population in the   276
Asheville MSA (Buncombe, Henderson, Madison and Haywood counties.)
For the U.S. as a whole, the rate was 387 per 100,000 and for North Carolina   NO
353 per 100,000.   950

Thus, violent crime rate in the Asheville area was about 42% lower
than in the country as a whole, and 36% lower than statewide. In 2012, the
Asheville Metro had a total of 976 violent crimes, while the country had   MET
more than 1.2 million and the state about 34,500.   prop

For property crimes (burglary, theft, auto theft and arson) the   crime
Asheville Metro area also has a lower rate than the U.S. and North Carolina,   2015:
but the differences are less striking. The property crime rate in the four-   5402
county Asheville Metro, FBI 2012 statistics show, is 2,802 per 100,000, just   per
2% lower than the national rate and 17% lower than the state average.   100,000

The crime rates for most small towns and rural areas in Western
North Carolina also are lower, often much lower, than national and state
averages.

The city of Asheville had in 2012, and in most other years, a higher
rate of both property and violent crime than does the four-county metro area.
In part at least this is due to the fact that each workday some 40,000 people
commute to work in the city. In addition, the city gets close to 3 million
visitors a year. All these extra people are magnets for crime. Even so,
Asheville city has a lower violent crime rate than a number of other cities in
the state, including Charlotte, High Point, Wilmington and even nearby
Hendersonville.

The bottom line is that most residents of the Asheville area and the
rest of Western North Carolina are not unduly concerned about crime. They
take the standard precautions – night lighting, locking doors and windows
when away from home, perhaps having a security alarm system or a dog that
barks at unknown visitors (or in rural areas, watch guinea fowl or geese) –
but with the exception of residents of a few blighted, low-income and drug-
infested areas, local citizens say they feel safe.

Local Guns Laws

North Carolina state law generally makes is easy for residents to buy
and carry rifles, shotguns and handguns.

There are no laws that require a license to buy or carry a "long gun" such as a rifle or shotgun, or that require that the long gun be registered. However, permits are required to buy a handgun or to carry a concealed handgun.

In general, North Carolinians are permitted to carry rifles, shotguns and handguns if they are not concealed. To carry a concealed handgun, an individual must get a concealed carry permit from the sheriff of his or her county, pay a fee of $5 and take a short course on handgun safety. In order to get that permit, residents undergo a background check, using state and federal databases.

Also, in order to buy a handgun, whether from a licensed dealer or a private individual, North Carolinians are supposed to obtain a pistol purchase permit from their local county sheriff or else already hold a concealed handgun permit. Fully automatic firearms, short-barreled shotguns and suppressors are legal to own as long as federal Department of Alcohol, Tobacco and Firearm regulations are followed.

ECONOMY OF ASHEVILLE AND THE MOUNTAINS

The economy of the four-county (Buncombe, Madison, Henderson and Haywood) metro Asheville, with a population of about 435,000, is diversified, with its main elements being **health care (the largest sector locally), government, tourism and hospitality, professional and business services, manufacturing and retailing/wholesaling.** The economy of the rest of Western North Carolina varies greatly from county to county.

While the Asheville area suffered, as did most of the rest of the country, from the severe recession that began in 2007-2008, the economy is rebounding strongly. As of the end of 2014, Asheville/Buncombe had the lowest unemployment rate – around 4% -- of any urban area in North Carolina, significantly lower than the state and national averages.

The unemployment rate dropped almost 2.5 percentage points in 2013 and another 1 percentage point in 2014. In some recent periods, the Asheville area has been creating jobs at the fastest rate in the state. Worker earnings growth surged in 2014, up an average of 6.2% in Asheville, far outpacing the national average of 2.2% and statewide average of 1.1%. Real estate sales and building activity are increasing at double-digit rates, though they are not yet back to the levels of 2004 to 2006.

Gross Domestic Product

The Gross Domestic Product (GDP) – that is, the total of goods and services produced within the area annually, including profits and income generated by companies and governments, all wages, salaries, profits, investment, dividend and interest income, and so on, of the four-county metro Asheville area – is around $15 billion, of which about $12 billion comes from the private sector.

Population and Demographics

According to the 2010 U.S. census, the Asheville Metropolitan Statistical Area (MSA), consisting of Buncombe, Henderson, Haywood and Madison Counties, had 424,858 people, making it the 117th largest MSA in the country. The population grew 15.1% from 2000 to 2010, a significantly faster growth rate than the national average but slightly slower than the state of North Carolina as a whole.

The population of the entire Western North Carolina mountains region, stretching from the Tennessee line to the edge of Piedmont North Carolina, is more than 1.4 million, spread out over an area of around 11,000 square miles, about the size of the state of Massachusetts.

Updated for the latest available projections, generally 2013-2014, populations are estimated as follows:

Asheville MSA:	438,000 (118th market)
City of Asheville (within city limits):	88,000
Buncombe County (including Asheville):	248,000
Henderson County:	110,000
Haywood County:	59,000
Madison County:	21,000
Western North Carolina Region:	1,450,000
State of North Carolina:	9,944,000

The median average age in Asheville-Buncombe is 41, above the state average of 37. A little over 16% of the Asheville-Buncombe population is 65 or over, while 23% are under age 20. About 87% of the Buncombe population is white, 7% of Hispanic ethnicity, 6% black, 3% of mixed race and 1% Asian. (Numbers are rounded and do not total 100%.)

In Asheville-Buncombe, the highest level of education achievement of the population 25+ is as follows: about 12% of the population have graduate degrees, 21% have four-year college degrees, 9% have two-year associate degrees and 26% have high school degrees, while 12% did not finish high school.

The four-county metro area currently has more than 57,000 students in primary and secondary schools, of which about 53,000 are in public schools and the rest in private and parochial schools.

The mountain region in and around Asheville has some 60,000 students enrolled in universities, colleges and community colleges. Most of these students are in the Asheville metro area at about a dozen tertiary schools and in Boone, home of Appalachian State University *(see Colleges and Schools section for more information.)*

Median household income in the four-county Asheville metro during the period 2008-2012 was $44,206, slightly below the state median of $46,410 and the national median of $51,517.

Tourism is big business in Asheville and WNC – shown here is the Omni Grove Park Inn, a mountain resort for more than a century, photo by Rose Lambert-Sluder

Employment

Of 205,000 employed workers (private and government) in the four-county metro area civilian labor force in 2014 about 19% were employed in health care and education, 16% in retailing and wholesaling, 16% in government, 13% in tourism and hospitality, 11% in manufacturing, 11% in professional and business services, 4% in construction, 3% in finance, 3% in transportation and 1% in information services. (Numbers rounded and do not total 100%.)

The unemployment rate for the Asheville metro area in early 2015 was 5%, lowest of any urban area in North Carolina and below the state and national rates. The unemployment rates for Asheville and Buncombe County, excluding surrounding counties that are in the Asheville MSA, were both below 5%.

The Asheville metro area began emerging from the recession in 2010. By the end of 2012, in terms of job creation Asheville was one of the fastest growing major urban areas in North Carolina, with employment growth higher than the state and national averages.

The area created almost 4,000 net new jobs in 2012, up 2.3% over 2011, another 4,500 jobs in 2013 and about 4,000 in 2014. Health care, tourism and professional/business services dominated job growth. As the health, education, tourism and commercial hub of the region, Asheville had seen strong growth in these sectors. The largest employer in the state west of Charlotte is Mission Hospitals.

The number of manufacturing firms in the Asheville metro area now is actually slightly higher than 20 years ago, but manufacturing employs far fewer workers. In 1990, the Asheville area had more than 32,000 factory jobs, or about one-fourth of the local workforce. Today, there are around 20,000 manufacturing jobs, representing around a 10th of local employment. Some of the new manufacturing jobs are in areas not usually associated with the South, such as craft beer making, wine distilling, mountain bike components manufacturing and specialty foods processing. Manufacturing still offers the best wages, with an average weekly paycheck locally of around $900 in 2012, compared with an average of $649 overall.

By 2014 the hospitality industry (hotels and restaurants) and retailing also were seeing growth. While service jobs are growing, wages tend to be low. About 56% of the region's retail sales take place in Buncombe County.

Western North Carolina has a number of niche sectors associated with hospitality and real estate, including summer camps --there are more than 60 summer camps for boys and girls in WNC -- retirement communities and senior active living communities, snow skiing resorts, river rafting and tubing outfitters, crafts schools and religious meeting and convention centers.

The four-county Asheville metro area has about 13,600 private businesses, of which around 7,300 are in Buncombe County. The vast majority of businesses in the area are small. Only about 200 Asheville area businesses have 100 or more employees, and about 95% of businesses in the area have fewer than 50 employees. The annual payroll in the in the Asheville metro is around $4.6 billion.

Largest Employers

Here are the largest employers in the metro area, with an estimate of employees. Employment levels can vary from year to year and even from month to month and that employment may be spread out among several cities and counties.

Mission Hospitals, 8,500
Buncombe County Schools, 4,000
Ingles Markets, 3,000
Buncombe Country Government, 2,500

Biltmore Company, 1,900
City of Asheville, 1,800
Henderson County Public Schools, 1,700
Charles George Veterans Affairs Medical Center, 1,500
CarePartners Health Services (Mission-affiliated), 1,200
Evergreen Packaging, Haywood, 1,200
Pardee Hospital, Henderson, 1,200
Park Ridge Hospital, Henderson, 1,100
Haywood County Public Schools, 1,050
State of North Carolina, 1,000
A-B Tech, 1,000
Walmart, 1,000
Omni Grove Park Inn, 900
Asheville City Schools, 750
MedWest Haywood, Health Care, 725
Eaton Corp., 700
Borg-Warner Turbo, 650
Thermo-Fisher Scientific, 500
UNC-A, 500
Guthy Renker Fulfillment Services, 500
Sitel, A Subsidiary of Onex Corp., 500
MB Haynes Corp., 500
Arvoto Digital Services, 500

Agriculture in Western North Carolina
Strawberries and tomatoes have replaced tobacco as the money crop in Western North Carolina. Vegetables, many grown naturally or organically, are becoming increasingly important on small farms in the mountains. Small farmers also keep cattle, goats and chickens. In Henderson County, apples are a major crop, and the county is the state's number one producer of apples.

In the five years between 2007-2012, Western North Carolina bucked long-time state and national trends of losing agricultural acreage, with WNC adding more than 10,000 acres of farmland, according to the recently released U.S. Department of Agriculture 2012 Census of Agriculture. In the five years prior to that, WNC had lost 11,300 acres of family farms.

The farm-to-table and organic farming movements have reinvigorated farming in Western North Carolina – photo by Sheila M. Lambert

Much of this gain in farming is due to the local food, farm-to-table movement. Entrepreneurs and small natural or organic farmers have started small farms around Asheville and WNC that sell directly to the consumer or to restaurants and supermarkets.

According to Appalachian Sustainable Agriculture Project, an Asheville-based local farm advocacy group, in 2013, WNC consumers spent more than $170 million on local farm products, a 42% increase over the previous year. By contrast, on a national basis direct sales from farms has been flat.

Direct sales made through tailgate markets and farm stands have increased by more than 60% in WNC, according to ASAP's Local Food Research Center, from $5 million in 2007 to $8 million in 2012. The total likely has increased even more in 2013-2014. ASAP says nearly 700 farms in WNC sell direct. On a per capita base that is about four times higher than the average nationally.

Buncombe County has 1,060 farms, according to the 2012 Census, with 71,480 acres in farmland. The median average farm size is 32 acres. Farmland in Buncombe was worth an average of $8,601 per acre in 2012, Census figures show. The average value of crops per farm in Buncombe was about $51,000.

Economic Trends

Here, based on local, regional and national forecasts, are our predictions of economic trends over the next several years in Asheville and Western North Carolina:

• Economic recovery is solidly underway in most key areas of the Asheville metro and WNC areas, and growth will continue over the next several years.

• Real estate, both existing home and home building, is recovering strongly in most areas of WNC and will continue to build steam in 2015-2016.

• Job creation will continue to increase, with a further drop in the unemployment rate

• The tourism sector in the Asheville area and regionally in WNC will see additional growth in the future, led by the region's outdoor attractions and activities – several new hotels have opened or are planned in Downtown Asheville.

• The new Republican control of the state legislature and governorship will lead to a more business-friendly climate, at the cost of a more regressive tax system, lower funding for the university system and public schools and a weaker social safety net for the less fortunate.

• Asheville's restaurant, specialty coffee and craft beer markets will continue to grow but at a slower rate than in the immediate past.

• With the improving national economy, retirement and relocation to Western North Carolina will regain momentum, driven by quality of life issues.

• Asheville will see a moderate increase in "creative" employment – in fields such as video, digital publishing, advertising, media, art and crafts, design and other "knowledge industries."

• Asheville will continue to see growth in the health care field, with nearly 50,000 patient admissions per year at Mission Hospital alone, on top of 100,000 emergency room admissions – Mission announced plans in mid-2013 for a new $350 million tower to replace the old St. Joseph's Hospital facility.

• The regional and national convention market in Asheville has great potential but is limited by the lack of a first-rate convention and meeting center and performing venue.

HEALTH CARE

Access to quality medical care is an important consideration in any relocation decision, but especially so for older transplants or anyone with chronic health conditions.

Happily, this area has very good health care. Of course, you don't have access to multiple nationally known teaching hospitals as in Boston, Washington, D.C., Chicago or New York. Nor do you have world-class cancer care as in Dallas or heart care as in Cleveland. But given the realities of population, health care in Asheville and across the Western North Carolina region is far better than most would expect.

In Asheville, the medical hub of WNC, you have access to excellent, nationally recognized health care. The main hospital in the Asheville area is **Mission Hospitals** *(509 Biltmore Ave., Asheville, 828-213-1111, www.mission-health.org)*, a not-for-profit independent community hospital. It is the tertiary referral center for the Western North Carolina region.

Together with its sister campus, St. Joseph Hospital, (St. Joseph was merged into Mission in 1998) it is licensed for 800 hospital beds and currently has 730 beds. Mission has around 550 physicians on the medical staff licensed in some 50 specialties, plus more than 1,800 RNs. Mission currently has about 40,000 hospital admissions per year, and that's expected to grow to nearly 50,000 over the next 10 to 15 years. The hospital, on a 90-acre campus on Biltmore Avenue just south of the main Downtown area, has more than 8,500 employees in the region, making it the largest private employer in WNC. In mid-2013, Mission announced plans to build a new $350 million tower to replace aging facilities on the old St. Joseph Hospital campus. It recently opened a new cancer center and a new office complex.

The Mission system includes **Blue Ridge Regional Hospital** in Spruce Pine, **McDowell Hospital** in Marion, **Transylvania Regional Hospital** in Brevard and **Mission Children's Hospital** in Asheville. In 2013, **CarePartners Health Care,** a 1,200-employee company that offers rehabilitation services, affiliated with Mission.

Mission is the state's sixth largest hospital system and is the busiest surgical hospital in North Carolina. Its centers of excellence include cancer, heart, orthopedics, pediatrics, women's health and neurosciences.

Thomson Reuters has ranked Mission Health Systems as one of the top 15 hospital systems in the U.S. Based on surveys of recently discharged patients, about 84% of patients would recommend Mission to friends and family, well above state (71%) and national averages (70%). Only 2% of recent patients would not recommend Mission.

The **Mission Hospital Emergency Room** *(509 Biltmore Ave., 828-213-1948, www.missionmd.org)* is busy, with more than 100,000 visits a year, but generally patients are seen quickly. Drive to the main entrance off Biltmore Avenue and a valet attendant will park your car. Mission has a Level II trauma center. (Level I offers the highest level of surgical care whiles Levels IV and V offer the lowest.) Mission's is the only Level II center in Western North Carolina, with two helicopters for quickly transporting trauma patients to Asheville from 17 WNC counties. The nearest Level I trauma center is at **Carolina Medical Centers** *(www.carolinashealthcare.org/cmc)* in Charlotte.

In addition, **Sisters of Mercy Urgent Care** walk-in health care services have several locations in the greater Asheville area *(1201 Patton Ave., West Asheville, 828-210-2121; 1833 Hendersonville Rd., South Asheville, 828-274-1462; 155 Weaver Blvd., Weaverville, 828-645-5088; 22 Trust Lane, Brevard, 828-883-2600; www.urgentcares.org).* Anther doc-in-a-box clinic is **FastMed Urgent Care** (*160 Hendersonville Rd., Asheville, 828-210-2835; www.fastmed.org*).

Asheville also has a large veterans hospital, **Charles George VA Medical Center** *(1100 Tunnel Rd., 828-298-7911; www.ashevilleva.gov)* serving the approximately 100,000 military veterans living in Western North Carolina. Services at the VA hospital include hospital and home-based primary care, extended care and rehab, emergency services, pharmacy and hospice care. The hospital was named after a Cherokee Indian U.S. Army veteran, Charles George, a Medal of Honor recipient killed in Korea.

Hospitals in other areas around Asheville include **Margaret R. Pardee Memorial Hospital** in Hendersonville *(800 N. Justice St., Hendersonville, 828-790-9355; www.pardeehospital.org);* **Park Ridge Hospital** in Fletcher, *(100 Hospital Dr., Hendersonville, 828-684-8501; www.parkridgehealth.org);* **MedWest-Haywood** in Clyde *(262 Leroy George Dr., 828-456-7311; www.haymed.org)* and **MedWest-Swain** in Bryson City *(45 Plateau St., Bryson City, 828-488-2155; www.westcare.org).*

The Buncombe County area has more than **1,000 practicing physicians.** There are large practice groups in cardiology, arthritis, oncology, orthopedics, family medicine, endocrinology, dermatology, various surgical specialties and in other areas. Buncombe County also has more than **200 dentists.**

For those with limited English proficiency, the Western Carolina Medical Society operates and helps fund **Western North Carolina Interpreter Network** (WIN), which offers trained medical interpreter services in approximately two dozen languages.

With so many health care providers, it's impossible to provide information on more than a small fraction of the larger and better known practice groups, nor are we as laypersons capable of evaluating professionals, but here are some of the representative larger practices in various specialties. The fact that a practice is not listed here is in no way a negative reflection on that practice.

MEDICAL PRACTICES

Advanced Dermatology and Skin Surgery *(16 Medical Park Dr., South Asheville, 828-274-4880, www.advancedskindoctor.com)* is a dermatology practice with five physicians on staff.

Allergy Partners of Western North Carolina *(www.allergypartners.com)* is part of the nation's largest single-specialty practice in allergy, asthma and immunology. This group has eight offices in WNC, including in Asheville, Hendersonville, Brevard, Franklin and Spruce Pine.

Asheville Cardiology Associates *(5 Vanderbilt Park Dr., South Asheville, 828-274-6000, www.missionmd.org/physicians-practices/asheville-cardiology-associates)* has about 35 cardiologists and more than 200 support staff. It is a part of Mission Health Systems and has its own cardiac care floors and cath labs at Mission Hospital. Full disclosure: My cardiologist, Dr. Robert Hanich, is with Asheville Cardiology, and I am confident that he has my best interests at heart.

Asheville Arthritis & Osteoporosis Center *(4 Vanderbilt Park Dr., Suite 200, South Asheville, 828-258-9533, www.ashevillearthritis.com)*, the largest rheumatology practice in the area, has six rheumatologists on staff. Full disclosure: My rheumatologist, Dr. Ellison Smith, is a physician at Asheville Arthritis, and I feel he has helped me.

Asheville Family Health Centers *(206 Asheland Ave., Downtown Asheville, 828-258-8681, www.fhonline.com)* is a primary care group established in 1978. It has around 18 physicians at the main Asheville office and in offices in Arden and Candler.

Asheville Family Medicine *(41 Oakland Rd., Suite 300, South Asheville, 828-252-8885, www.missionmd.org/asheville-family-medicine)* is a primary care practice established in 1981. It has five physicians and is associated with Mission Hospital. Full disclosure: Dr. William Snoddy, a partner in Asheville Family Medicine, has been my personal family physician for about 20 years, and I believe he, like the other partners in his practice, are caring physicians who have done a good job despite the fact that I am not always the ideal, compliant patient.

Asheville Gastroenterology *(191 Biltmore Ave., South Asheville, 828-254-0881, www.ashevillegastro.com)* has 17 board-certified gastroenterologists on staff.

Asheville Internal Medicine *(60 Livingston St., Suite 200, Downtown Asheville, 828-253-4851, www.avim.com)*, established in 1985, has four internists on staff.

Asheville Radiology *(534 Biltmore Ave., South Asheville, 828-213-0801, www.ashevilleradiology.com)* is a multi-specialty practice with 37 radiologists, five vascular surgeons and more than 200 other staff. Asheville Radiology is the largest practice of its kind in Western North Carolina. It provides a wide range of imaging services including women's imaging, CT, interventional radiology, MRI, neuroradiology, nuclear medicine, body imaging, musculoskeletal radiology and general and vascular ultrasound.

CarePartners Health Services *(68 Sweeten Creek Rd., South Asheville, 828-252-2255, www.carepartners.org)* offers extensive rehabilitation, day care, home health and hospice services. It is affiliated with Mission.

Carolina Internal Medical Associates *(4 Vanderbilt Park Dr., South Asheville, 828-258-0397, www.carolinaim.com)* is an internal medicine practice with nine physicians on staff.

Carolina Spine and Neurosurgery Center *(7 Vanderbilt Park Dr., South Asheville, 828-255-7776, www.csandnc.com)* has 10 physicians and surgeons on staff. It is affiliated with Mission Hospitals. Carolina Spine has six satellite offices around WNC, along with physical therapy services. Full disclosure: I visited a physician with Carolina Spine and spent several months in physical therapy at their facility.

Carolina Vascular *(222 Asheland Ave., Downtown Asheville, 828-213-9090, www.carolinavascular.net)*, a division of Asheville Radiology, specializes in peripheral vascular disease. It has a team of 14 of interventional radiologists, vascular surgeons and neurointerventional radiologists. Full disclosure: I have had procedures conducted by a Carolina Vascular interventional radiologist, Dr. Toby Cole, and I think the procedures helped me.

Community Family Practice *(260 Merrimon Ave., North Asheville, 828-254-2444, www.communityfamilyonline.com)* is a primary care group with five physicians.

Mission Neurology *(Inpatient Neurology, Mission Hospital, 509 Biltmore Ave., South Asheville, 828-213-1439; Outpatient Neurology, 890 Hendersonville Rd., Suite 200, South Asheville, 828-213-9530, www.missionmd.org/physicians-practices/mission-neurology)* has both inpatient and outpatient components.

The inpatient service is part of Mission Hospital's Neurosciences Center of Excellence, which includes a 14-bed neuro-trauma ICU and a 36-bed, neurosciences unit/stroke center.

Mission SECU Cancer Center *(21 Hospital Dr., South Asheville, 828-213-2500, www.cancer.mission-health.org)* has the following services as the new SECU Cancer Center on the Mission campus: pediatric hematology/oncology program, Zeis Children's Cancer Center, radiation therapy, Mountain Radiation Oncology (828-213-0100), infusion center for adult patients, palliative care offices, medical oncology through Cancer Care of Western NC.

Mission Wound Healing & Hyperbaric Center *(1 Hospital Dr., Suite 4100, South Asheville, 828-213-4600, www.missionmd.org/physicians-practices/mission-wound-healing-hyperbaric-center)* is the longest-established wound care center in WNC. Full disclosure: On two occasions I was a patient of Mission Wound Healing and Dr. David Humphrey, and he and his talented staff successfully resolved my lower extremity problems.

Our Family Doctor *(43 Oakland Rd., South Asheville, 828-252-2511, www.ourfamilydoctorasheville.com)* is a primary care practice with four physicians.

Vickery Family Medicine *(15 Yorkshire St., Suite 201, South Asheville, 828-274-1600, www.vickeryfamilymedicine.com)* is a primary care practice with two physicians. Founder Dr. David "Gus" Vickery also is medical director of the Biltmore Estate's Medical Practice.

Weaverville Family Medicine *(63 Monticello Rd., Weaverville, 828-645-3066, www.weavervillefamilymed.com)* is a primary care practice with five physicians.

WNC Dermatological Associates *(281 McDowell St., South Asheville, 828-252-5676, www.wncderm.com)* is a dermatology practice with five physicians on staff.

DENTISTS

Because there are so many local dentists, most in small practices of one to three dentists, it is impossible to recommend a particular dentist. Instead, I am listing two dentists to whom I have gone for many years.

Steven Adams, DDS *(26 Reynolds Mountain Blvd., North Asheville, 828-484-4469, www.reynoldsmountaindentistry.com)* practices general dentistry.

Jody S. Harrison, DDS *(201 E. Chestnut St., North Asheville, 828-255-8100, www.ashevilleimplantperio.com)*, practice limited to periodontics. Formerly the practice of Richard Howell, DDS, who retired.

For more information on medical professionals or to locate a physician or dentist, check these websites:

Buncombe County Dental Society *(304 Summit St., Asheville, 828-274-0498, www.bcdentalsociety.org)* has more than 200 member dentists.

North Carolina Dental Society *(www.ncdental.org)* lists more than 3,600 members in Western North Carolina and the rest of the state.

Western Carolina Medical Society *(304 Summit St., Asheville, 828-274-0493, www.mywcms.org)*, formerly the Buncombe County Medical Society, was established in 1885.

Angie's List *(www.angieslist.com)* lists more than 550 physicians in the Asheville area and gives more than 225 of them top ratings.

Health Grades *(www.healthgrades.com)* is one of the online services that attempts to provide ratings of health professionals by patients.

Insurance

Blue Cross and Blue Shield of North Carolina dominates the health insurance business in Western North Carolina and the state. According to the North Carolina Department of Insurance, Blue Cross has 96% market share in the direct to consumer comprehensive health insurance segment and an 82% share of the group comprehensive health insurance segment. The company also totally dominates the Medicare supplemental care segment.

LGBT ASHEVILLE

Asheville is a gay-friendly small city. Period.

According to the latest United States census, the Asheville area has 83% more lesbian, gay bisexual and transgendered (LGBT) identified people than the typical American city or town. Another study, in 2011, also based on census results found that Buncombe County (with 15.5 same sex couples per 1,000) and Asheville (19.7 per 1,000) are the most gay-friendly county and city in the state of North Carolina, on a per-capita basis well ahead of places like Charlotte, Raleigh, Durham, Chapel Hill and Carrboro. In 2010, the gay-oriented publication, *The Advocate,* ranked Asheville as the "12th gayest city in America." Atlanta was ranked #1.

LGBT visitors increasingly are discovering Asheville, with its great natural beauty, innovative dining and drinking gigs, heavy-duty gallery, arts and crafts scene, interesting shops and numerous gay-owned or gay-welcoming B&Bs and inns and businesses. You are likely to see a number of openly lesbian and gay couples around town, especially Downtown and in West Asheville.

Downtown Asheville has several LGBT bars, including **Scandals,** the largest gay and lesbian club in the city, with three dance floors and four bars, **O. Henry's** (one of the oldest gay bars in the state, perhaps *the* oldest) and **Smokey's After Dark.** *(See Clubs and Nightlife section for more information.)*

Nearly all the many B&Bs and small inns in the Asheville area are welcoming to gays, and more than a dozen local B&Bs are gay-owned. *(See Lodging section for more information.)*

Many businesses in Asheville are LGBT-owned. Perhaps the best known is the lesbian-owned **Malaprop's** bookstore, one of the best independent bookstores in the South. Gay-owned **Edna's of Asheville,** a specialty coffee shop in North Asheville, draws a diverse crowd, with many LGBT patrons.

Blue Ridge Pride *(www.blueridgepride.com)* is an umbrella organization promoting gay pride. It holds a variety of events and meet-and-greets year-round, including a pride event in October that draws more than 10,000 attendees. In July it sponsors a Gay 5K run and "Rainbow Romp" in Carrier Park. **GayAshevilleOnline** *(www.gayashevilleonline.com)* is a directory of gay local businesses. The **Association of Lesbian Professionals** *(www.alpsofasheville.com)* brings together Asheville's lesbian professionals.

Asheville QFest *(www.ashevilleqfest.com)* is Asheville's LGBT film festival, held in October.

Asheville has no one gay residential neighborhood or "gayborhood." Downtown, Montford, North Asheville and West Asheville are all popular with LGBT residents, but you may just as easily find LGBT couples living in a rural mountain cove.

The City of Asheville has offered domestic partner benefits to same-sex couples since 2011, and Buncombe County began doing so in 2013. Mission Hospital, by far the largest employer in the region, has offered same-sex domestic partner benefits to its employees since 2012.

North Carolina as a whole is not as LGBT-friendly as cities like Asheville. In 2012, about 61% of state voters approved a constitutional amendment defining marriage solely as being a union between a man and a woman. The amendment won due to a coalition of conservatives and churches, including large numbers of African-American churches. More than 25 other U.S. states have similar laws or constitutional amendments. Asheville and Buncombe County citizens voted against the anti-same sex marriage amendment.

In October 2014, same-sex marriage became legal in North Carolina, thanks to a ruling by U.S. Federal District Court Judge Max Cogburn in Asheville, citing the U.S. Fourth Circuit Court of Appeals ruling in July 2014 that nullified Virginia's ban on marriages between two men or two women.

North Carolina is part of the U.S. Fourth Circuit. The North Carolina legislature has tried to make an end run around the law by making it legal for magistrates and other officials to deny same-sex marriage licenses based on their personal religious beliefs, but even if such laws are passed it is believed they will not stand up to judicial review.

THE ARTS IN ASHEVILLE AND WNC

The arts in Asheville have a rich past, a vibrant present and a promising future. Whether it's the visual arts, crafts, music, dance or theatre, Asheville is magnetic and dynamic.

The Studies Building also known as "The Ship" at Lake Eden, second and final home of the radical experimental school, Black Mountain College

Black Mountain College

Black Mountain College was one of the biggest things ever to happen to the Asheville area, but at the time few people paid any attention. It is only in retrospect that it became clear that the radical, experimental college was a major force in American arts and culture of the 20th century.

There's little point in going into the details here of the the struggles of the college from 1933, when it was established by disgruntled former faculty members of Rollins College in Florida in rented quarters at Blue Ridge Assembly near Black Mountain, until 1957, when it whimpered to its end at Lake Eden northwest of Black Mountain.

Many of the depressing details are mired in the college's financial morass, academic politics and intellectual backbiting.

Even at its peak in the 1940s, Black Mountain never had more than 90 students at one time. Perhaps 300 people taught at the college over the course of its 34 years.

What is important to understand is that there were two distinct and separate impacts of the college, impacts that eventually reverberated nationally. One was in the visual arts. Through its faculty and students, Black Mountain College helped develop some of the major art movements of the 20th century, including abstract impressionism and performance art.

The other impact was more diffuse, and more about personal freedom, lifestyle and pop culture. It led directly to the Beat Movement and then indirectly to the watershed years of the 1960s – hippies, drugs and rock n' roll.

In the 1930s and 40s, many refugees from Nazi Europe and from America's Babbittvilles came to Black Mountain College, attracted by its free spirit and experimental environment. The faculty and student body (sometimes it was difficult to tell one from the other) included some who would become the great abstract artists of the century such as **Robert Motherwell, Willem and Elaine de Kooning, Jacob Lawrence, Franz Kline, Robert Rauschenberg, Kenneth Noland (an Asheville native), M.C. Richards, Robert DeNiro Sr.** and **Josef and Anni Albers.** *Avant garde* composer and musician **John Cage** and dancer **Merce Cunningham** collaborated on the first "happenings," the beginning of performance art. **Buckminster Fuller,** who taught engineering at Black Mountain, created his first geodesic dome at the college. **Albert Einstein** was on the school's board and lectured at the college. **Max Dehn,** the noted German-American mathematician, taught at the college for seven years.

Walter Gropius, the founder of the Bauhaus school of architecture (Josef Albers had been a Bauhaus instructor in Germany), designed buildings for the Lake Eden campus, though the college never had the money to construct them.

Another prominent architect and architectural historian, **Lawrence Kocher,** did design and manage the construction, in great part by students and faculty, of the Studies Building, called "the Ship." It is still a striking building today.

In its later years, Black Mountain became better known for its poets and writers than for painters, musicians and performers. **Charles Olson,** the intellectual (and physical) giant taught at the college, founding the so-called Black Mountain School of poets.

Among Olson's students were poets **Robert Creeley, Fielding Dawson, Jonathan Williams** and **Ed Dorn,** and *Village Voice* columnist **Joel Oppenheimer.**

Openly gay novelists **James Leo Hirlihy** and **Michael Rumaker** attended Black Mountain, as did filmmaker **Arthur Penn. Alfred Kazin, William Carlos Williams** and **Henry Miller** lectured there.

Through the little magazine founded by Robert Creeley, *Black Mountain Review,* which early on published Allen Ginsberg and Jack Kerouac, the college developed a connection with the Beat poets in San Francisco, and with the larger Beat movement in the 1950s.

The college's radical approach to education inspired a number of experimental colleges, including New College, Goddard College, Bennington, Warren Wilson College (located in Swannanoa near Black Mountain) and Shimer College in Chicago.

The communal lifestyle, sexual freedom and experimental approach to education and life at Black Mountain College undoubtedly, if not always admittedly, contributed to the radical changes that took place in American culture in the 1960s.

For an in-depth look at Black Mountain College, read Martin Duberman's *Black Mountain, An Exploration in Community.* First published in 1972, it remains by far the best book on Black Mountain. *See Resources section.*

EXPERIENCING BLACK MOUNTAIN COLLEGE TODAY

Today, with some planning, you can visit the two campuses of Black Mountain College and imagine what it was like to be a student there. Black Mountain College Museum + Arts Center in Downtown Asheville has exhibits on the college, puts on lectures and presentations and publishes monographs and books on Black Mountain.

Black Mountain College Museum + Arts Center (*56 and 67 Broadway St., Asheville, 828-350-8484, www.blackmountaincollege.org, open noon-4 Tues.-Wed., 11-4 Thurs.-Sat., admission fees vary depending on event, exhibition or conference)* has the mission of preserving and continuing the unique legacy of educational and artistic innovation of Black Mountain College. In a small space revamped in early 2015, it does a big job with programs, publications and exhibits. The museum has leased additional space diagonally across the street at 67 Broadway, opening mid-2015.

YMCA Blue Ridge Assembly *(84 Blue Ridge Assembly Rd., Black Mountain, 828-669-8422, www.blueridgeassembly.org)* was the original home of Black Mountain College. The college occupied Robert E. Lee Hall and some other buildings on the religious retreat's 1,200-acre grounds for about eight years. The YMCA hosts many programs at the Assembly, but normally you can visit the Assembly grounds without charge. *Directions: Blue Ridge Assembly is about 14 miles east of Asheville. From Asheville, take I-40 East to Exit 64, Black Mountain/Montreat and turn south on Highway 9. Proceed about .5 mile and go straight on Blue Ridge Rd. Travel .9 mile and turn left at small Blue Ridge Assembly sign, then proceed to Assembly entrance.*

In 1941, Black Mountain College moved across the valley to Lake Eden, which is now a summer camp, **Camp Rockmont** *(375 Lake Eden Rd., 828-686-3885, www.rockmont.com)*. Rockmont operates as a 550-acre Christian camp for boys from early June to mid-August and at other times rents parts of the camp to organizations and groups.

Permission should be sought in advance to visit the grounds of the private camp. Among the original buildings from the college's time are the Studies Building ("the Ship"), the dining hall with a large meeting room, the Round House (where musicians practiced) and two residential lodges. The Ship and other buildings are visible from Lake Eden Rd. Twice a year, in mid-May and mid-October, the **Lake Eden Arts Festival** or **LEAF** *(377 Lake Eden Rd., 828-686-8742, www.theleaf.org)* stages a weekend music and arts festival on the grounds of Camp Rockmont. Buy your tickets in advance as they always sell out. *Directions to Lake Eden: From Asheville take I-40 East and exit at Swannanoa, Exit 59, to US Hwy. 70. Turn right toward Swannanoa/Black Mountain. Turn left at the first traffic light in Swannanoa to cross a bridge, then right on Old US 70. It is 1.9 miles to Lake Eden Rd., where you turn left at the traffic light. Go 1.5 miles and you will see Rockmont's front gate on the left.*

Asheville Art Museum *(2 S. Pack Square, 828-253-3227, www.ashevilleart.org; Tue.-Sat. 10-5, Sun. 1-5, $8 adults, $7 seniors and students)* has a collection of about 500 works on Black Mountain College and by artists associated with the college. Some of these are available for viewing in digital form on the museum's website at www.ashevilleart.org/collection/black-mountain-college.

Western Regional Archives *(170 Riceville Rd., East Asheville, 828-296-7230, www.history.ncdcr.gov/wo; open to the public Mon. 1-4, Tue.-Fri. 9-noon, other times by appointment, free)* in a building formerly used by the VA Hospital, is a branch of the Office of Archives and History, North Carolina Department of Cultural Resources. It houses various archives related to Western North Carolina history and culture, but currently about three-fourths of the archives focus on Black Mountain College. There are boxes and boxes of old photos, original BMC art work and college academic records.

The River Arts District is home to hundreds of artists and crafters – shown here is the Jonas Gerard studio and gallery on Clingman Avenue, one of two of the artist's locations in the RAD – photo by Sheila M. Lambert

River Arts District

What is now the amazing River Arts District, a thriving and always-growing collection of art studios and galleries, plus business offices, restaurants, clubs, beer breweries and residential condos along the east side of the **French Board River** near Downtown was once one of the region's main industrial zones.

Anchored by the river and **Southern Railway,** the Riverside industrial area developed in the late 19th and early 20th centuries as a center for tanneries, livestock sales, cotton and other mills, ice and coalhouses, grain storage facilities and warehouses.

The worst flood in Asheville history in 1916 damaged many buildings in the low-lying river plain, but gradually the area recovered. Other serious flooding has occurred once every 10 or 15 year, including bad floods in 1928 and 2004 that damaged buildings in the Riverside area and Biltmore Village.

The Riverside industrial area thrived for several decades, but with changing economic conditions by the 1950s and 1960s many of the warehouses and businesses in the district had closed and were abandoned.

Wilma Dykeman, in her classic 1955 book, *The French Broad,* called by one critic "a love poem" to the river, laid out the history and importance of the 117-mile long French Broad, which flows north from its headwaters in Rosman, N.C., through Asheville to Tennessee, eventually flowing into the Mississippi. She presented a vision of what the then-polluted river could become again for the region.

In 1989, **RiverLink,** then known as the French Broad Riverfront Planning Committee, a group of volunteers interested in the preservation and enhancement of the French Broad River – notably **Jean Webb,** an Asheville native who became the first chair of the Riverfront Planning Committee (an Asheville riverside park has been named for her) and **Karen Kragnolin,** a lawyer who move to Asheville in the 1990s, now executive director of RiverLink (a park is also named for her)-- came together under the auspices of the Asheville Chamber of Commerce to develop a plan for the Asheville riverfront.

Volunteers, including experts from the University of North Carolina at Asheville and Warren Wilson College, plus interested local organizations such as Quality Forward (now Asheville Greenworks), an environmental organization, and the Preservation Society of Asheville, in association with American Institute of Architects consultants, developed *The Riverfront Plan* outlining ideas for greenways and responsible riverfront development, mainly on the west side of the river. The plan is now called the *Wilma Dykeman RiverWay Plan*, honoring the author and conservationist.

In 1991, Carolina Power & Light Company (today Progress Energy, which merged with Duke Energy in 2012) helped jumpstart redevelopment along the riverfront by donating to RiverLink a 1.9 mile-section of riverfront property on the west bank of the river for use as the first link in the urban riverfront greenway. The former Asheville Speedway stock car race track became a part of **Carrier Park,** now a popular site for walkers, joggers and bikers. Carrier Park is named for Edwin Carrier, a Pennsylvania entrepreneur who started Sulpher Springs resort near what today is Malvern Hills in West Asheville.

Also in the 1990s, **Mountain Housing Opportunities,** a community organization dedicated to affordable housing, became involved in what would become the River Arts District, helping fund renovations in the district and eventually redeveloping the old **Glen Rock Hotel** property across from what had been the **Southern Railway Passenger Depot** *(see below).*

In the 1980s and 1990s, artists and craftspeople rediscovered the former Riverside industrial zone, drawn by inexpensive rents for large industrial and loft spaces, perfect for studios. In an unusual development, some artists and craftspeople bought buildings and renovated them for their own studios, renting out space to other artists. Currently more than a dozen artists in the River Arts District own the buildings where they have studios.

Pioneers in the River Arts District include Brian and Gail McCarthy who moved their **Highwater Clays** business to the district in 1985 (they later bought a section of buildings on Clingman Avenue for their **Odyssey Center for the Ceramic Arts,** now **Odyssey Clayworks,** and, later, **Odyssey Gallery**), Lewis and Porge Buck, who bought an old warehouse and opened **Warehouse Studios** in 1987 and Pattiy Torno, who bought three buildings on Riverside Drive and opened **CURVE Studios** in 1989.

Today the River Arts District is home to more than 160 art and craft studios, most of which are open to the public. There also are art and craft galleries and at least a dozen restaurants, coffee shops and bars. A number of creative businesses such as ad agencies and design studios also have relocated to the area. Residential apartments are also available in the district.

The boundaries of the River Arts District are not strictly fixed, but generally the district is an area of about one mile by one-half mile bounded by the French Broad River on the west and Clingman Avenue and the Depot Street corridor on the east. The north and south ends of the district are somewhat fluid.

Among the notable structures in the industrial area was the **Han Rees Tannery** on 22 acres at Lyman Street. The group of about 30 brick buildings, built around 1898-1902, housed massive tannery operations once among the largest in the country.

At one point Hans Rees employed some 3,000 workers and processed 30,000 pounds of cattle hides a day. You can imagine the stench! As the 20th century progressed, tanneries went into decline and by the 1940s Hans Rees and other Asheville tanneries were out of business. Several of the tannery buildings still stand, and the brick buildings with distinctive saw-tooth roof lines now are home to **Riverview Station,** at 191 Lyman Street, a community of about 50 artists and businesses.

Farmers Federation, a cooperative organization with the goal of improving agriculture in Western North Carolina, was established in 1920 by James G. K. McClure, whose family now runs **Hickory Nut Gap Farm.** Local farmers bought shares in the Federation, which purchased feed and seed and farm supplies and equipment at wholesale, selling them to members at discounted prices. The co-op also hatched and sold chicks and poults (baby turkeys). The Farmers Federation building on Roberts Street, one of several warehouses and stores operated in WNC by the organization, is now home to **Wedge Brewery** and **Wedge Studios.** The original six-story Farmers Federation building at 125 Roberts Street, considered fire proof, was destroyed in a fire in December 1925. James McClure's wife's painting and many McClure heirlooms, stored in the warehouse, were consumed by the blaze, in which several carloads of beans and hundreds of turkeys were also lost.

The **Asheville Cotton Mill** was the industrial district's most prominent building. Its towering smokestacks, visible from the Smoky Park Bridge (recently renamed the Captain Bowen Memorial Bridge after a firefighter who died in a fire on Biltmore Avenue) on the west side of Downtown, were symbols of the district. The 122,000 square foot building, occupying over 3 acres, was destroyed in a fire in 1995. It was arson, but the culprit or culprits were never found. (Another suspicious fire burned an empty part of the Cotton Mill in April 2013.)

The fire, however, seemed to act as a catalyst for further revitalization of the River Arts District. One part of the Cotton Mill that was not destroyed in the fire was bought and renovated by Eileen Black, a potter from Greensboro, and her husband, Marty Black, turning the building into the **Cotton Mill Studios.**

Asheville Stockyards were a fixture of the region's agricultural life from the 1930s to 1970s. New Belgium, a leading national crafts beer brewer, is building its East Coast brewery and distribution center at the site of the old stockyards.

The **Southern Railway Roundhouse,** built around 1926, is among the few surviving railroad roundhouses in the South. Southern Railway was the successor to the Western North Carolina Railroad, the original railroad in the region.

In 1982, Southern merged with the Norfolk Railroad to form the Norfolk Southern Railway. The Roundhouse at 70 Meadow Road is still in operation.

The **Southern Railway Passenger Depot** on Depot Street was one of two hubs of railroad passenger service in the region, the other being the Biltmore Depot on Brook Street in Biltmore Village. (During the Vietnam War days, this writer took a train between Fort Riley, Kan., and Asheville, arriving and departing from Depot Street).

Across from Southern Railway Passenger Depot was the **Glen Rock Hotel**, built of wood around 1890 in the Queen Anne style. It was condemned as unsafe in 1929 and rebuilt in 1930, designed by Asheville architect Henry Irven Gaines, later to become one of the founders of the Six Associates architectural firm.

By the early 1970s the Glen Rock had become a home mostly for derelicts and then for a time was occupied by a food canning business. Passenger service to Asheville ended in 1975, and the Depot Street passenger terminal, sadly, was torn down by Southern Railway.

Today, **Glen Rock Depot** is a multi-used development with residential, commercial and office space. It consists of the **372 Depot Building**, a 90,000 square-foot building with 60 affordable housing apartments and 9,000 square feet of commercial space.

STUDIOS AND GALLERIES IN RAD

Here are some of the largest and best studios and galleries in the River Arts District. For more information, visit www.riverartsdistrict.com where you can download a 40-page booklet on the district.

District-wide "studio strolls" are held twice yearly, in mid-June and mid-November, when nearly all studios are open, many with special sales, free refreshments, entertainment and demonstrations. "Second Saturday" events are held on the second Saturday of each month, April through December, with artist demos and free refreshments. Many studios are open year-round. Admission is free, so you can see the artists and craftspeople at work and buy art and crafts direct from the source.

Cotton Mill Studios *(122 Riverside Dr., 828-252-9122, www.cottonmillstudiosnc.com)* houses about 15 artists in textiles, pottery, weaving, jewelry and painting.

Curve Studios *(6, 9 and 12 Riverside Dr., 828-388-3526, www.curvestudiosnc.com)* is home to more than a dozen artists in fabric, jewelry, clay and metal.

Hatchery Studios *(1 Roberts St., www.hatcherystudios.com)* features more than a half dozen painters, sculptors and clay artists, plus a gallery, **Bluerain Fine Art.**

Northlight Studios *(357 Depot St.,*
www.northlightstudiosasheville.com) is home to five artists in photography,
painting, jewelry and other media.

Odyssey Clayworks *(236 Clingman Ave., 828-285-0210,*
www.odysseyceramicarts.com), for years called Odyssey Center for Ceramic
Arts, is one of the pioneering studios in the River Arts District. It focuses on
pottery and ceramic arts, with a large number of clay classes and workshops,
plus studio rentals. More than 50 ceramic artists work at Odyssey, the largest
concentration in one place in the region. It also has a gallery, the **Odyssey
Gallery.** Under the same family ownership is **Highwater Clays** *(600
Riverside Dr., 828-252-6033, www.highwaterclays.com)*, the largest clay and
pottery equipment and supply company in the region.

Phil Mechanic Studios *(109 Roberts St., 828-254-2126,*
www.philmechanicstudios) is home to about 16 local artists working with
paint, metal, mixed media, ceramics, glass and wood. Also here are two
galleries, **Pump Gallery** and **Flood Gallery Fine Art Center.**

Pink Dog Creative *(342-348 Depot St., 828-216-1311,*
www.pinkdog-creative.com) is home to around eight artists, mostly painters.
The Gallery at Pink Dog Creative, Asheville Area Arts Council and **The
Junction** restaurant also are located here.

Riverview Station *(191 Lyman St., 828-231-7120,*
www.riverviewartists.com) is a community of artists in painting, sculpture,
mixed media, jewelry, photography, ceramics, and wood, along with a
number of businesses. **310 Art Gallery** is also located here.

Roberts Street Studios *(140 Roberts St.)* has several artists in
paint, glass and wood.

Wedge Studios *(111-129 Roberts St.)* has nearly 30 artists
working in paint, fabrics, mixed media, sculpture, clay and wood, although a
recent change in ownership has put the artist studio in flux.

This is only a partial listing of the studios and galleries in the River
Arts District. Also check out the studios of individual artists such as **Jonas
Gerard** *(240 Clingman Ave., www.jonasgerard.com)* and **Daniel
McClendon** (349 Depot St., *www.theliftstudios.com*).

Grayline Tours include the River Arts District on their hop-on/hop-
off trolley tours. *See Tours section.*

Asheville Area Art and Crafts

Asheville was named the number one small city in America for art
by *AmericanStyle Magazine* in 2011 and tied for number two in 2012.

Other top five small cities included Sarasota, Key West and Bradenton, Fla., and Santa Fe, N.M.

Several thousand artists and craft artists live in the Asheville area and around Western North Carolina.

Crafts Schools and Organizations

With a tradition of hand-made crafts going back hundreds of years, the presence of several nationally known crafts schools and crafts organizations, a huge influx of talented craftspeople to Asheville and the region and the opening of many first-rate crafts galleries, Asheville and the mountains have become one of the top crafts centers in the United States.

The area has particular strength in pottery and ceramic arts, glass, fabric arts and wood.

Folk Art Center *(Blue Ridge Parkway Milepost 382, 828-298-7928, www.southernhighlandguild.org, Jan.-Mar. 9-5 daily; Apr.-Dec. 9-6 daily, free),* headquarters of the Southern Highland Craft Guild, is a terrific place to see historical and contemporary mountain crafts. There are three crafts galleries, craft demonstrations and an Allanstand Craft Shop, which sells quality local and regional craft items.

Handmade in America *(125 S. Lexington Ave, 828-252-0121, www.handmadeinamerica.org),* established in 1993, is dedicated to helping support craftspeople in Western North Carolina. The community organization has published a popular guide, *The Craft Heritage Trails of Western North Carolina.* Its online Craft Registry is the region's most comprehensive directory of craft artists, galleries, craft resources and craft events.

North Carolina Homespun Museum *(111 Grovewood Rd., 828-253-7651, www.grovewood.com, Apr.-Dec. Mon.-Sat. 10-6, Sun. 11-5, closed Jan.-Mar., free),* a part of the Grovewood Gallery adjacent to the Grove Park Inn, focuses on the history of Biltmore Industries and its wool cloth. Biltmore Industries originally was a weaving and woodworking education program started by Edith Vanderbilt of the Biltmore Estate.

Southern Highland Craft Guild *(Folk Art Center, Milepost 382, Blue Ridge Parkway, 828-298-7928, www.southernhighlandguild.org).* Begun in Asheville in 1930, and second in age only to the Boston Society of Arts and Crafts, the Southern Highland Craft Guide is one of the preeminent craft organizations in the country. It represents more than 900 craftspeople in nine Southeastern states.

Guild membership is based on a juried process. The Guild operates the Folk Art Center on the Blue Ridge Parkway *(see above)* along with several first-rate crafts shops. Twice a year it puts on the Craft Fair of the Southern Highlands, with 200 craftspeople exhibiting in the U.S. Cellular Center in Asheville *(see Festivals section)*.

AROUND WESTERN NORTH CAROLINA
Crossnore Weavers *(Crossnore, 828-733-4660, www.crossnoreweavers.org, open Mon.-Sat. 9-5, free)* near Linville is a "working museum" of weaving.

It is an outgrowth of a boarding school for impoverished children established in 1913. Today, local women still weave blankets, scarves, napkins and other items. The **Crossnore Fine Arts Gallery,** located in what formerly was the weaving room, sells regional art and crafts to support the school, which is now a day school. Miracle Grounds, a specialty coffee shop selling organic coffees, is nearby, with profits also going to the school. *Directions: From Asheville, take I-40 East to Exit 105 Morganton. Go north on Hwy. 181 about 30 miles to Pineola at the intersection of Hwy. 181 and US Hwy. 221. At Pineola, turn left on US Hwy 221 S and go 1.5 miles, then turn right onto Crossnore Dr. Go .6 miles and turn right onto Johnson Ln. at the Blair Fraley Sales Store. Crossnore Gallery is third building on the left.*

John C. Campbell Folk School *(1 Folk School Rd., Brasstown, 828-837-2775 or 800-365-5724, www.folkschool.org; campus open daily during daylight hours, Craft Shop and History Center open Mon.-Sat. 8-5, Sun. 1-5, free)* dates to 1925. The school, in the far western part of the state near Murphy about two hours from Asheville, offers more than 800 weekend and weeklong classes for adults in everything from blacksmithing and basketry to cooking, quilting and woodworking.

Students can live in school housing and take meals at the school. The **Craft Shop** has items from some 300 local and regional craft artists, and the **History Center** is a small museum of mountain crafts with information on the school's history. The work of school co-founder Olive Dame Campbell is celebrated in the 2000 film *Songcatcher*. The campus is a Historic District on the National Register of Historic Places.

Visitors are welcome to explore the 300-acre campus on a self-guided tour during daylight hours. *Directions: From Asheville take I-40 West to exit 27, US Hwy. 19/23/74. Take 23/74 to Waynesville/Sylva. At Exit 81 take US Hwy. 23/441 south to Franklin. In Franklin, the US Hwy. 441 Bypass merges with US Hwy. 64 west.*

Follow US Hwy. 64 West from Franklin towards Hayesville. Eight miles west of Hayesville, turn left on Settawig Rd. (a brown Folk School sign points in that direction). Follow the signs to the Folk School.

Museum of North Carolina Handicrafts *(49 Shelton St. at US Hwy. 276, Waynesville, 828-452-1551, www.sheltonhouse.org; open May-Oct. Tue.-Sat. 10-4, admission $5, seniors $4, children $3)* is located in Shelton House, a two-story white Charleston-style farmhouse built in 1875 and now on the National Register of Historic Places. The house alone is worth a visit. The museum has exhibits of regional folk art, pottery, baskets, quilts, weaving and other crafts.

Penland School of Crafts *(67 Doras Trail, Penland, 828-765-2359, Gallery 828-765-6211, www.penland.org; campus open daily March-early Dec., Gallery open March-early Dec., Tue.-Sat. 10-5, Sun. noon-5, free admission)* is arguably the best crafts school in the country. Penland, on 460 acres in a beautiful rural area near Spruce Pine about an hour from Asheville, offers one- and two-week adult workshops in the summer and eight-week classes in spring and fall, in clay, books & paper, metals, glass, photography, printmaking, textiles and wood. Students live on campus in simple, rustic dormitory facilities. Around 1,400 students take classes at Penland each year. Most classes are oversubscribed, with waiting lists.

The school has no standing faculty; instructors are rotating full-time studio artists and college professors. Visitors are welcome on the Penland campus, although teaching studios usually are closed to the public during classes. The **Penland School Gallery,** which exhibits and sells the work of present and former students and faculty, most of it of very high quality and some of it extraordinary, is open to visitors from March to early December. Visitors are welcome to walk through the grounds. Note especially Craft House, one of the largest log structures in North Carolina. You can also visit The Barns, which houses the studios of the Penland's resident artists, fulltime craftspeople who live and work at the school.

There also is a café (which sells Asheville's Mountain City Coffee Roasters coffee) and gift shop. Free guided tours of the campus are offered March-early December Tuesday at 10:30 and Thursday at 1:30, reservations necessary – call 828-765-6211. If you're visiting Penland, you may want to stop at some of the nearby craft studios.

The area around Penland is home to about 100 craft artists. Watch for signs of open studios and galleries. An annual auction in August to support the school usually raises about a half million dollars.

Directions to Penland: Take US Hwy. 19/23 (future I-26) North past Mars Hill, then take Exit 9. Stay on US Hwy. 19 towards Burnsville. This road will become US 19E (do NOT take US Hwy. 19W). Go through Burnsville and continue about 10 miles. Turn left at the green Penland School sign onto Penland Rd. (a BP gas station is on the right). Follow Penland Rd. for 3 miles, when you will cross a bridge and railroad tracks. One mile past the railroad tracks, bear left at the big curve onto Conley Ridge Rd. Go all the way up the hill to Penland.

Qualla Arts and Crafts *(645 Tsali Blvd., Cherokee, 828-497-3103, www.quallaartsandcrafts.com; Jun.-Aug. Mon.-Sat. 8-7 and Sun. 9-5 pm, Sep.-May daily 8- 5 except closed Sun. Jan. and Feb.)* is the nation's oldest Native American cooperative, dating to 1946. The mutual co-op has more than 300 members. This is not a souvenir junk stand but a gallery of mostly high-quality crafts by master Cherokee crafts artists. The Qualla showroom displays and sells only locally handmade Cherokee crafts, including baskets, pottery, dolls, masks and woodcarvings. There also are exhibits of crafts that are not for sale.

ASHEVILLE ARTS AND CRAFTS GALLERIES

Asheville and environs has around 40 art galleries, plus another 25 or more galleries that focus primarily on crafts. The art galleries and studios are concentrated in the Downtown and River Arts District areas, with some in Biltmore Village *(www.biltmorevillage.com)* and Kenilworth *(www.kenilworthartists.org)* and a few in surrounding towns including Black Mountain, Hendersonville, Highlands and Brevard.

Here is a selection of some of the larger and better galleries.

Of course, the line between art and crafts is difficult to define and even more difficult to mark. Some craftspeople create work that is at least as skillful and expressive as that of the best painters and sculptors.

However, for purposes of this guide we have attempted, whether successfully or not, to divide those galleries that lean toward more functional work in ceramics, wood, jewelry, glass, fabric and other media and those that are inclined toward the traditional fine arts of painting and sculpture.

Downtown Art Walks are held five or six Fridays a year at around two dozen Downtown galleries, with many exhibit openings and appearances by artists. A brochure on art galleries is published by the Art Galleries Association, and copy can be downloaded from their website at www.ashevilledowntowngalleries.org.

Asheville Art Museum *(2 S. Pack Square, 828-253-3227, www.ashevilleart.org, open Tue.-Sat. 10-5, Sun. 1-5, admission $8 adults, $7 for students and seniors)* focuses on American art in the 20th and 21st centuries. The permanent collection of the recently expanded 53,000 square feet museum has more than 3,500 works in all media, plus another 5,000 architectural drawings. It includes a collection of about 500 works on Black Mountain College and by artists and photographers associated with the college. *See Black Mountain College above.*

Most Asheville galleries are clustered on and near Biltmore Avenue Downtown, in the River Arts District and in Biltmore Village. Hours vary, but most galleries are closed on Sundays and many don't open until late morning on weekdays and Saturdays. Many sell art crafts as well as paintings and other art. The following is a comprehensive but not complete list of galleries:

Aesthetic Gallery (6 College St., 828-398-0219, www.aestheticgallery.com) represents about a half dozen artists in photography, painting and fiber arts. In addition it imports fabric and ceramics and other items from Africa, Asia and Australia.

American Folk Art and Framing *(64 Biltmore Ave., 828-281-2134, www.amerifolk.com)* is a small gallery devoted to the work of about two dozen contemporary folk artists, plus the work of potters, jewelers and sculptors. It also has a wide selection of frames.

Ariel Gallery *(19 Biltmore Ave. 828-236-2660, www.arielcraftgallery.com)* is an artist-owned and run gallery next to Mast General Store with about a dozen member artists in ceramics, wood, glass and jewelry.

ARTery (346 Depot St., 828-258-0710, www.ashevillearts.com) is a multipurpose gallery, exhibition and event center that also serves as the headquarters of the Asheville Area Arts Council, a non-profit arts advocacy group that was established in 1952. The Arts Council moved to the River Arts District in 2011. Exhibits featuring local artists rotate roughly monthly.

ArtEtude Gallery (89 Patton Ave., 828-252-1466, www.artetudegallery.com), new in 2012, represents about 10 contemporary artists from around the country.

Asheville Gallery of Art *(16 College St., 828-251-5796, www.ashevillegallery-of-art.com)* has more than two dozen artist members who exhibit and sell their work at this gallery. Most are local residents.

Bella Vista Art Gallery *(14 Lodge St., 828-768-0246, www.bellavistaart.com)* in Biltmore Village represents more than three dozen contemporary painters, sculptors and ceramic artists.

Bellagio *(5 Biltmore Plaza, 828-277-8100,*
www.bellagioarttowear.com) in Biltmore Village, a part of the John Krum
arts empire, showcases what it calls "art to wear" in women's clothing,
jewelry and accessories. A sister gallery, **Bellagio Everyday** at 40
Biltmore Avenue, features somewhat less expensive designer clothing and
accessories.

Bender Gallery *(12 S. Lexington, 828-505-8341,*
www.thebendergallery.com) is devoted entirely to high-quality art glass,
exhibiting the work of about 80 nationally known glass artists in what the
gallery calls the largest collection of museum-quality art glass in the region.

Blue Spiral 1 *(38 Biltmore Ave., 828-251-0202,*
www.bluespiral1.com), owned by Asheville arts magnate John Krum, Blue
Spiral usually is considered the premier gallery in Asheville and is one of the
largest. It exhibits the work of leading contemporary artists and craftspeople
from Asheville and all over the South.

Castell Photography *(2C & D Wilson Alley, 828-255-1188,*
www.castellphotographygallery.com) exhibits only photo-based work.

The Compleat Naturalist Wildlife Art Gallery *(2 Brook St.,*
828-274-5430, www.compleatnaturalist.com) in The Compleat Naturalist
Natural History Store in Biltmore Village has a gallery with limited edition
wildlife prints by local and national artists.

Courtyard Gallery *(109 Roberts St., 828-273-3332,*
www.ashevillecourtyard.com) in the Phil Mechanics building in the River
Arts District features contemporary art, local crafts and film events.

Desert Moon Designs *(372 Depot St., 828-575-2227,*
www.desertmoondesigns-studios.com) in the River Arts District has an
eclectic gallery with jewelry, fabric art, sculpture and paintings by around a
dozen mostly local artists.

Edge Gallery *(58 College St., 828-257-3065,*
www.edgeofasheville.com) has functional but artistically designed furniture
of wood and metal.

Flood Fine Art Center *(109 Roberts St., 828-254-2166,*
www.floodgallery.org), on the second floor of the Phil Mechanics Building
in the River Arts District, is run by a non-profit arts organization. It exhibits
contemporary artists from around the U.S. and the world and also exhibits
some local artists. In the same building, on the first floor, **Pump Gallery** has
frequent exhibits by local artists, and on display also is the private collection
of Mitch and Jolene Mechanic.

Gallery Minerva *(8 Biltmore Ave., 828-255-8850, www.galleryminerva.com)* represents about 30 contemporary world and local artists.

Grand Bohemian Hotel Art Gallery *(11 Boston Way, 828-398-5555, www.grandbohemiangallery.com)* in the Grand Bohemian Hotel in Biltmore Village is one of a group of seven galleries operating at hotels in this small upscale chain. Among the items for sale are representational art works, jewelry and photographs.

Grovewood Gallery *(111 Grovewood Rd., 828-253-7651 or 877-622-7238, www.grovewood.com)* on grounds adjoining the Grove Park Inn is a large (9,000 square feet) high-quality crafts gallery showcasing furniture, jewelry, fiber, glass and ceramics by about 500 craftspeople from around the country.

The Haen Gallery *(52 Biltmore Ave., 828-254-8577, www.thehaengallery.com)* has works by about 20 contemporary national and international artists.

Henco Reprographics *(54 Broadway St., 828-253-0449, www.hencrorepro.com)* is not really an art gallery, but it does use its window on Broadway to display photos and art on a rotating basis. Dawn Roe is the artist and educator behind the project. Roe divides her time between Asheville and Winter Park, Fla., where she teaches at Rollins College.

Jonas Gerard Fine Art *(240 Clingman Ave., 828-350-7711, www.jonasgerard.com)* is a gallery in the River Arts District devoted to the bold, colorful abstract and representational art of Jonas Gerard. You'll see his work also displayed in several restaurants, hotels and shops in Asheville, and he has a second location in RAD in Riverview Station at 191 Lyman Street, Studio 144.

Kress Emporium *(19 Patton Ave., 828-281-2252, www.thekressemporium.com)* features the work of around 80 local and regional craftspeople and artists who rent sales space in the 1928 terra cotta-faced, colorful Renaissance style building that one housed a five-and-dime store. (As a child, this writer used to have lunch at the Kress lunch counter on the lower level.) Also in Kress are some antique and collectibles stalls. Kress is not air-conditioned, so it can be warm in summer.

New Morning Gallery *(7 Boston Way, 828-274-2831 or 800-933-4438, www.newmorninggallerync.com)* another John Krum venture in Biltmore Village, has garden art, jewelry, ceramics, glass and other crafts, all carefully selected and nicely presented. There's limited covered free parking next to the gallery.

Odyssey Gallery *(238 Clingman Ave., 828-285-0210, www.odysseyceramicarts.com)* is a ceramics gallery at the Odyssey Clayworks complex. It generally features the work of Odyssey resident artists and instructors.

Overström Studio *(35 Wall St., 828-258-1761, www.overstrom.com)* is a jewelry design studio and jewelry store.

The Potter's Mark *(122 Riverside Dr., 828-252-9122, www.pottersmark.com)* is a pottery studio and gallery in the Cotton Mill Studios in the River Arts District. It has operated in the Cotton Mill since 2003.

Sassafrass Studio *(191 Lyman St., www.sassafrassstudio.net)* displays work of artist owners Bet Kindley (encaustic or hot wax painting, photography and mixed media) and Mary Alice Ramsey (painting, drawings and mixed media works).

Seven Sisters Craft Gallery (117 Cherry St., Black Mountain, 828-669-5107, www.sevensistersgallery.com), in downtown Black Mountain since 1981, has work by about 250 local and national craft artists in ceramics, wood, glass and other media.

Stuart Nye Handwrought Jewelry *(940 Tunnel Rd., 828-298-7988 or 800-456-1933, www.stuartnye.com)* has been a fixture in East Asheville since 1933. The distinctive Stuart Nye and affordable jewelry, made from silver, copper and brass, often features designs based on local flora such as dogwood blossoms, oak and maple leaves and pine cones. Nye jewelry also is sold in other stores.

Thomas Kincade Gallery *(10 Biltmore Plaza, 828-277-0850, www.thomaskincadeasheville.com)* in Biltmore Village sells prints and other merchandise developed by the late mass merchandiser and artist, using his trademarked glowing highlights. One of every 20 American households is said to own a Kincade print.

310 Art Gallery *(191 Lyman St., 828-776-2716, www.310art.com)* in the River Arts District represents about 20 Western North Carolina artists.

The Village Potters *(191 Lyman St., 828-253-2424, www.thevillagepotters.com)* is a collective of seven potters in the River Arts District, with a gallery, studios and a clay teaching center.

Woolworth Walk *(25 Haywood St., 828-254-9234, www.woolworthwalk.com)* is billed as the largest crafts gallery in the area, with work by about 160 craft artists in 20,000 square feet of air-conditioned and heated space. The former five-and-dime store, with terra cotta facing and Art Deco motifs, originally opened in 1939. Inside Woolworth Walk is a functioning old-fashioned soda fountain, heavy on the stainless steel.

Working Girls Studio and Gallery *(30 Battery Park Ave., 828-243-0200, www.workinggirlsstudio.com)* displays the work of two local artists, Eli Corbin and Lynne Harty.

Zapow! *(21 Battery Park Ave., 828-575-2024, www.zapow.net)* says it is the only gallery in the Southeast specializing in Pop Art.

Theatre and Drama

Live theatre is going on somewhere in the Asheville area all the time. For up-to-date calendar of theatre, music and other arts events, check out the **LiveWire** website at www.livewireasheville.com.

Here are some of the drama companies and venues:

Altamont Theatre *(18 Church St., 828-348-5327, www.myaltamont.com)* is a 120-seat theatre and music listening room with gallery space and bar in the lobby and six short-term rental condos on the two top floors. The Altamont Theatre Company is a not-for-profit that puts on occasional off-Broadway type productions.

Asheville Community Theatre *(35 E. Walnut St., 828-254-1320, www.ashevilletheatre.org)*, founded at the end of World War II (Charlton Heston was a manager of the theatre in 1947) is one of the oldest community theatres in the country. It puts on about a dozen productions annually, some on the Main Stage and some at its smaller black box theatre, **35 Below.** Main Stage tickets are around $20-$25, with discounts for seniors and students.

Asheville Playback Theatre *(www.globalplayback.org)* is part of the global Playback Theatre Network. At Playback, personal stories from audience members are transformed into performance pieces, accompanied by improvised music.

Asheville Playback Theatre, around since 1996, currently appears at the **Altamont Theatre** and **North Carolina Stage Company.**

Asheville Puppetry Alliance *(73 Dye Leaf Rd., Fairview, 828-628-9576, www.ashevillepuppetry.org)* produces puppetry shows for both adult and children's audiences. The group hosts festivals, workshops, "puppetry slams" and a puppet club and stages shows at Diana Wortham Theatre and other venues.

Diana Wortham Theatre *(2 N. Pack Square, 828-257-4530, www.dwtheatre.com)* is an intimate 500-seat venue for music, drama and dance, with orchestra and balcony seating. The farthest seat is only 60 feet from the stage. A private parking deck is attached to the theatre.

Flat Rock Playhouse *(2661 Greenville Hwy., Flat Rock, 828-693-0731 or 866-732-8008, www.flatrockplayhouse.org)* is the official State Theatre of North Carolina, though the state provides only 2% of funding. The theatre draws nearly 100,000 patrons to its original Main Stage, a barn-like (but now air-conditioned and comfortable) theatre in Flat Rock, dating to 1952, and to its 250-seat **Playhouse Downtown** location in Hendersonville. Flat Rock puts on 10 productions a year in Flat Rock and another eight or nine in Hendersonville, plus occasional productions in Asheville, all highly professional and featuring many Equity actors and often elaborate sets. Many of the Main Stage productions are musicals or comedies. In 2012, Flat Rock debuted an original play on Zelda Fitzgerald, who died in a fire at a psychiatric hospital in Asheville. The theatre also operates a college apprentice and intern residence program in the summer and fall. Tickets for Main Stage productions are around $35-$40, with a variety of discounts available.

Haywood Arts Regional Theatre *(Performing Arts Center at Shelton House, 250 Pigeon St., Waynesville, 828-456-6322, www.harttheatre.com)* is a community theatre in Waynesville that stages about a half dozen productions each year. Tickets are around $20-24, with discounts available.

Masonic Temple *(80 Broadway St., 828-252-3924, www.masonic18.com)*, though still a functioning Masonic temple, in recent years has been opened to the public as a venue for plays, music and other performances. The exterior of 1915 four-story brick building at the intersection of Broadway and Woodfin, designed by the firm of Smith & Carrier, is something of a conglomeration of styles – Romanesque and Beaux-Arts with Greek Revival classical touches in the Ionic columns over the entrance. Inside, there's a charming 270-seat horseshoe-shaped theatre with balcony and orchestra seating.

Montford Park Players *(92 Gay St., 828-254-5146, www.montfordparkplayers.org)* is known for its Shakespeare in the Park productions. The Players have a 20-week summer season, staging about a half-dozen productions at the outdoor **Hazel Robinson Amphitheatre** behind the Montford Recreation Center off Pearson Ave., plus a 10-week winter season at the **Masonic Temple.** In summer, many patrons bring a picnic to enjoy before the play. All actors are volunteers. Summer productions are free, but a hat is passed at intermission, and a donation of $5 is suggested. Winter season productions cost around $12 to $15.

North Carolina Stage Company *(15 Stage Lane, 828-239-0263, www.ncstage.org)* puts on professional-level productions in an intimate 99-seat theatre. NC Stage tends to do edgier, more innovative productions than most other local theatres. An example in 2012 was the staging of a new play about Buckminster Fuller, who was associated for a time with Black Mountain College. Tickets usually are around $25-$28, with discounts on Wednesdays and for students. The first night of each production is "pay what you can" with a minimum of $6.

Southern Appalachian Repertory Theatre *(Owen Theatre, 44 College St., Mars Hill College, Mars Hill, 828-689-1384, www.sartplays.org)* stages about a half-dozen professional-quality productions annually. Some SART productions are classic Broadway and off-Broadway shows, but others have a connection with Appalachian culture. In most years at least one of the productions is a world premiere. Tickets are around $25-$28.

UNC-Asheville *(Carol Belk Theatre, UNC-Asheville, 1 University Heights, 828-251-6610, www.drama.unca.edu)* and its drama department stages several productions annually. Long-time department chair and noted theatre director Arnold Wengrow, now retired, made a name for drama at the university. General admission is $10.

Warren Wilson Theatre *(Kettridge Theatre, 701 Warren Wilson Rd., Warren Wilson College, 828-771-3040, www.warren-wilson.edu)* stages two or three productions each year. General admission is $10.

Music and Dance

Beginning in the 18th century Scots-Irish settlers brought their folk songs, reels and Elizabethan ballads to the mountains, and "old-timey mountain music" with fiddles, mandolins, banjos and guitars is still heard in the hills today. Traditional songs such as "Barbara Allen," "Wayfaring Stranger" and "Pretty Saro" were preserved by the isolated mountaineers. Today, a number of festivals including the **Mountain Dance and Folk Festival** in Asheville *(see Festivals section)* celebrate the heritage of Appalachian mountain music.

In some ways, the 1920s and 1930s were the heyday of "hillbilly" music in the region. Radio stations such as Asheville's **WWNC** (the call letters stood for "Wonderful Western North Carolina"), which went on the air in 1927, broadcast live the music of Jimmie Rodgers, often called the father of country music. WWNC also was one of stations carrying the "Crazy Water Crystals" program, which featured some 100 amateur country musicians from North and South Carolina.

Banjo picker **Earl Scruggs** (from Shelby, N.C.) and **Doc Watson** (born in Deep Gap, N.C., near Boone) with his flat-picking guitar style were among the pioneers of bluegrass music. WWNC Radio broadcast the first live session of **Bill Monroe and the Bluegrass Boys** in 1939. Both bluegrass pioneers died in 2012.

While far less popular than country and bluegrass, avant-garde and art music also have a history in the Asheville area. In 1952, at Black Mountain College, radical composer **John Cage** put on what was considered to be the first "happening."

During the *Black Mountain Piece*, as it has come to be known, Cage was on a ladder at the side of the room reading various texts, Robert Rauschenberg's now-famous white paintings hung from the ceiling, composer and pianist David Tudor played the piano and radio and **Merce Cunningham** danced around the room. This was a precursor to **"4'33,"** one of the most important avant-garde pieces of the 20th century. It was written by Cage and performed by Tudor. At a performance in Woodstock, N.Y., Tudor sat without playing in front of a piano for four minutes and thirty-three seconds.

Fiddler playing old-time mountain music – photo courtesy of Library of Congress

Noted Hungarian composer **Béla Bartók** spent the winter of 1943-44 in Asheville. Bartók worked on his "Third Concerto for Piano," also known as the **"Asheville Concerto,"** while residing at the Albemarle Inn *(86 Edgewood Rd., North Asheville),* now operating as a B&B.

More recently, **Robert Moog,** the inventor of the Moog synthesizer and electronic music pioneer, moved to Asheville where he spent his final years. His company is still in business in Asheville, and each October MoogFest, a festival of electronic music, is held in Asheville. *See Festivals section.*

Asheville Ballet *(4 Weaverville Hwy., 828- 252-4761, www.ashevilleballet.com)* headed by choreographer Ann Dunn has a ballet school and puts on many performances in the Asheville area.

Asheville Chamber Music Series *(performances held at Asheville Unitarian Universalist Congregation at 1 Edwin Place, 828-575-7427, www.ashevillechambermusic.org),* founded in 1952, has put on more than 240 classical music performances in Asheville by leading chamber ensembles including the Amadeus, Budapest, Julliard, Jupiter and Emerson Quartets, duos such as Janos Starker and Jean-Pierre Rampal and David Finckel and Wu Han, and other ensembles. Tickets are around $35.

Asheville Choral Society *(1 Battery Park Ave., 828-232-2060, www.ashevillechoralsociety.org),* founded in 1977, is a volunteer choral group with about 100 singers. It usually puts on three concert events a year.

Asheville Contemporary Dance Theatre *(20 Commerce St., 828-254-2621, www.acdt.org)* is a professional contemporary dance company and dance school that puts on up to 80 dance performances a year, in Asheville and elsewhere. ACDT owns the **BeBe Theatre,** a 69-seat black box theatre at 20 Commerce Street where most of the dance group's productions are staged.

Asheville Lyric Opera *(39 S. Market St., 828-236-0670, www.ashevillelyric.com)* puts on three or four operas and other musical performances each year at the Diana Wortham Theatre. Most productions feature nationally known singers. Tickets are $30 to $53, with discounts for students.

Asheville Symphony Orchestra *(U.S. Cellular Center, 87 Haywood St., 828-254-7046, www.ashevillesymphony.org),* founded in 1960, is a community orchestra of 80 to 100 musicians, depending on the concert.

Robert Hart Baker, the Symphony's first full-time conductor, led the ASO from 1981 to 2004, and during his tenure the Symphony grew in size and reputation.

Current conductor and music director is Daniel Meyer, formerly conductor of the Pittsburgh Symphony. The Asheville Symphony presents seven concerts a year, each with a nationally known guest artist. Concerts are held in the Thomas Wolfe Auditorium at U.S. Cellular Center. Single-concert tickets are $20 to $58, with discounts for students.

Brevard Music Center *(349 Andante Lane, Brevard, 828-862-2100, www.brevardmusic.org)*, on a 180-acre campus near Brevard, is a summer music institute for high school and college students, and it puts on a nationally known summer music festival. Each summer, from mid-June to early August, the Center puts on about 80 musical performances for an audience totaling more than 30,000. Artistic director is **Keith Lockhart,** conductor of the Boston Pops, principal conductor of the BMC Concert Orchestra and a Brevard Music Center alumnus.

Thomas Wolfe Auditorium *(U.S. Cellular Center, 87 Haywood St., 828-259-5544, www.ashevillenc.gov/Departments/CivicCenter.aspx)* in the U.S. Cellular Center (formerly Asheville Civic Center) with 2,400 seats is the venue for mid-size musical events and also for the Asheville Symphony Orchestra. Larger country and rock music concerts are held in the Arena of the U.S. Cellular Center. Although this is an old auditorium, acoustics in Thomas Wolfe are surprisingly good. The original Municipal Auditorium opened in 1940 and was renovated and renamed for the Asheville author in 1974, the same year the main Civic Center Arena opened. Seating has been upgraded in recent years. Still, it's not up to top regional standards, and Asheville loses many concerts and other events to facilities in Knoxville, Charlotte, Greenville, S.C., and elsewhere.

WCQS Radio *(73 Broadway St., 828-210-4800 or 800-768-6698, www.wcqs.org)* at 88.1 FM is Asheville's National Public Radio classical music station, programming classical music and NPR news, with jazz in the late evening.

HISTORIC ARCHITECTURE OF ASHEVILLE & WNC

View east from the BB&T Building of Pack Square Park with Art Deco
Asheville City Building at the far right top – photo by Sheila M. Lambert

Downtown Asheville

Downtown Asheville is perhaps best known for its Art Deco
architecture.

Asheville has more Art Deco buildings than any other city in the South except for Miami Beach.

However, the Asheville area also has impressive examples of other commercial and residential architectural styles, including Beaux Arts, Gothic, Greek Revival, Renaissance, Romanesque, Arts and Crafts, Queen Anne and others.

Altogether, the Downtown Asheville Historic District comprises about 170 buildings, mostly from the 1890s to 1940s.

Art Deco

Art Deco is a visual arts style that first appeared in Paris after the end of World War I and made an impact around the world during the 1920s and 1930s on the design of consumer products and in the exterior and interiors of buildings, fading away after World War II. Its name, not coined until the 1960s, came from the Exposition Internationale des Arts Décoratifs et Industriels Modernes held in Paris in 1925.

Bold, colorful geometric shapes –chevrons, spheres, trapezoids and rectangles -- often with a crafts-related theme characterize Art Deco. The Chrysler Building and RCA Building (now the GE Building) in New York and the Bullocks Wilshire Building in Los Angeles are classic Art Deco. The 1934 Chrysler Airflow and 1937 Cord automobiles were influenced by Art Deco design.

New York, Detroit, Chicago and most famously Miami Beach and Los Angeles have large collections of Art Deco buildings. Miami Beach has the largest collection of Art Deco buildings in the world, with hundreds buildings in the Art Deco and Streamline Moderne (a late stage of Art Deco featuring curved forms) styles in the South Beach Art Deco District. Outside of Miami, the largest number of Art Deco buildings is in Mumbai, India.

In architecture Art Deco isn't so much a building style as a style of ornamentation to the structures. Art Deco buildings may be designed in any style, from Beaux Arts to Gothic to Romanesque, and sometimes a combination of several styles; it is the striking ornamentation that makes the Art Deco style easy to recognize.

That Asheville has Art Deco architecture is a result both of the building boom in the city in the 1920s and the bust beginning in the Great Depression that stopped development and kept the old Art Deco structures extant.

Asheville City Building *(338 Hilliard Ave. at Pack Square Park, www.ashevillenc.gov, 828-251-1122),* completed in 1928, the eight-story masterpiece by Douglas Ellington is literally the symbol of Asheville, its abstracted form appearing as a logo on city graphics.

Ellington blended Beaux Arts design with Art Deco motifs, with a mass of orange-pink brick rising from a base of pink Georgia marble to the octagonal roof, tiled in green and pink terra cotta. The design uses feather motifs inspired by Native Americans.

Asheville High School *(419 McDowell Ave., www.ashevillecityschools.net, 828-350-2500),* completed in 1929, with later additions, was designed by Douglas Ellington. The hexagonal main building, of North Carolina pink granite, with three wings in a Y pattern radiating from it, sits elegantly on a terraced low hill just south of Downtown.

Originally known as Asheville Senior High before being renamed Lee Edwards High in 1935, the school was merged in 1969 with the local African-American high school (called Stephens-Lee and then South French Broad High) and given its present name of Asheville High. The 20-acre campus has suffered from a number of ungainly additions in recent years.

Biltmore Hospital *(8 Village Lane, now Festiva Biltmore Village, www.festiva-biltmorevillage.com, 828-337-3140)* was completed and opened in 1900 as Clarence Barker Memorial Hospital from designs by Richard Sharp Smith, with additions in 1902 and 1916 by local architect William Henry Lord.

Then, after a fire, a four-story, stone and brick 65-bed wing, in the Gothic Revival style with some Art Deco detailing including the entrance and the tile with concrete coping at the top of the building, was designed by Douglas Ellington, completed in 1930 and renamed Biltmore Hospital.

For four years beginning in the mid-1940s, it served as the maternal unit of Memorial Mission Hospital, although it was still called Biltmore Hospital. The old Biltmore Hospital was purchased by Imperial Life Insurance Company in 1951 and since has been used for insurance company offices and as a nursing home. It is now part of an international vacation rental and timeshare company, Festiva Travel, based in Asheville. The author was born in this hospital.

Coca-Cola Building *(345 Biltmore Ave.),* completed in 1940, was designed by local architect Henry I. Gaines, a founder of Six Associates. With its glass-block tchotchkes it was a fine example of late Art Deco and Art Moderne design. In its two-story lobby it had a curving staircase of stainless steel and aluminum. A remodel by new owner Mission Hospitals did not improve the building.

Federal Courthouse *(100 Otis St., www.ncwd.uscourts.gov, 828-771-7200),* was completed in 1930 as a U.S. Post Office and Federal Courthouse, and now is used only as the Federal District Courthouse and U.S. Bankruptcy Court.

It was designed by Washington supervising architect James A. Wetmore in a Classical style but with Art Deco touches, especially over the front entrance. The exterior is limestone with a granite base. The main Asheville Post Office moved to a pathetically undistinguished building on Coxe Avenue.

First Baptist Church *(5 Oak St., www.fbca.net, 828-252-4781),* completed in 1927, with later additions, is the building that brought Douglas Ellington to Asheville. Ellington designed the church in Beaux Arts and Renaissance styles with distinctive Art Deco ornamentation. The octagonal building of marble and brick has a massive two-story entrance with six brick columns, topped by a large tiled dome with a copper cupola. The sanctuary is a large, circular auditorium seating 2,000 on two levels.

Kress Building *(now Kress Emporium, 19 Patton Ave., www.thekressemporium.com, 828-281-2252),* completed in 1927, technically according to some architectural historians is not Art Deco, but the tan brick and cream terra cotta four-story, Renaissance-style building, with floral rosettes, definitely has an Art Deco feel. It is now occupied by a large craft shop with a number of vendors' stalls.

Pearlman's Furniture Building *(25 Page Ave.),* completed in 1940, is an Art Moderne structure opposite the Grove Arcade. Now housing an executive search firm, Kimmel and Associates, and renovated by Glazer Architecture, the front of the building features yellow brick, glass blocks, glass windows and stainless steel panels.

S&W Cafeteria *(60 Patton Ave. at Haywood St.),* completed in 1929, is another extraordinary work of Douglas Ellington. The design employs gold, black, blue and cream terra cotta facing, capped by blue terra cotta chevrons. The S&W Cafeteria, part of a regional chain owned by Frank Sherrill and Fred Webber, stayed in the building until it moved to the Asheville Mall in 1974. It has since been occupied by various businesses, including a steak house.

Shell Service Station *(now Wick and Greene Jewelers, 121 Patton Ave., www.wickandgreene.com, 828-253-1805),* completed in 1928, was designed by architect W. Stewart Rogers, one of the founders of Six Associates architectural firm.

Later an Exxon station, the little Art Deco building, with a two-story central cube and one-story side wings, all of creamy limestone, was beautifully restored in the mid-1980s by the owners of Wick and Greene jewelry store.

Tench and Francis Coxe Building *(20-22 College St.)*, a minor Art Deco building designed by Henry I. Gaines and completed in the 1930s, has a terra cotta facade with fountain and pyramid decorative elements.

Woolworth Building *(now Woolworth Walk, 25 Haywood St., www.woolworthwalk.com, 828-254-9234)*, completed in 1939, was designed by local architect Henry I. Gaines. Now used as a collection of craft shops and galleries, it has a facade of cream and orange terra cotta with plant and fountain designs over the upper-story windows.

In addition to the buildings in Downtown and nearby, there are several Art Deco buildings in West Asheville, notably two old service stations *(see below)*. Also, **Boyd Chapel** (360 School Rd., completed 1928) on the campus of The Asheville School near West Asheville is a Gothic stone building with Art Deco details.

Other Notable Buildings

All Souls Episcopal Cathedral *(9 Swan St., Biltmore Village, www.allsoulscathedral.org, 828-274-2681)*, completed in 1896 (with a 1954 addition) is one of the most striking church buildings in the South.

It was designed by Biltmore House architect Richard Morris Hunt in the Romanesque Revival style, inspired by abbey churches in Northern England. It features the short nave of the Greek cross rather than the long nave of the Latin cross. Hunt used the rough pebbledash (small stones imbedded in stucco) exterior he had used in other Biltmore Estate buildings, but here he set it off with dark red brick quoins and buttresses below dominating red-tile roofs.

Asheville Art Museum *(2 S. Pack Square, www.ashevilleart.org, 828-253-3227; 10-5 Tues.-Sat., 1-5 Sun., $8)*, completed in 1926, originally as Pack Memorial Library, was designed by New York architect Edward L. Tilton, who specialized in libraries. The three-story Renaissance Revival building with graceful arched windows on the second level and an arched two-story entrance has an exterior clad in Georgia marble. It is now the Asheville Art Museum, a part of the Pack Place complex. The library moved to a new building on Haywood Street in 1978.

Asheville Savings Bank Building *(11 Church St.,*
www.ashevillesavingsbank.com, 828-250-8430), combined into one V-shaped building from three separate building by Ronald Greene in 1922, is a fine example of Neo-Classical architecture. A misguided renovation in the mid-1960s hid the good points of the building, but Classical details were restored in 2005. The main part of the building exterior is concrete made to resemble stone; a part at the south end is brick.

Two-story Tuscan columns flank the dramatic corner entrance, with a clock and a pair of windows above the door, with a Doric entablature between the columns and the roof. James M. Westall, a lawyer who was president of what was then Asheville Federal Savings and Loan in the 1960s and 70s, was the grandson of builder J. M. Westall, brother of Julia Westall Wolfe, mother of Thomas Wolfe. An Asheville advertising agency co-owned by the author represented the bank in the 1970s.

Basilica of St. Lawrence (97 Haywood St.,
www.saintlawrencebasilica.org, 828-252-6942), completed in 1909, is a masterpiece of Spanish Baroque Revival architecture. It is the creation of engineer-architect Rafael Guastavino (1842-1908), who came to the U.S. from Barcelona in 1881.

He developed and enhanced a Catalonian style of fireproof construction with self-supporting vaulted dome roofs using courses of lightweight tiles fastened with Portland cement.

His company constructed more than 1,000 buildings in the U.S., including Grand Central Terminal, Grant's Tomb and the Cathedral of St. John the Divine in New York and the Boston Public Library.

In the 1890s, Guastavino worked briefly on the Biltmore Estate and then, in association with Richard Sharp Smith, designed and built the St. Lawrence Basilica. No wood or steel is used in building. The Basilica has a granite base and walls of brick with terra cotta inserts, topped by a self-supporting 58-by-82-foot oval dome. Floors are tile. Twin towers at the front, originally roofed with tile, are now covered in copper. Guastavino is buried in the church. Self-guided and guided tours of the Basilica are available – see the website for details. Note that there are plans for a new hotel across the street from the Basilica.

Battery Park Hotel *(1 Battle Square, now Battery Park Senior Apartments, www.nationalchurchresidences.org, 828-252-5277),* completed in 1924, stands on the site of the 1886 Queen Anne-style hotel by the same name. The original hotel was the first hotel in the South with an elevator.

It suffered a fire the early 1920s and was razed. E. W. Grove, who had built the Grove Park Inn and before his death in 1927 had planned and started building the Grove Arcade, just to the south of the Battery Park, hired W. L. Stoddart of New York to design the 14-story, 220-room hotel. Stoddart designed a number of other hotels in North Carolina including the Sir Walter Hotel in Raleigh.

Grove had the hill on which the original Battery Park Hotel leveled, a massive undertaking that required almost two years of work. The Neoclassical building, faced with brick with limestone and terra cotta highlighting, is relatively undistinguished. In his novel *Look Homeward, Angel,* Thomas Wolfe called the Battery Park the work of a "gigantic biscuit-cutter." It was in the Battery Park Hotel where Tony Buttitta in the mid-1930s owned a bookshop and in the summer of 1935 met F. Scott Fitzgerald, writing about him in his memoir *After the Good Gay Times.* The hotel operated until 1972; in the 1980s it was converted to 122 apartments for seniors and remains so today.

BB&T Building *(1 W. Pack Square, 828-210-8155, www.towerassoc.com),* completed in 1965, at 17 stories above ground level was for many years the tallest building in Western North Carolina. Tower 3 of the Harrah's complex in Cherokee, completed in 2012, at 22 stories is now the tallest.

Originally named the Northwestern Bank Building, the BB&T Building is a stark, rectilinear concrete, steel and glass form typical of skyscrapers built in the 1950s and 1960s in the International style

It was designed by the Charlotte architectural firm of Whittington & Associates and in some ways is a bad copy of the famous Seagram Building in New York designed by Mies van der Rohe.

A big difference is the way the two buildings treat the ground floor and the space around the building. The Seagram Building is distinctive because it has a large plaza with fountains at the base and is set back from the street, with expansive public space, whereas the BB&T building has only a small setback, just a tiny plaza and very little public space on the ground floor. The glass and exterior finishings of the BB&T Building were done on the cheap, unlike the Seagram Building. The proportions are also grossly different, in that the BB&T at 18 stories looks squat and the Seagram Building at 35 stories is elegantly tall.

Today, the interior and exterior of the building are overdue for renovation and upgrading, although an advanced new elevator system has been stalled. The higher floors have dramatic views of Asheville and the surrounding area, but at present there are no public areas in the building from which to view the city. In 2013, an interest in the BB&T Building was sold to a Charlotte developer, and plans have been announced for the office tower to be turned into a boutique hotel with some retail and possibly some residential uses, with the former parking garage across the street also being the site of a new seven-story hotel.

Biltmore Building *(1 N. Pack Square, www.biltmore.com, 828-225-6776, now headquarters for the Biltmore Companies),* completed in 1980, was originally built for Akzona, a textile company that then owned American Enka, and named the Akzona Building. It was acquired by the Biltmore Company in 1986 and renamed. The prominent I.M. Pei & Partners firm of New York, which was also responsible for the glass Pyramids at the Louvre in Paris, the John Hancock Tower in Boston and the National Gallery of Art in Washington, DC, designed the seven-story Modernist building, but there is little evidence Pei himself worked on the design. The coated-glass windows reflect the Vance Monument obelisk, the Jackson Building and the Pack Park scene. The building is now signed as the Merrill Lynch building.

Buncombe County Courthouse *(60 Courthouse Plaza, www.buncombecounty.org, 828-250- 4100),* completed in 1928, isn't actually ugly, but the 17-story Neoclassical structure, clad in limestone and brick, sits next to the elegant and stylish Asheville City Building, making it appear chunky and pedestrian like an overweight car salesman escorting a stylish young model.

It was designed by the Washington, DC, firm of Milburn & Heister after Buncombe County commissioners rejected the Art Deco ideas of Douglas Ellington.

Milburn & Heister specialized in courthouses and had designed at least a dozen in North Carolina alone. One of the principals of the firm, Frank Milburn, had retired to Asheville in 1926.

Citizen-Times Building *(14 O. Henry Ave., www.citizen-times.com, 800-672-2472),* completed in 1939, was designed in the International style by Asheville architect Anthony Lord, a founder of Six Associates. The ink-stained wretches of Asheville's only remaining daily newspaper (now owned by Gannett) work in this four-story building, with limestone relieved by small glass-block windows. Printing and production of the paper was moved to a plant near Enka and then to Greenville, S.C.

Central United Methodist Church *(27 Church St., www.centralumc.org, 828-253-3316),* completed in 1905, is of Gothic Revival design, with some Romanesque Revival elements. The architect was Reuben H. Hunt of Chattanooga. Central's builder J. M. Westall was a brother of Julia Westall Wolfe, mother of Thomas Wolfe. Built on the site of Asheville's first church, constructed in 1837, Central United Methodist is the oldest continuously operating church in Asheville. It has some 3,000 members.

Drhumor Building *(48 Patton Ave.),* completed in 1895, is a four-story brick building with limestone accents designed by Allen L. Melton in the Romanesque Rival style popularized by Henry Hobson Richardson. Note especially the frieze at the top of the first floor, with carved British lions, human faces and other designs by sculptor Fred Miles, who worked on the Biltmore House. The charming, restored building is now offices for what is claimed to be the oldest continuously practicing law firm in Asheville, McGuire, Wood & Bissette. Drhumor is pronounced either Drummer or Dru-MORE, depending on whom you ask, but it is *not* pronounced Doctor Humor.

Eagles Building *(73 Broadway St., now WCQS, www.wcqs.org, 828- 210-4800),* completed in 1914, is a three-story brick and limestone building designed in a Neo-Classical style by Richard Sharp Smith for the Fraternal Order of Eagles. It was rehabbed and the original facade restored by Patti Glazer of Glazer Architects of Asheville. Local public radio station WCQS occupies the first floor, with offices and apartments on upper levels.

Enka Village *(off Sand Hill Rd. and Lake Drive in the Enka-Candler area),* built 1928-30, was a company town developed by American Enka.

Enka (the "e" is pronounced as in pen, not like Inca, as many locals think it is) was owned by a Dutch company that in 1928 began constructing the largest rayon plant in the U.S.

Eventually the Enka plant would become one of the largest employers in the region, with some 3,500 workers. Enka Village was a planned residential community, part of the European garden city movement that was meant to provide attractive housing near the workplace for workers and managers. For the managers, large red brick homes with tile roofs in Tudor and Colonial Revival styles were built along a road overlooking 62-acre Enka Lake -- now Biltmore Lake -- by local architect William Waldo Dodge, who designed many homes in Biltmore Forest.

For workers, one- and two-story homes, in brick and frame, were built off Sand Hill Road across from the Enka plant by Lockwood, Green Engineers. By 1930, about 100 homes had been constructed. While the factory continued to produce rayon and then nylon the village was never completed due to the impact of the Depression. In 1958 the homes were sold to individual owners. In 1985, American Enka was purchased by what is now BASF. Limited manufacturing continues at the Enka plant.

Some 1,300 acres of Enka land was sold to Biltmore Farms, a development and hotel company owned by a branch of the Vanderbilt family, but not now directly affiliated with Biltmore Estate. In 2002, the company began building the upscale Biltmore Lake development, with some homes in the $1 to $2 million-range and with a total of more than 550 homes sold and occupied.

Flatiron Building *(10-20 Battery Park Ave.),* completed in 1926, gets our vote as one of the most charming buildings in Asheville, though it's hardly the most original, as most cities have a wedge-shaped building similar to this one. Designed by Asheville architect Albert C. Wirth in the Neoclassical style, the eight-story building has long been home to local physicians and dentists (the author's pediatrician had offices here). The elevator in the Flatiron Building still has a real, live operator. Also look for the flatiron – literally a flat iron -- sculpture nearby on Asheville's Urban Trail.

Grove Arcade *(1 Page Ave., www.grovearcade.com),* opened in 1929, is the creation of the drive and imagination of Edwin Wiley Grove, a Tennessee-born health tonic magnate who also built the Grove Park Inn. Grove's vision was for a large city arcade, similar to those in Europe, that would have stores and shops in an enclosed, sky-lit mall, with rooftop gardens and offices in a 14-story skyscraper rising above the arcade. Beside it would be a large hotel.

Grove hired Asheville architect Charles N. Parker to help him execute his vision. The Battery Park Hotel (architect William L. Stoddart) was completed in 1924.

The massive three-story arcade, under construction from 1926 to 1929, covering 257,000 square feet, or around 6 acres, was completed, along with the first two stories of the planned office tower. Grove, however, did not live to see his project come completely to fruition. He died in 1927, and the main part of the tower was never built, due to the Depression.

The Grove Arcade was occupied by shops and offices until 1942, when the U.S. government took over the building for a division of the General Accounting Office. From 1951 to 1995 the Arcade was home to the National Weather Records Center, now the National Climatic Data Center located in the Veach-Bailey Federal Building on Patton Avenue. The government bureaucrats bricked in the windows of the building. In 1994, the Feds transferred the Grove Arcade back to the City of Asheville for one dollar.

It was renovated and reopened in 2002 as a city market patterned after Pike Place Market in Seattle. While never as successful as the Seattle market, the building, leased to the Grove Arcade Public Market Foundation, now is nearly fully occupied, with shops on the first floor, a number of restaurants with outdoor seating on the Page Avenue side, and offices and 42 luxury apartments on upper levels. The number of visitors to the Arcade isn't known, but about half a million people annually pass by the south end of the Arcade on Battery Park Avenue.

The Arcade stretches over an entire city block. The exterior is covered in cream-colored terra cotta and granite. The style is an amalgam of Palladian, Renaissance, Gothic and Tudor elements. The interior has marble floors, beautifully lit by skylights, and the floor slopes downward from north to south, with a total of 16 feet drop. The north end of the Arcade (near what is now the Battery Park Senior Apartments) is guarded by plaster-winged lions, sometimes incorrectly referred to as griffins. The mythological griffins have the body of a lion but the wings and head of an eagle, usually with front legs with eagle talons. The Arcade has many gargoyles, 88 on the exterior and 50 inside. In addition there four cherubim-like grotesques and eight rams' heads.

Grove Park Inn, an Omni Resort *(290 Macon Ave., www.groveparkinn.com, 828-252-2711, parking fees of $10 to $12, and $15 for valet, may apply),* completed in 1913, with later additions, is one of the country's great resort hotel buildings. It was designed by E.W. Grove, who also built the Grove Arcade and the second Battery Park Hotel, and his son-in-law, Fred Seely, with some consultation with New York architect Henry Ives Cobb. Seely, however, was mostly responsible for the design.

The idea for the six-story, 150-room hotel owed much to the New Canyon Lodge in Yellowstone Park (opened in 1911 and demolished in 1962) and to other national park lodges in the West. Like the Canyon Lodge, the original part of Grove Park Inn used local natural materials – in the case of the Grove Park huge uncut granite boulders from Sunset Mountain, chestnut, oak and other local wood timbers and a roof of red clay tile – and features a large, rustic lobby.

The Grove Park's 80 by 120-foot (9,600 square feet) lobby, a victim in some ways of later renovations, retains the original large fireplaces bookending the room. The fireplace openings are each 10 feet wide and 6 feet high. An elevator runs up the back of one fireplace chimney.

The Sunset Terrace off the lobby offers views of downtown Asheville and of the golf course designed by Donald Ross. The furnishings in the lobby and in the rooms of the original section are by Roycrofters, the famous Arts and Crafts collective in East Aurora, N.Y., near Buffalo. The lobby has paddle arm sofas and chairs of wormy chestnut. The Grove Park Inn has the largest collection of Arts and Crafts furniture in the world.

On the grounds of the inn is the **Biltmore Industries** complex, a group of pebbledash cottages completed in 1917, now housing shops and weaving and antique auto museums. Ten United States presidents (Taft, Wilson, Coolidge, Hoover, Roosevelt, Eisenhower, Nixon, Bush, Clinton and Obama) have stayed at the inn, along with many famous entertainers and writers. F. Scott Fitzgerald spent the summers of 1935-36 at the inn, staying in rooms 451 and 453. After the U.S. entered World War II, several hundred foreign diplomats were interned at the inn until they could be sent to a neutral country. In 1942, Philippine president Manuel Quezon, forced to flee his country due to the Japanese invasion, established the government of the Philippines in exile in the Anne Hathaway Cottage at the Grove Park.

A self-guided walking tour of the hotel and grounds takes at least two hours.

The Grove Park has gone through a series of owners since E. W. Grove's day. The longest-tenured owner was Charles Sammon, an insurance multi-millionaire, who bought the inn in 1955 and whose company owned it until 2012. Sammons added the 202-room Sammons Wing in 1984 and the 166-room Vanderbilt Wing in 1988.

The current number of rooms and suites totals 551. The additions, along with the purchase of the Asheville Country Club golf course in 1976 and the opening of a large spa in 2001, has made the resort much more viable as a business, but the new wings are architecturally inferior to the original section, bad modern imitations of the classic original construction.

In 2012, the Grove Park Inn was sold by the Sammons company to KSL Capital Partners, a private equity firm in Denver. Then, in mid-2013 it was sold by KSL to Omni Hotels, which operates a number of hotels and resorts around the U.S. and in Mexico.

Hotel Asheville Building *(55 Haywood St. at Walnut St., now Malaprop's Bookstore, www.malaprops.com, 828-254-6734),* completed in 1914, was originally built for the BPO Elks. The four-story brick building then became the Jenkins Hotel and from 1932 until 1965 the Hotel Asheville. It is now home to the best bookstore in the region, with apartments on higher floors. Note the second floor with its arcaded veranda.

Jackson Building *(22 S. Pack Square)* completed in 1924, at 13 stories is usually considered the first skyscraper in Western North Carolina. With its thin profile (the front is on Pack Square is only 27 feet wide) it remains the most stylish. It was designed in the Gothic style by local architect Ronald Greene for real estate developer L.B. Jackson, using terra cotta and brick over a steel frame. Gargoyles near the top guard the building. It was built on the site of the monument shop of W.O. Wolfe, Thomas Wolfe's father, where, it is said, the angel of *Look Homeward, Angel* was displayed. Over the years, it has been the home of several local banks, including in the 1970s Western Carolina Bank. It shares elevators with the **Westall Building** next door.

Legal Building *(10-14 S. Pack Square),* completed in 1909, is five-story Renaissance design by Smith & Currier. It was originally the headquarters of the Central Bank & Trust, which collapsed during the Depression.

Lewis Memorial Park Office *(415 Beaverdam Rd., North Asheville, 828-252-5081)* is a small but striking work by Douglas Ellington. The stone Art Deco office at the entrance to the cemetery uses Ellington's trademarked octagonal design for its cupola and roof. There's now also a pet cemetery here, for dogs and cats with good taste.

Log Cabin Motor Court *(330 Weaverville Hwy./U.S. Hwy. 25, www.theashevillecabins.com, 828-645-6546),* about 6 miles north of Downtown Asheville, opened around 1930. This well-preserved collection of log cabins -- now 21 one- and two-bedroom cabins made from round logs with prominent white-painted chinking between logs -- is a classic from the early days of automotive tourism. Scenes from the 1958 movie *Thunder Road* starring Robert Mitchum were filmed in one of the cabins, Goldview. It rents for $130 a night.

The Manor *(265 Charlotte St.),* completed in 1898 with additions in 1903 and 1913 is an example of an Asheville tourist resort from the late 19th century. The rambling old hotel, designed in the Queen Anne and Shingle styles by New York architect Bradford Gilbert, was originally marketed as an English inn in America.

There is a Tudor Revival gatehouse at the entrance and a group of cottages in several styles, including Craftsman, Shingle and Tudor on the grounds. At one time, the author's office was in a Georgian Revival house adjoining the Manor grounds.

Ravenscroft *(29 Ravenscroft Dr.)*, completed in the late 1840s, with addition in the early 1900s, is thought to be the oldest building in Downtown Asheville, and the second-oldest brick house in Asheville after the **Smith McDowell House** *(see below)*. It has a three-story center tower with two-story wings, all in brick with entablatures on the wings and tower, in the Greek Revival style. Originally Ravenscroft was a school, later a boarding house and now it houses offices. Except for its age (Asheville isn't an old city), Ravenscroft is undistinguished.

Scottish Rite Cathedral and Masonic Temple *(80 Broadway St.)*, completed in 1913 and designed by Smith & Carrier, who must have been on laudanum at the time, is one of the ugliest and most awkward buildings in Asheville. The four-story brick fortress, with limestone trim, has an astonishingly monstrous portico over the entrance with a brace of Ionic columns on each side. This building is so grotesque and unappealing that it is almost worth seeing.

Vance Monument on Pack Square with I.M. Pei firm-designed building in background – photo by Rose Lambert-Sluder

Vance Monument *(Pack Square),* completed in 1896, is a 65-feet high granite obelisk -- the granite was quarried in nearby Henderson County -- designed by Richard Sharp Smith. It honors the Buncombe-born Zebulon Baird Vance (1830-1894), who was governor of North Carolina during the Civil War and afterwards, and later also a U.S. Senator.

The legacy of Vance, a Democrat, is now somewhat controversial because he was a slaveholder and a segregationist, though he also reached out to Jewish residents and spoke out against the anti-Semitism of the time.

Veach-Bailey Federal Building *(151 Patton Ave. at Otis St.),* completed in 1995, is home to the National Climatic Data Center *(www.ncdc.noaa.gov, 828-271-4800),* the largest depository of weather and climate information in the United States. In front of the six-story, Post-Modern building is a controversial iron sculpture, "Passages," by Albert Paley. Some artistically illiterate Asheville residents think it should be called "Junkyard."

West Asheville Aycock School Historic District *(400 block of Haywood Rd. on both sides of I-240)* consists mostly of low-rise commercial buildings built in the 1920s and 1930s. Among the notable structures here are the **McGeachy Filling Station** *(405 Haywood Rd., completed in 1936),* a one-story Art Deco-style building with stucco exterior, now operating as a convenience store and alternative fuel station – unfortunately this property is in poor condition and badly needs some TLC; **West Asheville Bank & Trust Building** *(414 Haywood Rd., completed in 1927),* a Neoclassical building of light-colored brick – the bank closed in 1932 during the Depression and now is used as offices; **West Asheville Fire Station** *(421-423 Haywood Rd., completed in 1922),* a two-story Mission Revival brick building; and **Universal Motors** *(428 Haywood Rd., completed in 1928),* a one-story brick building with a parapet (a low wall on the roof) with concrete coping and circular cast stone medallion, originally built as a Ford and Lincoln dealership and in the early 1940s home to a Willys Americar dealership co-owned by the author's father – the Americar, produced from 1937 to 1942, sold new for around $600. The **Charles B. Aycock School** *(441 Haywood Rd.)* after which the Historic District is named, a 1953 one-story, flat-roofed building designed by Six Associates, the fourth school at this site, is of little architectural interest.

West Asheville End of the Car Line Historic District *(700 and 800 blocks of Haywood Rd.)* features a collection of mostly early 20th century low-rise brick commercial buildings. It is designated by the National Register of Historic Places as the West Asheville End of Car Line Historic District. From 1911 to 1934, the Asheville street car line ended at a turn-around point at the intersection of Haywood and Brevard roads.

Among the more interesting buildings in this area are the **Bledsoe Building** *(771-783 Haywood Rd., completed in 1927),* the largest commercial building on Haywood Road; the Art Deco **Isis Theater** *(743 Haywood Rd., completed in 1937),* renovated and reopened in 2012 as the Isis Restaurant & Music Hall; and **Pure Oil Gas Station** *(784 Haywood Rd., completed in 1947)* with a steeply pitched and gabled roof covered in blue terra cotta tile, now the Universal Joint restaurant.

YMI Building *(39 S. Market St., corner of Eagle and Market Sts., www.packplace.org, 828-257-4500; exhibit area open Tues.-Fri. 10-5, $5)* was completed in 1893, under the direction of Richard Sharp Smith. George Vanderbilt funded the construction of the Young Men's Institute as a community center for Asheville's African-American community.

It is located in the heart of what was the Eagle-Market Streets African-American business district. However, far from reflecting any African-American tradition, the three-story building is in Richard Morris Hunt's English vernacular style used in Biltmore Village and for auxiliary buildings on the Biltmore Estate, with pebbledash exterior walls and brick window and door trim. After serving for a time as a YMCA branch, it sat idle until becoming the home in 1988 of the YMI Cultural Center, now a part of the Pack Place complex. However, in recent years its future as a repository of black culture has been put in doubt.

For information on the Biltmore House and Biltmore Estate buildings, see the Top Attractions section; for information on buildings in the River Arts District, see the Arts in Asheville section; for information on architecture in towns near Asheville, including Black Mountain, Brevard, Highlands and Hendersonville, see the Nearby Small Towns and Villages section.

Notable Houses and Residential Historic Districts

Biltmore Forest In 1920, Edith Vanderbilt sold 1,500 acres on the south side of the Biltmore Estate to a company set up to develop a residential area for "persons of moderate means" (by Vanderbilt standards, one supposes.) Several local developers began building houses, mostly in Tudor and Colonial Revival styles. Edith Vanderbilt herself in 1925 moved into one called **The Firth** on Firth Drive. Donald Ross designed the golf course for the Biltmore Forest Country Club.

A number of beautiful homes were built around the golf course, including the **Judge Junius Adams House** *(11 Stuyvesant Rd., 1921)* and the William Dodge-designed **William Knight House** *(15 E. Forest Rd., 1927).*

Biltmore Forest remains one of Asheville's most elite neighborhoods. Some homes in Biltmore Forest are valued at $2 million to $4 million or more. Actress Andie MacDowell had a home here for many years, before moving back to Los Angeles. She still owns property near Asheville.

Chestnut-Hill Historic District This historic neighborhood just north of Downtown Asheville is centered around East Chestnut and North Liberty streets. Most of the buildings in this area were built from 1880 to 1930, in the Craftsman, Queen Anne and Colonial Revival styles.

Beaufort House Inn *(61 N. Liberty St., www.beauforthouse.com, 828-254-8334, completed 1895),* a Queen Anne style home built for North Carolina attorney general and Asheville mayor Theodore Davidson and for a short time in the 1940s the home of actor Charlton Heston, is the most striking building in the district. The architect was Allen L. Melton, who also designed the Drhumor Building Downtown. Beaufort, by the way, is pronounced BO-fort, as with the North Carolina coastal town, not pronounced like the South Carolina town. **Princess Anne Hotel** *(301 E. Chestnut, www.princessannehotel.com, 828-258-0986, completed in 1924)* opened as a hotel for the families of tuberculosis patients but went through several owners and uses until the three-story Shingle-style building was renovated in 2003-2005 by local preservationist Howard Stafford and returned to being a 16-suite hotel. The **Tennant-Pritchard House** *(223 E. Chestnut, completed 1895)* was designed in the Queen Anne style by architect James A. Tennant as his own home. U.S. Senator Jeter Pritchard also lived in the house. **Chestnut Street Inn** *(176 E. Chestnut, www.chestnutstreeinn.com, 828-285-0705, completed 1905)* is a restored Colonial Revival style house now used as a B&B.

Grove Park Historic District *(See also the Grove Park Inn above.)* The jewel of the Grove Park and Proximity Park area is the **Dr. Carl V. Reynolds House,** now the **Albemarle Inn** *(86 Edgemont Rd., www.albemarleinn.com, 828-255-0027, completed in 1909).* The two-story Neoclassical building is a charmingly restored B&B. The most famous resident of the house was Hungarian composer Béla Bartók, who spent the winter of 1943-44 in Asheville and completed his "Third Concerto for Piano," also known as the "Asheville Concerto," here.

The **William Jennings Bryan House** *(107 Evelyn Place, completed in 1917)* was designed in the Colonial Revival style by Smith & Carrier as a retirement home for the populist presidential candidate, who lived here for several years before moving to Florida.

The **Reuben Robertson House** *(1 Evelyn Place, completed in 1922)* was designed by New York architect James Gamble Rogers for Robertson, the president of Champion, the paper mill in Canton (naturally the president wouldn't live near his odiferous factory). Richard Sharp Smith designed **St. Mary's Episcopal Church** *(337 Charlotte St. at Macon Ave., www.stmarysasheville.org, 828-254-5836, completed in 1914)* in the Gothic Revival style. Smith also designed the adjoining English cottage style rectory, completed in 1925 after Smith's death.

Kenilworth This neighborhood in southeast Asheville was established in the late 19th century and early 20th century. It was named for the original **Kenilworth Inn** -- completed in 1891 and destroyed by fire in 1909 -- that stood nearby. The "new" **Kenilworth Inn** *(60 Caledonia Rd.)* was completed in 1918 in the Tudor Revival style, under the direction of architect Ronald Greene. It later became a psychiatric hospital, Appalachian Hall, and then Charter Hospital, another psychiatric institution. It is now an apartment building, Kenilworth Inn Apartments. Many of the older homes in Kenilworth are in the Tudor Revival style, although the area also has Prairie, Bungalow and even Spanish Colonial homes, along with some homes built in the mid-20th century. The **Annie Reed House** *(68 Kenilworth Rd., completed 1948)* is a notable example of International style, by Ronald Greene.

Lakeview Park This 1920s subdivision in North Asheville curves around man-made Beaver Lake and the Donald Ross golf course, now operated by the **Asheville Country Club**. Most of the original 100 or so homes, as in Biltmore Forest, are in pretentious Tudor Revival and Colonial Revival styles. Lakeview Park was planned by noted landscape architect **John Nolen** (1869-1937), a student of Frederick Law Olmsted who also designed Myers Park in Charlotte and worked on plans for a number of cities in Florida including Clearwater and St. Petersburg.

Among the grander homes in Lakeview Park are the **Campbell House** *(144 Marlborough Rd., completed 1925)* and **Stratford Towers** *(193 Stratford Rd., completed 1925),* originally the residence of the president of Central Bank & Trust, which failed in 1930 after making too many bad real estate loans. Less ambitious homes were built in Lakeview Park after World War II. The **Dixie Highway** (now U.S. Highway 25), a collection of paved roads constructed and expanded from 1915 to 1927 connecting the Carolinas with Florida and the Midwest, passed through the Lakeview Park community. Beaver Lake is owned collectively by the residents of Lakeview Park, not by the City of Asheville. The area around the lake is a bird sanctuary.

Montford Historic District, just north of Downtown Asheville, is a 300-acre neighborhood that dates from 1893. It has some 600 homes, including a number designed by Richard Sharp Smith. Nearly all of the homes in the district were built before 1930. Architectural styles of homes in Montford range from Queen Anne to Craftsman to Neoclassical and Colonial Revival. The 87-acre Riverside Cemetery, where Thomas Wolfe, O. Henry, Richard Sharp Smith and Zebulon Vance are buried, is within the Montford Historic District.

Montford is also Asheville's "B&B District," with more than a dozen licensed bed and breakfast inns. Near the north end of Montford is the new Asheville Area Chamber of Commerce building, with its excellent **Asheville Visitor Center** *(36 Montford Ave., www.exploreasheville.com, 828-258-6129)*. The Visitor Center can provide information on a walking tour of Montford and other areas and a free map guide to the architecture of the district.

The main streets in Montford are Montford Avenue, the spine of the neighborhood, along with Cumberland Avenue and Flint Street, all running more or less north-south.

Among the many exceptional residential buildings in the district are: **Carolina B&B** *(177 Cumberland Ave., www.carolinabb.com, 828-254-3608, completed in 1901)* is a simple but pleasant pebbledash stucco house by Richard Sharp Smith, in the English vernacular style, with what the owner calls an Arts and Crafts front porch. Inside, the rooms have heart pine floors. **Lion and Rose B&B** *(276 Montford Ave., www.lion-rose.com, 828-255-7673, completed 1896)* is an elegant rose-colored house, beautifully restored and maintained and with extensive landscaping. It combines Colonial Revival, Neoclassical and Queen Anne elements. A special detail is the large stained glass Palladian window at the top of the oak stairs. Tommy French, one of the characters in Thomas Wolfe's *Look Homeward, Angel*, was said to live in this house.

Black Walnut B&B *(288 Montford Ave., www.blackwalnut.com, 800-381-3878, completed 1899)* was designed by Richard Sharp Smith in the English vernacular style, with half-timbered pebbledash exterior. It also has elements of Queen Anne architecture. Also known as the Ottis Green House (Green was a mayor of Asheville), it has been graciously restored and superbly maintained. **1900 Inn on Montford** *(296 Montford Ave., www.innonmontford.com, 800-254-9569, completed 1900)*, another Richard Sharp Smith work in the same area of Montford Avenue, features pebbledash and shingled walls. It has been lovingly restored and furnished in style. A cottage in the back is a later addition.

Abbington Green B&B *(46 Cumberland Circle, www.abbingtongreen.com, 828-251-2454, completed in 1908)* is a Colonial Revival house designed by Richard Sharp Smith. **Wright Inn** *(235 Pearson Dr., www.wrightinn.com, 828-251-0789, completed in 1899)* is an excellent example of Queen Anne style by architect George Barber. It has multiple gables and a charming side gazebo with conical roof. It has been completely restored.

Homewood at Highland Hospital *(19 Zillicoa St., completed in 1922, with later additions)* is part of the original Highland Hospital complex. The large stone house was built in the pretentious Gothic style similar to that of parts of Duke University in Durham. Homewood was the home of Zelda Fitzgerald's psychiatrist, Dr. Robert Carroll, founder of what was then called a mental hospital and tuberculosis sanatorium. Zelda died in a 1948 fire that destroyed the main building at the hospital. Homewood is now used as an event venue. **Rumbough House** *(49 Zillicoa St., completed in 1892)* is an impressive example of the Queen Anne and Colonial Revival styles. On the second floor is a five-sided central bay with windows. The house was purchased by Duke University in the 1950s to serve as an administrative building for Highland Hospital. Duke closed and sold Highland Hospital in 1981.

Frances Apartments *(333 Cumberland Ave., completed 1926)* is a charming, gabled three-story apartment building with an unusual rough brick and concrete exterior. The author's favorite high school English teacher lived here. Small studio apartments in the building start at around $600.

Smith-McDowell House *(283 Victoria Rd., www.nchistory.org, 828-253-9231, completed c. 1840 with a 1913 renovation; Wed.-Sat. 10-4, Sun. noon-4; $8 adults, $10 during Christmas season)* is believed to be the oldest surviving house in Asheville and the oldest brick house in Buncombe County. Bricks for the walls, which are up to 20 inches thick, are thought to have been made locally.

It's a two-story Federal style house, with Greek Revival interiors, although the early 20th century renovation by Richard Sharp Smith added Neoclassical elements. Frederick Law Olmsted's firm did the landscaping around 1900. The house was restored in the late 20th century under the direction of architect Henry I. Gaines and is now operated as a museum by the WNC Historical Society. It is especially known for its Christmas decorations.

Asheville's Famous Architects

The most prominent exponent of Art Deco in Asheville was architect **Douglas Ellington** (1886-1960), who arrived in Asheville from Pittsburgh in 1926. He had trained at the École des Beaux-Arts in Paris. During the next six years, Ellington designed several of the most striking buildings in the city, including the Asheville City Building, S&W Cafeteria, First Baptist Church and Asheville High School. Several of his buildings use octagonal shapes, with decorative elements from Native American culture.

Richard Morris Hunt (1827-1895), the first American to attend the École des Beaux-Arts in Paris, designed the Biltmore House, then as now the largest private home in America, along with a number of buildings in Biltmore Village including All Souls Episcopal Cathedral. Following the wishes of George Vanderbilt, a long-time client, Hunt based Biltmore on the Renaissance chateaux of France. Among other Hunt designs are the Fifth Avenue facade of the Metropolitan Museum of Art in New York and the Fogg Museum at Harvard.

At the Biltmore Estate, Hunt worked closely with pioneering landscape architect **Frederick Law Olmsted** (1822-1903). By the time Olmsted came to Asheville to design the Biltmore Estate, he was already world-famous for his designs of Central Park in New York (along with Riverside Park, Prospect Park, Forest Park and Morningside Park in that city), the Emerald Necklace parks in Boston, the 1893 Chicago World Exposition and parts of the campuses of Auburn University, Bryn Mawr College, Cornell University, Oregon State University, Smith College, Stanford University, Washington University, Yale University and others. Olmsted had 125,000 acres to work with at Biltmore, including the formal gardens around the main house, along with miles of roads to the house and tens of thousands of acres of managed forestland. Olmsted recommended that George Vanderbilt hire Gifford Pinchot, who with Dr. Carl Schenck would establish the first forestry school in the United States and help develop what would become the Pisgah National Forest. Pinchot later served as the first chief of the USDA Forest Service.

Six Associates was established in 1942 by six prominent Asheville architects, who until then each had their own practices. The motivation behind the founding of the collective practice was to achieve a size large enough to qualify for bidding on wartime architectural commissions. The six architects were **William Waldo Dodge Jr., Henry Irvin Gaines, Anthony Lord, William Stewart Rodgers, Erle G. Stillwell** and **Charles Waddell.**

Individually and as a firm they designed dozens of well-known Western North Carolina commercial and residential buildings, mostly in the International style. Among the buildings are the Asheville Citizen-Times Building, American Enka Administration Building, the UNC-A's Ramsey Library, Woolworth Walk and many of the buildings at Mars Hill College and Western Carolina University. None of the founders is still alive, but Six Associates remained in business under that name until the mid-1990s. The firm was bought by Ellis/Naeyaert/Genheimer Associates and eventually became a part of what is now CJMW Architecture, but that firm no longer has an Asheville office.

Yorkshire-born **Richard Sharp Smith** (1852-1924) came to Asheville from New York in 1890 at age 37 to be the Biltmore House on-site supervising architect for chief architect Richard Morris Hunt. Smith designed several outbuildings on the Biltmore Estate and a number of buildings in Biltmore Village. He stayed in Asheville after the completion of Biltmore House and opened an architecture office. Before his death here in 1924, Smith designed more than 700 homes and commercial buildings in the Asheville area, some as sole architect and after 1906 in partnership with **Albert Heath Carrier** (Smith & Carrier). It's nearly impossible to overstate the impact Smith had on the look of Asheville. Many of the commercial buildings constructed in Asheville between 1900 and 1920 were designed by Smith or by Smith & Carrier. Among Smith's works are the Vance Monument on Pack Square and the Masonic Temple and Legal Building Downtown. He also designed distinctive homes in the Montford, Biltmore Village, Grove Park and Chestnut-Liberty areas of Asheville. Much of his residential work is in the English vernacular style, using half-timbered exteriors with pebbledash (pebbles embedded in stucco), but he also was a master of Queen Anne, Colonial Revival, Craftsman and several other styles.

MUSEUMS

There are around 100 museums in Asheville and Western North Carolina. Here are the most interesting, noteworthy and unusual ones in Asheville and nearby.

A reproduction of the Thomas Wolfe angel in front of the Asheville Art Museum – photo by Rose Lambert-Sluder

Most museums have free or reduced admission for members, and most are free for young children (ages vary).

Small museums run by volunteers from the local historical society often offer free admission, but donations are welcomed and sometimes actively requested. Remember, hours for some of these museums, especially small local ones, are subject to change. Most museums are closed on major holidays such as Christmas, New Years and Thanksgiving. It is best to call ahead to confirm open days and times.

ASHEVILLE & ENVIRONS

Asheville Art Museum *(2 S. Pack Square, 828-253-3227, www.ashevilleart.org; Tue.-Sat. 10-5, Sun. 1-5, $8 adults, $7 students and seniors),* established in 1948, focuses on 20th and 21st century art, especially the work of Southeastern artists. The museum has a permanent collection of about 3,500 works, plus an additional 5,000 architectural drawings. Of particular note are about 500 works on Black Mountain College by artists associated with the experimental school. The museum has 12 galleries and about 54,000 square feet of space in a 1926 Renaissance Revival building, formerly Pack Memorial Library and now a part of the Pack Place complex.

Asheville Pinball Museum *(1 Battle Square, Downtown Asheville, 828-776-5671, www.ashevillepinball.com, $10 admission allows unlimited free play, open Wed.-Thu. 4-9, Fri. 2-9, Sat. noon-9, Sun. 1-6)* may be more of a pinball game place than a true museum, but it does have more than 30 pinball machines from 1947 to 2003. It's popular enough that in 2015 it moved to a larger location near its original site.

aSHEville Museum *(35 Wall St., Downtown Asheville, 828-785-5722, www.ashevillemuseum.com, admission by donation on a sliding scale of $5 to $15, children 13 and under free, open Sun.-Mon., Wed-Thu. 11-5, Fri.-Sat. 11-7, closed Tue.*) is a women's cultural museum. Core exhibits include Appalachian Women, 100 Years of Sexism in Advertising and A History of Hysteria, and there are rotating exhibits.

Big Ivy Historical Park *(540 Dillingham Rd., Barnardsville, 828-626-2522; hours vary, free)* has a restored 19th century log cabin. On the first Saturday in October, a syrup mill on the site makes molasses.

Black Mountain College Museum + Arts Center *(56 Broadway St., Asheville, 828-350-8484 with an additional space across the street at 67 Broadway St., www.blackmountaincollege.org; open noon-4 Tue.-Wed., 11-5 Thu.-Sat., closed Sun.-Mon., free admission but admission fees charged on some events, exhibitions or conference)* focuses on preserving the legacy of educational and artistic innovation of Black Mountain College.

This radical experimental college near Asheville that from 1933 to 1957 attracted leading artists, writers and thinkers including Buckminster Fuller, Robert Motherwell, Willem and Elaine de Kooning, Robert Rauschenberg, M.C. Richards, Josef and Anni Albers, John Cage, Merce Cunningham, Charles Olson, Robert Creeley, James Leo Hirlihy and Arthur Penn. In a small space, the Downtown museum does a big job with exhibits and programs about the college.

Blue Ridge Parkway Visitor Center *Blue Ridge Parkway Milepost 384, approx. 2 miles south of US Hwy. 70 Parkway entrance in East Asheville, 828-298-5330, www.nps.gov/blri; daily 9-5, free*), opened in 2009, is the main parkway visitor information center. It has high-tech exhibits on the parkway and its history, including the I-Wall, a 22-foot long interactive map of the parkway, and a 24-minute film. The center is as green as it can be, with a 10,000 square-foot "living" roof covered in drought-resistant local plants.

Colburn Earth Science Museum *(2 S. Pack Square, 828-254-7162, http://colburnmuseum.wordpress.com; Tue.-Sat. 10-5, Sun. 1-5, adults $6, students, military and seniors $5, children 5 and under free),* part of the Pack Place complex, has displays on gems from North Carolina and elsewhere, including more than 350 minerals found in the state. It also has exhibits on the geology of the region and the history of mining in North Carolina. An exhibit on fossils is being developed.

Estes-Winn Antique Automobile Museum *(828-253-7651 or 877-622-7238, www.grovewoodgallery.com; Mon.-Sat. 10-5, Sun. 11-5, closed Jan.-Mar., free),* a part of the Grovewood Gallery adjacent to the Grove Park Inn, has on display 18 old cars, from a 1913 Model T Ford to a 1959 Edsel, along with a 1925 Asheville La Salle fire truck. This is a small, low-key museum, but it's fun to wander around and admire the fine old vehicles.

Folk Art Center *(Milepost 382, Blue Ridge Parkway, 828-298-7928, www.southernhighlandguild.org; Jan.-Mar. 9-5 daily; Apr.-Dec. 9-6 daily, free),* headquarters of the Southern Highland Craft Guild, is a terrific place to see historical and contemporary mountain crafts. There are three crafts galleries, craft demonstrations and an Allanstand Craft Shop, which sells quality local and regional craft items.

Moog Music Factory *(160 Broadway St., Five Points, North Asheville, 828-251-0090, www.moogmusic.com, open Mon.-Fri. 10-6, tours Mon.-Fri. at 10 and 3)* is a shop, factory and memorial to the late Robert Moog, a pioneer in electronic music. Here you can play Moog instruments and take a factory tour – for tour reservations call 828-239-0123 in advance. The Moog Music Festival is held annually in Asheville in spring.

The Quilt Garden at the North Carolina Arboretum – photo courtesy of the Arboretum

North Carolina Arboretum *(100 Frederick Law Olmsted Way off Brevard Rd./Hwy. 191 and the Blue Ridge Parkway at Milepost 393, 828-665-2492, www.ncarboretum.org; 8 am – 9 pm Apr.-Oct., 8-7 Nov.-Mar., gates close an hour before closing time, free admission but $12 per car parking fee, free first Tue. of the month)* is a 434-acre nature park with 65 acres of cultivated gardens and 10 miles of hiking and biking trails. It is affiliated with the University of North Carolina system and is located in the Bent Creek Experimental Forest on Pisgah National Forest land. Highlights include a quilt garden (flowering plants arranged in a quilt pattern), local heritage garden, holly garden, native azalea garden, permanent and rotating exhibits in the Baker Exhibit and Education Center buildings, one of the best bonsai exhibits in the U.S., and a wonderful trail system. A ¾-mile mulched trail connects the Baker building and the Education Center, with trailheads easily reached from either building. Interpretive signs along the trail explain plant, animal, ecologic and environmental topics. There is a café and gift shop in the Education Center and an art and crafts gallery in the Baker Exhibit Center. The Arboretum conducts many classes and holds a number of plant and flower shows annually, including ones on bamboo, orchids, roses, dahlias and mums. You can easily spend an entire day visiting the Arboretum. Picnics on the grounds and dogs on leash are permitted.

North Carolina Homespun Museum *(111 Grovewood Rd., 828-253-7651 or 877-622-7238, www.grovewood.com, Apr.-Dec. Mon.-Sat. 10-6, Sun. 11-5, closed Jan.-Mar., free)*, a part of the Grovewood Gallery adjacent to the Grove Park Inn, focuses on the history of Biltmore Industries and its wool cloth. Biltmore Industries originally was a weaving and woodworking education program started by Edith Vanderbilt of the Biltmore Estate.

Smith-McDowell House *(283 Victoria Rd., www.nchistory.org, 828-253-9231; Wed.-Sat. 10-4, Sun. noon-4; $8 adults, $10 during Christmas season)* is believed to be the oldest surviving house in Asheville and the oldest brick house in Buncombe County. It's a two-story Federal style house, with Greek Revival interiors, although the early 20th century renovation by Richard Sharp Smith added Neoclassical elements. Frederick Law Olmsted's firm did the landscaping around 1900. The house was restored in the late 20th century under the direction of Asheville architect Henry I. Gaines and is now operated as a museum by the WNC Historical Society. It is especially known for its Christmas decorations.

Southern Appalachian Radio Museum *(Room 315, Elm Building, Asheville-Buncombe Technical Community College, Victoria Rd., www.saradiomuseum.org; open Fri. 1-3 except Dec. and Jan., free, other times by appointment, $5)* is a tiny museum with displays on amateur radio.

Joshua P. Warren's Asheville Mystery Museum *(basement of Masonic Temple Building, 80 Broadway St., 828-335-6764, www.ashevillemystery.com; by appointment, included at no extra charge with Asheville tours, $20 adults, $15 children 9-14)* is a collection of "artifacts" on ghosts and mysterious goings on in Asheville, put together by local "ghostwriter" and TV personality Joshua P. Warren.

Western North Carolina Nature Center *(75 Gashes Creek Rd., 828-259-8080, www.wncnaturecenter.org; daily 10-5, adults $8, seniors $7, with $2 discount for Asheville City residents, children 3-15 $4)* in East Asheville is a 42-acre zoological and nature park focused on the fauna of the Southern Appalachians. Displays include ones on red and gray wolves, bobcats and coyotes, black bears and snakes of the region, plus a farm with donkeys, goats, rabbits, chickens and sheep.

Thomas Wolfe Memorial *(52 N. Market St. and 48 Spruce St., 828-253-8304, www.wolfememorial.com; visitor center open Tue.-Sat. 9-5, Sun. 1-5; $5 adults, $2 children, guided tour of the house included, tours begin at bottom of hour)* is a North Carolina State Historic Site. The rambling 29-room boarding house, operated by Wolfe's mother Julia Wolfe, is where Thomas Wolfe grew up.

The "Old Kentucky Home," called "Dixie" in Wolfe's novel, *Look Homeward, Angel,* is directly behind the visitor center at 48 Spruce Street. The Wolfe home was extensively damaged in a 1998 fire (the arsonist was never caught), but it was meticulously restored as it might have looked in the early 20th century when Wolfe lived there before heading off to college at Chapel Hill.

The house, a Queen Anne style structure built in 1883 with later additions, is painted a bright canary yellow. The visitor center exhibits artifacts and personal effects of the author, including some of his clothes, his Remington typewriter and his diploma from Harvard. There's also a 22-minute film on the author's life and work.

Vance Birthplace *(911 Reems Creek, Weaverville, 828-645-6706, www.nchistoricsites.org; Tue.-Sat. 9-5, free, donations accepted)* is the birthplace of 19th century North Carolina three-time governor Zebulon B. Vance (1830-1894). A reconstructed log cabin (the chimney and fireplaces are original), furnishings (some original) and outbuildings evoke a prosperous mountain farm in the early 1800s. This is also a good place for a picnic.

YMI Cultural Center *(39 S. Market St., corner of Eagle and Market Sts., www.packplace.org, 828-257-4500; exhibit area open Tue.-Fri. 10-5, $5)* was funded by George Vanderbilt as a community center for Asheville's African-American community, many of whom worked building the Biltmore House. The 1893 building, designed by noted architect Richard Sharp Smith, is located in the heart of what was Asheville's black business district. Over the years it housed a public library, drugstore, funeral parlor and doctor's office. After serving for a time as a YMCA branch, it sat idle until becoming the home in 1988 of the YMI Cultural Center, now a part of the Pack Place complex. Exhibits include African masks, drawings by African-American artist Charles W. White and photographs that tell the history of the YMI.

NEARBY

Allison-Deaver House Museum *(2753 Asheville Hwy., Pisgah Forest near Brevard, 828-884-5137, www.tchistoricalsociety.com; Sat. 10-4, Sun. 1-4 mid-May to late summer, $5 adults or donation),* operated by the Transylvania County Historical Society, is one of the oldest standing frame houses in Western North Carolina. It was built in 1815, with significant additions in the 1830s and 1850s, and restored in the 1980s and 1990s by the Historical Society.

Avery County Historical Museum *(1829 Shultz Circle, Newland, 828-733-7111, www.averymuseum.com; Fri.-Sat. 11-3, Sun. 1-3, free)* has exhibits on the history of Avery County and the Toe River area. The museum is located in the 1912 Avery County Jail. Behind the museum is the 1917 Linville Depot building, once a stop on the East Tennessee and Western North Carolina Railroad. It was moved here from its original location on Grape Street in Linville. The Depot is being restored, complete with a bark exterior.

Banner House Museum *(7990 Hickory Nut Gap Rd., Banner Elk, 828-898-3634, www.bannerhousemuseum.org; Tue.-Sat. 11-4 mid-June-mid-Oct., guided tours adults $5, children 6-12 $1)* is in the 1860s-vintage home of Samuel Henry Banner, one of Banner Elk's original settlers. The museum is furnished in the style of the 1870s and 1880s.

Bennett Classics – Antique Auto Museum *(241 Vance St., Forest City, 828-247-1767, www.bennettclassics.com; Mon.-Fri. 10-5, Sat. 10-3, $10 adults, $8 seniors, children $4)* has more than 50 antique cars and trucks on display. It also offers antique cars for sale – recently a restored 1955 Pontiac Chieftain was offered for $15,500.

Blowing Rock Pictorial History Museum *(1094 Main St., Blowing Rock, 828-295-6114; Mon. and Sat. 1-4 May-Dec., free)*, in an 1894 building once part of the now-closed Watauga Inn, displays antiques, photographs and memorabilia from the town of Blowing Rock.

Bostic Lincoln Center *(112 Depot St., 828-245-9800, www.bosticlincolncenter.com; Thu. 1-4, Fri. and Sat. 10-1, free, donations accepted)* is an eccentric little museum dedicated to the idea that Abraham Lincoln, the 16th U.S. president, was not born in Kentucky but in a log cabin on Puzzle Creek near Bostic in Rutherford County. Some local residents and a few historians believe that Abe was born out of wedlock to Nancy Hanks of Puzzle Creek, who lived in Western North Carolina until the future president was about six years old.

John C. Campbell Folk School *(1 Folk School Rd., Brasstown, 828-837-2775 or 800-365-5724, www.folkschool.org; campus open daily during daylight hours, Craft Shop and History Center open Mon.-Sat. 8-5, Sun. 1-5, free)* is one of the leading folk and crafts schools in the country. It dates to 1925. The school, in the far western part of the state near Murphy about two hours from Asheville, offers more than 800 weekend and weeklong classes for adults in everything from blacksmithing and basketry to cooking, quilting and woodworking.

Students can live in school housing and take meals at the school. The **Craft Shop** has items from some 300 local and regional craft artists, and the **History Center** is a small museum of mountain crafts with information on the school's history. The work of school co-founder Olive Dame Campbell is celebrated in the 2000 film *Songcatcher.* The campus is a Historic District on the National Register of Historic Places. Visitors are welcome to explore the 300-acre campus on a self-guided tour during daylight hours.

Canton Area Historical Museum *(36 Park St., Canton, 828-646-3412, www.cantonnc.com; Mon.-Fri. 8-5, free)* has collections of late 19th and early 20th century local artifacts and a large collection of photographs and memorabilia of the town and its long-time main industry, the Champion Paper Mill. The museum also serves as a visitor center.

Cherokee County Historical Museum *(87 Peachtree St., Murphy, 828-837-6792, www.cherokeecounty-nc.gov; Mon.-Fri. 9-5, adults $3, children $1)* has on display 800 dolls dating from 1865, along with 2,000 artifacts of the Cherokee Indians and a collection of local minerals.

Clay County Historical and Arts Council Museum *(21 Davis Loop, Hayesville, 828-389-6814, www.clayhistoryarts.org; Tue.-Sat. 10-4 Memorial Day to Labor Day, Fri. and Sat. 10-4 Sep.-Oct., free)* has interesting displays on local history, including a collection of feed sacks, spinning wheels, farm equipment, Cherokee Indian masks and gems and minerals of Clay County. In the museum is a replica of the office and medical equipment of a local physician, Dr. Paul Killian. The museum is located in the Old County Jail, built 1912.

Cradle of Forestry in America *(11250 Pisgah Hwy. /Hwy. 276, Pisgah Forest, near Brevard, 828-877-3130, www.cradleofforestry.com, daily 9-5, mid-Apr.-early Nov., $5 adults, children under 16 free, free for everyone on Tues., free at all times for National Park Senior Pass holders)* is a 6,500-acre site within the Pisgah National Forest devoted to the history of America's first school of forestry. The school was established by George Vanderbilt who, upon the recommendation of his landscape architect Frederick Law Olmsted, hired Gifford Pinchot as forest manager of the 125,000-acre Biltmore Estate. Pinchot later would become the first head of the USDA Forest Service and governor of Pennsylvania.

In 1895, Vanderbilt hired German forester Dr. Carl A. Schenk to succeed Pinchot. Together, Pinchot and Schenk created the modern concept of forestry management and conservation. In the visitor center are 15 hands-on exhibits on forestry, including a simulated ride in a firefighting helicopter.

A 1-mile trail winds through the original forestry campus, where you can explore a general store, one-room schoolhouse, blacksmith shop, cabins and a vegetable garden. Another trail, 1.3 miles long, has a sawmill and 1915 steam locomotive used in logging.

Crossnore Weavers *(Crossnore, 828-733-4660, www.crossnoreweavers.org; open Mon.-Sat. 9-5, free)* near Linville is a "working museum" of weaving. It is an outgrowth of a boarding school for impoverished children established in 1913.

Today, local women still weave blankets, scarves, napkins and other items. The **Crossnore Fine Arts Gallery,** located in what formerly was the Weaving Room, sells regional art and crafts to support what is now a day school.

Dry Ridge Historical Museum *(41 N. Main St., Weaverville, 828-250-6482; Sat. 10-2, mid-Mar.-mid-Dec., free)* is a small museum on the history of what the Cherokee called the Dry Ridge, the Reems Creek and Flat Creek areas of northern Buncombe County.

The Fine Art Museum at the John W. Bardo Fine and Performing Arts Center at Western Carolina University *(199 Centennial Drive, Western Carolina University, Cullowhee, 828-227-3591, www.wcu.edu/museum; Mon.-Wed. and Fri. 10-4, Thu. 10-7; free)* gets our vote for the clumsiest name for a museum in the region. The permanent collection of the museum has around 1,200 works from artists from around the country and the world, with no particular area of specialization.

Franklin Gem and Mineral Museum *(25 Phillips St., Franklin, 828-369-7831, www.fgmm.org; Mon.-Sat. noon-4 May-Oct., Sat. noon-4, Nov.-Apr., free)* has displays of local minerals and gems from the Cowee Valley, as well as from other areas. The museum is located in the Old Macon County Jail.

Grandfather Mountain Nature Museum *(2050 Blowing Rock Hwy. /US Hwy. 221, Linville, off Blue Ridge Parkway Milepost 305, www.grandfather.com; spring 8-6, summer 8-7, fall 8-6:30, winter 9-5; adults $18, seniors $15, children 4-12 $8—fees include admission to all parts of the park including the swinging bridge and zoo),* part of the Grandfather Mountain complex, has exhibits on the history of Grandfather Mountain, local gems and minerals and birds and wildflowers found in the area.

Granite Falls History and Transportation Museum *(107 Falls Ave., Granite Falls, 828-396-2792, www.granitefallshistorymuseum.org; Sat. noon-4, Sun. 2-4, free)* is located in a renovated 1790s house, the second oldest house in Caldwell County. The museum has exhibits on Caldwell County history.

Great Smoky Mountains National Park Mountain Farm Museum *(Oconaluftee Visitor Center, US Hwy. 441/Newfound Gap Rd. about 2 miles north of Cherokee, 865-436-1200, www.nps.gov/grsm; daily 8-4:30 Jan.-Feb. and Dec., daily 8-5 Mar. and Nov., daily 8-6 Apr.-May and Sep.-Oct., daily 8-7 June-Aug., free)* is a mountain farmstead with nine historic buildings re-assembled and recreated from original buildings in the Smokies.

It is the best example of a late 19th/early 20th century mountain farm in the region. Among the buildings are a chestnut log house, apple house, corncrib, springhouse and a large barn with some 16,000 hand-split roof shingles. You can do a self-guided tour (tour booklet and map $1 at adjacent visitor center), and rangers are available to put on demonstrations and answer questions.

Hands On! A Child's Gallery *(318 N. Main St., Hendersonville, 828-697-8333, www.handsonwnc.org; Tue.-Sat. 10-5; $5 for adults and children)* is an activity center for children ages 1-10. Among the interactive displays are a grocery store, music room, costume theatre and a Lego ramp.

Henderson County Heritage Museum *(1 Historic Courthouse Square, Hendersonville, 828-694-5007, www.hendersoncountymuseum.org; Wed.-Sat. 10-5, Sun. 1-5, free)* has exhibits on Henderson County history, including exhibits on local residents who fought in the Civil War and in World War I and a recreation of a local one-room schoolhouse.

Hickory Ridge Living History Museum *(591 Horn in the West Drive, Boone, 828-264-2120, www.hickoryridgemuseum.com; spring and fall, Sat. 9-1, summer Tue.-Sun. 5-8 and Sat. 9-1, closed for winter starting mid-Oct.; $3 suggested donation)*, located on the grounds of the Horn in the West outdoor drama facility, tells the story of Daniel Boone and early settlers in the region. Interpreters in 18th century clothing give visitors a glimpse of the daily lives of these hardy mountaineers.

Highlands Historic Village *(524 N. 4th St., Highlands, 828-787-1050, www.highlandshistory.org; late May-Oct. Fri.-Sat. 10-4, Sun. 1-4, free)* consists of the 1877 Boynton-Trapier-Wright Home, the oldest existing house in Highlands and the Highlands Historical Museum and Archives in a building that dates from 1915.

It also includes Bug Hill Cottage, a recreation of an early 20th century tuberculosis sanitarium outdoor cubicle where patients took the mountain airs. There are exhibits about Highlands history including historic homes in the area, moonshining, golfer Bobby Jones and a collection of photographs of Highlands by George Masa, best known for his photographs of the Great Smoky Mountains National Park.

Historic Burke Foundation Heritage Museum *(Old Burke Country Courthouse, on the Square bounded by Green, Union, Meeting and Sterling streets, Morganton, 828-437-4104, www.historicburke.org; Mon.-Fri. 10-4, free),* located in the mid-1830s vintage county courthouse, has a permanent exhibit on the local court system and displays on Morganton and Burke County history.

Historic Johnson Farm *(3346 Haywood Rd./NC Hwy. 191, Hendersonville, 828-891-6585, www.historichendersonville.org; open Tue.-Fri. 8-2:30 Sep.-May, Mon.-Thu. 8-2:30 June-Aug., visits to grounds free, guided tours, usually at 10:30 am on days the farm is open, are $5 for adults and $3 for students K-12)* is a late 19th century farmstead once owned by a wealthy tobacco farmer and now operated as a museum and activity center by the Henderson County Board of Education. The property, which is on the National Register of Historic Places, consists of 15 acres and a dozen buildings, including a large two-story 1880 house built of bricks fired on site from mud from the French Broad River. It has bee hives, and the Henderson County Bee Club frequently offers beekeeping demonstrations on Saturdays.

History Museum of Burke County *(Old City Hall, 201 W. Meeting St., Morganton, 828-437-1777, www.thehistorymuseumofburke.org; railroad depot Sat. 2-4, free, museum Tue.-Fri. 10-4, Sat. 10-2, free)* includes the Morganton Railroad Depot, built in 1886 and restored to its appearance in 1916, and a museum in the Old Morganton City Hall. The museum is dedicated to the preservation of Burke County's memorabilia and artifacts.

House of Flags Museum *(33 Gibson St., Columbus, 828-894-5640, www.houseofflags.org; Tue. and Thu. 10-1, Sat. 10-4, free)* has a collection of 300 flags.

KidSenses Children's Museum *(172 N. Main St., Rutherfordton, 828-286-2120, www.kidsenses.com; Tue.-Thu. and Sat. 9-5, Fri. 9-8, adults and children $5, seniors $3)* is an interactive museum and activity center for children ages 1-12.

Macon County Historical Society and Museum *(36 W. Main St., Macon, 828-524-9758, www.maconnchistorical.org; Mon.-Fri. 10-4, free)* is in the Pendergrass Building, a dry goods and grocery store dating to the early 20th century. Many of the items in the museum are from this old store, now in the National Register of Historic Places. Other exhibits are on Cherokee Indian artifacts, old medical instruments and period clothing from the early 20th century.

Mineral and Lapidary Museum of Henderson County *(400 N. Main St., Hendersonville, 828-698-1977, www.mineralmuseum.org; Mar.-Dec. Mon.-Fri. 1-5, Sat. 10-5, Jan.-Feb. Tue.-Fri. 1-5, Sat. 10-5, free)* has collections of North Carolina and world gems and minerals, including many geodes, along with Cherokee Indian artifacts.

Mountain Farm and Home Museum *(101 Brookside Camp Rd., Hendersonville, 828-697-8846, www.mflmuseum.com; call for times when open, free)* has a fascinating small collection of old farm tractors and antique farm equipment.

Mountain Gateway Museum *(102 Water St., Old Fort, 828-668-9259, www.mountaingatewaymuseum.org; Tue.-Sat. 9-5, Sun. 2-5, Mon. noon-5, free)* has permanent exhibits on mountain folk medicine, moonshining and spinning and weaving. There are two reconstructed 19th century cabins on the grounds of the museum. The 1890 Old Fort train station depot and museum, renovated and reopened in 2005, and associated with the Mountain Gateway Museum, is nearby at 25 East Main Street. The museum complex is part of the North Carolina Museum of History system in the state Department of Culture.

Mountain Heritage Museum at Western Carolina University *(150 H. F. Robinson Administration Building, Western Carolina University, Cullowhee, 828-227-7129, www.wcu.edu; Mon.-Wed. and Fri. 8-5, Thu. 8-7, open selected Sat. in summer and fall, free)* focuses on the cultural and natural history of the Southern Appalachians. The museum has an excellent permanent exhibit on the history of the Scots-Irish who settled the mountains, plus two traveling and temporary exhibit halls. A recent temporary exhibit was on Horace Kephart and the camping equipment he used in the Great Smokies. The museum's entrance area is paneled in wormy chestnut.

Museum of Ashe County History *(301 E. Main St., Jefferson, 336-846-1904, www.ashehistory.org; Mon.-Sat. 10-4, free)* is dedicated to restoring and using the old Ashe County Courthouse, built in 1904 in the Beaux Art style, as a museum devoted to the county's history.

Museum of North Carolina Handicrafts *(49 Shelton St. at US Hwy. 276, Waynesville, 828-452-1551, www.sheltonhouse.org; open May-Oct. Tues.-Sat. 10-4, admission $5, seniors $4, children $3)* is located in Shelton House, a two-story white Charleston-style farmhouse built in 1875 and now on the National Register of Historic Places. The house alone is worth a visit. The museum has exhibits of regional folk art, pottery, baskets, quilts, weaving and other crafts.

Museum of North Carolina Minerals *(Milepost 331 Blue Ridge Parkway at NC Hwy. 226, Spruce Pine, 828-765-9483, daily 9-5, free)* showcases some 300 gems and minerals found in the Spruce Pine area and elsewhere in North Carolina. If you're on the Parkway in the Spruce Pine area, this little museum is worth a stop.

Museum of Rutherford Hospital *(288 S. Ridgecrest Ave., Rutherfordton, 828-286-5000, www.rutherfordhosp.org; Mon.-Fri. 8-5, free)* is a small museum on the history of Rutherford Hospital. It has medical equipment and furniture used at the hospital in the past. There's also a 45-foot mural by artist Clive Haynes depicting the history of the hospital.

Museum of the Cherokee Indian *(589 Tsali Blvd./U.S. Hwy. 441, Cherokee, 828-497-3481, www.cherokeemuseum.org; daily 9-5 with extended summer hours 9-7 Mon.-Sat. Memorial Day to Labor Day, adults $10, children 6-12 $6)* is a world away from the tacky plastic gift stores of Cherokee. This serious and professional museum has permanent exhibits on Cherokee history from 12,000 years ago through today and on the Trail of Tears. It also sponsors cultural and literary events and publishes books and other research on the Cherokee.

Mystery Hill *(129 Mystery Hill Lane, Blowing Rock, 828-263-0507, www.mysteryhill-nc.com; daily 9 am-8 pm June-Aug., 9-5 Sep.-May, $9 adults. $8 seniors, children 5-12 $7, children 4 and under free)* is a group of commercial, for-profit museums, including the Appalachian Culture Museum (formerly associated with Appalachian State University) with antiques and what the website calls "household" furnishings, a Native Artifacts Museum with a claimed 50,000 Native American artifacts and a "Mystery House" that purports to defy the laws of physics.

North Carolina School for the Deaf Museum *(517 W. Fleming Dr., Morganton, 828-433-2971, www.ncsdmuseum.net; call for hours, free)* covers the history of the North Carolina School for the Deaf in Morganton, which was established in 1894.

Old Depot Gallery and Caboose Museum *(207 Sutton Ave., Black Mountain, 828-669-6583, www.olddepot.org; Tue.-Sat. 10-5 Apr.-Dec., free)* is primarily a crafts gallery in the early 20th century Black Mountain train depot, with a small museum in a Norfolk & Western Railroad caboose.

Orchard at Altapass *(1025 Orchard Rd., Spruce Pine, off Blue Ridge Parkway Milepost 328.3, 828-765-9531, www.altapassorchard.com; Mon.-Sat. 10:30-5:30, Sun. noon-5:30, closed Tue. some weeks May-Oct., free)* is a century-old, 80-acre apple orchard.

The orchard, organized as a non-profit, offers hayrides and holds Bluegrass and mountain music concerts some days. There's a gift shop and in season you can buy apples or pick your own.

Penland School of Crafts *(67 Doras Trail, Penland, 828-765-2359, Gallery 828-765-6211, www.penland.org; campus open daily March-early Dec., Gallery open March-early Dec., Tues.-Sat. 10-5, Sun. noon-5, free; free guided tours of the campus offered March-early Dec. Tues. at 10:30 and Thurs. at 1:30, reservations necessary – call 828-765-6211)* is arguably the best crafts school in the country. Penland, on 460 acres in a beautiful rural area near Spruce Pine about an hour northeast of Asheville, offers one- and two-week adult workshops in the summer and eight-week classes in spring and fall, in clay, books & paper, metals, glass, photography, printmaking, textiles and wood. Students live on campus in simple, rustic dormitory facilities. Around 1,400 students take classes at Penland each year. Visitors are welcome on the Penland campus, although teaching studios usually are closed to the public during classes. Penland pottery instructor Cynthia Bringle was named a "North Carolina Living Treasure" by the Museum of World Cultures at UNC-Wilmington, and the school itself received special recognition from the Museum in 2011 as a national center for craft education dedicated to helping people live creative lives.

The **Penland School Gallery,** which exhibits and sells the work of present and former students and faculty, most of it of very high quality and some of it extraordinary, is open to visitors from March to early December. Visitors are welcome to walk through the grounds. Note especially **Craft House**, one of the largest log structures in North Carolina. You can also visit **The Barns,** which houses the studios of the Penland's resident artists, fulltime craftspeople who live and work at the school. There also is a café and gift shop. If you're visiting Penland, you may want to stop at some of the nearby craft studios. The area around Penland is home to about 100 craft artists. Watch for signs of open studios and galleries.

Piedmont & Western Railroad Club and Old Rock School Railway Museum *(400 W. Main St., Valdese, 828-879-2129, www.pwrr.org; usually 8-5 Mon.-Fri., or by appointment, free)* is an HO-scale model of the fictitious Piedmont & Western Railroad, built by the Valdese model railroad club. The model railroad layout covers an area from Marion through Asheville to East Tennessee. The museum has many photos of real North Carolina railroads and train depots, along with railroad artifacts.

Pisgah Astronomical Research Institute *(1 PARI Drive, Rosman, 828-862-5554, www.pari.edu; Mon.-Fri. 9-4 for self-guided tours, free, public tours Wed. at 2 pm, $5 for those 10 and over)* an astronomical research and education facility that has displays on space and holds a variety of events related to stargazing and space. PARI has several optical and radio telescopes, including two large 26-meter radio telescopes. Some are available for rent by students and researchers. The facility also has a planetarium. PARI is an offshoot of the Rosman Satellite Tracking Station, which was established in 1962 and used until the 1980s by NASA as part of an international network of stations tracking manned and unmanned space flights. Later it was run by spooks at the Defense Department for intelligence gathering. The tracking station closed in 1995 and was turned over to the U.S. Forestry Service. In 1999 it was purchased for use as an astronomical research and education facility. PARI has about 30 buildings on its campus located in a beautiful remote setting on 200 acres in the Pisgah National Forest near Brevard.

Presbyterian Heritage Center at Montreat *(318 Georgia Terrace, Montreat, 828-669-6556, www.phcmontreat.org; Fri. 10-4, Sat. 1-4, Sun. 1:30-4, free)* is a small museum covering the history of the Presbyterian Church and of Montreat.

Rural Life Museum at Mars Hill College *(Montague Building, Mars Hill College, Mars Hill, 828-689-1262, www.mch.edu)*, which has artifacts and displays from local farms, is currently closed for extensive renovations.

Carl Sandburg Home National Historic Site *(81 Carl Sandburg Lane, for GPS use 1800 Little River Rd., Flat Rock, 828-693-4178, www.nps.gov/carl/index.htm; guided tour fee $5 adults, $3 seniors, children 15 and under free, admission to grounds and barn free, daily 9-5 year-round, tours of house every half hour starting at 9:30, last tour 4:30)* is operated by the National Park Service. It's the first national park to honor a poet. You enter the grounds via a short walk up a winding driveway lined with white pines.

The house, a white one-and-a-half story on a raised basement, with Greek Revival columns on the front porch, built around 1839 as a summer cottage by a South Carolina railroad owner, sits on a knoll above a lake. On the guided tour, you'll see the Sandburg house much as it was in the 1960s, as if the family had stepped out for a walk.

Carl Sandburg home – photo courtesy of the National Park Service

There are magazines on the floor, a guitar leaning against the piano and shelves of books. Sandburg's book-filled study has his typewriter. There's a bookstore with a good selection of books by and about Sandburg on the basement level of the house. Don't miss a visit to the barn and outbuildings, where you'll see descendants of Paula Steichen Sandburg's herd of dairy goats. The farm has some 5 miles of hiking trails.

Scottish Tartans Museum *(86 E. Main St., Franklin, 828-524-7472, www.scottishtartans.org; Mon.-Sat. 10-5, adults $2)* focuses on the traditional dress of the Scottish Highlands. The museum displays kilts, some over 200 years old, and more than 500 traditional Scottish tartans. It is an extension of the Scottish Tartans Society in Edinburgh, Scotland.

Senator Sam J. Ervin, Jr. Library and Museum *(Phifer Learning Resources Center Library, Western Piedmont Community College, 1001 Burkemont Ave., Morganton, 828-448-6198; Mon.-Fri. 8-5, free)* contains some 10,000 items from the career of the U.S. Senator (Democrat, 1954-1974) and constitutional expert from Morganton who headed the Watergate hearings.

Although a graduate of Harvard Law School, Ervin called himself a "simple country lawyer." Once a political conservative and defender of racial segregation, Ervin became a civil liberties champion and helped bring down both Senator Joseph McCarthy and President Richard Nixon. The museum has an exact replica of Senator Ervin's home library.

Shook House Museum *(178 Morgan St., Clyde, www.shookmuseum.org; Tue., Fri. and Sat. 1-5, tour $5)* is probably the oldest frame house in the region, believed to have been constructed around 1810 and possibly earlier, with a later addition in the 1890s.

Smoky Mountains Trains Museum *(100 Greenlee St., Bryson City, 828-488-5200, www.smokymountaintrains.com; 9-5 daily with reduced hours and days seasonally, $9 adults, $5 children, free with Great Smoky Mountains Railroad ticket purchase)* is a commercial museum with 7,000 Lionel model train cars and engines on display.

Swain County Heritage Museum *(112 Everett St., Bryson City, 828- 488-9273, daily 10-5, free)*, located in on the second level of 1908 Swain County Courthouse in downtown Bryson City, the delightful little museum tells the story of the county and its people. There's a restored log cabin porch, an 1887 church organ and a reconstruction of a one-room schoolhouse. The Bryson City/Swain County visitor center is on the first floor, and there's an elevator to the museum. Free parking is at the back of the museum.

Swannanoa Valley Museum *(223 W. State St., Black Mountain, 828-669-9566, www.swannanoavalleymuseum.org; Tue.-Sat. 10-5 Apr.-Oct, donation requested)* focuses on the history of the Swannanoa Valley and of Buncombe County. It is housed in the old Black Mountain firehouse, designed by architect Richard Sharp Smith and built in 1921.

Transylvania County Heritage Museum *(189 W. Main St., Brevard, 828-884-2347, www.transylvaniaheritage.org; Wed.-Sat. 10-5, Mar.-mid-Dec., free)* covers the history and culture of Transylvania County. It is located in an 1890s house.

Turchin Center for the Visual Arts *(423 W. King St., Boone, 828-262-3017, www.tcva.org; Tue.-Thu. and Sat. 10-6, Fri. noon-8, free)*, part of Appalachian State University, has six art galleries and two small sculpture gardens. The center has a permanent collection of more than 1,600 regional, national and international works.

Waldensian Heritage Museum *(208 Rodoret St. South, Valdese, 828-874-1111, www.waldesianheritagemuseum.org; call for information on tours, free)* celebrates the heritage of the Waldenses, a European Calvinist religious group dating to the Middle Ages.

Members of the group settled Valdese beginning in 1893. Eleven families left Europe for the U.S. and bought a tract of land in Valdese. Later these settlers were joined by other families. The museum is located at the Waldensian Presbyterian Church.

Western North Carolina Air Museum *(1340 E. Gilbert St., Hendersonville, 828-698-2482, www.wncairmuseum.com; Wed. and Sun. noon-5 and Sat. 10-5, Apr.-Oct., Wed., Sat. and Sun. noon-5 Nov.-Mar., free)* has a collection of about 15 vintage aircraft from 1930 to the 1970s. The airplanes are on display in a hangar adjoining the Hendersonville Airport.

Wheels Through Time Museum *(62 Vintage Lane, Maggie Valley, 828-926-6266, www.wheelsthroughtime.com; Thu.-Mon. 9-5 Apr.-Nov., adults $12, seniors $10, children $6)* displays more than 300 classic and antique motorcycles. Also on exhibit are antique automobiles and 25,000 pieces of art and junque relating to cars and bikes.

World Methodist Council Museum *(545 N. Lakeshore Dr., Lake Junaluska, 828-456-9432, ext. 4, www.lakejunaluska.com; Tue.-Sat. 9-noon and 1-4 year round, free)* has the world's largest collection of materials on early Methodism. Also on the grounds of the Lake Junaluska Assembly is the related **SEJ Heritage Center,** with exhibits on the Southeast Jurisdiction of the United Methodist Church and also on Lake Junaluska.

Rush Wray Museum of Yancey County History *(11 Academy St., Burnsville, 828-682-3671, Wed.-Sat. 10-4, free)* is devoted to the history of Yancey County. The museum is located in the McElroy House, built around 1840.

Zachary-Tolbert House Museum *(1940 Hwy. 107 South, Cashiers, 828-743-7710, www.cashiershitoricalsociety.org; guided tours of house Fri.-Sat. 11- 3 mid-May-mid-Oct., $5 donation requested, grounds open daily, free)* is in an eight-room Greek Revival house completed around 1852. The house has been left in its original state, with unpainted interior walls and no running water, central heat or electricity. In the house is a large collection of Southern plain-style furniture, wood furniture handmade in Western North Carolina during the 1800s and early 1900s.

ASHEVILLE AUTHORS AND THE LITERARY SCENE

"Oh, I remember so well the day I arrived in Mountain City. It was spring of 1937."

-- Gail Godwin, *A Southern Family*

In terms of the authors who have lived and worked in the area, a small city such as Asheville doesn't begin to compare with New York, San Francisco, New Orleans, Chicago or other larger and perhaps more exciting cities. Nonetheless, Asheville has been fertile ground for writers.

The "Big Three" in the Asheville area are native son **Thomas Wolfe,** Jazz Age novelist **F. Scott Fitzgerald,** who spent summer here in the 1930s and who lost his love, Zelda Fitzgerald, to a fire at an Asheville psychiatric hospital, and poet and historian **Carl Sandburg,** who spent the last 22 years of his life on a farm in Flat Rock.

Thomas Wolfe

Thomas Wolfe (1900-1938) was born in Asheville at 92 Woodfin Street. His father carved gravestones, and his mother ran a boarding house at 48 Spruce Street, where Wolfe lived until he went to Chapel Hill to attend the University of North Carolina. At UNC, Wolfe had several plays produced by the Carolina Playmakers and rose to become editor of the *Tar Heel,* the university's newspaper, which under his leadership began publishing twice a week. (It is now the *Daily Tar Heel*.) After finishing at Chapel Hill in 1920, he went to Harvard to study playwriting.

After getting a master's degree at Harvard, Wolfe spent time in Europe and in Brooklyn. He had a five-year love affair with Aline Bernstein, a married woman 18 years his senior who helped support him financially.

Wolfe's first and arguably best novel, *Look Homeward, Angel,* is autobiographical. Eugene Gant is Wolfe, and scores of the many characters in the novel are thinly disguised real people in Asheville, which in the novel is called Altamont. Later Wolfe called Asheville Libya Hill.

Angel was edited by the great Maxwell Perkins who also was the long-time editor of Hemingway and Fitzgerald. It was published by Scribner's just days before the 1929 stock market crash and did not do well commercially in the United States, though it was critically acclaimed and sold well in Europe.

The boarding house in Downtown Asheville where author Thomas Wolfe grew up, called it "Dixie" in his novel, Look Homeward, Angel *-- photo by Rose Lambert-Sluder*

Many in Asheville took issue with the book and its author, and Wolfe did not return to Asheville until near his death at age 37. Of the town's reaction to Wolfe's first book, Wilma Dykeman wrote, "With the usual perverseness of humanity, the people of Asheville did not seem shocked at much of the deceit and folly and wickedness and waste that Wolfe found – they were shocked only that he exposed it."

The author's second novel, *Of Time and the River,* did better commercially. His next, and last, two books, both over 700 pages long, *The Web and the Rock* and *You Can't Go Home Again*, were published posthumously.

Wolfe died in Baltimore in 1938 of tuberculosis of the brain. He is buried next to his father, W.O. Wolfe, and mother, Julia Wolfe, at Asheville's Riverside Cemetery.

During his professional lifetime and in the years afterward, Wolfe was – with Hemingway and Faulkner – considered one of the best serious novelists of the century. Some critics put him at the very top of the list. Since then, his reputation has been in decline, and his sprawling books are no longer widely read except in college English classes, but he remains Asheville's best-known literary figure. The cycle may one day turn again; readers and critics may rediscover Wolfe.

Today, you can visit Wolfe landmarks including the boarding house he called "Dixie" in *Look Homeward, Angel,* the marble angel of the title at the Oakdale Cemetery in Hendersonville and his grave at Riverside Cemetery. *(See below.)*

Another Tom Wolfe, the white-suited New York sophisticate, also wrote unflatteringly about Western North Carolina in his 2004 novel, *I Am Charlotte Simmons.* His fictional main character is a student at elite Dupont University – said to be a combination of Harvard, Yale, Princeton, Duke and Stanford -- who is from Sparta in Alleghany County.

F. Scott Fitzgerald

F. Scott Fitzgerald (1896-1940) had a fairly brief but intense relationship with Asheville.

Born in St. Paul, Minn., Fitzgerald was the chronicler of the "Jazz Age" in the 1920s. One academic wrote, "the dominant influences on F. Scott Fitzgerald were aspiration, literature, Princeton, Zelda Sayre Fitzgerald, and alcohol."

Fitzgerald briefly mentioned Asheville in his 1920 short story "The Ice Palace" and in his 1925 novel *The Great Gatsby,* but he didn't spend time in the city until the summer of 1935, when he visited seeking relief for what probably was tuberculosis. At that time, in the days before antibiotics, Asheville's climate and elevation were believed to be helpful to victims of the disease. Some biographers, however, believe that he was suffering mainly from overconsumption of demon alcohol.

At the height of his career, Fitzgerald earned the equivalent today of $50,000 or more for a single story in the *Saturday Evening Post.* By the mid-1930s the Roaring 20s were long gone, the country was mired in the Great Depression, Fitzgerald's novels were seen as relics of the past and Fitzgerald was an alcoholic.

In 1935 Fitzgerald took a room at the Grove Park Inn, spending the summer trying to overcome his alcoholism, drinking beer by the case instead of his usual gin. It was during that summer that Fitzgerald met Tony Buttitta, the owner of a bookstore at the George Vanderbilt Hotel (now Vanderbilt Apartments). Buttitta kept a record of his talks with Fitzgerald, which he published many years later, in 1974, in *After the Good Gay Times*. A graduate of UNC, Buttitta also had co-founded the much-loved Intimate Bookshop in Chapel Hill, now sadly closed.

Of Fitzgerald that summer Buttitta wrote, "He was a physical, emotional, and financial bankrupt. He smoked and drank steadily, but ate very little; he took pills to sleep a few hours, and he could scarcely write what he thought was a decent line. He was a stranger in Asheville...."

After staying at the Grove Park Inn, Fitzgerald moved in November 1935 to the Skyland Hotel in Hendersonville (now condominiums) where he began his collection of essays, *The Crack-Up*.

Returning to Asheville in April 1936, Fitzgerald brought his wife Zelda, who was by then deep in mental illness. Fitzgerald installed Zelda at a local psychiatric hospital, Highland Hospital (now closed). Fitzgerald again stayed at the Grove Park Inn, in rooms 441-443. Fitzgerald himself wasn't all that stable. At one point, he threatened suicide and fired a pistol while at the inn.

In July 1937, Fitzgerald left Asheville for good, moving to Hollywood where he lived until his death in 1940. Zelda died in a fire at Highland Hospital in 1948.

Fitzgerald's literary reputation was at its nadir in the 1930s and 40s, but since then it has been rising and rising, eclipsing even that of Faulkner and Hemingway. Two of his novels, *The Great Gatsby* and *Tender Is the Night*, and some of his short stories, such as "The Diamond as Big as the Ritz" and "The Ice Palace," are now viewed as among the greatest works of the 20th century.

Each year, around the anniversary of Fitzgerald's birth September 24, the Grove Park Inn holds an F. Scott Fitzgerald Weekend, when you can tour Fitzgerald's suite with a literary critic.

Carl Sandburg

Carl Sandburg (1878-1967) was already famous for his down-to-earth poetry celebrating industrial and agricultural America and for what eventually would become his six-volume biography of Abraham Lincoln, when in 1945 he moved to Connemara, a 264-acre farm in Flat Rock

Carl Sandburg's study at his home in Flat Rock, left as it was when he died -- photo courtesy of National Park Service

near Hendersonville. There he lived with his wife Paula Steichen Sandburg, brother of the photographer Edward Steichen, until his death.

At Connemara, Sandburg continued to write – several volumes of poetry, the novel *Remembrance Rock* and his autobiography, *Always the Young Stranger.* About one-third of his published work was completed at the farm.

Sandburg's best-known poem is "Chicago," published in 1916. In it he famously describes the city where he worked as a newspaper reporter as "Hog Butcher for the World, Tool Maker, Stacker of Wheat, Player with Railroads and the Nation's Freight Handler, Stormy, husky, brawling, City of the Big Shoulders." Children know Sandburg for his *Rootabaga Stories.* Sandburg won three Pulitzer prizes, two for his poetry and one for his Lincoln biography.

In the 2012 PBS documentary, *The Day Carl Sandburg Died,* filmmaker Paul Bonesteel relates Sandburg's radical politics and anarchist writing during World War I. The Sandburg home and farm in Flat Rock are now maintained as a National Historic Site, operated by the National Park Service. *(See below.)*

Black Mountain Poets and Other Black Mountain Writers

For the first two decades of its too-short existence, Black Mountain College was known for its painters and other visual artists who taught or were students there.

These included Josef and Anni Albers, Willem and Elaine de Kooning, Franz Kline, Robert Rauschenberg, Robert Motherwell, Kenneth Noland and M.C. Richards.

After World War II and especially in the early 1950s, Black Mountain College was better known for its poets and writers than for painters, musicians and performers. **Charles Olson** (1910-1970) taught and served as rector at the college from 1951 to 1956. Olson, who began writing poetry in the early 1940s, is considered a transitional figure between earlier modern poets such as Ezra Pound and the New American Poets such as Elizabeth Bishop and the Beat Poets such as Allen Ginsberg.

Olson founded the so-called Black Mountain School of poets. Among his students were poets **Robert Creeley** (1926-2005), the author of more than 60 books, **Fielding Dawson** (1930-2002), **Jonathan Williams** (1929-2008), whose company published several of the Black Mountain Poets, **Ed Dorn** (1929-1999) and **John Joseph Wieners** (1934-2002). Olson also influenced many other poets including Denise Levertov and Paul Blackburn.

Through a magazine founded by Robert Creeley, *Black Mountain Review,* which early on published Allen Ginsberg and Jack Kerouac, Olson and Black Mountain College developed a connection with the Beat poets in San Francisco and with the larger Beat movement in the 1950s.

Novelists **James Leo Hirlihy** (1927-1993), who wrote *Midnight Cowboy,* and **Michael Rumaker** (1932-) attended Black Mountain, as did filmmaker **Arthur Penn** (1922-2010). *(See below and also The Arts in Asheville section.)*

Other Notable Writers Who Served Time Here

William Bartram (1739-1823), the famed natural historian, explored Western North Carolina in 1776. His classic work, published in 1791, is *Travels in North and South Carolina, Georgia, East and West Florida, the Cherokee Country, etc.* The Bartram Trail, honoring his travels in five Southern states, runs a little over 78 miles in the mountains of North Carolina.

Wilma Dykeman (1920-2006), born in Buncombe County, was the author of 18 books including T*he French Broad,* published in 1955 as part of the Holt Rinehart Rivers of America series.

The French Broad is a history of the river, which runs from near Brevard to Tennessee, and an oral history of the people who lived along the river.

Ernest Hemingway (1899-1961) stayed in a log cabin at Pine Crest Inn in Tryon on a hunting trip.

DuBose Heyward (1885-1940), author of the 1925 novel *Porgy,* which he and George Gershwin transformed into the opera *Porgy and Bess,* lived in Charleston, S.C., but had a summer home in Hendersonville. Heyward died in Tryon.

Henry James (1843-1916), the American-born realist writer, and his friend, **Edith Wharton,** (1862-1937) both visited the Vanderbilts at their Biltmore Estate in 1905 (but separately). Neither appeared much taken with Biltmore House, yet both now have suites there named for them.

Horace Kephart (1862-1931) is best known for *Our Southern Highlanders,* his 1913 study of mountain people in what would become the Great Smoky Mountains National Park. Born in Pennsylvania, he came to Western North Carolina in 1904 and lived in Hazel Creek, Bryson City and Dillsboro.

With photographer **George Masa,** Kephart was instrumental in establishing the national park in the Smokies. He also helped plot the route of the Appalachian Trail through the Smokies. His 1910 book, *Camp Cookery,* on how to cook game and other food during camping trips, is still in print.

Caroline Miller (1903-1992), a Georgia native, lived for several years in Waynesville. Her 1933 novel, *Lamb in His Bosom,* won the Pulitzer Prize for fiction.

John Parris (1914-1999) was one of the great keepers and historians of mountain culture. Born in Sylva, Paris became a foreign correspondent with United Press and the Associated Press. Then, for almost four decades wrote a daily column in the *Asheville Citizen* called "Roaming the Mountains." The columns were prose poems, sometimes sentimental but always engaging, about the mountains and mountain people. Many of the columns were collected into books, including *Roaming the Mountains* (1955), *My Mountains, My People* (1957), *Mountain Bred* (1967), *These Storied Mountains* (1972) and *Mountain Cooking* (1978). Sadly, these books are now out of print. They deserve to be republished and cherished by all who love the mountains. John Parris and his wife, Dorothy Luxton Paris, helped launch the Mountain Heritage Center at Western Carolina University.

Walker Percy (1916-1990), who lived in St. Tammany Parish near New Orleans, in the 1970s and 1980s spent part of most summers in Highlands. His novel, *The Second Coming* (1980), is set in Western North Carolina.

William Sydney Porter (1862-1910), wrote short stories with surprise endings under the pen name O. Henry. He married a childhood friend from Weaverville and spent a short time in Asheville near the end of his life, though he found the city too quiet. O. Henry, a heavy drinker who died in New York of complications of alcoholism and diabetes, is buried at Riverside Cemetery in Asheville. Occasionally, diehard O. Henry fans leave $1.87 on his grave, in memory of the amount of money that features prominently in "The Gift of the Magi," O. Henry's best-known story, about a young couple who are short of money but want to buy each other Christmas presents. The avenue that runs between the Asheville Citizen-Times Building and the Grove Arcade was named after O. Henry.

Marjorie Rawlings (1896-1953) wrote much of her classic Florida novel, *The Yearling,* holed up in a cabin at Lees-McRae College in Banner Elk. *The Yearling* won a Pulitzer Prize. She met Scott Fitzgerald in Asheville in 1936.

Contemporary Writers

Sarah Addison Allen (1971-) grew up in Asheville and was graduated from UNC-Asheville. She is the author of five popular and well-reviewed novels, plus an early romance novel written when she was a teenager under the pen name Cathie Gallagher. Her 2007 debut novel under her own name, *Garden Spells,* is set in Balsam, N.C., a town that resembles Asheville. Her latest work, *Lost Lake,* was published in 2014.

Cathy Smith Bowers (1949-), a poet who lives in Tryon and has taught at UNC-Asheville, was North Carolina Poet Laureate from 2010 to 2012. She has published four books of poetry, including *Like Shining from Shook Foil* in 2010.

Wayne Caldwell (1948-), who grew up in Enka-Candler, is the author of two of the best novels ever written about mountain life. *Cataloochee* (2007) and *Requiem by Fire* (2010) are both mostly set in the Cataloochee Valley before the coming of the Great Smoky Mountains National Park. *Cataloochee* follows several generations of mountain people from the Civil War to 1928, while *Requiem by Fire* takes place in the late 1920s when the government begins to remove residents to make way for the park. Caldwell gets the setting, the people and mountain speech exactly right.

Canton native and former North Carolina Poet Laureate **Fred Chappell** (1936-) has written a series of novels, including *Look Back All the Green Valley* (1999), set in Haywood County. In the novels Canton is called Tipton.

Tony Earley (1961-), a short story writer and novelist, was born in San Antonio but grew up in Rutherfordton and graduated from Warren Wilson College. His best-known novel is *Jim the Boy,* set in the 1930s in a fictional small town of Aliceville, N.C. He now lives in Nashville and teaches at Vanderbilt.

John Ehle (1925-), an Asheville native, has authored 11 novels, most set in Appalachia. A member of the North Carolina Literary Hall of Fame, Ehle and his wife have a home in Penland.

Asheville-born **Charles Frazier** (1960-) had a huge success with his 1997 novel, *Cold Mountain,* which won the National Book Award and was made into a movie in 2003. It was filmed in Romania, however, not in Western North Carolina. *Cold Mountain* tells the story of a Confederate deserter making his way back to his home in the mountains. To view the real Cold Mountain (elevation 6,015 feet) in the Shining Rock Wilderness section of the Pisgah National Forest, drive to the overlook at Milepost 412 of the Blue Ridge Parkway. An even better view of Cold Mountain is available from the top of Mt. Pisgah. It's a 3-mile roundtrip hike from the parking area at Milepost 407 of the Blue Ridge Parkway to the top of Pisgah. Frazier's second novel, *Thirteen Moons* (2006), also set in Western North Carolina, traces the story of a white man's involvement with the Cherokee Indians in the early 19th century. His latest novel, *Nightwoods* (2011), a thriller, is also set in the mountains. Frazier now lives on a farm near Raleigh.

Gail Godwin (1937-) was born in Birmingham, Ala., but raised in Asheville. Several of her 11 novels, including *A Mother and Two Daughters* and *A Southern Family* have been at least partly set in or near Mountain City, a town that resembles Asheville. Godwin's most recent novel, *Unfinished Desires* (2010), is set almost entirely in Mountain City. A tale of the girls and nuns at a local Catholic school for girls, now closed, St. Genevieve's, (which Godwin attended), the story features area landmarks such as the S&W Cafeteria, the Man's Store, the Asheville School and the American Enka plant.

Billy Graham (1918-), whose home is in Montreat, has published 30 books on religion and spiritual advice. His wife, **Ruth Graham** (1920-2007), was author or co-author of 14 books, including volumes of poetry and personal recollections.

Jan Karon (1937-), born in Lenoir, retired from advertising and lives in Blowing Rock, the setting (as the mountain town of Mitford) of the nine-book Mitford series, which began with 1994's *At Home in Mitford.* Karon also has authored two books in the Father Tim series, several books for children and other books.

Novelist **Elizabeth Kostova** (1964-), best known for her first novel, *The Historian,* published in 2005, lives in Asheville. One of the settings for Kostova's second novel, *Swann Thieves,* is Warren Wilson College.

Valerie Ann Leff co-founded the Great Smokies Writing Program at the University of North Carolina at Asheville. Her wonderfully titled 2005 first novel, *Better Homes and Husbands,* follows the lives of the residents of a posh New York City co-op building from the 1970s to the present. She now lives in Weston, Mass.

Robert Morgan (1944-), born in Hendersonville, is a poet, short-story writer, novelist and historian who teaches at Cornell. Several of his novels, including the best-seller *Gap Creek,* are set in Western North Carolina. He is a member of the North Carolina Literary Hall of Fame.

Heather Newton (1963-) was born in Raleigh. Her first published novel, *Under the Mercy Trees,* won the 2011 Thomas Wolfe Memorial Literary Award. She has finished a collection of related short stories set on the campus of a boarding school in the North Georgia mountains and is working on a new novel that she describes as a women's friendship story set in Western North Carolina. Newton practices law in Asheville.

Asheville poet **Glenis Redmond** (1963-) is best known for her poetry performances, but she has published a book of her poetry, *Backbone.*

Joshua Warren (1978-) of Asheville has created a writing career out of the paranormal. He penned his first book at age 13 and has since written more than half a dozen books on ghosts in Asheville and elsewhere. He appears in a ghost hunters show, "Paranormal Paparazzi," on the Travel Channel.

Allan Wolf (1963-) is a Connecticut-born poet and writer who lives in Asheville. He authored a notable history of the Lewis and Clark expedition, *New Found Land: Lewis and Clark's Voyage of Discovery.* Wolf is active in local poetry slams and theatrical poetry.

Among **mystery writers** with an Asheville area connection are **Mart Baldwin** of Hendersonville, author of *A Diary to Die For* and other novels; **Rick Boyer,** who moved to Asheville after doing the *Places Rated Almanac,* the author of 11 mystery novels, some under pseudonyms; **Lilian Jackson Braun** (1913-2011), author of 29 highly popular *The Cat Who ...* mystery novels featuring newspaper reporter James Qwilleran and his two Siamese cats KoKo and Yum-Yum – Braun for many years lived part of each year in Tryon;

Patricia Cornwell (1956-), who spent part of her childhood in Montreat, author of 20 popular mysteries on medical examiner Dr. Kay Scarpetta; **Mark de Castrique**, born in Hendersonville but now living in Charlotte, author of eight mystery novels set in Western North Carolina, including *The Sandburg Connection,* about poet Carl Sandburg;

Sharyn McCrumb, who has written extensively about the Appalachian mountains, including a retelling of the Tom Dooley ballad; **Brenda J. Moody**, author of *More Than Murder* in 2009, based on a true-life murder of three men in 1960s Hendersonville, two of them gay lovers; **Ann B. Ross**, creator of the spunky, funny *Miss Julia* series, which now totals 13 novels, lives in Hendersonville (Abbotsville, N.C. in her books); **Alexander Skye's** astrologer-sleuth Charlotte McCrae lives in a small North Carolina mountain resort town; **Elizabeth Daniels Squires** (1926-2001), of Weaverville, granddaughter of Josephus Daniels, founder of the *Raleigh News and Observer*, author of series of mysteries set in the Carolina mountains featuring Peaches Dann, a smart, absent-minded, middle-aged woman.

For more on the literati of Western North Carolina, see *Literary Trails of the North Carolina Mountains* by Georgann Eubanks and *Scribblers: Stalking the Authors of Appalachia* by Stephen Kirk.

LITERARY LANDMARKS
Black Mountain College Lake Eden Campus In 1941, Black Mountain College moved from rented quarters at Blue Ridge Assembly to Lake Eden, which is now a summer camp, **Camp Rockmont** *(375 Lake Eden Rd., 828-686-3885, www.rockmont.com)*. Rockmont operates as a 550-acre Christian camp for boys from early June to mid-August and at other times rents parts of the camp to organizations and groups. Seek permission in advance to visit the grounds of the private camp. Twice a year, in mid-May and mid-October, the **Lake Eden Arts Festival** or **LEAF** *(377 Lake Eden Rd., 828-686-8742, www.theleaf.org)* stages a weekend music and arts festival on the grounds of Camp Rockmont. Buy tickets in advance, as they usually sell out. You can walk around and see the buildings that remain of the original campus, including the Studies Building, dining hall and two lodge dormitories. Some attendees camp out on the grounds or rent cabins or a bed in dorms used by Black Mountain College.

Black Mountain College Museum + Arts Center *(56 Broadway St., Asheville, 828-350-8484, www.blackmountaincollege.org; open noon-4 Tues.-Wed., 11-4 Thurs.-Sat., admission fees vary depending on event, exhibition or conference)* is dedicated to preserving and continuing the legacy of educational and artistic innovation of Black Mountain College. ___

Grove Park Inn, an Omni Resort *(290 Macon Ave., 828-252-2711, www.groveparkinn.com)* hosted F. Scott Fitzgerald in during the summers of 1935 and 1936. Capitalizing on the writer's fame, the hotel now holds a Fitzgerald weekend annually around the time of Fitzgerald's birthday, September 24. It's possible to tour or even stay in the rooms Fitzgerald occupied, rooms 451 and 453, if they are available. Over the years, many other writers have stayed at the Grove Park Inn, including Margaret Mitchell, Alex Haley, George Plimpton, Will Rogers, Pat Conroy, Charles Kuralt and Charles Frazier. The inns developed the luxury condominiums nearby named The Fitzgerald.

Homewood at Highland Hospital *(19 Zillicoa St.)*, at the northwestern edge of the Montford section, is part of the original Highland Hospital complex where Zelda Fitzgerald died in a 1948 fire that destroyed the hospital's main building. Eight other patients also perished. The remains of the four-story frame and stone building, owned by Duke University, was razed. Homewood was the residence of Zelda's psychiatrist, Dr. Robert Carroll, founder of what was then called a mental hospital and tuberculosis sanatorium. The large stone house was built in 1922 in the Gothic style. Homewood is now used as an event venue, and the psychiatric hospital no longer exists. See Homewood Event and Conference Center *(828-232-9900, www.mybelovedhomewood.com)*.

Oakdale Cemetery *(U.S. Hwy. 64W and Valley St., Hendersonville, 828-697-3088, www.cityofhendersonville.org)* is the site of the marble angel owned by W. O. Wolfe, Thomas Wolfe's father, that is featured in *Look Homeward, Angel*. It marks the grave of Mrs. Margaret Bates Johnson. There is a wrought iron fence surrounding the grave and angel. Look for a state historic marker.

Riverside Cemetery *(53 Birch Ave., 828-350-2066, www.ashevillenc.gov; daily 8-5, gates open 7 am-8 pm, free)* is an 87-acre cemetery where writers Thomas Wolfe and O. Henry are buried. George Masa, the Japanese photographer who worked with Horace Kephart in promoting the idea of the Great Smoky Mountains National Park, also is buried here. You can download a Riverside Cemetery map and walking tour from the City of Asheville website.

Carl Sandburg Home *(81 Carl Sandburg Lane, for GPS use 1800 Little River Rd., Flat Rock, 828-693-4178, www.nps.gov/carl/index.htm; guided tour fee $5 adults, $3 seniors, children 15 and under free, admission to grounds and barn free, daily 9-5 year-round, tours of house every half hour starting at 9:30, last tour 4:30)* is operated by the National Park Service.

It's the first national park to honor a poet. You enter the grounds via a short walk up a winding driveway lined with white pines. The house, a white one-and-a-half story on a raised basement, with Greek Revival columns on the front porch sits on a knoll above a small lake. The house was built around 1839 as a summer cottage by a South Carolina railroad owner. On the guided tour, you'll see the Sandburg house much as it was in the 1960s, as if the family had stepped out for a walk. There are magazines on the floor, a guitar leaning against the piano and shelves of books. Sandburg's book-filled study has his typewriter. There's a bookstore with a good selection of books by and about Sandburg on the basement level of the house. Don't miss a tour of the barn and outbuildings, where you'll see descendants of Paula Steichen Sandburg's herd of dairy goats. The farm has some 5 miles of hiking trails.

Thomas Wolfe Memorial *(52 N. Market St. and 48 Spruce St., 828-253-8304, www.wolfememorial.com; visitor center open Tues.-Sat. 9-5, Sun. 1-5; $5 adults, $2 children, guided tour of the house included)* is operated as a North Carolina State Historic Site. The rambling 29-room boarding house, operated by Wolfe's mother Julia Wolfe, is where Thomas Wolfe grew up. The "Old Kentucky Home," called "Dixie" in Wolfe's novel, *Look Homeward, Angel,* is directly behind the visitor center at 48 Spruce Street. The Wolfe home was extensively damaged in a 1998 fire (the arsonist was never caught), but it was meticulously restored as it might have looked in the early 20th century when Wolfe lived there before heading off to college at Chapel Hill. The house, a Queen Anne style structure built in 1883 with later additions, is painted a bright canary yellow. The visitor center exhibits personal effects of the author, including some of his clothes, his Remington typewriter and his diploma from Harvard. There's also a 22-minute film on the author's life and work.

BLUE RIDGE PARKWAY

"The mountains are calling and I must go."
--John Muir

• One of nation's most-visited National Park Service units, with 13 million visitors in 2013 -- in previous years it has been the most-visited unit, but bad weather and road closures cut visitation in 2013, so Golden Gate Bridge recreation area in San Francisco with 14 million visitors temporarily edged out the Blue Ridge Parkway • One of the most beautiful drives in the country • Free admission • Winds along mountain crests for 469 miles, 256 in North Carolina and 213 miles in Virginia • Took 52 years to complete • Elevation ranges from 650 feet to 6,053 feet • More than 200 scenic overlooks • Maximum 45 mph speed limit • Access the parkway at many road intersections, including 7 in Asheville area • Great bicycling • Excellent hiking on 100 trails • 9 campgrounds along the parkway with more than 1,000 tent and RV sites • 3 lodges on the parkway • Picnic at many developed picnic areas or along most parts of roadway • Home to 74 species of mammals, 160 nesting birds, more than 585 species of amphibians and reptiles and 1,300 kinds of wildflowers

Parkway Headquarters: 199 Hemphill Knob Rd., Asheville, 828-271-4779 or 828-298-0398 for recorded information; www.nps.gov/blri, free.

The Blue Ridge Parkway often is considered the most beautiful drive in the East and one of the most beautiful in all of North America. It passes through the city limits of Asheville, and visiting at least part of the parkway is an absolute must when vacationing in Asheville.

The parkway technically is not a national park, but it is a national parkway nearly half a thousand miles in length with many access points along the way. As such it normally gets more annual visitors – around from 13 to 22 million a year – than any other unit of the entire system operated by the National Park Service.

Of course, many of these parkways "visitors" are local people who use the park to commute short distances.

Connecting the **Skyline Drive** and **Shenandoah National Park** in Virginia and the **Great Smoky Mountains National Park** in North Carolina, the parkway winds its way 469 miles, mostly along or near the crests of mountain peaks, 213 miles in Virginia and 256 in North Carolina.

It's often called the country's longest and narrowest park. Although the parkway consists of more than 81,000 acres, at some points the parkway lands are only a few hundred yards wide, with farms and private homes visible near the two-lane park road; in others areas, though, especially as it passes through the Pisgah National Forest, the vistas spread out over vast horizons of mountains, with small towns and communities only specks in the far distance.

The **Blue Ridge Mountains** are part of the **Appalachian Mountains.** From Blue Ridge Parkway Milepost 0 at Rockfish Gap, Va., to Milepost 355 near Mt. Mitchell State Park, N.C., the parkway follows the crest of the Blue Ridge Mountains, averaging about 3,000 feet in elevation. At Mt. Mitchell, the parkway veers westward through the **Black Mountains,** then into the **Craggies** before descending toward Asheville. From there, the road climbs to elevations over 6,000 feet in the **Balsam Mountains** before entering the Great Smoky Mountains National Park near Cherokee near MP 469.

History of the Parkway

The history of the planning and construction of the Blue Ridge Parkway is fascinating. The idea for a motor parkway through the Southern Appalachians dates from the early part of the 20th century, but there were lengthy and complex debates about the route of the road, especially as to whether it would run from Virginia to North Carolina or to eastern Tennessee. (Western North Carolina of course won.) Then there were debates about whether the parkway should follow the crests of the mountains or the valleys. In the end, most of it was built to follow the mountain crests. Obtaining land for the road was a long and disputatious process.

Construction finally began on September 1935, near Cumberland Knob in North Carolina, and construction in Virginia began in February 1936. On June 30, 1936, the U.S. Congress formally authorized the project as the Blue Ridge Parkway and placed it under the jurisdiction of the National Park Service. Much of the construction was done by private contractors, but some of it was carried out by government New Deal agencies, including the Work Projects Administration and Civilian Conservation Corps.

Work progressed rapidly during the 1930s but slowed during World War II. It resumed after the war, and by the late 1950s most of the parkway had been completed. However, the last section, Linn Cove Viaduct at Grandfather Mountain, wasn't finished until 1987.

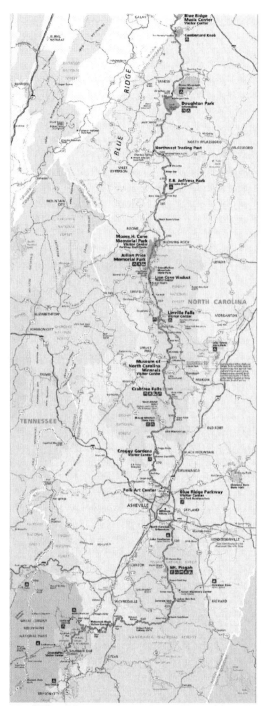

*North Carolina section of the Blue Ridge Parkway—
courtesy of National Park Service*

If you're interested in the history of how the parkway came about, you'll enjoy the best book on the planning and construction of this magnificent national treasure: *Super-Scenic Motorway: A Blue Ridge Parkway History, by* Anne Mitchell Whisnant, published in 2006 by the University of North Carolina Press.

"Driving Through Time" is a remarkable, if somewhat clunky to navigate, website *(www.docsouth.unc.edu/blueridgeparkway/)* that includes more than 5,000 digitized historic photographs, maps, drawings, newspaper articles, oral histories and other documents related to the parkway's construction and development. The site is based partly on the work of historian Dr. Anne Mitchell Whisnant.

Planning Your Visit

The official website of the Blue Ridge Parkway is that of the National Park Service, www.nps.gov/blri. It is less comprehensive than the Park Service's website on the Great Smoky Mountains National Park, but it is nonetheless useful in planning your visit. Be sure to download the parkway map at www.nps.gov/blri/planyourvisit/maps.htm. Also, many private guidebooks to the parkway have been published – *see Resources.*

Because the parkway is accessible from many major crossroads along its length, you can enter at a large variety of different points and take the scenic roadway in chunks of a few hours or even a few minutes.

Marker at the site of the highest point on the Blue Ridge Parkway – 6,053 feet

Most parkway aficionados say that the most scenic parts of the parkway are from around Boone and Blowing Rock to Asheville, and then from Asheville to the Great Smokies. These are the highest elevation areas of the parkway and offer dramatic mountain views and a diverse selection of types of trees, shrubs and wildflowers.

The parkway is in theory open year-round, but in winter the higher elevations of the parkway, especially north and south of Asheville, often are closed due to ice and snow. Some sections also close periodically for maintenance or to remove rockslides. The Folk Art Center in Asheville, the main Blue Ridge Parkway Visitor Center adjacent to park headquarters near Asheville and the Museum of North Carolina Minerals at Spruce Pine are open year round. Most other facilities, including visitor centers, campgrounds, inns, restaurants and picnic areas, typically begin opening in April and stay open through the fall leaf color in October or early November.

The **Blue Ridge Parkway Association** is the officially designated marketing partner of the Blue Ridge Parkway. Its members, mostly tourist-related businesses near the park, have worked together more than six decades to promote the park. The website is very helpful, and it has an excellent planning guide to the parkway, available either in paper or as an online download from the association website at www.blueridgeparkway.org. Both versions are free. A free mobile app is also available for many smartphones and tablets. The **Blue Ridge Parkway Foundation** (www.brpfoundation.org) is a non-profit established in 1997 that helps raise money to support the parkway.

Driving the Parkway

The vast majority of visitors to the Blue Ridge Parkway see it from their autos. Commercial vehicles are banned on the parkway without specific advance permission. You can even be stopped for having a magnetic business sign attached to the door of your car or truck.

The speed limit on the parkway is 45 mph, and in some areas lower. Often you'll be traveling at 30 mph or slower, so to drive the entire parkway in Virginia and North Carolina will take 12 hours, without stopping. To drive the length of the parkway in a leisurely fashion, with stops for sightseeing and meals, plan at least three or four days.

Access Points

The 105-mile long Skyline Drive in Virginia, with which the Blue Ridge Parkway connects. has only four access points.

However, the Blue Ridge Parkway has dozens of access points along its entire length, typically with an entrance at every major crossroad.

In the Asheville area, there are seven access points – the easiest entrances are from U.S. Highway 70 east of Asheville at Milepost 382, from U.S. Highway 25 at MP 389 and from NC Highway 191 near I-26 at the North Carolina Arboretum at MP 393. You also can access the parkway at Bull Gap (MP 375) via Elk Mountain Scenic Highway or via Reems Creek and Ox Creek roads; Craven Gap (MP 377) via Webb Cove Road; via U.S. Highway 74A in East Asheville/Fairview (MP 385); and via NC Highway 151/Pisgah Highway near Candler that takes you on a very curvy ascent to MP 405 near Elk Pasture Gap.

You can also enter near many other towns and cities along its path, including Cumberland Knob, Sparta, Mount Airy, Blowing Rock, Boone, Linville, Little Switzerland, Spruce Pine, Brevard, Waynesville, Maggie Valley and Cherokee in North Carolina and Waynesboro, Lynchburg, Roanoke and Galax in Virginia.

Don't-Miss Sights

Here are some of the top sights on the Blue Ridge Parkway, listed from north to south. Many of the visitor centers have gift shops.

Humpback Rocks (Milepost 5.8) – visitor center, museum of 19th century log buildings, picnic area, access to Appalachian Trail and trail to summit of Humpback Mountain.

James River and Otter Creek (MP 60-63) – visitor center, restored canal locks on the James River, campground and hiking trails along Otter Creek.

Peaks of Otter (MP 86) – lodge and restaurant, visitor center, 1930s restored Johnson farm, campground, picnic area, and access to Appalachian Trail, extensive trail system. The museum at the visitor center has good information on the Native American history of the mountains.

Roanoke (MP 106-120) - access to the parkway's largest neighboring city, hiking and horse trails and campground.

Mabry Mill (MP176.2) – the Mabry Mill Trail features a blacksmith shop, wheelwright's shop and whiskey still, as well as one of the most photographed structures on the parkway, Mabry Mill itself. This is a working gristmill. There are three picnic areas, a visitor center, campground and hiking into Rockcastle Gorge.

Blue Ridge Music Center (MP 215) – outdoor amphitheater, visitor center and museum. This is the parkway's premier site for interpreting and featuring the musical heritage of the region.

Moses H. Cone and Julian Price Parks (MP 295-298) – the Cone house is a 23-room, 13,000 square feet mansion completed in 1900 on a 3,500-acre estate near Grandfather Mountain. Moses Cone was a textile manufacturer and was called the "denim king of America." His company was a major supplier of denim to Levi Strauss for about 100 years. At one time, the Cone estate had 25 miles of carriage roads, several lakes, extensive rose gardens, four orchards with 32,000 apple trees, stables, barns, carriage and apple houses, a bowling alley and a carbide plant that provided gas and lighting to the manor. The house now contains a Southern Highland Handicraft Guild craft store. There is a 47-acre lake at Price Park, along with many hiking trails, picnic area and campground.

Linn Cove Viaduct (MP 304) -- the 1,243-foot-long Linn Cove Viaduct is a dramatic feat of engineering on the slopes of Grandfather Mountain. This was the last section of the Parkway to be completed, in 1987. Here you can visit the bridge museum and visitor center maintained by National Park Service and hike on a trail that runs under the viaduct.

Linville Falls (MP 317) – visitor center, campground, picnic area and access to popular wilderness area, Linville Gorge.

Museum of North Carolina Minerals (MP 331) – visitor center and museum highlighting the geology and gems of the region, open year-round. Kids especially will enjoy it.

Crabtree Falls (MP 349) - campground, picnic area and access to Crabtree Falls, in the Black Mountain Range.

Mt. Mitchell (off MP 355), the highest peak in the East, is at the end of a 4.8-mile access road. At Mt. Mitchell State Park, there's a visitor center, restaurant and snack bar open seasonally, along with walk-in and hike-in campsites. The restaurant, snack bar and restrooms are open May through October.

Craggy Gardens (MP 364) – Craggy Gardens is a high elevation heath bald. There is a visitor center here and a picnic area. Spectacular displays of rhododendron blooms occur in June and early July.

Asheville (MP 382-393) – Asheville is home to park headquarters and is the region's major tourist destination. The parkway runs through part of the Biltmore Estate. If you exit the parkway at U.S. Highway 25 North (MP 389), you're only about 3 miles from the entrance to Biltmore. The Folk Art Center (MP 382), open year-round, is one of the best crafts centers in the region. The main Blue Ridge Parkway visitor center (MP 384), open year-round, has exhibits and films. Near MP 394, adjacent to the parkway, is the wonderful North Carolina Arboretum.

Pine Mountain Tunnel (MP 399.3) -- the longest tunnel on the parkway, at 1,320 feet long.

Mt. Pisgah (MP 408) – the section around Mt. Pisgah has a campground, picnic area and the Pisgah Inn lodge and restaurant. The Cradle of Forestry, the birthplace of forestry in America, Sliding Rock and the largest trout hatchery in North Carolina are nearby – to reach these attractions go south toward Brevard on U.S. Highway 276 into the Pisgah National Forest at MP 412.

Cold Mountain (MP 412) – two overlooks offer views of the mountain made famous in Charles Frazier's best-selling 1997 novel and the 2003 movie of the same name. For the best view, stop at Wagon Gap Road parking area at MP 412.2, then walk north a short distance on the parkway. There also is a view, somewhat obstructed by trees, of Cold Mountain from the overlook at MP 412.2. The movie made from the novel was not filmed in Western North Carolina but in Eastern Europe.

Graveyard Fields (MP 419) – has views quite different from what you see on most of the rest of the parkway, in that there are few tall trees. The spooky name of this popular site comes from the tree stumps and dirt mounds left after a windstorm and later forest fire. There's a popular hiking trail (Graveyard Fields Loop) here that passes three waterfalls and a nice swimming hole. In August, Graveyard Fields is a good place to pick wild blueberries – Park Service rules permit the picking of one gallon per person per day. On busy weekends, the Graveyard Fields parking lot can be full. However, in 2014, the Park Service expanded the parking lot and made other improvements.

Waterrock Knob (MP 451) – visitor center near the Cherokee Reservation and near the parkway's highest elevation, featuring views over the Great Smokes region.

Terminus of Parkway (MP 469) – connects with US Highway 441, the main road through the Great Smoky Mountains National Park, near Oconaluftee visitor center and the Mountain Farm Museum.

Bicycling

Biking is permitted the entire length of the parkway, and bicycling is popular. Keep in mind, however, that automobile drivers may have trouble seeing bikes on curves and especially in long, unlit tunnels. Always wear high-visibility clothing and equip your bike with front and rear lights and reflectors. Even if you're an experienced rider and you're in good shape, you should plan on seven to eight days to bike the entire length of the parkway. That's 60 to 70 miles a day, with much of it up steep grades. At that pace, you won't have much time to stop and smell the flowers.

Hiking

The parkway offers about 100 hiking trails, ranging from short nature walks to multi-mile hikes. There is access to the Appalachian Trail at several points in Virginia, including near Roanoke and Peaks of Otter.

Some of the most popular trails with trailheads on or near the parkway in North Carolina include Linville Falls Trail (Milepost 316.4, 0.8 mile to view of lower and upper falls), Crabtree Falls Loop Trail (MP 339.5, 2 miles to waterfall), Craggy Pinnacle Trail (MP 364.2, 0.7 miles to panoramic high mountain view), Mountain-to-Sea Trail (MP 382, parallels parkway, 7.2 miles), Bent Creek-Walnut Cove (MP 393.7, 3.1 miles), Graveyard Fields Loop Trail (MP 418.8, 2.3 miles passes two waterfalls), Black Balsam Knob (MP 420.2, 2 miles to mountain bald) and Waterrock Knob Trail (MP 451.2, 1.2 miles to view over Smokies).

Camping

There are nine National Park Service campgrounds along the parkway with more than 700 tent sites and nearly 350 RV sites:

Otter Creek (MP 61) is near Virginia's James River.

Peaks of Otter (MP 86) is near the Peaks of Otter Lodge, Abbott Lake, the restored 1930s Johnson Farm and an excellent trail system.

Roanoke Mountain (MP 120) has easy access to the largest city along the Parkway corridor.

Rocky Knob (MP 167) has easy access to Rockcastle Gorge and is just nine miles from Mabry Mill.

Doughton Park (MP 241) is near Basin Cove and an extensive trail system.

Julian Price Park (MP 297) is near Boone and Blowing Rock and close to the Moses Cone Estate and a lake. This is the Parkway's largest campground, with 129 tent sites and 68 RV sites.

Linville Falls (MP 316) is on the Linville River and with access to the trail system into Linville Gorge Wilderness Area.

Crabtree Falls (MP 340) campground is near the Crabtree Falls Trail and within 15 miles of Mt. Mitchell State Park.

Mt. Pisgah (MP 408) is the highest parkway campground at almost 5,000 feet elevation.

Camping along the parkway is permitted only in designated campgrounds. Fees are $20 per night, with group camping at Linville Falls $35 a night.

Senior lifetime national park pass holders pay $8 to $10 per night. (The Senior pass, by the way, is a terrific deal, available to those 62 and older. It costs just $10 and allows admission to most federal parks and recreations areas in the United States at no charge. It's sold at many national park units.)

You are limited to camping a total of 21 days between June 1 and Labor Day. RVs and trailers are limited to 30 feet in length. Dump stations are available at all campgrounds, as are toilets, but there are no water or electric hook ups. There are many private, commercial campgrounds near the parkway, some with amenities such as hot showers and swimming pools.

For the most popular campgrounds -- Peaks of Otter, Mt. Pisgah, Price Park, Doughton Park and Linville Falls -- reservations can be made on-line at www.recreation.gov or by calling toll-free 877-444-6777. The advance reservation charge is an extra $3 per night. Otherwise, camping is first-come, first-served. Campgrounds tend to fill up on holidays and weekends in summer and fall.

Lodging

There are three lodging options on the parkway, along with hundreds of motels, inns and lodges in towns and cities near the parkway:

Peaks of Otter Lodge *(Milepost 85.6, 85554 Blue Ridge Pkwy., Bedford, VA 24523; 540-586-1081 or 866-387-9905, www.peaksofotter.com; rates start at $135 plus tax including breakfast, higher on some weekends and holidays, with discounts available for advance booking).* The 60-room motel-style lodge was built in 1963 and opened in 1964. While the setting is beautiful – it is right beside Abbott Lake with its reflection of Sharp Top Mountain -- not much has been done to update or refurbish the lodge since the 1970s and 1980s. A new concessionaire took over in 2013 and some changes may be ahead. There are no televisions, no internet, no room phones and no cell phone reception. Some furniture and furnishings need replacing. There is a restaurant that most guests describe as good but not exceptional. The restaurant is open from early April through November. Bed and breakfast rates start at $135, with discounts of 15 to 25% for booking and paying from 7 to 14 days in advance. Peaks of Otter Lodge is 9 miles from Bedford and 25 miles from Roanoke.

Rocky Knob Cabins *(Milepost 174.1 near the town of Floyd, 20 Rock Church Rd., Meadows of Dan, VA 24120; as of late 2014 the concessionaire status of these cabins was pending – check locally.* Eight rustic cabins, each with two double beds and a kitchenette but no bathroom (except for one ADA-compliant cabin that has one bed and an ensuite bathroom), were built in the 1930s by members of the Civilian Conservation Corps. Toilets and showers are in two sex-segregated bathhouses about 100 feet from the cabins. Consider this basic but clean and pleasant cabin camping in a get-away-from-civilization setting.

Pisgah Inn *(Milepost 408.6 near Mt. Pisgah, Mail: P.O. Box 749, Waynesville, NC 28786, tel. 828-235-8228, www.pisgahinn.com; rates $138 plus tax single or double weekdays, higher on weekends, holidays and in October, breakfast included; some discounts available in April and May; open Apr.-Oct.).* This is more of a motel than an inn, and the rooms are basic, but the setting at 5,000 feet and the dramatic mountain views are the reasons to stay here. The inn is directly on the parkway near the 5,721-foot Mt. Pisgah about 26 miles from Asheville, 20 miles from Brevard and 24 miles from Waynesville.

Once part of the vast Biltmore Estate, the site of the Pisgah Inn along with some 80,000 acres was sold by Edith Vanderbilt in 1914 and became the basis of what is now Pisgah National Forest. The present day inn is not far from George Vanderbilt's beloved late 19th century Buck Springs Lodge, visited frequently by horse and wagon by Vanderbilt and friends. Sadly, the chestnut-log lodge was later disassembled and razed by the U.S. government, over the objections of preservationists. A short walk down the Buck Spring Trail from the Mt. Pisgah parking lot takes you to a historic exhibit located at the foundation stone remains of the hunting lodge.

The original Pisgah Inn opened in 1919, but it closed and, in disrepair, was torn down in the 1990s. The current two-story inn was constructed in 1964. On the grounds are a restaurant – the food here is surprisingly good and reasonably priced, and the views from the dining room are fabulous – and a gift shop and small convenience store.

Nearby is a 137-site park campground, operated separately from the inn. You can make reservations for the campground in advance on-line at www.recreation.gov or by calling toll-free 877-444-6777.

Keep in mind that the weather at this elevation can be unpredictable. A storm in early May 1992 dropped 5 feet of snow on the inn and stranded guests for several days.

Picnics

You can stop anywhere on the parkway and picnic, except at designated and signed watersheds including a section north of Asheville and a section near Waynesville. Be sure to pull completely off the roadway to park. In addition, there are many developed picnic areas, including ones at Humpback Rocks (Milepost 5.8), Peaks of Otter (MP 86), Rocky Knob (MP 167), Mabry Mill (MP 176.2), Doughton Park (MP 241), Moses Cone Park (MP 294), Julian Price Park (MP 296.4), Linville Falls (MP 316.5), Crabtree Falls (MP 364), Folk Art Center (MP 382), Parkway Visitor Center (MP 384) and Mt. Pisgah (MP 407). This is not an exhaustive list of developed picnic areas on the parkway.

Flora and Fauna Along the Parkway

Wildlife and birds are plentiful along the parkway, including 74 species of mammals, more than 50 species of amphibians and 35 species of reptiles. About 160 species of birds nest along the parkway with many others passing through. Having said that, many wild creatures have learned to avoid the traffic on the roadway, and you may never spot most of them unless you get out and hike.

At least 1,600 species of vascular plants grow along the parkway, and nearly 1,300 of these are wildflowers. More than 130 species of trees are present, about as many as are found in all of Europe. In addition, it is estimated there are almost 400 species of mosses along the parkway and around 2,000 species of fungi.

Blue Ridge Parkway by the Numbers

$2.5 billion	Annual tourism spending generated by parkway
13-22 million	Annual visitors to parkway (includes commuters)
82,000	Acres of government land along parkway
6,053	Highest elevation in feet on parkway, at MP 431
1,300	Types of wildflowers along the parkway
650	Lowest elevation on parkway, at MP 64
469	Total miles of parkway
256	Miles of parkway in North Carolina
250+	Number of auto wrecks on parkway annually
200+	Number of overlooks on parkway
174	Number of bridges and viaducts on parkway
160	Number of species of birds that nest along parkway
74	Number of species of mammals along parkway
52	Years required to complete parkway (1935 to 1987)

45	Maximum speed limit in mph
26	Number of tunnels on parkway
25	Number of tunnels on parkway in NC
20	Nightly fee in dollars for parkway campgrounds
12	Hours to drive entire parkway without stopping
4	Park-service owned restaurants on the parkway
3	Lodging on parkway
0	Gas stations on parkway; entrance fee to parkway

GREAT SMOKY MOUNTAINS NATIONAL PARK

"It is one of the blessings of wilderness life that it shows us how few things we need in order to be perfectly happy."
–Horace Kephart, *Camping and Woodcraft*, 1917

• Nation's most visited national park with more than 9 million visitors annually • Free admission • More than 800 square miles in size • One of the most biologically diverse places on earth, with 6,000 known species of wildflowers, plants and trees, 66 species of mammals including black bears, elk, bobcats and deer, more than 250 varieties of birds, 50 native fish species, more than 80 types of reptiles and amphibians and possibly 100,000 different life forms • 1,500 to 2,000 black bears in the park • Elevation "On Top of Old Smoky" at Clingmans Dome is 6,643 feet • Excellent hiking on 900 miles of trails with 150 different routes • Camp at 10 developed campgrounds with almost 950 sites, plus hundreds of backcountry camping sites • Only a single lodge in the park, the hike-in Mt. Le Conte Lodge • Picnic at 11 developed picnic areas or at any beautiful spot (but protect food from bears) • Fish 2,100 miles of streams • More than 380 miles of scenic drives including Newfound Gap Road, Cades Cove Loop and Cataloochee Valley • 5 historic districts with 100 preserved buildings

Park Headquarters: 107 Park Headquarters Rd., Gatlinburg, TN 37738, visitor information line 865-436-1200; www.nps.gov/grsm; park open 24 hours daily, weather permitting; free.

Directions: From Asheville, take I-40 West to Exit 27 to U.S. Hwy. 74 West towards Waynesville. Turn onto U.S. Hwy. 19 and go through Maggie Valley to Cherokee. Turn onto U.S. Hwy. 441 North at Cherokee and follow the road into the park. Alternatively, enter the Blue Ridge Parkway at any Asheville area entrance point – *see below* – and follow it south to the parkway terminus at U.S. Hwy. 441 at Cherokee. The parkway route takes about 2 ½ hours, while the I-40/Hwy.19 route takes about an hour, but the parkway route is far more scenic.

There are about 1,500 to 2,000 black bears in the Great Smokies – photo courtesy of the National Park Service

The Great Smoky Mountains National Park is **America's most-visited national park,** with about twice as many visitors – more than 9 million a year -- as the second most-visited park, the Grand Canyon.

The Great Smokies is one of the largest remaining wild areas of Eastern America, roaming over some **521,000 acres or more than 800 square miles** in Western North Carolina and East Tennessee. Slightly more of the park is on the North Carolina side than on the Tennessee side.

Some of the tallest mountains in the East are here, including 16 peaks over 6,000 feet. **Clingmans Dome,** the highest peak in the park, soars 6,643 feet above sea level and 4,503 feet above the valley floor.

Although many visitors just zip through the park on the main east-west road, U.S. Highway 441, also known as **Newfound Gap Road,** the park has enough to keep you busy for a week or longer. The Great Smoky Mountains National Park offers extraordinary opportunities for outdoor activities. It has world-class hiking on around 900 miles of trails, from easy nature walks to multi-day backpacking treks.

The **Appalachian Trail** goes through the park, and North Carolina's 1,000-mile **Mountains-to-Sea Trail** (only about one-half finished) begins here. However, some of the most interesting sights in the park are viewable from the comfort of your vehicle. The park has more than 380 miles of roads, paved and unpaved.

Also in the park are the fascinating remains of several communities including **Cataloochee, Cades Cove, Roaring Fork** and **Elkmont.** Altogether there are nearly 100 restored historical buildings in the park, including the best collection of old log cabins in the East.

You can camp at **10 developed front country campgrounds** in the park with a total of 947 tent and RV sites, or hike in and camp at around **100 backcountry campsites,** each with a capacity of 4 to 20 campers, plus **15 backcountry shelters** with a total capacity of near 200. There are no cabins for rent in the park, but many privately operated ones are available on both the North Carolina and Tennessee sides. You also can hike in and stay at rustic **Le Conte Lodge,** the highest-elevation mountain lodge east of the Rockies. Fish hundreds of miles of trout streams in the park, go tubing in cold mountain streams, explore some of the 40 waterfalls in the park, picnic at any of 11 developed picnic areas or anywhere you find a pleasant spot, or go bicycling or mountain biking. Hire a horse and ride some of the 550 miles of trails open to horses, and if you have your own animal there are five horse camps.

Where there are modest fees for camping ($14-$23 a night for developed frontcountry campsites, $4 for backcountry sites) and a few other activities in the park, such as hayrides, overall the Great Smoky Mountains National Park is a great bargain, because access to the park and most of its facilities is always **free.** This is one of the few major national parks in the country that doesn't charge admission.

The Great Smoky Mountains National Park has one of the richest and most diverse collections of flora and fauna in the world. It is home to **6,000 known species of wildflowers, plants and trees.** About 95% of the park is forested. The Smokies sometimes is called the **"wildflower national park,"** as it has more flowering plants than any other U.S. national park. You can see wildflowers in bloom virtually year-round, although spring and summer are the best times.

Living in Great Smoky Mountains National Park are **66 species of mammals, more than 250 varieties of birds, 50 native fish species and more than 80 types of reptiles and amphibians**.

The **American black bear** is the symbol of the Smokies. At least **1,500 to 1,600 bears** are in the park (some estimates are as high as 2,000), a density of about two per square mile. There are more than **6,000 white-tailed deer** in the park. The Park Service also has helped reintroduce **elk, river otters** and **peregrine falcons** to the Smokies.

For a few short weeks, usually from late May to mid-June, **synchronous fireflies** put on a light show. In this illuminated mating dance, the male *Photinus* fireflies blink 4 to 8 times in the air, then wait about 6 seconds for the females on the ground to return a double-blink response.

Probably 100,000 different organisms exist in the park, although so far only about 17,000 have been identified and named.

Planning Your Trip

The official National Park Service website for the Great Smokies (www.nps.gov/grsm) has a tremendous amount of useful information on the park. Before you go, download the **Smokies Trip Planner** from the NPS site. Once in the park, at a visitor center pick up a copy of *Smokies Guide,* a free tabloid newspaper published four times a year by the Park Service. For sale at park visitor centers for $5, the **Smokies Starter Kit** is a useful collection of maps, pamphlets, brochures and other material on the park. Also worth considering is the **Smokies Explorer Packet** ($19.95), which includes two guidebooks. The **Great Smoky Mountains Association** is a non-profit group that has been supporting the park since 1953. It runs the bookstores and gift shops in the park. Its website at www.smokiesinformation.org has a wealth of information and many photos, along with an online store. There also are free Smokies **visitor guide apps** for iPhone and Android smartphones downloadable from the GSMA website.

History of the Park

More than 10,000 years ago, nomadic people called Paleo-Indians occupied the mountain valleys of the region, including what is now the Great Smoky Mountains National Park.

About 3,000 years ago, Eastern Woodland Indians took up a more settled agrarian life in the mountains. At the time the Europeans arrived in the 16th century, the Cherokee nation had a population of about 100,000 in eight Southeastern states.

The Spanish explorer, **Hernando de Soto,** came through the Smokies in 1540. In the early 1700s, sizeable numbers of white settlers, mostly from Scotland and Northern Ireland, arrived and began subsistence farming in the Smokies and elsewhere in the mountains.

Conflict between Native Americans and white settlers was an ongoing concern. In response, President Andrew Jackson ordered the removal of all Native American people from the Southern states, relocating them to reservations in Oklahoma. The forced march of the Cherokee that took place in 1838-39 is now known as *"Nunna daul Isunyi"* in the Cherokee language, or **"The Trail of Tears."**

About 600 Cherokee Indians remained in North Carolina. They became the basis of the Eastern Band of the Cherokee Nation, based today on the Qualla Boundary reservation adjoining the Great Smokies Park.

In the late 1800s and early 1900s, large timber companies moved into the southern Appalachians, clear cutting the mountains and erecting sawmills and paper factories. Railroads were built, and roads were cut through the mountains.

To preserve the natural beauty of the mountains, people in Asheville and in Knoxville began promoting the idea of a park. There was debate as to whether the park should be in North Carolina or in Tennessee, but eventually a compromise was reached that it would straddle the border of the two states.

In 1904, **Horace Kephart,** a librarian from St. Louis, arrived in Hazel Creek, in what is now the Smokies, with plans to study the wilderness areas of the Southern Appalachian highlands. Kephart moved into a cabin at the old Adams mining camp just above Sugar Fork. Kephart's book *Our Southern Highlanders,* published in 1913, was the first major study of Southern Appalachian culture. He also wrote guides to camping in the park and a history of the Cherokee. Later Kephart, with his friend and nature photographer **George Masa,** campaigned for the establishment of the Great Smokies park. Although Kephart died in a car accident in 1931, before the park was dedicated (he is buried in Bryson City), he is now known as a father of the Smokies.

Earlier national parks established in the west, such as Yellowstone, were simply carved out of land already owned by the U.S. government, but the situation in the Southern Appalachians was different. Most of the land was in private hands, and money to purchase the land had to be raised privately. Fund raising began in 1925, with money from private individuals trickling in. A John D. Rockefeller family charity saved the day for the park, giving $5 million to be matched with state funds.

Beginning in 1929, land for the park was acquired from the timber companies and from more than 6,000 individual landowners.

In 1934, the Great Smoky Mountains National Park was officially established with some 300,000 acres. However, it took several years to complete the purchase of additional land and to resettle most of the landowners outside the park. **President Franklin D. Roosevelt** dedicated the park in a ceremony September 2, 1940, at Newfound Gap.

The construction of the **Blue Ridge Parkway** in 1940s and 1950s (its southern terminus is near the entrance of the Smokies at Cherokee) and of **Interstates 40, 26, 85, 65** and other parts of the national highway system in the 1960s and 1970s made the Smokies more accessible to millions of people all over the East and Midwest.

Entering the Park

There are two main entrances to the park, both on U.S. Highway 441. One is at **Oconaluftee** about 2 miles from Cherokee on the North Carolina side, about 50 miles or a little over one hour by car from Asheville, and the other at **Sugarlands** near Gatlinburg on the Tennessee side. Three main visitor information centers are in the park, at **Oconaluftee, Sugarlands** and **Cades Cove.** In addition, there is a small visitor station at **Clingmans Dome** and four information centers outside the park in Tennessee, in **Sevierville, Townsend** and two in **Gatlinburg.** On the North Carolina side there are a number of other places where you can enter the park, typically on unpaved roads, including at Balsam Mountain, Big Creek, Bryson City, Fontana and Waynesville.

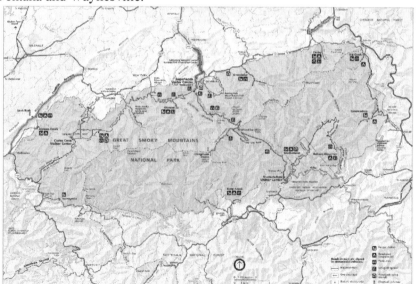

Map of Great Smoky Mountains National Park – courtesy of National Park Service

Weather

Elevations in the park range from 875 feet to 6,643 feet. This difference in elevation can affect local weather in significant ways. It can be 15 to 20 degrees F. cooler at Clingmans Dome or Mt. Le Conte than at park entrances. Driving from the Oconaluftee or Sugarlands entrance to Clingmans Dome is the equivalent, in terms of climate and flora, of driving from the Mid-Atlantic U.S. to northern Canada. July and August are the warmest months, while January and February are the coldest.

Precipitation averages 55 inches per year in the lowlands to 85 inches per year at Clingmans Dome. About one day in three in the Smokies sees some precipitation, either rain or snow. Precipitation is pretty well spread out over the year, with September and October generally being the driest months.

It's advisable to dress in layers, especially from fall through spring and if you are planning to hike or backpack. At higher elevations, a sunny day can quickly turn cold and windy, with ice or snow.

Early **spring** sees variable weather conditions, with mild temperatures in the lower elevation areas but snow possible at higher elevations. Later in the spring, in April and May, the Smokies warm up, with temps frequently in the 70s or 80s except at the highest elevations.

We hate to tell you, but **summer** tends to be humid and fairly hot in the Smokies, especially at the lower elevations, where temps can reach the high 80s or low 90s, with rain showers or thunderstorms common in the afternoons. The highest temperature ever recorded in the Smokies was 100 degrees, in 1983. However, evenings generally are much cooler, and at higher elevations it's always chillier. Mt. Le Conte, for example, has only once in recorded history (in July 2012) seen 80 degrees, and the average high temperature at Clingmans Dome in July is just 65. You'll experience more haze -- the blue "smoke" for which the park is named, although today much of that haze is due to pollution from electrical power plants than from natural conditions -- in the summer than at any other time.

Fall is glorious in the Smokies, typically with brisk, clear days and cool to chilly nights, depending on elevation. The first frosts in the park usually happen in September. October is the peak time for leaf peeping, and the month is usually dry, with invigorating temperatures. By November, you'll probably experience freezing temperatures at night even at the lower elevations.

In **winter,** snow is light and infrequent at lower elevations, but Newfound Gap with an elevation over 5,000 feet receives an average almost five feet of snow a year.

About half the days in the winter have high temperatures of 50 degrees or more, but at night temps are typically below freezing and can drop to as low as minus 15 to 20 degrees F. at the higher mountain peaks. The coldest temperature ever recorded in the Smokies was minus 23 degrees F. in 1985.

Call 865-436-1200, extension 630 for park weather information. The National Park Service has two webcams in the park, one at Purchase Knob at 5,000 feet and another at Look Rock at around 2,670 feet, so you can get a live peek at the weather before you go.

Best Times to Go

The biggest month for visitation in the park is July, followed by June, and then October, peak fall-color season. Weekends in October are especially crowded -- expect traffic delays on Newfound Gap Road and serious traffic backups on Cades Cove Loop Road. Beat the crowds by visiting on weekdays rather than weekends and also by arriving early in the day. Late spring is a great time to visit the park -- wildflowers are in bloom, and it's before the heat and crowds of summer. Winter in the park can be beautiful, especially when there's snow on the ground or rime frost on trees. Some park roads, including Clingmans Dome Road are closed in winter, and at times even the main Newfound Gap Road closes. Call 865-436-1200 for road closure and weather information. Dial extension 631 for updates on road closures and extension 630 for weather conditions.

Scenic Drives

The park has 384 miles of roads, most but not all paved. Even the unpaved roads in the park are suitable for two-wheel drive vehicles except after severe weather. Primary roads including **Newfound Gap Road, Little River Road** and the **Cades Cove Loop Road** are open year round, weather permitting. Some roads, including **Clingmans Dome Road, Balsam Mountain Road, Heintooga Ridge Road, Parson Creek Road** and **Roaring Fork Road** are routinely closed in winter, and any road may be closed temporarily due to ice and snow.

The main road through the park, and the only road that completely traverses the park from one side to the other, is the paved two-lane **U.S. Highway 441,** also known as **Newfound Gap Road.** It runs 33 miles from the eastern entrance at Cherokee to the western side near Gatlinburg.

The speed limit on this road is 45 mph, lower in places. It passes a number of the park's picnic sites and campgrounds, and it has numerous scenic overlooks. After more than 10 inches of rain in three days drenched the Smokies in January 2013, a 100-yard-long segment of Newfound Gap Road slumped off the mountainside, closing the road across the park for more four months, reopening in April 2013. The road is also closed at times during winter due to ice and snow.

Clingmans Dome Road is a 7-mile paved spur off Newfound Gap Road leading to the trailhead that takes you to the peak of Clingmans Dome. This road is closed to vehicles in winter, from December to March, although it is open to hikers and, when there's snow, to cross country skiers.

Cove Creek Road to Cataloochee Valley The Cataloochee Valley is one of the most remarkable parts of the Smokies. Here you can see some of the approximately 140 elk reintroduced into the park and a number of late 19th and early 20th century structures that were here before the valley became part of the park. By car you can visit five historic buildings, including two homes, two churches and a school. Several other buildings require a hike. To get to Cataloochee from Asheville, take I-40 West, exit at North Carolina Exit # 20 and go 0.2 miles on N.C. Highway 276. Turn right onto Cove Creek Road and follow the signs 11 miles into the Cataloochee Valley. Most of this road is unpaved, narrow and curvy. It has some blind curves and steep drop offs with no guardrails. Drivers may need to stop or back up their vehicles to allow oncoming motorists to pass. It is definitely not suitable for large RVs or other oversized vehicles. From Asheville, plan for it to take about 75 minutes to get to Cataloochee.

Little River Road is an 18-mile paved road that runs along the Little River from Sugarlands visitor center to the entrance to Cades Cove. In itself it is not particularly scenic, but it passes several popular camping and picnic spots and connects two of the most scenic drives in the park, Newfound Gap Road and Cades Cove Loop Road.

Cades Cove Loop Road is an 11-mile paved, one-lane road that passes the historic houses, churches and schools in the 6,800-acre Cades Cove Valley near Townsend, Tennessee. You almost always see deer along this route and often black bears and wild turkeys. From May to September the road is closed to vehicular traffic on Wednesday and Saturday mornings until 10 am, making it ideal for biking or walking. On weekends in the fall this road can be one long traffic jam. Stop near the entrance to the Loop and pick up a copy of the driving tour booklet ($1).

Heintooga Ridge/Balsam Mountain Road, accessible from the Blue Ridge Parkway at Milepost 458.2, is paved for the first 9 miles, then unpaved for the next 14 miles until it connects with Big Cove Road near Cherokee. This scenic road is closed in winter. The unpaved section is not suitable for big RVs.

Roaring Fork Motor Nature Trail, on the Tennessee side near Gatlinburg, is a 6-mile, paved, one-way scenic road that passes a number of historic buildings.

Foothills Parkway is a 71-mile parkway in Tennessee that runs just outside the park on the northern and western edges. Only two sections of the parkway, totaling around 23 miles, have been completed and opened to the public. The 17-mile western section is particularly scenic. U.S. 129, known as "Tail of the Dragon" for its 318 curves in 11 miles and popular with motorcycle and sports car enthusiasts, connects with the end of the Foothills Parkway at Chilhowee, Tennessee. The speed limit on the Dragon is 30 mph.

For more information on auto touring in the park, get a copy of *Smokies Road Guide,* available at park visitor centers and from the Great Smoky Mountains Association online. It costs $11.95.

Cataloochee Creek in fall – photo courtesy of NPS

Picnics

Visitors to the park have a choice of **11 developed picnic grounds,** ranging in size from 10 to 182 picnic tables.

Two of the picnic areas, Collins Creek and Chimneys, are easily accessible from the main road through the park, Newfound Gap Road.

Four of them – at Cades Cove, Metcalf Bottoms and Greenbrier in Tennessee and Deep Creek in North Carolina – are open year-round; the rest are closed from late fall to early spring. When open the hours are usually around daybreak to sundown.

Our favorite picnic grounds are **Heintooga** off the Blue Ridge Parkway, located at over a mile high and set in evergreen forest; **Deep Creek,** on a stream near Bryson City where you can go tubing; and **Chimneys,** a shady (and very popular) picnic area beside the Pigeon River off Newfound Gap Road on the Tennessee side.

However, you're not limited to picnicking only at designated picnic areas. You can spread out your food and enjoy a gourmet lunch most anywhere you find a pleasant site. Do keep in mind that bears are attracted to the smell of food, so don't leave your coolers and picnic baskets out, and clean up the picnic site completely after your meal. Feeding bears is illegal and eventually can cause the death of the bear, as well as the potential injury and legal prosecution of humans.

Except for a convenience store at Cades Cove campground, there's no place to buy picnic supplies in the park. However, there are supermarkets near the park entrances. In North Carolina, **Ingles** is the dominant supermarket chain, with stores in Asheville, Bryson City, Waynesville, Sylva and Robbinsville, among other places. **Bi-Lo,** another Southeastern chain, has a location in Waynesville. There are several independent grocery stores around Cherokee, and **Food Lion,** a regional supermarket, has a location in Whittier near Cherokee. In Asheville, besides many regular chain groceries you'll find **Greenlife** (owned by **Whole Foods**) and **Earth Fare,** two natural-foods supermarkets, and **Fresh Market,** part of a gourmet supermarket chain. The Asheville area also has many tailgate markets and the largest farmers' market in North Carolina.

There are no restaurants in the park, except for a snack bar at Cades Cove campground and the remote Le Conte Lodge. Le Conte Lodge on the Tennessee side offers lunch for day visitors. Overnight guests can get breakfast and dinner at the lodge. However, access to Le Conte is by foot only, and it's a 15-mile roundtrip hike.

Hiking

The Great Smoky Mountains National Park has some 900 miles of hiking trails.

The park about 150 different official trails, ranging from short, paved trails and nature walks accessible to just about everyone to hikes of 20 miles or longer, requiring a high level of fitness and multi-night stays.

Around 71 miles of the 2,179-mile **Appalachian Trail** are in the park, and North Carolina's **Mountains-to-Sea Trail** (only partially completed) begins at Clingmans Dome and travels about 1,000 miles to Jockey's Ridge on the Outer Banks.

HIKING SAFETY TIPS

Because of elevation gain and the fact that trails may be rough in places, don't expect to set any speed records. Figure that even if you're fit you'll cover only about a mile and a half per hour. Never hike alone. Pace yourself. Recognize your limitations. Use a hiking stick and wear shoes or boots with good ankle support. Take plenty of water, especially when hiking in summer. Water from streams in the Smokies may contain Giardia, a parasite that can cause intestinal infection – treat water by boiling at least two minutes or with a 1-micron filter. Take a paper map with you. GPS units can be helpful in the backcountry, but the Park Service warns that, especially in vehicles, navigation systems sometimes provide inaccurate information about the Smokies, sending you the wrong way on one-way roads or leading you to a dead end in a remote area.

Be aware of possible severe changes in weather that may occur suddenly. Depending on elevation, the Smokies can be hot and humid in summer and bitterly cold and snowy in winter (and in early spring and late fall), so dress in layers. Take a small flashlight and matches and, especially on longer hikes, a first-aid kit. Pack as lightly as possible. Be aware that you may encounter potentially dangerous wildlife including bears, elk and snakes. On overnight hikes, register in advance. Advise friends and family of your hiking plans and your expected return time. When leaving your vehicle at a trailhead, avoid leaving notes or other information that suggest you will be gone for a long time, and don't leave valuables in your vehicle. Remember, cell phones don't work in most parts of the Smokies – if you get in trouble you can NOT depend on a cell phone to call 911.

Dogs or other pets are NOT allowed on trails in the Smokies, except for the Oconaluftee River Trail at the Oconaluftee Visitor Center and the Gatlinburg Trail at Sugarlands. An exception is working service animals, which are allowed throughout the park. Pet dogs are allowed on trails in the Pisgah and Nantahala national forests.

Because there are so many hiking trails in the Smokies, and nearly every hiker has a favorite, we list just a representative sample of some of the best trails:

Alum Cave Trail is a 4.4-mile roundtrip hike (moderate) that begins at a parking lot on the Tennessee side of Newfound Gap Road about 9 miles from Sugarlands and ends at a large concave bluff. It's called a cave, but it's really not one. In the mid-1800s, Epsom Salts were mined here, as was saltpeter used to make gunpowder. You may see peregrine falcons enroute. Alum Cave is one of the routes to Le Conte Lodge.

Andrews Bald Trail is a moderate 3.5-mile roundtrip hike starting at the parking lot of Clingmans Dome. At the grassy meadow or bald, you'll enjoy spectacular views of the mountains. It's also a great area to see rhododendron and flame azalea in bloom in the late spring and early summer.

Deep Creek Loop is a moderate 4.6-mile roundtrip hike near Bryson City. You'll see waterfalls and, in spring and early summer, a large variety of wildflowers including trilliums, Jack-in-the-pulpit, crest dwarf iris and flame azalea.

Gregory Ridge Trail is a strenuous 11.3-mile hike from Cades Cove with an elevation gain of more than 3,000 feet. Gregory Bald is world-famous for its flame azaleas, usually in bloom here in great variety, color and profusion in mid-June. The 10-acre grassy bald is one of only two balds maintained by the Park Service. From the bald are great views of Cades Cove and Fontana Lake.

Oconaluftee River Trail is an easy 3-mile mostly level walk beginning at the Oconaluftee Visitors Center near Cherokee. It passes the wonderful Mountain Farm Museum and then meanders along the Oconaluftee River. A bonus is that dogs and bicycles are permitted on this trail. About 40 species of wildflowers have been identified along this trail – how many can you spot?

Porters Creek Trail is a fairly easy to moderate 4-mile roundtrip hike from Greenbrier on the Tennessee side. The trail passes historic old cabins and a waterfall.

Several excellent guides to hiking in the Smokies and nearby are available from park visitor centers or online from the Great Smoky Mountains Association store at www.shop.smokiesinformation.org. Among these are *Day Hikes of the Smokies* by Carson Brewer ($9.95), which covers 34 of the best day hikes, and *Hiking Trails of the Smokies* ($20.95), which covers all 150 official trails in the park. Also available are a series of booklets (most 50 cents to $2) on hiking in specific areas of the park. Be sure to buy or download (from www.nps.gov/grsm a copy of the park's trail map and get a copy of the booklet *Day Hikes of the Smokies* ($1) at visitor centers or from the GSMA online.

A commercial website with a lot of information on hiking in the part is www.hikinginthesmokys.com, with detailed information on 80 hiking trails in the park and an online store with books and maps.

Public Transportation

Unfortunately, there is no regular public transportation to the national park from major cities in the area. On the Tennessee side, the city of **Gatlinburg** *(865-436-4178 or 800-588-1817;* www.gatlinburg.com*)* offers a **bus trolley** from Gatlinburg to Sugarlands Visitor Center, Laurel Falls parking area and Elkmont June-October for a fee of $2 round-trip. At times there has been seasonal shuttle and tour service to Cades Cove from Gatlinburg – check locally to see if it is in operation when you are there.

Cherokee Transit *(828-554-6300 or 866-388-6071;* www.cherokeetransit.com*),* operated by the Eastern Band of the Cherokee Indians, offers bus service from Cherokee to Gatlinburg and Pigeon Forge, Tenn., during summer and fall.

Camping

The Great Smokies park is a paradise for campers. Whether you're a backcountry backpacker or prefer your camping in a deluxe RV, you'll be happy in the park.

Developed Campgrounds

The park has **10 frontcountry developed campgrounds** with a total of 946 tent and RV sites: **Balsam Mountain, Big Creek, Cataloochee, Deep Creek** and **Smokemont** on the North Carolina side, and **Abrams Creek, Cades Cove, Cosby, Elkmont** and **Look Rock** on the Tennessee side. In addition, there are five horse camps in the park. *(See section on horseback riding below.)*

Elkmont is the largest campground, with 220 sites, while Big Creek is the smallest, with just 12 sites. All campgrounds have tent sites, and all except Big Creek also have trailer and RV sites, though size limits vary. Tents must be pitched on the pad, if provided. Each RV or tent site is limited to a maximum of six occupants. Pets are allowed at developed campgrounds but must be leashed and are not permitted on trails. Alcohol in the campgrounds is okay if you're 21 or over.

Fees at campgrounds range from $14 to $23 per night per site.

All campgrounds have restrooms with cold running water and flush toilets. Each individual campsite has a fire grate and picnic table.

Cades Cove, Smokemont and Elkmont have firewood for sale, as do stores in towns outside the park. Due to the risk of importing tree diseases into the park, beginning March 1, 2015, only heat-treated firewood that is bundled and certified by the United States Department of Agriculture (USDA) or a state department of agriculture may be brought into the park. Certified heat-treated firewood is packaged and clearly marked with a state or federal seal. Campers may also collect dead and down wood found in the park for campfires. You can collect firewood in the park only if it is on the ground and dead.

All food and equipment used to prepare and store food must be kept sealed in a vehicle. Balsam Mountain, Big Creek, Cades Cove, Cataloochee, Cosby, Deep Creek, Elkmont and Smokemont campgrounds have bear-proof storage lockers.

There are no showers or electrical or water hookups in the park, although there are 5 amp electric hookups at a few sites in Cades Cove, Elkmont and Smokemont for those with medical needs. RV dump stations with potable water are available at Cades Cove, Cosby, Deep Creek, Look Rock and Smokemont campgrounds, and at the Sugarlands visitor center. Quiet hours are in effect from 10 pm to 6 am, and generator use is prohibited from 8 pm to 8 am.

Campsites at Cades Cove, Cataloochee, Cosby, Elkmont and Smokemont may be reserved online at www.recreation.gov or by phone at 877-444-6777. Advance reservations are *required* at Cataloochee. All remaining park campgrounds are first-come, first-served. Signs at park visitor centers note the campgrounds with available space. Stays are limited to 14 consecutive days at a specific campground. After that, you can move to another campground in the park.

Cades Cove and Smokemont campgrounds are open year-round. The others are open spring through fall; dates vary.

For detailed information on frontcountry campgrounds, including site maps, visit www.nps.gov/grsm/planyourvisit/frontcountry-camping.htm.

In addition to campgrounds in the park, there are many commercial campgrounds in communities around the park, including Asheville, Bryson City, Cherokee, Gatlinburg, Townsend and Waynesville. Nearly all of these campground have water and electric hook ups, many offer hot showers and some have resort amenities such as swimming pools and playgrounds.

Backcountry Camping

Hiking and camping in the backcountry is the best way to experience the true beauty of the park.

The park has about 100 backcountry campsites, each with from four to 20 tent sites. Also in the park are 15 shelters, each with a capacity of around a dozen campers. Tent camping isn't allowed at the shelters. All of these campsites and shelters are hike-in, and some require a hike of many miles. Some sites are available to those riding horses.

Camping is permitted ONLY at designated campsites and shelters. You can camp in the backcountry as long as you like, but maximum stay at any campsite is three nights, and one night at a specific shelter. Maximum group size is eight persons, except at a few sites where the maximum is 12. Open fires are prohibited except at designated areas, and you may use only wood that is dead and on the ground. Food and backpack storage cable systems are at all backcountry sites.

Human feces must be put in a six-inch-deep hole and covered with soil. Do not urinate or defecate within 100 feet of a campsite, water source or trail. All garbage and items such as used tampons must be packed out.

Advance reservations are required at more than two dozen backcountry campsites and at all 15 shelters. Currently, reservations may be made up to one month prior to the first day of your camping trip. To reserve sites, call 865-436-1231. Backcountry camping registration is available at all visitor centers and a few other areas in the park.

Permits are required for all backcountry camping. Until 2013, backcountry camping permits were free. Beginning in 2013, a fee of $4 per person per night (up to a ceiling of $20 for seven days) was introduced.

For more on backcountry camping, visit www.nps.gov/grsm/planyourvisit/backcountry-camping.htm.

Le Conte Lodge

(Mailing address: 250 Apple Valley Rd., Sevierville, TN 37862; 865-429-5704; www.lecontelodge.com, email reservations@lecontelodge.com; open late March to late November.) The only accommodations in the park (other than camping) are at Le Conte Lodge, a hike-in lodge at 6,360 feet on the Tennessee side. Le Conte, built in 1926, has seven rustic wood cabins, plus three dormitory cabins. Rooms have no running water or bathrooms. You do your business in shared privies with flush toilets, but there are no showers. Kerosene lamps provide the light. Hot water is available from a spigot near the dining room. Bring your own towel and washcloth. Bed sheets are provided.

The appeal here obviously is not luxury but the extraordinary setting and the views, although be advised that at this elevation clouds and fog sometimes obscure the scenery. It can be chilly here, even in summer, and some snow in spring and fall is to be expected. You sleep under wool blankets, and the cabins have propane heaters. The temperature at the lodge has only once reached 80 degrees F., one summer day in July 2012. Five hiking trails lead to the lodge. They range in length from 5.5 to 8 miles one-way. The shortest but steepest trail is Alum Cave, which a hiker in good condition can do in about four hours. Start early enough to reach the lodge by 6 pm, dinnertime.

Supplies for the lodge are brought up three times a week on the 6.5-mile Trillium Gap Trail by llama pack train. This trail, while longer than some, is considered the easiest hike, as it is less steep. Rates in the cabins are $272 per night double, including a hearty breakfast and dinner (lunch is included for those staying more than one night), plus staff tips and 9.75% Tennessee tax. Meals are served family-style, and wine is available (for those 21 and over) for $10 per person per night. Vegetarian meals are offered, with advance notice. A sack lunch, available even if you are not staying at the lodge, costs $10. Demand for accommodations here exceeds supply. Reservations for the following year open October 1, and by Christmas most of the rooms are booked. There is a wait list, and a lottery system applies for heavily requested dates.

Wildlife Spotting

The Great Smoky Mountains National Park arguably is the best place in the East to see the greatest number and variety of wild creatures. Here are some of the wild animals you can see and the best places to see them:

American Black Bear *(Ursus americanus)*: The black bear is the symbol of the Smokies. Many visitors feel slighted if they come to the park and don't see one. With some 1,500 to 2,000 bears in the park, depending on who is doing the estimating, your chances are pretty good. Bears in the park weigh 250 to 600 pounds when fully mature. They can stand and walk on their hindquarters but usually walk on all fours.

Fast runners and excellent tree climbers, if a bear wants to catch you, it can. However, serious incidents between humans and bears are rare. The only known fatal attack by a bear on a human in the park was in 2000 in the Elkmont area. Bears have a shaggy black coat and a long snout, with an excellent sense of smell. They are omnivorous with their diet including insects, nuts, berries, fish and small mammals.

Contrary to popular belief, in the Smokies bears do not fully hibernate in winter, although they become less active and may sleep for long periods. Black bears in the wild normally live 8 to 12 years, though some live 20 years or longer. Probably the best place to see bears from your car is in **Cades Cove,** although they also frequent campgrounds in search of food; often, due to campers not taking care to protect their food, bears become a nuisance at campgrounds and may have to be relocated. It is illegal – and stupid – to feed bears. Bears also are often seen on the **Roaring Fork Motor Trail.**

Bat: The park has 11 species of bats, including the endangered Indiana bat (*Myotis sodalist*). Seven of the park's bat species live in the park year-round, while the others migrate south. The bats you are most likely to see in the park are the big brown bat, eastern red bat and the eastern pipistrelle. Bats play a vital role in the park's ecosystem by eating flying insects by the millions. Note that the white-nose syndrome in bats is now present in the park and is spreading. This fungus disease can be deadly to bats but is not known to have any impact on humans. However, bats with white-nose syndrome may act erratically, such as swooping down toward you. Erratic actions were noticed particularly in the winter of 2012-2013, when bats that normally hibernate came out of their caves. Do not touch or handle bats, as they can carry rabies. To help stem the spread of white-nose syndrome, which has killed millions of bats in the U.S., the Smokies closed all caves to the public in 2009. The U.S. Forest Service in 2012 closed caves and abandoned mines to the public in national forests in 13 Southeastern states, including those in Pisgah and Nantahala national forests in Western North Carolina.

Bobcat *(Lynx rufus)*: The bobcat is believed to be the only native wild cat remaining in the Smokies, although mountain lions, or "panthers" as mountain people call them, occasionally are reported. Bobcats are about twice the size of a housecat, have grayish-brown coats, black-tufted ears and a short tail with a spot of black at the tip. They prey primarily on rabbits, along with rodents, birds and squirrels. Solitary and territorial, they occasionally can be spotted at dawn or at twilight. You are most likely to see a bobcat on a backcountry trail rather than along a main road. Bobcats pose no threat to humans.

Coyote *(Canis latrans)*: Coyotes have returned to the Southeast in large numbers and can be found in the park. Reddish-gray with a buff underside, coyotes resemble medium-sized dogs, but their yellow eyes, alert ears and bushy, black-tipped tails give are markers.

They run in packs or as loners, roam either day or night and eat nearly anything – freshly killed rabbits, squirrels and other meat, carrion, insects, fruits and vegetables. Coyotes have a varied vocal repertoire filled with barks and wails. If you're in the backcountry at night their calls, which seem to come from all sides at once, can be chilling. They are more often heard than seen. You may occasionally spot them in open fields at Cades Cove or Cataloochee or on backcountry trails. On rare occasions (but not in the Smokies) coyotes have been known to attack humans.

Elk *(Cervus canadensis)*: The last native elk in the Southern mountains was believed to have died more than 200 years ago. In 2001, in an experimental reintroduction program, the park imported more than 50 elk, and a number have since had calves. Today, there are some 150 elk in the park. At least a dozen elk calves are born in the park each year. Males reach 700 pounds and at the shoulders stand as tall as a large SUV. Mature males have antlers up to 5 feet wide, which they use when competing with other males during rutting season. Their bugling mating call is common in autumn. The best place to see elk is in the open fields of the Cataloochee valley, although you can see them elsewhere. In fact, the author has seen elk on the main road through Maggie Valley. It is illegal to get closer than 150 feet to elk. Mating males or females protecting calves have been known to charge humans.

Gray Fox *(Urocyon cinereoargenteus):* Foxes are primarily nocturnal but sometimes can be seen foraging along roadsides or in fields, especially in Cades Cove, during the day. This small fox has grayish-brown fur, sports a white belly and facial markings and has a black stripe on its back and tail. It can climb trees and feeds on small mammals, insects, birds, eggs, nuts and berries. The **red fox** *(Vulpes fulva)* also is present in the park.

Northern Copperhead *(Agkistrodon contortrix):* This pit viper is, with the timber rattlesnake, one of only two venomous snakes in the park. Copperheads have a pale tan to pinkish tan ground color overlaid with a series of tan or light brown bands. They rarely grow to more than 3 feet in length. Visitors often confuse the northern water snake or other harmless snakes for a copperhead. You're unlikely to actually see a true copperhead, although they are present throughout the park.

Salamander: The park is known as the "salamander capital of the world." There are at least 30 species of salamanders in the park. In fact, salamanders outnumber all other vertebrates (that is, backboned animals) in the Smokies. You'll find them in creeks, streams and wetlands all over the park. Mountain people refer to salamanders as "spring lizards," although salamanders are not true lizards.

Synchronous Firefly *(Photinus carolinus)*: The Great Smokies park is one of the few places in the world where you can see fireflies blinking in unison. For a few weeks, usually from late May to mid-June, these fireflies put on an amazing light show. Entire hillsides seem to blink in rhythm as if they were covered with Christmas tree lights. In this illuminated mating dance, the male fireflies blink 4 to 8 times in the air, then wait about 6 seconds for the females on the ground to return a double-blink response. Elkmont and Cades Cove are two good places to see them.

Timber Rattlesnake *(Crotalus homidus)*: This rattlesnake is variable in color, ranging from yellow and brown to nearly black, with W-shaped lateral markings across its back. The rattles at the end of the tail distinguish it, but individual snakes sometimes lose their rattles. In the park, these rattlesnakes typically reach about 3 feet in length. While not commonly seen, they are present in most parts of the park.

White-tailed Deer *(Odocoileus virginianus)*: There are at least 6,000 deer in the park. They live throughout the park but are most common in areas with open fields, especially Cataloochee and Cades Cove. Usually, does give birth to their fawns in June; it takes about two years for the young deer to fully mature. Bucks fight for mating rights in the late summer and mate in November, and November is the most likely month of the year for vehicle collisions with deer.

Wild European Boar *(Sus scrofa)*: The wild boars were brought from Europe to a private game preserve in Western North Carolina over 100 years ago. Some of the hogs escaped, interbred with domestic hogs, and eventually, in the 1940s, made their way to the Smokies. Mature males can weigh several hundred pounds. At their peak, in the 1970s, wild hogs in the park numbered several thousand. After years of the Park Service removing them from the park, today only a few hundred boars remain. The wild boars (both female sows and males are called boars) travel in packs, called sounders, of 10 to 20 or more. Though rarely seen anymore in the park, wild boars can be dangerous to humans, especially if they are protecting young piglets.

In addition to the above, five species of squirrels (gray, red, fox and two types of flying squirrels), two species of skunks, Northern river otters, beavers, muskrats, long-tailed weasels, possums, raccoons, groundhogs and 16 species of rats and mice.

BEAR SAFETY TIPS

Black bear attacks are humans are extremely rare, and only one death has ever been reported in the park from a bear attack. Still, bears are wild creatures and can be unpredictable. By the way, it is legal to have bear pepper spray in the park, but if you are smart you should never need to use it (and who knows if it really would work?!)

This is what the National Park Service says about co-existing with bears in the Smokies:

If you see a bear remain watchful. Do not approach it. If your presence causes the bear to change its behavior (stops feeding, changes its travel direction, watches you, etc.) you're too close. Being too close may promote aggressive behavior from the bear such as running toward you, making loud noises or swatting the ground. The bear is demanding more space. Don't run, but slowly back away, watching the bear. Try to increase the distance between you and the bear. The bear will probably do the same. If a bear persistently follows or approaches you, without vocalizing, or paw swatting, try changing your direction. If the bear continues to follow you, stand your ground. If the bear gets closer, talk loudly or shout at it. Act aggressively and try to intimidate the bear. Act together as a group if you have companions. Make yourselves look as large as possible (for example, move to higher ground). Throw non-food objects such as rocks at the bear. Use a deterrent such as a stout stick. Don't run and don't turn away from the bear. Don't leave food for the bear; this encourages further problems.

Most injuries from black bear attacks are minor and result from a bear attempting to get at people's food. If the bear's behavior indicates that it is after your food and you're physically attacked, separate yourself from the food and slowly back away. If the bear shows no interest in your food and you're physically attacked, fight back aggressively with any available object--the bear may consider you as prey! Help protect others, report all bear incidents to a park ranger immediately. Above all, keep your distance from bears!

Birding

Around **250 species of birds** have been identified in the park, but only about 60 are year-round residents. About 120 species breed and nest in the park.

Elevation determines what birds you are likely to see. At the highest elevations, in the spruce-fir forests, you'll find birds that live in the boreal forests of Canada, such as the Blackburnian and Canada warblers, northern saw-whet owl and common raven.

The higher-elevation hardwood forests have a mix of northern and southern birds, while the middle and lower elevations have mostly southern birds such as the Carolina chickadee, eastern screech owl, downy woodpecker and scarlet tanager. The few open fields in the park, such as in Cades Cove and Cataloochee, are home to wild turkeys, bobwhites, eastern bluebirds and barn swallows.

Among the most striking large birds in the park are these:

Common Raven *(Corvus corax)*: The raven resembles a crow but has a bigger bill and wider wingspan. It is found mostly in the higher elevations of the Smokies. You can also recognize the raven by its deep, baritone croak, rather than the caw of a crow.

Great Horned Owl *(Bubo virginianus)*: The largest owl in North America, the great horned owl can have a wing span of more than 4 feet. The owl's hearing is so acute, it generally locates its prey in the undergrowth by sound alone, hooting to panic mice and rabbits into betraying their position. This nocturnal predator can swivel its head 270 degrees, which gives it wider range of motion to detect prey without moving and giving away its position.

Ruffed Grouse *(Bonasa umbellus)*: Males make a drumming sound, like an engine starting. If you happen to walk too close they will suddenly explode out of the leaves and fly away.

Wild Turkey *(Meleagris gallopavo)*: Wild turkeys are common in the park, especially in Cades Cove and Cataloochee. They travel in flocks of up to 60 and roost at night in trees. Smaller than their domesticated counterparts, which are bred for their breast meat, wild turkey males may reach 16 or 18 pounds, while females are somewhat smaller.

Wildflowers

The Great Smokies has **more flowering plants than any other U.S. national park.** You can see wildflowers in bloom virtually year-round, from trillium and columbine in late winter and early spring to red cardinal flowers, orange butterfly weed and black-eyed Susans in summer to Joe-Pye weed, asters and mountain gentian in the fall. The best time to see wildflowers in the park is the spring, especially April and early May. From early to mid-June to mid-July, the hillsides and heath balds are on fire with the orange of flame azaleas, the white and pink of mountain laurel and the purple and white of rhododendron. Note: It is illegal to pick any wildflower, plant or tree in the park.

A nationally known five-day **Wildflower Pilgrimage** is held annually in late April. More than 140 different hikes, classes and events explore the park's unique fauna, wildflowers and natural ecology. Online registration usually begins in mid-February. Most programs are conducted on the trails in the park, while indoor classes and events are held in Mills Conference Center and at the Sugarlands Visitor Center in Gatlinburg.

Registration is $50 for one day and $75 for two to five days and covers everything except an optional welcome luncheon, which is $25. Students are $15 for the entire event, and children under 12 are free.

The 2015 Pilgrimage, the 64th, was April 21-25. For information, registration or to download a program, visit www.springwildflowerpilgrimage.org.

The Disappearing Trees of the Smokies

You'll see many dead or dying trees in the Smokies. Here are some of them, and why they are dying.

American Chestnut *(Castaneda dentata)*: Until the early 20th century, the American chestnut was the dominant tree in the Smokies and in much of the Eastern U.S. It represented up to one-third of *all* trees in the Smokies. Its mast provided plentiful food for animals, its insect-resistant wood was widely used for building and its tannic bark was used in tanning leather. Then, in the early 1900s, a fungus was accidentally brought in from Asia. It quickly spread throughout the entire range of the American chestnut. In Asia, this fungus and the local chestnuts had evolved to co-exist with each other, but in the U.S. the American chestnut had no defenses, and the fungus proved devastating.

By the late 1940s, virtually every chestnut tree in the Smokies and elsewhere in America had been killed. Some four billion trees died. The virulent pathogen still remains in American forests. Sprouts from wild American chestnut roots still spring up, but when they reach 10 or 20 feet tall, they are killed back by the blight. The American Chestnut Foundation (www.acf.org), based in Asheville, began a breeding process that in 2005 produced the first potentially blight-resistant trees. Now assisted by some 6,000 members and volunteers in 16 state chapters, the organization is undertaking the planting of restoration chestnuts in the Eastern United States.

Eastern Hemlock *(Tsuga canadensis)*: Also known as the Canadian hemlock, the stately eastern hemlock commonly stands 100 feet tall. It grows well in shade and likes moist areas near streams. It can live hundreds of years, with the oldest known specimen being over 500 years old.

Sadly, most hemlocks in the Smokies and elsewhere in the region are now infested with the hemlock wooly adelgid, which first arrived in the U.S. in 1924 from Asia. Individual trees can be treated against this adelgid, but it is impractical to do so in large wild stands. In recent years, tens of thousands of hemlocks have died. An effort is under way to save the largest and tallest remaining eastern hemlocks in the Great Smokies.

Fraser Fir *(Abies fraseri)*: Named after the 18th century Scottish botanist John Fraser, the Fraser fir is best known as a Christmas tree. In the Smokies, it lives only at the highest elevations, typically above 4,000 ft. It is usually mixed with red spruces. The Fraser firs in the Smokies and elsewhere in the mountains have been hit a double blow: First, acid rain killed many high-elevation trees. Second, a tiny alien from Asia, the balsam wooly adelgid, has killed up to 90% of the trees. The firs regenerate from seedlings, but in a few years the maturing trees also are struck by this destructive adelgid. At the higher elevations of the Smokies, you'll see thousands of dead firs.

Fishing

The Smokies have some of the best trout streams in the East. The National Park Service doesn't stock trout streams. However, through natural reproduction many park waters are at capacity, with **2,000 to 4,000 trout per mile.** Many of the more than 2,100 miles of streams in the park are loaded with rainbow, brown and brook trout. The "brookie" *(Salvelinus fontinalis)* or speckled trout or specks as locals call it, is the only native trout in the streams of the Smokies. It's not a true trout but a char. Rainbow trout and brown trout, originally brought here from other areas, are more common. Among the best trout streams are **Deep Creek, Big Creek, Palmer Creek, Noland Creek, Little Cataloochee** and **Hazel Creek** on the North Carolina side, and **Little River, Abrams Creek** and **Little Pigeon River** on the Tennessee side. Often, the best fishing is in higher-elevation streams, in areas that are more difficult to reach. Lower-elevation streams that are easily accessible have greater fishing pressure. Nearly all streams are open to fishing year-round.

On the North Carolina side, persons 16 and over and on the Tennessee side persons 13 and over must have a state fishing license, either from North Carolina or Tennessee. For trout and other fishing in the Great Smokies, your best bet is to buy a North Carolina comprehensive inland fishing license.

You can order a North Carolina inland fishing license online from the **North Carolina Wildlife Resources Commission** *(888-248-6834,* www.ncwildlife.org*)*, or you can buy one from fishing shops or from wildlife agents. A 10-day nonresident inland fishing license good in the Smokies and elsewhere in North Carolina is $10, and an annual fishing license is $20, or $35 if you want to include coastal fishing.

Licenses for North Carolina residents cost $5 for a 10-day inland fishing license and $20 for an annual license good in the Smokies and statewide including coastal fishing. If you're 65 or over and a North Carolina resident, you can get a real bargain – a lifetime comprehensive coastal and inland fishing license plus comprehensive hunting license good for the lifetime of the license holder for just a one-time fee of $30.

Tennessee fishing licenses are available from **Tennessee Wildlife Resources Agency** offices, most county clerk offices, sporting goods stores, hardware stores, boat docks and online *(www2.tn.wildlifelicense.com)*. A Tennessee nonresident fishing license including trout, good throughout the Smokies, is $16 for a one-day license, $33.50 for a three-day license and $50.50 for a 10-day license. For Tennessee residents, the one-day fishing license is $11 and $46 for an annual combined fishing (all types including trout) and hunting license. Separate licenses are available for fishing in Gatlinburg-area waters only.

Daily possession limits in the park are five brook, rainbow or brown trout, smallmouth bass, or a combination of these, regardless of whether they are fresh, stored in an ice chest or otherwise preserved. The combined total must not exceed five fish. Twenty rock bass may be kept in addition to the above limit. Size limits: brook, rainbow, and brown trout, 7-inch minimum; smallmouth bass, 7-inch minimum; rockbass, no minimum. Fishing is allowed in the park from a half hour before official sunrise to a half hour after official sunset.

Fishing is permitted only by the use of a hand-held rod. Only artificial flies or lures with a single hook may be used. Use or possession of any form of fish bait (minnow, worm, corn, cheese, bread, etc.) or liquid scent is prohibited. Disturbing and moving rocks to form channels and rock dams is illegal.

To fish in the Cherokee Reservation, those 12+ need a separate permit, available at shops on the reservation for $10 for one-day, $17 for a two-day, $27 for a three-day, $47 for a five-day, or an annual license for $250.

The season on Cherokee waters is year-round for catch-and-release, and May through late March for other types of fishing. Daily limit in Cherokee water is 10 trout. Some streams in the reservation are for reservation residents only. Note that the Cherokee reservation waters are outside the Smokies, so only the Cherokee permit is needed, not a state license.

Historic Sites

There are five historic districts in the Smokies: **Cataloochee, Mountain Farm Museum** at the Oconaluftee Visitor Center, **Cades Cove, Roaring Fork** and **Elkmont.**

The park contains about 100 historical buildings and 200 old cemeteries. Cades Cove is the most popular historic site in the park, with the auto traffic to prove it, but our favorite is the remote Cataloochee.

Caldwell House in Cataloochee is a 19th century farmhouse that has been maintained much as it was when the Cataloochee Valley became part of the Great Smokies park – photo courtesy of National Park Service

Cades Cove Historic District: Cades Cove on the Tennessee side of the park near Townsend is the most visited part of the park (other than the main road through the park). An 11-mile, one-way loop road circles Cades Cove. You'll pass a number of preserved old houses, barns, churches and a working gristmill.

Among these are the **John Oliver Cabin**, the oldest building left in the cove, constructed around 1822-1823 by the cove's first permanent European settlers; the **Primitive Baptist Church** (1887); the **Cades Cove Methodist Church**, constructed in 1902; **Cades Cove Missionary Baptist Church**, (1915-16); the **Elijah Oliver Place** (1866) and nearby **Meyers Barn;** the **John Cable Grist Mill** (1868); the **Becky Cable House** (1879), adjacent to the Cable Mill; the **Henry Whitehead Cabin**, (1895-96); the **Dan Lawson Place** (1840s); the **Tipton Place** (1880s).

The paneling on the house was a later addition. Along with the cabin, the homestead includes a carriage house, a smokehouse, a woodshed and a double-cantilever barn; and the **Carter Shields Log Cabin** (1880s). Although the loop is relatively short, allow at least two to three hours to tour Cades Cove, longer if you walk some of the area's trails. Traffic is heavy during the tourist season in summer and fall and on weekends year-round. A visitor center (open daily) and restrooms near the Cable Mill are located about half way around the loop road.

Cataloochee Historic District: In this beautiful valley you'll see old homesteads, a school, churches and barns that were here when the park opened in the early 1930s. These buildings have been preserved as they were in the early 20th century and thus most have a more "modern" look than the log cabins in some of the other historic districts. Among the structures in Cataloochee are the **Hannah Cabin** in Little Cataloochee, probably built in the 1850s; the **Cook Cabin** in Little Cataloochee, also built in the 1850s but dismantled in the 1970s after being vandalized and restored to its original site in 1999; the **Palmer House** in Big Cataloochee (1869) -- originally as a log cabin -- a framed addition and weatherboarding were added later, and the house now contains a small self-guided museum in what was once a room used as a post office; the **Palmer Chapel** in Big Cataloochee (1898); the **Caldwell House** in Big Cataloochee, built 1898-1903 by Hiram Caldwell, with a barn adjacent to the house that dates from 1923; the **Steve Woody House** in Big Cataloochee (1880) was originally built of logs, with paneling and extra rooms added later; and the **Little Cataloochee Baptist Church** (1889). Surrounded by 6000-foot peaks, the Cataloochee Valley was one of the largest settlements in what is now the Smokies. Some 1,200 people lived here before the coming of the park. In Cataloochee you also are likely to see elk, deer, wild turkeys and possibly black bears. There is a horse camp and popular developed campground here, along with many good areas to picnic.

Elkmont Historic District: Originally a small logging community, Elkmont, on the Tennessee side of the park, eventually became a summer cottage colony and hunting and fishing club, with its own clubhouse, the **Appalachian Club,** for wealthy families from Knoxville. There was a passenger and logging railroad from Gatlinburg to Elkmont.

A 26-room hotel called **Wonderland Club Hotel** was built here, in 1911. In poor repair and partly burned in a fire, it finally ceased operation in 1992, and in 2006 it was dismantled by the National Park Service. All that remains now are a rock staircase and part of a fireplace.

With the coming of the national park in the 1930s, the Elkmont community became part of the park, although long-term leases were granted to owners. A 60-acre section of Elkmont was put on the National Register of Historic Places in 1974. As the leases expired in the late 20th century, a debate within the National Park Service developed as to what would be done with the more than 70 old cottages and other buildings in the historic district – raze them and let the area return to its natural state or restore them as part of the history of the park. A compromise was reached whereby about 18 cottages and the Appalachian Club would be restored and preserved, while the remainder of the buildings would be torn down. The newly restored Appalachian Clubhouse, near Elkmont campground, reopened in 2011. The 3,000 square feet building is available April to mid-November for public rental for group meetings, weddings and family reunions. Rental fee is $400 per day. Renovation of some of the cottages is underway. The historic **Spence Cabin** on Little River already has been restored and can be rented as meeting space for $150 to $200 a day. Reservations can be made online at www.recreation.gov or by calling 877-444-6777.

Mountain Farm Museum Historic District: Located adjacent to the **Oconaluftee Visitor Center** at the entrance to the park near Cherokee, the Mountain Farm Museum is a mountain farmstead with nine historic buildings re-assembled and recreated from original buildings in the Smokies. It is the best example of a late 19th/early 20th century mountain farm in the region. Among the buildings are the **John Davis Cabin**, a chestnut log house that dates from around 1900, the **Messer apple house** with its rock base, two corncribs, springhouse, hog pen, sorghum mill and the **Enloe Barn,** a large barn with some 16,000 hand-split roof shingles that was originally built around 1880 just a few hundred yards from where it now stands. You can do a self-guided tour (tour booklet and map $1 at adjacent visitor center), and rangers are available to put on demonstrations and answer questions. The museum is at the start of the Oconaluftee Trail that follows the Oconaluftee River into Cherokee. Nearby is the 1886 **Mingus Mill,** a turbine-driven gristmill that was restored by the Civilian Conservation Corps in 1937 and still operates today.

Roaring Fork Historic District: This historic district, only a short distance from Gatlinburg on the Tennessee side of the park, has several well-preserved log cabins, gristmills and other historic buildings. The **Roaring Fork Motor Nature Trail** is a 6-mile paved one-way scenic road that passes a number of the historic buildings.

Among the notable old structures along the trail are **Noah "Bud" Ogle Place,** with a "saddlebag" cabin (two cabins joined in the middle by a fireplace, along with a barn and tub gristmill; the **Jim Bales Place,** with the original barn and corn crib dating from the 1860s; the **Emphraim Bales Place,** with a double or "dog trot" cabin from the early 1900s (a dog trot cabin is two cabins with a few feet of space between them but with the space covered by a roof, and with each of the cabins having a fireplace); the **Alfred Reagan Place,** with a tub gristmill and sawed-board cabin; and the **Alex Cole Cabin** that was moved here from the Sugarlands area.

Horseback Riding

The Great Smoky Mountains National Park is one of the best places in the East for horseback riding. Park concessionaires at Smokemont near Cherokee on the North Carolina side and at Cades Cove and near Gatlinburg on the Tennessee side offer guided rides. Rides (around $30 for a one-hour ride) are suitable for even inexperienced riders. There are weight limits, typically 225-250 pounds.

You can also bring your own horse. There are five horse camps in the Smokies, three on the North Carolina side and two in Tennessee. Fees are $20 to $25 per site. Advance reservations are required and can be made by calling 877-444-6777 or online at www.recreation.gov. About 550 miles of the park's hiking trails are open to horses.

River Tubing

Although officially frowned on by the National Park Service due to the possibility of accidents, tubing on some streams in the Smokies is popular. Just rent a tube and pop in the water and float down the stream. On the North Carolina side, the best tubing is at **Deep Creek** near Bryson City. You can rent a tube for around $5 from one of several commercial outfitters near the Bryson City entrance to the park.

Little River is the most popular tubing river on the west side of the Smokies. You can tube on the Little River within the park, but several outfitters outside the park in Townsend, Tennessee, rent tubes and life jackets and provide shuttle buses that drop you at an entry point from which you can float a mile or two downriver to the outfitter's store. Expect to pay from around $8 to $14 per person, which includes a full day's tube and life jacket rental plus unlimited use of the shuttle.

Smokies by the Numbers

9 million+   Visitors annually to Great Smokies Park

2 million	Visitors to Cades Cove annually
1.4 million	Visitors in busiest month of year (July)
522,000+	Acres of land in the park
500,000	Visitors who hike part of a park trail annually
300,000	Visitors in slowest month of year (January)
100,000	Estimated umber of species of life forms in park
77,000	Annual number of backcountry campers
17,000	Number of species so far identified in park
6,643	Elevation of highest peak in park, Clingmans Dome
6,000	White-tailed deer in the park
4,000	Trout per mile in some park streams
2,115	Miles of rivers, streams and creeks in the park
1,700	Kinds of flowering plants in park
1,500+	Black bears in park
946	Individual campsites in developed campgrounds
900+	Miles of hiking trails in park
874	Lowest elevation in park, at Lake Chilhowee
816	Square miles of land in park
784	Picnic tables in park
384	Miles of road in park
250+	Species of birds in park
160+	Elk in park
150	Hiking trails in park
115+	Backcountry camping areas and shelters in park
100+	Historic buildings preserved in park
95	Percent of park that is forested
71	Miles of Appalachian Trail in park
69	Average inches of snow annually at Newfound Gap
66	Species of mammals found in park
55	Average precipitation annually in Cades Cove
45	Maximum speed in mph in park
30	Salamander species in park
23	Maximum cost in dollars per night to RV camp
16	Mountain peaks in park higher than 6,000 feet
14	Elk born in park in 2012
11	Developed picnic grounds in park
10	Developed campgrounds in park
3	Main visitor centers in park
2	Bears per square mile; types of poisonous snakes
1	Lodges in park; fatal bear attacks in park history
0	Entrance fee to park

Movies Filmed in the Great Smokies

Among the movies filmed in the Smokies are parts of the popular TV series *Davy Crockett* (1954-55), starring Fess Parker; *A Walk in the Spring Rain* (1970), starring Ingrid Bergman and Anthony Quinn; *The Dollmaker* (1983), starring Jane Fonda and Levon Helm; *A Smoky Mountain Christmas* (1986), starring Dolly Parton; *Blaze* (1989), starring Paul Newman; and *Christy* (1994), starring Kellie Martin. A number of other movies, including *The Last of the Mohicans* (1992), starring Daniel Day Lewis, and *The Fugitive,* (1993) starring Harrison Ford and Tommy Lee Jones were filmed near the Smokies with the parts of the park in the distance.

BILTMORE HOUSE AND ESTATE

Biltmore House is the most-visited attraction of its type in North Carolina – photo courtesy of Biltmore

• Biltmore House is the largest private home in America, with 250 rooms – including 34 bedrooms and 43 bathrooms -- in more than 4 acres of floor space, nearly the size of four football fields • The house has its own bowling alley, gymnasium, indoor swimming pool and three kitchens and incorporated all the latest technologies of the time, including elevators, telephones and refrigerators – the estate generated its own electrical power, hot water and central heat • It took 1,000 workers over five years to build • While the exact cost of construction was never calculated, it ran into the many millions, and to duplicate the house, its furnishings and art work, land, estate grounds and gardens today would easily cost $2 billion dollars or more • Designed by one of the leading architects of the 19th century, Richard Morris Hunt and with the grounds created by the leading landscape architect in America, William Law Olmsted, in 2007 Biltmore House ranked eighth in the list of America's Favorite Architecture by the American Institute of Architecture, just behind the Lincoln Memorial and the U.S. Capitol

• Originally the estate comprised some 125,000 acres or 191 square miles of land ranging from Asheville to the peak of Mt. Pisgah and beyond -- today, the estate consists of "only" 8,000 acres, the bulk of the estate's original acreage sold to the federal government to form the basis of Pisgah National Forest • To manage the vast estate, Biltmore established the first forestry school in the United States • The house and grounds get more than a million visitors a year • The winery, which produces almost 2 million bottles of wine a year, gets more visitors than any other winery in America including those in the Napa Valley • The grounds have 75 acres of formal gardens and a winding driveway 3 miles long • On the estate are a 212-room, award-winning hotel and several restaurants • More than a dozen major movies have been filmed on the estate • The property is still owned by the family of the Gilded Age multi-millionaire, George Washington Vanderbilt, who built it – Vanderbilt also was an intellectual who spoke eight foreign languages fluently and had a library of 23,000 books • William A. V. Cecil, grandson of the founder, was instrumental in turning Biltmore House from a financial failure into an economic and tourism success.

How Biltmore Came About

George Washington Vanderbilt (1862-1914), who would build Biltmore House and establish the Biltmore Estate, was the youngest child of Maria Kissam and William Henry Vanderbilt (1821-1885). William Henry Vanderbilt was believed to be the **wealthiest man in the world at the time,** with a wealth in today's buying power of about $50 billion, having inherited most of his moolah from his father, **Cornelius "Commodore" Vanderbilt** (1784-1877). The Vanderbilt fortune came initially from shipping and railroads. The Commodore, like some other 19th century multi-millionaires (multi-*billionaires* in today's dollars), later in life became a philanthropist. On his money **Vanderbilt University** was established. Son William Henry continued running railroads and shipping lines and added new investments.

Now, back to George. A fave of his dad William Henry, young George grew up shy and introverted. He was interested in books and ideas, not in business. He was never involved in the running of any of the family railroad and shipping businesses. Eventually he would become fluent in eight foreign languages and amass a library of 23,000 books at Biltmore House.

Following his grandfather's death in 1877 and his father's death in 1885, George inherited a total of around $13 million, plus a mansion on New York's Fifth Avenue and other real estate.

Although $13 million doesn't sound like all that much today, it is the equivalent of around $1.8 billion in today's dollar in terms of actual purchasing power, although you can calculate it in different ways.

George, with his mother, first visited Asheville in early spring of 1888. By that time he had built a yacht and owned a house or two, spending time in Bar Harbor, Maine, New York City and Saratoga, N.Y. Asheville was then a small town of around 12,000, but it was becoming known as a fashionable mountain resort town, and, because of its climate and elevation as a healthy place good for the treatment of tuberculosis, malaria, asthma and other ailments. In summer its population swelled to as many as 40,000, with visitors staying at one of eight hotels and about 30 guesthouses. George and his mom stayed at then nearly new and tony 125-room **Battery Park Hotel,** which had all the modcons of the time including electric lights and elevators. The original Battery Park Hotel, on a hill overlooking the city and with views from the porches of the mountains around, later burned. It was razed and replaced, on a leveled site, by a newer edition constructed by E. W. Grove. Now it is apartments for seniors, just north of the Grove Arcade.

It is not entirely clear why George took such a liking to Asheville, but he appeared to enjoy the climate and the mountain views. Later, he would tell Frederick Law Olmsted: "I came to Asheville with my mother. We found the air mild and invigorating and I thought well of the climate. I enjoyed the distant scenery. I took long rambles and found pleasure in doing so."

Unlike the better-established fashionable resorts of the time, such as Bar Harbor, Newport, R.I., and Saratoga, the Asheville area still had plenty of undeveloped and cheap land. In 1888 George Vanderbilt began acquiring land, through a straw party, Charles McNamee, a New York attorney related to him by marriage. Soon he had accumulated about 2,000 acres, at prices of from $5 to $20 an acre, mostly purchased from local subsistence farmers.

In late 1888, George Vanderbilt asked **Frederick Law Olmsted** (1822-1903), by then a highly successful landscape artist responsible for New York's Central Park (constructed from 1857 to 1873) and many other projects, to come to Asheville and assess the potential of the land for a house, gardens and forest. Olmsted had worked for George on the plans for the grounds of a home he owned in Bar Harbor and for other members of the Vanderbilt family.

Olmsted's first reaction was not entirely positive. He saw the land as "worn out" and "sterile" with "miserable woods and eroded hillsides." However, Olmsted was not completely negative, and he advised Vanderbilt to create a small park for the house, farm the bottomlands nearby and turn the rest of the land into a tract of managed forest and gameland.

Vanderbilt considered Olmsted's advice and took it. He instructed his attorney to continue buying large tracts of land in the mountain areas nearby. By 1895, **the estate comprised some 125,000 acres,** including large areas around Mt. Pisgah, about 16 miles from Biltmore House as the crows fly.

Building of the House

Biltmore historians believe that originally George Vanderbilt intended to build a relatively modest house in Asheville, perhaps of less than 10,000 square feet. Several architects were involved in the early plans, but fairly quickly Vanderbilt decided on using **Richard Morris Hunt** (1827-1895), one of the greatest architects of the time and the founder of the American Institute of Architecture. Hunt had worked on several Vanderbilt family projects including mansions in New York City and Newport.

Hunt did not visit the Biltmore site until March, 1889, after Olmsted's plans for the estate were well advanced. In May and June of 1889, Vanderbilt and Hunt traveled together to England and France, visiting some of the great baronial estates of those countries, including the newly built Rothschild estate in Buckinghamshire, England, called Waddesdon Manor, a French Renaissance structure constructed between 1877 and 1899. They also visited Knole, Sevenoaks, Haddon Hall and Hatfield in England. In France, Hunt and Vanderbilt visited estates near Paris and in northern France, including the Château de Chantilly, a 16th century mansion that had been destroyed in the French Revolution and just recently been rebuilt by the Duke of Chantilly.

After the trip, Hunt's assistants began refining Hunt's plans for a large mansion in the **French Renaissance style.** Sketches were presented to Vanderbilt in beginning in the summer of 1899. Hunt modeled Biltmore on the ornamented style of the French Renaissance and adapted elements, such as the stair tower and the steeply pitched roof, from several 16th-century châteaux in the Loire Valley including Blois, Chenonceau and Chambord.

Vanderbilt named Biltmore by combining two words – "Bildt," the region in Holland where the Vanderbilt family originated, and "more," an Old English word meaning rolling countryside.

A scale model of the grand four-story house, with its towers, gables and sharp roofs, was delivered to Asheville in October 1889. Construction began soon after, in early 1890, although the first bricks and limestones weren't laid until 1891.

During the more than five years of construction, Vanderbilt came to Asheville several times a year, usually for a week or two at a time. He often was accompanied by Hunt and Olmsted. They traveled in Vanderbilt's private railroad car, complete with a chef.

Richard Sharp Smith, an Englishman who had relocated to the U.S. in 1882, was hired as supervising architect, which meant that he was on site much of the time supervising the actual construction. When Smith wasn't available due to illness or vacation, another associate of Hunt, Warrington Lawrence, acted as supervising architect. Attorney Charles McNamee was named estate manager.

It goes without saying that construction of the huge house was a massive undertaking. More than 11 million bricks, made at a brick factory on the estate, were used in the house. Six-inch facings of Indiana limestone covered the bricks.

By 1893, the state employed 580 construction workers, plus another 200 workers on contract. The workforce varied seasonally and as the various stages of construction progressed. At one point, there were 200 masons and stonecutters on site.

About the same time, the landscape department employed 215. By 1893 the estate had planted almost 3 million trees and plants. Biltmore Estate, Olmsted's last major private commission, is often cited as the crowning achievement of his career, summing up his important ideas on landscape design and forest management.

Unskilled laborers were mostly hired locally and included many African-Americans. Typical laborers earned $1 a day. Skilled masons and cabinetmakers generally were recruited from Northern cities. Stonecutters and masons earned about $3.50 a day, while cabinetmakers received up to $2.75 a day.

Two schools, segregated by race, were started and subsidized by Biltmore for the children of workers

The mechanical systems of the building were complex. The entire house was wired for electricity, with power coming from a generator driven by a gasoline engine. A switchboard channeled power to two Otis elevators, the first installed in the Southeast, to refrigerators, electrical outlets and telephones. Hot water was available in the kitchens and 43 bathrooms, generated by two coal-fired boilers in the basement.

Central heat was generated by three steamship boilers, fired by either wood or coal. Even before the house was constructed, six miles of telephone wires were installed and eventually all the main parts of the estate were connected by telephone.

Hunt commissioned **Rafael Guastavino** (1842-1908) to construct the arched, fireproof tile ceilings. Guastavino, originally from Catalonia in Spain, later designed the St. Lawrence Cathedral in Asheville. The Austrian sculptor **Karl Bitter** (1867-1915) was hired to do the major ornaments on the house. Furnishings and furniture for the house were sent by the train carload from New York and Europe.

The chateau was the centerpiece of the estate, but many other things – barns, cottages, the plant conservatory, not to mention the roads, gardens and forest plantings and 24 homes in Biltmore Village – also had to be completed.

Completion of Biltmore House had long been set for Christmas 1895. In October of that year, George Vanderbilt moved in, but the house was still unfinished, as were other important parts of the estate, such as the gatehouse. Vanderbilt, then age 33, lived in the north wing, while work continued on the main rooms on the first floor.

Work on the estate continued long after 1895. A large dairy barn begun in 1898 wasn't completed until 1902. The forestry school, the first in the U.S., opened in 1898 under the leadership of the German-born **Dr. Carl Schenck.**

The arboretum, with a nine-mile drive and a science museum, a key part of Olmsted's landscape plan, was never built. **Chauncey Beadle** succeeded Olmsted as head of the landscape department, which continued to do major work on the estate for more than a decade after the house was completed. **Buck Springs Lodge at Mt. Pisgah,** an expansive Adirondack-style complex of buildings made of native chestnut logs, begun by Richard Morris Hunt and completed by his son Richard Howland Hunt, opened in 1902.

For an extraordinary history of the design and construction of Biltmore, see *Biltmore Estate, The Most Distinguished Private Place* by John M. Bryans. The large-scale photos are remarkable. *See the Resources section.*

Biltmore Through the Years

George Vanderbilt met **Edith Stuyvesant Dresser** (1873-1958), a descendant of Peter Stuyvesant, the first colonial governor of New York, while on a trip to London. He married her in Paris in 1898. **Their only child, Cornelia Vanderbilt,** was born in 1900. The couple lived in Biltmore House about six months of each year.

However, **in the early 1900s financial problems began to plague George Vanderbilt and Biltmore.** A number of planned projects were never undertaken due to lack of money.

In one of the periodic panics of the time, George lost considerable money in the failure of a local bank. A recession in 1907 further eroded his capital. By some estimates, creating Biltmore consumed at least one-half of Vanderbilt's fortune.

The Great Hall is one of the most stunning of the 250 rooms at Biltmore House – photo courtesy of Biltmore

Vanderbilt began cutting back on maintenance and staffing at Biltmore. He closed some of the farm operation and leased forestland for hunting. Though he sold part of his art collection and put much of the Biltmore Estate lands up for sale, his fortunes didn't improve (and the land didn't sell.) Some rooms in the house, such as the first floor music room, were left unfinished.

In 1908, George and Edith closed the house, dismissed the servants and moved to Europe, where they could live more cheaply. In 1909, Vanderbilt stopped underwriting the forestry school Dr. Schenck had started and had run for him since 1898. Vanderbilt was late with his property tax payments on the house, causing Asheville schoolteachers to be unpaid for a time. The Vanderbilts were, however, able to buy a mansion in Washington, D.C.

In 1912 Vanderbilt opened discussions with the federal government about selling most of the estate's forestlands for a planned national forest, but negotiations failed.

The Vanderbilts spent the Christmas holidays of 1913 at Biltmore House. After returning to their home in Washington, George fell ill, and his doctor diagnosed appendicitis.

George Vanderbilt died March 6, 1914, as a result of complications of the appendectomy. He was 51.

Wasting no time, **Edith reopened negotiations with the government on the sale of Biltmore lands.** The sale of 86,700 acres at $5 an acre was agreed upon in May 1914. She later sold some 1,500 acres for the Biltmore Forest subdivision and a few hundred acres of other estate land.

With this money and the remaining part of George's estate, Edith Vanderbilt was able to live well. She spent considerable time at Biltmore, dividing her time between Asheville and Washington, and became immersed in North Carolina affairs, advocating for adult literary and better roads. Edith promoted **Biltmore Estate Industries,** involved in wool spinning and woodworking, as a way to provide work for local people.

George and Edith's daughter, **Cornelia,** following in her mother's footsteps, also became involved in local community work. In 1924, **Cornelia married John Francis Amherst Cecil,** a member of English royalty educated at Eton and Oxford and third in line to a lordship. The couple made their home at Biltmore House. **They soon had two sons, George Henry Vanderbilt Cecil and William Amherst Vanderbilt Cecil.**

A year later, in 1925, Edith herself remarried, to **U.S. Senator Peter Gerry** of Rhode Island.

For a few years, in the boom days of the 1920s, Cornelia and John Cecil lived the good life at Biltmore, much like George and Edith Vanderbilt had in the late 1890s. **Then came the crash of 1929.** Real estate went bust, and even spiffy Biltmore Forest homes sat unsold or foreclosed.

In 1930, for the first time, Biltmore House was opened to the public. The opening was spun as an effort by the Cecils to help boost tourism to Asheville, but in fact it was a way for them to generate much-needed cash to operate the house, which cost $150,000 a year to maintain, with a property tax bill of $50,000 a year, huge sums during the Depression. Admission initially cost $1.50, and in the first year Biltmore attracted almost 39,000 visitors, generating $64,000 in much-needed cash for the family. Later admission was raised to $2.

In 1932, the Biltmore Company was organized, with Junius Adams, an Asheville attorney who had won the trust of Edith Vanderbilt, as president of the corporation that owned the house and estate.

Cornelia owned one-half the shares, and sons George and William owned the other half. For the next 30 years, Biltmore Estate was run not directly by the Cecil family or Edith Vanderbilt Gerry but by Junius Adams. Day-to-day management of the estate was delegated to Chauncey Beadle, the former assistant to Frederick Law Olmsted and head of the Biltmore landscape department.

As the Depression worsened, Asheville's fortunes declined. Most of the local banks failed. Bonds issued by the city went into default, and it was decades before they were paid off. Biltmore also suffered. Admissions dwindled to an average of just 30 a day.

Cornelia and John Cecil eventually divorced, but John stayed on at the house until his death in 1954.

Junius Adams believed that the future of the estate was not in tourism but in the dairy business, producing milk, ice cream and other dairy products. The Biltmore system included 14 tenant dairy farmers, each with his own "farm" on the estate. Each tenant farmer was responsible for a certain quota of milk production. A 15th farm was run by hired hands. Biltmore had a herd of more than 1,000 registered Jersey cows and 25,000 square feet of dairy barns. A fleet of Biltmore Dairy Farm trucks delivered milk to homes and stores in Asheville, Charlotte and cities in North Carolina. The black and yellow Biltmore Dairy logo was well known in the region.

The system, though perhaps feudal, worked. By 1936, after several years of losses, Biltmore Dairy Farm showed a profit and continued to do so for about the next 30 years. Junius Adams was key in saving Biltmore from financial ruin. Tourist admissions to Biltmore varied year to year, increasing in the late 1930s before declining sharply during World War II due to gasoline restrictions. The house was closed to the public for a time during the war, and the house was used to store paintings from National Gallery in Washington.

Though revenues increased in the 1950s, due in part to the appearance of Biltmore House in the 1956 movie, *The Swan,* starring Grace Kelly, the house continued to lose money.

William Cecil, who had grown up mostly in Europe, attended Harvard ("I was glad to make Cs as long as they let me stay at Harvard," he once told this writer) and worked for Chase Manhattan Bank, **returned to Asheville in 1959. He and his wife, Mimi, lived at The Firth, his mother's old home in Biltmore Forest. His job was to try his hand at running the tourist side of the estate.** Junius Adams continued as president of Biltmore Company until his death in 1962. William's brother, George Cecil, then took over management of the highly profitable dairy operations.

At first, William Cecil knew little about running a business, and even less about running a tourist attraction and historic home. However, **William's goal from the beginning was to combine historic preservation with a successful tourist attraction,** according to *Lady on the Hill, How Biltmore Estate Became an American Icon,* by Howard E. Covington Jr.

While this is an "official" history of the estate in the 20th century, it is very well researched and written by a Pulitzer Prize-winning journalist. *See the Resources section.*

William Cecil said he didn't preserve Biltmore to make money. Instead, he wanted to make money to preserve Biltmore.

William **invested heavily in advertising and promotion.** He even attended meetings of the local Ad Club to learn more about public relations and advertising. Cecil's ad budget was as much as 25% of each year's total operating expenses. He cultivated relationships with the local and national press, attracting national television network coverage and more films on location at Biltmore.

Biltmore House itself was showing its age and badly needed maintenance and upgrading, and William Cecil invested money in improvements. He also opened up additional sections of the house and grounds to the public.

By the mid-1960s, admissions had increased to 94,0000 from about 35,000 in the late 1950s. **Biltmore House was listed on National Register of Historic Places in 1964. By 1969, the tourist side of the business made its first profit under William Cecil,** albeit only of $16. Admissions continued to increase, and despite the impact of the 1973 gasoline crisis Biltmore hosted 283,000 guests.

New ideas were tried, and some of them, such as **Christmas at Biltmore,** with the house lavishly decorated for the holidays, worked. In 1975, only about 900 visitors came to Biltmore in December. By 1979, December attendance had jumped to 12,000. Today, the six-week-long Christmas season is the busiest time of year for Biltmore.

In mid-1979, George and William Cecil came to an agreement over the division of their property. William got the house, gardens and 8,000 acres of the estate. George got the dairy operations and about 4,000 acres.

Revenues from estate admissions at that time were only a fraction of those of the dairy operations – roughly $3 million compared to $41 million for the dairy.

Today, George Cecil's company, Biltmore Farms, is no longer in the diary business but is involved in developing upscale housing developments including Biltmore Park, Biltmore Lake and The Ramble, along with the Biltmore Town Square shopping complex in South Asheville and a number of hotels.

By the early 1980s, visitor admissions to the House had risen to around 420,000 and annual revenues were about $3½ million. William Cecil was constantly on the lookout for ways to create additional revenues. He started an ad agency to do the estate's advertising and created an historic conservation company that failed. He had tried to sell flowers and bedding plants. He leased land to farmers for growing tomatoes and other crops.

In 1985 came the biggest event yet: the opening of the Biltmore winery. Cecil had been investigating the idea of Biltmore vineyards and a winery for 15 years. About 30 acres of French-American hybrid grapes were planted in 1971. Biltmore produced its first wines, 5,000 bottles, in 1979. It turned out the wines were terrible. Cecil kept on, however. With Biltmore's first winemaster, **Philippe Jourdain,** he expanded his vineyard to 150 acres on the west side of the estate using **European vinifera grapes grafted onto hybrid roots** grown on the estate. He built a new 30,000 square-foot winery adjoining the old Biltmore dairy barn, with an initial capacity of 32,000 cases.

The winemaking did not always go smoothly. A 1985 cold front dropped local temperatures to 23 below zero, and 70% of Biltmore's vines were killed.

William Cecil made more improvements to the house and opened restaurants and a gift shop. In 1987, he **bought the former Akzona headquarters building on Pack Square Downtown,** designed by the I.M. Pei company. According to local reports, he got a huge bargain, paying only a small fraction of the building's $15 million cost.

By the early 1990s, the estate had revenues of more than $28 million and was profitable. Admissions increased to more than 700,000 a year. By the turn of the 21st century, the Biltmore winery had sold more than 1 million bottles of wine.

Grapes grown on the estate today in about 94 acres of vineyards include cabernet sauvignon, cabernet franc and merlot for red varietals, and Riesling, chardonnay and viognier for white varietals. Other grapes are purchased from vineyards in North Carolina, California and Washington State. **Today, the estate's wine business is owned by Cecil's children, Bill and Dini. Production has reached about 140,000 cases of more than 45 kinds of wine, including 15 varietals.**

A new welcome center for the estate opened in 1994. More restaurants were added, including Deer Park and The Stable.

In 1995, on the centennial of Biltmore, William A. V. Cecil announced he was transferring management of the company to his son, Bill. Among son Bill's innovations on the estate was the construction of a new 210-room, $32 million hotel, the Inn at Biltmore.

It is probably not an overstatement to say that **William A. V. Cecil is the most important figure in Biltmore history other than George Washington Vanderbilt. In just three decades, he turned a money-losing small business into a successful, high-achieving national brand.**

Today, revenues of The Biltmore Company -- the house, estate activities, inn, restaurants, winery, wine sales, retail stores and brand licensing -- likely **exceed $140 million**. (As a private company, Biltmore does not release detailed financial results.) Estate attendance is over a million a year, and the company employs about 1,900 people. Biltmore was the most-visited museum or historic attraction in North Carolina for eight straight years, from 2004 to 2011, but in 2012 the **North Carolina Museum of Natural Sciences** and its newly opened **Nature Research Center** in Raleigh, with 1.2 million visits, edged out Biltmore, with 1.1 million visits, according to a study by Carolina Publishing Associates. The other most-visited museum and historic sites (the list excludes national parks and other natural attractions) are **Discovery Place** in Charlotte, the **North Carolina Zoo** in Asheboro and **Fort Macon State Park** in Atlantic Beach.

Biltmore Today

Biltmore Estate today is a complex of facilities with a variety of activities. Here's an overview of what you can see and do on the estate. Everything is included in the admission price except where noted.

Biltmore House: The centerpiece of the estate remains the 250-room French Renaissance-style Gilded Age chateau, with self-guided tours offered daily. Open for the tour are most of three floors plus the basement. Allow about 1½ to 2 hours to see the house. Specialty guided tours and a recorded audio guide also are offered at additional cost.

Biltmore Winery: Guided tours of the 90,000 square-foot winery are included in estate admission, followed by a wine tasting (available for those 21 and over, some wines free, premium wines for a fee). On exhibit is the 1913 Stevens-Duryea Model "C-6" automobile owned by George and Edith Vanderbilt. The Winery is in the Antler Hill Village area.

Antler Hill Village: Antler Village opened in 2009, with a group of restaurants, shops, barn and displays. There is a small exhibition on the Biltmore history and legacy. At the village are three restaurants (Cedric's Tavern, Smokehouse and Bistro), an ice cream shop and a wine bar. An area of the village presents farm life exhibits from the early 1900s, a kitchen garden and farm animals. Among the stores in the village are a wine shop, outdoor shop, interior decor and crafts shop and a gift shop.

Visits to Antler Hill are included in regular estate admission. In addition, elsewhere on the grounds of the estate are five other shops, five other places for meals and light snacks plus the Deerpark Restaurant. A new hotel is being built in this area of the estate, with completion planned for late 2015.

Formal Gardens: Frederick Law Olmsted designed the 75-acre formal gardens at Biltmore. A **rose garden** has about 250 rose varieties. There also is a **shrub garden, azalea garden, butterfly garden, scented plant wall, spring garden** and several garden loops and trails. Apples, pears, apricot and other trees and shrubs are espaliered along the original stone walls of the Walled Garden. The **glassed-in conservatory** houses thousands of tropical plants and has areas devoted to orchids and to succulents. A **Festival of Flowers** is held annually in the spring, with more than 100,000 tulips and other spring bulb plants in bloom. The gardens and conservatory are included with regular admission to the estate.

Estate Grounds: You can drive paved roads and walk on unpaved trails around the estate, at no extra charge. Olmsted planted hundreds of thousands of plants and trees. Many of the trees are just now coming to full maturity, and some are over-mature. Among the trees are virtually all native varieties, plus many exotic trees such as a 100-foot tall redwood. Birding is permitted on the grounds. Look for bluebirds (the estate has about 100 bluebird nesting boxes), Canada geese in the lagoon, great blue herons along the French Broad River and migrating hawks in the fall.

Inn at Biltmore Estate: *(1 Antler Hill Rd., Biltmore Estate, Asheville, 866-336-1245 or 828-225-1600; www.biltmore.com)* This luxury hotel with 210 rooms and suites opened in 2001. In-season rates start at around $325, but discounts are available off-season. The hotel has an upscale restaurant (typical entree at dinner is about $28-$35). A seven-course degustation menu is $135.

Village Hotel *(Antler Hill, Biltmore Estate, www.biltmore.com)* A new, 209-room, four-story, 130,000 sq. ft. hotel is under construction in the Antler Hill section of the estate. It is set to open in late 2015 and is accepting advance reservations in spring 2015. Final rates have not been set, but they are expected to be somewhat lower than at the Inn at Biltmore.

Activities: You can take part (most at extra cost) in a large variety of other activities on the estate, including horseback riding and bicycling estate trails, carriage rides, fly fishing classes, Land Rover driving school, guided Segway tours, river float trips and others. Music concerts by national entertainers are held in the summer and fall.

Visiting Biltmore

Biltmore Estate main entrance: 1 Lodge St., Asheville, 800-411-3812 or 828-225-1333, www.biltmore.com

Biltmore House and the Biltmore Estate, to coin a phrase, will blow your mind. Asheville would still be Asheville without Biltmore, and the mountains certainly would be just as beautiful and appealing without Biltmore, but Biltmore adds another layer of "amazingness" that is difficult to overestimate.

Yes, admission to Biltmore is expensive, and while there are many opportunities at the estate to spend extra money, the basic admission ticket allows you to see the house, gardens, winery, Antler Hill village and much of the 8,000-acre estate grounds. You can also enjoy a free wine tasting.

The admission price structure is also a little complicated, with prices varying depending on the time of year and whether or not you buy your ticket in advance. **Currently, prices for adults range from around $35 to $74,** though more typically with advance purchase and other discounts admission is rarely over $50. Tickets for youth 10-16 are free to $39.50. Children 9 and under are always free. **Lowest rates** are 7-day advance purchase for visits in January, February and March. **Admission rates during the Christmas season,** with an extra fee for candlelight Christmas tours, are the highest of the year, and this is the most crowded time of the year. Behind-the-scenes and other guided tours range mostly from $17 to $20, plus admission. The recorded audio tour is $10 (free January-February). A premium tour with guide is $150 plus admission. Parking on the estate is free. Free shuttles are available from the parking lots to the main house.

How much time should you plan for seeing the estate? Of course it varies depending on your interests and ability to get around (there's a good deal of walking required), but figure on these times:

Self-guided tour of the house: 1½ to 2 hours
Self-guided tour of formal gardens and conservatory: 1 to 2 hours
Winery tour and wine tasting: 1½ hours to 2 hours
Antler Village: 1 hour+
Driving and sightseeing on estate grounds: 1-2 hours +

These times are minimums and will be increased significantly if you spend time shopping, dining, exploring the grounds or taking part in extra-cost activities and tours.

Tips on Seeing Biltmore

• Buy your tickets online at www.biltmore.com or by phone at 800-411-3812 **at least seven days in advance and you'll save $10 to $15 per adult ticket.**

• **Print your ticket at home** in advance, which will save you time on getting the ticket at day of arrival.

• To avoid big crowds, skip visits on summer and fall weekends, the Christmas period and Easter weekend. **Christmas weekends are especially busy.** Consider **attending on a weekday, especially Tuesday or Wednesday.**

• Consider **attending from January to mid-March,** when crowds are smallest and admission prices are cheapest, plus for most of the period you get a free recorded audio guide.

• For eating at the estate, **Cedric's** has good pub food (about $20 per person for lunch, $40 for dinner); the **Bistro** (about $20-$25 per person for lunch, $50 for dinner) has a farm-to-plate philosophy; **Stable Cafe** (about $15-$20 for lunch) has burgers, sandwiches and BBQ; **Deerpark** (around $30 per person) has a nice buffet; in winter there's only a weekend brunch. You can also pack a picnic lunch and dine al fresco on the grounds at no charge. The restaurant at the **Inn at Biltmore** is top-notch, but pricey -- with drinks and tip expect to pay around $75-$85 per person, and you can easily spend more. The new Village Hotel, set to open in late 2015, will offer new food and beverage options.

• **On most weekends and other busy days, you will need to make a reservation in advance for a specific time for the self-guided house tour** – at Christmas the wait to get into the house may be several hours, although you can use the time to tour other parts of the estate.

• **Plan on a minimum of a full day on the estate to see the highlights** and two days to see everything in more depth (you can purchase admission for the second day for only $10, as long as you do so before leaving the grounds).

• **Bargain alert!** If you plan to visit on several occasions during the year, or if you live in the area and would like to visit the grounds frequently, get the **Twelve-Month Pass**, which allows unlimited daytime admissions to the estate (doesn't include nighttime visits during the Christmas season), plus discounts on restaurants, shopping and tickets for guests. It also provides very significant discounts for stays at the Inn at Biltmore Estate during the off-season. Regular price for the pass is $129 to $149, but significant discounts – to around $89 -- are available at times. You can usually upgrade your regular admission to a Twelve-Month Pass for an extra fee.

• If you're a **senior 65+** you'll save $10-$15 on same-day admission on Tuesdays and Wednesdays.

• Due to the historic architecture of the house, **only the first and second floors are accessible by wheelchair.** All shops and restaurants on the estate are handicap-accessible. Parking assistance is available for guests with state-issued handicap parking permits. Guests with hearing difficulties can visit the front desk of Biltmore House (near the main house entrance) to request a neckloop telecoil coupler or a printed transcript of the audio guide. Guests with vision difficulties can receive the use of a free audio guide at the front desk.

• **Free shuttles are available from parking lots** to Biltmore House. However, a car is needed to get around on most of the estate.

• **Wear comfortable shoes,** as the tours involve a good deal of walking and standing.

• If you decide a one-day visit isn't enough, you can **come back the next day for only $10** (you must pay in advance at one of the guest services location before leaving the grounds).

Biltmore by the Numbers

$2 billion	Estimated cost to duplicate Biltmore today
$140 million	Estimated annual revenues of The Biltmore Company, 2012
11 million	Bricks used in building Biltmore House
1.8 million	Bottles of wine produced annually by Biltmore
1.2 million	Visitors to Biltmore in 2013
600,000	Visitors to Biltmore winery annually
125,000	Acres of land of original Biltmore Estate
8,000	Acres of land of Biltmore Estate today
1,900	Employees of The Biltmore Company
1,000	Jersey milk cows on Biltmore Farms in 1950s

500	Number of Angus cattle on estate today; also, number of sheep on estate
419	Rooms and suites at the Inn on Biltmore Estate and planned Village Hotel
250	Rooms in Biltmore House
94	Acres of vineyards at Biltmore
68	Number of Christmas trees in Biltmore House during the holidays
65	Fireplaces in Biltmore House
45	Varieties of wines produced by Biltmore
43	Bathrooms in Biltmore House
34	Bedrooms in Biltmore House
20	Percent of grapes grown on Biltmore for its wines
12+	Restaurants, snack shops and eating/drinking spots on the grounds
6	Years required to build Biltmore House
3	Length in miles of the Biltmore House driveway
0	Number of family members who currently live in Biltmore House

Movies Filmed on Location at Biltmore

Here are some of the movies filmed at least in part at Biltmore House and/or Biltmore Estate:

The Swan (1956) starring Grace Kelly

Being There (1979) starring Peter Sellers and Shirley MacLaine

The Private Eyes (1980) starring Don Knots and Tim Conway

Mr. Destiny (1990) starring James Belushi

The Last of the Mohicans (1992) starring Daniel Day-Lewis

Forrest Gump (1994) starring Tom Hanks

Richie Rich (1994) starring Macaulay Culkin

My Fellow Americans (1996) starring James Garner and Jack Lemmon

Patch Adams (1998) starring Robin Williams

Hannibal (2001) starring Anthony Hopkins

The Clearing (2004) starring Robert Redford and Helen Mirren

ASHEVILLE & WNC OUTSIDE ... NATURALLY

"I felt my lungs inflate with the onrush of scenery—air, mountains, trees, people. I thought, 'This is what it is to be happy.' "
-- Sylvia Plath, *The Bell Jar*

Max Patch Bald in Madison County – photo by Rose Lambert-Sluder

• Enjoy nearly unlimited opportunities for hiking, backpacking, camping, fishing, hunting, boating, river rafting, canoeing, kayaking, splashing in swimming holes at waterfalls and in lakes and streams, rock climbing, birding, wildlife and wildflower spotting, road and mountain biking, gem mining, golfing, snow skiing, snow boarding and snow tubing, skateboarding, horseback riding, hot air ballooning, ziplining and many other activities. • In addition to the Blue Ridge Parkway and Great Smoky Mountains National Park (both among the nation's most visited National Park Service units), the Asheville area also offers more than a million acres of national forests plus state forests, state parks, city parks and lakes

• Highlights include Pisgah National Forest, Nantahala National Forest, DuPont State Forest, Mt. Mitchell State Park, Joyce Kilmer Memorial Forest, North Carolina Arboretum and Cradle of Forestry

For scenic beauty and variety in outdoor activities, few if any other area in the Southeastern United States matches Asheville and Western North Carolina. Near Asheville are two of the most-visited units in America's national park system (the Blue Ridge Parkway and Great Smoky Mountains National Park), two huge national forests (Pisgah and Nantahala), numerous state parks (including Mt. Mitchell, Grandfather Mountain, Gorges and Chimney Rock), two state forests (DuPont and Holmes), scores of mountain peaks over a mile high, several large lakes for boating and other watersports (including Fontana, Lure, Santeetlah, Hiwassee, Chatuge and James), thousands of miles of hiking trails and trout fishing streams, hundreds of waterfalls and many other wonderful places for outdoor adventures of all kinds.

The region abounds in opportunities for hiking, backpacking, camping, fishing, hunting, boating, river rafting, canoeing and kayaking, rock climbing, birding, wildlife and wildflower spotting, bicycling and mountain biking, golfing, snow skiing and snow boarding, horseback riding, hot air ballooning and many other activities.

Even the most active outdoor enthusiast will find many activities to test his or her physical abilities in many sports. On the other hand, if you have mobility challenges or are just a couch potato, you can still enjoy many of the Asheville area's scenic wonders, either from your car or via short, easy walks.

The two main units of the U.S. national park system, the **Great Smoky Mountains National** Park and the **Blue Ridge Parkway,** are covered extensively in their own chapters. This chapter covers the many outdoor recreational opportunities in the Asheville area, including the places and outdoor activities for which the region is well known.

National Forests

What's the difference between a national park and a national forest?

National parks emphasize strict preservation of pristine areas, while national forests permit a wider number of public uses. For example, national parks usually forbid hunting, while national forests usually allow it. Pets can be taken on national forest trails, but not on most trails in national parks. National forests may provide trails for motorcycles or ATVs; national parks do not.

National park rangers work for the National Park Service (NPS) under the Department of Interior; national forest rangers are with the US Forest Service (USFS) under the Department of Agriculture.

Under the national forest "multiple use" concept, national forests are managed to provide a variety of services and commodities, including lumber, livestock grazing, mineral products and recreation with and without vehicles.

There are four national forests in North Carolina, two in the mountains (Pisgah and Nantahala), one near the coast (Croatan) and one in the Piedmont (Uwharrie), together totaling around 1.25 million acres. All four national forests in the state are administered from an office in Asheville *(160 Zillicoa St. Suite A, Asheville, 828-257-4200; www.fs.usda.gov/nfsnc).*

Pisgah National Forest *Pisgah National Forest is divided into three administrative districts: Appalachian Ranger District, U.S. Hwy. 19E Bypass, Burnsville, 828-682-6146; Grandfather Ranger District, 109 East Lawing Dr. at Exit 90 of I-40, Nebo, 828-652-2144; and Pisgah Ranger District, 1001 Pisgah Hwy./U.S. Hwy. 276, Pisgah Forest near Brevard, 828-877-3265; www.fs.usda.gov/nfsnc.*

The basis of the Pisgah National Forest was the 85,000 acres purchased in 1914 from Edith Vanderbilt and the Biltmore Estate, one of the first purchases under a 1911 law, the Weeks Act, that eventually established national forests all over the East. National forests already had existed in the West.

Today, the Pisgah National Forest consists of about 513,000 acres north, northeast, northwest and southwest of Asheville, divided into two main sections. The larger section north of Asheville is J-shaped, running from the eastern edge of the Great Smoky Mountains National Park along the Tennessee line past Hot Springs to Valle Crucis and Blowing Rock and then back to near Marion and Old Fort. The section southwest of Asheville runs from the Enka-Candler area southwest past Brevard to the Nantahala National Forest and south near the South Carolina line. Pisgah lands are not all in one piece, and there are privately owned areas within some national forest sections, and as you drive around the area you may go in and out and then back in national forest land.

Pisgah National Forest offers a vast number of outdoor recreation and adventure experiences, including hiking, camping, birding, swimming, fishing, hunting, mountain biking and waterfall visiting. Most of these activities are free.

Within the forest are some of the highest mountain peaks in the East, along with three wilderness areas – Shining Rock, Linville Gorge and Middle Prong. Also on Pisgah lands are a number of educational, historic and recreational sites, including the North Carolina Arboretum, Cradle of Forestry, Sliding Rock and the Pisgah Center for Wildlife Education *(see listings below)*.

Cradle of Forestry in America *(11250 Pisgah Hwy. /Hwy. 276, Pisgah Forest, near Brevard, 828-877-3130, www.cradleofforestry.com, daily 9-5, mid-Apr.-early Nov., $5 adults, children under 16 free, free for everyone on Tues., free at all times for National Park Senior Pass holders)* is a 6,500-acre site within the Pisgah National Forest devoted to the history of America's first school of forestry. The school was established by George Vanderbilt who, upon the recommendation of his landscape architect Frederick Law Olmsted, hired Gifford Pinchot as forest manager of the then 125,000-acre Biltmore Estate. Pinchot later would become the first head of the USDA Forest Service and governor of Pennsylvania. Later, in 1895, Vanderbilt hired German forester Dr. Carl A. Schenk to succeed Pinchot. Together, Pinchot and Schenk created the modern concept of forestry management and conservation.

In the visitor center of the Cradle of Forestry are 15 hands-on exhibits on forestry, including a simulated ride in a firefighting helicopter. A 1-mile trail winds through the original forestry campus, where you can explore a general store, one-room schoolhouse, blacksmith shop, cabins and a vegetable garden. Another trail, 1.3 miles long, has a sawmill and 1915 steam locomotive used in logging. Adjoining the Cradle of Forestry main grounds are the **Pink Beds.** The name comes from the rhododendron, mountain laurel and azalea that bloom in the spring and summer. The Pink Beds area has 21 picnic tables and flush toilets. The picnic area is open all year, but the restrooms are closed in winter.

North Carolina Arboretum *(100 Frederick Law Olmsted Way off Brevard Rd./Hwy. 191 and the Blue Ridge Parkway at Milepost 393, 828-665-2492, www.ncarboretum.org; 8 am–9 pm Apr.-Oct., 8-7 Nov.-Mar., gates close an hour before closing time, free admission but $12 per car parking fee, parking free first Tue. of the month, parking always free for members)* is a 434-acre nature park with 65 acres of cultivated gardens and 10 miles of hiking and biking trails. It is affiliated with the University of North Carolina system and is located in the Bent Creek Experimental Forest on Pisgah National Forest land.

Highlights include a quilt garden (flowering plants arranged in a quilt pattern), local heritage garden, holly garden, native azalea garden, permanent and rotating exhibits in the Baker Exhibit and Education Center buildings, one of the best bonsai exhibits in the U.S., and a wonderful trail system. A ¾-mile mulched trail connects the Baker building and the Education Center, with trailheads easily reached from either building.

Interpretive signs along the trail explain plant, animal, ecologic and environmental topics. There is a café and gift shop in the Education Center and an art and crafts gallery in the Baker Exhibit Center. The Arboretum conducts many classes and holds a number of plant and flower shows annually, including ones on bamboo, orchids, roses, dahlias and mums. You can easily spend an entire day visiting the Arboretum. Picnics on the grounds and dogs on leash are permitted.

Mt. Pisgah *(Blue Ridge Parkway Mileposts 407-409, free),* about 16 miles away from Asheville's Downtown as the crow flies, is probably the most-recognizable mountain peak in Western North Carolina, because a huge television transmission tower for WLOS-TV perches on top of it, at 5,721 feet. Despite this unnatural attribute, the Mt. Pisgah area is popular and truly scenic. Near the peak are the Pisgah Inn (one of three lodges directly on the parkway), a large campground, picnic area, convenience store, paved parking areas and several hiking trails including a 3-mile roundtrip trail to the summit. Mt. Pisgah was once a part of the vast Biltmore Estate. The mountain was named after the mountain in the Bible near the Dead Sea from which Moses was said to have first spied the Promised Land. There also are peaks named Mt. Pisgah in Oregon, Massachusetts, Pennsylvania and Vermont, as well as in Australia and Antarctica.

Pisgah Center for Wildlife Education and Bobby Setzer Trout Hatchery *(1401 Fish Hatchery Rd., Pisgah Forest, off U.S. Hwy. 276 near Brevard, 828-877-4423; www.ncwildlife.org; open Mon.-Sat. 8-4:45 year-round, free)* has a small museum on wildlife in the Pisgah National Forest and a short hiking trail. Here also is a trout hatchery, the largest in the state. Rainbow, brown and native brook trout are raised in more than 50 concrete tanks or raceways. The hatchery stocks about a half a million trout each year in more than 80 mountain trout streams. Trout fishing is popular in the Davidson River that runs past the center and hatchery.

Sliding Rock *(U.S. Hwy. 276 about 7.6 miles from the intersection with U.S. Hwy. 280 in Brevard or about 8 miles south on Hwy. 276 from Blue Ridge Parkway Milepost 412; open Memorial Day to Labor Day, with lifeguards on duty 10 to 5:30, but the natural water slide is open at other times of day and during other warm days in the late spring and early fall, at your own risk; admission $2 adults)* is a 60-feet long slippery, slick rock fed by 11,000 gallons of water a minute ending in a 7- to 8-feet deep pool. It's like a water slide at an amusement park, but in a beautiful natural setting. Both kids and adults enjoy slipping and sliding down the rock.

Bring shorts or old jeans, tee shirt and shoes suitable for getting wet – there's a changing area at the site. Children under 7 must slide with an adult. Pets are allowed at Sliding Rock but are not permitted to slide. Remember, the mountain water is COLD even on a warm summer day, and since the pool at the bottom has water deeper than your head you need to know how to swim. No alcohol permitted. No picnicking allowed at Sliding Rock, but a picnic area at the Pink Beds is about 4 miles south on U.S. Highway 276, toward Brevard. Note that on holidays and hot summer weekends Sliding Rock can be very crowded, with long waits to get into the parking area and for the rock slide.

Nantahala National Forest *(Nantahala National Forest is divided into three administrative districts: Nantahala Ranger District, 90 Sloan Rd., Franklin, 828-524-6441; Cheoah Ranger District, 1070 Massey Branch Rd., Robbinsville, 828-479-6431; and Tusquitee Ranger District, 123 Woodland Dr., Murphy, 828-837-5152; www.fs.usda.gov/nfsnc)* in the far southwestern tip of North Carolina, at more than 531,000 acres is the largest of the state's four national forests. Nantahala is a Cherokee word meaning "land of the noon-day sun," an appropriate moniker given that on the floor of the deep Nantahala Gorge, a river gorge with 5,000-feet mountains on either side, there is full sun only in the middle of the day.

Like the Pisgah National Forest, Nantahala offers a huge variety of outdoor activities, including hiking on some 600 miles of trails, camping, picnicking, fishing, horseback riding, hunting and water activities. Nantahala is particularly known for its excellent mountain biking in the **Tsali Recreation Area** near Fontana Lake and for whitewater rafting on the **Nantahala River** near Bryson City. Most activities are free.

Among the highlights of the Nantahala National Forest are the **Joyce Kilmer Memorial Forest,** where old-growth poplars, never subject to a saw or axe in 400 years, stand in towering magnificence; the Nantahala River with its superb white-water rafting in the East; and the great mountain biking trails of Tsali.

Joyce Kilmer Memorial Forest *(about 15 miles from Robbinsville in western Graham County.)* Directions: From Robbinsville, take NC Hwy. 129 North for 1.5 miles to the junction with NC Hwy. 143 West (Massey Branch Rd). Turn left and go west on Hwy. 143 for 5 miles to a stop sign. Turn right onto Kilmer Rd. Go 7.3 miles to the junction with the Cherohala Skyway. Bear right and continue on another 2.5 miles to the entrance of the Joyce Kilmer Memorial Forest. Turn left into the entrance and go 0.5 miles to the parking area.

Trees
By Joyce Kilmer (1886-1918)
I think that I shall never see
A poem lovely as a tree.

A tree whose hungry mouth is prest
Against the sweet earth's flowing breast;

A tree that looks at God all day,
And lifts her leafy arms to pray;

A tree that may in summer wear
A nest of robins in her hair;

Upon whose bosom snow has lain;
Who intimately lives with rain.

Poems are made by fools like me,
But only God can make a tree.

Joyce Kilmer Memorial Forest is a 3,500-acre tract of national forest land that is mostly old-growth forest. In 1934, the forest was dedicated as a memorial to the poet Joyce Kilmer, who was killed in World War I. Kilmer, of course, is famous for his short, simple but moving poem, "Trees."

The largest trees here are poplars, some 400 years old or even older, with circumferences of 20 feet or more. It is truly amazing to see what the virgin forests of Eastern American must have looked like several hundred years ago. Here also are huge red oaks and Eastern hemlocks, but many of the hemlocks have been killed by the hemlock wooly adelgid, as the giant chestnuts here before them were killed by an alien fungus.

There are two trail loops: the 1.25-mile lower loop passes the Joyce Kilmer Memorial plaque. To view a grove of the biggest trees, take the upper 0.75-mile Poplar Cove loop. Both are moderately easy, but there are some steeper sections. Allow one to two hours for the complete figure-eight trail, depending on your level of fitness and pace. The parking area of the Kilmer Memorial is also a good place to see synchronous firefly displays, usually in June.

Joyce Kilmer Memorial Forest is a part of the 18,000-acre **Joyce Kilmer-Shining Rock Wilderness,** a primitive area left as much as possible in its natural state. Admission is free. Vehicles and bicycles are not permitted here, and trails are not blazed. It's easy to get lost in this wilderness, and in fact more hikers are reported lost here than in any other area of the state. The Benton MacKaye Trail on the western and northern edges of the wilderness is fairly easy to follow, but other trails are not. Primitive camping is permitted. Remember that in the fall deer, bear and wild boar hunting is permitted here (and in most other national forest areas in the mountains) so wear blaze orange colors.

North Carolina State Forests

DuPont State Forest *(Cedar Mountain; 828-877-6527; www.ncforestservice.gov or the unofficial site of Friends of DuPont State Forest, www.dupontforest.com, free).* Directions from Asheville: Take I-26 East toward the Asheville Regional Airport. Exit at the airport (Exit 40) and go south on NC Hwy. 280 for about 16 miles. Turn left (east) onto U.S. Hwy. 64 and go 4 miles. In Penrose, turn right onto Crab Creek Rd. for 4 miles to DuPont Rd. Turn right on DuPont Road and continue for 3.1 miles. There are several access points to the state forest.

DuPont State Forest is a 10,400-acre recreational forest in Transylvania and Henderson counties about 40 minutes by car from Asheville. It is a favorite area for hikers and mountain bikers who want fairly easy trails and access to beautiful waterfalls. The state purchased the majority of the land in the recreational area in 1996-97 by the state from E.I. du Pont de Nemours company, and obtained another large tract in 2000 by its right of eminent domain from a real estate developer who was trying to build a big residential project near waterfalls in the middle of the forest. DuPont, which is managed by the North Carolina Forest Service, has elevations from 2,240 to 3,620 feet.

It has about 90 miles of dirt roads and trails open to hikers, mountain bikers and horseback riders. Little River runs through the forest, with four major waterfalls along its course, including Triple Falls and High Falls, and there are other waterfalls on Grassy Creek. DuPont also contains five lakes and ponds, the largest being 99-acre Lake Julia.

The state forest offers fishing for largemouth bass, sunfish and bluegill in the lakes and trout fishing in cold-water streams (a state license is required). Hunting on a limited basis for deer, wild turkey and small game is also allowed in season, but a special permit is required and some areas are off limits to hunting.

A map of DuPont State Forest is sold at area outdoor and outfitters stores, and a version can be downloaded at www.dupontforest.com. For information on mountain biking trails and routes, see the Pisgah Area Southeast Offroad Bicycling Association (SORBA) website at www.pisgahareasorba.org. Bikers and equestrians should stay on trails marked with brown wooden signs. Motor vehicles are prohibited in the state forest except at the entrance parking areas and on signed public roadways.

Holmes Educational State Forest *(1299 Crab Creek Rd. off Kanuga Rd., Hendersonville, 828-692-0100; www.ncforestservice.gov, open Tue. -Sun. mid-Mar.-late Nov., free)* is mainly designed to teach school children about managed forests, although adults interested in learning more also are welcome. Holmes has a ½-mile trail with "talking trees" and tree identification signs, plus other trails totaling around 5 miles on the 235-acre site just west of Hendersonville. Also on site are picnic tables and grills. Holmes is one of six educational forests in the state.

North Carolina State Parks

North Carolina has 39 state parks and recreation areas, including several important ones in the Asheville area. Entrance to the parks in Western North Carolina is free, except for Chimney Rock State Park, currently managed by a private company, and the commercial part of Grandfather Mountain, which also is under private management. Several of the parks have developed camping, for which generally a fee is charged, and primitive hike-in camping, which is free. Alcohol is prohibited at all state parks. Pets are allowed if on leash. Firearms and other weapons are prohibited except that those with a proper permit may possess a concealed handgun where allowed.

Mt. Mitchell State Park *(2388 State Highway 128, Burnsville, 828-675-4611; www.ncparks.gov; open Mar., Apr., Sep. and Oct. 8-8, May-Aug. 8 am-9 pm, Nov.-Feb. 8-6 weather permitting; restaurant and concession stand open May-Oct., hours vary; free).* Directions: From Asheville, take the Blue Ridge Parkway north to Milepost 355 and turn left onto NC 128, which leads 3.5 miles to the park. The parkway and NC 128 may close at times in winter. There is a parking area, from which you can hike 850 feet to an observation deck (erected in 2009) at the summit, with panoramic views.

Established in 1916, this was North Carolina's first state park. Within the boundaries of the 1,946-acre park in the Black Mountains is the highest peak in Eastern America, Mt. Mitchell, at 6,684 feet. An exhibit hall (open May-October 10-6) has a replica log cabin, wildlife dioramas and 3D topographical maps.

The park has a shady picnic area with 40 picnic tables with stone fire grills, open year-round (weather permitting). There also are two large picnic shelters for up to 16 people each. A pleasant, moderately priced restaurant (open May-October) is at the park, along with a concession stand and restrooms (May-October) at the main parking area near the summit.

In 1787, French botanist Andre Michaux journeyed to the Black Mountains to seek plants for the French royal gardens. Michaux collected more than 2,500 specimens of trees, shrubs and other plants. About the same time, Englishman John Fraser collected plants to take back to England. The Fraser fir was named for this explorer.

In 1835, Dr. Elisha Mitchell, a science professor at the University of North Carolina in Chapel Hill, visited the area to measure the mountain elevations. At the time, Grandfather Mountain was assumed to be the highest point in the region, but previous trips had persuaded Mitchell that the Black Mountains were higher. On this and follow-up trips, Dr. Mitchell calculated the height of the peak at 6,672, only 12 feet off modern calculations. In 1857, Dr. Mitchell returned to the Black Mountains to verify his measurements. While hiking across the mountain, he fell from a cliff above a waterfall, was knocked unconscious and drowned. In honor of his work, the highest peak in the Black Mountain range was given his name in 1858. Originally buried in Asheville, Mitchell's body was reburied atop Mount Mitchell a year later.

At the state park are nine walk-in campsites with picnic grills, tent pads, running water and restrooms ($20 a day, $15 for those age 62 and older, $12 a day for winter rates without running water starting November 1). In addition, there are two primitive hike-in campsites (free).

The NC State Parks Guide app for mobile devices including iPad and iPhone is available online free from the iTunes store (https://itunes.apple.com).

Grandfather Mountain State Park *(Linville, 828-963-9522;*
www.ncparks.gov; Mar., Apr., May, Sep., Oct, 8 – 8, Jun.-Aug., 8 am- 9 pm,
Nov. – Feb. - 8 – 6; free). Directions: From Asheville: Take 40 East to Exit
72 to merge onto U.S. Hwy. 70 toward Old Fort. Turn left at NC 226
Bypass/U.S. Hwy. 221 and follow to U.S. Hwy. 221. Turn right at Newland
Hwy. Continue straight onto U.S. Hwy. 221. Turn left at Grandfather
Mountain Rd.

Listen up, because the situation with Grandfather Mountain is a little
complicated. In 2008, the state of North Carolina reached an agreement to
acquire almost 2,500 acres of private land on Grandfather Mountain. That,
along with conservation easements on around 4,000 acres on the mountain
owned by The Nature Conservancy, became in 2009 the basis of Grandfather
Mountain State Park.

Entrance to the state park is free. The process of developing the state
park is ongoing, but hikers have access to 12 miles of challenging trails in the
park, some of which require the use of the trails' ladders and cables in steeper
sections. Camping (free) is allowed with a permit at 13 backpack camping
sites along the trail system.

However, a private company still operates the 749-acre **Grandfather
Mountain Attraction** *(2050 Blowing Rock Hwy./U.S. Hwy. 221, Linville,*
828-733-4337 or 800-468-7325; www.grandfathermountain.com; park open
daily 8-6 spring, 8-6 summer, 8-5:30 early fall, 8-4:30 late fall, winter 9-5,
adults $20, seniors 60+ $18, children 4-12, $9). Directions: The Blue Ridge
Parkway links Grandfather at Milepost 305 with Asheville at MP382. Plan
on a 2 ½ - to 3-hour drive if you take the parkway. A faster route is to take I-
40 East to Exit 85 at Marion. Turn left at the bottom of the ramp and go 1
mile to a stoplight. At the stoplight turn left and follow U.S. Hwy. 221 North
30 miles to the entrance of Grandfather Mountain.

The commercial part of Grandfather Mountain has the famous "mile
high swinging bridge," zoo, nature center and other tourist facilities. The
5,946-foot mountain is topped by a 228-foot suspension bridge, built in 1952,
that connects two peaks. On clear days it's possible to see Charlotte, more
than 100 miles away. Although the bridge is perfectly safe to cross (you can
even take an elevator up to it), and it is designed to hold 3 million pounds,
when it swings in the wind most people can't help feeling a little frightened.
And it can be very windy – record wind gusts of more than 120 mph were
recorded in December 2012. Wind speeds exceeded 60 mph on 61 different
days in 2012. In high winds the bridge is temporarily closed to visitors.

This private tourist attraction charges admission fees. Owners of the attraction, the heirs of Grandfather Mountain founder Hugh Morton, a photographer and conservationist who died in 2006, say that they have decided to pursue the conversion of the company to a 501(c)(3), not-for-profit entity. The acquisition agreement gives North Carolina a conservation easement on the 749 acres where the attraction is located and has operated since the 1950s. At this time, though, the state parks system has no management responsibility for the Grandfather Mountain commercial attraction and its facilities.

Parts of the movie *Forrest Gump* were filmed at Grandfather.

Chimney Rock at Chimney Rock State Park *(Chimney Rock, 828-625-1823; www.ncparks.gov or www.chimneyrockpark.com; ticket plaza hours Jan.-mid-Mar., 10-4:30 Fri.-Tue., mid-Mar.-early Nov. 8:30-5:30 daily, rest of Nov.-Christmas 10-4:30 Fri.-Tue., week after Christmas 10-4:30 daily, park remains open 1 ½ hours after ticket plaza closes; access to Rumbling Bald climbing area is free, but the main part of the park charges fees – adults, $15, children 5-15 $7, reduced fees off-season).* Directions: From Asheville take I-240 East to Exit 9 (U.S. Hwy. 74A East). Stay on Hwy. 74A East for 20 miles to the park entrance, on the right.

The situation at Chimney Rock State Park in some ways is similar to that at Grandfather Mountain State Park. As at Grandfather, the state of North Carolina purchased, mostly from 2005 to 2007, much of a private tourist attraction and is gradually turning it into a traditional state park. At present, however, commercial management still operates much of the park and charges admission fees. Chimney Rock State Park currently occupies about 5,700 acres on both the north and south sides of Hickory Nut Gorge and efforts are underway to add additional acreage.

The eponymous Chimney Rock at Chimney Rock State Park is a 315-feet high outcropping of rock above Hickory Nut Gorge at an elevation of 2,280 feet. Most visitors ride the 26-story elevator to the top of the rock, although for a workout you can walk up the steep stairs and trail to the top. It has been a tourist destination in western North Carolina since a stairway was built to the rock's summit in 1885. In 1902, Lucius B. Morse of Missouri bought the site. The Morse family developed park facilities including a tunnel and elevator to the rock summit, nature center and a network of hiking trails including one to the 404-foot-high Hickory Nut Falls. There's a café and gift shop at the park.

Some scenes of the 1992 movie, *Last of the Mohicans,* were filmed at Chimney Rock.

Gorges State Park *(976 Grassy Ridge Rd., Sapphire, 828-966-9099; www.ncparks.gov; Mar., Apr., May, Sep., Oct, 8 – 8, Jun.-Aug., 8 am- 9 pm, Nov. – Feb. - 8 – 6; free).* Directions: From Asheville take I-26 East to Exit 9, NC Hwy. 280 toward Brevard. Turn west on U.S. Hwy. 64 and travel toward Sapphire. To reach the Frozen Creek access (east side of the park), turn left onto Frozen Creek Rd., 2 miles past NC 178. The east entrance is 3 miles on the right. To reach the Grassy Ridge access (west side of the park), turn south on NC Hwy. 281 in Sapphire; the western park entrance is 0.7 miles on the left.

In 1999, the state of North Carolina purchased more than 10,000 acres from Duke Energy Corporation in Transylvania County near the South Carolina state line, creating a 2,900-acre gameland managed by the N.C. Wildlife Resources Commission and almost 7,500 acres for Gorge State Park. The park offers hiking, horseback riding, mountain biking, waterfall overlooks, bass fishing in Lake Jocassee and trout fishing in streams. Horses and mountain bikes, as well as hikers, are permitted on the Auger Hole Trail from the Frozen Creek access to Turkey Pen Gap on the western boundary of the park.

Gorges State Park opened a new 7,100 square-foot visitor center and two large picnic shelters in late 2012. Six primitive campsites (free) are in the park at Lake Jocassee, with fire rings and picnic tables. Access is via the 5.5-mile Cane Brake Trail.

Lake James State Park *(see Lakes section below).*

Other Notable Outdoors Spots

Highest Mountain Peaks in Western North Carolina There are more than 50 mountains in Western North Carolina over 6,000 feet high.

Here are the 10 highest peaks:

1. Mt. Mitchell, Yancey County -- 6,686 ft.
2. Mt. Craig, Yancey County -- 6,637 ft.
3. Mt. Guyot, Haywood County -- 6,614 ft.
4. Balsam Cone, Yancey County -- 6,585 ft.
5. Blue Ridge, Allegheny County -- 6,581 ft.
6. Mt. Buckley, Swain County -- 6,568 ft.
7. Big Tom, Yancey County -- 6,568 ft.
8. Cattail Peak, Yancey County -- 6,516 ft.
9. Clingmans Peak, Yancey County -- 6,499 ft.
10. Mt. Gibbes, Yancey County -- 6,467 ft.

LAKES

All the lakes in Western North Carolina are man-made. There are no natural lakes in the region. Keep in mind that some of the lakes, including Fontana, Chatuge and James, are used for power generation. At certain times the year, the Tennessee Valley Authority raises or lowers the water level, making a considerable difference in the size and shoreline of the lakes. That's especially true for Fontana. Here are some of the WNC lakes of greatest interest:

Beaver Lake *(bounded by Merrimon Ave. and Lakeshore Dr. about 2 miles north of Downtown Asheville)* is a small, 40-acre lake in a residential area of North Asheville. Designed by noted urban landscape architect John Nolen and completed in 1923, Beaver Lake and the nearby Lakeview Park residential area are privately owned and maintained. The lake is used by local residents and guests as a place to picnic, walk or jog on trails around the lake or go birding. Swimming is not permitted, and fishing and boating (in canoes or kayaks) are by permit only. Pets must be leashed. There is a small parking area on the west side of Merrimon Avenue, just beyond the North Asheville Library, for the public to visit the 10-acre Beaver Lake bird sanctuary (free), co-owned and managed by the Elisha Mitchell Audubon Society. From the sanctuary parking area, from dawn to dusk, you can bird watch on a 3/8-mile boardwalk through a wetland area and by the lake, with spots to sit along the way. Around 160 species have been sighted in the sanctuary, including 19 kinds of geese and ducks and four species of herons. Residential developments and communities near the lake include Lakeview Park, the Asheville Country Club, Reynolds Mountain and Ciel.

Lake Chatuge (*U.S. Hwy. 64 and NC Hwy. 69, Hayesville, about 2 hours southwest of Asheville, 828-837-7395 for water conditions and information on TWA release times.*) Directions: From Asheville take I-40 West. Take Exit 27 and merge onto U.S. Hwy. 74/19 West toward Waynesville/Murphy. Go 25 miles and take Exit 81 and merge onto U.S. Hwy. 23/441 toward Franklin/Dillsboro. This becomes U.S. Hwy. 64. Stay on Hwy. 64 for 28 miles and take left onto NC Hwy. 175 to Hayesville. In Hayesville, turn left onto NC Hwy. 17/69 and follow it to the end. Turn left onto Hwy. 76 to Lake Chatuge area.

In 1942, the Tennessee Valley Authority constructed a dam across the Hiawassee River, forming 7,200-acre Lake Chatuge (pronounced Sha-toog), which is about one-half in North Carolina and one-half in North Georgia. You can walk across the dam for a spectacular view of the lake and surrounding mountains.

With around 133 miles of shoreline, the lake has numerous fingerlike projections of land forming coves for fishing, swimming, boating and other water sports. There are three boat ramps on the NC side: Jackrabbit Mountain Campground, off NC 175; Gibson Cove Campground, off Myers Chapel Road and Ledford Chapel Wildlife access, on U.S. Highway 64.

Bass fishing is the thing here, with largemouth, smallmouth, spotted and striped bass the main targets for anglers. Altogether there are around three dozen kinds of fish in the lake. Fishing licenses are required. Chatuge is around 144 feet deep at the dam, but lake levels vary by 9 feet or more, depending on TVA water releases. Real estate agents in the Hayesville, N.C., and Hiawassee, Ga., areas have listings for vacation rentals and for lakefront property.

Fontana Lake (*Fontana Dam Visitor Center, Fontana Dam Rd., off NC Hwy, 28, 32 miles from Bryson City, TVA headquarters in Knoxville, Tenn., 865-632-2101; www.tva.gov; dam visitor center open daily 9-7 May-Nov., lake open daily year-round; dam visitor center and boat access areas free, various charges for private marinas and services.*) Directions: From Asheville take I-40 west to the exit for U.S. Hwy. 74, a four-line divided highway also known as Great Smoky Mountain Expressway. Stay on U.S. Hwy. 74, and 8 miles past Bryson turn right on NC Hwy. 28. Continue on Hwy. 28 for 25 miles.

Fontana Lake is the largest lake in Western North Carolina, comprising about 10,300 acres. It lays along the southern boundary of the Great Smoky Mountains National Park near Bryson City. The lake is 17 to 29 miles long, depending the water level, and has around 240 miles of shoreline. Depth ranges to 440 feet and averages about 135 feet. Each September, TVA begins its annual draw down, which lowers lake levels as much as 55 to 65 feet.

More than 90% of the land around the lake is owned either by the National Park Service or the U.S. Forest Service, so shoreline development has been relatively limited.

Fontana offers boating, fishing, swimming, water skiing and beautiful views of the Smokies from the water. You can also take boats across the lake for great hiking and trout fishing in the Smokies. There are several public boat access ramps – on Old NC Route 288, Lemmons Branch, Cable Cove, Flat Branch, Lewellyn Branch and elsewhere -- plus several private marinas, including **Fontana Marina, Alarka** and **Almond.** The lake has some of the best bass fishing in the region, with large populations of black bass, white bass and smallmouth and largemouth bass. Some large walleye and muskie also have been caught in the cold, deep waters of the lake.

At 480 feet high, **Fontana Dam** is the highest dam east of the Rockies and the fourth tallest in the country. The Appalachian Trail crosses the dam, which stretches 2,365 feet across the Little Tennessee River.

The dam and reservoir were built by TVA from 1942 to 1944 during World War II to provide electric power for aluminum production by ALCOA. Today, the dam provides 241 megawatts of hydropower. What was once the construction village of 5,000 people working 24 hours a day for almost three years is now the resort and timeshare **Fontana Village Resort** *(300 Woods Rd., Fontana Dam, 828-498-2211 or 800-849-2258; www.fontanavillage.com; cabins cost around $99-$300 depending on size and time of year, lodge rooms are $79-$129, tent camping is $20-$30 and RV/trailer sites with hook-ups are $25-$40.)* Fontana Village Marina at the resort has boat slips and rents pontoon boats, canoes, kayaks and jet skis.

Lake Junaluska *(91 Lakeshore Dr., Lake Junaluska, 800-222-4930 or 828-452-2881; www.lakejunaluska.com.)* Directions: From Asheville, take I-40 West to Exit 27 onto US Hwy. 19-23. Drive about 3.5 miles on Hwy. 19-23. Take Exit 103 and go about 1 mile until you see Lake Junaluska Conference and Retreat Center front entrance gates on the right. Bear right and follow the main road to the Bethea Welcome Center.

Lake Junaluska Assembly is a 1,200-acre conference center and retreat of the United Methodist Church on a small, 200-acre lake about 30 minutes west of Asheville. On the grounds are several inns, lodges, apartments, cottages, campsites and other accommodations with a total of about 400 rooms and spaces. Rates are moderate, but most accommodations are occupied by participants at conferences, which can total up to around 3,000 per day in summer. The Aquatic Center is open to the public daily from Memorial Day to Labor Day and includes an outdoor pool and rentals of canoes, kayaks and paddle boats ($5 per hour) for use on the lake. On the grounds also are tennis courts, mini-golf and shuffle board.

Lake James *(883 NC Hwy. 126, Nebo, about 45 minutes east of Asheville, 828-584-7728; www.ncparks.gov; state park facilities including swimming area, bathhouse, concession stand and canoe/kayak rentals are open May-Sep. Campsites open Mar.-Nov. Hidden Cove boat access is open Mar.-Oct. while Canal Bridge boat access is open year-round. Swimming, fishing and boating are free except for pertinent licenses.)* Directions: From Asheville, take I-40 East, turn the Nebo/Lake James exit (Exit 90) and head north. After 0.5 mile, turn right onto Harmony Grove Rd. and follow for 2 miles to a stoplight. Proceed straight across the intersection past Nebo Elementary School to a stop sign. Turn right onto NC 126 and follow the signs to the park entrance 4.8 miles on the right.

Lake James is a 6,812-acre reservoir with more than 150 miles of shoreline, at the base of Blue Ridge mountains between Marion and Morganton, at around 1,200 feet elevation.

An area on the west side of the park makes up Lake James State Park, but other parts of the shoreline are private. The lake was created between 1916 and 1923 as a source of hydroelectric power. Among the activities available at the lake are boating (the Canal Bridge boat access ramp is open year-round); fishing for large and smallmouth bass, walleye, bluegill, bream, sunfish, perch and others – a fishing license is required; lifeguarded swimming at Paddy Creek May-September 10-6 with a fee per day of $5 for adults and $3 for children 3-12; camping at 20 walk-in tent sites off Campground Road with fire circles and picnic tables March-November, fees $20 per day ($15 per day for those 62 and better) – reservations strongly advised; canoe and kayak rentals are $5 per hour for first hour, then $3 per hour for additional hours. Hiking also is available on several trails around the lake.

Private lakefront lots (mostly $100,000 to $200,000) and homes on or near the lake ($200,000 to $2 million) are offered in a number of private developments on the lake. Rental cottages and houses are also offered on the lake. See Vacation Rentals by Owner (www.vrbo.com) for a number of options. Local real estate agents in the area also have vacation home rentals.

Lake Lure *(2724 Memorial Hwy., Lake Lure, 828-625-1373.)* Directions: From Asheville, take I-240 East to Exit 9 (Bat Cave/Blue Ridge Parkway) and continue on U.S. Hwy. 74A to Chimney Rock. Lake Lure is about 1 mile past Chimney Rock.

Lake Lure is a 720-acre lake with about 27 miles of shoreline near Chimney Rock. There's fishing for bass and other fish, boating and swimming. A beach and water park, open from Memorial Day to Labor Day, offers fun on the lake. Across the road from the lake is the 1927-vintage **Lake Lure Inn** *(2771 Memorial Hwy. Lake Lure, 828-625-2525 or 888-434-4970; www.lakelure.com; rates for 69 rooms and 3 cabins vary but generally are overpriced; closed Sun.-Wed Dec.-Feb.),* which was renovated in 2005 but is still nothing special. The 17-room lakefront **Lodge at Lake Lure** *(361 Charlotte Dr., Lake Lure, 800-733-2785 or 828-625-2789; www.lodgeonlakelure.com, rates $135-$300),* originally built in the 1930s as a retreat for North Carolina Highway Patrol officers, is more expensive but worth it. Breakfasts daily and dinner Wednesday-Saturday seasonally.

The 1987 cult movie *Dirty Dancing* was shot partially in Lake Lure. Many of the scenes were filmed at the old Boys Camp, which is now part of a private residential community, Firefly Cove. Boat tours from Lake Lure Inn (from $15) take you by the filming sites. Local real estate agents in the area have vacation rentals.

Though not a lake, **Hot Springs** *(U.S. Hwys. 25/70 North off I-26)*, in the Pisgah National Forest in Madison County about 45 minutes north of Asheville, has 108-degree mineral springs. These are the only hot-water mineral springs known in the state. The area has been a resort for about 200 years and in the 19th century was home to the 350-room Warm Springs Hotel. After the hotel burned, the area went into decline, but Hot Springs -- at the junction of the Appalachian Trail and the French Broad River -- has made something of a comeback, with B&Bs, new eateries, river rafting and funky mineral water "hot tubs."

SPORTS AND OUTDOORS ACTIVITIES

Many of the outdoor activities listed below are covered in detail in the PLACES sections of this chapter *(above)*, and in the Great Smoky Mountains National Park or Blue Ridge Parkway chapters. Please refer to them. Information on the activities below primarily relates to service providers and, in some cases, to our top picks for selected activities.

Baseball in Asheville

Returning Civil War soldiers supposedly brought the game of baseball to Asheville. Semi-professional baseball in Asheville dates back to at least 1897, to a team called the Asheville Moonshiners (who according to old-timers wore, of all things, purple uniforms). Pro ball in Asheville began in earnest in 1909. Other early names for the Asheville teams included the Redbirds, the Mountaineers and the Skylanders, and the Tourists name goes back at least to 1915.

Built during one of Asheville's real estate booms, McCormick Field has been the home of the Asheville Tourists since 1924, except for a few years of hiatus during wars, when leagues folded or when the team suffered financial problems. The Tourists, then officially called the Asheville Skylanders, beat the Detroit Tigers 18-14 on April 3, 1924, the formal opening game in McCormick Field. Ty Cobb was center fielder and manager of the Tigers.

In April 1925, Babe Ruth and the New York Yankees arrived in Asheville to play the Brooklyn Dodgers. Unfortunately, on arrival by train at the Southern Railway Depot Ruth was taken ill with a stomach ailment.

By some accounts, he had consumed too many hot dogs and too much beer on the train. Even without the Babe, on April 7, 1925, the Yankees beat the Dodgers 16-8 at McCormick Field.

McCormick Field is located at 30 Buchanan Place off Biltmore Avenue just south of the main Downtown area.

As befits one of the classic minor league parks in the country, McCormick Field has a rich baseball history. Besides Babe Ruth and Ty Cobb, baseball greats Lou Gehrig, Pee Wee Reese, Roberto Clemente, Gil Hodges, Roy Campanella and Dizzy Dean have made exhibition appearances here.

In 1930, the Yankees with Lou Gehrig in addition to Babe Ruth returned to Asheville to play three exhibition games. Supposedly a New York sportswriter claimed that 2,000 people were inside McCormick Field and 15,000 outside the park watched the games. The Yankees won all three games.

A crowd of 5,500 including 2,000 African-Americans watched Jackie Robinson and the Brooklyn Dodgers play an exhibition game at McCormick Field in 1948, and the Dodgers returned for another game in 1951. Willie Stargell, Eddie Murray and all Cal Ripken Sr. (sons Cal Jr. and Billy played Little League in Asheville) were with the Tourists in one capacity or another. Legendary manager Sparky Anderson won a league champion here, in 1968. University of North Carolina head basketball coach Roy Williams, who grew up in Asheville, was a batboy for the Tourists.

All together more than 400 players who played for Asheville have moved on, if only briefly, to the Bigs. Among the alumni of the Tourists who went on to the major leagues besides Stargell and Murray include Craig Biggio, Dennis Martinez, Todd Helton, Curtis Wilkerson, Danny Darwin, Shane Reynolds, Wayne Tolleson, Ian Stewart and many others.

Willie Stargell, who played for the Tourists in 1961, a year when eight Tourists players graduated to the major leagues, is the only former Tourist player in the Baseball Hall of Fame, inducted in 1988. As a first baseman and leftfielder, Stargell played 21 years for the Pittsburgh Pirates. A powerful hitter who at one time held the record for the longer home runs in almost one-half of all the National League stadiums, he was known for standing in the on-deck circle and warming up with a sledgehammer instead of a weighted bat.

Branch Rickey, legendary baseball executive, numerous times referred to Asheville's McCormick Field as one of his favorite ballparks in the country, and Rickey made the Tourists a farm club for three different major league teams he was with, St. Louis, Brooklyn and Pittsburgh.

The Tourists played in the North Carolina State League until 1917, when the league was disbanded due to the war. Baseball came back to Asheville in 1924 (the team was temporarily called the Skylanders before reverting to the Tourists nickname.) The Tourists played in the old South Atlantic Association until 1930, before moving to the Piedmont League in 1932.

After a couple of years' absence, baseball returned to Asheville in 1934 when the Columbia, S.C., Sandpipers moved to Asheville, changing their name to the tried-and-true Asheville Tourists. The Piedmont League suspended operations in 1942.

After World War II, baseball returned to the Land of the Sky in 1946, when a new tourist franchise began playing in the Tri-State League. In the 1940s and early 1950s, the Tourists shared McCormick Field with the Asheville Blues, a Negro Southern League team. The Blues were owned and managed by C. L. Moore, a prominent baseball coach and teacher at Stephens-Lee, the segregated black high school in Asheville.

The Asheville High football team, then called the Maroons, played some home games at McCormick field during this period. The Maroons' best player was Charlie "Choo Choo" Justice, who went on to star at the University of North Carolina and with the Washington Redskins.

From 1955 to 1959, partly due to the popularity of the new medium of television, which kept people at home glued to the flickering black-and-white screens, again the city was without a professional baseball team. For three summers, from 1956 to 1958, McCormick Field was used as a stock car racetrack. A quarter-mile asphalt track was laid on the field and a concrete block wall was built around the park. Banjo Matthews, driving a '37 Ford, was the local racing sensation, at one time winning 13 weekly races in a row.

In 1959, a new South Atlantic League (later the Class AA Southern League) team began playing at the remodeled McCormick Field. In 1968, the team won the Southern League championship under manager Sparky Anderson, who went on to manage the Cincinnati Reds and Detroit Tigers. In 1972, the Tourists became affiliated with the Baltimore Orioles. The O's renamed the team the Asheville Orioles, under which name the team played until 1975, when the O's moved its farm team to Charlotte.

In 1976, a new franchise took over, using the historic Tourists name, operating as a farm club for the Texas Rangers.

Over the years, the Tourists have been affiliates of various major league teams.

These include the Detroit Tigers (1920s), Boston Red Sox (1934), St. Louis Cardinals (1935-42), Brooklyn Dodgers (1946-51 and 1953-55), Philadelphia Phillies (1959-60), Pittsburgh Pirates (1961-66), Houston Astros (1967 and 1982-93), Cincinnati Reds (1968-70), Chicago White Sox (1971, in the Class AA Dixie Association, a league that stretched from Albuquerque to San Antonio to Charlotte), Baltimore Orioles (1972-75) and Texas Rangers (1976-81).

Continuously since 1994 the Tourists have been a Single A affiliate of the Colorado Rockies.

In 2010, a prominent Ohio family, the DeWines, headed by former Republican Congressman and U.S. Senator and current Ohio Attorney General Mike DeWine, purchased the Asheville Tourists Baseball Club. The team operates under the name DeWine Seeds Silver Dollar Baseball, LLC. The seeds name is a reference to Mike DeWine's father, Dick DeWine, who with wife Jean built a national seed company. It is also a reference to an event that supposedly occurred during the 1939 World Series, when as the story goes Dick DeWine wrapped a ticket he had bought to the game around a silver dollar and threw the coin to a friend waiting outside Crosley Field in Cincinnati, enabling the friend to join him to see the Reds and Yankees play. (The Yankees won the game and swept the Series in four games.)

Brian DeWine, a son of Mike DeWine, is general manager of the Tourists. Joe Mikulik, a former minor league baseball player, managed the team from 2000 to 2012, when he was fired. Mikulik is possibly best known for a rant at a 2006 Tourists game with the Lexington Legends, when he pulled up second base and threw it down on the field and then threw bats from the dugout and poured water on home plate. The extended tirade went viral on the internet and on TV. Mikulik was suspended for seven days and given a $1,000 fine.

During Mikulik's tenure, however, some 60 Tourist players went on to the major leagues. He now manages the Class Advanced Myrtle Beach Pelicans. Fred Ocasio, a former minor league infielder who played two years for the Tourists in the 1990s, currently is the manager of the Tourists.

The Tourist's team mascot is Ted E. Tourist. The latest logo illustrates a baseball flying over the moon, with an alternate logo being a moon-faced tourist in sunglasses swinging a bat with a hobo's bag tied to it.

McCormick Field

McCormick Field, the quintessential minor league stadium, was named after Dr. Lewis McCormick, an Asheville bacteriologist.

Dr. McCormick gained a national reputation for his campaign to raise awareness about the dangers of the common housefly, called appropriately enough "Swat That Fly."

Originally constructed mostly of wood, McCormick Field was remodeled in 1959 and more substantively in 1991-1992. The venerable stadium – which until then could claim to be the oldest minor league stadium and the fifth oldest stadium (after Fenway Park, Wrigley Field, Tiger Stadium and Yankee Stadium) in the country – was razed and rebuilt in concrete, with a brick exterior and metal roof. However, the playing field was left much as it had always been.

After the 2012 season, new grass was put on the field, using a type of Bermuda grass that is supposed to hold up well to mountain weather.

The stadium seats 4,000, and most seats are sheltered from the rain and sun under a cantilevered roof. McCormick Field is a hitter's park, with left field 326 feet from home plate, center field 373 feet and right field only 297 feet. The right field fence stands 36 feet high, only about a foot lower than Fenway Park's Green Monster and 5 feet closer to home plate.

McCormick Field is said to be home to the closest-to-the-batter-box seats in all of professional baseball. These are box suites just to the inside of the dugouts, in front of the existing backstop, protected by netting completely surrounding the boxes. Additionally there are regular box seats. General admission seats are in plain concrete bleachers.

The stadium is set part way up a low hill. It doesn't enjoy great views of surrounding mountains, but you can see part of 1920s-era Asheville Memorial Stadium, now used for local soccer and football.

McCormick Field had a minor role in the 1988 film, *Bull Durham.* Crash Davis, played by Kevin Costner, is cut from the Durham Bulls but then breaks the minor league home run record as a member of the Tourists. Some scenes will filmed at McCormick Field.

One negative to McCormick Field is lack of parking. The stadium has only limited parking (mostly reserved for season ticket holders and VIPs) in front of the stadium. Fans park in the free lot at Memorial Stadium just above McCormick Field or on the street on Biltmore Avenue and nearby, or at the lots of businesses closed during the ballgames. For a well-attended game, you may need to walk quite a distance to the park.

In 2012, the Asheville Tourists defeated the Greensboro Grasshoppers in the South Atlantic League championship series three games to one. That Sallie League title is the first won by the Tourists since 1984.

For more on the history of baseball in Asheville, see Bob Terrell's *The Old Ball Yard* (1997) and Bill Ballew's *A History of Professional Baseball in Asheville* (2007).

Attending a Game:

Asheville Tourists, 30 Buchanan Place, 828-259-5800, www.asheville.tourists.milb.com

Ticket prices: general admission $7 advance, $8 day of game; box seats $10 advance, $11 day of game; dugout box seats $29 advance, $30 day of game. Because the stadium is small and seating is close to the field, there are really no bad seats in this park.

The season runs from early April to early September. The Tourists play in the South Atlantic League along with Savannah, Greensboro, Charleston, S.C., Augusta and other teams.

Most Thursdays are Thirsty Thursdays, when beer at the park is only a buck ($2 for premium beers). Hot dogs usually are $1 on Fridays.

Bicycling and Mountain Biking

Asheville is an increasingly bicycle-friendly town. The area has many bike trails and an increasing number of designated bike lanes on city streets. Asheville currently offers more than 4 miles of developed greenways -- multi-use paths used for recreation and alternative transportation – and is working towards its goal of a 15-mile system composed of 12 interconnected corridors. Keep in mind that the terrain ranges from fairly flat around town to hilly and rolling to screaming mountain climbs. For road cycling, the **Blue Ridge Parkway** is primo *(see Blue Ridge Parkway chapter).*

The **Blue Ridge Bicycling Club** (www.blueridgebicycleclub.org/) is the area's largest biking club, with more than 300 members. The club offers a variety of rides weekly and the club's website has detailed information on some of the best rides in the area.

Asheville has many good bicycle shops. Among them are **Liberty Bikes** (1378 Hendersonville Rd., Asheville, 828-274-2453, www.libertybikes.com); **Pro Bikes** (610 Haywood Rd., West Asheville, 828-253-2800, www.pro-bikes.com); **BioWheels Asheville** (81 Coxe Ave., Asheville, 828-236-2453, www.biowheels.com); **Carolina Bike Mechanic** (1500 Brevard Rd., Asheville, 828-670-0091, www.carolinabikemechanic.com); **Motion Makers Bicycle Shop** (878 Brevard Rd., Asheville, 828-633-2227, www.motionmakers.com); **The Bicycle Company,** 779 Church St., Hendersonville, 828-696-1500, www.thebikecompany.net); and **REI** (Biltmore Park, 31 Schenck Parkway, Asheville, 828-687-0918, www.rei.com).

Several of the bike shops also offer rentals – expect to pay around $45 to $65 a day for a quality mountain bike, usually less for a road bike.

The three main **mountain biking** areas in Western North Carolina are the **Bent Creek Experimental Forest** in Pisgah National Forest just west of Asheville, **DuPont State Forest** near Brevard and **Tsali Recreation Area** near Fontana Lake in the Nantahala National Forest.

Bent Creek Experimental Forest *(1577 Brevard Rd., Asheville, 828-667-5261, www.srs.fs.usda.gov/bentcreek/)* has miles of mountain biking trails for beginning and intermediate riders in a 6,000-acre section of the Pisgah National Forest. It is easily accessible via I-26 and Brevard Road or the Blue Ridge Parkway off Milepost 393.

DuPont State Forest *(www.ncforestservice.gov)* has more than 80 miles of trails open to mountain bikers, as well as to hikers and horseback riders. Some of the trails, with steep inclines and big drops, are appropriate only for advanced riders. Parking for all of the bike trails in the 10,400-acre forest is at the Corn Mill Shoals Access Area on Cascade Lake Rd. From Brevard, take U.S. Hwy. 276 south to Cedar Mountain. Turn left on Cascade Lake Rd. to access area.

Tsali Recreation Area *(in Nantahala National Forest off NC Route 28 near Robbinsville, www.fs.usda.gov/)* has a national reputation as a prime mountain biking area. There are more than 42 miles of trails open to bikes (as well as to hikers and horseback riders). The four main riding loops enjoy dramatic views of the Smokies and Fontana Lake. Due to the popularity of the area, biking is limited to only certain days, varying depending on the trail. There is a $2 per day trail use fee. Directions: From Robbinsville take NC Hwy. 143 East. Turn right (south) on NC Route 28 and go about 8 miles. The Tsali Recreation Area entrance is on the north side of the road. Go about 1.5 miles to a parking lot with entrances to the various trail heads.

Birding

Birders will find an unexpectedly rich environment for birding in Western North Carolina, due to the large differences in elevation and habitats in a relatively small area. At the highest elevations, 4,500 to 6,500 feet and higher, in the coniferous forests (at least where the Fraser firs and red spruces have survived acid rain and alien infestations), you can find nesting birds that you would usually see in the northeastern U.S. and in Canada, including a number of warblers and owls normally seen farther north.

Deciduous forests dominate most of Western North Carolina – 95% of the **Great Smoky Mountains National Park** is forested, for example – but within these wooded areas are several different types of forests, each with different types of birds:

On elevated moist slopes there are warblers, grosbeaks and vireos and dry slopes with chickadees and titmice and other birds common in the Piedmont; hardwood cove forests in the moist, fertile coves are home to many birds including tanagers; cool streams with hemlocks and an understory of rhododendron are where a variety of warblers live; lower-elevation dry slopes with Virginia and other pines and birds similar to those in the Piedmont of North Carolina offer jays and chickadees; and, finally, cliff and rock faces such as **Whiteside Mountain** and **Chimney Rock, are** home to ravens and even peregrine falcons and eagles.

More than 460 bird species have been identified in the state of North Carolina, and at least 300 in the Western North Carolina mountains. In Asheville and Buncombe County alone 266 species have been identified.

You can even see birds in Downtown Asheville – photo by Jessamyn Weis

The **Blue Ridge Parkway** is popular for birders, because it traverses such a wide range of habitats and elevations. The **Great Smokies** and **Pisgah and Nantahala national forests** also are popular with birders. Small land birds stream through the deciduous forests during spring migrations, and birding here is spectacular in the spring. Most of the fall migration, however, occurs on or near the coast, not through the mountains.

However, the migration of hawks in the autumn is exciting, especially at areas such as Mt. Pisgah and Chimney Rock. Summer may not provide the same large variety of species, but the Smoky Mountains park alone has more than 120 nesting species, including at least 23 species of warblers. Even in winter there are many local birding opportunities, and you may see finches and buntings as well as many year-round species.

Here are a few areas of special interest to birders. For more ideas and information, check with local birding clubs such as the **Elisha Mitchell Audubon Society** (http://emasnc.org), which is the Asheville chapter of the Audubon Society, and the **Carolina Bird Club** *(www.carolinabirdclub.org)*, which has members all over North and South Carolina.

Also refer to one of the excellent local birding guides, such as *The North Carolina Birding Trail, Mountain Trail Guide,* which describes 105 birding destinations in the mountains, and *Birds of the Carolinas*, which exhaustively describes the birds of both North and South Carolina. Both are published by the superb University of North Carolina Press. Also consider *Birding North Carolina,* published by Globe Pequot. The national field guides – *Sibley, Stokes, Peterson* and others – are also helpful. *See Resources section for recommendations.*

Birding Ventures Tours *(828-253-4247, www.birdventures.com)* runs day birding tours in the Asheville area. Some of the trips concentrate on a specific family of birds, such as woodpeckers or owls. One of the guides who operates Birding Ventures also is a co-owner of **Wild Birds Unlimited** *(1997 Hendersonville Rd., Asheville, 828-687-9433)* a birding and bird-feeding store.

Beaver Lake Bird Sanctuary *(U.S. Hwy 25 North/Merrimon Avenue, about 2.5 miles north of Downtown Asheville)* is a 10-acre bird sanctuary managed by the local chapter of the Audubon Society. It is notable for migrating waterfowl and some wintering waterfowl, including the great blue heron and green heron.

Biltmore Estate *(off Exit 50 of I-40, with entrance in Biltmore Village south of Downtown Asheville)* is an appealing spot for birding, as there are a number of different habitats – mature pine forests, hardwood forests, rivers, small lakes and wetlands, open fields, farmland, vineyards – in an area of about 8,000 acres. The downside is that you'll have to purchase admission to the estate, expensive on a daily basis but a bargain for an annual pass (from $89) that permits unlimited daytime admissions to the grounds, house, winery and other facilities.

Carl Sandburg Home National Historic Site *(3 miles south of Hendersonville in Flat Rock on Little River Rd. off U.S. Hwy. 225, free admission to grounds)* is a 264-acre site, mainly oak and mixed hardwoods, with miles of hiking trails, but there are about 40 acres of pasture and two small lakes. More than 120 species of birds have been identified here. There is a small admission charge to tour the Sandburg home, but admission to the grounds and farm is free.

Chimney Rock State Park *(on U.S. Hwy. 74A about 25 miles southwest of Asheville)* has a 315-foot rock outcrop surrounded by hardwood cove forests and with a stream and waterfall. The touristy rock chimney is still privately managed, although the entire area is gradually becoming a more traditional state park. There are nesting peregrine falcons here, and the rarely seen Swainson's warbler. In the fall, don't miss the hawk migrations where you can see hundreds of broad-winged and other hawks.

Craggy Gardens *(along the Blue Ridge Parkway about 20 miles north of Asheville, between Mileposts 364 to 367, free)* is a high-elevation area of spruce-first forests, hardwood cove forests and heath balds, home to a variety of breeding songbirds from May through September, especially warblers. Also look for sharp-shinned and other hawks and common ravens.

DuPont State Forest *(southeast of Brevard off U.S. Hwy. 276, free)* is a 10,400 acre forest area with some 80 miles of hiking trails with a variety of bird habitats including small lakes, rivers with waterfalls, hardwood cove forests, oak forests and rock outcroppings. You can see bluebirds, warblers, finches, grebes along with wild turkeys, several kinds of hawks, bald eagles and a variety of waterfowl including herons and ducks. You do have to share most trails with mountain bikers and horseback riders, and hunting is permitted in the fall.

Grandfather Mountain *(off the Blue Ridge Parkway at Milepost 305 near Linville)* is one of the tallest mountains in the region. It is a nature sanctuary and most of the mountain is now a North Carolina state park. More than 200 bird species have been identified here. There is an admission charge to the privately managed Grandfather Mountain attraction, but the state park is free.

Heintooga Spur Road *(off Blue Ridge Parkway at Milepost 458)* is a remote, high-elevation area where you can see red crossbills, least flycatchers, pine siskins, ruffed grouse and many warblers. The best birding is May to early July. Heintooga is closed in winter, spring comes late and autumn arrives early.

Jackson Park *(off East 4th Ave. near downtown Hendersonville)* is a small park with a lot of songbirds, especially in the spring and fall. About two dozen different warblers have been identified here in a single day.

Max Patch *(on Max Patch Rd. in northern Madison County, near the Tennessee line)* is a grassy bald in the Pisgah National Forest at around 4,600-feet elevation. The bald has marvelous views. Look for swallows, hawks and bobwhites on the bald, with a variety of warblers and other songbirds in the hardwood cove forests and other woods below the bald.

Boating

Boat rentals and boat ramps are available at several of the larger lakes in Western North Carolina including Fontana, James, Chatuge, Hiwassee and Santeetlah.

Marinas usually require boating experience for those renting boats. Under North Carolina law those under age 26 must have completed a boating education course before they can operate a boat with an engine over 10 horsepower. Unless otherwise stated, full-day boat rentals are for an 8-hour day.

Also see the River Rafting, Kayaking and Canoeing section below.

Alarka Dock, Fontana Lake *(Lower Alarka Rd., Bryson City, 828-488-3841, www.alarkadock.com)* offers pontoon boat rentals for $250 a day and small powerboat rentals for $50 a day (rates do not include fuel). Boat slip rentals are $75 a month or $400 for the season. Alarka also has fishing supplies and bait for sale and can arrange guides and transport to the Smokies side of the lake.

Fontana Marina, Fontana Lake *(Peppertree Fontana Village Resort, 300 Woods Rd.*
Fontana Dam, 828-498-2211or 800-849-2258, www.fontantavillage.com) has pontoon boats for rent starting at $60 an hour or $295 a day, bass boats from $35 to $40 an hour/$150 to $200 a day and jet skis for $85 an hour, along with canoes and kayaks for $50 to $75 for 24 hours. Uncovered boat slip rentals are $10 a day, $75 a week and $1,225 a year. The marina also offers lake cruises and transport to the Smokies side of the lake. The Fontana Village Resort has rooms, cabins, tent camping, dining and other resort services.

Chatuge Cove Marina, Lake Chatuge *(2397 NC Hwy. 175, Hayesville, 828-389-6155, www.chatugecovemarina.com)* rents pontoon boats for $220 to $270 a day including fuel and boat slips for $1,500 to $1,800 a year. It has boat and fishing supplies store and RV/trailer campsites.

Mountain Harbour Marina, Lake James *(9066 NC Hwy. 126, Nebo, 828-584-0666, www.mountainharbourmarina.com)* has 18-foot pontoon boats for rent for $175 a day, uncovered boat slip rentals from $1,600 a year and covered slips from $2,400, a marine store and other services.

Mountain View Marina, Lake Hiwassee *(Bear Paw Resort, 200 Dean Aldrich Dr.*
Murphy, 828-644-5451, www.mountainviewmarina) has 20- to 24-foot pontoon boat rentals for $160 to $175 per day, not including fuel or tax, and rents boat slip for $10 to $15 a day or around $1,200 to $1,400 a year.

Santeetlah Marina, Lake Santeetlah *(1 Marina Dr., Lake Santeetlah, 828-479-8180, www.santeetlahmarina.com, open Apr.-Oct.)* rents pontoon boats for $280 to $320 per day and canoes and kayaks for $60 to $75 a day. Slip rentals are $20 to $50 a day, and a seven-month seasonal rental is $875 to $1,475. The marina also has a ship store with boat and fishing equipment, bait and snacks. Note that Graham County is a dry county, so you can't buy beer or other alcohol here.

Camping

The two most popular areas for camping in the region, the **Great Smoky Mountains National Park** and along the **Blue Ridge Parkway** are covered in their own chapters, with detailed information on camping opportunities and costs. There are many other popular areas for camping, including **Pisgah National Forest, Nantahala National Forest, Mt. Mitchell State Park** and **DuPont State Forest.** These areas offer both developed and primitive or backcountry camping. *See information on those areas above.*

Western North Carolina also has hundreds of private campgrounds. Most are focused on RV and trailer camping, with water and electric hook-ups and dump stations. It is beyond the scope of this book to list all the private campgrounds in the region. *Woodall's Campground Directory* and *Trailer Life RV Parks Directory* merged in 2012 and now appear as a combined directory, the *Good Sam RV Travel Guide & Campground Directory,* which includes some 16,000 listings in the U.S., Canada and Mexico. A version is available online, the **Good Sam Trailer Life Directory** (*www.trailerlifedirectory.com*)**.**

Here are a few of the better private campgrounds in the immediate Asheville area:

Asheville Bear Creek RV Park and Campground *(81 South Bear Creek Rd., Asheville, 828-253-0798; www.ashevillebearcreek.com)* has 25 paved pull-through and 65 back-in spaces with 30 and 50 amp service, plus tent sites, a swimming pool, showers, game room, clubhouse, small laundry, Wi-Fi and other amenities. Sites are rather tightly packed together. Nightly rates are $44 to $60, with discounts for RV club and AAA members. Monthly rates start at $650. There's is also a cottage for rent. The campground is easily accessible from I-40 or I-26 just west of Asheville, and just one exit from Biltmore Estate. Open year-round.

Indian Creek Campground *(1367 Bunches Creek Rd., Cherokee, 828-497-4361; www.indiancreekcampground.com)* is off Big Cove Road near Cherokee. Rates are $28 to $34 for RV and trailer sites with 30 amp electric and water; some with water, electric, sewer and cable TV. Tent sites also available for $25 to $30 per site. Bath house, camp store. Trout fishing available in stocked stream beside campground (tribal permit required at around $10 per day). Small cabins available for rent. Open year-round.

Lakewood RV Resort (55+) *(15 Timmie Lane, Flat Rock, 828-697-9523 or 888-819-4200; www.lakewoodrvresort.com)* is near Hendersonville off I-26 about 30 minutes south of Asheville. It is limited to adults 55 and over. Lakewood has 69 pull-through and back-in sites, as well as permanent sites. Amenities include a swimming pool, gym, rec room, clubhouse, restrooms and showers, picnic tables, small pond, Wi-Fi and cable TV. Rates $35 to 40, with discounts for weekly and monthly stays, and for RV club and AAA members. Lakewood is open year-round and also offers apartment rentals.

Rutledge Lake Travel Park *(170 Rutledge Rd., Fletcher, 828-654-7873; www.rutledgelake.com)* bills itself as a "luxury" campground on a small lake, with a few lakefront RV and trailer sites, plus pull-through and back-in sites, along with tent sites. Most sites are gravel, not paved. There's a swimming pool, rec room, park store, laundry, free cable TV and Wi-Fi throughout the campground. Rates are around $40 to $60 a night, depending on the site and time of year, with discounts for weeklong stays, RV club and AAA members and off-season. Rutledge also has cottage rentals. Open year-round.

Turkey Creek Campground *(135 Turkey Creek Rd., Almond, 828-488-8966; www.turkeycreekcampground)* is a small campground in a beautiful rural setting near Fontana Lake and the Great Smokies. Shady tent pad sites, nice bathhouse, full hook-ups with 20 to 50 amp service, some on the creek. Rates $10 per person plus $4 per vehicle, maximum $40. Closed November-March.

Caving

Western North Carolina is not one of the major caving areas of the U.S., but there are numerous limestone and other caves in the mountains. Neighboring Tennessee has more than 8,000 caves, more than any other state. Bull Cave, White Oak Sinks and Gregory Cave are in Cades Cove area of the Smokies. Altogether the national park has 17 caves, plus two old mining shafts.

As of spring 2013, caves in the Great Smokies and in Pisgah and Nantahala national forests are closed due to the presence of white-nose syndrome in bats, to avoid spreading it further.

The condition, named for a fungus around the muzzles and on the wings of hibernating bats, has killed millions of bats in the U.S., most in the Northeast and Southeast. That's serious, because bats help control noxious insects such as mosquitoes. A colony of 100 bats can consume up to 600 million insects in a single year.

River & Earth Adventures in Boone *(1655 Hwy. 105, Boone, 866-411-7238 or 828-355-9797; www.raftcavehike.com)* offers trips to Worley's Cave in East Tennessee and to other limestone caves for around $45-$75 per person, depending on the size of the group. **High Mountain Expeditions** *(3149 Tynecastle Hwy., Banner Elk, 828-898-9786 or 800-262-9036; www.highmountainexpeditions.com)* also has trips to Worley's Cave for around $75.

The only commercial cave in WNC is **Linville Caverns** *(19929 U.S. Hwy. 221, Marion, 828-756-4171 or 00-419-0540; www.linvillecaverns.com; open daily at 9 am Mar.-Nov. with varying closing times, open weekends only Dec.-Feb., adults $8, seniors over 62 $7, children 5-12 $6)* near Linville Falls about 75 minutes from Asheville. Directions from Asheville: Take I-40 East to Exit 72 (Old Fort), staying straight off exit ramp onto U.S. Hwy. 70 East for about 12 miles. Turn left at intersection with U.S. Hwy. 221 and go north for 18 miles. The caverns entrance is on left. It is also accessible via the Blue Ridge Parkway at Milepost 317 -- turn left onto US Hwy. 221 South for 4 miles. Open since 1937, Linville Caverns inside Humpback Mountains offers 35-minute guided tours.

The caverns have limestone stalactite and stalagmite formations and an underground stream. Temperature in the cave is a constant 52 degrees F. year-round. Most of the cave is handicap-accessible. Flash photography is permitted. White-nose syndrome disease has been found in a few bats in the cave, but as of this writing it remains open to the public.

Fishing

Western North Carolina has around 4,000 miles of trout streams with rainbow, brown and the native brook trout (locally called specks or speckled trout), and more than a dozen lakes (all man-made) with fishing for various kinds of bass, bluegill, crappie, walleye and other freshwater fish.

WNC has at least seven different kinds of trout stream and reservoir designations, ranging from stocked streams where there is creel limit of seven but no size limit or bait or lure restrictions to catch-and-release only streams restricted to single-hook artificial flies or lures.

Some streams are open year-round, while others are closed in March to early April. Check with the **North Carolina Wildlife Resource Commission** (www.ncwildlife.org) and look for diamond-shaped signs that describe the type of fishing allowed.

Trout in some streams are rare as hens' teeth, while other streams have trout loads of 4,000 or more trout per mile. Every angler will have an opinion on the best trout streams, but here are some considered by many as the best: **Bradley Fork, Forney Creek, Cataloochee Creek, Deep Creek** and **Hazel Creek**, all in the Great Smokies; **Nantahala River** (especially the lower reaches) in the Nantahala National Forest; **Davidson River** in the Pisgah National Forest near Brevard; **South Mills River,** also in Transylvania County; **Tuckasegee River** in Jackson County; and **Big Snowbird Creek** in Graham County. The headwaters of this creek are good for native brook trout.

In general for native brookies you'll need to hike to colder, purer streams at higher elevations. Once abundant here, they were almost wiped out by the money-hungry lumber company operators that clear cut thousands of square miles of the mountains in the late 19th and early 20th centuries. Brook trout are small, rarely over 8 inches in length and a half pound in weight, but they are considered even better eating than rainbow (which can weigh up to 6 pounds here) and brown (which go up to 4 pounds).

For lake fishing, most would agree **Fontana**, **Santeetlah** and **James** are top choices. Note, however, that the best bass fishing in North Carolina is at lakes in the central part of the state, not in WNC.

Except on your own private land, or on the Cherokee Indian Reservation, where you'll need a tribal permit, anyone 16 and over must have a state fishing license to fish in North Carolina waters. For trout and other fishing consider a North Carolina comprehensive inland fishing license.

You can order a North Carolina inland fishing license online from the North Carolina Wildlife Resources Commission *(888-248-6834, www.ncwildlife.org)*, or you can buy one from fishing shops or from wildlife agents. A 10-day nonresident inland fishing license is $10, and an annual fishing license is $20, or $35 if you want to include coastal fishing. Licenses for North Carolina residents cost $5 for a 10-day inland fishing license and $20 for an annual license good statewide including coastal fishing. If you're 65 or over and a North Carolina resident, you'll enjoy a real bargain – a lifetime comprehensive coastal and inland fishing license plus comprehensive hunting license good for the lifetime of the license holder for just a one-time fee of $30.

An excellent website on Western North Carolina fly fishing is www.flyfishingnc.com, which has fishing reports and listings of dozens of fishing guides and outfitters in Western North Carolina.

Gem Mining

Western North Carolina is rich in minerals and gems, especially in the Cowee Valley near Franklin and the area around Spruce Pine. Most of the precious and semi-precious stones – rubies, sapphires, emeralds, opals, garnets, kyanite crystals and others -- found here have only sentimental value, although occasionally a large and truly valuable sapphire, emerald or other gem is found. For example, in 2009 a 65-carat emerald was found on a farm in the rural community of Hiddenite, about 50 miles northwest of Charlotte. It is said to be worth several hundred thousand dollars.

Gold was mined commercially for a time in the region. According to experts at N.C. State University, North Carolina was the nation's only gold-producing state from 1803 until 1828 and continued as a leading producer until 1848 when gold was discovered in California. In the 19th century, although most of the gold mines were in the Piedmont around Charlotte, there were small gold mines in Ashe, Buncombe, Cherokee, Clay, Henderson, Jackson, Transylvania and Watauga counties in Western North Carolina. You're unlikely to find more than a few flakes, but you can pan for gold in privately owned mountain streams with the permission of the owner (it's illegal in national park streams but may be permitted in national forests). It is said that the best places to find gold in streams is where they begin to widen or change in velocity, such as along the insides of bends or in slow-water areas below rapids. Gold also accumulates in crevices and potholes in rock under the streams.

However, let's face it: Some of the commercial gem and gold mining outfits here, especially those that seed their buckets so you are "guaranteed" to find a gem or gold, are little more than tourist traps. You pay an admission fee, buy buckets of dirt often seeded with non-local stones, wash them in flume with a sieve and then get hustled to have your "find" mounted as a souvenir.

For a better experience, start with a visit to one of the leading gem and mineral museums in the region (most are free or have modest entry fees) so that you will know something about the type and quality of gems and minerals found in the area. Then, if you want to try your hand, go to one of the better gem mining operations. Kids especially will find them a lot of fun, and you might find a stone that you'll want to have set, not for its monetary value but for its memory value.

You may want to join **MAGMA, the Mountain Area Gem and Mineral Association** *(www.wncrocks.com)*. The club has about 2,500 members from around the world, and standard membership is free. MAGMA members go on field trips and hold meetings in Western North Carolina and elsewhere in region. Most of these trips are digs on private land or old mines, and members do find interesting and sometimes valuable gems and minerals.

Also, see the book *Rock, Gem, and Mineral Collecting Sites in Western North Carolina* by Richard James Jacquot Jr., which provides information on more than 50 locations in the region for gem mining.

MUSEUMS
Colburn Earth Science Museum *(2 S. Pack Square, Asheville, 828-254-7162, http://colburnmuseum.wordpress.com; Tue.-Sat. 10-5, Sun. 1-5, adults $6, children, military and seniors $5, children 5 and under free),* part of the Pack Place complex in Downtown Asheville, has informative displays on gems from North Carolina and elsewhere, including more than 350 minerals found in the state. It also has exhibits on the geology of the region and the history of mining in North Carolina.

Franklin Gem and Mineral Museum *(25 Phillips St., Franklin, 828-369-7831, www.fgmm.org; Mon.-Sat. noon-4 May-Oct., Sat. noon-4, Nov.-Apr., free)* has displays of local minerals and gems from the Cowee Valley, as well as from other areas. The museum is located in the Old Macon County Jail.

Mineral and Lapidary Museum of Henderson County *(400 N. Main St., Hendersonville, 828-698-1977, www.mineralmuseum.org; Mar.-Dec. Mon.-Fri. 1-5, Sat. 10-5, Jan.-Feb. Tue.-Fri. 1-5, Sat. 10-5, free)* has collections of North Carolina and world gems and minerals, including many geodes, along with Cherokee Indian artifacts.

Museum of North Carolina Minerals *(Blue Ridge Parkway Milepost 331 at NC Hwy. 226, Spruce Pine, 828-765-9483, daily 9-5, free)* showcases some 300 gems and minerals found in the Spruce Pine area and elsewhere in North Carolina.

GEM MINING

Cherokee Ruby & Sapphire Mine *(41 Cherokee Mine Rd., Franklin, 828-349-2941; www.cherokeerubymine.com, adults $15, children 6-11 $10 including two starter buckets of dirt, additional bucks $2.50 each)* does not salt buckets with out-of-area gems. You may find rubies, sapphires and garnets.

Crabtree Emerald Mine at Emerald Village *(331 McKinney Mine Road, Spruce Pine near Little Switzerland, 828-765-6463, www.emeraldvillage.com; open daily Apr.-Oct., admission for digging in emerald mine dumps $20 per day, admission to Mining Museum $7 adults, $6 seniors and $5 students)* is owned by Mineral City Mining Company and leased to Mountain Area Gem and Mineral Association or MAGMA. This mine produced emeralds from 1895 until it closed in the 1990s. The actual mineshaft went underground several hundred feet but is now flooded under a small pond. There are some extensive dumps around the mine, piles of dirt that were excavated from the original mine. Some emeralds were overlooked in these dirt piles. Dig through the dumps at Emerald Village for $20 per day, by permit only. You can keep any emeralds you find. You can also take a mine tour, visit the Mining Museum and buy prepared buckets for $10 and up.

Mason's Ruby & Sapphire Mine *(6961 Upper Burningtown Rd., Franklin, 828-369-9742; www.masonmine.com; open daily Mar.-Nov., adults $30, children 6-11 $15 for all day, cash only)* is a mine that dates back to 1895. You dig your own dirt and wash it in one of four flumes. Native stones only.

Golf

Western North Carolina has more than 55 golf courses, if you include all country club courses, private courses at real estate developments and those at resorts where play is limited to guests only. Here we've provided detailed information only for public courses or those at resorts open for play by non-guests, with the emphasis on courses in and near Asheville.

The top private courses in WNC include **Grandfather Golf & Country Club** in Linville, designed by Ellis Maples; **Elk River Club** in Banner Elk, designed by Jack Nicklaus; **Linville Golf Club** in Linville, designed by Donald Ross; **Biltmore Forest Country Club** in Asheville, another Donald Ross design; **Wade Hampton Golf Club** in Cashiers, designed by Tom Fazio; **Linville Ridge** in Linville, designed by George Cobb; **The Cliffs at Walnut Cove** in Arden near Asheville, designed by Jack Nicklaus; **Lake Toxaway Country Club** in Lake Toxaway, designed by Chris Spence; and **Asheville Country Club** in North Asheville, designed by Donald Ross. These are all highly ranked by leading golf and business publications. If you can wangle an invitation to play any of these clubs, go for it.

Asheville Municipal Golf Course *(226 Fairway Dr., Asheville, 828-298-1867; www.ashevillenc.gov; open daily year-round, green fees including golf cart $36 during Daylight Savings Time, $31 the rest of the year)* is an 18-hole, 6,420-yard par 72 course along the Swannanoa River in East Asheville. It was designed by Donald Ross and opened in 1927. The front nine has a flat, open layout, while the back nine is wooded and hilly and is generally tougher to play. After losing money on operations of the course for several years, in late 2012 the City of Asheville reached an agreement with Pope Golf, a private golf management company in Sarasota, Fla., on a seven-year contract to manage the public course. Rates and amenities may change.

Black Mountain Golf Club *(17 Ross Dr., Black Mountain, 828-669-2710; www.blackmountaingolf.org; open daily, fees walking are $20 to $22 or $27 to $39 including cart for 18 holes depending on the day, lower rates for seniors and members)* was designed in 1929 by Donald Ross as a 9-hole course and turned into an 18-hole course in 1962. The par 71 6,215-yard public municipal course is known for its well-maintained greens and low rates, as well as its inexpensive memberships ($550 for residents and $750 for non-residents). It's also known for its 747-yard, par 6 17th hole, one of the five longest holes in the U.S. It's about 30 minutes east of Asheville.

Connestee Falls Golf Club *(98 Overlook Clubhouse Dr., Brevard, 828-885-2005; www.connesteefallsgolf.com; open year-round, rates for public are $40 May-Oct. and $30 the rest of the year)* is a 6,440-yard par 72 semi-private course open for public play year-round. It was designed by George Cobb. It's around an hour from Asheville.

Omni Grove Park Inn Golf Course *(280 Macon Ave., Asheville, 800-438-5800; www.groveparkinn.com; open year-round, golf fees including carts and taxes are $140 for 18 holes weekdays and $160 weekends mid-Apr.-mid-Nov., lower off-season, resort memberships available)*, formerly the Asheville Country Club course, was designed by Donald Ross in 1926 and restored in 2001. The 6,720-yard, par-70 resort course, set just below the hotel in North Asheville, has tree-lined fairways, challenging bunkers and bent grass greens. While tee time preferences are given to resort guests, non-guests can play here. President Barack Obama played this course while on vacation in Asheville.

Mount Mitchell Golf Club *(11484 State Hwy. 80 South - Burnsville, 828-675-5454; www.mountmitchellgolf.com; open Apr.-Nov., golf rates for the public are $49 to $80 depending on the day, with lower rates for seniors and early and late in the season, and also lower rates for guests of members)* is a public course about an hour from Asheville.

It has been ranked 4 ½ stars by *Golf Digest* and usually is considered one of the top 10 public courses in the state. The par 72 course is flat with bent grass greens and great views of the surrounding mountains. It plays to 6,495 yards from the blue tees.

Sequoyah National Golf Club *(79 Cahons Rd., Whittier, 828-497-3000, www.sequoyahnational.com; open year-round to the public and Harrah's Cherokee guests, golf rates vary but including carts are about $65 to $110 mid-Apr.-Oct. and $35 to $65 rest of the year, depending on time of play and discount cards; 90-day advance bookings start at $40)* is the course associated with Harrah's Cherokee Resort & Casino. Designed by Robert Kent Jones II and opened in 2009, Sequoyah is a par 72 course, playing to 6,600 yards, with bent grass greens and bluegrass fairways. It is a challenging course, especially for novice golfers, because it's steep with few flat areas and a lot of fairway bunkers. Mountain vistas all around.

Hiking

The Asheville area and Western North Carolina region are lucky to have thousands and thousands of miles of hiking trails. The **Great Smokies National Park, Pisgah and Nantahala national forests, the Blue Ridge Parkway, North Carolina Arboretum and Bent Creek Experimental Forest and DuPont State Park** are among the favorite areas for local hikers. Dozens of guidebooks have been written about the best trails. *See Resources section for recommendations.*

Here are some local hiking organizations that you may want to investigate, especially if you are an avid hiker.

Carolina Mountain Club *(828-738-3395,*
www.carolinamountainclub.com) was formed in 1923 by a group of outdoor enthusiasts in Asheville. It is one of the most active clubs in the nation with a membership of more than 900. CMC has at least three hikes each week: two all-day hikes and a half-day hike. Membership costs $20 for an individual or $30 for a family. The club's website provides excellent information on hiking trails, frequent hiking reports and opportunities to join group treks or to participate in trail maintenance work. You can participate in some of the club's hikes even before becoming a member.

Asheville Amblers Walking Club *(www.amblers.homestead.com)*, a part of the German-inspired American Volkssport Association, has around 200 members. They have relatively short hikes or walks and then often meet for a meal and perhaps a *bier.*

Asheville Hiking Group *(www.meetup.com/asheville-hiking),* founded in 2008, offers a couple of dozen hikes a month.

Great Smoky Mountains 900-Miler Club *(www.900miler.com)* is an elite club for those who have hiked all 900 miles of trails in the Smokies. Currently there are around 375 members.

Horseback Riding

Western North Carolina is one of the best places in the East for horseback riding. The area has many rent-a-horse **stables.** If you have your own horse there are horse camps in several areas. The **Great Smoky Mountains National Park** has five horse camps and about 550 miles of trails open to horses. The **Pisgah and Nantahala national forests** have many old logging roads and bridal trails for horseback riding. The **Tsali Recreation Area** near Fontana Lake in the Nantahala National Forest is an excellent riding area with 18 miles of bridal trails, though you have to share the trails with mountain bikers. In the Pisgah National Forest the 12-mile **Mills River Trail** is a popular riding trail. Many of the 80 miles trails in **DuPont State Forest,** including some that go by waterfalls, are open to horses. You can even go horseback riding at the **Biltmore Estate.**

Horse shows are put on regularly at the **WNC Agricultural Center** *(1301 Fanning Bridge Road, Fletcher, 828-687-1414;* *www.wncagcenter.org)* across from the Asheville Regional Airport. The town of **Tryon** is known for its horse shows and for the **Block House Steeplechase** *(www.blockhouseraces.com),* a social as well as equestrian event that has been held annually in April since 1947.

Here are a few of the riding options in and around Asheville:

Biltmore Equestrian Center *(Biltmore Estate, Asheville, 828-225-1454 or 800-411-3812; www.biltmore.com)* has about 80 miles of riding trails. You can bring your own horse and ride on your own (a day ride pass is $25 plus regular estate admission, and an annual equestrian pass including estate admission is $220 for adults and $87 for youth 6-16,) or take a guided trail ride using Biltmore horses. Biltmore also offers lessons, riding clinics, summer youth camps, horse boarding and dressage and endurance events.

Cedar Creek Stables *(542 Cedar Creek Rd., Lake Lure, 828-625-2811 or 877-625-6773; www.cedarcreekstables.com)* has guided trail rides from $35 to $65 per person. Weight limit 240 to 260 pounds. For young riders 8 and under there's a pony ride for $10. Cedar Creek Stables also operates a gem mine.

Pisgah View Ranch *(70 Pisgah View Ranch Rd., Candler, 828-667-9100 or 866-252-8361; www.pisgahviewranch.net)* is a 2,000-acre "dude ranch" in the same local family since 1790. It primarily offers vacation packages that include lodging in cabins and cottages, meals and a variety of activities including horseback riding. However, non-guests can ride horses on an extensive network of private trails, with 24-hour advance reservations. One-hour group rides are $40 and two-hour rides are $75. Higher rates for private rides and lessons. Pisgah View Ranch is located off Pisgah Highway about 30 minutes west of Asheville.

Sandy Bottom Trail Rides *(1459 Caney Fork Rd., Marshall, 828-649-3464 or 800-959-3513; www.sandybottomtrailrides.net)* has one- to four-hour guided trail rides for $40 to $150 on a remote ranch in Madison County. Longer rides include a stop at a mine to look for garnets.

Smokemont Riding Stable *(135 Smokemont Riding Stable Rd., Cherokee, 828-497-2373; www.smokemontridingstable.com)* is a concessionaire in the Great Smoky Mountains National Park, near the Smokemont Campground, open late March through October. Rides of one to four hours in the park cost $30 to $100. Weight limit 225 pounds. Wagon rides also are available for $10 per person.

Smoky Mountain Trail Rides and Bison Farm *(1959 Walnut Creek Rd., Marshall, 828-768-9339; www.smokymountaintrailrides.com)* offers one-hour rides for $35 and two-hour rides for $60. Longer rides are available. Also at the site in Madison County is a farm with buffaloes.

Hot Air Ballooning

Balloons Over Asheville *(Grove Arcade, 1 Page Ave., #322, Downtown Asheville, 828-545-2329, www.balloonsoverasheville.com)* offers group rides from $99 per person and private rides for $599.

The balloons generally leave from the Candler area – you'll be notified by email of the time and place to meet.

Go up a mile high and experience Asheville and the nearby mountains from the sky with **Asheville Hot Air Balloons** (*909 Smoky Park Hwy., Candler, 828-667-9943, www.ashevillehotairballoons.com*). Sunrise balloon flights -- winds are usually calmer at daybreak than at other times -- last about an hour, and the whole ballooning process takes about 2 to 3 hours. Cost for a shared flight is around $235 per person. Private flights for a couple are more expensive, around $600.

Rock Climbing

Asheville is not exactly a mecca for rock climbers, but there are enough places to keep you occupied on weekends. Here are some of the more popular spots for climbing:

Linville Gorge *(nearest town is Morganton)* is a 14-mile, 2,000-foot-deep gneissic gorge in the Pisgah National Forest with dozens of climbing routes from single- to multi-pitch. **Table Rock** *(off NC Route 183 and Ginger Cake Rd.)* in the Linville Gorge is one of the most popular climbing areas in the gorge, with several rock faces and traditional climbing of mostly moderate difficulty.

Looking Glass Rock *(near Brevard, of U.S. Hwy. 276 and Fish Hatchery Rd.)* is a white granite cone with mostly traditional climbing.

Rumbling Bald *(near Lake Lure, off Boys Camp Rd.)* has boulder, traditional and sport climbing. It is especially well known for its bouldering.

Shiprock Mountain *(near Blowing Rock, accessible from the Blue Ridge Parkway at Milepost 303)* has climbing for those of all skill levels.

Snake Den *(near Barnardsville, off Dillingham Rd. at the end of a Forest Service dirt road in Pisgah National Forest)* is a small rock outcropping about 150 feet high.

Whiteside Mountain *(near Highlands -- from U.S. Hwy. 64 between Highlands and Cashiers follow Whiteside Mountain Rd., then follow signs to parking area and trailhead)* has a large wall with many pitches.

A couple of local climbing **guidebooks,** including *Selected Climbs in North Carolina* by Yon Lambert and Harrison Shull, and *Rumbling Bald Bouldering Guide* by Chris Dorrity, will be helpful. *See Resources section.*

ClimbMax Climbing *(43 Wall St., Asheville, 828-252-9996; www.climbmaxnc.com)* is the region's leading climbing store. It has an **indoor climbing center** and also offers guided local, national and international climbs, classes for those of all ages and skill levels, summer climbing camps and other activities. Owner Stuart Cowles is an expert guide who has been involved with climbing for more than 25 years.

Appalachian Mountain Institute *(21 Cherry Ridge Rd., Pisgah Forest, 828-553-6323; www.appalachianmountaininstitute.com)* offers climbing instruction and guided trips for climbers of all skill levels. Also offered are guided ice climbing trips.

River Rafting, Kayaking and Canoeing

In 2006, *Outside Magazine* named Asheville the number one white water town in the country, and the region is afloat with rafting companies.

The granddaddy of them all is **Nantahala Outdoor Center** *(Nantahala Outdoor Center, 13077 U.S. Hwy. 19 West, Bryson City, 888-905-7238 or 828-488-2176; www.noc.com)*.

NOC offers rafting on seven rivers in the region, including the Nantahala, Oconee, French Broad, Pigeon, Cheoah, Nolichucky and Chattooga. It also offers river float trips, lake kayaking, mountain biking, ziplining, jet boat rides, wilderness survival schools, hiking and other activities. NOC's rafting trips leave from several different locations, but NOC's 500-acre main campus in the Nantahala Gorge near Bryson City has lodging, restaurants, shops and rental gear. NOC also has a location in Gatlinburg, Tenn.

Among other rafting, canoeing, kayaking and tubing outfitters and providers in the Asheville area are **1-866-USA-RAFT** *(13490 U.S. Hwy. 25/70, Marshall, 866-872-7238; www.myusaraft.com)*; **Asheville Adventure Rentals** *(704 Riverside Dr., Asheville, 828-505-7371; www.ashevilleadventurerentals.com)*; **Asheville Outdoor Center** *(521 Amboy Road Asheville, 828-232-1970 or 800-849-1970; www.ashevilleoutdoorcenter.com)*; **French Broad Rafting Expeditions** *(9800 U.S. Hwy. 25/70 Bypass, Marshall, 828-649-0486 or 800-570-7238; www.frenchbroadrafting.com)*; **Huck Finn Rafting** *(158 Bridge St., Hot Springs, 800-303-7238; www.huckfinnrafting.com)*; (**Wildwater Adventure Centers** *(10345 Hwy. 19 West, Bryson City, 866-319-8870; www.wildwaterrafting.com)*.

River rafting rates vary according to the outfitter, river, length of trip and season, but expect to pay $45 to $80 for a half-day trip and $65 to $150 for a full-day, guided trip. Family-friendly rafting trips generally have a 7- to 8 year-old and 60-or 70-pound minimums, while more adventuresome white water trips typically have 13- to 16-year-old minimums.

Scenic Drives

Part of the fun of exploring the Asheville area and Western North Carolina region is striking out on your own. You'll find many rural roads and byways with a quiet beauty. To help you get started, here are some of the best scenic drives in the region, but don't limit yourself to these popular routes. Remember, many of these routes are narrow and curvy mountain roads. Most of the time, it will take you longer than you expect to drive these roads, especially if you stop along the way to enjoy the views, as you should.

Blue Ridge Parkway For mile-high views and dramatic mountain scenery, a drive on the parkway tops any other route. Especially scenic is the section from **Asheville south past Mt. Pisgah to the terminus of the parkway at Cherokee.** This is around 85 miles, depending on where in Asheville you enter the parkway. Plan on 2 ½ hours, plus stops.

Another highly scenic, high-elevation section is from **Asheville north to the Blowing Rock/Boone area**, a distance of about 95 miles. Expect this drive to take close to 3 hours, plus stops.

Cades Cove Loop, Great Smokies This 11-mile, one-way loop road circles **Cades Cove** on Tennessee side of the **Great Smoky Mountains National Park.** You'll pass a number of preserved old houses, barns, churches, schools and a working gristmill. Along the road and in the broad fields of the valley, you'll likely see deer, wild turkeys and, often, black bears. Although the loop is relatively short allow at least two to three hours to tour Cades Cove, longer if you walk some of the area's trails. Traffic is heavy during the tourist season in summer and fall and on weekends year-round. Some 2 million people visit Cades Cove each year. A visitor center (open daily), restrooms, and the Cable Mill historic area are located half way around the loop road. Numerous hiking trails originate in the cove, most with backcountry campsites, and there also is a large developed campground and picnic area near the start of the loop. Only bicycle and foot traffic are allowed on the loop road until 10 am every Saturday and Wednesday morning from early May until late September. Otherwise the road is open to motor vehicles from sunrise until sunset daily, weather permitting.

Cataloochee Valley, Great Smokies From Asheville take I-40 West to Exit 20. Go 0.2 miles on U.S. Hwy. 276. Turn right onto **Cove Creek Road** and follow the signs about 11 miles into the Cataloochee Valley in the **Great Smoky Mountains National Park.** The first 1.5 miles of Cove Creek Road are paved; the remainder are hard packed dirt. This narrow route, mostly one-lane, is not recommended for large RVs. Bear right for an extraordinary drive past old homesteads, a school, church and barn that were here when the park opened in the early 1930s. These buildings have been preserved as they were in the early 20th century. Surrounded by 6000-foot peaks, the Cataloochee Valley was one of the largest settlements in what is now the Smokies. Some 1,200 people lived here before the coming of the park. In Cataloochee you also are likely to see elk, deer, wild turkeys and possibly black bears. From Asheville, the roundtrip mileage is around 80 miles and requires at least two hours, plus stops. Bring a picnic and spend the day. Several hiking trails with primitive campsites begin in Cataloochee, and there's a popular developed campground and horse camp (advanced reservations required for both).

Cherohala Skyway connects the **Cherokee National Forest** in Tennessee with the **Nantahala National Forest** in North Carolina, so you can guess where the name came from. Begin the Skyway drive (also known as NC Route 143) at **Santeetlah Gap** near **Robbinsville** in Graham County and the **Joyce Kilmer Memorial Forest.**

It winds its way westward along mountain ridges, with a number of overlooks with beautiful views. The Skyway in North Carolina is around 45 miles in length and takes around 1 ½ hour. If you like, you can continue your drive in Tennessee. Tractor-trailer trucks are prohibited on the Cherohala Skyway, and it is not recommended for large RVs.

Forest Heritage National Scenic Byway A short, 17-mile (about 35 minutes without stops) section of this Scenic Byway follows U.S. Highway 276 between the town of **Brevard** (junction of U.S. Highways 280 and 64) and the **Blue Ridge Parkway** at Milepost 412. The route passes the **Cradle of Forestry,** home of the first forestry school in America, the **Davidson River** and the **Pink Beds** picnic area. Just off this route is the **Pisgah Wildlife Education Center and Trout Hatchery.** You can extend this drive to the full 79-mile route, which with stops takes essentially a full day, by adding the section from Brevard to Rosman on U.S. 64, then Balsam Grove, Sunburst, Lake Logan and connect back with U.S. 276 near Waynesville.

General Store Drive Start this drive in **Cranberry** in Avery County and follow NC Route 194 through the Elk River Valley to **Banner Elk.** The road then descends into the Watauga River Valley and passes through **Valle Crucis**, home to the original **Mast General Store,** one of the most authentic of old general stores in the mountains, and the 19th century **Mast Farm Inn.** The route ends in the Watauga County community of Vilas at the intersection of N.C. 194 and U.S. Highways 321/421 north of **Boone.** The drive is about 17 miles in length and takes from 45 minutes to an hour.

Interstate 26 from Mars Hill to Tennessee State Line You don't usually think of an interstate as a scenic drive, but this 9-mile section of I-26 from around Exit 3 at Mars Hill through Madison County to the Tennessee line offers beautiful mountain vistas. You get an even better view coming from Tennessee toward Asheville. You can do the out-and-back in about half an hour, plus stops. The **North Carolina Welcome Center** has an overlook with views of **Mt. Mitchell, Grandfather Mountain** and the **Blue Ridge Parkway.** Near the Welcome Center is the highest point on any interstate in North Carolina, Buckner Gap at around 5,000 feet. The **Appalachian Trail** runs *under* the I-26 highway at the North Carolina-Tennessee line.

Nantahala River and Gorge Drive The 7-mile river drive on U.S. Highway 74 runs beside the **Nantahala River** through the **Nantahala Gorge.** The river part of the drive is between the communities of **Nantahala** and **Wessner.** In the warmer times of year, you'll see many rafters on the river, and even in cold weather you may see canoes and kayaks.

You may also spot the **Great Smoky Mountain Railroad** train, which snakes through the gorge on a route that begins in **Bryson City.** If you wish to drive the entire Nantahala Gorge, it runs about 43 miles between the town of **Marble** near **Murphy** to **Whittier** near **Cherokee** and takes about 1½ hours to drive, without stops.

Newfound Gap Road Through Great Smokies U.S. Highway 441, also known as Newfound Gap Road, is the only east-west main road through the Great Smoky Mountains National Park. Even though it can be crowded with cars, especially on summer and fall weekends, it's a beautiful drive with scenery that changes dramatically depending on elevation. As it often said, driving this 33-mile road is like driving from the Upper South to Canada in less than an hour. The highest elevation is at the North Carolina-Tennessee line at **Newfound Gap,** and a 7-mile spur road to **Clingmans Dome** takes you to the highest elevation peak in the Smokies, at 6,642 feet. Newfound Gap Road was closed to through traffic for several months in early 2013 due to a slide after heavy rains, and it's sometimes closed in winter due to snow and ice.

Pisgah Highway This route combines rural landscapes with a curvy mountain drive through heavy forest and ends at the Blue Ridge Parkway near Mt. Pisgah. Begin at the intersection of NC Highway 151/Pisgah Highway at U.S. Highway 19/23 in Candler, at what is locally known as Boone's Corner. Drive 12 miles on the Pisgah Highway, past many small farms and rural homes in the **South Hominy community.** At around the 7-mile point you'll enter a heavily forested area and the road turns steep, with many sharp curves and switchbacks. Avoid it if your passengers easily get carsick. The **Stoney Point Park** picnic area on the left at around mile 7 is claimed by some to be haunted. The Pisgah Highway then enters the Pisgah National Forest and ends at Milepost 405 on the parkway, about 3 miles from Mt. Pisgah.

Tail of the Dragon, near Robbinsville Definitions of the start and end of this extraordinarily winding and curvy drive on U.S. Highway 129 vary, but we say it begins in North Carolina at **Fugitive Bridge,** from which Harrison Ford jumped in the 1993 movie *The Fugitive*. The Dragon ends 14 miles ahead across the mountain in Tennessee at the **Tabcat Creek Bridge.** The Tail has more than 350 curves and switchbacks. It has become a popular drive for motorcyclists and sports car enthusiasts – expect at least 1,000 vehicles a day on the road in season. The speed limit on The Tail has been reduced to 30 mph, so figure it will take you at least 30 minutes to drive one-way. There are few crossroads or pullouts, so keep your eye on the road.

Whitewater Falls Byway This short (9-mile), scenic drive begins at the intersection of U.S. Highway 64 and NC 281 in Sapphire and passes several waterfalls. Follow NC 281 through Nantahala National Forest to reach the entrance to **Whitewater Falls Scenic Area** about 8.5 miles from Sapphire. An overlook for this 411-foot waterfall, the highest in the East, is a short stroll from the parking area. Drive time is around 20 minutes, without stopping to visit any waterfalls.

Mountain Waters Scenic Byway begins in Highlands and follows U.S. Highway 64 and NC Route 28, Old Highway 64, State Road 1310 and U.S. Highway 19, first going through the **Cullasaja Gorge** in the **Nantahala National Forest,** past several waterfalls including **Bridal Veil Falls** and **Dry Falls** to Franklin, then climbing to **Wayah Gap** passing **Nantahala River** and **Nantahala Lake** and ending at **Fontana Lake.** A short side trip to nearby **Wayah Bald** is worth it for its display of flame azaleas in late spring to early summer. The total route is about 61 miles and requires at least two hours, not including stops and detours.

Touring the Western North Carolina Backroads by Carolyn Sakaowski is the unmatched, and probably unmatchable, guide to drives in the region. It was originally published in 1995 and is now in its third edition. Note that it does not include drives in the Smokies or on the Blue Ridge Parkway. *(See Resources section of this guide.)*

Running

Running in Asheville is no cakewalk, due to the hilly and mountainous nature of the terrain. Many roads and streets don't have sidewalks, much less jogging and walking trails.

Still, there are many runners in Asheville, and most visitors find a good place to jog.

Many hiking trails are also good for running. In fact, a local writer, Trish Brown, has authored *Asheville Trail Running,* a guide to running on trails around Asheville. *See Resources section.* Many of the best running trails near Asheville are in **Bent Creek Experimental Forest** and the **North Carolina Arboretum** just southwest of Asheville, and these are covered extensively in Brown's book. One of her easy running trails is the **"Obama Hike Out-N-Back,"** (3.48 miles), Craven Gap to Rice Knob/Ox Creek Road north of Asheville, a part of the **Mountains-to-Sea Trail.** President and First Lady Obama hiked this section in 2010. About a dozen parks in Asheville maintained by the Asheville Parks and Recreation Department have fitness walk or jog trails.

Richmond Hill Park, a 183-acre city park north of Asheville on Richmond Hill Drive off Riverside Drive, has a number of jogging trails. **Carrier Park** on Amboy Road near West Asheville has a multi-used paved track and paved and unpaved jogging and walking trails. The **French Broad River Greenway Extension,** a 2.8-mile bicycle and pedestrian trail that connects Carrier Park with **French Broad River Park** and **Hominy Creek Park** in West Asheville, has on-road and off-road sections and winds along the north bank of the French Broad River, providing views of the Biltmore Estate. The **Botanical Gardens at UNC-A** also has jogging trails.

The Asheville area hosts many 5K, 10K, half-marathon and marathon races. Asheville's running club, the **Asheville Track Club** *(www.ashevilletrackclub.org)* maintains a list of races and provides other running information.

Skateboarding

Asheville has its share of young skateboarders, but skateboarding technically is illegal on Downtown sidewalks, parks and streets.

An effort to allow skateboarding failed in a 4-3 vote by the Asheville City Council in mid-2012. Fortunately for enthusiasts, there's a state-of-the-art skateboard park in town. **Food Lion SkatePark** *(50 Cherry St. N., Asheville, 828-225-7184, www.ashevillenc.gov; daily until dark, but time of opening varies from 10 am to noon, $2 residents/$4 non-residents weekdays, $3 residents/$5 non-residents weekends and holidays)* is a 17,000 square feet concrete skateboard park just north of Downtown at Cherry and Flint streets. It has three areas: the beginner bowl, intermediate street course and an advanced vertical bowl. The Asheville Parks and Recreation Department operates it; there isn't actually a Food Lion supermarket at the site. North Carolina regulations require helmets and pads to be worn by skaters. The area has several skateboarding shops, including **Flipside Skateboards** *(88 N. Lexington Ave., Asheville, 828-254-9007, and 1712 Asheville Hwy, Hendersonville, 828-693-0900; www.flipsideboardshop.com)*.

Snow Skiing

The elevation of Asheville itself is too low for skiing, but some of the high mountains around Asheville, at higher elevations and with more natural snow, have **ski resorts.** All the resorts, most of which opened in the 1960s, have snowmaking equipment, but to be candid the snow skiing is Western North Carolina isn't usually up to the standards of New England, the Rockies and Northwest. Still, it's a lot of fun, and most of the resorts are within a short drive of Asheville.

Ski season in the mountains around Asheville typically is **mid-November or early December through late March,** but warm weather can interrupt skiing at any time, especially at the beginning and end of the season. Typically, the six ski resorts in the area get in about 100 to 125 days of skiing a year. Several of the ski areas offer snowboarding, snow tubing and ice skating. One former ski resort, **Hawksnest,** is now entirely devoted to snow tubing. In warm-weather months, some of the resorts offer golf, mountain biking, tennis, ziplining or other sports. All of the ski areas rent skis, poles and other equipment if you don't have your own.

Cross-country skiing also is possible in some high-elevation areas. Clingmans Dome Road in the Smokies, closed to vehicles winter, is one area where people come to try out their cross-country skis and snow shoes.

Here are the ski resorts in the WNC mountains:

Appalachian Ski Mountain *(940 Ski Mountain Rd., Blowing Rock, 828-295-7828 or 800-322-2373; www.appskimtn.com; open Dec.-late Mar., weather permitting, day ski tickets 9-5 $56 weekends, $37 weekdays, day/night tickets 9 am-midnight $65 weekends, $45 weekdays, reduced rates for seniors, children under 12 and in late Mar., season passes available)* near Boone has been operating since the winter of 1962. The resort is at elevations of 3,635 to 4,000 feet, a vertical drop of 365 feet. It has 12 slopes, with the longest run about one-half mile. There are three chairlifts and two conveyor and one tow lifts. Beside snow skiing, App Mountain offers snowboarding, ice skating and rentals of all kinds. Chalets near the slopes are offered for rent, and there's a 46,000 square feet clubhouse with shops, restaurants, fireplaces and other amenities.

Beech Mountain *(1007 Beech Mountain Pkwy., Beech Mountain, 828-387-2011 or 800-438-2093; www.beechmountainresort.com; open mid-Nov.-late Mar., full-day or evening weekend ski/lift tickets are $63 for adults, $45 for seniors 65-69 and children under 13, weekday tickets are $35 and $30, lower prices for half-day tickets, and seniors 70 and over ski free anytime)* is the highest ski resort in the East, at up to 5,506 feet, with a vertical drop of 830 feet. It has seven lifts and a total of 16 ski trails, with an extensive array of snowmaking equipment in all ski areas. Opened in 1967, Beech also offers equipment rentals, several restaurants, two terrain parks for snow boarding and an ice-skating rink. In warm weather, Beech offers mountain biking. Rental chalets and condos are near the slopes. Special bargain alert: Geezers and geezerettes 70 and better ski free.

Cataloochee Ski Area *(1080 Ski Lodge Rd., Maggie Valley, 828-926-0285 or 800-768-0285; www.cataloochee.com; open early Nov.-late Mar., weekend tickets are $50 to $79 for adults and $37 to $59 for children, with reduced rates early and late in the season, season passes available)* was the first ski area to open in Western North Carolina back in the early 1960s. It is at elevations of up to 5,400 feet, with a vertical drop of 730 feet. Cataloochee has 17 slopes, the longest of which is 3,500 feet, with three chair and two conveyor lifts. Rentals are available and the ski area has two different types of snowmaking equipment. The ski area is about 40 minutes from Asheville, depending on weather and road conditions.

Sapphire Valley Ski Area *(127 Cherokee Trail, Sapphire Valley, 828-743-7663; www.skisapphirevalley.com; full-day ski/lift tickets any day of the week are $36 adults and $16 for children 12 and under, lower rates for those staying on-site)* is the smallest ski area in the region, with just two slopes, two lifts, about 8 acres of ski area and a vertical drop of just 200 feet; however, it also has the lowest rates.

While Sapphire Valley is a timeshare resort, its ski area is open the public. There is a ski rental shop and snowboarding. A separate 700-feet frozen course for snow/ice tubing is open to the public for $24 for a 1¾ -hour session.

Sugar Mountain Resort *(1009 Sugar Mountain Dr., Sugar Mountain, 828-898-4521 or 800-784-2768; www.skisugar.com; open Nov.-Mar., full-day ski/lift tickets weekends $68 adults, $45 children under 12, weekdays $41 and $32; lower rates for half-days and twilight, for North Carolina and Tennessee college students and for March)* opened in 1969 and now has 20 slopes and trails – the longest 1½ miles – on 115 acres, five chairlifts and two surface lifts. Elevation is 4,100 to 5,300 feet, a vertical drop of 1,200 feet. Sugar also has snow tubing on a 700-foot course and a 10,000 square foot outdoor ice skating rink. Equipment rentals, shops, bar and cafeteria food service are in the base lodge. There are chalets and condos for rent at the slopes, along with a number of other rentals and motels nearby.

Wolf Ridge Ski Resort *(578 Valley View Circle, Mars Hill, 828-689-4111 or 800-817-4117; http://www.skiwolfridgenc.com; open Dec.-mid-Mar., weekend ski/lift rate for adults 18-64 is $54 and $49 for students 9-18, weekdays $39 and $34, seniors 65 and over ski free, reduced rates for twilight skiing, half-days and consecutive days)* is the closest ski resort to Asheville, around half an hour depending on weather conditions. The resort is 5 miles off Exit 3 of I-26. It has 21 ski runs, four chair lifts and one surface lift.

There are two ski lodges, one at the base and one at the top of the mountain. Both have rental equipment, gift shops and food service. The elevation ranges from 4,000 to 4,700 feet, with 72 acres of ski area and a vertical drop of 700 feet. Wolf has two snow tubing courses near the ski resort, each 800 feet long; a two-hour session is $35. A few townhouse rentals are available at the slopes. Wolf Ridge is in Madison County, one of North Carolina's few remaining dry countries where alcohol can't be sold. Another big bargain for seniors: Those 65 and over ski free anytime.

Hawksnest *(1058 Skyland Dr., Seven Devils, 828-963-6561 or 800-822-4295; www.hawksnesttubing.com; open Nov.-Apr., sessions are 1 ¾ hours; rates are $30 per session weekends and $25 weekdays, and $32 for two sessions Mon.-Thu., discounts for military and in Mar. and Apr.),* formerly a ski resort, is now entirely devoted to snow tubing and claims to be the largest snow tubing park in the East, with 20 lanes from 400 to 1,000 feet in length and two conveyor lifts.

Hawksnest also has a zipline (www.hawksnestzipline.com) that operates year-round, even when it's snowing, with 19 ziplines and what it says are 4 miles of lines over 200 feet high with speeds of up to 50 mph. Two zip tours are available, one with 10 and one with 9 ziplines, with per-person rates of $70 to $85. The Eagle Tour with 9 lines and a swinging bridge is limited to those at least 10 years old, weighing no more than 220 pounds and with a waist line of 40 inches or less.

If you're a frequent skier and are in the area over the winter, check out the **Gold Card** season pass from the **North Carolina Ski Areas Association** *(828-898-4521, www.goskinc.com)*. The Gold Card allows unlimited skiing and snowboarding at all six North Carolina ski areas for $800. However, only a small number of these passes, about 100, are available each year. The cards go on sale to the public in early August; previous cardholders can buy cards in July.

Summer Camps

Summer camps for boys and girls are a major seasonal industry in Western North Carolina. The area has more than 60 camps. Most of the camps, around 50, are in just three counties: Buncombe, Transylvania and Henderson. The camps draw more than 55,000 campers annually. The **North Carolina Youth Camp Association** *(P.O. Box 282, Black Mountain, NC 28711, 828-669-2145, www.nccamps.org)* maintains a list of camps, mostly in Western North Carolina.

Tennis

Asheville has about a dozen public tennis court facilities operated by the City of Asheville Parks and Recreation Department, with a total of 30 courts. There also are six public courts at the University of North Carolina at Asheville. The largest public facility is **Aston Park Tennis Facility** *(313 Hilliard Ave, Asheville, 828-251-4074; www.ashevillenc.gov)* near Downtown, with 12 lighted Har Tru outdoor clay courts. Fees are $5 an hour for city residents, and $7 an hour for others. Season passes are available for unlimited play ($160 for resident individuals or $200 for families; $130 for senior individuals or $160 for senior families). Reservations are encouraged, but walk-ins are accepted when possible.

The private **Asheville Racquet Club** *(828-274-3361 or 828-253-5874; www.ashevilleracquetclub.com)* has two locations, one south on Hendersonville Road and one at the Crowne Plaza Resort just west of Downtown, with a total of 46 indoor and outdoor courts.

Fees vary, but a comprehensive family membership is $120 a month, plus a one-time $250 enrollment fee. Indoor courts have fees of $30 per court per hour. Depending on availability, non-members can play for $40 per court per hour, plus a $15 guest fee.

The **Omni Grove Park Inn Resort & Spa, Country Club of Asheville, Biltmore Forest Country Club** and several apartment complexes in Asheville also have private tennis courts. Some may be open to guests. Resorts, lodges and real estate developments in the mountains around Asheville including **Highland Lake Inn** in Flat Rock, **Greystone Inn** at Lake Toxaway, **High Hampton Inn** in Cashiers, **Sapphire Valley Resort** in Sapphire, **Hound Ears Club** in Blowing Rock, **Bear Lake Reserve** in Highlands, **Yonahlossee Resort** in Boone, among others, also have tennis courts.

Waterfalls

We doubt that anyone knows for sure exactly how many waterfalls there are in Western North Carolina. The Great Smokies Park has at least 40. The Pisgah National Forest has more than 250, Nantahala National Forest has several dozen and Du Pont State Forest has at least a half dozen. Many more are on private lands.

Several guidebooks have been written to the waterfalls of the region. *(See Resources section for recommendations.)*

Here are some of the roadside waterfalls you can see from your car or with just a short walk:

Looking Glass Falls, on U.S. Highway 276 between the Blue Ridge Parkway and Brevard, is 60 feet high and easily viewed from a roadside parking area.

Dry Falls is a 75-feet high waterfall on U.S. Highway 64 west of Highlands about 3 miles from the junction with NC Route 106. It's called Dry Falls because you can walk behind it without getting wet. At least sometimes that's the case.

Soco Falls is a beautiful double waterfall (the higher of the two is 120 feet tall) just off U.S. Highway 19 between Maggie Valley and Cherokee. From the roadside parking area, it's about a 5-minute walk to the viewing platform.

Bridal Veil Falls on U.S. Highway 64 about 2.5 miles from Highlands is unusual because you can drive your car on an old road behind the falls.

Viewing these waterfalls requires a hike:

Abrams Falls is a 5-mile roundtrip hike from a trailhead on Cades Cove Loop Road in the Smokies. Although the falls is only 20 feet high, it has a huge volume of water. The pool below the falls is beautiful, but it can be dangerous to swim in, due to undertow. Several swimmers have died here.

Crabtree Falls, off Blue Ridge Parkway Milepost 339.5, requires a 2.5-mile loop hike of moderate difficulty. The area gets its name from the crab apple trees in the area. The falls are about 70 feet high.

Graveyard Fields at Blue Ridge Parkway Milepost 418 has a 4-mile loop with two accessible waterfalls, Second Falls and Upper Falls.

Hickory Nut Falls is about 400 feet high. It's accessible via an easy ¾-mile hike at Chimney Rock (admission to the park required).

Laurel Falls is a 2.6-mile roundtrip hike on a paved trail (figure two hours or more) off Little River Road on the Tennessee side of the Great Smokies. Laurel Falls is about 80 feet high.

Linville Falls is a very popular 90-feet high waterfall off Blue Ridge Parkway Milepost 316.4. There are several trails totaling about 4 miles with five different views of the falls.

Skinny Dip Falls is about a 1/2-mile fairly easy hike from Blue Ridge Parkway Milepost 417, the Looking Glass Overlook. While actual skinny dipping isn't encouraged here (it's a popular site, and there are families), there is a beautiful swimming hole with a jump-off rock and a few areas that are somewhat secluded.

Whitewater Falls, at 411 feet, is among the tallest waterfalls in the East. To get to the falls, an hour's drive from Asheville, take I-26 East to U.S. Hwy. 64. Continue on Hwy. 64 past Brevard to NC Route 281 at Sapphire and go south about 8 miles to the parking area for the falls. There's a paved 1/4-mile walkway to an upper overlook, accessible to wheelchairs and those with limited mobility. A lower overlook requires walking down (and back up) 154 wooden steps.

Wildflower Walks

The diverse habitats and differences in elevation around Asheville and in Western North Carolina contribute to the abundance of wildflowers from early spring to late fall. This short list only begins to highlight some of the flowers you'll see through the year.

Early in the spring (or even in late winter) you'll see the white blooms of several different wildflowers including **bloodroot** (the name comes from the color of the sap of the root, used by the Cherokee in baskets), **wood anemone, hepatica** and **Carolina spring beauty.**

As spring progresses and any lingering snow leaves the ground, you'll spy more colorful wildflowers including several varieties of **trilliums** (yellow, red and other colors), **firepinks** (crimson), **larkspur** (blue or purple), **columbine** (red and other colors) and **dwarf crested iris** (purple).

Later in spring and early summer come some of the showiest wildflowers, including **mountain laurel** (pinkish white), **flame azalea** (intense bright orange) and other **wild azaleas** (in a rainbow of colors) and purple, white and pink Catawba, rosebay and other **rhododendrons** in bold, wonderful profusion. Later in the summer in open fields look for the showy orange **butterfly weed** and the quietly beautiful **phlox,** of which there are nearly a dozen species in the area, ranging from spreading beds on sunny rocks to tall phlox. As summer gets long in the tooth, look for the brilliant red **cardinal flower** in boggy places and the happy yellow of **black-eyed Susan** in open fields.

Fall is just about everyone's favorite season in the mountains. Autumn brings a surprising measure of lovely wildflowers, including several species of **asters** (mostly blue or violet, including the beautiful but invasive **chicory**, a sky-blue aster that is prolific on roadsides), the bright **goldenrod** (contrary to popular opinion few people are allergic to it), the tall, gangling purplish **Joe-Pye weed** that stands higher than almost any other field plant, **bittersweet** with its orange berries (we have a native version, but the alien Asiatic bittersweet seems to be taking over) and the dwarfish **mountain ash** tree with stunning orange-red berries (not a true ash but a member of the rose family that grows only at the highest elevations).

As to where to go to see wildflowers, the better question is where can you NOT see them? Drive the **Blue Ridge Parkway** or the main or back roads in the **Great Smoky Mountains National Park,** stop frequently and walk among the native wildflowers of the season (but do NOT break the law by picking them!) More than 1,600 types of wildflower and other flower plants are in the Smokies alone. The **North Carolina Arboretum** and the **Asheville Botanical Gardens** also are great places to see flowers.

A five-day **Wildflower Pilgrimage** is held annually in late April in the Great Smoky Mountains National Park. More than140 different hikes, classes and events explore the park's unique fauna, wildflowers and natural ecology. Most programs are conducted on the trails in the park, rain or shine, while indoor classes and events are held in Mills Conference Center and Sugarlands Visitor Center in Gatlinburg, Tenn. Registration is $50 for one day and $75 for two to five. Students are $15 for the entire event, and children under 12 are free. For information, registration begins in February) or to download a program., visit www.springwildflowerpilgrimage.org.

Elk in Cataloochee in the Great Smokies, tagged so rangers can keep track of them – photo courtesy of the National Park Service

Wildlife Spotting

The **Great Smoky Mountains National Park** with more than 800 square miles of protected wilderness is without a doubt the top spot in the region for wildlife spotting, including black bear, elk and white-tailed deer.

Cades Cove and Cataloochee Valley are two top areas for seeing these large mammals. But on just about any hiking trail, riverside or country road you may stumble upon raccoons, possums, bobcats, coyotes, beavers, otters, red and gray foxes, skunks, groundhogs and red, gray, flying and fox squirrels.

Ziplining

Ziplines have become ubiquitous in forested areas around the world. The Asheville area has several ziplines, and the more popular ones average 50 to 75 admissions a day.

Asheville Treetops Adventure Park and Asheville Zipline *(1 Resort Dr., Asheville, 828-225-2921 or 877-247-5539; www.ashevilletreetopsadventurepark.com; daily spring to fall, open in winter on Wed., Fri. and Sat.; the zipline is $79, with discounts for groups, the adventure park is $49 adults and $44 youths and a combo pass to both the zipline and adventure park is $99.)*

The newest zipline in the area, and the only one within the city limits of Asheville, opened in late 2012. The zipline, on 125 acres, is just west of Downtown, across the French Broad River adjacent to the Crowne Plaza Resort. It includes 10 zipline sections, up to 1200 feet long, nine treetop platforms, three tower platforms and three sky bridges. Besides being up close and personal with trees, you'll also see views of Downtown. The zipline is part of **Asheville Treetops Adventure Park,** at the same site, which has about 50 climbing, walking, jumping, swinging and rappelling facilities. The park contains four trails to choose from with various levels of difficulty. Each trail includes 10 to 15 different challenges to complete the circuit. To participate you must be at least 10 years old and weigh 70 to 250 pounds. The Asheville company is owned by Adventure America, the largest zipline company in the Southeast. It also operates ziplines in Nantahala and Pigeon River.

French Broad Ziplines *(9800 U.S. Hwy. 25/70 Bypass, Marshall, 828-649-0486 or 800-570-7238; www.frenchbroadrafting.com)*, associated with French Broad Rafting in Marshall has 10 ziplines from 75 to 1,000 feet. Day zips are $79 and night zips are $89. Participants must be at least 10 years old, be in good health and weigh from 70 to 250 pounds.

Hawksnest *(2058 Skyland Dr., Seven Devils, 828-963-6561 or 800-822-4295; www.hawksnestzipline.com*) operates year-round, even when it's snowing, and advertises 19 zip lines and 4 miles of lines over 200 feet high with speeds of up to 50 mph. Two zip tours are available, one with 10 and one with 9 ziplines, with per-person rates of $70 to $85.

The Eagle Tour with 9 lines and a swinging bridge is limited to those at least 10 years old, weighing no more than 220 pounds and with a waist line of 40 inches or less. The Hawk Tour with 10 lines is limited to those weighing no more than 250 pounds with a waist of 40 inches or less. Formerly a ski resort, Hawksnest has now gone totally tubular (www.hawksnesttubing.com) in cold weather, with snow tubing on 20 lanes open November or December through early April, weather permitting.

Nantahala Gorge Canopy Tours *(10320 US 19 West, Bryson City, 866-319-8870; www.wildwaterrafting.com, daily Mar.-Nov, $79 with discounts for groups)* has 13 zipline sections and 8 swinging bridges on 20 acres in the Nantahala Gorge. To participate you must be at least 10 years old and weigh 70 to 250 pounds.

Navitat Canopy Adventures *(242 Poverty Branch Rd., Barnardsville, 828-6263700 or 855-628-4828; www.navitat.com; open daily late Mar.-early Nov., $99 weekends, $89 weekdays, group, military and local resident discounts available, night tours $109).* Located on 242 acres in Madison County about 25 minutes north of Downtown Asheville, Navitat offers a 3 ½-hour experience that includes 10 zip lines (the longest is 1,100 feet, though a longer mountain-top to mountain-top line is being planned), 2 bridges, 2 rappels and 3 short hikes. To participate you must be at least 10 years old and weigh between 90 and 250 pounds.

NOC Zipline Adventure Park *(888-905-7238; www.noc.com; daily year-round, $49.99)* is the newest addition to the Nantahala Outdoor Center's list of adventures. It opened in mid-2012. The zipline is located near NOC's 500-acre main campus in the Nantahala Gorge near Bryson City. It takes about 2 ½ hours to complete and includes ziplines, spider webs, sky bridges and tight ropes. Participants must weigh between 75 and 275 pounds.

Pigeon River Canopy Tours *(10320 US 19 West, Bryson City, 866-319-8870; www.wildwaterrafting.com, daily Mar.-Nov, $59 for the Pigeon River zipline and $79 for a gorge canopy tour, with discounts for groups)* has two different options, a gorge option with 12 ziplines, 4 sky bridges and a cliff perch, on 15 acres along the Pigeon River, and a shorter river option with 7 ziplines. This is operated by the same company that has ziplines in Asheville and the Nantahala Gorge. Participants must be at least 10 years old and weigh 70 to 250 pounds.

CLUBS AND VOLUNTEER ORGANIZATIONS

Getting involved in clubs and organizations in your new community is one of the best ways to meet people with mutual interests and become more integrated into the area. Here is information on some of the clubs and organizations in the Asheville area. It is by no means a comprehensive list. In nearly all cases, these groups eagerly welcome new members. Many of the groups listed also welcome volunteers.

Many of the organizations have no permanent local office address, and the contact phone may be for the current president or membership chair, which change frequently, so in a lot of cases we have included only the organization's website address.

Some of the groups are affiliated with national organizations, while others are entirely local. International and national organizations may have multiple groups in a number of towns around Western North Carolina. It would be impractical to list each location individually, so in most cases we have provided information only the Asheville group, with a website address to help you find other locations in the region.

National and international social networking organizations such as MeetUp *(www.meetup.com)* have many affiliated groups in the Asheville area. MeetUp claims it has more than 13 million members in 125,000 groups in around 200 countries. Not all MeetUp groups in the Asheville area are listed here.

Local chambers of commerce often have club listings for their area.

Athletic, Sports and Outdoor Clubs
American Singles Golf Association, Asheville Chapter
(www.singlesgolf.com) holds membership dinner meetings at various local restaurants at 5:30 pm the second Tuesday of each month, and members play golf as a group as often as they would like. Membership is open to single men and women who enjoy playing golf or who want to learn to play. The club plays at a number of area public and semi-private courses; in cold weather, the club often makes outings to warmer weather clubs in South Carolina. Membership in the Asheville chapter is $79 a year, not including meals and course fees.

Asheville Amblers Walking Club *(www.amblers.homestead.com)*, a part of the German-inspired American Volkssport Association, has around 200 members. The club has loop hikes or walks of around 3 to 5 miles, suitable for members of almost any fitness level, and then members often meet for a meal and perhaps a *bier*. Dues are $10 a year for individual membership, $15 for household membership.

Asheville Bicycle Racing Club *(www.abrc.net)*, founded in 1984, has about 100 members who participate in all forms of competitive bike racing. The three-day French Broad Cycling Classic, usually held the third weekend in July, is the club's major local race. It typically attracts more than 500 racers from around the Southeast. Annual racing club dues are $40, or $25 for students and those under 18.

Asheville Hiking Group *(www.meetup.com/asheville-hiking)*, founded in 2008, offers a couple of dozen hikes a month. Participation in hikes is free. It is part of the international social networking organization MeetUp.

Asheville Rowing Club *(www.ashevillerowing.org)* is an athletic and social club dedicated to fitness and fun through rowing. It has club rows five times a week at Lake Julian in South Asheville. Newcomers are welcome, but they should contact the club in advance. The club also puts on classes for beginners. Asheville Rowing Club has about 40 boats at its boathouse on Lake Julian, from one-person trainers to eight-person boats. Full membership is $250 a year, and members must have experience or have completed the club's learn-to-row course. A complete, multi-part learn-to-row course costs $220. Members compete in various regional and national regattas (rowing races), and the club has held an Asheville regatta.

Asheville Sports & Social Club *(828-761-1401, www.ashevillessc.com)* provides recreational sports leagues and social events for adults. Kickball, dodge ball, bowling, softball, volleyball and flag football are some of the sports played. The club also has parties, pub crawls and charitable events. ASSC says it emphasizes recreational play and doesn't take the score too seriously. Typically you'll play a minimum of eight league games over eight weeks, plus playoffs if your team qualifies, plus a preseason party and socials at a local sponsor bar after every game where you can enjoy social time with teammates and opponents. Some pickup games and events are free; others have fees, typically no more than around $50 to $75 for a league.

Asheville Table Tennis Club *(www.attcnc.com)* attracts a membership of fairly serious table tennis players, including some highly rated USATT players. However, other members are just basement recreational players, and prospective members are invited to come to a couple of evenings of play to see the level of play and to learn more about the game. Currently, play is on Tuesday and Thursday evenings at The Asheville School. Annual membership fee is $40.

Asheville Track Club *(www.ashevilletrackclub.org),* the area's largest running organization, maintains a list of races and provides other information for runners. It is an inclusive club with members of all ages and experience in running. Annual membership costs $22.50 for individuals and $32.00 for families. Among the benefits of membership are discounts of 10 to 20% at local running and outdoor stores.

Blue Ridge Bicycle Club *(P. O. Box 309, Asheville, NC 28802, www.blueridgebicycleclub.org)* is a local biking club with more than 300 members that offers around 175 rides a year, open to both members and non-members. Rides vary in length and difficulty, ranging from around 15 to 100 miles. Memberships, which include discounts at a number of local bike shops, cost $25 for individuals, $30 for families and $10 for students.

Boy Scouts of America, Daniel Boone Council *(333 West Haywood St., Asheville, 828- 254-6189, www.danielboonecouncil.org),* established in 1920, serves 14 Western North Carolina counties through five districts and hundreds of Scout packs. It has a permanent camp, Camp Daniel Boone, in Haywood County about 14 miles south of Canton, where about 4,000 local Boy Scouts attend summer camp.

Carolina Mountain Club *(828-738-3395, www.carolinamountainclub.com)* was formed in 1923 by a group of outdoor enthusiasts in Asheville. It is one of the most active hiking clubs in the nation with a membership of more than 900. CMC has at least three hikes each week: two all-day hikes and a half-day hike. Membership costs $20 for an individual or $30 for a family. The club's website provides excellent information on hiking trails, frequent hiking reports and opportunities to join group treks or to participate in trail maintenance work. You can participate in some of the club's hikes even before becoming a member.

Girl Scouts Carolinas Peaks to Piedmont *(64 W.T. Weaver Blvd., North Asheville, 828-252-4442 or 800-672-2148, www.girlscoutsp2p.org)* serves around 24,000 girls and adults with five offices in North Carolina, including Asheville.

Mountain High Hikers *(www.mountainhighhikers.org)*, though based in Young Harris, Ga., has among its nearly 200 members a number from Western North Carolina. The club, founded in 1993, is active in trail maintenance, and there are usually several hikes a week. Membership is $20 for individuals and $30 for couples. You can go on up to three club hikes before joining.

Nantahala Hiking Club *(www.nantahalahikingclub.org)*, based in Franklin, is one of 31 volunteer clubs that maintain the Appalachian Trail. The Nantahala Club maintains about 57 miles of the AT in North Carolina. The club also conducts two hikes each weekend during most of the year and has monthly meetings March through December in Franklin. Membership is $15 annually for singles or families.

Outdoor Club South *(www.meetup.com/oacs-asheville)*, which claims to be the largest outdoor club in the Southeast, has an Asheville chapter that organizes hiking, biking, camping, rock climbing and river paddling trips in Western North Carolina. It is affiliated with the social networking company MeetUp.

Pisgah Area Mountain Biking Meet-Up *(www.meetup.com/pisgah-area-mountain-biking-asheville-hendersonville-brevard)* is a networking group set up to get people together who enjoy mountain biking. It says it has about 800 participants, though many are not active.

Business Clubs and Organizations

American Association of University Women, Asheville Branch *(www.asheville-nc.aauw.net)* dates to 1915 when 16 local college grads founded what would become the Asheville branch of AAUW. Membership is open to women with at least associate or bachelor degrees. Annual dues are $73. The club usually holds monthly luncheon meetings with a speaker at the First Baptist Church on Charlotte Street in Downtown Asheville. The AAUW raises money for college scholarships for women.

American Business Women's Association, Sky-Hy Chapter of Asheville *(www.abwaskyhy.com)* has the mission of bringing together businesswomen to provide opportunities for personal and professional growth, networking and to provide college scholarships. Nationally, the group has some 60,000 members. In Asheville, monthly dinner meetings are held the second Thursday of each month from around 5:30 to 8 pm at the Crowne Plaza Resort. Cost is $25 for each dinner meeting. In addition, combined national and local dues are $125 a year.

Asheville Area Chamber of Commerce *(36 Montford Ave., Downtown Asheville, 828-258-6101, www.ashevillechamber.org)* is the leading business organization in the Asheville metro area. It has a membership of about 1,800 businesses, large and small. Among its objectives are to attract new business and industrial investment in Asheville and Buncombe County and to act as a voice for business. However, the Asheville Chamber is nonpartisan and does not endorse political candidates, operate a PAC or engage in political campaigns. Under the auspices of the Buncombe County Tourism Development Authority, which is funded to the tune of more than $6 million a year by the state-authorized 4% hotel room tax in Asheville and Buncombe County, the Asheville Chamber operates the Asheville Convention & Business Bureau *(www.exploreasheville.com and www.ashevillecvb.com)* and occupies the same building on Montford Avenue. Although it often works with government agencies, especially in economic development, the Chamber is a private organization and has no affiliation with any government. The Asheville Chamber also has no affiliation with other chambers of commerce, including the national US Chamber of Commerce. In recent years, it has taken positions on some legislative and cultural issues that are variance with – and generally more liberal than -- those of the national Chamber. For those considering a move to the area, the Asheville Chamber sells a relocation package for $19.95, available through the Chamber's website. The relocation package includes a map, an Asheville area telephone directory on DVD, a magazine on Asheville, a variety of brochures and real estate sales and rental information. Dues for Chamber membership depend on the number of employees in your business. Annual dues start at $350 for businesses with one to five local employees and range up to $1,415 for businesses with 76 to 100 employees. Large companies with more than 100 employees pay higher rates.

Asheville Toastmasters International

(www.ashevilletoastmasters.com), the oldest Toastmasters International club in the state, nearing 70 years old, helps member improve their speaking and leadership skills. There are three other Toastmasters clubs in Asheville and several others in Western North Carolina – visit www.toastmasters.org for locations and information on meetings. The Asheville club is unusual in that meetings are conducted strictly under Robert's Rule of Order, allowing members to practice these meeting procedural skills. Meetings are held weekly on Thursdays from 6:15-7:45 pm at the Small Business Center at the Enka campus of Asheville-Buncombe Technical Institute.

Speeches are a required part of the Toastmasters curriculum and are the way in which members are able to measure their progress. New members are given a manual and usually assigned a mentor. International dues are $36 every six months, plus $20 initial fee for new members; some local clubs have additional dues.

Downtown Asheville Association *(29 Haywood St., Downtown Asheville, 828-251-9973, www.ashevilledowntown.org)*, established in 1987, is dedicated to the preservation and improvement of Asheville's central business district. DAA also sponsors a number of Downtown events including Downtown After 5 and the Holiday Parade. Annual membership dues range from $25 for individuals and $35 for families (these members need not be involved in Downtown businesses) to $350 for businesses with 20 or more employees.

River Arts District Association *(www.riverartsdistrict.com)* is open to those who rent and maintain an art or crafts studio in the River Arts District. Associate membership is open to those who own a business or building in the district. Members are listed in a RADA brochure, attend meetings and may participate in semi-annual RAD Studio Strolls. RAD's website, www.riverartsdistrict.com, promotes individual members as well as the district at large. Regular membership is $75 a year; associate status is $100. Additionally, both classes of members pay 15% of their gross sales receipts (less sales tax) that occur during the Studio Strolls to RADA as a commission.

Young Professionals of Asheville *(36 Montford Ave., Downtown Asheville, www.ypasheville.org)*, affiliated with the Asheville Chamber of Commerce and similar to the Jaycees, is a networking organization for younger business and professional people age 21-40. The YPA has monthly social meetings, a holiday party and other events. Annual dues are $20.

Vibrant Asheville Business *(www.meetup.com/vibrantashevillebusiness)* is a MeetUp group for Asheville business people. The group's motto is "Networking opens online but closes in person."

West Asheville Business Association *(www.west-asheville.com)*, founded in 1950, is an organization for businesses located in Asheville west of the French Broad River. Dues are $50.

Civic, Patriotic and Service Clubs

American Legion *(www.legion.org)*, chartered in 1919, is the country's largest veterans organization.

Membership is open to current U.S. armed forces members and to veterans of World War I, World War II, Korea, Vietnam, Lebanon/Grenada, Panama, the Gulf War and today's so-called "War on Terrorism." Members don't necessarily have to have been in a war campaign but only to have served during that period. The Legion has various patriotic and veterans support programs and also sponsors American Legion Baseball leagues. The American Legion has about 25 posts in Western North Carolina, including three in Asheville (Posts 002, 070 and 526). For information on local posts, see the North Carolina state Legion website *(www.nclegion.org)*. The state has about 40,000 Legion members. National membership is $25 a year. Most posts also have local membership dues.

Daughters of the American Revolution *(http://www.ncdar.org)*, open to women who can prove lineal descent from "an ancestor who aided in achieving American independence." The DAR, whose current mission involves patriotic education and service, is organized by state. North Carolina has more than 100 chapters with some 6,000 members, including 11 chapters in Western North Carolina and two in Asheville.

Benevolent and Protective Order of Elks *(www.elks.org)* has a lodge in Asheville *(Elks Lodge #608, 232 Haywood St., Downtown Asheville, 828-253-4731)*. The lodge meets on the first and third Mondays of each month at 6:30 pm. The Elks is a fraternal order founded in New York in 1868. It now has about 2,000 chapters and around 850,000 members. Membership in the Order is only by invitation of a member in good standing. To be accepted as a member, one must be an American citizen, believe in God, be of good moral character and be at least 21 years old. Besides Asheville, there also are Elks lodges in Hendersonville and Waynesville. Membership dues vary by lodge but generally are under $100 a year.

Junior League of Asheville *(www.juniorleagueasheville.org)*, one of about 265 Junior League groups around the world with 160,000 members, focuses on charitable efforts and volunteering to improve the community. It is open to women only. Among the local chapter's projects are Homeward Bound, an effort to end homelessness in Asheville and Buncombe County. Dues for new members are $135. New members attend monthly training sessions along with regular monthly club meetings, complete at least seven hours of volunteer work during the year and attend either an Asheville City Council or Buncombe Board of Commissioners meeting, or a city or county school board meeting. There also is a social aspect to Junior League, with the club holding a fund-raising ball each fall and other social events.

Kiwanis Club of Asheville *(www.kiwanisofasheville.org)* is one of about 16,000 Kiwanis Clubs around the U.S. and in some 80 other countries, with 600,000 members. Kiwanis (a word that comes from the Ojibwa Native American-First Nation language and means "fool around" but was mistranslated by Kiwanis organizers as "we build") today focuses on helping children. Locally, the club is actively involved in supporting education, including distributing school supplies to needy children, providing college scholarships and awarding bicycles to students with perfect attendance and no tardiness. The Asheville club holds a luncheon meeting weekly at noon on Tuesday at St. Mark's Lutheran Church at the corner of Merrimon Avenue and East Chestnut Street in North Asheville. Kiwanis also organizes and sponsors clubs for students from middle school to university. Asheville club dues are $150 a quarter, which includes the weekly lunches. The Carolinas district of Kiwanis covers both North and South Carolina with more than 200 clubs and 8,000 members. There are Kiwanis clubs in many other towns in Western North Carolina.

League of Women Voters of Asheville-Buncombe *(www.ablwv.org)* is a non-partisan political organization that supports informed participation in government and education about public policy. The League does not support or oppose any individual party or candidates. Membership is open to all, not just to women. The Asheville League currently is working to support several issues, including redistricting reform, voting rights and gun safety. It also surveys candidates on key issues and publishes a voter guide. Dues are $50 for an individual, $75 for a household and $20 for students. Also in WNC are two other League chapters, in Henderson County *(www.lwvhcnc.org)* and a member-at-large unit in Madison County.

Lions of North Carolina *(7050 Camp Dogwood Dr., Sherrills Ford, NC 28673, 828-478-2135 or 800-662-7401, http://script.nclionsinc.org)* has around 45 local Lions Clubs in Western North Carolina, including more than 15 in the Asheville area. Most meet once or twice a month. The Lions is a well-known community-service organization that focuses on helping the sight-impaired. With 46,000 clubs and 1.4 million members worldwide, Lions says it is the world's largest service club. The North Carolina Lions, with a membership of about 10,000, have a 56-acre recreation center on Lake Norman near Charlotte where the blind and visually impaired can come for retreats offering fishing, swimming, boating and other water sports. Each year, the North Carolina Lions VIP Fishing Tournament attracts more than 500 blind and visually impaired people, along with their guests.

Loyal Order of Moose *(www.mooseintl.org)* has around 15 chapters and lodges in Western North Carolina, including two in Asheville. This international fraternal and service organization, founded in 1888, has around 800,000 male members in 1,800 lodges, in all 50 U.S. states. It also has 500,000 female members in 1,600 chapters of Women of the Moose. Nationally, the Moose run Mooseheart in Illinois, a school for disadvantaged children, and Moosehaven, a retirement home in Florida for Moose members. Locally, Moose Lodge 781 in Leicester has bingo, beanbag tosses and, for traveling members, recreational vehicle hookups.

Mt. Herman Blue Lodge 188, Masonic Temple Fraternal Order of Masons *(80 Broadway St., Downtown Asheville, 828-252-3924, www.masonic118.com),* founded in 1848, is one of the older Masonic lodges in the U.S. The lodge is in a four-story brick building completed in 1915 and designed by noted architect Richard Sharp Smith. The building is an amalgam of several architectural styles, with Ionic columns over a Norman arched front entry. The massive building was constructed with 600,000 bricks made in Knoxville. Although some Mt. Herman lodge meetings are now held elsewhere, the Masonic Lodge building on Broadway, now open to the public including for theatrical and musical events in its 270-seat theater, is still maintained by the Masons. It contains a Masonic library and a collection of historic Mason photographs and artifacts. After a period of declining membership, the Asheville lodge now has a membership of several hundred. There are eight Masonic lodges in the Asheville area, and several others around Western North Carolina.

The Asheville lodge is named after Mt. Herman, on the border of Syria and Lebanon. Mt. Herman, actually a group of three mountain peaks all over 9,000 feet, is the northern bounder of the Biblical "Promised Land" and may also have been site of the "Transfiguration" of Jesus. Many conspiracy theories have sprung up around the secretive Masons, which may date back to stonemason guilds in the Middle Ages, but essentially it is a social and fraternal organization devoted to personal and societal improvements. Its official mission states: "The mission of Freemasonry in North Carolina is to raise the moral, social, intellectual, and spiritual conscience of society by teaching the ancient and enduring philosophical tenets of Brotherly Love, Relief, and Truth, which are expressed outwardly through service to God, family, country, and self under the Fatherhood of God within the Brotherhood of Man."

You'll never be asked to become a Mason, because Masons are prohibited by their own rules to solicit members. Prospective members must actively seek membership. A committee investigates the prospective member, and membership is granted only by a unanimous vote of the lodge members present. This approach has been partly responsible for the decline in Masonic membership. In 1959, there were 4 million Masons in the U.S.; today, there are only around 1.5 million. After joining, members work through three degrees of Masonry.

Optimist Club International *(www.optimist.org)* has three clubs in the Asheville area *(www.ashevilleoptimists.com)* plus nine other clubs in Western North Carolina. The oldest and largest local club, Asheville Optimist Club, chartered in 1923, has meetings every Thursday at 12:30 pm at the Asheville Renaissance Hotel. The local club is a part of Optimist International, an association of 2,600 Optimist Clubs around the world dedicated to "Bringing Out the Best in Kids." Asheville Optimists have been operating Santa Pal *(www.santapal.org)* in Asheville since 1936. Santa Pal operates a seasonal store at the Innsbruck Mall on Tunnel Road in East Asheville where underprivileged families can come and pick out a toy for a child 2 to 12 at no cost. Optimistic Club members really are supposed to be optimists. Part of the Optimist Creed states, "talk health, happiness and prosperity to every person you meet ... look at the sunny side of everything and make your optimism come true."

Rotary Club of Asheville *(www.rotaryasheville.org)* says that it is one of the oldest and largest service clubs in North Carolina. The Downtown Asheville club has been involved in many worthy charitable works, including building a rehabilitation hospital, establishing a Boy Scout camp and, more recently, providing meals for 300,000 North Carolinas through Rotarians Against Hunger. Rotary clubs are made up of members, typically local leaders in each field of business and the professions. Some clubs are exclusivist, in that they accept only one member from each field. When the author was a member of the Rotary Club of Asheville, it was for men only, but Rotary is now open to all, regardless of gender, race, religion or other attributes. Members are required to attend all club meetings or make them up by attending another club or online.

The Asheville Club meets weekly on Thursdays at noon at the Asheville Renaissance Hotel in Asheville. Lunch is $17 (you can attend the meeting without buying lunch.) It is the home club of 1958 Rotary International President Buzz Tennant.

Asheville Rotary was the first Rotary club in Western North Carolina, established in 1915. There are seven other Rotary clubs in the Asheville area and in many towns in Western North Carolina. Check the Rotary International website (*www.rotary.org*) for locations and meeting times. Rotary International says it has 1.2 million members in 34,000 clubs in 200 countries.

Land of the Sky Shrine Club *(Jim Branch Rd., Swannanoa, East Asheville, www.landoftheskyshrineclub.com)* is recognizable for its members' fez hats, funny costumes and frequent participation in parades in miniature vehicles or scooters. Formerly called the Ancient Arabic Order of the Nobles of the Mystic Shrine, in 2010 the parent organization changed its name to Shriners International. It is an 1870 offshoot of the Freemasons, and still today only Master Masons can become Shriners. The fraternal organization is now best known for its support of Shriners Hospitals for Children, a network of 22 hospitals in the U.S., Canada and Mexico. The hospitals deal with orthopedic care, burn treatment, cleft lip and palate care and spinal cord injury rehabilitation. They now bill insurance companies for services, but they accept children under 18 at no charge if the child does not have insurance.

Shriners has about 200 shrines or temples in North and South America, Europe and Southeast Asia. Despite its original name, the terminology of the buildings and the fez hats, Shriners International has no relationship with Islam or any other formal religion. The local Shrine Club puts on several fund-raising events each year for the Shriners Hospitals, including a golf tournament, circus and car show. Dinner meetings are held at the club's building in Swannanoa the second Monday of every month, starting with social hour at 6 pm. The building also is rented out for social functions.

Sons of Confederate Veterans *(www.scv.org)*, an organization for male descendants of any veteran who served honorably in the Confederate armed forces during the Civil War. The SVC has a "camp" in Asheville, the Zebulon Baird Vance Camp #15 (. The camp is one of the oldest in the country, established in 1896. It is part of the Southern Highland Brigade, one of 11 brigades with 99 camps comprising the North Carolina Division of the national Sons of Confederate Veterans; altogether there are about 18 SCV camps in Western North Carolina.

The Asheville camp closed during the Great Depression but was reactivated in the mid-1960s. Members of SCV must prove lineage from a Confederate veteran through generally accepted genealogical methods.

They salute the Confederate States of America flag "with affection, reverence, and undying devotion to the cause for which it stands." However, the CSA says that it disavows any organization based on racial or social bias. The local group, which has around 45 members, meets on the fourth Thursday of most months at 6 pm at Ryan's Steakhouse on Brevard Road in West Asheville. National dues are $35 a year, and local camps may impose additional dues.

Veterans of Foreign Wars *(www.vfw.org)* has around 20 posts in Western North Carolina, including one in Asheville, Sgt. Daniel Frank Hyatt Sr. Post 891 *(626 New Leicester Hwy., West Asheville, 828-254-4277, www.myvfw.org/nc/post891)*. WNC posts have a total membership of more than 5,000, and the Asheville post has about 500 members. There are three main criteria for membership in the VFW: 1) be a U.S. citizen or U.S. national, 2) honorable service in the Armed Forces of the United States, 3) service entitling the applicant to the award of a recognized campaign medal for overseas service or having received hostile fire pay. National VFW dues are $35 a year; local posts may require additional dues.

Conservation and Ecology Clubs

Asheville Greenworks *(318 Riverside Dr., North Asheville, 828-254-1776, www.ashevillegreenworks.org)*, established in 1973 as Quality Forward and now an affiliate of the national Keep America Beautiful, is an environmental organization that works to improve the quality of life in Asheville-Buncombe through grassroots, community-based efforts often involving clean up and recycling. It has more than 400 members, and several thousand people volunteer with it annually. Greenworks is especially active in river clean up, tree planting and greenway building. You can sign up on the organization's website to become a Greenworks volunteer, working either on your own or in group projects.

Carolina Bird Club *(www.carolinabirdclub.org)* is a club for birders in both North and South Carolina. The club meets at least four times a year in different locations around the two states, with meeting sites usually offering good birding. There also are several field trips a year, plus a Christmas bird count in association with the Audubon Society. Members receive a newsletter six times a year plus an annual ornithological publication. Dues are $25 for an individual, $30 for families and $15 for students.

Elisha Mitchell Audubon Society *(P.O. Box 18711, Asheville, NC 28814, www.emasnc.org)* was formed in 1986 as the Asheville chapter of the national Audubon Society. The Elisha Mitchell Audubon Society owns and manages the Beaver Lake Bird Sanctuary, an 8-acre wildlife sanctuary in North Asheville, and depends on volunteers to maintain it and to lead bird walks there. Bird walks are held at the sanctuary on the first Saturday of every month at 9 am October through March, and 8 am April through September. The local group sponsors birding outings and publishes a digital newsletter, *The Raven,* eight or nine times a year. The chapter is named after the UNC-Chapel Hill scientist who first proved that Mt. Mitchell is the highest peak in the East. Annual membership includes membership in the national Audubon Society and costs $20.

Katuah Earth First! *(www.katuahearthfirst.org)* is the Asheville-based unit of the international Earth First! movement. Earth First! locally takes direct-action stands for wilderness and against threats to the mountain ecology. Participants are frequently arrested in protests, civil disobedience actions and demonstrations against genetically modified crops and trees, logging of national forests and large coal mining interests in the Southern Appalachians. Earth First! worldwide *(www.earthfirst.com)* says it is a movement, not an organization, and that it has no "members," just a diverse group of EarthFirst!ers with a belief in biocentrism and that life on earth comes first and who put their beliefs in action.

Preservation Society of Asheville and Buncombe County *(324 Charlotte St., North Asheville, 828-254-2343, www.psabc.org)* works to preserve the historic heritage of the area. It promotes the use of conservation easements to protect property with significant historic, architectural or archaeological resource. The easement limits changes that can be made to the property, or parts of it, in the future. Properties can include private homes, commercial buildings, landscapes and gardens, excavated foundations and other types of property The value of the easement – typically the difference between the unfettered market value of the property and the value of the property after the easement – is usually considered a charitable contribution and can be deducted on federal and state taxes. The Society publishes a monthly newsletter, holds special events such as tours of Black Mountain College campus at Lake Eden, the Log Cabin Motor Court or of notable historic homes and gives annual awards, the Griffin Awards, to notable local preservation projects. Individual memberships in the Preservation Society are $35 a year, and family members are $50.

Sierra Club of Western North Carolina *(www.wenoca.org)*, covering most of the counties in WNC from Buncombe west (except Henderson, Polk and Transylvania counties, which are part of the Pisgah Group, is one of ten groups in the North Carolina state chapter of the national Sierra Club. The local club usually meets at 7 pm the first Wednesday of each month at the Unitarian Universalist Congregation on Edwin Place in Asheville and holds frequent hikes around Western North Carolina. It endorses political candidates and takes public positions on political issues. Annual dues for membership in the national organization and local chapter begin at $15 for a single membership and $20 for a joint membership.

WNC Alliance *(29 North Market St., Ste. 610, Downtown Asheville, 828-258-8737, www.wnca.org)* is a community-based, grassroots environmental organization that focuses on sensible land use, restoring public forests and improving water quality. Although based in Asheville, it has chapters in several towns around Western North Carolina. The WNC Alliance actively seeks volunteers and interns to monitor streams, maintain the Alliance's paddle trail along the French Broad River and to clear trails in national forests, among other activities. Individual annual memberships start at $30, and family memberships at $50.

Hobby and Special Interest Clubs

Antique Auto Club of America, Great Smoky Mountain Region *(www.local.aaca.org/gsmr/)* is a club for vintage and antique car enthusiasts. The club publishes an online newsletter and holds numerous tours and show events. Membership in the national organization, required if you want to be a member of the local chapter, is $38 a year, and local membership is an additional $14.

Apple Valley Model Railroad Club *(650 Maple St., Hendersonville, www.avmrc.com)* is a club for model train enthusiasts. The club's office is the historic Hendersonville Railroad Depot on Maple Street downtown, which was built in 1902 with later additions. In the depot the club has a 22 ft. by 100 ft. HO-scale model train layout, based on actual railroads in Western North Carolina. The model railroad layout is open to the public on Saturdays from 10 am to 2 pm and Wednesdays from 1 to 3 pm. The approximately 40 members of the club can bring their own model train equipment to run on the tracks. In Hendersonville also is the **French Broad E 'N' Pire** club, a group that models in N scale.

Apple Valley Antique Engine and Tractor Association
(www.applecountry.org) is affiliated with the **Mountain Farm & Home Museum** *(www.mfhmuseum.homestead.com)* in Hendersonville. The club, founded in 1985, is dedicated to restoring and preserving vintage farm tractors and other engine-powered machines. It holds annual three-day show in late October at the WNC Ag Center and exhibits in early September at the Mountain State Fair also at the WNC Ag Fair. The club stages tractor pulls and other events. Membership is $20 a year.

Artists Clubs. The website of **Asheville Art** *(www.avlart.com)* maintains a list of art-related clubs and groups in Western North Carolina. Among the clubs are the **Kenilworth Artists Association, Western North Carolina *Plein Air* Painters, Blue Ridge Realists, Art Group of Waynesville** and **Appalachian Pastel Artists.** Asheville Art also has contact information for local galleries, art schools and other artist resources.

Asheville Beer Club *(www.meetup.com/asheville-beer-club/)* is an active MeetUp group that gets together to visit the area's two dozen or so craft breweries and for learning events.

Asheville Bridge Clubs *(www.web2.acbl.org/)* has more than 20 American Contract Bridge League-affiliated bridge clubs in Western North Carolina. There are eight in Asheville alone. Most Asheville clubs play and some offer bridge classes at River Ridge Marketplace in Fairview, South Asheville.

Asheville Humane Society *(16 Forever Friend Lane, West Asheville, 828-250-6430, www.ashevillehumane.org)* relies partly on volunteers to help care for animals brought to the Buncombe County Animal Shelter near Brevard Road, I-26 and the WNC Farmers' Market in West Asheville. The campus comprises two facilities: the Asheville Humane Society Adoption and Education Center and the Buncombe County Animal Shelter. Each year the Society, which recently merged with the local chapter of Animal Compassion Network, rescues, rehabilitates and places for adoption about 4,500 animals. The Humane Society operates the shelter under contracts with Buncombe County and the City of Asheville. The Society works closely with the Humane Alliance of Western North Carolina in West Asheville, a nationally known organization that performs some 24,000 spay/neuter surgeries a year. The Asheville Humane Society also has a free spay/neuter program and free rabies vaccinations for feral cats. Volunteers, who must be at least 18 years old unless accompanied by a parent, provide a variety of services depending on their interests and skills. One of the most popular services is Hiking Hounds, a program where volunteers take dogs on hikes. Volunteer orientations are held twice monthly.

Asheville Quilt Guild *(www.ashevillequiltguild.org)*, founded in 1988, holds monthly meetings at the Folk Art Center on the Blue Ridge Parkway, organizes a number of quilting bees, publishes a newsletter, maintains a lending library on quilting of nearly 800 volumes at the Folk Art Center and puts on an annual Quilt Show. Guild members make and donate hundred of quilts each year to local charitable agencies. The Guild's Asheville Quilt Show is held in late September at the WNC Ag Center in Fletcher and attracts exhibitors from around the country. Prizes for best quilts total around $8,000. Guild dues are $25 a year and $15 for junior members under 16 years old.

Asheville Scrabble Club *(www.ashevillescrabble.com)* is a club for Scrabble players of any level, although club and tournament play can be highly competitive. Scrabble dates to 1938, when an American architect, Alfred Mosher Butts, invented a game he called Criss-Crosswords. The name was changed to Scrabble in 1948. The game received a huge boost in 1984 when a daytime TV show called *Scrabble* debuted on NBC. Currently, the Asheville Tile Slingers club meets for Scrabble play Sundays from 2 to 6 pm at Atlanta Bread Company at 633 Merrimon Avenue in North Asheville and Wednesdays (newcomers' night) from 5 to 9 pm at Atlanta Bread Company at 484 Hendersonville Road in South Asheville. For the first three visits, attendees may use a "cheat sheet" and free challenges. Dues of $20 a year are payable after six months of participation in the club. Some Asheville Scrabble Club members travel to regional and national tournaments, and the club usually hosts a regional tournament annually in the fall in Asheville, with players from around the Southeast. Current co-directors of the Asheville Scrabble Club are Dr. Bill Snoddy and Jacob Cohen.

Asheville Ski Club *(www.ashevilleskiclub.com)* organizes national and international winter snow ski trips to places like Jackson Hole, Reno and Banff, Canada. The club, which is associated with the National Ski Council Federation, also sponsors a ski race team that competes at ski resorts mostly in Western North Carolina. In warm weather, the club holds hiking and biking outings in the Asheville area. Meetings are usually held the second Thursday of the month at 6:30 pm at the Asheville Country Club, 170 Windsor Road in North Asheville. Membership is $35 for singles, $60 for families and $15 for junior members. There's an additional $35 fee for racing.

Asheville Stamp Club *(828-692-9550)* meets the third Sunday of every month at 2 pm at Deerfield Episcopal Retirement Community in Arden (South Asheville).

Asheville Vegan Society *(www.meetup.com/the-asheville-vegan-society/)* is a MeetUp group with more than 600 members. It does monthly potluck vegan meals that attract 50 or so members and dine-outs that get around 20 members.

Asheville Wine Meet-Up *(www.meetup.com/asheville-wine-meetup/)* holds winetastings, usually at local restaurants or wine bars that attract up to 40 or 50 members. The MeetUp group organizer, Bob Bowles, has a website on local wines, www.wncwinetrail.com.

Book Clubs. Asheville and Western North Carolina have a large number of book clubs, too many to list here. To find a book club that meets your interests, check with local bookstores and libraries. **Malaprops** *(www.malaprops.com),* an independent book store in Downtown Asheville, has several book clubs (on general interest, mystery, politics, young adult, food, autism and other subjects) that meet at various times in the store's café at 55 Haywood Street in Downtown Asheville. Malaprops also maintains a list of some other area book clubs. Among other book clubs are **Eat Your Words** at Avenue M restaurant on Merrimon Avenue and **Women in Lively Discussion (WILD)** at the Battery Park Book Exchange & Champagne Bar in the Grove Arcade. Local public libraries often sponsor book clubs, as do some churches and social clubs.

British Car Club of Western North Carolina *(www.bccwnc.org)* is a sports car and enthusiast club for owners and admirers of British-made cars such as MG, Jaguar, Rolls-Royce, Bentley, Vauxhall, Austin-Healy, Land Rover, Lotus and others. Members get together for group drives, caravans to car shows and for dinner meetings. The club meets the first Tuesday of each month at 6 pm at J&S Cafeteria near the Asheville Regional Airport. Annual dues are $20 per household.

Buncombe County Beekeepers *(www.wncbees.org)* is a part of the North Carolina State Beekeepers Association *(www.ncbeekeepers.org),* which has 2,000 members around the state. The NCSBA, the largest state beekeeping organization in the U.S., works closely with the North Carolina Department of Agriculture and NC State University apiculture program. Because of funding cutbacks at NC State, the NCSBA now also runs the NC Master Beekeeper training and certification program. The Buncombe chapter currently meets most months on the first Monday of the month at 6:15 at Grace United Methodist Church at 954 Tunnel Road in East Asheville.

Also in Asheville is the Center for Honeybee Research *(22 Cedar Hill Rd., West Asheville, 828-779-7047, www.honeybeeresearch.org)*, an organization that focuses on natural beekeeping without chemicals or antibiotics; it worked to get Asheville designated as the first Bee City USA. Membership in the Buncombe County Beekeepers, open to both hobbyist and commercial beekeepers and also to those who aren't beekeepers but are interested in bees or in becoming beekeepers, is $10 individual, $15 family and $5 students. State association membership (optional) is an additional $15. There also are active beekeepers clubs in Henderson County *(www.hcbeekeepers.com)*, Haywood County *(www.hcbees.org)* and elsewhere. The Hendersonville Beekeepers Association offers a popular and excellent beekeeping class each year in the winter. The class usually attracts 100 or more current and would-be beekeepers. Other mountain counties also have beekeeping clubs.

Buncombe County Coin Club meets at 7 pm the second Monday of every month in the conference room of the Grove Arcade in Downtown Asheville. A local coin dealer and gold seller, Black Mountain Coins *(www.blackmountaincoins.com)* can provide information on the club.

Camera Club of Hendersonville *(www.cameraclubofhendersonville.com)* is open to anyone in Western North Carolina interested in photography at any level. The club has classes and mentoring programs for beginners. Meetings are on the fourth Tuesday of each month at 6:30 pm at the Hendersonville Chamber of Commerce building on Church and Kanuga streets in downtown Hendersonville. Annual dues are $20 per person.

Embroiders Guild of America *(www.egausa.org)* has a chapter in Western North Carolina near Hendersonville. The Guild, with about 10,000 members in almost 300 chapters nationally, fosters the art of needlework and associated arts. Membership starts at $25, and local chapters may have additional membership fees. The **Henderson County Laurel Chapter** has about 40 members. It meets at 9:30 am the first Thursday of each month, except December, at Cummings Memorial Methodist Church in Horse Shoe, about 6 miles from Hendersonville.

Ethical Society of Asheville *(www.meetup.com/ethical-society-of-asheville/)* is a humanist, non-theistic alternative to traditional religion and a member organization of the American Ethical Union. It is a part of the social networking group, MeetUp.

Meetings are held the first and third Sundays of each month from 2 to 3:30 pm at the visitor center in the YMI Community Center, 39 South Market Street in Downtown Asheville or the Asheville Friends Meeting House at 227 Edgewood Road in North Asheville. Members discuss topics of current interest, philosophy and education from a humanist perspective.

f/32 Photography Group *(www.f32nc.com)* is a club for lovers of photography, regardless of background or skill level. Meetings are usually the second Wednesday of the month at 7 pm at the Reuter Center at the University of North Carolina at Asheville in North Asheville. Besides monthly meetings, the group or its members have shows at local galleries, run an online forum and have a Christmas party. Dues are $25 a year for an individual and $35 for a couple or family. Dues are waived for members of the Osher Lifelong Learning Institute at UNC-A.

French Broad Mensa *(www.frenchbroad.us.mensa.org)* is the local WNC chapter of American Mensa, the "high IQ" society open to those in the top 2% of intelligence. Most months, the group has social dinner meetings, usually on a Thursday, at various restaurants in Asheville and surrounding towns. French Broad Mensa also fields a trivia team that plays at Juicy Lucy's restaurant in Downtown Asheville and has a monthly bowling night, along with other events including a holiday party in December. Mensa, with some 110,000 members in more than 100 countries, is non-political and free from all racial or religious distinctions. The society welcomes people from every walk of life who enjoy getting together for social, intellectual and cultural interaction. To qualify for membership in Mensa, you can take a test offered in Asheville and in many other locations, or you can submit qualifying results from standardized tests such as LSAT and GMAT. Annual membership is $70 and includes membership in a local group such as French Broad Mensa.

Garden Clubs thrive in the climate of Western North Carolina. The Asheville area has a number of clubs, including **Asheville Garden Club; Asheville E-Z Gardeners; Four Seasons Garden Club; Friends of the Earth Garden Club; Leicester Garden Club; Men's Garden Club of Asheville** *(www.mensgardenclubasheville.org);* and **Weaverville Garden Club.** Most of the local garden clubs don't have websites, but you may be able to find them on Facebook or Twitter. One of the oldest and most active clubs is the **French Broad River Garden Club** *(1000 Hendersonville Rd., South Asheville, www.fbrgc.org)*. It was founded in 1927 and has held an annual Christmas Greens sale for nearly 90 years. The sale is on the first two Saturdays in December at "Clem's Cabin" at the club's gardens at 1000 Hendersonville Road in South Asheville.

Hendersonville Kennel Club *(828-388-2565, www.hkc-nc.org)* is an all-breed dog club licensed by the national American Kennel Club. Established in 1977, the HKC promotes responsible dog ownership, public education, and seeks to protect the rights of dog owners in the community. It sponsors handling classes and health clinics. The club offers two local all-breed conformation, obedience and rally shows a year, open free to the public. It also supports Paws for Love, affiliated with Therapy Dogs.

Mountain Area Gem and Mineral Association or MAGMA *(www.wncrocks.com)* is an organization for gem hunters. The club has about 2,500 members from around the world, and standard membership is free. MAGMA members go on field trips and hold meetings in Western North Carolina and elsewhere in the region. Most of these trips are digs on private land or old mines, and members find interesting and sometimes valuable gems and minerals.

Mountain Flyers Flying Club *(www.mtnflyers.com)*, based in the general aviation area at the Asheville Regional Airport, is a member-owned association of pilots. The club owns four aircraft, two Cessna Skyhawks (172s) and two Cessna Skylanes (182s) that are rented to members starting at around $100 an hour including fuel and insurance. Club initiation fee is $975, and monthly dues are $45. Demo flights for prospective members are $49. Mountain Flyers also offers flight training for those who want to learn to fly and become licensed.

North Carolina Clay Club *(www.ncclayclub.blogspot.com)* is made up of clay artists who want to connect with other potters. It usually meets monthly on the second Wednesday of the month at a location in the River Arts District in Asheville.

Old Buncombe County Genealogical Society *(128 Bingham Rd., Suite 950, West Asheville, 828-253-1894, www.obcgs.com)*, established in 1979, promotes interest in family history in most of Western North Carolina. It maintains an extensive library of genealogical documents on what was the original Buncombe County, created by the state legislature in 1791. The original county covered what is now known as Buncombe, Haywood, Henderson, Jackson, Madison and Transylvania counties, plus the western part of Yancey, McDowell and Polk counties. The Society also covers Macon, Clay, Cherokee, Graham and Swain counties. It maintains a library of more than 12,000 books and documents about families in WNC. The Society's library and office are open to the public Monday-Saturday (hours vary) for assisted or unassisted research. It has a bookstore and publishes a free newsletter. Volunteers are welcome. Annual membership is $35 for an individual and $40 for a family.

Southern Appalachian Mineral Society *(828-628-2422, www.main.nc.us/sams/)* is one of the oldest mineral societies in the U.S., founded in 1933. Meetings are held at 7 pm on the first Monday of each month except January and September at Tuton Hall Community Center, Deerfield Retirement Community in South Asheville. The club also conducts field trips most months to collect gems and other minerals. Asheville is in the center of an area with the widest variety of gems and minerals in the U.S. Annual dues are $20 for individuals, $26 for families and $5 for students. The society publishes a monthly newsletter.

Western Carolina Chapter of National Association of Watch and Clock Collectors *(www.community.nawcc.org/chapter126/home/)* has members in both Western North and South Carolina. Among the membership are collectors, those interested in the history of watches and clocks and those interested in watch and clock repair. The horologist club undertakes volunteer repair and restoration projects of notable public clocks in the region, such as clocks in Hendersonville, Marshall and Clemson, S.C. Meetings are held the second Saturday of odd months at the Skyland Fire Department, 9 Miller Road in Skyland (South Asheville). The largest watch and clock museum in North America, with 12,000 items, is located in Columbia, Penn., in Lancaster County.

Western North Carolina Quilters Guide

(www.westernncquilters.org), based in Hendersonville, is a group of about 200 men and women interested in quilting. Monthly luncheon meetings and some workshops are held at Grace Lutheran Church at the corner of U.S. Highway 64 and Blythe Road in Hendersonville, while full-day workshops and shows are held elsewhere in the area. The Guide also holds a quilt show and sale at the North Carolina Arboretum off Brevard Road near Asheville. Annual dues are $25.

Western North Carolina Rock Climbing Meet-Up

(www.meetup.com/wnc-climbing-meetup/) is a MeetUp group organized by Fox Mountain Climbing School. The group runs several indoor and outdoor climbing trips a year. The cost per trip is usually under $80, with all equipment provided. Novice rock climbers are welcome on some trips.

WNC Chess Association *(www.wncchess.org)* is a confederation of chess clubs in the region. **Asheville Chess Club** meets weekly on Wednesday at 6:30-10:30 pm at the North Community Center at 37 Larchmont Lane in North Asheville behind Asheville Pizza on Merrimon Avenue. The **Hendersonville Chess Club** meets Tuesdays at 6-8:30 pm at the First Presbyterian Church, in downtown Hendersonville at the corner of King and 6th.

The **Smoky Mountain Chess Club** meets Thursdays at 2-4 pm at Blue Ridge Books, 152 South Main Street in Waynesville. Times and places of meetings are subject to change. Tournaments are held several times a year in Asheville and Hendersonville. The Land of the Sky tournament in Asheville, usually held in January, has cash prizes of up to $2,400 for section winners. For information on tournaments around the state, visit the North Carolina Chess Association website *(www.ncchess.org)*.

WNC Herb Club, formed in fall 2013, is for those interested in growing medicinal herbs. Initial meetings were at the Mountain Crops Research and Extension Center (828-684-7197, 74 Research Dr., Mills River between Asheville and Hendersonville). Call the Extension Center for current details.

WNC Model Railroaders *(www.wncmrr.org)*, founded in 1974 and affiliated with the National Model Railroad Association, promotes model railroading as a hobby. The club meets the first Thursday of each month except July at 7 pm in the administration building at Eliada Home in Leicester. It holds an annual model railroad show, usually in early March at the WNC Ag Center near the Asheville Airport. Many members participate in modular model railroading, building 2 x 4 feet HO-scale modules that can be put together at shows or at the club. The club publishes a monthly newsletter and sponsors field trips to nearby railroading sites. Membership in the National Model Railroad Association, which includes local club dues, is $44 without *NMRA Magazine* to $66 with the magazine, and $32 for students. A trial six-month membership, which provides full member rights except voting, is $9.95.

WNC Pilots Association *(www.flywncpa.org)* promotes aviation safety and interest in flying. The group holds monthly meetings, plans flying events, hosts social activities and funds an aviation education scholarship. Membership is open to anyone with an interest in flying, even if he or she doesn't have a pilot's license or an airplane. Meetings are the third Tuesday of each month starting at 6:15 pm with a light dinner and then a program on aviation. They are held in the O.D. "Lacy" Griffin building at the General Aviation area of the Asheville Regional Airport. Annual dues are $25, plus a one-time $5 initiation fee. There also is a flying club in Franklin, the **Smoky Mountain Flying Club** *(www.smokymtnflyingclub.com)*.

Writers' Groups. The Asheville area has a number of groups for writers and wanna-bes. **Asheville MeetUp** *(www.writers.meetup.com/cities/us/nc/asheville/)* has four or five MeetUp groups for writers, poets, songwriters and others, with a total membership, active or not, of around 400.

AsheNoWriMo *(www.ashenowrimo.org)* is a group that gets together about twice a month for two to three hours for "write-ins" at places like Green Sage South or French Broad Chocolate Lounge to write without disturbances or phone calls. **Asheville Christian Writers Group** *(www.ashevillechristianwriters.org)* meets from 9:30 to 11:30 am on the second Saturday of most months in South Asheville. Attendance is free, and participants may bring a sample, less than 3,200 words in length, of their writing, or email it in advance, and they also are asked to participate in critiquing the work of others at the meeting. **Asheville Writing Enthusiasts** *(www.davidpereda.com)*, led by novelist David Pereda, is dedicated to helping writers improve their writing while helping other writers do the same. It meets on the first and third Saturdays of the month from 10:30 am to 12:30 pm at the boardroom at Pack Place, 2 South Pack Square, Downtown Asheville. Meetings are free and open to the public. **Flatiron Writers** *(www.flatironwriters.com)*, founded in 1993, first met in the Flatiron Building in Downtown Asheville but now moves around to various locations in towns. Membership has varied from three to eight members. Most are published writers. Flatiron also puts on occasional workshops and seminars for writers, for which there is a small fee. The **Great Smokies Writing Program** *(215 Lipinsky Hall, CPO # 2260m One University Heights, North Asheville, 828-250-2353, www.agc.unca.edu/great-smokies-writing-program)* is a joint effort among the UNC-Asheville departments of Literature and Language, Creative Writing and the Asheville Graduate Center. The program offers university-level classes led by published writers and experienced teachers. Each course carries academic credit awarded through UNC Asheville. Each class incurs regular UNC-A class fees, which are lower for in-state residents, and there is a $20 application fee. Tuition and fees for a single class start at around $800-$1,050 per semester for in-state residents. Tuition and fees at UNC-A for full-time in-state residents are $4,200 to $5,200 per semester, and for out-of-state residents around $14,000 to $15,000. The program also offers readings and seminars and publishes a literary magazine, *Great Smokies Review*. It also sponsors a "Writers at Home" program, with readings by mostly local writers. **Mysterians** *(www.wncmysterians.org)* is for "serious mystery, suspense and thriller" writers. Members meet weekly to critique each other's works. Prospective members must submit a sample of their writing, and membership is limited to eight writers at any one time. The goal of **SCBWI Carolinas** *(www.scbwicarolinas.org/critique-groups)* is to bring together writers and illustrators of children's books. There are two groups in the Asheville area, but both are currently full and are not accepting new members. **Women Writing in Asheville** *(www.womenwritinginasheville.org)* was founded in

2008 as a place for women to share their writing. The group holds critique workshops twice a month. The **Writers' Workshop of Asheville** *387 Beaucatcher Rd., East Asheville, 828-254-8111, www.twwoa.org)*, established in 1985, puts on classes, seminars, workshops in Asheville and Charlotte, contests, readings, book signings and other events. Workshops typically cost around $75, and entry fees for contests are in the $25 range. The non-profit group says that since it was founded more than 21,000 people have participated in its programs and events. Among its editorial board are nationally known writers John Ehle, E. L. Doctorow and John le Carré. Annual individual membership is $35, family membership $65 and student membership $25. Members can attend local functions such as showings of foreign movies, potluck dinners and hikes usually at no charge.

Newcomers Clubs

Asheville Newcomers Club *(www.ashevillenewcomersclub.com)* is a club for women new to the Asheville area. The club meets on from 9:30 to 11:30 am on the second Wednesday of each month. Meeting locales vary and could be at a gallery, restaurant, historic site, coffee house or elsewhere. Annual dues are $30. Prospective members are encouraged to attend a meeting or two before joining and paying dues.

Asheville New Friends *(www.ashevillenewfriends.org)* is a group that that been here for more than three decades. The organization's purpose is to welcome newcomers and residents to the Asheville area and to introduce them to new friends. It also tries to introduce members to the numerous social and cultural activities in the Asheville area. The club sponsors Special Interest Groups (SIGS) to stimulate the mind (book clubs, an investment group, bridge, canasta), the body (hiking, golf) and social activities (outings to restaurants and concerts, home potlucks and parties.) There are two general membership meetings a year, plus at least two social events. Annual dues are $13 for singles or $26 for couples, plus any charges for events.

Senior Friendships of Henderson County

(www.seniorfriendships.com) is open to any Henderson County resident. Its purpose is to introduce newcomers to the area and to build friendships, to support worthy local causes and to encourage community involvement. Meetings are the third Thursday of the month except June, July and December at First Congregational Church, 1735 Fifth Avenue West in Laurel Park, Hendersonville. It also sponsors or organizes meetings for breakfast, lunch, danced bowling, bridge, golf, pinochle, walking and other activities for the club's nearly 200 members. Dues are $15 a year, plus any charges for events.

Urban Legends *(www.meetup.com/urban-legends)*, affiliated with MeetUp, is a social-minded group of around 300 who get together in all kinds of activities, from picnics to book clubs to seeing movies to hiking and other outdoor adventures. Membership is $5 a year.

Political Organizations

Amnesty International *(www.takeaction.amnestyusa.org)* has a student chapter at the University of North Carolina at Asheville.

Asheville Socialists *(www.internationalsocialist.org)* is the Asheville branch of the International Socialist Organization. It meets most Wednesdays at 5:30 pm at the Eagle Street Coffee Emporium at the corner of Eagle and Market streets Downtown.

Buncombe County Democratic Party *(951 Old Fairview Rd., East Asheville, 828-274-4482, www.buncombedems.org)* is the local unit of the North Carolina Democratic Party. It is funded by contributions from members. Membership is open to any registered Democrat. It holds a luncheon the first Wednesday of each month at noon, usually at the party headquarters building in Fairview. There's a charge for the catered meals. In addition, there are Democratic Party chapters in most other counties in Western North Carolina.

Buncombe County Democratic Men's Club *(951 Old Fairview Rd., East Asheville, 828-274-4482, www.buncombedems.org)* is open to any registered Democrat, not just men. Annual dues are $100 for members and an additional $50 for other family members. The Men's Club has monthly Saturday morning breakfast meetings, held at Democratic Party headquarters. The cost of the breakfasts is included in the annual dues.

Buncombe County Democratic Women's Club *(951 Old Fairview Rd., East Asheville, 828-274-4482, www.buncombedems.org)* is dedicated to supporting Democratic women in politics, encouraging all Democrats to vote and to actively participate in the local political process. Dinner meetings are held the third Thursday of each month at 6 pm at party headquarters in Fairview. Cost is $12 per meal.

Buncombe County Republican Party *(46 Haywood St #222, Downtown Asheville, 828- 253-5800, www.buncombegop.org)* is the local unit of the Republican Party. It meets the second Thursday of the month from 6:30-8:30 pm at the Renaissance Hotel in Downtown Asheville. Two Republican women's groups also meet monthly in Asheville. In addition, there are Republican Party chapters in most other counties in Western North Carolina.

Libertarian Party Buncombe County *(www.lpbuncombe.org)* is a unit of the national Libertarian Party. A Libertarian social group meets every Monday at 7 pm at La Chapala restaurant on Merrimon Avenue in North Asheville. There also is a Libertarian Party chapter in Henderson County *(www.henderson.lpnc.org)*.

Professional Organizations

American Advertising Federation Asheville

(www.adfedasheville.org) is one of about 200 units of the national American Advertising Federation, which has a membership of about 40,000 ad agency and other advertising practitioners. The Asheville group has about 35 members.

American Institute of Architects Asheville *(828-253-6014, www.aiaasheville.org)* is part of the 80,000-member national AIA and 2,000-member state professional organization. There are about 200 AIA members in Asheville and Western North Carolina. Full membership is available to licensed architects. Members pay annual dues to the national, state and local organizations. Total dues vary depending on several factors but typically are around $600-$700 per year.

Asheville Area Paralegal Association, established in 2004, no longer has an active website but is on Facebook.

Asheville Area Professional Pet Sitters Association *(www.ashevilleareapetsitters.com)* is for the owners of pet sitting businesses. The several dozen members of the association must attend at least one meeting or event per year. Annual membership is $65.

Buncombe County Dental Society *(www.bcdentalsociety.org)* is a unit of the North Carolina Dental Society. The local society has about 215 members. BCDS Meetings are held six times a year, on the second Tuesday of the months of January, February, March, April, October and November. The dinner meetings, which include an educational program, are usually at 6 pm at the Doubletree Hotel on Hendersonville Road in South Asheville. Annual dues for active members are $250.

North Carolina Nurses Association, Mountain Region *(103 Enterprise St., Raleigh, 919-821-4250 or 800-626-2153, www.ncnurses.org)* is a professional voice for registered nurses in the 15-country Western North Carolina area. North Carolina was the first state in the U.S. to register and license nurses. Annual membership dues in the North Carolina Nurses Association, a part of the American Nurses Association, are $180 for state-only membership and $307 for combined ANA/NCNA membership. Reduced rates are available for student nurses and those 62 and over.

North Carolina State Bar *(217 E. Edenton St., Raleigh, 919-828-4620, www.ncbar.gov)* is the official state agency responsible for regulating the practice of law in North Carolina. There are about 36,000 member of the State Bar. It is mandatory that all attorneys practicing in North Carolina be members of and pay their annual dues of $375 to the State Bar. Every active member of the State Bar who resides in North Carolina must also be a member of the judicial district bar where he or she practices. Asheville and Buncombe County comprise the **28th Judicial District Bar** *(62 Charlotte St., Suite F, Downtown Asheville, 828-252-5733, www.28thjdb.com)*. There are about 700 members of 28th Judicial District Bar, which is sometimes referred to as the Buncombe County Bar, since it covers Buncombe County. Annual dues are $125. The **North Carolina Bar Association** *(8000 Weston Pkwy, Cary, 919-677-0561, www.ncbar.org)*, by contrast, is a *voluntary* association serving the needs of the legal profession of North Carolina with member services such as continuing legal education, legislative lobbying, health insurance, specialty sections and public service activities. The state Association has around 14,000 members. State Bar Association dues are $275 a year, with lower rates for new attorneys.

Structural Engineers Association, Asheville Chapter *(www.seaofnc.org)* holds several meetings a year. Membership for professional engineers is $50.

Western Carolina Chapter of the North Carolina Association of Certified Public Accountants *(3100 Gateway Centre Blvd., Morrisville, 800-722-2836 or 919-469-1040, www.ncacpa.org)* has a membership of about 700 CPAs in 15 WNC counties including Buncombe and Henderson. The group holds quarterly meetings. Total membership of the state CPA association is about 13,000.

Western Carolina Medical Society *(304 Summit St., South Asheville, 828-274-2267, www.mywcms.org)*, founded in 1885 and formerly the Buncombe County Medical Society, is the professional voice for physicians (MDs and DOs) in the area. The society has a membership of around 1,000. Membership dues for active physicians are $300 a year for those in Buncombe County and $150 for those practicing elsewhere; reduced rates are available for interns, government-employed physicians and retired physicians. There also medical societies in most other counties in Western North Carolina.

Alumni Associations

Many colleges and some high schools and preparatory schools have alumni groups in the Asheville and Western North Carolina.

Among these are Asheville High School, The Asheville School, University of North Carolina at Chapel Hill, University of North Carolina at Asheville, North Carolina State University, Mars Hill University, Appalachian State University, Duke University, North Carolina A&T University, Western Carolina University, Asheville-Buncombe Tech, University of Georgia, Princeton University, Indiana University, University of Tennessee, University of Delaware, Virginia Tech, University of Alabama and others.

Search Google, Facebook and Linked-In for alumni groups for your school or university to see if there is a group in the Asheville area. Many colleges and high school have informal alumni groups and temporary groups organized to celebrate key reunions.

Support Groups

Asheville and Western North Carolina has support groups sufferers or victims of most diseases, dependencies and other special needs. If the support group you are seeking isn't listed here, check with local hospitals and health centers, specialist medical practices, churches and other referral sources. In listings where meeting times and places are shown, remember that these may change, so it's best to call ahead or visit the organization's website for updates. *Mountain Xpress* newspaper and several Asheville websites also provide listings of support group meetings. Most groups are free, while a few require a small fee or ask for a donation. The MeetUp social network *(www.meetup.com)* has many meetings that are similar to support groups.

Adult Children of Alcoholics & Dysfunctional Families (828-281-1314) meets Fridays at 7 pm at Grace Episcopal Church, 871 Merrimon Avenue in North Asheville.

Affordable Housing Coalition of Asheville and Buncombe County *(34 Wall St., Downtown Asheville, 828-259-9216, www.housingassistanceonline.com)* is a source of information on affordable housing in the community. It does not provide direct assistance.

Al-Anon *(800-286-1326 or 888-425-2666, www.al-anon.org)*, for families and friends of alcoholics, has meetings in Asheville, Hendersonville, Brevard and elsewhere in WNC.

Alcoholics Anonymous, District 70, Western North Carolina *(70 Woodfin Place, Suite 206, Park Place Office Bldg., Downtown Asheville, 24-hour hotline 828-254-8539, www.ashevilleaa.org)* has many meetings all over Asheville and WNC. You can search for meeting times and places on the local website.

Alzheimer's Association of Western North Carolina *(31 College Place, Downtown Asheville, 828-254-7363, 24-hour helpline 800-272-3900, www.alz.org)* has support groups for Alzheimer's caregivers in Asheville and in most Western North Carolina counties. See www.alz.org/northcarolina/in_my_community_support.asp for times and places of meetings.

Asheville Area Mothers of Multiples *(www.ashevillemom.com)* is a local group for mothers of twins, triplets and other multiples to find support, community, education and fun. It is affiliated with the North Carolina Mothers of Mulitiples *(www.ncmom.org)* and the National Organization of Mothers of Twins Clubs *(www.nomotc.org)*. The Asheville groups currently meets monthly at 7 pm on the first Thursday of the month at various locations. See the website for meeting information.

Asheville Debtors Anonymous *(www.debtorsanonymous.org)* helps people recover from "compulsive debting." It currently meets Mondays at 7 pm at First Congregational United Church at 20 Oak Street in Downtown Asheville.

Asheville Mommies *(www.ashevillemommies.com)* is group of around 200 mothers in Buncombe County who get together mostly on a private, free online forums for support and friendship.

CarePartners *(Main Campus, 68 Sweeten Creek Rd., South Asheville, 828-277-4800, www.carepartners.org)*, a part of Mission Health Systems, offers many support groups including ones for **ALS, Aphasia, Arthritis, Bereavement, Brain Injury, Burn Survivors, Caregivers, End-of-Life Care Planning, Essential Tremor, Grief, MS Caregivers, Parkinson's, Post-Polio, Spinal Cord Injury, Stroke** and others. Call CarePartners or see the website for information on when and where each group meets.

Exceptional Children's Assistance Center, Western Office *(70 Woodfin Place, Downtown Asheville, 828-255-1972, info line 800-962-6817, www.ecac-parentcenter.org)* is private, non-profit group operated by and staffed primarily with parents of children with disabilities and special health care needs. Parent training and other services such as webinars, a lending library and workshops are provided at no cost, with funding by the U.S. Department of Education.

Food Addicts Anonymous *(www.foodaddictsanonymous.org)* is for those recovering from a "biochemical disease of food addition.) The local group currently meets twice weekly in Asheville, at noon Monday and 7 pm Friday at Biltmore United Methodist Church at 376 Hendersonville Road in South Asheville.

GRASP Asheville *(www.grasp.org)* is a support group for adults with Asperger's Syndrome, Pervasive Development Disorder and other high-functioning autism. It currently meets the second Saturday of each month from 3 to 4:30 pm at Firestorm Café, 48 Commerce Street in Downtown Asheville.

The Healing Place *(722 5th Avenue West, Hendersonville, 24-hour crisis line 828-692-3931 in Henderson County or 800-656-4673 in other counties, www.thehealingplace.info),* an offshoot of the Buncombe County Rape Crisis Center, (now Our Voice) offers support for men, women and children who have been victims of sexual violence in Henderson County and elsewhere.

Henderson County Moms

(www.hendersonvillemomsclub.wordpress.com) is part of the International MOMS Club, a non-profit group with some 2,000 chapters with more than 100,000 members across the United States. The local club is a support group for moms who are home during the day, whether or not they also work outside the home.

Hepatitis C Support Group *(www.hepchope.org)* meets the fourth Monday of the month at 6 pm at Mountain Area Health Education Center (MAHEC), 121 Hendersonville Road in South Asheville.

MedWest Health *(68 Hospital Rd., Sylva, 828-586-7000; 45 Plateau St., Bryson City, 828-488-2155; 262 Leroy George Dr., Clyde, 828-456-7311, www.medwesthealth.org),* a group of associated hospitals serving Haywood, Jackson, Swain, Macon and Graham counties affiliated with Charlotte-based Carolinas HealthCare, offers a variety of support groups, including ones on **Breast Cancer, Prostrate Cancer, General Cancer, Grief** and others.

Mission Health *(509 Biltmore Ave., South Asheville, 828-213-1111, www.mission-health.org)* offers many support groups, including **Breast Cancer Survivors, Cancer** (including several American Cancer Society groups), **Cancer Caregivers, Caring for Aging Parents, Diabetes, Disordered Eating, Exercise, Heart, Leukemia and Lymphoma, Lung Transplant, Parenting, Prenatal and Birthing, Women's Issues** and others. Call Mission or visit its website for information on each group, including dates, times and places.

Narcotics Anonymous Western North Carolina Area *(help hotline 866-925-2148, www.wncna.org)* has meetings in Asheville, Hendersonville, Flat Rock and elsewhere. See the website for details on times and places.

National Multiple Sclerosis Society, Asheville
(www.nationalmssociety.org) meets every Thursday from noon to 3 pm at West End Bakery in West Asheville. There are a number of other formal and informal support groups for MS sufferers and caregivers in Western North Carolina.

Our VOICE *(44 Merrimon Ave. Suite 1, North Asheville, 828-252-0562, 24-hour crisis line 828-255-7576, www.ourvoicenc.org)*, established in 1974 as the Rape Crisis Center, provides free, confidential referrals and services for sexual assault victims, survivors and their close family and friends. Our VOICE also conducts a number of educational programs for teens, women and others. Volunteers who staff the crisis line and provide support to sexual violence victims at Mission Hospital Emergency Room must be at least 20 years old, go through a 30-hour training program and have a cell phone and reliable transportation.

Pardee Hospital *(800 N. Justice St., Hendersonville, 828-696-1000, www.pardeehospital.org)* sponsors support activity groups in **AARP Driver Safety, Bipolar, Diabetes, Fibromyalgia, Fitness General Cancer, Labor and Birth, Sjogren's Syndrome, Strength Training, TOPS Weight Management, Yoga, Yogalates** (yoga and pilates) and other. See the events calendar on the Pardee website for details on groups, including time and place.

Park Ridge Hospital (100 Hospital Dr., Hendersonville, 828-684-8501, www.parkridgehealth.org) offers several support groups in South Asheville and Henderson County including **Breast Cancer Survivors** and **Memory Caregivers**.

Sex Addicts Anonymous (828-258-5117 or 828-237-1332, www.orgsites.com/nc/saasheville) has more than a half dozen weekly meetings in Asheville, along with meetings in Hendersonville, Waynesville and elsewhere. These meetings are closed in the sense that they are open only to those seeking to overcome sexual addiction and to become sexually sober via a 12-step program.

WNC Brain Tumor Support *(828-691-2559, www.wncbraintumor.org),* for brain tumor survivors, their families and caregivers, currently holds monthly meetings at Mountain Area Health Education Building (MAHEC) at 121 Hendersonville Road in South Asheville.

WNC Down Syndrome Alliance *(www.wncdsa.org)* is an organization covering 17 Western North Carolina counties devoted to education, support and inclusion of people with Down Syndrome and their families.

Among the services of the Alliance is a free summer day camp (the Buddy Camp) for children 6 to 14 with Down Syndrome and also a family picnic.

Youth Villages *(38 Rosscraggon Road, Suite 38 C, East Asheville, 828-654-7700, www.youthvillages.org)* offers intensive in-home and transitional living services for troubled youth using therapies called Intercept and Multi-Systemic Therapy. It is certified by the NC Department of Health and Human Services. The goal of the private non-profit Youth Villages is to help emotionally and behaviorally troubled children and their families live successfully, preferably in their own homes.

COLLEGES, UNIVERSITIES AND SCHOOLS

Asheville is not really a college town, but there are nearly a dozen colleges in Asheville and Western North Carolina with a total enrollment of around 60,000. Of these, about 25,000 are in the immediate Asheville area, but that includes community college students who may attend just a few classes a year and may be employed full time.

The four-county Asheville metro area alone currently has more than 57,000 students in primary and secondary schools, of which about 53,000 are in public schools and the rest in private and parochial schools.

Tuition and fees costs at colleges shown below do not include room and board or the cost of books. Those costs vary but typically would be around $8,000 to $10,000 a year.

North Carolina's 59 two-year community colleges have an open-enrollment policy. All the community colleges have the same tuition and fees costs, around $2,300 a year for full-time in-state students and $8,500 for out-of-state students. These figures are for 2014-2015.

Most of the colleges and universities in Western North Carolina are not considered "highly selective."

Standardized test achievement scores in local high schools are significantly higher than the state and national averages. *(See below.)*

The North Carolina legislature, now controlled by conservative Republicans, has been accused of gutting the state's previously elite university system and keeping public school teachers lowly paid. North Carolina is 46th among all states in public school teacher pay. In the Southeast, pathetically, it ranks ahead of only Mississippi and West Virginia in teacher salaries.

COLLEGES AND UNIVERSITIES
Appalachian State University *(Boone, 828-262-2000; www.appstate.edu)* is part of the University of North Carolina system. On its main 410-acre campus in Boone, in the High Country, it has around 17,000 students, the largest number of any university in Western North Carolina. Including satellite campuses, App State covers around 1,300 acres and has about 18,000 students. It offers around 150 undergraduate and graduate majors, granting bachelor, masters and a small number of doctoral degrees.

The average SAT score of freshmen in the 2014 entering class (combined math and verbal, maximum score 1600) was 1180. In-state tuition at App State for 2015-2016 is around $6,700 and out-of-state about $20,000. The App State Mountaineers have 20 varsity sports teams in Division I of the NCAA; the school's football team competes in the Football Championship Subdivision, formerly I-AA. In what some sports writers called the ultimate upset, in 2007 App State defeated the then 5th ranked University of Michigan, the first time that an I-AA team beat a nationally ranked I-A team.

Asheville-Buncombe Technical Community *College (340 Victoria Rd., Asheville, 828-254-1921; www.abtech.edu)* is a large community college in Asheville founded in 1959. With satellite campuses in Enka-Candler and in Madison County, typical enrollment is around 8,000. Over the course of the year, some 27,000 people ranging from high school students to retirees take classes at A-B Tech. The main concentrations are courses leading to associate two-year degrees in nursing and allied health industries, business management, technical engineering and emergency services.

Blue Ridge Community College *(180 West Campus Dr., Flat Rock, 828-694-1700; www.blueridge.edu)* is a two-year community college near Hendersonville, with a satellite campus in Brevard. The community college offers nearly 40 two-year degree programs. In-state tuition is around $2,300 a year while out-of-state tuition and fees total about $8,500. The school has about 2,500 students, of which around 1,000 are full-time.

Brevard College *(1 Brevard College Dr., Brevard, 828-883-8292 or 800-527-9090; www.brevard.edu)* is a four-year private liberal arts college affiliated with the United Methodist Church. It has a 120-acre campus with about 700 students in the town of Brevard. Tuition and fees are around $26,000. Average SAT math and verbal scores are 965.

Caldwell Community College & Technical Institute *(372 Community College Dr., Boone, 828-297-3811; www.cccti.edu)* operates a satellite campus in Boone, with a total of about 1,800 students full- and part-time.

Haywood Community College *(185 Freedlander Dr, Clyde, NC, 828-627-2821; www.haywood.edu)* is a two-year community college about 25 miles west of Asheville in Haywood County. The school has about 3,000 students in some 30 diploma and other programs.

Isothermal Community College *(286 ICC Loop Rd., Spindale, 818-286-3636; www.isothermal.edu)* is a two-year community college in Spindale in Rutherford County, with a satellite campus in Columbus, N.C. About 2,500 students attend the school. WNCW-FM is based on the ICC campus.

Lees-McRae College *(191 Main St., Banner Elk, 828-898-5241;* *www.lmc.edu)* has about 900 students on a 460-acre campus at around 4,000 feet elevation in Banner Elk. Average SAT score on verbal and math (maximum 1600) is 969. Tuition and fees total about $24,000.

Mars Hill University *(100 Athletic St., Mars Hill, 866-642-4968;* *www.mhc.edu)* is a Baptist-affiliated four-year college in Mars Hill in Madison County, about 25 minutes north of Asheville. The college has about 1,200 students in about 30 majors, with another 200 adults in evening programs. Tuition and fees total about $28,000. The average SAT score (verbal and math) is 935.

Montreat College *(310 Gaither Circle, Montreat, 800-622-6968,* *www.montreat.edu)* is a Christian college on a 43-acre acre main campus near Black Mountain. The college has several other locations around North Carolina. There are about 450 students at the main campus, and about 750 at all its branches. Currently, Montreat offers baccalaureate and a small number of master's degrees. The average SAT scores of the middle 50% of students is 810 to 1030. Tuition at Montreat is around $25,000. Montreat College has been facing financial shortfalls, and its board at one point was looking at various options, including mergers or consolidations.

South College-Asheville *(140 Sweeten Creek Rd., 828-398-2500,* *www.southcollegenc.edu)* is a private, for-profit college that offers associate degrees in several medical, business and criminal justice areas, plus bachelor of science degrees in two fields. The school, with several hundred students, is located in a single building in South Asheville. Tuition costs are high, four to five times the cost of public community colleges.

Southwestern Community College *(447 College Dr., Sylva, 828-339-4000, www.southwesterncc.edu)* serves Jackson, Swain and Macon counties. The main campus is in Sylva, with satellite centers near Franklin, in Cashiers, Cherokee and in Almond. Enrollment is around 2,700. SCC offers more than 70 different two-year degree and other training programs.

University of North Carolina at Asheville *(1 University Heights, Asheville, 828-251-600, www.unca.edu)* is a liberal arts university in the University of North Carolina system. It has around 3,800 students, with about two-fifths living on campus and the rest commuting. The college offers bachelor and master's degrees. UNC-A has been ranked by several national publications as one of the best values in the country in a liberal arts public college. In 2014 *U.S. News & World Report* named UNC-Asheville the seventh best public liberal arts college in the nation. Average SAT scores (verbal and math) are 1166. In-state tuition and fees total around $7,700 and out-of-state tuition and fees about $22,000.

Warren Wilson College *(701 Warren Wilson Rd., Swannanoa, 828-258-4521; www.warren-wilson.edu)* is a private college that focuses on a "triad of education, work and service." All resident students put in 15 hours a week on one of about 100 farm and other college work crews, in addition to their academic courses. Students also are required to put in at least 100 hours over four years in community service. The college, on a 900-acre campus between Asheville and Black Mountain, has about 900 students and offers bachelor and MFA degrees. About 90% of students live on campus. Average freshman SAT scores (verbal and math) in 2014 were 1124. Tuition and fees run about $31,000. Around Asheville Warren Wilson is known as a "hippie" or alternative college.

Western Carolina University *(1 University Way, Cullowhee, 828-227-7321; www.wcu.edu)*, part of the University of North Carolina system, has about 10,000 students in undergraduate and graduate programs. The 600-acre campus in Cullowhee is an hour by car southwest of Asheville. In-state tuition and fees for 2015-2016 around $6,500 a year, and out-of-state about $20,000. Math and verbal SAT scores of the middle 50% of the 2014 entering freshman class were 920 to 1100.

PUBLIC HIGH SCHOOL SYSTEM
SAT SCORES 2014
US: 1497
NC: 1483
Buncombe County: 1543
Asheville City: 1601
Average SAT Scores Based on Verbal, Math and Writing Combined (Perfect Score = 2400)

U.S. NEWS AND WORLD REPORT RANKINGS, 2014
Hendersonville High School is ranked fourth in North Carolina in the *U.S. News and World Report's* "Best High Schools" rankings, released in 2014, while three Buncombe County high schools placed in the Top 20 in the state. Hendersonville High in Hendersonville was awarded a silver medal in the magazine's rankings. Also earning silver medals were Reynolds High School, Owen High School and Enka High School in Buncombe County, which ranked No. 12, No. 17 and No. 20 in the state, respectively, *U.S. News* awards gold, silver or bronze medals based on schools' performance on state assessments and how well they prepare students for college.

Which School Is Right for Your Kids?

If you have school-age kids, making a decision about the right primary, middle or high school comes down to the right fit for you, and, more importantly, for your kids. Big school, small school, public, private, charter – it all depends on how your kids will do in that atmosphere.

The author went to Enka High School in Buncombe County, back in the Dark Ages. At that time, it was just a country school, and few of the students came from families with more money than just to get by. However, we received what I thought was a very good education, with some superb, dedicated teachers (and some that were just doing their time.) My sincere and lifetimes thanks to wonderful teachers, like Mr. Paul Deason, Mr. Jerry Starnes and Miss Laura Harrell, to name a few. My class had a sizeable number of National Merit Semi-finalists and Finalists, and a number of my schoolmates went on to get PhDs or to become physicians, dentists, lawyers, engineers, college professors or other professionals.

Our own kids went to Asheville High School, and in my opinion they received a first-rate public school education. At that time, the late 20th and early years of the 21st century, Asheville High was actually two schools, and it is probably still so today. One school had the sons and daughters of much of Asheville's elite -- doctors, attorneys, successful businesspeople -- while the other had kids who were in many cases victims of poverty, broken families and of discrimination based on class, race and ethnic background. Still, many of Asheville High's teachers, administrators and coaches were truly excellent. Badly paid, overworked and often not appreciated, they deserve to be recognized as heroes and exceptional people. Our kids were admitted to some of the country's top private and public schools. Our son chose to go to Harvard, and our daughter chose to go to UNC-Chapel Hill and to the University of Oregon for graduate school.

Asheville also has very good private and parochial schools, including The Asheville School and Carolina Day School.

Notable Secondary Public and Private Secondary Schools in the Region

A. C. Reynolds High School
Asheville High School
The Asheville School
Carolina Day School
Charles D. Owen High School
Christ School
Enka High School

Hendersonville High School
T. C. Roberson High School
Watauga High School

SHOPPING IN ASHEVILLE

Grove Arcade in Downtown Asheville, built in the 1920s, supposedly was one of the country's first enclosed malls – photo by Rose Lambert-Sluder

Asheville is the shopping hub of Western North Carolina. While there are interesting shops in Hendersonville, Waynesville, Brevard, Bryson City, Black Mountain and other towns in WNC, Asheville gets about 60% of total retail dollars in the region.

Antiques

Asheville, like most cities, abounds with antique stores and shops. Probably the two best areas for antique shopping in Asheville are the **Biltmore/South Asheville** area, with more than a dozen shops and antique malls, and the **North Lexington Avenue** area of Downtown.

Swannanoa River Road near Biltmore has several large antique malls/barns, including **Antique Tobacco Barn** *(75 Swannanoa River Rd., South Asheville, 828-252-7291; www.atbarn.com)*, in a former burley tobacco warehouse, with 77,000 square feet of antiques and junque from 75 dealers. **ScreenDoor** *(115 Fairview Rd., 828-277-3667; www.screendoorasheville.com)* has about 100 vendors in 30,000 square feet.

Biltmore Village has several upscale antique shops. Downtown, check out antique shops along Lexington Avenue, Walnut Street, Rankin Avenue and Broadway Street. However, a couple of the longtime antique malls in this area have closed or relocated.

Art and Crafts Galleries

If you're a gallery junkie, Asheville is paradise. There are dozens of art and crafts galleries Downtown and in the River Arts District. *See the Arts chapter for information on the galleries.*

Bargains

Asheville Food Truck Lot *(51 Coxe Ave., Downtown Asheville),* next to the main Asheville Redefines Transit bus terminal, is a permanent spot for food trucks selling inexpensive food at lunch and dinner. Vendors vary, but you can get Vietnamese, Indian, Lebanese, Mexican, Korean, sandwiches, soul food and other eats. A few vendors stay open late, especially in summer. Food trucks also make appearances, on a rotating basis, at other venues including the Bywater bar, Wedge Brewery, Pisgah Brewery and elsewhere. A second, smaller food truck lot is on Broadway next to the Masonic Temple building.

Discount Shoes *(1266 Brevard Rd., Asheville West, 828-667-0085)* attracts shoppers from far and wide for its huge selection of name-brand boots and shoes at discounted prices. This warehouse-style, self-service store usually has large, wide and narrow sizes often not available in regular stores. Not every pair of shoes is a bargain, but there are many deals, and the selection is truly huge. Next door and owned by the same people is **Country Casuals** *(1255 Brevard Rd., 828-667-9776)* with discounted Carhartt work and outdoor clothing.

Enchanted Forrest Boutique *(235 Merrimon Ave., North Asheville, 828-236-0688 and 1800 Hendersonville Rd. South Asheville, 828-274-1591; www.theenchantedforrest.com)* is an upscale consignment shop specializing in designer label apparel and accessories for women. If you're lucky, you find brands like Prada, Gucci, Hermes, Louis Vuitton, Michael Kors, Fendi and Armani. Consignors get 40% of the sales price, or 50% if they take their loot in store credit.

Goodwill Industries Retail Store *(616 Patton Ave., West Asheville, 828-771-2192; www.goodwillnwnc.org)* has several outlets in the Asheville area, but this one, in a former Lowe's store, is huge, and it was renovated and expanded in late 2012. Along with the usual used clothes (displayed by size), appliances, furniture and such, it has a section of new, never-used items.

Habitat for Humanity ReStore *(31 Meadow Rd., South Asheville near Biltmore Village, 828-254-6706; www.ashevillehabitat.org)* is one of the best Habitat stores you'll see. It's been recently redone and has a large selection of furniture, antiques, housewares, appliances, sporting goods and electronics (no clothing).

Lulu's Consignment Boutique *(3461 Hendersonville Rd., Fletcher, 828-687-7565, www.ilovelulus.net)* is the biggest consignment shop in the area, with 6,000 consignors in 13,000 square feet of space. Lulu's has name-brand clothing, furniture, shoes and lots more. It doesn't accept many low-end brands or a number of items such as exercise equipment, real fur, knives or guns. Many items are available only seasonally. If the item sells, consignors get 40%, the store gets 60%.

Tanner Outlet *(214 Fashion Circle., Rutherfordton, 828-287-4205 and 119 Broadway, Black Mountain, 828-669-5117)* has clothes for professional women (mostly the Doncaster brand) at very serious savings.

WNC Farmers Market Truck Sheds *(570 Brevard Rd., Asheville West, 828- 253-1691; www.ncagr.gov/markets/facilities/markets/asheville/)* is the place to go if you're looking for a bushel of peaches, a peck of hot peppers, pumpkins and corn shocks for your Halloween decorations or a fresh-cut Fraser fir for Christmas. Some truck shed stalls (notably shed numbers 1, 4 and 5) are limited to farmers who only sell locally grown products, while stalls in other sheds others are rented by vendors who re-sell produce from out-of-state. The truck sheds are located below the main retail buildings that you'll pass first as you enter the market.

Bookstores

ASHEVILLE

Barnes & Noble *(Asheville Mall, 3 S. Tunnel Rd., Asheville, 828-296-7335, and 33 Town Square Blvd., Asheville, 828-687-0681; www.bn.com)* has locations at the Asheville Mall and Biltmore Park Town Square south of Asheville.

Battery Park Book Exchange & Champagne Bar *(Grove Arcade, 1 Page Ave., Asheville, 828-252-0020, www.batteryparkbookexchange.com)*, in a new location on the south end of the Grove Arcade, has wines by the glass and 22,000 books. "Dogs and their well-behaved owners welcome."

Biblio.com *(P.O. Box 1211, Asheville, NC 28802, 828-350-0744, www.biblio.com)* is a large used and rare bookstore based in Asheville that sells only on-line.

Established in 2003, it claims to offer 85 million used, rare and out-of-print books from more than 5,000 bookshops. Some sources say it is the third largest used book marketplace in the U.S.

Captain's Bookshelf *(31 Page Ave., Asheville, 828-253-6631, www.captainsbookshelf.com)* is the region's oldest and best antiquarian bookstore.

Downtown Books & News *(67 N. Lexington Ave., Asheville, 828-253-8654, www.downtownbooksandnews.com)*, associated with Malaprop's Bookstore, has an excellent selection of used and rare books and out-of-town newspapers and magazines.

Firestorm Cafe and Books *(www.firestormcafe.com)* is a worker-owned café with a small selection of independently published, offbeat books. Formerly on Commerce Street Downtown, it plans to reopen at 610 Haywood Road in West Asheville in 2015.

Malaprop's Bookstore/Café *(55 Haywood St., Asheville, 828-254-6734, www.malaprops.com)*, in business for more than 30 years, is Asheville's best bookstore, what an independent bookstore should be, with many local and regional books and a knowledgeable staff.

Montford Books & More *(31 Montford Ave., Asheville, 828-285-8805; www.montfordbooks.com)* has some 20,000 used books, CDs, DVDs and vinyl records. There's also a coffee bar.

Spellbound Children's Books *(21 Battery Park Ave., Asheville, 828-319-1907, www.spellboundchildrensbookshop.com)* is a bookshop with books for babies and toddlers to teens, located inside the ZaPow Art Gallery.

OUTSIDE ASHEVILLE

City Lights Bookstore *(3 East Jackson St., Sylva, 828-586-9499 or 888-853-6298; www.citylightsnc.com)* is a small, comfy bookshop with a good selection of regional books. However, it's not much like its famous namesake in San Francisco. Next door is the pleasant **City Lights Café.**

The Fountainhead Bookstore *(408 N Main St., Hendersonville, 828-697-1870; www.fountainheadbookstore.com)* is in downtown Hendersonville.

Car Dealers

Nearly all vehicle brands have dealerships in the Asheville area and around Western North Carolina. Toyota, Chevrolet, Buick, Cadillac, Ford, Chrysler, Dodge, Jeep, Nissan, Honda, Kia, Hyundai, Subaru and other major brands have multiple locations in the region.

Audi, Porsche, VW, Volvo, Mercedes, BMW, Jaguar and Land Rover also have dealers in the Asheville-Hendersonville area. The exceptions without local dealerships include Rolls-Royce, Bentley, Tesla, Ferrari and, oddly, Lexus; the nearest Lexus dealer currently is in Greenville, S.C.

A number of new car dealers have gravitated to Brevard Road in West Asheville, handy to both I-40 and I-26.

We give a nod toward **Jim Barkley Toyota** *(777 Brevard Rd., West Asheville, 828-667-8888, www.jimbarleytoyota.com),* not necessarily because they offer the lowest prices but because they have no-haggle pricing and no pushy salespeople. We've also found their service department to be generally competent and service-oriented, though sometimes a little pricey for repairs.

Funky Boutiques

North Lexington Avenue (on the north side of Patton Avenue) is the place for small funky boutiques, selling organic clothing, tie-dyed items, beads, crafts and New Age items. Lexington also has some not-so-funky but interesting shops. In fact, many sides of Asheville are represented on Lexington Avenue: subversive hippie, wholesome hippie, hipster, sexy-deviant, intellectual, with its almost self-caricaturizing shops; proudly organic clothing shops; funky resale hipster shops; an intellectual, gritty lesbian bookshop; the artsy; and DYI bead shop. There's even a lingerie store.

Among other places check out **Vintage Moon,** with gorgeous handmade clothes and aprons and elegant lacy vintage items; **The Honeypot,** a vintage, hipster shop with some handmade items; **Hip Replacements,** like The Honeypot, but even more hipster; **Chevron Trading Post and Beads; Downtown Books and News** *(see Bookstores, above);* **Natural Home** and **Dobra Tea,** with a Czech heritage and a great selection of teas along with sweet and savory snacks.

Not funky, but one of the great old-time Asheville stores, dating back to 1952, is **Tops for Shoes** *(27 N. Lexington Ave., Downtown Asheville, 828-254-6721; www.topsforshoes.com)***,** with a huge selection of adult and children's shoes, helpful sales people and a friendly atmosphere.

Groceries and Supermarkets

The major chain supermarket in the Asheville area is **Ingles** *(2913 US Hwy. 70 West, Black Mountain, 828-669-2941; www.ingles-markets.com),* a publicly held regional chain with more than 200 stores in the Southeast.

It was founded in Asheville 1963 (the first store was on Hendersonville Road near Biltmore) and is still based in the Asheville area. The largest and most appealing Ingles stores locally include those in North Asheville *(915 Merrimon Ave.)* and on Tunnel Road *(29 Tunnel Rd.)* **Bi-Lo, Go Grocery Outlet** and **Harris-Teeter** are among other regional chains with outlets in Asheville. **Publix** is opening in 2015 on Hendersonville Road in South Asheville. **Walmart** has several Supercenters with grocery sections in the area, plus a **Sam's** with bulk food items. **Costco** long has been rumored to be opening in Asheville, but so far that hasn't happened. **Target** stores also sell some groceries.

Among the organic and gourmet groceries in the Asheville area are **Earth Fare** *(66 Westgate Parkway, West Asheville, 828-253-7656, and 1856 Hendersonville Rd., South Asheville, 828-210-0100; www.earthfare.com),* founded and based in Asheville and now with about 30 locations in the Southeast and Midwest**; Fresh Market** *(944 Merrimon Ave., North Asheville, 828-252-9098 and 1378 Hendersonville Rd., South Asheville, 828-277-7023; www.thefreshmarket.com),* a publicly held upscale supermarket chain based in Greensboro, N.C. with around 130 stores in 26 states; **French Broad Food Co-op** *(90 Biltmore Ave., Downtown Asheville, 828-255-7650; www.frenchbroadfood.coop),* a local store specializing in locally grown organic foods and other products, open to the public although co-op members and co-op workers receive discounts; and **Greenlife** *(70 Merrimon Ave., North Asheville, 828-254-5440; www.wholefoodsmarket.com),* though now owned and operated by the **Whole Foods** chain, remains immensely popular locally. There is a second **Whole Foods**, this one under the Whole Food brand *(4 Tunnel Road, East Asheville, 828-239-9604, www.wholefoodsmarket.com/stores/asheville-kenilworth).* **Katuah Market** *(2 Hendersonville Rd., South Asheville, 828-676-2882; www.katuahmarket.com),* which opened in late 2013, is operated by Ashevillian John Swann, who was co-owner of the original Greenlife.

Trader Joe's *(120 Merrimon Ave., North Asheville; www.traderjoes.com),* the chain of neighborhood groceries with nearly 400 stores in 33 states, finally opened here in 2013. The rumor mill has it that the chain is also looking at a location in South Asheville. Fresh Market, Greenlife, Harris-Teeter, Ingles and Trader Joe's are among the groceries on **"Supermarket Mile"** on Merrimon Avenue.

Amazing Savings *(121 Sweeten Creek Rd., South Asheville, 828-669-898; 45 S. French Broad Ave., Downtown, 828-255-8858; and U.S. Hwy, 70, Black Mountain, 828-669-8988)* does have some truly amazing bargains on food items, although you have to look carefully at the expiration dates.

Malls

If you must go to a mall, the only one worth of the name is the **Asheville Mall** *(3 S. Tunnel Rd., East Asheville, 828-298-5080; www.asheville-mall.com)*, a large regional mall with one million square feet of retail space, more than 100 specialty stores and **Belk, Sears, Dillard's** and **JCPenney** as anchors. The **Barnes & Noble** bookstore here is the largest one in the state. Be forewarned that Tunnel Road traffic can be very bad. The other "major" mall, **Biltmore Square Mall** never achieved much success. It underwent a complete makeover, reopening in May 2015 as **Asheville Outlets** *(800 Brevard Rd, 828-667-2308, www.shopashevilleoutlets.com)* with about 75 outlet stores. The other "malls" around town, such as **Westgate, River Ridge, Southridge** and **Innsbruck Mall,** are just strip shopping centers.

A couple of other mallish places you might consider are **Biltmore Park Town Square** *(1 Town Square Blvd., South Asheville, 828-210-1660; www.biltmorepark.com)*, a planned mix-used community with a 15-screen movie theater, **Biltmore Grande,** some chain stores including **REI, Orvis** and **Barnes & Noble,** a **Hilton** hotel and a number of chain restaurants including **P.F. Chang's**, plus apartments and condos. The **Grove Arcade** *(1 Page Ave., Downtown Asheville, 828-252-7799; www.grovearcade.com)*, originally built in the 1920s as an one of the first enclosed malls in the country, is perhaps more for visitors than locals, but it has a nice selection of restaurants around the exterior, many with sidewalk seating, and a few interesting shops inside, along with apartments and offices. Don't miss the **Battery Park Book Exchange & Champagne Bar** *(1 Page Ave., #101, Downtown Asheville, 828-252-0020, www.batteryparkbookexchange.com)*.

Big Box stores including **Best Buy, Target, Home Depot** and **Lowe's** are scattered around the Asheville suburbs.

Tailgate Markets

The Asheville area is home to dozens of tailgate markets selling organic and natural produce, crafts, jams, jellies and other homemade foods and other items. The **Appalachian Sustainable Agriculture Project** or **ASAP** *(306 Haywood St., Downtown Asheville, 828-236-1282; www.buyappalachian.org)* maintains a complete list of tailgate and farmers markets in the region.

Among the larger Asheville tailgate markets are the following. Most markets close in winter or have reduced hours.

Asheville City Market *(161 S. Charlotte St., Downtown Asheville, Wed. 1-5; winter location atrium of Haywood Park Hotel, 46 Haywood St., Sat. 10-1)*

Asheville City Market South *(2 Town Square Park, Biltmore Town Square, South Asheville, Wed. 1-5 Apr.-Oct.)*

French Broad Co-Op Wednesday Tailgate Market *(70 Biltmore Ave., Downtown Asheville, Wed. 2-6, Apr.-Nov.)*

North Asheville Tailgate Market *(Parking Lot C, University of North Carolina at Asheville, North Asheville, Sat. 8-noon.)*

Oakley Farmers Market *(607 Fairview Rd., South Asheville near Biltmore Village, Thurs. 3:30-630, May-Sep.)*

River Arts District Tailgate Market *(175 Clingman Ave., River Arts District, Wed. 2-6, May-Nov.)*

Weaverville Farmers Market *(60 Lakeshore Dr., Weaverville, Wed. 2:30-6:30, Apr.-Oct.)*

West Asheville Tailgate Market *(718 Haywood Rd., West Asheville, Tue. 3:30-6:30, Apr.-Nov.)*.

Direct sales made through tailgate markets and farm stands have increased by more than 60% in WNC, according to ASAP's Local Food Research Center, from $5 million in 2007 to $8 million in 2012. The total likely has increased even more in 2013-2015. ASAP says nearly 700 farms in WNC sell direct. On a per-capita basis that is about four times higher than the average nationally.

Altogether according to ASAP, in 2013 WNC consumers spent more than $170 million on local farm products, a 42% increase over the previous year. By contrast, on a national basis direct sales from farms have been flat.

Asheville Souvenirs and Mementos

While you're trying to decide if you want to live in Asheville or not, you might as well buy a souvenir of your visit. The most meaningful souvenirs and mementos of Asheville and the mountains are locally and hand-produced items, including crafts, art, books and food and drink.

At or near the top of the list for souvenirs has to be **crafts.** The Asheville area is a nationally known center for crafts, **especially pottery and ceramics, woodworking, basketry and fabric crafts, especially quilts.** You'll want to start your search either at some of the **Downtown Asheville craft galleries and malls,** or at the studios and galleries the **River Arts District.** *See the Arts section of this book for comprehensive information.*

You can find collectible pottery starting from around $25 to $50, though some pieces sell for much more. Asheville and the surrounding area, especially near Penland School, has literally scores of talented potters, including many whose work is known nationally and is in museum collections.

In the Downtown galleries and River Arts District working studios also are many examples of hand-made wood crafts, both furniture and functional small pieces. Many are made from local cherry, maple, hickory, oak and black walnut woods.

Hand-made quilts have become highly collectible in recent decades. Prices often run into the thousands for fine examples of hand-made and antique quilts. The **Folk Art Center** on the Blue Ridge Parkway is a good place to begin looking at quilts, but some crafts galleries Downtown also have fine quilts. The **Asheville Quilt Show** is held at the **WNC Ag Center** *(1301 Fanning Bridge Rd. Fletcher, 828-687-1414; www.mountainfair.org)*, across from the Asheville Regional Airport. The Asheville area has about two dozen fabric and quilting shops, some of which can refer you to local quilters. The **Asheville Quilt Guild** *(www.ashevillequiltguild.org)* is an organization of more than 300 local quilters. The national **Alliance for American Quilts** *(www.allianceforamericanquilts.org)* is now based in Asheville.

Baskets, especially those made by Cherokee craftspeople, are another highly collectible category. Fine modern and antique examples of basketry can cost many hundreds, even thousands, of dollars. **Qualla Arts & Crafts Mutual** *(645 Tsali Blvd., Cherokee, 828-497-3103; www.quallaartsandcrafts.com)* displays and sells museum-quality work in baskets and other local Native American crafts.

Asheville has many fine artists working in all mediums. Local galleries display and sell their works. *See the Arts section of this book.*

Local mountain foods are another excellent idea for souvenirs of Asheville. Consider locally made **jams, jellies, preserves and canned vegetables.** Local honey is another great souvenir, especially the **sourwood honey** found almost nowhere else except Western North Carolina. Sourwood honey is very light in color and has a delicate taste. Sourwood trees typically bloom in June and July in the mountains, so the sourwood honey flow shows up in July.

Be sure to buy from a reputable honey producer or retailer, as other light honeys, such as black locust (which is produced by honeybees in May), is sometimes passed off for sourwood. Because of its rarity, sourwood honey costs more than most other honeys, retailing for around $20 a quart.

The **WNC Farmers Market** (*(570 Brevard Rd., Asheville West, 828-253-1691*) is a good place to buy sourwood honey, along with many locally put up jellies and vegetables. **Oates Produce** and **Haw Creek Honey** are two commercial beekeeping operations that sell at the WNC Farmers Market. Also visit local tailgate markets, usually held weekly at various locations around Asheville. *(See Tailgate Markets above.)*

If you're a gardener, **Sow True Seeds** *(146 Church St., Downtown Asheville, 828-254-0708, www.sowtrueseed.com)* has more than 500 varieties of heirloom, open-pollinated, GMO-free and organic vegetable, herb and flower seeds, some of them unique to the Western North Carolina area. The retail store, usually open daily except Sunday (hours vary seasonally), is in the company's warehouse. Sow True Seed also has paper and online catalogs.

For local and regional books, check out **Malaprop's** (*(55 Haywood St., Down Asheville, 828-254-6734, www.malaprops.com)*, or one of the other bookstores *listed above.*

Local beers, wines and liquors are other items to consider taking back home. Look for local craft beers and wines that may not be available in your hometown. **Biltmore** is by far the best-known winery in the region, producing some 140,000 cases a year, but there are many other small local winemakers in the mountains. Beers and ales from **Pisgah, Wedge, Highland, Green Man** and **Wicked Weed** are among the most interesting local brews. Moonshine is produced legally at least two local distilleries. **Troy and Sons** *(12 Old Charlotte Hwy., 828-575-2000, www.troyandsons.com)* distills and sells legal moonshine made from locally grown heirloom white corn. However, distilled spirits including Troy and Sons moonshine can only be purchased in ABC stores, not at the distillery. *For more information see the Beer and also the Wineries and Distilleries sections of this book.*

Local gems and minerals also make good souvenirs of your trip to Asheville. The area has many gem mines where you can dig or pan for precious and semi-precious gems. Some are tourist traps, and some are not. *For the best choices, see the rock hounding section of the Asheville Outside chapter.*

If you're a baseball fan, check out the souvenir shop at **McCormick Field,** *(30 Buchanan Place, Downtown Asheville, 828-259-5800, www.asheville.tourists.milb.com),* home of the Asheville Tourists minor league team (a Single A affiliate of the Colorado Rockies.)

Photographs of your trip help bring back memories that last forever. You'll find amazing photographic opportunities on the Blue Ridge Parkway, in the Great Smokies, on the Biltmore Estate, in Downtown Asheville and all over the Western North Carolina region.

WHERE WILL YOU LIVE?

Deciding where to move is a big decision, but deciding exactly where you will live there can be an equally big decision. Buying real estate is a major investment decision, of course. But beyond that, every city, town and village has pluses and minuses, and within each area often there are subtle differences within sections of neighborhoods, or even from one block to another. Each piece of land, home, condo or apartment has its own positives and negatives.

It's impossible for this or any other book to lead you to the perfect, ideal, platonic place for you to live. Our goal here is to give you a sense of the options available to you, the pros and cons of each one and an idea of the cost at the time of writing (2014). We'll also direct you to sources of more information and the best available data on up-to-date prices.

At the same time, we have no interest in selling you any particular property. When we mention a residential subdivision, a condo development or any community by name, we are just bringing it to your attention so you can evaluate it for yourself. What he hope is that we can help you come to your own decision, one that suits your needs best.

Please note: When it comes to real estate, there are statistics, statistics and statistics. Whether it's rental rate or home prices, you'll find significant variations in numbers. Some variations come from definitions – median versus average, listing versus selling price, gross versus net rent, and so on. Others variations come from the methodology used by various sources, whether it's the U.S. Census *(www.census.gov),* private real estate websites such as Zillow *(www.zillow.com)* or Trulia *(www.trulia.com)* or local real estate firms such as Beverly-Hanks *(www.beverly-hanks.com).* We use a diverse mix of sources of information. Just don't expect total consistency.

Rent or Buy?

In my articles and books on moving to Belize, I always recommend that prospective retirees or relocatees to Belize rent for a while, usually six months to a year, before they buy or build a home. Most other responsible advisors give the same advice. In the case of Belize, it's a new country, a new society, a new environment.

New arrivals may decide they don't like Belize after all, or for medical, family or financial reasons they need to be somewhere else. Just as important, because the Belize real estate market is thin, with relatively few local buyers and expensive or difficult to obtain mortgage loan options, it can take years to sell some properties.

Moving to another part of your home country, or perhaps within the same region or even the same state, the argument for renting for a time before you buy is less persuasive. From previous visits, you may know Asheville and the Western North Carolina mountains quite well and may be ready to buy as soon as you find the right place. Still, for some people renting first still makes sense, so in this chapter we have included information on renting, along with buying or building. No matter how many times you visited here on vacation, or have stayed here with friends or family, nothing can take the place of actually living here for several months or a year or two to give you a true local perspective on the area.

Typical Rental Rates

Overall, in the four-county Asheville MSA about 31% of households rent instead of own or have other living arrangements. Those figures are 2012-2013 estimates from the U.S. Census. Other estimates put the percentage of rentals in Asheville-Buncombe as high as 44%, being especially high in the city of Asheville. Home ownership rates vary in other parts of Western North Carolina but generally are slightly higher in small towns and rural areas, as opposed to Asheville and Buncombe County.

According to U.S. Census estimates for 2013, the median gross rent in the Asheville area was $797 a month, lower than the U.S. national median gross rent of $905 a month. Median means that one-half the rentals were above this figure, and one-half below it. Gross rent is contract rent plus the estimated average monthly cost of utilities (electricity, gas, water and sewer) and fuel (oil, kerosene, wood, etc.). These rental figures take into account all types and sizes of rentals.

The Asheville rental vacancy rate in 2013 was around 4.9%, almost 2 percentage points lower than the national average. There is usually strong demand for well-priced rentals in or near job and population centers such as Asheville, and landlords and property managers often report getting a high level of responses on rental advertisements in local newspapers or on Craig's List. A few years ago, the author put an ad for a small (600 square feet) house for rent in a rural area near Asheville on Craig's List. The monthly rent was around $500 (only water included), and I received more than 150 emails, calls and visits in a week. I could have rented a dozen such houses.

Rental rates vary greatly by geographical area and by size and type of property. The lowest rental rates tend to be in rural areas some distance from population centers, while the highest rates are for homes and large apartments in or near Downtown Asheville. Mobile homes almost always are the at the bottom end of the rental rates. According to the Asheville Area Chamber of Commerce, the average rental in the Asheville-Buncombe area for a 2-bedroom, 1-2 bath, unfurnished, 950 sq. ft. apartment is $865. Zillow *(www.zillow.com)* and Trulia *(www.trulia.com)* provide current rental listings, with rates, square footage and photos, in different geographic areas and neighborhoods in Western North Carolina.

1896 farmhouse owned by the author's family – restored by the author and Robert Rice in 2002

Typical Home Purchase Costs

For the Western North Carolina region, the median average home sale price for $194,500 in late 2014, according to data provided by Beverly-Hanks, the largest real estate firm in the region. There were about 4,700 properties on the market in the region. About 33% of sales in the region in 2014 were for cash, and about 12% of sales were "distress" sales due to foreclosures, short sales and related reasons. (In a short sale, the homeowner negotiates with the lender to sell the property for less than the total mortgage amount.) A total of more than $3 billion in real estate sales took place in the Western North Carolina region in 2014.

For Asheville and Buncombe County, which had about 1,500 properties actively on the market in late 2014, the median sales price was $215,000, up 4.8% from $205,000 at the same time in 2013, again according to Beverly-Hanks data. The largest number of homes sold in Asheville-Buncombe, a little over one-third, were in the $100,000 to $199,000 price range, while a little over one-fourth in the $200,000 to $299,000 price range, and about 19% were in the $300,000 to $499,000 range. Another 8% were in the $500,000 to $999,000 range, and less than 1% over $1 million.

At the $215,000 median sales price figure for Buncombe County, lenders typically would require a household annual income before taxes of about $50,000 to qualify for mortgage of around $172,000 (20% down). The monthly payment would be about $1,050 (including principal, interest, taxes and insurance) if your loan rate were 4%. Of course, since we're talking median averages, by definition one-half of the homes sold cost less than the amount shown.

Here are median average home sale prices in late 2014 in a number of WNC counties. Note that median sales prices can vary significantly from quarter to quarter, especially in the smaller counties with relatively few sales.

Buncombe	$215,000
Henderson	$187,000
Haywood	$160,000
Madison	$170,000
Transylvania	$190,000
Rutherford	$138,000
Polk	$180,000

Largest Real Estate Firms in Asheville Area

Obviously, it is not possible to list all the real estate firms and agents in the region. We have selected some of the largest firms, most located in and around Asheville, the largest city in the mountains.

We do not try to recommend the "best" real estate firms. Larger firms usually provide a wider range of services, but it all comes down to finding a firm and, perhaps more importantly, an agent with whom you feel comfortable and whom you trust.

Large Area Firms Ranked by Sales Volume
1. Beverly-Hanks & Associates, All Offices*
2. Keller Williams Realty Asheville
3. Keller Williams Realty Hendersonville
4. Coldwell Banker King

5. RE/MAX Mountain Realty
6. Preferred Properties
7. Carolina Mountain Sales
8. Town and Mountain Realty

Beverly-Hanks & Associates
300 Executive Park, Asheville, NC 28801
Toll-free: 800-868-7221 or 866-858-2257, 828-254-7221
www.beverly-hanks.com

History: Founded in 1976 through the merger of two local firms. Largest real estate brokerage firm in Western North Carolina and among top seven in the state. Beverly-Hanks belongs to Leading Real Estate Companies of the World network, which has members in more than 40 countries.

Real estate sales volume, 2014: Over $810 million

Number of offices in WNC: 14 (3 residential and 1 commercial Asheville offices, Hendersonville, Waynesville, Lake Lure and Lake James plus branches at selected new home communities including Biltmore Lake, Champion Hills and The Ramble)

Approximate number of local agents: 250+

Services: Residential, commercial, warehouse and land sales; represents about 20 new home communities in WNC; national, international and corporate relocation; mortgage services; title insurance services

Keller-Williams Realty Asheville
86 Asheland Ave., Asheville, NC 28801
Toll-free: 877-221-7253, 828-254-7253
www.kellerwilliamsasheville.com

History: Keller Williams is a national real estate franchise organization established in Texas in 1983. Based in Austin, it has some 700 offices in the U.S. and several foreign countries. It claims to be the largest U.S. real estate firm in terms of number (80,000) of agents.

Number of offices in WNC: 6 (Asheville, Hendersonville, Black Mountain, Waynesville, Brevard and Weaverville)

Approximate number of local agents: 200+

Services: Residential and land sales with both seller and buyer agents; commercial sales through KW Commercial division; mortgage services

Coldwell Banker King
20 Town Mountain Rd., Suite 100, Asheville, North Carolina 28801
828-398-5700

History: Coldwell Banker is a franchise real estate organization based in Madison, N.J., with about 3,000 offices in some 50 countries. It traces its founding as a real estate company back to 1906.

Number of offices in WNC: 1 in Asheville

Approximate number of local agents: 50+

Services: Residential and commercial sales; mortgage services

RE/MAX Mountain Realty

RE/MAX Mountain Realty Waynesville and Maggie Valley

RE/MAX All Stars Realty Asheville

RE/MAX Four Seasons Realty Hendersonville

303-770-5531 (national headquarters)

www.remax.com

History: RE/MAX is an international real estate franchise based in Denver with some 100,000 agents in 6,000 offices in about 90 countries. It claims to be the largest real estate company in the world in terms of market share as measured by residential transactions. Each office is independently owned, and some agents, who are independent contractors, work out of their homes or independent offices.

Number of offices in WNC: 4 (Asheville, Waynesville, Maggie Valley, Hendersonville)

Approximate number of local agents: 125+

Services: Residential, commercial and land sales

Preferred Properties

39 Woodfin St., Asheville, NC 28801

Toll free: 800-951-4646, 828-258-2953

www.preferredprop.com

History: Preferred Properties was founded in Asheville in 1968. It has the reputation of selling higher priced and luxury properties, especially in North Asheville and Biltmore Forest, and the vast majority of its agents are women.

Number of offices in WNC: 2 in Asheville

Approximate number of local agents: 40

Services: Residential sales with sellers', buyers' and dual agents

Carolina Mountain Sales

1550 Hendersonville Rd., Suite 210, Asheville, NC 28803

828-277-5551

www.carolinamountainsales.com

History: Carolina Mountain Sales bills itself as a boutique but full-service realty firm.

Number of offices in WNC: 1 in Asheville
Approximate number of local agents: 20+
Services: Residential sales

Town and Mountain Realty
261 Asheland Ave., Asheville, NC 28801
Toll-free: 800-238-7056, 828-232-2879
www.townandmountain.com

History: Town and Mountain Realty was established in Asheville in the early 2000s.

Number of offices in WNC: 1 in Asheville
Approximate number of local agents: 35+
Services: Residential sales

Properties for Sale in Western North Carolina

The **North Carolina Mountains MLS** (Multiple Listing Service) covers most of Western North Carolina with active real estate listings in 15 counties. There are more than 2,500 real estate agents in Western North Carolina that -- through four local MLS services and boards including Asheville MLS -- own the North Carolina Mountains MLS *(5030 Hendersonville Rd., B1, Fletcher, NC29732, www.ncmmls.com)*. Many thousands more agents use the services of NC Mountains MLS, though they are not owners.

The good news is that consumers also have access to the NC Mountains MLS, at no cost. You simply have to register with your name, email address and a password. You can then search by county, city or zip code for any type of property in which you're interested.

For example, recently we searched for a residential property for sale in Asheville and Buncombe County, with a minimum of three bedrooms and two baths in a house (not a condo) of at least 2,000 sq. ft., priced between $200,000 and $300,000. On this particular day, the system instantly turned up 102 homes that met all those criteria. They are shown on a map of the county, and in addition each listing is identified by address and asking price, with photos of the inside and outside of the home, and with details such as square footage, lot size, year built, style of home, type of heating and cooling, type of flooring in each room, the elementary, middle and high school districts, listing agent, a mortgage calculator and much more.

We then searched for a house in Henderson County, with a minimum of four bedrooms, three baths of at least 3,000 sq. ft., built since 1980, on a lot of 1 acre or more, and priced from $500,000 to $800,000. The MLS system found 10 properties for sale that fit those criteria on this particular date.

Altogether, including homes, condos, townhouses and properties under construction, NC Mountains MLS found 1,522 properties for sale in Asheville and Buncombe County on this particular date in 2014, from $78,400 for a one-bed, one-bath condo in Arden to $10,750,000 for a five-bedroom, seven bath, 16,000 sq. ft. home on 2 acres in Biltmore Forest.

Several other sites, including **Realtor.com** (www.realtor.com), **Zillow** (www.zillow.com) and **Trulia** (www.trulia.com) also are helpful in providing up-to-date data on recent sales and current homes and other property for sale.

Most of these sites also let you search for new listings, foreclosures, short sales and various permutations of historic sales information, so you can see both the big picture and very detailed information on properties of all types in Asheville and Western North Carolina. These sites usually also let you search for rentals.

Another, albeit commercial resource for buyers looking for a private community in Asheville and the WNC mountains is **Private Mountain Communities** (*Grove Arcade, One Page Avenue, Suite 150, Downtown Asheville, 888-517-3322, www.pmcdiscoverasheville.com*). This company acts as a buyer's agent for some 200 communities in the region.

Types of Property in Western North Carolina

Western North Carolina has the usual mix of housing options, including:

Single-family homes: These constitute by the largest category of housing in Asheville and Western North Carolina. Usually manufactured homes and mobile homes are included in this category. Prices for single-family homes in WNC vary tremendously, from under $50,000 for a used mobile home on a small lot to $10 million or more for super-luxury home in a prestigious neighborhood or development.

Condominiums and townhouses: In North Carolina, there are some legal differences between condominiums and townhouses. Condo owners own only the inside of their units. Townhouse owners own the complete unit, including exterior surfaces and the land on which the unit is built.

Condo or townhouse developments may also have "common areas" of the property such as swimming pools, recreation areas, sidewalks, parking lots, etc. Condo owners share ownership of the common areas with other owners; common areas in townhouse developments usually are owned by the homeowners' association for the benefit of unit owners.

With your condo or townhouse you may get deeded parking, or you may only have shared rights to a parking lot or garage, or in some cases, no guaranteed parking at all.

The condo category is most common in and around more urban areas, such as Asheville and Hendersonville. Townhouses are more common in suburban areas. There are many more townhouse developments than true condo developments.

Almost always with condos and townhouses there will be a monthly HOA (Home Owners Association) fee for maintenance and upkeep. Monthly fees vary, but typically will be several hundred dollars. The developer usually remains in control of the association until the developer no longer has the majority of the votes in the association, or until a predetermined deadline has passed.

In North Carolina, the creation, sale and management of condos are governed by specific statutes -- the Unit Ownership Act for condos created before October 1, 1986, and the North Carolina Condominium Act for condos created on or after that date. There are no specific statutes governing most townhouses. However, townhouse projects of more than 20 units and created on or after January 1, 1999, are covered by the Planned Community Act.

Generally, townhouses are less expensive than single-family homes (other than mobile homes), because more units can be packed to the acre. In Asheville, townhomes also usually are less expensive than condominiums, but there are exceptions, especially where former apartment buildings have been converted to condos. In WNC, condos and townhouses start under $100,000, and luxury condos in Asheville can range up beyond $2 million.

Mobile homes: Statewide, according to the U.S. Census Bureau, 14.3% of households lived in mobile homes, compared to 6.6% nationally. North Carolina ranks 5th highest in the U.S. in percentage of mobile homes, after South Carolina, New Mexico, Mississippi and Alabama. In most rural areas of Western North Carolina, including rural parts of Buncombe County, there is no zoning to prohibit mobile homes or to require that they must be in mobile home parks. Note that in North Carolina as of 2014 the sales tax on mobile and modular homes is 4.75% of the sales price, with no cap. That can be a substantial sum, given that the average price for a new single-wide (not including lot) is around $41,000 and $75,000 for a double wide.

Gated communities: In Western North Carolina, gated communities – developments that have a gated entrance to limit access to homeowners and their designees -- are relatively common. We estimate that there are at least 350 to 400 gated communities across the region. Typically, gated communities are at the top tier of lot and home prices. Many of the private **golf communities** in WNC are gated.

Intentional communities: These communities usually reflect some sort of cooperative and sustainable living arrangements. Intentional communities come in many flavors – cohousing, ecovillages, residential land trusts or even communes. There are believed to be more than 40 intentional communities in Western North Carolina. WNC has about two-thirds of all such communities in the state.

Active living adult communities: Adult communities usually require that all or a substantial majority of the units be occupied by at least one person who is over a certain age, typically 55. The "active living" component is used to try to distinguish them from retirement communities or nursing homes.

Retirement communities: These communities usually have three levels of living – independent living for those who don't need any special care, assisted living for those who may need assistance in bathing, dressing or getting meals, and skilled nursing/health center, for those who require 24/7 nursing or other medical care. The better retirement communities in WNC charge substantial prices, often ranging to $5,000 to $10,000 or more a month for a couple in assisted living. Under "Life Care" plans, payments are in a lump sum for the life of the single resident or couple. These plans may require payment of several hundred thousand dollars up to $1 million or more.

Farms and acreage: For some, the perfect mountain home includes some acreage, for a garden, fruit orchard, pastures to keep cattle, horses, goats and other domesticated animals, along with some woods for privacy and beauty. In the state of North Carolina as a whole, the price of farmland averaged $4,450 in 2014. However, acreage in the mountains of Western North Carolina can run much higher than that. The average price of land in parcels of 15 acres or more sold in 2014 was $6,638 per acre, according to a market study by Beverly Hanks & Associates. More than 4,500 acres of land were sold in tracts of at least 15 acres.

Overview of WNC Places to Live

It may seem unnecessary to provide an overview of the region's real estate options.

After all, nearly every region of the country has its cities, suburbs, rural areas and such. But Asheville and the mountains have their own particular, and in some cases, unique characteristics. For example, within the mountains are many, many different microclimatic zones. Elevation, obviously, is critical. The difference between living in a low river valley and on a mile high mountain can be similar to the experience you have driving from warm, sunny Georgia to snowy southern Canada. Even which side of the mountain you live on, say the northeast versus the southwest, can be very important in terms of precipitation and temperature.

Cities

Western North Carolina really has only one real city, Asheville. The Asheville city limits contain a population of around 88,000, while Buncombe County, of which Asheville is the county seat, has a population of 251,000. The four-county Asheville Metropolitan Statistical Area (MSA) consists of Buncombe, Henderson, Haywood and Madison counties, with a total population of around 444,000. These population numbers are estimates for 2014.

Asheville, though hardly a large city, is truly the hub of WNC. It is where many residents from surrounding areas come for entertainment, shopping, arts and culture, dining, medical care and air transportation. Only the town of Hendersonville, population 13,500, is at all competitive with Asheville for urban amenities, and although a lovely spot, it runs a distant second.

Asheville Neighborhoods

Here are **thumbnail sketches of neighborhoods in and around Asheville.** *For more information on the architectural history of the neighborhoods, see the Asheville architecture section.*

Biltmore Forest *(a residential area on the west side of Hendersonville Rd./US Hwy. 25 from Biltmore Village south to near the Blue Ridge Parkway entrance on Hendersonville Rd)* was a creation of the **Biltmore Estate.** In 1920, Edith Vanderbilt, wife of Biltmore founder George Vanderbilt (he had died in 1914) sold 1,500 acres on the south side of the Biltmore Estate to a company set up to develop an upmarket residential area, with lots of 2 acres or more.

Prominent local developers began building large houses, mostly in Tudor and Colonial Revival styles. Edith Vanderbilt herself in 1925 moved into one called **The Firth,** later the home of her son William A.V. Cecil, who reinvigorated and successfully ran the Biltmore House from the 1960s to 1990s.

Biltmore Estate landscape architect **Chauncey Beadle,** an associate of the Frederick Law Olmsted firm, helped plan the community. **Donald Ross** designed the golf course for the **Biltmore Forest Country Club.** A number of beautiful homes were built around the golf course, which opened in 1922. **William Dodge,** a leading local architect, designed many of the homes.

Today, Biltmore Forest remains **one of Asheville's most elite neighborhoods**, home to many prominent business people, physicians and other professionals. Some homes in Biltmore Forest are valued at $2 million to $9 million or more. However, the recession of 2007-2011 hit the upper end of the housing market in Asheville fairly hard, and assessed tax values of homes in Biltmore Forest fell an average of 16% from 2006 to 2012, while home values in most other parts of Asheville proper remained flat or increased slightly. According to the real estate website Zillow, in 2014 the median average home sales price in Biltmore Forest was $622,000.

Biltmore Village *(now predominantly a commercial area of small boutiques and restaurants directly east of the entrance to Biltmore Estate south of Downtown)* was **envisioned by George Vanderbilt as a manorial village,** housing Biltmore workers and necessary business services. The streets were laid out by 1896, and the homes and other buildings in the original village were completed by around 1910. Most of the buildings, designed by Biltmore House chief architect **Richard Morris Hunt**, his son **Richard Howland Hunt** and **Richard Sharp Smith,** were two- and three-story dwellings done in Tudoresque style with rough pebbledash exterior walls with half-timbering and red brick. The village also had shops, a post office, railroad depot, small hospital and **All Souls Episcopal Cathedral.** Today, most of Biltmore Village is commercial, with boutique shops, art galleries, restaurants and a few offices and banks.

A number of the old pebbledash dwellings have been converted for business use, and the village, anchored by the stunning All Souls Cathedral, remains quaint and, at least in the original section, walkable.

Many new structures were built over the years, including in recent times a large hotel, the **Grand Bohemian**, and a row of commercial shops, restaurants and condos along Sweeten Creek Road. Traffic often is heavy along Hendersonville Road, McDowell Street and Sweeten Creek Road, and it is sometimes backed up by a railroad crossing on Hendersonville Road. Street parking is somewhat limited in the main part of Biltmore Village.

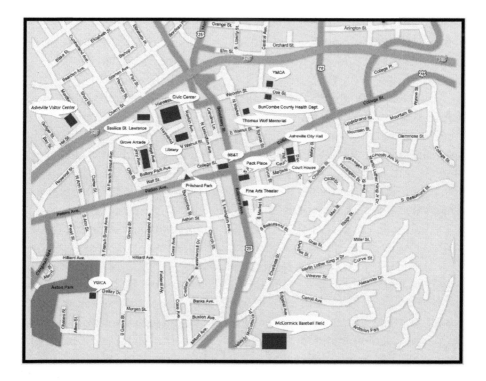

Downtown Asheville map

Downtown Asheville The hub of Asheville's fairly compact and highly walkable Downtown is **Pack Square,** and most of the city's major streets radiate out from it: **Patton Avenue to the west, Broadway Street to the north, Biltmore Avenue to the south and College Street to the east.** The Pack Square area is home to a number of popular restaurants, along with the Pack Place museum complex on the south side of the square and on the west side the **BB&T Building** (at 17 stories the region's tallest office building, but now outgrown by one of the hotel towers at Harrah's Cherokee Casino & Resort in Cherokee).

Plans are to convert the BB&T Building and its garage to two upscale hotels, likely with some condos and a limited amount of retail space, over the next several years. On the east side is the nicely planned and landscaped **Pack Square Park,** which faces the elegant Art Deco **Asheville City Building designed by Douglas Ellington** and the squat **Buncombe County Courthouse**. In warm weather the water fountains in the park are a favorite spot for kids to play. On the north side of the square the windows of the **I.M. Pei company-designed Biltmore Building** reflects the images of older buildings on the square, including the elegant **Jackson Building,** one of Asheville's first skyscrapers.

Biltmore Avenue *(the main north-south corridor from Pack Square south to Biltmore village)* was originally called Main Street. Many of the buildings in the first few blocks south of Pack Square were built from 1900 to 1920, as low-rise commercial structures, and now are home to a thriving selection of art galleries, restaurants and bars, several of them opening in 2012-2013. The new **Aloft Hotel** (which debuted in late 2012) has brought new tourism traffic to Downtown and also a new public parking lot under the hotel, making dinner parking easier for local residents. Farther south is **McCormick Field**, home of the **Asheville Tourists** minor league baseball team, and the main campus of **Mission Hospitals**, its St. Joseph campus. Mission is the largest private employer in the region. In addition to its 730-bed main campus facility it owns and operates many other medical support and physician offices along the Biltmore Avenue Corridor and elsewhere. Just to the west of Biltmore is the Asheland Avenue and McDowell Street areas. **Asheville High School,** a wonderful Douglas Ellington Art Deco design, is one of the top public high schools in the state.

Broadway Street Corridor *(the northerly extension of Biltmore Avenue, which runs from Pack Square north to the UNC-Asheville area, connecting with I-26)* is filled with restaurants, coffee houses, clubs and small shops. As it passes under I-240, Broadway becomes less retail-oriented, and the streetscape opens up. Broadway passes the east side of the Montford Historic District and the slightly funky but growing Five Points area before reaching the 360-acre **University of North Carolina at Asheville campus** and I-26.

East End *(a section just to the southeast of Pack Square and near the main Asheville police department and fire station)* was an **important African-American business and residential district,** with many black-owned shops, restaurants, a theater and a hotel. It heart was **Market and Eagle streets.**

The area contained at least 10 churches and **Stephens-Lee High School** (1924-64, the area's only black high school). It also was home to the **YMI Cultural Center,** built by George Vanderbilt as a community center for the city's black citizens, operating (somewhat tenuously) now as a museum of local black history. Today, the area is gentrifying, with new upscale restaurants, shops and condos.

Southside *(bounded roughly by the French Broad River, Biltmore Ave., Oakland Ave. and the Aston Park)* was one of Asheville's **premier African-American business districts**, surrounded by a large residential neighborhood. At over 400 acres, the urban renewal project that began in the 1960s was one of the largest in the Southeast. One observer noted that more than 1,100 homes, 14 grocery stores, 11 beauty parlors and barber shops, five filling stations, eight apartment houses, seven churches, one hotel, five funeral homes, one hospital and three doctor's offices were razed by urban renewal programs. Today the area is predominantly residential, a racially mixed neighborhood, although the expansion of Mission Hospitals and supporting medical offices continues to encroach on the area.

In recent years, the term **South Slope** has come into use to describe the area generally bounded by Ashland Avenue, Biltmore Avenue and Buxton Street and Coxe Avenue. This is an up-and-coming area for restaurants, bars and craft breweries.

Lexington Avenue *(a main north-south street that keeps the Lexington name as it crosses Patton Ave.)* is as **authentically Asheville** as you can get. In 2012, the North Carolina Chapter of the American Planning Association named it **one of the state's "Great Main Streets,"** along with Charlotte's Tryon Street, Hillsborough's Churton Street and Edenton's Broad Street. Lexington has some 40 small, local clothing and second-hand shops, clubs, restaurants, brewpubs, antique shops and street art installations. Eminently walkable and slightly funky, Lexington in many ways is an **icon of the resurgence of Asheville's Downtown since the 1980s,** a street with character and full of life day and night. At the north end of Lexington is a mural on the I-240 overpass celebrating Asheville. Here, you can continue on to the northern section of Broadway or bear right onto Merrimon Avenue.

Patton Avenue Corridor *(one of Asheville's first east-west thoroughfares, a main access corridor from the west – where it is variously called U.S. Hwy. 19/23 or Smoky Park Hwy. to Downtown's Pack Square)* is one of Asheville's bi-polar streets. It is both an **ugly commercial thoroughfare through Candler and West Asheville** -- high school kids still cruise some of the West Asheville strip on weekends -- and a **business and banking street in town.**

As it enters the main Downtown area it passes the **National Climatic Data Center** in the Veach-Baley Federal Building, home to the world's largest climate data archive; Pritchard Park, host to a Friday night **drumming circle;** and one of Asheville's Art Deco highlights, the old **S&W Building**. There are a few crafts galleries and restaurants before Patton reaches Pack Square.

Battery Park, Grove Arcade and Haywood Street *(a commercial area between I-240 to the north, North French Broad St. to the west, South Lexington Ave. to the east and Patton Ave. to the south)* in the early to mid-20th century was the heart of Asheville's retail Downtown. The **Grove Arcade**, between Page and O. Henry streets, was originally built in the 1920s as an enclosed multi-use urban mall. Despite the Depression it functioned as such until it was taken over by the federal government during World War II. In the early 21st century, it returned to its roots as a mixed-used market, office and residential building. Along Battery Park Avenue and Haywood Street were most of **Asheville's original department stores, including Ivey's, JC Penney and Bon Marché.** Today this area has become a lively combination of residential condos, boutiques, crafts shops, restaurants and hotels including the all-suites **Haywood Park Hotel** and the hip **Indigo Hotel**. Even though there are three large city parking lots in the area -- one across from the Grove Arcade, one on Rankin Avenue and one behind the main Pack Library -- plus considerable street parking, finding a space can occasionally be difficult when there is a major concert or other functions at the Asheville Civic Center (now **U.S. Cellular Center**) and **Thomas Wolfe Auditorium**. Asheville's best independent bookstore, **Malaprop's,** is located on Haywood Street.

Wall Street *(just north and above Patton Ave. with the main pedestrian entrance off Battery Park Ave.)* is a short, picturesque side street with a number of restaurants and small boutiques. Parking is easy due to a large city parking garage on the west end of the street.

The Downtown Asheville area has many small and mid-size condominium developments, including **21 Battery Park, 45 Asheland Avenue. The Ashton** and **37 Hiawassee,** with prices from around $150,000 to more than a million.

Kenilworth *(southeast Asheville between Biltmore Ave. on the west and Tunnel Rd. on the east)* was established in the late 19th century and early 20th century. It was named for the large resort hotel, the Kenilworth Inn -- completed in 1891 and destroyed by fire in 1909 -- that stood nearby.

Many of the older homes in Kenilworth are in the Tudor Revival style, although the area also has Prairie, Bungalow and even Spanish Colonial homes, along with a number of newer homes built in the mid-20th century. According to the real estate website Trulia in 2014 the median average home sales price in Kenilworth was $336,000.

Montford *(just north of Downtown Asheville and I-240)* is a **300-acre neighborhood historic district** that dates from the late 19th century. It has some 600 homes, including a number designed by **Richard Sharp Smith.** Nearly all of the homes in the district were built before 1930. Homes in Montford are in Victorian, Queen Anne, Craftsman, Neoclassical and Colonial Revival styles.

Plagued by crime and deteriorating properties in the mid-20th century, much of Montford was gentrified beginning in the 1970s. Part of its attraction is that most of Montford is within a short drive or walk of Downtown, yet the neighborhood is mostly single-family homes with porches, yards and sidewalked streets. Some larger homes in Montford now are valued at over $1 million. According to the real estate website Trulia in early 2014 the median home sales price in Montford was $495,000.

The 87-acre **Riverside Cemetery,** where Thomas Wolfe, O. Henry, Richard Sharp Smith and Zebulon Vance are buried, is within the Montford Historic District. Montford is also **Asheville's "B&B District,"** with more than a dozen licensed bed and breakfast inns.

The main streets in Montford are **Montford Avenue,** the spine of the neighborhood, along with **Cumberland Avenue** and **Flint Street,** all running more or less north-south.

Stumptown was a traditionally African-American neighborhood of around 30 acres near Riverside Cemetery that developed in the late 19th century, but by the 1970s urban renewal had changed the area, dispersing most of the 200 or so black families that had lived there.

North Asheville is a group of different neighborhoods and districts, including the Merrimon Avenue corridor, Broadway corridor, Kimberly, Grove Park, Charlotte Street, Chestnut-Hill and Lakeview Park/Beaver Lake.

Albemarle Park *(off Charlotte St. across from Edwin Place)* is a small but intriguing historic district comprised mainly of turn of the 20th century **Manor and Cottages.** The Manor, a resort with an English inn atmosphere conceived by Thomas Raoul and his father William Greene Raoul, was begun in 1898 on a 32-acre tract of land acquired by the elder Raoul, a railroad magnate.

Working in collaboration with the Raouls, architect **Bradford Gilbert** designed cottages that each bears a distinctive motif reflecting the eclectic character of the Manor with various combinations of Shingle, Tudoresque and Colonial Revival styles.

Chestnut-Hill (*located north of Downtown, centered around East Chestnut and North Liberty streets.*) Most of the 200 or dwellings in this historic district were built from 1880 to 1930, in the Craftsman, Queen Anne and Colonial Revival styles. Two locally important architects' works are represented here: **J.A. Tennent** and **Richard Sharp Smith.** A number of medical, dental and other professional offices have opened along East Chestnut.

Grove Park (*consisting of several blocks flanking the north end of Charlotte St.*) was the creation, in the early 1900s, of **E. W. Grove of Grove Park Inn and Grove Arcade fame.** He developed the Grove Park residential area with the help of landscape architect **Chauncey Beadle** of the Biltmore Estate. The design used curving streets rather than a rectangular grid pattern. Most of the early homes in Grove Park were in the Tudor Revival, Colonial Revival and Bungalow styles. Many were designed by **Richard Sharp Smith** and his firm, **Smith & Carrier.**

A landmark in the Grove Park and Proximity Park area (Proximity Park already existed when E. W. Grove began his development, but the park area is now considered a part of the Grove Park neighborhood) is the **Dr. Carl V. Reynolds House,** now the Albemarle Inn at 86 Edgemont Road, a bed and breakfast. The two-story 1909 Neoclassical building is charmingly restored. The most famous resident of the house was Hungarian composer **Béla Bartók,** who spent the winter of 1943-44 in Asheville and worked on his "Third Concerto for Piano," also known as the **"Asheville Concerto,"** here.

According to the real estate website Trulia in 2014 the median average home sales price Grove Park area sold for $482,000.

Kimberly Avenue/Norwood Park (*residential corridor from Charlotte St. to Beaverdam Rd.*), sometimes considered as part of the Grove Park area, in effect begins at Edwin Place, which turns off Charlotte Street. Edwin Place becomes Kimberly Avenue, which then runs by the Grove Park Inn's golf course on the east, with a row of upscale homes across Kimberly on the west. These homes, in the $500,000 to $1 million+ range, are an eclectic mix of Colonial Revival, Mediterranean and other styles, mostly built from the 1920s to 1940s. This part of Kimberly is lined with sugar maples, which often are stunning in their fall gold colors.

Farther on, some of the homes on Kimberly were built in the mid-20th century. **Norwood Park** is a 26-acre National Historic District on the west side of Kimberly, with many Craftsman bungalows, along with Colonial Revival and other home styles, built in the first half of the 20th century. Most of the Norwood Park lots are relatively small. Kimberly Avenue eventually intersects with Beaverdam Road, a long and winding residential road with attractive homes and a number of condominium developments. Beaverdam leads to Webb Cove Road, which winds up to the **Blue Ridge Parkway**. Noted author **Wilma Dykeman** was born in and spent much of her life in the Beaverdam Valley of North Asheville. In 2014, the real estate website Trulia reported that the median average listing price in the Norwood Park area was $435,000.

Lakeview Park/Beaver Lake *(on both sides of Merrimon Ave./U.S. Hwy. 25 with Beaver Lake on the west and the Asheville Country Club on the east)* is a 1920s-era residential subdivision. It curves around Beaver Lake and the **Donald Ross golf course,** now a part of the **Asheville Country Club.** Most of the original 100 or so homes, as in Biltmore Forest, are in Tudor Revival and Colonial Revival styles. Homes and condos built later are in a variety of styles. Lakeview Park was planned by Charlotte landscape architect **John Nolen**, a student of Frederick Law Olmsted. Beaver Lake is owned collectively by the residents of Lakeview Park. Part of the lake is a **10-acre bird sanctuary** owned and managed by the local chapter of the Audubon Society, open free to the public. According to the real estate website Trulia in 2014 the average home sales price in Lakeview Park was $408,000.

The **Merrimon Avenue Corridor** *(along Merrimon Ave./US Hwy. 25 from Downtown north toward Weaverville)* is primarily commercial, with offices, stores and restaurants lining the busy street (mostly two lanes each way). Merrimon is becoming known as **Supermarket Row,** with locations for **GreenLife** (owned by Whole Foods), **Harris-Teeter, Trader Joe's, Ingle's, Fresh Market** and others. On side streets east and west of Merrimon are many appealing homes, many dating from early 1900s to 1920s, some modest bungalows and others more substantial.

River Arts District *(an area of about one mile by one-half mile bounded by the French Broad River on the west and Clingman Ave. and the Depot St. corridor on the east, with the north and south ends of the district somewhat fluid)* was **once one of the region's main industrial zones.** Anchored by the French Broad River and Southern Railway, the Riverside industrial area developed in the late 19th and early 20th centuries as a center for tanneries, livestock sales, cotton and other mills, ice and coalhouses, grain storage facilities and warehouses.

Although in 1916 the worst flood in Asheville history damaged many buildings in the low-lying river plain, the area recovered. Riverside thrived for several decades, but with changing economic conditions by the 1950s and 1960s many of the warehouses and businesses in the district had closed and were abandoned.

In the 1980s and 1990s, **artists and craftspeople rediscovered the former industrial zone,** drawn by inexpensive rents for large industrial and loft spaces, perfect for studios. Today the River Arts District is home to more than 160 art and craft studios, most of which are open to the public. There also are art and craft galleries and at least a dozen restaurants, coffee shops and bars. A number of creative businesses such as ad agencies and design studios also have relocated to the area. Residential apartments and condos also are in the district.

RAD Lofts, a new seven-story, 200-unit apartment complex with 300-450 vehicle parking deck is under development at the former Dave Steel site, at the corner of Clingman Avenue and Roberts Street. One-bedroom units are expected to go for $900, with two-bedrooms at $1,350.

West Asheville *(bounded roughly by the French Broad River on the east, I-40 on the south, the Enka area on the west, with Patton Avenue on the north, although parts of what is considered West Asheville also lay north of Patton)* has been a part of the City of Asheville since 1917, but it continues to be seen by locals as a separate area. It has been considered as Asheville's cheap real estate date, with homes costing a fraction of what they do in some other areas of the city, such as North Asheville. Residents tended to be older and blue collar. In the 1980s, young people discovered the cheaper house prices and rents in Asheville and migrated here, creating an increasing vibrant and diverse restaurant, retail and bar scene. By the early 21st century, parts of West Asheville became known as **hipster neighborhoods.**

Many of the homes here date from the early part of the 20th century, some in the late Queen Anne and bungalow style. Sizeable numbers of dwellings, mostly frame or red brick bungalows, were built in the post-World War II period. In the last couple of decades, small clusters of new construction have taken place in West Asheville, with the focus on moderately priced starter and second homes.

Established neighborhoods such as **Malvern Hills**, along Brevard Road and Virginia Avenue, are solidly middle class, while some other areas, especially those near I-240, are still a little scruffy, but gentrifying.

Haywood Road (as distinguished from Haywood Street Downtown) is a commercial spine of West Asheville. It connects the River Arts District and South French Broad areas with Patton Avenue. Many of the commercial buildings are two-story brick structures dating from 1900 through the 1920s. Small shops, boutiques, second-hand stores, restaurants, coffee houses and bars have opened in recent years.

A prominent co-educational prep school, **The Asheville School** (founded 1900) is at the far west end of what is considered West Asheville.

Prices have risen all over West Asheville, but it's still possible to find attractive buys in the $150,000 to $250,000 range. According to the real estate website Trulia, in 2014 the median average home sales price in the Malvern Hills area of West Asheville was $170,000, and in the Westwood Place development the average listing price was $244,000.

Suburban Areas

"Suburbia" in Western North Carolina mainly means the areas in Buncombe County surrounding the city of Asheville. This would include Woodfin and Weaverville to the north, with I-26 being the main traffic artery; Haw Creek, Swannanoa and incorporated areas to the east, with I-40 and US Highway 70 the primary transportation routes; to the south Arden, Fletcher, Fairview and various unincorporated areas, some in northern Henderson County, with I-26, U.S. Highway 25 and NC Highway 191 the main arteries; and Leicester and Enka-Candler to the west, with I-40 and US Highway 19/23 being the primary travel routes.

Here is more information on *some* of the suburban communities around Asheville:

East Asheville *(from Town Mountain and Chunn's Cove at the east edge of Asheville past the Tunnel Road mega retail strip to Oteen and Swannanoa)* is a sprawling area that includes the major retail strip along and near Tunnel Road, anchored by the **Asheville Mall**, a regional mall that ranks as the eighth largest in the state, after malls in Charlotte, Raleigh, Durham and Winston-Salem (the largest in the state is Hanes Mall in Winston-Salem). But it also includes many well-established, middle-class subdivision and residential areas including **Town Mountain**, with wonderful views over Downtown, **Chunn's Cove, Haw Creek** and **Beverly Hills,** with many of the homes built between the 1940s and 1970s, along with areas farther out including **Oteen** and **Swannanoa.**

According to the real estate website Trulia *(www.trulia.com)* in 2014 the typical home sales price in Haw Creek was $240,000.

Home sales prices in the Asheville/Buncombe area are on average about 6% less than the listed asking price.

Enka-Candler *(a non-incorporated area in southwest Buncombe County in what is called the Hominy Valley)* is an amalgam of small farms, middle-class subdivisions, modest homes, condos, trailer parks, small businesses and a large upscale planned community around a lake. The main commercial spine of the Enka-Candler area is the **Smoky Park Highway** (U.S. Highway 19-23), housing an unruly collection of small businesses suffering from lack of zoning controls.

Enka Village, off Sand Hill Road, was begun in 1928 as a planned company town developed by American Enka, a European-owned rayon-nylon factory that became one of the largest employers in the region. By 1930, about 100 homes, both small homes for workers and large brick homes with lake views for managers, had been constructed, but the village was never completed due to the impact of the Depression. In the late 1950s the homes were sold to individual owners. American Enka eventually was purchased by what is now BASF, an international conglomerate, and limited manufacturing continues at the Enka plant.

A typical house out in the country southwest of Asheville

Some 1,300 acres of Enka land was sold to Biltmore Farms, a development and hotel company owned by a branch of the Vanderbilt family but not directly affiliated with Biltmore Estate.

In 2002, the company began building the upscale **Biltmore Lake** development, with homes in the $500,000 to $2 million range, and condos/townhouses generally priced from $150,000 to $800,000. There are now more than 600 homes in the development, with additional ones planned.

Candler has many different communities, including some located near the main public schools in the area (especially Hominy Valley Elementary, Enka Middle and Enka High) and others along a scenic rural stretch of the Pisgah Highway/NC Highway 151 that eventually winds it way through the Pisgah National Forest to the Blue Ridge Parkway and Mt. Pisgah.

According to real estate website Zillow, the median sales price of homes in Candler in 2014 was $183,000.

Leicester *(an unincorporated area in Buncombe County northwest of Asheville),* locally pronounced "Lester" rather than "Lee-cester," is a mix of suburban subdivisions, modest homes, trailer parks and rural areas, with a total population of about 12,000. The commercial spine is **Leicester Highway,** which can be heavily trafficked at rush hours. According to Zillow, the median sales price of homes in Leicester in 2014 was $215,000.

South Asheville *(a hard-to-define area primarily along the I-26 and US Highway 25 corridors from the south edge of Asheville city limits to Skyland, Arden and Fletcher near the Asheville Regional Airport, then blending into northern Henderson County, in particular the Mills River area)* has seen more growth in recent decades than any other area of Buncombe County. One reason is that land here tends to be flatter than in most other areas around Asheville, thus making it easier for building. Large strip malls have sprung up here, turning rural pastureland into sites for Big Box stores and fast food chains. **Biltmore Park,** a large mixed-use residential, office and retail planned community, was developed by **Biltmore Farms** of Asheville and Crosland of Charlotte. The development has an 800,000 square-foot retail center, **Biltmore Park Town Square,** designed along New Urbanism principles, that includes a 15-screen movie theater, Biltmore Grande, and many restaurants and stores including Barnes & Noble and REI, plus a Hilton Hotel, YMCA and condos and apartments. In this area Biltmore Farms also developed the Biltmore Park residential subdivision, with more than 550 upscale homes and the 1,000-acre Ramble development. According to the real estate website Trulia in 2014 the median average home in the Biltmore Park development sold for $701,000.

Weaverville *(off I-26 about 15 minutes north of Asheville)* is a small community with several sizeable manufacturing plants, a commercial area with many small businesses and a thriving arts community. The incorporated town has a population of about 2,500, but additional residents live in the areas around the town. North Carolina's Civil War governor, Zebulon Vance, was born in the **Reem's Creek** community, and his family cabin is now a state historic site. Most homes in the Weaverville area are in the $150,000 to $400,000 range.

Options for Living in the Asheville Area

Note that the following are only **representative samples** of the options for each type of housing in the Asheville area. *For living options in towns and villages outside Asheville, see the next chapter.*

Planned Residential Developments

Here is information on some of the larger and more prominent planned residential subdivisions and developments in the Asheville area. This is only a fraction of the developments available. To see other options, check with local real estate firms or see information on websites such as Zillow *(www.zillow.com)*, Trulia *(www.trulia.com)* or Asheville Real Estate *(www.ashevillerealestate.com)*.

Biltmore Lake *(Beverly-Hanks Biltmore Lake Sales Center, 80 Lake Drive, Biltmore Lake aka Enka-Candler, 828-209-5253 or 877-232-5253, www.biltmorelake.com)* is a 1,300-acre planned community around a 62-acre lake, formerly Enka Lake and now called Biltmore Lake. It adjoins Enka Village, which was established in the late 1920s as housing for workers and managers at American Enka Company. Biltmore Lake is being developed by Biltmore Farms, which became a separate entity in 1979 when the Biltmore Estate was divided between the two brothers, George and William Cecil, who had inherited the estate. Biltmore Farms, which received the dairy farm and about 4,000 acres of land in the split, purchased the Enka property for the lakeside community in 2001 and began building the development the next year. Biltmore Lake, about 15 minutes from Downtown Asheville, says it has around 600 occupied homes and townhouses.

Home sizes range from around 1,300 square feet to more than 6,000 square feet. There are a variety of architectural styles, but most homes show Craftsman (Arts and Crafts) design influence. Biltmore Lake offers completed single-family home and lot packages from around $500,000 to more than $1 million and townhouses from around $300,000.

Some sections of the development are gated, while others are not. At first glance, the location of Biltmore Lake seems unusual, as it is literally across the road from a large industrial complex and has limited shopping and dining options nearby. However, once inside the development, the property is beautiful, and it is the only Asheville-area modern development on a sizeable lake. Amenities include a clubhouse with outdoor tennis courts and a basketball court, a boathouse with canoes, kayaks, pedal boats and small sailboats, playgrounds, pocket parks and 4 miles of walking and jogging trails. Biltmore Lake is in the Enka school district, and Enka High, Enka Middle and Hominy Valley and Sand Hill primary schools are close to the development. The Asheville School, a private day and boarding prep school founded in 1900, is nearby. The Enka campus of Asheville-Buncombe Technical Institute is also close by. Exclusive sales agent for Biltmore Lake is Beverly-Hanks & Associates. If you want to build your own home, Biltmore Lake has a list of approved builders, emphasizing those that use "green building" techniques. The development has a stringent design review process to approve construction design and plans.

Biltmore Park *(Off Long Shoals Rd. and I-26, South Asheville, www.biltmorepark.com)* is a 750-acre mixed-use development in fast-growing South Asheville, about 20 minutes from Downtown Asheville. The original 700-acre single-family home section was established in the 1990s and is now built out with around 550 homes. However, resales are available through local real estate companies, usually ranging from around $500,000 to more than $2 million. Biltmore Square Town Park, comprising about 42 acres, has townhouses, condos and rental apartments, along with retail space including Barnes & Noble and REI, a 15-screen movie theater called Biltmore Grande, a Hilton hotel, office space, a number of restaurants and a branch of the Asheville YMCA. *See below for more information on condos and apartments.* Biltmore Park is in the T.C. Roberson High, Valley Springs Middle and Estes Elementary school district. Western Carolina University offers undergraduate and graduate programs at Biltmore Park Town Square, including doctoral programs in education and nursing.

Hawks Landing *(Weaverville)* is a 230-acre residential community being developed near Weaverville. Homes and lots, offered through Asheville MLS members, are priced in the $400s for homes and for around $40,000 to more than $100,000 for lots.

Moore's Valley *(Moore's Valley Rd., Leicester, 828-771-2396, www.mooresvalleync.com),* located west of Asheville in the Leicester community, has about 100 1- to 3-acre homesites for sale from around $50,000 to the low $100s. Log home construction packages are offered, but you can use your own builder if you want.

The Ramble *(5 Valley Springs Rd., South Asheville, 828-274-1336,* www.ramblebiltmoreforest) is a 1,000-acre planned gated community off Hendersonville Road in South Asheville. It is being developed by Biltmore Farms, which also developed Biltmore Park, Biltmore Park Town Square and Biltmore Lake. Completed home and lot packages range from near $1 million to $2 million or more. Building lots here are expensive, ranging from around $150,000 to almost a million. When built out, The Ramble will have about 400 single-family homes. As of this writing, the development has about 125 owners. Amenities include a network of parks and green spaces, walking and jogging trails and clubhouse with salt-water pool, fitness center and outdoor barbecue area. The Ramble is in the T.C. Roberson High, Valley Springs Middle and Estes Elementary school district, and the private Carolina Day School is nearby.

Reynolds Mountain *(Off U.S. Hwy. 25/Weaverville Hwy., North Asheville)* is a 250-acre planned mountainside community in North Asheville with about 200 homes and townhomes. Remaining building lots start in the low $100s and range up to more than $500,000. Resale homes typically are in the $500,000 to $2 million range. Most homes have outstanding views of Asheville and the mountains. It is about 15 minutes from Downtown Asheville and is near Beaver Lake and close to upscale shopping and restaurants.

Condos and Townhouses

45 Asheville Avenue *(45 Asheville Ave., Downtown Asheville, owners' agent Beverly-Hanks & Associates, 828-251-1800,* www.45asheland.com) is a new condominium project about four blocks south of Patton Avenue in Downtown Asheville. When complete, it will have 27 two- and three-bedroom units of 1,100 square feet and larger, priced from the low $400s. Units have deeded parking and balconies.

The Aston *(61 Church St., Downtown Asheville, offered through MLS agents)* has a marvelous location in the heart of Downtown. The original building dates to 1928. It has 14 2-bedroom units on four levels, with secure parking and a rooftop garden. A 2-bedroom, 2-bath resale of almost 1,500 square feet was recently offered at $500,000, and other units have sold in the $400s. Homeowner association fees are around $400.

Beaucatcher House *(9 Kenilworth Knoll, East Asheville, managed by Baldwin Real Estate, 828-684-3400,* www.beaucatcherhousecoa.com) is a 106-unit, four-story condo development in East Asheville in the Reynolds school district. Built in 2007, it has 2-bedroom, 2-bath units of around 1,200 to 1,300 square feet along with smaller 1-bedroom, 1-bath apartments.

Most 2-bedroom units for re-sale are offered through the Asheville MLS in the mid to high $100s. There is parking in outdoor lots, a swimming pool and fitness center.

Biltmore Park Town Square Condos and Townhouses *(Beverly-Hanks, Suite 140, One Town Square, Biltmore Park, 828-654-0660, www.biltmorepark.com),* located in the Biltmore Park mixed-used development, offer access to a clubhouse, fitness center and outdoor swimming pool. Most units are priced from around $200,000 to over $400,000. This development is in the Estes, Valley Springs and T. C. Robertson school district. Resales are available through Asheville MLS brokers. Homeowner fees vary but expect to pay around $300 a month for a typical unit.

Creekside Village *(Weaverville, offered through MLS agents)* is a development of about 250 townhouses (when completed) in the Weaverville/North Buncombe school districts. Three-bedroom, 2-bath units of around 1,300 square feet and larger are priced in the high $100s to mid $200s.

Fitzgerald Condominiums *(288 Macon Ave., North Asheville, 828-251-1140, www.groveparkinn.com/fitzgerald-residences)* is a group of 24 2- and 3-bedroom luxury condominiums developed by the Grove Park Inn, next door to that *grande dame* resort, in a building that formerly housed WLOS-TV. As of 2014, all units reportedly had been sold. Resales may be available from time to time.

Pioneer Building *(190 Broadway St., North Asheville, 828-255-4663, www.recenter.com)* is a four-story, mixed-use building in the Five Points area On Broadway north of I-240. The neo-Arts and Crafts-style building has two-bedroom condos with high ceilings and balconies. Units are in the 1100-1300 square foot range, priced in the $400s.

Vistas of Westfield *(61 Westfield Way, Candler, 828-274-1004, www.lifestylehomes.net)* offer a more rural version of condo living, with lower county taxes. Located off US Highway 19-23 in West Buncombe in the Sand Hill/Enka school district, about 20 minutes from Downtown Asheville, Vistas of Westfield when built out will have around 80 townhomes and 40 condos, starting at around $273,000. There's a clubhouse, pool and fitness center.

Woodland Trails *(Candler, sales agents Beverly-Hanks & Associates, 828-254-7221, www.woodlandtrailscondo.com)* has homes and condos in a rural area between Queen Road and the Pisgah Highway in Candler. Small condos start at around $105,000.

Active Adult Communities/Retirement Communities

Crowfields *(Crowfields Condominium Association, 1745 Hendersonville Rd., South Asheville, 828-274-5068, www.crowfieldsasheville.com)* is a long-established 55-and-over adult community on 72 wooded acres, of which 80% were left undeveloped. The 192 condo units, most build in the 1970s and 1980s and arranged in clusters of four to eight, have 1,300 to 3,600 square feet. There's a clubhouse and heated pool. Resales available recently through Asheville MLS brokers ranged from just under $200,000 to $375,000. Homeowner association dues are a little over $400 per month. Occasionally units are available for lease. Association by-laws require that 90% of the units at Crowfields must have at least one occupant who is 55 or over.

Deerfield Episcopal Retirement Community *(1617 Hendersonville Rd., South Asheville, 828-274-1531, www.deerfieldwnc.org)* is considered one of the best retirement communities in the region. There are more than 600 residents at Deerfield, and the community's occupancy rate is over 90%. Established in 1955, it has expanded to its present size of 475 units in three mid-rise buildings and a number of townhome/cottage clusters on 125 acres. Red roofs, stucco and stonework echo the Arts and Crafts architectural style. There is a wellness center, community center, spa, several food service options, a glass-enclosed aquatic center and a health services center. Three types of retirement living are available at Deerfield: independent living in 351 cottages, townhomes and freestanding homes; assisted living in Haden Hall, which has 62 apartments where residents can receive help in bathing, dressing and monitoring of medications, along with three meals a day; and a skilled nursing center with a capacity of 62 for those who need care 24 hours a day. Admission to Deerfield is limited to those 62 and over. Residents must have Medicare A and B plus one supplemental insurance. A physical examination may be required before admittance. Life Care and Fee-for-Service contracts are available.

The cost structure is complex, but quality retirement centers are not cheap. Under Fee-for-Service fees for independent living units range from around $2,500 to $4,000 per month for one person with a second-person fee of about $1,200, plus a maintenance fee of a little over $1,000 per month. For assisted living, there is a monthly service fee for assisted living range from $4,200 to almost $6,000 for one person and $3,333 for a second person. Plus, there is a one-time admission fee of around $24,000 for assisted living and $8,000 for skilled nursing. Other fees may apply.

Under Life Care programs, a lump sum payment of from $180,000 to $1 million is made, plus about $51,000 to $94,000 for a second person, depending on the unit and the type of refund plan. See the disclosure statement that is provided, as required by law, on the Deerfield website.

Givens Estates Retirement Community *(2360 Sweeten Creek Rd., South Asheville, 828-274-4899, www.givensestates.org)* is a not-for-profit continuing care retirement community. It is located on a 215-acre campus in South Asheville. There are about 800 residents of Givens Estates; independent living, assisted living and health care facilities. Givens Estates is associated with the Western North Carolina Conference of the United Methodist Church, and the main retirement community is associated with Great Laurels of Junaluska near Waynesville, for residents with lower financial abilities. The main Givens campus includes 86 single-family cottages, 40 duplexes, 82 villas and 192 independent living apartments; 78 HUD-assisted apartments; 47 assisted living beds; and an 84-bed health care center, Medicare/Medicaid certified, with short-term rehab beds and skilled nursing care beds. Givens has nearly 60 different floor plan options, ranging from 1-bedroom 550 square feet apartments to 2-bedroom cottages with almost 1,900 square feet. As at other retirement communities, it is not cheap to live here. Entrance to Givens Estates includes a one-time zero-refund entrance fee ranging from about $33,000 to $384,000, depending on type of accommodations. Refundable plans, at higher rates, are available. There is also a monthly service fee, ranging from about $1,200 to $3,500 per month. This is for single residency; there are additional fees for a second person. Fees generally include weekly housing, maintenance, water, sewer and garbage pick-up, insurance, several meal plan options, utilities except internet, cable TV and telephone, and access to a pharmacy and health care on-site.

Intentional Communities

Fellowship for Intentional Community *(www.ic.org)* is a good reference source for finding intentional communities in Western North Carolina and elsewhere.

Earthaven Ecovillage *(5 Consensus Circle, Black Mountain, 828-669-3937, www.earthaven.org)* was established in 1994-96 "as an aspiring ecovillage on 329 acres." Currently, Earthaven has 56 members, 50 adults and 6 children. It is open to visitors and new members. Several dwellings are currently available for rent. Earthaven plans to eventually grow to 150 members.

More than 40 homes have been built in 14 "neighborhoods," while others are under construction. The land is owned collectively by the community. Most members work in their own small businesses.

The ecovillage is "spiritually eclectic." Elementary school children are usually home-schooled. All decisions are made by consensus. Members say they are seeking "seeking hardworking, entrepreneurial people, including but not limited to organic growers and farmers; people with solar system, electrical, plumbing, and mechanical skills; healers, artists, and families with children." Most Earthaven members eat dinner two to five times a week with other members, some of which are vegetarians and others omnivores. Members are completely financially independent of each other. The joining fee amount for is $4,400 per adult; the fee is adjusted up or down each year to reflect the consumer price index. There is a one-time site lease fee (99-year, renewable, transferrable site lease). A full site (which can be shared by up to four members and children) is $21,000, and smaller sites are $10,500 to $12,600. In addition, annual dues miscellaneous fees are $600 to $900 each year.

Villages at Crest Mountain *(30 Ben Lippen School Rd., West Asheville, 828-252-7787, www.crestmtn.com)* is a co-housing community in the Woodfin. The initial phase of the co-housing community has 12 acres, of which 2 acres are not developed. A second phase of an additional 24 acres is planned. As of this writing 24 lots have been sold, and 18 homes completed with three others under construction. Lot prices start at $57,000 and home/lot packages start at $210,000. Currently there are 29 members of the community, of which 22 are full-time residents. The initiation fee is $1,250, and monthly home-owner dues are $60. If you build, the minimum size is 2,200 square feet, and there are architectural guidelines. The co-housing segment is part of a 165-acre, multi-use community that includes banquet facilities, vacation rentals, office studios, a gated residential community, luxury condos and a small girls school, the Hanger Hall School for Girls.

Westwood Cohousing *(56 Millpond Rd., West Asheville, www.westwoodcohousing.com)* is an intentional community in West Asheville, in a wooded 4-acre setting with 23 clustered dwellings and a common house in the center of the community.

Established in 1998, the Planned Unit Development (PUD) community now has 61 members, 50 adults and 11 children. Members share meals on average twice a week, and there are no dietary rules. Children go to public schools. Residents are members of a community association that owns the common building and common areas; houses are individually owned. Members are expected to work one or two hours a week for the community.

The community is open to new members when a house is for sale. Homes values vary, but a recent proposed sale was in the $200s. However, there is a waiting list and at the time of this writing there are no homes in the community for sale. Occasionally, units are available for rental. Visitors are welcome with advance notice. A $5 donation is requested. Email contactwestwood@gmail.com to arrange a tour.

Golf Communities

Cliffs at Walnut Cove *(Cliffs Land Partners, 22 South Main St., Greenville, SC, 866-411-5771, www.cliffscommunities.com)* is one of seven large Cliffs developments in Western North Carolina and Upstate South Carolina and the only one still in business in WNC. Walnut Cove is between Asheville and Hendersonville. Another ambitious Cliffs development near Asheville, Cliffs at High Carolina, is at best on life support and is unlikely to continue with the planned Tiger Woods golf course, according to Silver Sun Partners, the group that bought The Cliffs out of bankruptcy in 2012 when the high-end residential/golf course company went bust under mountains of debt and lawsuits. However, Cliffs at Walnut Cove has restarted building. The Cliffs claims that it sold more than $23 million of real estate at its seven Carolina communities during the first half of 2013. The 1,300-acre gated Walnut Cove development has a Jack Nicklaus Signature golf course completed in 2005 before the Great Recession. Homes offered for sale range from around $1 million to over $4 million. Building lots start at $150,000 and go up to about $750,000.

Reems Creek Golf Community *(Golf course: 36 Pink Fox Cove Rd., Weaverville, 828-645-4393, www.reemscreekgolf.com)* is an established golf course and residential development on 300 acres near Weaverville. The 18-hole course was designed by Hawtree & Son of England. The course is now open to the public with daily greens fees or annual memberships. Homes in the development go for around $300,000 to more than $800,000, and building lots range from around $50,000 to $100,000. Lots and homes in the development are sold through Asheville MLS brokers.

Note: For information on real estate in small towns and villages in Western North Carolina, and in rural areas, see the next chapter.

Building Your Own Home

The typical building lot (up to 3 acres, usually with some deed restrictions) in WNC sold for around $79,000 in 2014, and 80% of the approximately building 750 lots sold in the region in 2014 went for less than $100,000.

Supply far outstrips demand for building lots. There is a five-year supply of building lots available in the region.

It is difficult if not misleading to specify a particular per-square-foot cost for building in the mountains, due to the differences in designs, site conditions, quality of finish desired, materials, sewerage and water considerations and other factors. In general, however, standard to moderate quality construction ranges from $115 to $175 per square foot, while higher quality custom construction runs from $200 to $325 per square foot. Construction costs in the mountains tend to be higher than in areas where buildable land is cheaper and where builders don't have to deal with hillside construction.

Construction prices per square foot fell sharply in the 2007-2010 period during the peak of the Great Recession. Since then, pushed up by rising materials costs, construction prices have been increasing.

OTHER PARTS OF WNC: SMALL TOWNS AND VILLAGES

Former Swain County Courthouse in the small town of Bryson City, near the Great Smokies

Here is information on some of our favorites towns and villages in Western North Carolina. To make it easier for you to visit these places on a scouting trip, we've include information on lodging and dining, as well as a profile of the place and real estate information.

Black Mountain

Distance from Asheville: 16 miles east, 20 minutes by car
Population: 8,000
Visitor and Relocation Information: *Black Mountain-Swannanoa Chamber of Commerce, 201 E. State Street, Black Mountain, 828-669-2300 or 800-669-2301, www.blackmountain.org*

    If you're looking for a quaint, almost idyllic little mountain town, with a pleasant downtown, away from the hurly-burly but with a nice choice of restaurants and activities, you couldn't do better than Black Mountain.

It is short, easy drive from Asheville via I-40, but once you take Exit 64, you're soon in the town's small, easy-to-get-around downtown. The main street, West State Street, and side streets from and near it, Cherry Street, Church Street, Sutton Avenue, Broadway and others, are lined with boutiques, galleries and small dining spots. **Town Hardware & General Store** *(103 West State St., 828-669-7723, www.townhardware.com)* is a big, old-fashioned hardware store that has added gifts and other items. **The Old Depot** is a non-profit art and crafts shop in the Black Mountain train depot *(207 Sutton Ave., 828-669-6583, www.olddepot.org)*. **Tyson's Furniture** and **Penland Furniture** are locally popular places to shop for furniture at good prices.

Just west of Black Mountain is the final site of the experimental arts college open from 1933 to 1957, **Black Mountain College.** This is now a summer boys camp and the site of the twice-a-year music and arts festival, **Lake Eden Arts Festival (LEAF).** *See the Arts and Festivals sections for more information.* Also near Black Mountain is **Montreat College** *(310 Gaither Circle, Montreat, 800-622-6968, www.montreat.edu)*, worth visiting for its wooded campus with many early 20th century buildings constructed of river rock.

For lunch, go directly to the **Veranda Cafe** *(119 Cherry St., 828-669-8864, www.verandacafeandgifts.com)*, very popular for its fresh-made soups and sandwiches. Soups are $3 to $5, and most sandwiches around $8. Next door to the Veranda is the **Black Mountain Ale House** *(117 Cherry St., 828-669-9090, www.blackmountainalehouse)*. Down a short flight of stairs, in a rathskeller-type setting, though there's an outdoor patio in the back, you'll find good drink and bar food – good burgers, fish and chips and sandwiches. For something more at dinner, check out **Que Sera** *(400 E. State St., 828-664-9472, www.queserarestaurant.com)*, nondescript on the outside but with appealing dishes like mountain trout almandine and coffee-rubbed filet mignon with spinach and shoestring potatoes (entrees around $13 to $30). Good pizza, too. For something caffeinated, check out **Dynamite Coffee, Dripolator Coffee** and **Dobra Tea.** For craft beer, **Pisgah Brewing Company** is the place.

Staying overnight? Black Mountain has more than a half dozen B&Bs, the best of which are the **Inn Around the Corner** *(109 Church St., 828-669-6005 or 800-393-6005, www.innaroundthecorner.com)* and **Arbor House** *(207 Rhododendron Ave., 866-669-9303, www.arborhousenc.com)*, both moderate with rooms in the $135 to $200 range.

Inn Around the Corner, in a restored 1915 house, is close to downtown, while Arbor House, built recently but in the Arts and Crafts style, is a bit farther away, near Lake Tomahawk (more of a pond than a lake), with the 18-hole Black Mountain municipal golf course, tennis courts and half-mile, lighted walking path.

According to the real estate website Trulia.com the median average home selling price in Black Mountain in 2014 was $161,500.

Blowing Rock

Distance from Asheville: 93 miles northeast, almost 2 hours by car
Population: 1,500, growing to 8,000 in summer
Visitor and Relocation Information: *159 Chestnut St., Blowing Rock, 828-295-4636 or 877-750-4636, www.blowingrock.com*

Blowing Rock, though only about 9 miles from Boone, is about as different from the sprawling college town as it can be. The little town of Blowing Rock is compact, and you get the sense that a lot of the summer residents and visitors have money to spend. Main Street and other streets of the village are lined with upscale shops and galleries. Restaurants skew to the expensive side, though there are some value eateries, too. The visitor information center is in the **Blowing Rock Art and History Museum** *(159 Chestnut St., Blowing Rock),*

With an elevation near 3,600, the town is usually cool in summer, and over the course of winter you can expect up to 3 feet of snow.

Among places to stay in the Blowing Rock area, **Westglow Resort & Spa** *(224 Westglow Circle, Blowing Rock, 828-295-446, www.westglowresortandspa.com)* gets the top nod, and its restaurant, **Rowland's,** is highly rated, too (though expensive, with dinner entrees starting at $35, and with a full meal, drinks and tip expect to pay at least $100 a person). Westglow Resort rates are sky high -- $850 to $1,000 a night double in-season, with meals. Spa charges can add hundreds more.

One of our favorite spots to stay and eat in Blowing Rock is **The Inn at Ragged Gardens** *(203 Sunset Dr., Blowing Rock, 828-295-9703, www.ragged-gardens.com).* It's in the center of the village, within walking distance of most things. The rustic lobby has stone floors and a chestnut-paneled reading room. The guest rooms are cozy, and the restaurant, **The Best Cellar,** at several different locations has been a fixture in this area for almost 40 years. Inn rates are around $140 to $250, more for a suite or cottage, and the restaurant dinner entrees run about $20 to $45.

The **Village Cafe** *(146 Greenway Ct., Blowing Rock, 828-295-3769, www.thevillagecafe.com) is* down a short path from Main Street, with a garden patio, open only for breakfast and lunch late April to early November. The Village Cafe is moderately priced (lunch is around $10 to $15, eggs Benedict for breakfast $10), has long been popular and is often crowded. Another casual, moderately priced spot, just outside the village, is **Canyons** *(8960 Valley Blvd., Blowing Rock, 828-295-7661, www.canyonsbr.com).* The food here is just so-so, and the place needs an upgrade, but the views are terrific.

According to the real estate website Trulia.com the median average home selling price in Blowing Rock in 2014 was $347,500.

Among the real estate developments in the Blowing Rock area are:

Blue Ridge Mountain Club *(1098 Main St., Suite 11, Blowing Rock, 828-295-8667, www.blueridgemountainclub.com)* has lots from $90,000 to $400,000, while home/lot packages cottages start from the mid-$300s.

Firethorn *(Blowing River Rd., Blowing Rock, 828-264-8062 (agent), www.firethornblowingrock.com)* located off U.S. Highway 321 between Blowing Rock and Boone. The development offers 96 homesites. Lots are from around $200,000 to $600,000.

Sweetgrass *(agent Blowing Rock Realty, 855-528-2528, www.sweetgrass.com)* has lots at elevations up to about 3,600 feet priced from around $100,000 to $200,000. There's a 22-acre stocked trout lake on the property.

Boone

Distance from Asheville: 100 miles northeast, about 2 hours by car
Population: 19,000
Visitors and Relocation Information: *Boone Area Chamber of Commerce, 870 W. King St., Suite A, Boone, 828-264-2225, www.boonechamber.com or High Country Host, 1700 Blowing Rock Rd., Boone, 800-438-7500, www.highcountryhost.com*

Boone is the only true college town in Western North Carolina. **Appalachian State University,** with some 17,000 undergrad and graduate students at the main campus, totally dominates the town. Some App State students live in nearby towns such as Blowing Rock, and some are not included in the population estimates for the town. Also in Boone is a satellite campus of **Caldwell County Community College & Technical Institute,** with about 1,800 students in Boone. Watauga County, where Boone is located, has a population of around 52,000.

The main street through Boone, West King Street, has small shops and restaurants and gives off a college town vibe, but the suburban areas around Boone, especially Blowing Rock Road (U.S. Highways 221/321) sprawl with fast food and motel chains. The center of the ASU campus is Sanford Mall, a grassy quad named for former North Carolina governor and Duke University president Terry Sanford. Rivers Street divides the campus into east and west sections. The **Turchin Center for the Visual Arts** *(423 W. King St., Boone, 828-262-3017, www.tcva.org)* has six art galleries and two small sculpture gardens. Admission is free.

In 2012, Boone was listed among the **10 best places to retire** in the U.S. by *US News & World Report.*

The town is named for pioneer and explorer Daniel Boone, who in the 1770s camped in what is now the city of Boone. In the summer, an outdoor drama, **Horn in the West** *(591 Horn in the West Dr., Boone, 828-264-2120, www.horninthewest.com)* tells the Boone story. Tickets are $18 for adults and $9 for children. The adjoining 3-acre **Daniel Boone Native Gardens** has native plants (open daily May-October, admission $2).

At an elevation of around 3,300 feet, Boone is in what is called the High Country of Western North Carolina. The surrounding mountains offer snow skiing, boarding and tubing, rock climbing, hiking, fishing, rafting and camping, and the Blue Ridge Parkway route comes near Boone and Blowing Rock. **Appalachian Ski Mountain** and the snow tubing resort, **Hawksnest,** are near Boone. **Sugar Mountain** and **Beech Mountain** ski resorts also are fairly close by. *(See the Asheville Outside section for more information.)*

For dining in Boone, **Vidalia Restaurant & Wine Bar** (831 W. King St., Boone, 828-263-9176, www.vidaliaofboonenc.com) is a small street-front spot with creative versions of Southern dishes such as smoked chicken with potato gnocchi dumplings. Dinner entrees are around $14 to $25, and lunch is around $12. For family-style home cooking, with heaping plates of fried chicken, country ham, along with country vegetables, the **Dan'l Boone Inn Restaurant** *(130 Hardin St., Boone, 828-264-8657, www.danlbooneinn.com),* the oldest restaurant in Boone, will still fill you up. Nuanced it ain't, but sometimes we just want to stuff ourselves with ham biscuits, overcooked green beans and peach cobbler. Dinner is $17 for adults and breakfast is $10. No credit cards, no reservations except for large groups. For a casual lunch or dinner, we still like **Red Onion Café** *(227 Hardin St., Boone, 828-264-5470, www.theredonioncafe.com),* which has loads of salads, soups, pizzas, burgers and sandwiches at moderate prices, mostly $8 to $17.

For a more upscale dinner, try the **Gamekeeper** *(3005 Shulls Mill Rd., Boone, 828-963-7400, www.gamekeeper-nc.com)*, in a woodsy rural setting outside of town. The menu includes ostrich, bison and duck entrees, along with beef, pork chops and lamb. Entrees are around $22 to $30, but with appetizer or salad, drinks, dessert and tip you'll likely pay closer to $75 to $90 a person. Another upmarket dinner option is **Joy Bistro** *(115 New Market Centre, Boone, 828-265-0500, www.joybistroboone.com)*, which offers Italian and French dishes, along with good steaks burgers. Entrees range from $11 to $32.

Note that at long last Boone voted in liquor by the drink, so you can have a cocktail with dinner, as well as wine or beer.

Lodging choices in Boone are mostly chain motels. Among your better options in the suburban sprawl outside downtown are **Holiday Inn Express, Fairfield Inn, Courtyard by Marriott, Hampton Inn, La Quinta** and **Country Inn & Suites.**

For something more interesting, your best bet in a B&B is **Lovill House Inn** *(404 Old Bristol Rd., Boone, 800-849-9466, www.lovillhouseinn.com)*, run by the same innkeepers for many years. At the edge of town on 11 acres, this charming B&B has rates from around $130 to $220 a night, and all six rooms have cable TV, Wi-Fi, air-conditioning. Some rooms have fireplaces. Rates include a full hot breakfast.

According to the real estate website Trulia.com the median average home selling price in Boone in 2014 was $223,000.

Among the real estate developments in the Boone area:

Councill Oaks *(agent App Real Estate, 215 Boone Heights Dr., Suite 100, Boone, 828-264-4330, www.apprealestate.com)* is a 92-acre gated residential neighborhood with 81 home sites and is conveniently within walking distance to the campus of Appalachian State University. Lots start at $145,000.

Powder Horn Mountain *(1568 Powder Horn Mountain Rd., Deep Gap, 828-264-2072, www.powderhornmountain.com)* is a 1,250-acre established development with clubhouse, hiking trails, three small lakes and trout streams. Lot and home sales are offered through various real estate brokers in Boone, including Parker Mountain Properties *(www.parkermountainproperties)*.

Lots range from under $15,000 to more than $150,000. Existing homes are priced from under $100,000 to the mid $300s.

Brevard

Distance from Asheville: 35 miles southwest, 50 minutes by car

Population: 8,000

Visitor and Relocation Information: *Brevard-Transylvania County Chamber of Commerce (175 East Main St., Brevard, 828-883-3700, www.brevardncchamber.org or Land of Waters, www.visitwaterfalls.com*

Brevard is a gateway to some of the best attractions in the **Pisgah National Forest,** including the **Cradle of Forestry** and **Sliding Rock,** to dozens of waterfalls – Brevard and Transylvania County are known as "The Land of Waterfalls" -- and to great hiking, fishing, mountain biking and camping in the **DuPont State Forest** and Pisgah National Forest.

The town itself, at about the same elevation as Asheville, has a Mayberry-type vibe, and indeed one of the best-known shops in Brevard, a toy store, is called **O.P. Taylor's** (get it?). There are a number of art and crafts galleries, clothing boutiques and such.

Brevard Music Festival *(349 Andante Lane, 828-862-2100, www.brevardmusic.org)* is a nationally known classical music festival held at the **Brevard Music Center** from mid-June to early August. The **Brevard Music Center Orchestra,** made up of talented high school and college musicians, and guest musicians present about 80 symphony concerts, chamber music sessions, operas and other classical music events. Attendance at the various events totals around 30,000. Keith Lockhart is artistic director.

Princeton has its famous black squirrels, but Brevard is known for its white squirrels. These are not albinos but a variant of the Eastern gray squirrel. The story goes that in the 1950s a couple of white squirrels escaped after arriving in town in a circus truck, but who knows? About one-fourth of the squirrels in Brevard are white, and each spring around Memorial Day in late May the town holds a **White Squirrel Festival** *(www.whitesquirrelfestival.com),* with music and a soapbox derby. A good place to see them is the campus of **Brevard College,** a small liberal arts school near downtown.

Square Root Cafe *(33 Times Arcade Alley, Brevard, 828-884- 6171, www.squarerootrestaurant.com)* is a friendly, popular spot for lunch, hidden in an alley downtown, with wraps, salads, burgers and sandwiches, most around $10. Dinner is a good bit more expensive, with entrees including salmon, Cornish game hen and trout from $15 to $22.

Bracken Mountain Bakery *(42 S Broad St., Brevard, 828-883- 4034, www.brackenmountainbakery.com)* has excellent breads and other baked goods. **Rocky's Soda Shop & Grill** *(50 S. Broad St., Brevard, 828- 862-4700, www.ddbullwinkels.com)* has an old-fashioned soda fountain and good hot dogs. It adjoins D. D. Bullwinkel's gift shop. Hokey, but your kids will probably like it.

Hob Knob *(192 W. Main St., Brevard, 828-966-4662, www.hobknobrestaurant.com) Southern* cuisine with a lot of seafood dishes, and **Marco Trattoria** *(204 W. Main St., Brevard, 828-883-4841, www.marcotrattoria.com)*, mostly Northern Italian and wood oven pizzas, sit side-by-side on Main Street. Both are pleasant spots for lunch or dinner. Dinner entrees at Hob Knob are around $16 to $32, and at Marco Trattoria $12 to $17. Lunch is less expensive at both.

Should you want to stay overnight, there are several chain motels outside the downtown area, including **Hampton Inn, Holiday Inn Express** and **Rodeway.** For something more interesting, the **Red House Inn** *(266 W. Probart St., 828-884-9349, www.brevardbedandbreakfast.com)* is the best B&B in town. Built in 1912, with some elements from an earlier 1851 structure, the two-story stucco house with two-tiered porches has five bedrooms, plus there are three separate cottages offered by the B&B owners. Rates are around $135 to $300, depending on the date, including breakfast.

According to the real estate website Trulia.com the median average home listing price in Brevard and Transylvania County in 2014 ranged from $133,000 to more than $1.1 million, depending on the zip code.

Among the real estate developments in the Brevard area:

Straus Park *(agent Fisher Realty, 10 Park Place West, Straus Park Brevard 828-883-9895, www.fisherrealtybrevardnc.com)* is an established planned community within the Brevard city limits. It has a 6-acre pond, swimming pool and hiking and walking trails. Home resales range from around $300,000 to more than $1 million.

Sylvan Heights *(agent Steve Owen and Associates, 6 East Main St., Brevard, www.sylvanheights.net)* is a 64-homesite development established in 2005 about 10 minutes from Brevard with most lots from 2 to 4 acres. Prices range from around $50,000 to $275,000. More than one-half of the lots have been sold.

Bryson City

Distance from Asheville: 65 miles west, about 1¼ hours by car
Population: 1,500
Visitor and Relocation Information: *Bryson City-Swain County Chamber of Commerce & Visitor Center, 210 Main St., Bryson City, 828-488-3681 or 800-867-9246, www.greatsmokies.com*

Bryson City is one of the North Carolina gateways to the Great Smoky Mountains National Park. The **Deep Creek** entrance to the park, only about 2 miles from Bryson City, is popular for river tubing and also has a nice picnic area and campground. There are three waterfalls just a short hike away from the Deep Creek entrance. Lakeview Drive, which was to have stretched some 30 miles along the north shore of **Fontana Lake,** was never finished. It is better known as the **Road to Nowhere** and takes you 6 miles from Bryson City into the Smokies, ending at a tunnel mouth. *(See Great Smoky Mountains National Park section.)*

The early 20th century **Bryson City business district,** mainly along Main and Everett streets, seems to have been mostly taken over by the **Great Smoky Mountains Railroad** *(226 Everett St., 828-586-8811, www.gsmr.com)* and businesses trying to cash in on it. The tourist railroad makes Bryson City its headquarters and main depot, running sightseeing train trips along the Tuckasegee River to Dillsboro and through the Nantahala Gorge to the Nantahala Outdoor Center. Schedules and fares vary seasonally, and on whether you ride in open-air cars or first class enclosed cars, but adults usually pay from $51 to $67 and children 2-12 pay $29 to $38, plus 13.75% sales and historic preservation taxes. Meals, if you want to dine on the train, are extra. Tickets on the railroad include admission to **Bryson City Model Railroad Museum,** good for kids though a bit commercial. **Bryson City Train Depot** on Everett Street, a one-story frame building, was constructed in 1895 by Southern Railway, a successor to the Western North Carolina Railroad. In the early 20th century there were four passenger trains daily between Asheville and Murphy, stopping in Bryson City. The original depot now serves as part of the headquarters of the Great Smoky Mountain Railroad.

Horace Kephart, author of *Our Southern Highlanders* and who with Dr. Kelly Bennett of Bryson City helped lead the effort to establish the Great Smoky Mountains National Park, lived in an apartment above the former Bennett's Drugstore *(32 Everett St.)*. The drugstore, which closed in 2010 after some 100 years in the same family, is now a used bookstore called Friends of the Marianna Black Library Book Store.

The former **Swain County Courthouse** *(Main and Everett Sts.),* designed by architects Frank Pierce Milburn and Richard Sharp Smith and completed in 1908, is a small but striking example of Neoclassical Revival architecture, with a gold-colored octagonal cupola. The columns at the front are Ionic. The courthouse building is now used as a visitor center and houses the charming **Swain County Heritage Museum** on the second floor.

Kituwa or **Kituwah** *(off U.S. Hwy. 19 between Bryson City and Cherokee, near the confluence of the Tuckasegee and Oconaluftee rivers)* is considered one of the "mother towns" and a mythical birthplace of the Cherokee. Kituwah was probably occupied starting around 8000 BC. British soldiers burned the town during the Anglo-Cherokee War in 1761. The Eastern Band of the Cherokee repurchased the 309-acre Kituwah site, where today only an earthen mound remains, in 1996.

The former **Bryson City Bank,** a handsome brick building completed in 1908, houses a specialty coffee shop, wine bar and restaurant, **Bryson City Cork & Bean** *(16 Everett St., 828-488-1934, www.brysoncitycorkandbean.com)*. The Cork & Bean offers excellent baked goods and crepes. Amazingly, this is one of three specialty coffee shops in little Bryson City. For lunch, don't miss The **Filling Station Deli Sub Shop** *(145 Everett St., 828-488-1919, www.thefillingstation.com)*, in an old gas station. This joint (counter service only, with a few seats outside on the sidewalk) does sandwiches as they should be done. The Cuban, called High Test, is *muy bueno*. Most sandwiches and subs are around $6 to $7.

Places to stay: **Fryemont Inn** *(245 Fryemont St., 828-488-2159 or 800-845-4879, www.fryemontinn.com)*, a rustic inn on a hill above Bryson City, completed in 1923, has poplar bark shakes on the outside, and a large stone fireplace and chestnut paneling inside. The inn has 37 rooms in the main lodge. The original owners were Amos and Lillian Reginia Rowe Frye, both attorneys. Lillian Frye was the first woman to graduate from the University of North Carolina School of Law and the first woman to be admitted to the bar in North Carolina. Rates at the Fryemont Inn range from around $135 to $275, including breakfast and dinner. The main lodge is closed December-March, although cottages and cabins are open year-round.

Hemlock Inn *(Galbraith Creek Rd., 828-488-2885, www.hemlockinn.com)* won't suit everybody, but it you want to be out in the country and you don't mind no-frills rooms, with no TV, phones or Wi-Fi, and country cooking served family style, you may be among those who become repeat guests here. Rates are around $200 for a double room with breakfast and dinner. There's something of a Christian atmosphere, and alcohol can be consumed only in rooms.

According to the real estate website Trulia.com the median average home listing price in Bryson City and Swain County in 2014 was $222,000.

Alarka Highlands *(agent Bryson City Realty Group, 264-4 US Highway 19 South*
Bryson City, 828-508-4391, www.alarkahighlands.com) is a 350-acre development bordering the Nantahala National Forest near Bryson City. Lots, which have been reduced from original asking prices, are now mostly offered for around $100,000 to $150,000. Completed lot and log home packages are from the low $200s to high $500s.

The Woodlands *(agent Great Smokys Realty, 184 Everett St., Bryson City, 828-488-2200, www.4smokys.com)* has building lots from $35,000 to $100,000, including roads and septic systems. Minimal homeowners dues for road maintenance.

Burnsville/Spruce Pine

Distance from Asheville: Burnsville is 36 miles northeast of Asheville, about 45 minutes by car; Spruce Pine is about 50 miles northeast of Asheville, about an hour by car

Population: Burnsville 1,700, Spruce Pine 2,200

Visitor and Relocation Information: *Yancey County Chamber of Commerce, 106 West Main St., Burnsville, 828-682-7413, www.yanceychamber.com and Mitchell County Chamber of Commerce, Spruce Pine, 828-765-9483 or 800-227-3912, www.mitchell-county.com*

We lump these two mountains towns together, because although Burnsville is in Yancey County, and Spruce Pine is in Mitchell County, they are only about 15 minutes apart. If you visit one, you'll probably also visit the other.

Confusingly, Mt. Mitchell, the highest mountain in the East, is in Yancey County, not Mitchell County.

One of the main reasons to visit the area is **Penland School** *(67 Doras Trail, Penland, 828-765-2359, Gallery 828-765-6211, www.penland.org)*, a nationally known crafts school on a 460-acre campus, with many crafts studios in the area. Penland is about equidistant from Spruce Pine and Burnsville. Spruce Pine is a mineral and gem mining area, with several dig-it-yourself mines. *(See the Asheville Outside section for more information.)* Both Spruce Pine and Burnsville have small, quaint downtown areas with decidedly unquaint suburbs along U.S. Highway 19.

In Spruce Pine the **Knife and Fork** *(61 Locust St., Spruce Pine, 828-765-1511, www.knifeandforknc.com)* is doubtless the best restaurant in the area and worth a stop for dinner. It's a small, 30-seat restaurant with a rigorous farm-to-table philosophy.

——

The chef, Nate Allen, puts together some interesting taste combinations, such as the parsnips and kettle popcorn small plate as an appetizer. Hanger steak with crispy potatoes and arugula is $22 and local trout is $18. You'll pay around $40 per person for dinner, including wine (no cocktails available).

Buck House Inn on Bald Mountain Creek *(5860 Bald Mountain Rd., Burnsville, 828-536-4140 or 855-405-5005, www.northcarolina-mountain-vacation.com)* is a restored 1904-vintage country house with Colonial Revival stylings. It has chestnut walls, ceilings and floors, and the property is on 8 acres in a beautiful rural setting. Rates in the B&B's four rooms are around $129 to $169 double and include breakfast.

According to the real estate website Trulia.com the median average home listing price in Burnsville and Yancey County in 2014 ranged from $154,000 to more than $367,000 depending on the zip code.

Among the developments in the area:

Mountain Air Country Club *(311 Club House Dr., Burnsville, 828-682-3600 or 800-247-7791, www.mountainaircc.com)* is on top of Slickrock Mountain near Burnsville at about 4,900 feet. It's built as a "fly-in" community because it has a 2,875-foot mountaintop paved airstrip, but of course you can also drive in. There's a golf course, clubhouse, swimming pool, tennis courts and community organic garden. Homesites are priced from around $50,000 to more than $1 million. Condos go from the mid $100s to high $800s, and homes from around $300,000 to $1.6 million.

Cherokee

Distance from Asheville: 51 miles west of Asheville, about 1¼ hours by car; the route via the Blue Ridge Parkway takes about two hours

Population: population of town of Cherokee 2,000; population of Qualla Boundary Reservation 9,000; membership in Eastern Band of the Cherokee 14,000; population of Swain County 14,000

Visitor and Relocation Information: *Visit Cherokee, 498 Tsali Blvd. Cherokee, 800-438-1601, www.visitcherokeenc.com*

Cherokee is a tourist-oriented town that is the main gateway to the North Carolina side of the Great Smoky Mountains National Park. It is on the Qualla Boundary Reservation, home to the Eastern Band of the Cherokee.

For decades, Cherokee has been known for its tacky "faux Indian" motifs, "Indian chiefs" in Hollywood style dress standing in front of tourist gift shops, black bears in cages and mom 'n pop motels and restaurants. We admit it: As kids we used to love to go to Cherokee on our way into the Smokies. We'd stop and buy a toy bow and arrow or spear.

But times change, at least in some ways. Unfortunately there are still some caged bears on display and plenty of tacky tourist gift shops. But there has been a resurgence of interest by local Cherokee in their own history, and the town of Cherokee now has several decidedly non-tacky sights including a museum, high-quality Cherokee crafts co-op and gallery, an updated outdoor drama and a replica 18th century Native American village.

Qualla Arts and Crafts *(Tsali Manor Dr. Cherokee, 828-497-3103, www.quallaartsandcrafts.com)* is the best place to buy high-quality Cherokee art and crafts, including baskets, dolls, masks, pottery and carvings. Probably the best-known Cherokee craft is basket making. The Cherokee used river cane, white oak and honeysuckle to weave baskets, either leaving them in their natural colors or colored with boiled black walnut or bloodroot to produce darker colors. Top contemporary examples of baskets sell for $50 to $1,000 or more, and historical museum-quality examples are virtually priceless. The store also has a museum gallery of Cherokee art and crafts, with displays that are not for sale.

Museum of the Cherokee Indian *(589 Tsali Blvd., Cherokee, 828-497-3481, www.cherokeemuseum.org; daily 9-5 year-round with extended hours 9-7 Memorial Day to Labor Day, $10 adults, children 6-12 $6)* has self-guided tours of permanent interactive exhibits on the Cherokee from the Paleo period through the Trail of Tears and modern times.

Oconaluftee Indian Village *(NC 1361, Cherokee, 828-497-2111; www.visitcherokeenc.com, open daily 10-5 May-mid-Oct., adults 13+ $18.40, children 6-12, $10.40)* is a replica of a Cherokee settlement of around 1760. Cherokee guides knowledgeable about local culture, history and crafts give you a tour.

Unto These Hills *(Drama Rd. off U.S. Hwy. 441/Tsali Blvd., Cherokee, 828)-497-2111, www.visitcherokeenc.com; Jun.-mid-Aug, adults $18-$22, children 6-12 $8-$12)* is an outdoor drama in the 2,800-seat Mountainside Theater. It traces the Cherokee people from their earliest days through the peak of their power to the heartbreak of the Trail of Tears, when in 1838 the U.S. government forcibly removed most of the Eastern Cherokee to Oklahoma, and ending in the present day. Some 6 million people have seen the play since it first opened in 1950.

But the biggest practical change in Cherokee in recent times has been the coming of the **Harrah's Cherokee Casino & Hotel** *(777 Casino Dr., Cherokee, 828-497-7777, www.harrahscherokee.com),* the only casino in North Carolina. The complex employs more than 2,500, making it one of the largest private employers in Western North Carolina. Dealers at the casino can make up to $60,000.

One of the three hotel towers rises 21 stories, the highest building in North Carolina west of Charlotte. Following a recent $650 million expansion, the 150,000 square-feet casino has more than 5,000 video gaming slot machines. Live games including roulette, blackjack and craps were introduced in late 2012. The hotel has more than 1,100 rooms, making it the largest hotel in the state. Rooms – the ones in the new Creek Tower are the nicest -- are a good value at around $130 to $150 but many are comped to regular gamblers. The complex's 3,000-seat Events Center draws national entertainers. Caution: Smoking is allowed in most of the casino, though not in the restaurants, and the tobacco smoke can be overwhelming.

Harrah's Cherokee has a golf course, **Sequoyah National,** and several restaurants including the 404-seat **Paula Deen's Kitchen, BRIO Tuscan Grill** and a **Ruth's Chris Steak House.** The casino and hotel complex is the only place on the Qualla reservation where liquor by the drink, wine and beer are available. The hotel complex also has a spa, fitness center and a new heated, glass-enclosed swimming pool, open year-round, added in 2014.

In addition to the huge casino hotel, Cherokee has a number of chain motels including **Hampton Inn, Fairfield Inn**, **Comfort Suites, Baymont** and **Holiday Inn Express** along with some 1950s and 60s-vintage independent motels. **Two Rivers Lodge** *(5280 Ela Rd., Cherokee, 828-488-2284, www.tworiverslodgenc.com)* between Cherokee and Bryson City, is a well-run 16-room motel with low prices starting at $49 double off-season and $59 in-season. Dining in Cherokee is mostly limited to buffets and fast food due to the unavailability of alcohol outside the casino. One local dining institution is **Peter's Pancakes & Waffles** *(1384 Tsali Blvd., Cherokee, 828-497-5116 or 800-697-0752, www.peterspancakesnc.com),* very popular for its breakfasts. It's open from 6:30 am to 2 pm.

The Great Smokies park entrance and the Oconaluftee visitor center are just 2 miles from Cherokee.

According to the real estate website Trulia.com the median average home listing price in Cherokee and Swain County in 2014 was $222,000.

Dillsboro
Distance from Asheville: 50 miles southwest, about an hour by car
Population: 250
Visitor and Relocation Information: www.visitdillsboro.org

You can see most of Dillsboro in about 15 minutes. The whole downtown is about five square blocks. All that's there are a few craft and gift shops and a Great Smoky Mountains Railroad depot.

The **Jarrett House** *(100 Haywood Rd., Dillsboro, 828-586-0265 or 800-972-5623, www.jarretthouse.com)*, an inn since 1884, is a place to eat and, perhaps to stay, in Dillsboro if you want a historic, three-story Victorian inn with not a whole lot of amenities and Southern country food that can vary from time to time from good to not so good. Open March to late fall. Room rates are around $129 double including breakfast. The dining room offers country basics like fried chicken, country ham and trout for $15-$18 for dinner.

If you want a modern motel, your best bet is the **Best Western Plus River Escapes Inn** *(248 WBI Dr., Dillsboro, 828-586-6060, www.bwriverescape.com)* near town on the Tuckasegee River.

According to the real estate website Trulia.com the median average home listing price in Dillsboro and Jackson County in early 2014 ranged from $209,000 to more than $1 million, depending on the zip code.

Franklin

Distance from Asheville: 70 miles southwest of Asheville, 1½ hours by car

Population: 4,000 in Franklin, about 35,000 in Macon County

Tourism Information: *Discover Franklin, 828-524-2516, www.discoverfranklinnc.com*

Franklin is an entry point into Western North Carolina from Hotlanta, so it and Macon County have seen recent growth. Frankly Franklin doesn't offer much to visitors beyond some touristy gem mining (it bills itself as the "Gem Capital of the World," an example of municipal self-promotion beyond rational comprehension), a **Scottish Tartan Museum** *(86 East Main St., Franklin, 828-524-7472, www.scottishtartans.org)* and a lot of fast food restaurants. But go take a look at it if you desire.

According to the real estate website Trulia.com the median average home listing price in Franklin and Macon County in 2014 ranged from $158,000 to $707,000, depending on the zip code.

Hendersonville/Flat Rock

Distance from Asheville: 26 miles south, about 30 minutes by car

Population: 17,000 in Hendersonville and Flat Rock, 109,000 in Henderson County

Visitor and Relocation Information: *Visitors Information Center, Historic Hendersonville, 201 S. Main St., Hendersonville, 828-693-9708 or 800-828-4244, www.historichendersonville.org*

If you include the suburbs just outside Hendersonville proper, this is the second-largest city in Western North Carolina, after Asheville. Henderson County also is the second-largest county in Western North Carolina.

Hendersonville and Flat Rock have attracted visitors from the South Carolina Lowcountry and elsewhere in the South for more than a century. More recently, Henderson County has become a retirement destination, and the mayor of Hendersonville proclaimed it "the Friendliest City for Retirees in America." Population growth in Henderson County is the fastest in the four-county Asheville metro area, increasing by more than 18% between national censuses in 2000 and 2010, a rate of growth that's about twice the national average. From 1970 to today, Henderson County's population jumped from 52,000 to almost 109,000.

For visitors, Hendersonville has a well-preserved Main Street lined with shops, boutiques and restaurants. Parking is free along Main Street, though sometimes it's difficult to find an empty space. In summer many of the shops have bear statues on the sidewalk, cleverly decorated by local artists to make a statement about the shops. (The Bearfootin' bears are a fund-raiser for local non-profits.) There are historic neighborhoods near downtown, including the Fifth Avenue and Druid Hills neighborhoods. The commercial strips along U.S. Highway 25 and U.S. Highway 64 are more typical examples of suburban sprawl, with chain stores, strip malls and fast food restaurants galore.

In part because of the relatively flat land near Hendersonville, many residential developments have sprung up in the area, including around **Flat Rock,** long a resort destination for wealth South Carolina planters, in the incorporated township of **Laurel Park** and between Hendersonville and South Buncombe.

Henderson County is known for its apples, with around 200 apple growers producing about two-thirds of the state's apple crop. The **North Carolina Apple Festival** *(www.ncapplefestival.org)* celebrates Henderson County's leading crop. Held **Labor Day weekend** in early September for more than 60 years, the Apple Festival occupies most of Main Street in downtown Hendersonville, with music, craft booths, freshly picked apples and cooked products like cider and apple pies.

The festival has a parade that often attracts 50,000 people. President George H.W. Bush attended one year. The festival is free.

Carl Sandburg was already famous for his poetry when in 1945 he moved to Connemara, a 264-acre farm in Flat Rock near Hendersonville. There he lived with his wife Paula Steichen Sandburg, brother of the photographer Edward Steichen, until his death in 1967. The **Carl Sandburg Home National Historic Site** *(81 Carl Sandburg Lane, Flat Rock, 828-693-4178, www.nps.gov/carl/index.htm)* is the first national park site devoted to a poet. The house, a white one-and-a-half story on a raised basement with Greek Revival columns on the front porch, was built around 1839 as a summer cottage by a South Carolina railroad magnate. It sits on a knoll above a small lake. On the National Park Service guided tour, you'll see the Sandburg house much as it was in the 1960s, as if the family had stepped out for a walk. At the barn and outbuildings you'll see descendants of Paula Steichen Sandburg's herd of dairy goats. The farm has some 5 miles of hiking trails. Admission to the farms and grounds is free; a guided tour of the house $5 adults, $3 seniors, children 15 and under free.

Hendersonville doesn't have the quantity or quality of restaurants of Asheville, but it has several good dining choices. **West First Wood-Fired** *(101B First Ave. West, Hendersonville, 828-693-1080, www.flatrockwoodfired.com)* has some of the best pizza in the region. The main dining room is a large rectangle, anchored at the far end by the open wood-fired pizza oven blazing away. Dominating the left side of the room are two large, striking paintings, said to be portraits, more or less, of the owner's grandparents. The other long wall is brick. The ceiling is high, in the standard industrial restaurant style with ductwork showing. There is also a pleasant small dining area in a covered patio outside, and a second level loft. A personal pizza and beer at lunch will set you back about $12. At dinner there are additional entrees in the $11 to $22 range. The same owners operate **Flat Rock Village Bakery. Mezzaluna** *(226 N. Main St., Hendersonville, 828-697-6575, www.mezzaluna-hendersonville.com)* is another very popular wood-fired pizza spot downtown. Pizzas are around $14 to $24 with toppings, and Mezzaluna also serves other Italian dishes – entrees at dinner are $11 to $18. Lunch subs and sandwiches are $6 to $8.

Lime Leaf Thai Fusion *(342 N. Main St., Hendersonville, 828-692-3300, www.lifeleaf101.com)* does acceptable Thai, nicely presented, in a pleasant atmosphere, at slightly above-average prices. Most dinner entrees around $9 to $15, though some seafood dishes are over $20. Avoid the fried calamari. The Singha Thai beer is deliciously cold and served in a chilled glass.

Hendersonville also has a well-run outpost of **Papas and Beer** *(1821 Asheville Hwy., Hendersonville, 828-692-9915)* for a Mexican food fix, and a Japanese restaurant, **Umi** *(633 N Main St., Hendersonville, 864-698-8048)* with good sushi.

If you're staying overnight, the U.S. Highway 64 strip off I-26 has a number of chain motels, including **Hampton Inn, Best Western, Red Roof, Comfort Inn** and **Ramada.** Of these, the Hampton Inn is probably the best choice. Hendersonville has more than a dozen B&Bs. Among the best are the elegant **Melange Bed and Breakfast,** *(1230 Fifth Ave. West, Hendersonville, 828-697-5253, www.melangebb.com),* the 1893 **Elizabeth Leigh Inn** *(908 5th Ave. West, Hendersonville, 828-808-5305, www.elizabethleighinn.com),* **Inn on Church Street** *(201 Third Ave. West, Hendersonville, 828-696-2001, www.innonchurch.com),* close to everything downtown, and **1898 Waverly Inn** *(783 N Main St., Hendersonville, 828-693-9193, www.waverlyinn.com),* a comfortable 15-room inn at the end of Main Street.

According to the real estate website Trulia.com the median average home sales price in Hendersonville in 014 was $165,000. In Henderson County as a whole, the median sales price ranged from $95,500 to $315,000, depending on the area of the county and the zip code.

Among the many real estate developments in and near Hendersonville are the following;

Grand Highlands at Bear Wallow *(10 Autumn Sky Drive, Hendersonville, 828-233-1017, www.grandhighlands.com).* This is a 288-acre development at an elevation of 3,300 to 3,800 feet. It is planned as a gated community with miles of walking trails, parklands, a 12,000 square foot clubhouse, pool and hot tub, tennis and a community barn. Ready-to-build home sites are priced from $65,000 to $350,000. Custom homes are offered from $425,000 to $2,500,000.

Champion Hills *(15 Club View Dr., Hendersonville, 800-633-5122, www.championhills.com)* is a 700-acre private golf community about five minutes from downtown Hendersonville. It has an excellent Tom Fazio-designed 18-hole course with clubhouse, pool, tennis courts and fitness center. The golf club is member-owned and is said to be debt-free. The upscale homes, typically dating from the 1990s and early 2000s sell in the $400,000 to $4 million range. Lots also vary greatly in price according to location and size, from around $15,000 to more than $200,000. Home and building lots are sold by WNC MLS members and by the developer through Beverly-Hanks & Associates. According to the developer, about one-half of Champion Hills residents live there year-round, and the golf course is also open year-round.

Cummings Cove *(20 Cummings Cove Parkway, Hendersonville, 800-958-2905, www.cummingscove.com)* is a 650-acre gated golf community about 15 minutes from Hendersonville. Home sites start in the $60s and range to more than $300,000. Lot/home packages range from near $400,000 to over $1 million.

The Orchards at Flat Rock *(90 Summerfield Place, Flat Rock, 828-243-8800, www.lifestylehomes.net/communities/orchards-flat-rock)* is a 45-acre development with 200 homes plans. Current prices for lot/home packages range from the mid $270,000 with 2-bedrooms, 2 baths and a 2-car garage. Packages top out at about $350,000.

Highlands/Cashiers

Distance from Asheville: 73 miles southwest of Asheville, about 2 hours by car

Population: 1,000, swelling to 15,000 in summer

Visitor and Relocation Information: *Highlands Chamber of Commerce, 269 Oak St., Highlands, 866-526-5841; www.highlandschamber.org*

If you know people from Palm Beach or Atlanta's Buckhead, you may run into them in Highlands. This small town, whose population swells by 10 to 15 times in summer and fall, is the tony top of the mountains, both in elevation and finance. Though no longer the highest incorporated town in the East (Beech Mountain now takes that honor at over 5,500 feet), Highlands' elevation of around 4,100 feet gives it cooler summers than Asheville. The typical home for sale in Highlands in recently listed for over $850,000, and many homes go for $1 to $2 million or more.

Main Street downtown is lined with boutiques, gift shops, antique stores and upmarket restaurants. The little town has four different theater groups, ten golf courses (mostly private), a chamber music series and several spas.

For upscale dining, think about **Ristorante Paoletti** *(440 Main St., 828-526-4906, www.paolettis.com)*, the Italian favorite in Highlands for about three decades; **Wolfgang's** *(474 Main St. 828-526-3807, www.wolfgangs.net)*, with an eclectic menu and, like Paoletti's, an excellent wine list; or, out of town on Harris Lake, **Lakeside Restaurant** *(Smallwood Ave, Highlands, 828-526-9419, www.lakesiderestaurant.info)* with excellent steaks and other items.

Cyprus Restaurant *(470 Dillard Rd., Highlands, 828-525-4429, www.cyprushighlands.com)* is a happening spot with an eclectic "international" menu, with dishes from Cambodia, China, Mexico, India, Japan and elsewhere, along with American entrees such as a cowboy ribeye and Prime New York strip. Figure you'll drop $75 or so per person, or more, at any of these spots.

The top place to stay in Highlands is the totally redone **Old Edwards Inn** *(445 Main St., Highland, 866-526-8008, www.oldedwardsinn.com)* with a variety of upscale options including the restored historic main inn, nearby cottages and houses. The inn's main restaurant, **Madison's,** is very good, and the inn has a nationally recognized spa and golf packages. Rooms in season start at round $300, and the inn is often fully booked weeks in advance. Just across Main Street yet far less fancy, but with character and affordable prices, is the historic 130-year-old **Highlands Inn** *(420 Main St., Highland, 828-526-9380 or 800-964-6955, www.highlandsinn-nc.com)*, with rates starting at $139, plus tax.

Highlands also has a number of good B&Bs, including **4½ Street Inn** *(55 4-1/2 St., Highlands, 828-526-4464, 888-799-4464, www.4andahalfstinn.com)* and **Colonial Pines Inn B&B** *(541 Hickory St., Highlands, 828-526-2060 or 866-526-2060, www.colonialpinesinn.com)*. Both are reasonably priced.

While in Highlands, take a quick side trip to **Cashiers** (pronounced CASH-ers), about 20 minutes or 10 miles away, an even tinier village (year-round population just 250). **High Hampton Inn** *(1525 NC 107 South, Cashiers, 888-647-0820, www.highhamptoninn.com)* may be too old-fashioned and 1950ish for your tastes, but some families have been coming here for generations. Frankly, we are charmed by the 1,400-acre mountain resort with the main inn, shingled in poplar and chestnut, dating from 1932. There is a golf course and tennis courts. Motorcycles and RVs aren't permitted on the property. There's good food at **The Orchard** *(905 NC 107, Cashiers, 828-743-7614, www.theorchardcashiers.com)* and, for less money, at **Cornucopia** *(16 Cashiers School Rd. off NC 107, Cashiers, 828-743-3750, www.cornucopianc.com)*.

According to the real estate website Trulia.com the median average home sales price in Highlands in 2014 was $300,000, but numerous homes are valued at many times that figure. In Jackson County as a whole, the median listing price ranged from $209,000 to more than $1 million.

Among the residential developments near Highlands/Cashiers are the following:

Cullasaja Club *(1371 Cullasaja Club Dr., Highlands, 828-526-3531, www.callasajaclub.org)* is a private gated golf community on 685 acres at around 4,200 feet elevation. Plans are for 300 homeowners. Arnold Palmer designed the par-72, 6,900 yard course. On the grounds are Ravenel Lake and the Cullasaja River. Homesites mostly are in the $200s and $300s. Homes range from around $450,000 to more than $4 million.

Trillium *(One Trillium Center, Cashiers, 828-743-6161 or 888-464-3800, www.trilliumnc.com)* is a residential, lake and golf community near Cashiers. For the Cashiers-Highlands area, this a "mid-range" gated community. The 18-hole Trillium Links was designed by Morris Hatalsky. Homesites rate from $75,000 to over $600,000. Condos and townhomes are from the high $200s to high $500s. Custom-built homes range from the mid $200s to about $1.6 million.

Wade Hampton Golf Club *(68 Golf Dr., Cashiers, 828-743-5465, www.wadehamptongc.com)* is a well-established and very golf-focused club and community near Cashiers. The 300-acre property has a lake and a highly rated Tom Fazio-designed 18-hole course but no swimming or tennis facilities. Only residents can have a golf club member; there are no social memberships. Both the clubhouse and golf course have dress standards. Lots range from $150,000 to $1.6 million, and homes on the re-sale market are offered from $800,000 to more than $3 million.

Hot Springs

Distance from Asheville: 37 miles northwest of Asheville, 50 minutes by car

Population: 600

Visitor and Relocation Information: www.hotspringsnc.org

Hot Springs is one of the small mountain villages that leaves us cold, but in the 19th century it was a leading mountain resort with a big resort hotel, Warms Springs Hotel. It was named 2012's "Best Small Mountain Town" by *Blue Ridge Outdoors* magazine, so we guess we're missing something. It does have 108-degree hot mineral springs (the hottest in North Carolina) and is at the junction of the Appalachian Trail and the French Broad River. We do like the nearby **Max Patch Bald,** a high-elevation heath bald on the Appalachian Trail with panoramic views of the mountains. Avoid the bald during thunderstorms – in 2010 a woman was killed by lightning just as her partner was about to propose marriage to her.

Mountain Magnolia inn *(204 Lawson St., Hot Springs, 828-622-3543 or 800-914-9306, www.mountainmagnoliainn.com)* is the best place in the area to stay and eat.

According to the real estate website Trulia.com the median average home listing price Hot Springs in 2014 was $279,000.

Robbinsville

Distance from Asheville: 90 miles southwest of Asheville, about two hours by car

Population: 650

Visitor and Relocation Information: *Graham County Travel and Tourism, 387 Rodney Orr Bypass Robbinsville, 828-479-3790 or 800-470-3790, www.grahamcountytravel.com*

The little town of Robbinsville itself has little to recommend it to visitors. However, Robbinsville is the county seat of Graham County, two-thirds of which is national park or national forest. Two-thirds of Graham County is National Forest Lands. Graham County is the home of the wonderful **Joyce Kilmer Memorial Forest** with its ancient virgin trees and the **Nantahala National Forest**, and it borders the **Great Smoky Mountains National Park**. The **Appalachian Trail** crosses the county. **Fontana Lake** and **Lake Santeetlah** are both a short drive Robbinsville. The county has several scenic roads, including the **"Tail of the Dragon"** (Highway 129) with 318 curves in 11 miles, beloved by motorcycle and sports car fans, and the 50 mile-long **Cherohala Skyway.**

The classic place to stay in Graham County is **Snowbird Mountain Lodge** *(4633 Santeetlah Road, Robbinsville, 828-479-3433 or 800-941-9290, www.snowbirdlodge.com)*, a mountainside lodge that dates to 1940. The main lodge building is built of stone with paneling of chestnut, cherry, sourwood, maple and other native woods. The dining room serves excellent meals. Another option is **Fontana Village Resort** *(300 Woods Rd., Fontana Dam, 828-4982211 or 800-849-2258, www.fontanavillage.com)* in the Nantahala National Forest near Fontana Lake. The resort, parts of which were originally constructed during World War II to house workers building Fontana Dam, has a variety of accommodations including cabins, rooms in the main lodge and an RV and tent campground. There is also a marine with boat rentals.

According to the real estate website Trulia.com the median average home listing price in Robbinsville and Graham County in 2014 ranged from $237,000 to $272,000, depending on the zip code.

Sylva

Distance from Asheville: 48 miles southwest of Asheville, about an hour by car

Population: 2,600

Visitor and Relocation Information: *Jackson County Chamber of Commerce, 773 W. Main St., Sylva, 828-586-2155, www.mountainlovers.com*

Sylva is dear to our hearts because it was the birthplace of mountain writer **John Parris,** whose daily columns in the *Asheville Citizen-Times* were collected in many books, beginning with *Roaming the Mountains* in 1955.

Other than that, it's just a little mountain town. The old Jackson County Courthouse in Sylva, set on hill, is worth a look. Sylva is the closest town to **Western Carolina University in Cullowhee,** so it draws a few students and others for shopping and eating. It does have a good microbrewery, **Heinzelmannchen Brewery** *(545 Mill St., Sylva, 828-631-4466, www.yourgnometownbrewery.com)*, and a good independent bookstore, **City Lights** *(3 East Jackson St., Sylva, 828-586-9499 or 888-853-6298, www.citylightsnc.com)* with an adjoining café and coffeehouse. In fact, the entire little town is caffeinated, with three or four coffee houses.

According to the real estate website Trulia.com the median average home listing price in Sylva and Jackson County in 2014 ranged from $208,000 to more than $1 million, depending on the zip code.

Among the real estate developments near Sylva is the 4,400-acre **Balsam Mountain Preserve** *(81 Preserve Rd., Sylva, 866-452-3456, www.balsammountainpreserve.com)*. More than 3,000 acres of the development have been put aside for conservation only. It is claimed that Balsam Mountain is the least-dense development in Western North Carolina. The community has an Arnold Palmer-designed golf course at 3,700 feet, tennis courts, more than 30 miles of hiking trails and an equestrian center. Cottages here start in the $600s, with most homes priced from $800,000 to $3.5 million. Home sites start at around $175,000. Balsam Mountain is about 45 minutes from Asheville.

Waynesville

Distance from Asheville: 31 miles west of Asheville, about 35 minutes by car

Population: 10,000

Visitor and Relocation Information: *Haywood County Tourism Development Authority, 44 N. Main St., Waynesville, 828-452-0152 or 800-334-9036, www.visitncsmokies.com*

Waynesville is an engaging small town with a walkable downtown with brick sidewalks, many shops, galleries and eateries. It has drawn a sizeable number of retirees.

Probably the biggest event of the year in Waynesville is **Folkmoot USA** *(www.folkmootusa.org)*, which brings dance and folk music groups from several countries to downtown Waynesville. It is held during the last two weeks of July.

Near the main downtown is **Frog Level,** which is trying to evolve into the town's entertainment area. So far there's not too much there beyond **Frog Level Brewing Company** *(56 Commerce St., Waynesville, 828-254-5664, www.froglevelbrewing.com)* and **Panacea Coffee House Cafe** *(66 Commerce St., Waynesville, 828-452-6200, www.panaceacoffee.com)*.

The best places to eat in town are **Chef's Table** *(30 Church St., Waynesville, 828-452-6210, www.thechefstableofwaynesville.com)*, which leans toward fine dining with fresh-made pastas, appetizers like fried quail legs in a bourbon glaze and entrees from $17-$35 for dinner, with an extensive wine list. A local favorite is the much more casual and homey **The Sweet Onion** *(39 Miller St., Waynesville, 828-456-5559, www.sweetonionrestaurant.com)*, focused on updated Southern dishes such as bacon-wrapped meatloaf and mac and cheese with blue crab. Sandwiches and salads at The Sweet Onion for lunch are around $6 to $12, while dinner entrees are mostly in the $13 to $20 range. **Frogs Leap Public House** *(44 Church St., Waynesville, 828-456-1930, www.frogsleappublichouse.org)* is enjoyable for its farm-to-plate New Southern menu ($17 to $36 for dinner entrees).

For overnight stays, Waynesville has more than a dozen B&Bs. Among the best are **Andon-Reid Inn** *(92 Daisy Ave., Waynesville, 828-452-3089 or 800-452-3089, www.andonreidinn.com)*, a 1902 house with five bedrooms about a mile from downtown; **Yellow House on Plott Creek** *(89 Oakview Dr., Waynesville, 828-452-0991 or 800-563-1236, www.theyellowhouse.com)*, a lovely old house with 10 rooms and suites with beautiful grounds, in a rural area just outside Waynesville (the Plott hound, a coonhound by trade, is the state dog of North Carolina); **Herren House** *(94 E. Waynesville St., Waynesville, 828-452-7837, www.herrenhouse.com)*, a restored Victorian boarding house, is the closest B&B to the downtown area; **Oak Hill on Love Lane** *(224 Love Lane, Waynesville, 828-456-7037, www.oakhillonlovelane.com)*, a 1900 home within strolling distance of downtown. You'll generally pay around $120 to $200 a night at these little inns, breakfast included. **The Swag Country Inn** *(2300 Swag Rd., Waynesville, 828-926-0430 or 800-789-7672, www.theswag.com)* on 250 acres on a mountain top outside Waynesville adjoining the Great Smoky Mountains National Park, has won national acclaim for its beautiful grounds, good food and rustically appealing lodging, but it comes at a price -- $500 to $800 a night double, including meals.

According to the real estate website Trulia.com the median average home listing price in Waynesville in 2014 was $290,000.

Among the planned real estate developments near Waynesville is **Avalon at Junaluska Highlands** *(866-936-5263, www.avalonwnc.com)*. About 5 minutes from Waynesville, Avalon is Avalon has about 100 home sites on some 400 acres. Lot sizes range from .75 to 5 acres, with elevations around 3,200 feet and higher. Lots in this gated community start at around $35,000.

ASHEVILLE BY THE NUMBERS

14-22 million	Visitors to Blue Ridge Parkway annually
9 million+	Visitors to Great Smoky Mountains National Park annually
3 million+	Overnight visitors to Asheville annually
1.4 million	Acres of national parks, national forests, state and local parks in WNC
1.2 million	Annual visitors to Biltmore Estate
438,000	Population of 4-county Asheville metro area, 2014 =
248,419	Population of Buncombe County, 2014 (est.)
215,000	Median sales price of existing home in Asheville area in 2014
88,000	Population of Asheville (within city limits) 2014
44,331	Median annual household income in dollars in Buncombe
7,200	Private businesses in Buncombe County
6,686	Height of highest mountain in WNC, Mt. Mitchell
6,638	Average sales price per acre of land in larger tracts, WNC 2014
4,000+	Miles of trout streams in WNC
3,554	Homes sold in Buncombe in 2014
2,165	Average elevation in feet in Asheville
1,520	Number of public parking spaces in Asheville
1,000	Number of physicians in Buncombe County area
963	Number of eating places in Asheville area
797	Average gross rental in Asheville area, 2013
714	Average weekly wage in Buncombe County, 2012
656	Square miles of land in Buncombe County
363	Population density per square mile, Buncombe County
350+	Number of waterfalls in WNC
266	Bird species identified in Asheville and Buncombe County
252	Miles of Blue Ridge Parkway in North Carolina
125+	Number of hotels, motels and inns in Asheville area

111	Average daily hotel rate in Asheville
101.2	Cost of living index in Asheville (national = 100)
99	Highest temperature ever recorded in Asheville (July 1983)
90	Percent of Asheville/Buncombe population that is white
87	Percent of 25+ population who completed at least high school
85	Average daily high temperature in July (hottest month)
69	Annual hotel occupancy rate (percentage) in Asheville, 2013
68	Number of Christmas trees at Biltmore House
65	Average daily low temperature in July (hottest month)
60	Art and crafts galleries in Asheville
58	Average annual temperature
55.31	Percentage of vote for President Obama, Buncombe 2012
55	Number of golf courses in WNC
50+	B&Bs in Asheville area
50	Average annual rainfall, in inches
47	Average daily high temperature in January (coldest month)
44	Average cost for two of meal in mid-price restaurant
41	Median age of population
40	Micro beer breweries/brewpubs in Asheville area
32	Percent of population 25+ with at least B.A. degree
30	Number of specialty coffee houses in Asheville area
28	Average daily low temperature in January (coldest month)
21	Average daily commute from home to work, in minutes
18.82	Living wage in dollars per hour of work of single adult with 1 child
16.2	Percent of population in Buncombe 65 and over (national = 13.3%)
15.6	Percent of population under poverty line, Buncombe, 2012 (national = 14.3%)
14	Average annual snowfall, in inches
7.30	Average cost in dollars of movie ticket

7.20	Average cost in dollars for brand-name pack of cigarettes
7	Blue Ridge Parkway entrances around Asheville
6.7	Percent of Asheville/Buncombe population that is black
6.2	Percent of Asheville/Buncombe population of Hispanic descent
6	Snow ski resorts around Asheville
2.50	Average price in dollars for single espresso
0	Naturally formed lakes in WNC
-16	Lowest temperature ever recorded (January 1985

MOVING CHECKLIST

About 2-3 Years Before Your Move
Begin researching areas you're considering for a move

About 1-2 Years Before Your Move
Begin making scouting visits to areas you're considering for a move
Make decision on whether you'll initially rent, buy or build

About 1 Year Before Your Move
Depending on market conditions and your specific situation, consider putting your present home on the market
Start researching specific developments and properties in your chosen community or area
If you're hiring a buyer's agent, make decision on agent
Begin looking at properties or apartments

About 4-6 Months Before Your Move
Make decision about which property you'll buy or rent
If you're financing the property, apply for loan or make other arrangements for buying or renting

About 2-3 Months Before Your Move
Make a budget for your move
Collect estimates from moving companies, if you are using one
Create a "move file" to keep track of dates, quotes, receipts and other important information
Conclude closing or other arrangements on your new home

8 Weeks Before Your Move
Start compiling medical, dental, shot and prescription records
Ask your medical providers or friends for referrals in your new location
Arrange to have school records and veterinarian records transferred
Gather copies of legal, financial and other important records
Talk to your insurance agents about your old and new policies
Contact fitness clubs, civic organizations and groups to cancel or transfer memberships

Decide what you'll throw out, give away or sell – you may want to have a garage sale

6 Weeks Before Your Move
Start using up frozen foods and other food items you don't want to move
Order boxes and moving supplies
Begin packing up personal items and items you don't use often – label boxes with information on what they contain and which room in your new home they should be placed
Make a final determination of your exact move date with the moving company or do-it-yourself moving truck
Make hotel reservations in your new city, if necessary

3-4 Weeks Before Your Move
File a change of address with the Postal Service and ask that your mail be held at the post office in your new city
Notify all utilities (electric, gas, water, telephone, cable or satellite, internet provider, sewerage, trash) in your old and new cities of the date of service stop and start
Notify the following of your move and discuss any issues that may arise: accountant, attorney, church, temple or synagogue, physicians, dentist, financial planner, health insurance provider, insurance agents, pharmacy, schools
Notify or file change of address with these providers: auto finance company, banks and credit unions, credit card companies, exterminator, fitness club, home care service providers such as lawn mowers, laundry service, magazine and newspaper subscriptions, local charge accounts
Notify pertinent government offices of your move: tax assessor, state department of motor vehicles, Social Security, local, state and federal tax offices, Veterans Administration, voter registration office
Notify friends and family of your new address and other contact information
Have a garage sale

2-3 Weeks Before Your Move
Have your motor vehicles serviced
Confirm or reconfirm all travel arrangements, including for pets
Plan meals to use up your food
Assemble a folder of important info about your house for the next homeowner, if applicable

1 Week Before Your Move

Review your moving plans with your moving company or moving consultant; if moving yourself, pack as much as you can in advance, with each box clearly labeled and with a destination room designated
Notify your bank or credit card company if you are planning to use debit or credit cards in your new area – this avoids having your account blocked by the banks' fraud department
Refill any prescriptions you will need during your move
Pack an essentials box to keep with you during the move
Drain gas and oil from lawn equipment, gas grills, heaters, etc.
Empty and defrost refrigerator at least 24 hours before the move
Prepare your houseplants and valuable household items for moving
Visit your bank safety deposit box, clear it out and close the account
Make a decision on how you will transport or ship valuables such as gold coins, jewelry and bearer bonds

Moving Day Checklist
Get up early, eat a good breakfast and prepare yourself mentally for little problems that often happen with any move
Personally supervise hired labor
Place carpet, floor and door frame protectors throughout your home
If moving yourself, load goods in a pre-designated order, saving "last-in, first-out" items for the rear of your shipment
Check every room and closet one last time to make sure nothing is left behind
Leave a note with your new address so that future residents can forward stray mail

Moving In
Confirm that all utilities are on and operating properly
Meet with any hired labor for the move in
Clean your new home, make sure everything is in working condition and make any needed repairs, preferably before your household goods arrives
Unload your items and begin organizing your new home
Pick up mail being held at the local post office
Get a new driver's license and automobile tags, register to vote, start local newspaper, etc. *(see Practicalities in Establishing Residency in North Carolina section for detailed information)*
Enjoy your new home!

SCOUTING TRIPS

If you haven't already done so, you'll want to make a scouting trip – and preferably several trips at different times of the year – to the area or areas you're considering for your new home. Stay as long as you can on your trips. After all, relocating to any area is a big decision and costly in both time and money.

Among the many things you'll probably want to accomplish on your scouting trips are:

• See the destination in all four seasons.

• Try to find a real estate agent with whom you're comfortable, ideally one who is friendly, helpful and knowledgeable. If possible, start looking at homes, condos or apartments, to see in person what you're likely to get for your money.

• Investigate options for medical care, especially if you are older or have chronic health concerns.

• Try to establish networking contacts through civic clubs, professional groups, churches or other religious organizations, hobbies and activities that you are active in back home.

• Be sure to look for negatives, aspects of the destination that you may not like.

• If you plan to work here, begin the early stages of your job hunt, and investigate what business or professional licenses you may need.

• Start trying to make new friends here. Some ideas: Attend meetings of clubs and organizations of which you are a member; stay in bed and breakfasts and small inns where you are likely to have interactions with the innkeepers and with other guests; take part in sports and outdoor activities, especially those of a group nature; get in touch with local newcomers clubs.

• Explore as many communities and neighborhoods as you can – you may find the perfect place you didn't even know existed.

• Try to figure out if you and your family are a good "fit" with the where you may live – socially, politically, educationally and otherwise.

• Be a tourist! Seeing the sights, taking tours and doing the fun, touristy things are a fine way to learn about the area. Frankly, if and when you become a resident, you may never do some of those touristy things again.

The chapters that follow – on travel practicalities, lodging, dining, drinking and other matters – are designed to help you make the most of your visits to Asheville and Western North Carolina.

TRAVEL PRACTICALITIES

This section covers the basic practical information -- such as getting cash from ATMs, cell phone service, local media and emergency medical care -- that you need when you travel in Asheville and the mountains. More comprehensive coverage of these subjects are found in other parts of this book.

ASHEVILLE AREA CODE

The area code for Asheville and the rest of Western North Carolina is **828.**

BANKING AND GETTING CASH

You'll have no problems getting cash from ATMs in Asheville and Western North Carolina. National and large regional banks with locations in the Asheville include **Bank of America, Wells Fargo**, **BB&T, SunTrust, TD Bank** and **First Citizens Bank,** all with ATMs. Among the larger locally based banks and thrifts are **Asheville Savings Bank** and **Hometrust Bank,** which also have ATMs. There are other smaller local banks, credit unions and savings banks, nearly all with ATMs that accept cards on the major networks such as Plus, Cirrus, MasterCard and Visa. Keep in mind that you will usually be charged a fee for using an ATM that is not a part of your home bank's system.

CELL PHONE SERVICE

AT&T and **Verizon** have the best cell coverage in Asheville and Western North Carolina. Note, however, that the mountain terrain can play havoc with cell service. In a deep valley cell service suddenly may drop out. Service in national park and national forest areas with few if any cell towers may be limited or non-existent.

CRIME AND SAFETY PRECAUTIONS

The crime rate in the Asheville and Western North Carolina is generally low. Based on Uniform Crime Report statistics by the Federal Bureau of Investigation, most major crime rates in Buncombe County and in surrounding counties in WNC are somewhat to significantly lower than the national average.

The usual precautions for visitors to the Asheville area are the same as those given to travelers elsewhere: Be aware of your surroundings, noting people or places that just don't "look right." At night, park and walk in well-lighted areas. Don't flash large amounts of cash. Avoid walking alone in isolated areas late at night. Protect your PIN when using ATMs. Don't leave valuables such as purses, cameras or cell phones in view in parked vehicles. If you see a crime or fear being involved yourself, call 911 immediately. Remember, though, Asheville and Western North Carolina generally are safe, friendly places for visitors, and it is highly unlikely that you will experience any crime.

DRUGS

Asheville is more "dope-friendly" than most other cities in North Carolina or the South, but possession and distribution of even marijuana is still against the law – it has not been legalized or even decriminalized here -- and North Carolina does not yet have medical marijuana laws. In most cases, in Asheville police do not arrest for possession of a small amount of weed, as long as you don't go out of your way to flaunt it, or if arrested charges will be dismissed. At most you will be charged with a misdemeanor. But using weed in Asheville is still a risk. A good number of people in Asheville smoke fairly openly at outdoor music events and sometimes on rooftops of garages. Outside of Asheville, including in rural Buncombe County, law enforcement may be more rigid.

Technically, in North Carolina possession of ½ ounce or less of marijuana is a misdemeanor, punishable by 30 days in jail and a $200 fine. Possession of ½ to 1½ ounces is a misdemeanor, punishable by up to 120 days in jail and a $500 fine. Community service is possible for these offenses, and the maximum sentence is 45 days if the offender has no priors. Possession of more than 1½ ounce is a felony, punishable by 1 year in jail and a discretionary fine. Distributing or cultivating 5 grams to 10 pounds is a felony, punishable by up to 1 year in jail and a $5,000 fine.

Psychedelic mushrooms and acid also are fairly common in Asheville, but police do arrest and charge for possession. Police pursue use and distribution of harder drugs fairly aggressively. Meth labs are a problem in some rural areas of the state.

GETTING TO ASHEVILLE

The vast majority of visitors to Asheville – around 95% – arrive by car.

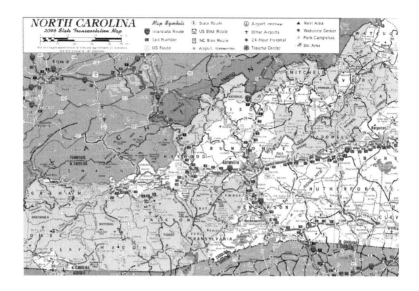

Two interstates go through Asheville: **I-40** (a major east-west highway, 2,559 miles long, that connects Wilmington, N.C., with Barstow, Calif., running through Tennessee, Arkansas, Oklahoma, Texas, New Mexico and Arizona) and **I-26** (a newer interstate connecting Kingsport, Tenn., and Charleston, S.C.) As it crosses the country, I-40 connects with eight of the 10 major north-south interstates.

I-26 to the northwest connects with I-75 and U.S. Highway 23 through Ohio to the Great Lakes, and to the southeast connects with interstates 20, 77, 85 and 95.

The most scenic route to Asheville is the 469-mile **Blue Ridge Parkway,** which connects Shenandoah National Park in Virginia with the **Great Smoky Mountains National Park** in Western North Carolina. The parkway has seven entrance/exits in the Asheville area. *(For more information, see the Blue Ridge Parkway section.)*

You can also reach Asheville via **U.S. Highways U.S. 19/23, 25, 25A, 70 and 74** as well as on a number of secondary North Carolina roads.

GPS NAVIGATION

GPS navigation devices generally work well here, but there are some important exceptions. First, mountainous terrain, long tunnels and heavy tree canopies can at least temporarily disrupt contact with satellites. Second, because Western North Carolina is predominantly a rural area, not all destinations have a specific street address.

Your GPS navigation system may tell you that you've arrived at a destination when it fact you could be hundreds of yards or even miles away from the true location. Finally, and perhaps most importantly, roads and trails in national and state forests, in the Great Smoky Mountains National Park and on the Blue Ridge Parkway may not be adequately or accurately mapped in GPS databases. Use an extra dose of common sense when interpreting GPS navigation directions in remote government lands.

EMERGENCIES

For **all crime, fire, health and other emergencies** in Asheville and the rest of the region, **dial 911.** In addition, here are other direct numbers for selected first responders:

Asheville Police Department *(100 Court Plaza, Asheville, 828-252-1110; www.ashevillenc.gov/Departments/Police.aspx)* has about 250 employees, plus around 150 volunteers.

Asheville Fire Department *(100 Court Plaza, Asheville, 828-259-5636; www.ashevillenc.gov/Departments/Fire.aspx)* has a total of 12 fire stations. Buncombe County has an additional 24 fire stations and volunteer fire departments.

Buncombe County Health Department *(40 Coxe Ave., Asheville, 828-250-5000; www.buncombecounty.org)* is primarily for Buncombe County residents. In rankings of all 100 North Carolina counties, Buncombe's overall health rankings have steadily increased from #25 to #14.

Buncombe County Sheriff's Department *(202 Haywood St., Asheville, 828-255-5555; www.buncombecounty.org)* has around 360 full-time employees. In 2011, the department answered 58,000 calls for service. As in other North Carolina counties, the sheriff, currently Van Duncan, is elected by county voters. Elections are every four years.

Carolinas Poison Control Center *(800-222-1222; www.ncpoisoncenter.org)* is a 24-hour hotline that provides advice on what to do in case of a possible poisoning.

Federal Bureau of Investigation *(151 Patton Avenue, Suite 211, 828-253-1643; www.fbi.gov)* has a small satellite office in Asheville, working out of its main regional office in Charlotte.

North Carolina State Highway Patrol *(600 Tunnel Rd., 828-296-7260; www.ncdps.gov)* has around 1,800 officers in North Carolina who patrol the state's 78,000 miles of roads, the most roadways of any other state except Texas. North Carolina had 912 traffic fatalities in 2012.

The Highway Patrol made almost 24,000 arrests in 2012 for driving while impaired. The legal blood alcohol level in North Carolina is 0.08. For a 200-pound male, that's about four to five 12-ounce beers, or the equivalent, consumed over a two-hour period; for a 140-pound female, that's about two to three 12-ounce beers or the equivalent consumed in a two-hour period. The exact blood alcohol level depends on the percentage of alcohol in beer or wine, on the amount of alcohol and its proof in mixed drinks and on other factors. Driving while impaired is a very serious offense -- always err on the side of being conservative.

INTERNET SERVICE WHILE TRAVELING

In Asheville, the major internet service providers are **AT&T** and **Charter Cable.** AT&T (www.att.com) has DLS service with downstream speeds of up to 18Mbps. Charter (www.charter.com) offers downstream speeds of up to 30Mbps.

Most lodging places provide internet service for guests, with the vast majority providing it at no charge. Many coffee houses and bookstores and some bars and restaurants have free internet service, as do some fast food restaurants including McDonald's, Wendy's, Dunkin' Donuts and Bruegger's Bagels.

The **Asheville-Buncombe Library System,** with 12 locations in Asheville and Buncombe County, has computers and internet service at all locations, free for local library cardholders and with a small charge ($1 per hour) for guests without local library cards.

MEDICAL CARE

In Asheville, whether as a resident or a visitor, you have access to excellent, nationally recognized health care. The main hospital in the Asheville area is **Mission Hospital** *(509 Biltmore Ave., Asheville, 828-213-1111, www.mission-health.org)*, a not-for-profit independent community hospital. It is the tertiary referral center for the Western North Carolina region. Together with its sister campus, St. Joseph Hospital, it is licensed for 800 hospital beds and currently has 730 beds. Mission has around 550 physicians on the medical staff licensed in some 50 specialties, plus more than 1,800 RNs.

The hospitals, with a main, 90-acre campus on Biltmore Avenue just south of the main Downtown area, has more than 8,500 employees in the metro area, making it the largest private employer in the region.

Mission has announced plans to build a new $350 million tower to replace aging facilities on the old St. Joseph Hospital campus. It recently opened a new cancer center and a new office complex.

Mission is the state's sixth largest hospital system and is the busiest surgical hospital in North Carolina. Its centers of excellence include cancer, heart, orthopedics, pediatrics, women's health and neurosciences.

For emergency care in Asheville, the hub of medical care in Western North Carolina, you can go to **Mission Hospital Emergency Room** *(509 Biltmore Ave., 828-213-1948, www.missionmd.org)*. The emergency room is busy, with more than 100,000 visits a year, but generally patients are seen quickly. You can drive to the main entrance off Biltmore Avenue and a valet attendant will park your car. Mission has a Level II trauma center. (Level I offers the highest level of surgical care whiles Levels IV and V offer the lowest.) Mission's is the only Level II center in Western North Carolina, with two helicopters for quickly transporting trauma patients to Asheville from 17 WNC counties. The nearest Level I trauma center is at **Carolina Medical Centers** *(www.carolinashealthcare.org/cmc)* in Charlotte.

In addition, **Sisters of Mercy Urgent Care** walk-in health care services have several locations in the greater Asheville area *(1201 Patton Ave., West Asheville, 828-210-2121; 1833 Hendersonville Rd., South Asheville, 828-274-1462; 155 Weaver Blvd., Weaverville, 828-645-5088; 22 Trust Lane, Brevard, 828-883-2600; www.urgentcares.org)*. Anther doc-in-a-box clinic is **FastMed Urgent Care** *(160 Hendersonville Rd., Asheville, 828-210-2835; www.fastmed.org)*.

Asheville also has a large veterans hospital, **Charles George VA Medical Center** *(1100 Tunnel Rd., 828-298-7911; www.ashevilleva.gov)* serving the approximately 100,000 military veterans living in Western North Carolina. It also serves visiting veterans, including with emergency care.

Hospitals in other areas around Asheville include **Margaret R. Pardee Memorial Hospital** in Hendersonville *(800 N. Justice St., Hendersonville, 828-790-9355; www.pardeehospital.org);* **Park Ridge Hospital** in Fletcher, *(100 Hospital Dr., Hendersonville, 828-684-8501; www.parkridgehealth.org);* **MedWest-Haywood** in Clyde *(262 Leroy George Dr., 828-456-7311; www.haymed.org)* and **MedWest-Swain** in Bryson City *(45 Plateau St.,Bryson City, 828-488-2155; www.westcare.org)*.

The Mission Hospitals system includes **Blue Ridge Regional Hospital** in Spruce Pine, **McDowell Hospital** in Marion, **Transylvania Regional Hospital** in Brevard and **Mission Children's Hospital** in Asheville. **CarePartners Health Care,** a 1,200-employee company that offers rehabilitation services, is affiliated with Mission.

The Buncombe County area has more than **1,000 practicing physicians.** There are large practice groups in cardiology, arthritis, oncology, orthopedics, family medicine, endocrinology, dermatology, various surgical specialties and in other areas. Buncombe County also has more than **200 dentists.**

For medical and dental emergencies, your hotel may also have the names of physicians and dentists on call.

For those with limited English proficiency, the Western Carolina Medical Society operates and helps fund **Western North Carolina Interpreter Network** (WIN), which offers trained medical interpreter services in approximately two dozen languages.

NEWSPAPERS

Here are the chief print newspapers you may want to read in the Asheville area.

Asheville Citizen-Times (14 O. Henry Ave., Asheville, 800-672-2472, www.citizen-times.com), owned by Gannett ("with the emphasis on the net,") is the largest daily newspaper in the region. *The Scene,* a tabloid section devoted to local entertainment, is published on Friday. Daily circulation is around 58,000 and Sunday about 68,000. The on-line edition has a pay wall. As with many newspapers, it has cut its editorial staff and is not the paper it used to be.

Mountain Xpress (2 Wall St., Asheville, 828-251-1333, www.mountainx.com) is a popular free alternative tabloid with extensive coverage of local entertainment, restaurants, clubs and music. It is published weekly on Wednesday.

Print circulation of *Mountain Xpress* is around 25,000, distributed at restaurants, bars, shops and elsewhere around the area. The on-line edition also is free.

Hendersonville Times-News (106 Henderson Crossing, Hendersonville, 828-692-5763, www.blueridgenow.com), is a daily formerly owned by the New York Times Company and now a part of the Halifax Media Group. It has a circulation of around 15,000.

RADIO AND TV STATIONS

Here are some of the radio stations you may want to listen to when drive to or around Asheville.

Note that **Sirius/XM satellite radio** *(www.siriusxm.com)* may drop out in heavy tree canopies along roadways and in the steep mountain terrain.

WCQS Asheville, 88.1 FM, National Public Radio programming mostly classical music and NPR news. WCQS also broadcasts on the following frequencies in towns around Asheville:

88.5	WMQS, Murphy
89.7	Cullowhee, Waynesville, Clyde, Webster
91.3	WFQS, Franklin and North Georgia
91.5	Dillsboro, Sylva
94.7	Bryson City
95.3	Cherokee, Waynesville
101.7	Highlands
105.1	Brevard
107.5	Black Mountain/Montreat

WFLA Asheville-Greenville, S.C. 91.3 FM, Christian contemporary

WHKP Hendersonville, 1450 AM, local news, talk, sports and country music

WISE Asheville, 1310 AM, sports

WKSF Asheville, 99.9 FM, owned by Clear Channel, programs country music

WMIT Black Mountain, 106.9 FM, religious station affiliated with Billy Graham organization

WNCW Spindale, 88.7 FM, a Public Radio community station licensed to Isothermal Community College, programming an eclectic "crossroads" mix of independent, alternative and other music

WOXL Asheville/Biltmore Forest, 96.5 FM, adult contemporary

WPVN Asheville, 103.5 FM, progressive talk radio

WWNC Asheville, 570 AM, owned by Clear Channel, is a talk/news radio affiliated with Fox News – it has a right-wing slant with syndicated programs by Rush Limbaugh and Sean Hannity.

Television stations in Asheville:

WLOS-TV (Channel 13), owned by Sinclair Broadcast Group, is the dominant Western North Carolina TV station. It is an ABC-TV affiliate. WLOS-TV also operates WMYY-TV through a local marketing agreement.

WHNS-TV (Channel 22) is a Fox affiliate.

WUNF-TV (Channel 33) is the Public Television station, a part of the University of North Carolina system.

Asheville is part of the **Greenville-Spartanburg-Anderson (S.C.)- Asheville television market,** the 36th largest television market in the country.

WYFF-TV (Channel 4, NBC, Greenville), **WSPA-TV** (Channel 7, CBS, Spartanburg) and six other South Carolina stations have service in the Asheville area. **Charter Communications** is the major cable company in the Asheville area.

HOTEL AND SALES TAXES

Visitors primarily will be interested in sales and hotel room taxes.

North Carolina's statewide sales tax is 4.75%, and in addition local counties and municipalities charge local sales taxes. In Asheville and Buncombe County the **total state and local sales tax is 7%.** It is slightly lower in neighboring Henderson and Madison counties, at 6.75%. Most grocery food items are subject only to a 2% sales tax, and prescription drugs are exempt from sales taxes. The Republican-controlled North Carolina legislature has been considering raising grocery tax rates, as part of a package to reduce or eliminate state income taxes.

Hotel or room taxes in Asheville and Buncombe County are the 7% sales tax plus 4% local room occupancy tax, for a **total of 11% tax on the hotel room rate.** The 4% local occupancy tax mostly goes to fund tourism promotion.

TRAVEL AND TOURISM INFORMATION

Amazing Asheville *(www.amazingasheville.net),* affiliated with the *Amazing Asheville* guidebook and with this book, is a comprehensive online travel guide to Asheville and Western North Carolina. Information is updated several times a week.

American Automobile Association *(local AAA offices at 178 Merrimon Ave., Asheville, 828-252-5376 and 1550 Hendersonville Rd., Asheville, 828-274-2555; www.aaa.com)* offers free travel maps, trip planning and guidebooks for members.

Asheville Convention and Visitors Bureau *(36 Montford Ave., 828-258-6129; www.exploreasheville.com; open Mon.-Fri. 8:30-5:30, Sat.-Sun. 9-5, a satellite visitor pavilion is in Pack Square Park, open 9-5 daily)* is a terrific source of information on Asheville and the mountains. Visit online or in-person at the modern visitor center near Downtown on Montford Avenue.

A **Downtown satellite visitor** pavilion is in Pack Square Park. A free travel guide to Asheville is available in both digital and paper versions. The main visitor center offers a souvenir shop, The Asheville Store, and a concierge to help you find accommodations. A relocation package is available for $19.95.

Blue Ridge Parkway (*Parkway headquarter is 199 Hemphill Knob Rd., Asheville off Milepost 384, 828-271-4779 or 828-298-0398 for recorded information; www.nps.gov/blri; open daily 9-5*) has helpful staff, informative literature and a 3-D map of the parkway.

Great Smoky Mountains National Park (*Park headquarters: 107 Park Headquarters Rd., Gatlinburg, TN 37738, visitor information line 865-436-1200) www.nps.gov/grsm*) has a complete visitor information center on the North Carolina side of the park at Oconaluftee on U.S. Highway 441 near Cherokee (open daily, hours vary seasonally).

Hendersonville Tourist Information Center (*201 S. Main St., Hendersonville, 828-693-9708 or 800-828-4244; www.historichendersonville.org*; open weekdays 9-5, weekends 10-5) offers a free travel planner brochure both online and in a paper version. A relocation package is available for $25.

High Country Host (www.highcountryhost.com) is a non-official online guide to Boone, Blowing Rock and other areas of the North Carolina High Country.

Romantic Asheville (www.romanticasheville.com) is a non-official online travel guide to Asheville with more than 600 pages of information and 2,500 photographs. Besides covering Asheville, it has information on the area within about 85 miles of Asheville.

PARKING IN ASHEVILLE AND ELSEWHERE

Finding parking in **Downtown Asheville** can sometimes take a bit time, but you can always find a space somewhere. Parking is at a premium during weekday business hours when the population of downtown swells, as about 40,000 people commute to downtown for work. It's also often the case in the evenings when Asheville's restaurants and nightlife attract crowds. Friday and Saturday nights in summer and fall are particularly sticky times for finding a convenient space on the street, notably on Lexington Avenue, Broadway, Biltmore Avenue, Haywood Street, Wall Street, Battery Park Avenue and around the Grove Arcade, Pack Square and U.S. Cellular Center (formerly Asheville Civic Center). Still, with many public and private parking garages and lots, you can always find a spot if you look hard enough.

You can try doing what a friend and co-worker of mine in New Orleans, Victoria Slind-Flor, used to do. When searching for a spot on the notoriously narrow and crowded streets of the Vieux Carré she would dredge up memories of the Catholic Rosary from her childhood and whisper "Hail Mary, full of grace ..." and, miraculously, Victoria always found a parking space.

Street Parking

The City of Asheville has about 700 metered on-street parking spaces downtown. All spaces are for short-term parking, for two hours or less. Cost is $1 per hour, and most meters accept coins only (no pennies). About 100 meters will let you pay with your smart phone, although you have to set an account in advance and there's a 25 cents an hour surcharge. Meters are monitored from 8 am to 6 pm Monday-Saturday, and street parking is free on Sundays, holidays and between 6 pm and 8 am. The fine for overtime parking is $10 ($50 for parking in a fire lane or beside a fire hydrant, and $100 for parking illegally in a handicap zone.) You have 15 days to pay the fine, or a late penalty of $25 is assessed, with further late penalties of $25 for each additional 30 days the fine is overdue. Parking fines can be paid online through the City of Asheville website at www.ashevillenc.gov, or at City Hall. For more information on public parking in Asheville, go online or call the city's Parking Services division at 828-259-5792.

Public Parking Garages

Asheville has four public parking garages, with a maximum total of around 1,450 spaces. City parking garages are attended Monday-Friday, 10 am to 7 pm (may be later during special events). During other hours, payment is made when exiting from the garages using the exit pay-in-lane stations. Both the attendants and stations accept coins, cash, validation tickets (from some restaurants and merchants) and MasterCard or Visa credit or debit cards. Some of the garage parking spaces are taken by those with monthly parking permits, which cost $80 to $100 a month.

Buncombe County operates one large public parking garage downtown with 650 parking spaces.

Biltmore Avenue Garage, under Aloft Hotel at 51 Biltmore Avenue at Alston Street. With 450 spaces (the number may be reduced to as few as 289 depending on usage by the hotel, this is the newest of the city's four public garages and is convenient to shopping, dining and other activities on the north end of Biltmore Avenue, on the south end of Broadway and around Pack Square and the Market Street area. Rates: First hour free, then $1 an hour (maximum $10 per day). Special events $7.

Civic Center Garage, off Haywood Street, behind the Pack Memorial Public Library at 67 Haywood Street next to U.S. Cellular Center. This is the largest of the public garages, with 550 spaces. It is convenient to events in the U.S. Cellular Center and for shopping, dining and other activities on Haywood Street and nearby. Rates: First hour free, then 75 cents an hour (maximum $8 per day). Special events $7.

Rankin Avenue Garage, with 262 spaces, is between Haywood Street and Rankin Avenue just north of College Street. This garage can handle overflow from U.S. Cellular Center events and is handy for shopping, dining and other activities on Haywood Street and Lexington Avenue. Rates: First hour free, then 75 cents an hour (maximum $8 per day). Special events $7.

Wall Street Garage, with 232 spaces, is located off Otis Street between Wall Street and Battery Park Avenue, directly across the street from the Grove Arcade. The entrance to this garage is on Otis Street. It is convenient for shopping, dining and other activities at the Grove Arcade and on Wall Street and Battery Park Avenue. Rates: First hour free, then 75 cents an hour (maximum $8 per day). Special events $7.

College Street Parking Deck, 164 College Street across from Asheville City Hall and Buncombe County Courthouse. This 650-space, seven-story parking garage is operated by Buncombe County. Rates: $1 an hour (maximum $8 per day).

Private Parking Lots and Garages

Asheville has many small private surface parking lots and a few private garages. Rates and parking rules vary. Note that some of the lots are for tenants of specific office buildings or for certain stores or restaurants only. Violators may be towed.

Among the larger private garages is **Pack Place Biltmore Avenue Parking Deck,** 12 Biltmore Avenue, next to Diana Wortham Theatre. Rates $2 for first hour, then $1 per hour. Evening flat rate $5.

Parking in Biltmore Village

Park in unmetered street parking spaces in Biltmore Village, and in strip center lots near the edge of the Village.

Parking in West Asheville

Park in unmetered street parking spaces along Haywood Road and on side streets. Some private business lots are available for public parking after 6 pm, but watch for tow-away signs.

Other Towns

Free street parking is available in downtown Hendersonville, Black Mountain, Brevard, Bryson City, Highlands, Waynesville and most other small towns and villages in Western North Carolina. As in Asheville, during peak visiting times from late spring to late fall you may have to drive around a while to find a park spot near your destination.

LODGING IN ASHEVILLE AREA

Lobby of Aloft Hotel in Downtown Asheville

The Asheville area has a gorgeous mix of **resort hotels** such as the **Grove Park Inn, chain motels and hotels** from most of the major brand families including **Hilton, Holiday Inn, Starwood** and **Marriott, bed and breakfasts, mountain lodges** and small **owner-operated inns and motels**. There are more than 50 B&Bs in the metro area, one of the largest concentrations in the South. Most bed and breakfasts are in the **Montford** area near Downtown, around the Biltmore Estate and in the Grove Park and other North Asheville areas.

With the opening of the **Aloft** and **Indigo** hotels, several new urban hostels and vacation apartment/rental condo complexes, the renovation of **Haywood Park Hotel** and the planned opening of the **Hilton Garden Inn, Hyatt Place, Cambria Suites** and two hotels at the site of the BB&T Building and its garage across the street, plus older existing properties such as the **Renaissance,** you'll find a good selection of places to stay Downtown, within walking distance of restaurants and bars.

Our view is that choice of lodging is a very personal decision. Some travelers live by the old adage "sleep hard, eat well."

These travelers say they spend little time in their room; they're looking for the cheapest acceptable lodging options so they'll have more money to spend on dining and activities.

Others like the convenience and standardization of the chain motels. We aren't among those who sniff that staying in a chain motel is being a tourist, not a traveler. This writer was a Hilton Honors Diamond member for many years, an elite status with this chain that requires a minimum 60 nights a year or 30 different stays. Frankly, we like knowing exactly what we're going to get in a room and services, and we enjoy the amenities that are becoming more common, especially for frequent stayers, such as included breakfasts, free drinks at afternoon cocktail hours, free internet access and room upgrades.

More than 100 chain motel properties are located around the Asheville metropolitan area, with large clusters on Tunnel Road near the Asheville Mall, on U.S. Highway 25 and Biltmore Avenue near the Biltmore Estate and along I-40 and I-26. While we've included listings of some of the best of these, due to their generally standardized facilities and services we don't attempt to describe each one individually, only calling attention to particularly noteworthy differences, such as location or a heated indoor pool.

Still others love the pampering they get at unique small inns and B&Bs. Asheville is fortunate in having some of the best B&Bs in the region, if not the country, in all price ranges.

In rural areas around the city are lodges, mountain cabins and even a couple of dude ranches.

Increasingly, an option for nightly or weekly (or longer) stays are rentals from private owners. For weekly rentals, including mountains cabins, **Vacation Rentals by Owner** (www.VRBO) is an excellent source. There are more than 450 properties in the Asheville area listed on VRBO and well over 4,000 rentals in the Western North Carolina Mountains. You can search rental options by area, number of bedrooms and other characteristics. While VRBO is the best-known service, **HomeAway** (www.homeaway.com) and other online vacation rental services also are worth checking out.

Air BnB (www.airbnb.com) is another popular service for matching homeowners and guests for short-term stays. This online service, with private accommodations in some 34,000 cities in 192 countries, offers both entire houses and apartments and also single rooms. Asheville has about 450 listings, starting at under $40. Guest satisfaction levels are rated on a one-to-five-star system, based on reviews of properties by people who have stayed there.

Another option is **couchsurfing.** Local hosts offer accommodations in their homes, typically free of charge (although it costs members $25 to sign up and become "verified), in more than 100,000 cities around the world. You can join more than 1 million other couchsurfers, either as a traveler or a host, or both (www.couchsurfing.org). The Asheville area has about 3,500 couchsurfing members; however, not all open their homes to visitors.

We recommend you use the **American Automobile Association (AAA)** *Tour Books* to help when making lodging decisions. AAA *(www.carolinas.aaa.com)* is often a poor source of information on restaurants, but it is almost always reliable in its lodging descriptions and ratings. We would note that it is not always as good, or as comprehensive, on B&Bs as it is with hotels and motels. Inspectors for AAA personally visit listed lodging places regularly – usually annually – to provide first-hand and up-to-date information. There is an AAA *Tour Book* that covers North Carolina exclusively. The books and also local maps are free for AAA members. AAA members also often get a discount on lodging stays, typically around 10%. AARP members get a similar discount.

For crowdsourcing information on lodging, naturally you can't ignore **TripAdvisor** *(www.tripadvisor.com).* Generally, the ratings by TripAdvisor members of Asheville area lodging seem spot on. However, lodging owners and their friends, not to mention competitors, can game the system with phony reviews. TripAdvisor catches some – but definitely not all – of them. The algorithms TripAdvisor uses to rate and rank hotels, restaurants and attractions are not very transparent. Cheaper properties, and those located close to major attractions such as Biltmore Estate, may enjoy higher ratings than perhaps they deserve. Use TripAdvisor to help you decide on lodging, but use it with a healthy dose of skepticism.

We list what we consider the best and best-value lodging options in the Asheville area. In no way is this list a complete or comprehensive listing of all properties. In some cases we have personally stayed at these properties, and in other cases we have toured and inspected them. Occasionally we rely on contract employees and friends to provide reports. We do take into account first-person reports on TripAdvisor and other social network sites. **For this guide we do NOT accept free accommodations or other consideration, so even if you don't agree with our assessment, you know it is our candid opinion.**

Lodging properties are listed alphabetically within each neighborhood. The exception is for rental cabins, which are in a separate section, listed alphabetically, not geographically.

Price categories are for two persons (a double) in high season (usually late spring to early fall) for a regular room, not including the sales and accommodations tax, which varies slightly depending on area but generally totals 11.75%. Service, if any, also is not included in the rate. If the weekend rate is generally higher, we use that as the rate basis. Rates may be higher on certain peak holiday weekends and during fall color season in October; rates may be lower in winter. Lowest lodging rates in the Asheville area are usually January through March. Unless otherwise stated, rates do not include meals, except in those cases where breakfast in included in the room rate.

Remember, increasingly, as with airlines and their yield management systems, hotel rates vary considerably from day to day depending on demand and occupancy. They also vary depending on how far ahead, or how near to the stay date, you book. Discounts may also be available for multiple night stays or for member in AAA, AARP or other organizations. Call the lodging facility or check the property's website for the exact rates available for the dates you plan to stay. Always ask for the lowest available rate for the room and time of stay. Don't be shy about asking, "Do you offer any other discounts?" or "Is that the lowest rate available?"

>*Very Expensive* Over $300 double
>*Expensive* $200-$299 double
>*Moderate* $100-$199 double
>*Inexpensive* $50-$99 double
>*Very Inexpensive* Under $50 double
>*(Rates shown do not include sales and accommodations tax, usually 11.75%, or service charge, if any.)*

Listings show address, phone, web address, type of lodge (motel, hotel, B&B, etc.) and typical rate range, along with a review of the property.

Many Asheville-area lodging properties, even some B&Bs, do allow pets, though some assess a pet cleaning charge. Most properties now offer only non-smoking rooms, the exception being a few of the chain motels that have some smoking rooms. Wi-Fi is available at almost all properties listed, free at B&Bs, inns and most motels, although a few hotels and motels still charge a fee.

See also the section above on Towns and Villages near Asheville for recommendations on places to stay outside Asheville.

Downtown Asheville

Once a near urban desert for accommodations, with the opening of the Aloft and Indigo hotels, the renovation and upgrading of the Haywood Suites and Renaissance hotels, along with the debut of several small independent suites places and even a hostel or two, Downtown now offers visitors a number of excellent choices for lodging, in all price ranges. Another five Downtown hotels are either under construction now or are planned within the next several years.

Aloft Asheville Downtown *51 Biltmore Ave., Downtown Asheville, 828-232-2838 or 877-462-5638, www.starwoodhotels.com,* **Hotel, Expensive to Very Expensive**

This 115-room Starwood property opened in late 2012. The location is excellent, near many of Asheville's best restaurants on Biltmore Avenue and Pack Square. There's handy parking in a new public garage under the hotel (some spaces are reserved for hotel guests). You usually enter through a "sub-lobby" at the garage level (though you can also take a garage elevator directly to the main lobby). This sub-lobby has a huge blackboard where guests and others scribble their thought of the day. You can then take an elevator or a flight of stairs up to the main lobby, with its colorful decor, a bar and mini-restaurant. The hotel targets a younger, hipper crowd, although we've seen many older folks here, too. Rooms are not overly large but have 42" LCD TVs. The decor leans toward a Scandinavian minimalism. Not a part of the hotel but in the main level retail space is the Blackbird restaurant, and many other top Asheville restaurants, including Cúrate, Limones, Chestnut, Wicked Weed Brewery and Seven Sows are within a block or two. Asheville's largest nightclub and private music venue, The Orange Peel, is close by, so you can rock late if you so desire. There's an art movie theater across the street and plenty of bars, coffee houses and shops nearby. With some in-season rates over $300 a night, this hotel is priced higher than you'd expect.

Asheville Hostel *16 Ravenscroft Dr., Downtown Asheville, 828-423-0256, www.aahostel.com;* **Hostel, Inexpensive**

In an older house a few blocks south from the center of town, within walkable distance of most restaurants and attractions, Asheville Hostel has clean private rooms in the $60 double range. There's a common kitchen and free make-your-own waffles, coffee and tea. Free Wi-Fi. Minimum stay two nights on weekends, maximum stay seven days. The owner also has the Asheville Arthaus Hostel in the same area.

Four Points by Sheraton *22 Woodfin St., Downtown Asheville, 828-253-1851 or 866-716-8133, www.fourpointsashevilledowntown.com*; **Hotel, Moderate**

Across the street from the Renaissance Hotel at the north edge of Downtown, this 150-room Four Points by Sheraton property might be an option for you if you want to be within hiking distance of most Downtown attractions. That is, if you are willing accept dated decor, some down-at-the-heels hallways and other spaces and lack of first-class amenities such as an indoor pool. Moderate priced most times of year – a few high-season weekends are in the Expensive range and occasionally weekday rates are in the Inexpensive range.

Haywood Park Hotel *1 Battery Park Ave., Downtown Asheville, 828-252-2522, www.haywoodpark.com*; **Hotel, Expensive to Very Expensive**

The location of this boutique, 33-suite, four-story hotel can't be beat. It's centrally located, near many restaurants, galleries and the Grove Arcade. Formerly the site of Ivey's and Bon Marché department stores, the hotel references that with canned elevator announcements like "Third Floor, Children's Department." It's an all-suite property, and the accommodations (from about 400 to 1,200 square feet) recently received a much-needed upgrade and renovation. There are flat-screen TVs in the main room and also in the bathroom. On arrival in the lobby, you're saluted with a player piano and receive a glass of complimentary champagne. The hotel has two dining venues, the Haywood Park Café in the atrium, which opened in early 2013, and Isa's Bistro, the hotel's main restaurant at the corner of Haywood and Battery Park, which opened in April 2013. The chef at Isa's Bistro, Duane Fernandes, who worked for Per Se in New York before moving to Asheville as chef at Gabrielle's at Richmond Hill Inn (which was destroyed in a fire) and at Horizons at the Grove Park Inn. Isa's serves food influenced by the cuisine of Mediterranean France, Spain and Italy and features locally sourced seasonal dishes. Free valet parking and Wi-Fi.

Hotel Indigo *151 Haywood St., Downtown Asheville, 828-239-0239 or 877-846-3446, www.ihg.com/hotelindigo*; **Hotel, Moderate**

Indigo is the InterContinental and Holiday Inn group's attempt to reach a younger, hipper audience. The Asheville edition is right at the north edge of town, overlooking to the north the I-240 Expressway.

It is within easy walking distance of the Grove Arcade and the restaurants, shops and clubs in the northwest part of Downtown. What were supposed to be condos on the upper floors didn't sell and have been converted to hotel suites.

Renaissance Asheville Hotel 31 Woodfin St., Downtown Asheville, 828-252-8211 or 800-741-5072, www.marriott.com; **Hotel, Expensive**

This 12-story, 277-room Marriott property is one of the older Downtown properties, but a renovation was completed in early 2013, making the hotel much more appealing. The location, which faces the north edge of Downtown rather than facing into Downtown, is convenient to many businesses, some restaurants and the Buncombe Courthouse and government offices. Rates in-season are in the mid to high $200s double, but some do include buffet breakfast. It's what you'd expect in a large Marriott property, with decent-size rooms with first-rate beds, bar, a new restaurant, gift shop, indoor pool and fitness room. Free parking.

Sweet Peas Hostel *23 Rankin Ave., Downtown Asheville, 828-285-8488, www.sweetpeashotel.com;* ***Hostel, Very Inexpensive to Inexpensive***

Under the same ownership as Lexington Avenue Brewery (LAB), though the entrance is on Rankin Avenue above LAB, Sweet Peas is a somewhat upmarket Euro-style hostel with loft-style accommodations with bunk beds ($28), private pods ($35) and private rooms ($60 single or double). There's a fully equipped common kitchen, a living room with TV and a coin laundry. The best thing is the handy location in the middle of Downtown. The brewpub below can be noisy, but the hostel provides free earplugs. Free Wi-Fi. Breakfast not included but many breakfast spots and restaurants are nearby.

Windsor Boutique Hotel *36 Broadway St., Downtown Asheville, 844-494-6376, www.windsorasheville.com;* ***Small Suites Inn, Expensive to Very Expensive***

In a beautifully renovated 1907 building, the newly opened Windsor is a small, boutique hotel with 14 suites in a primo location Downtown. Suites, which vary in size, feature designer furnishings, exposed brick, wood floors, Wi-Fi and lots of artwork. Each has a kitchen and washer and dryer. You're only a few steps away from some of Asheville's best restaurants and bars. On the downside, there's no pool and no parking lot at the hotel (public parking is about three blocks away), but the great location makes up for it.

Biltmore Village/Biltmore Estate Area

The Biltmore Village/Biltmore Estate area is a mixed bag of accommodations, ranging from a group of chain motels to two upscale hotels to several B&Bs. Be aware that with only a few exceptions, most of the lodging options are not directly in Biltmore Village. Given the heavy traffic on Biltmore Avenue/U.S. Highway 25 and nearby streets (though the Village itself is fairly quiet and walkable) you'll probably still want a car to get to the Village and to Biltmore Estate. On the Biltmore Estate grounds itself is one of the premier hotels in the region, with prices to match. Note that a number of the properties listed here are not within easy walking distance of Biltmore Village or of Biltmore Estate – you will need a car or go by taxi.

Asheville Green Cottage *25 St. Dunstans Circle, South Asheville near Biltmore Village, 828-707-6563, www.ashevillegreencottage.com;* **B&B, Moderate**

Located near the Biltmore Estate and Mission Hospital, in a residential area off Biltmore Avenue, Asheville Green Cottage is a house originally constructed in the 1920s in the Arts & Crafts style, built from granite blocks. The B&B strives to be as eco-friendly as possible, using natural materials, and is a member of the Green Hotels Association. The four rooms are decorated in themes from the owners' world travels in Africa, India and elsewhere. Rates are $115 to $165 for weekends in-season, slightly lower at other times.

Baymont Inn & Suites *204 Hendersonville Rd., South Asheville near Biltmore Village, 828-274-2022 or 800-337-0550, www.baymontinns.com;* **Motel, Moderate**

If you want a moderately priced motel within a few blocks of the Biltmore Estate entrance, and a short walk to the main part of Biltmore Village, this is a good option. The 71-room Baymont, part of the Wyndham chain, is modern, clean and a continental breakfast is included. Note that this motel has a policy of not accepting guests who live within 50 miles of the inn.

Biltmore Village Inn *119 Dodge St., Biltmore Village, 828-274-8709 or 866-274-8779, www.biltmorevillageinn.com;* **B&B, Expensive to Very Expensive**

This B&B is on a low hill above Biltmore Village and the old Biltmore Hospital.

It's a bit of a hike to some of the restaurants in Biltmore Village and to the Biltmore Estate entrance, but you'll likely have a car anyway. The three-story 1892 Queen Anne-style Victorian house, redone in 1973 and in 2007, was originally known as the Samuel Harrison Reed House and is listed on the National Register of Historic Places. For a time it was the Thoms Rehabilitation Hospital. The inn has five spacious, deluxe rooms in the main house, plus two rooms in the carriage house. All the rooms are luxuriously decorated and all but one have gas or electric fireplaces. Rates, which include gourmet three-course breakfasts, range from around $200 to $335 double.

Cedar Crest Inn *674 Biltmore Ave., South Asheville, 828-252-1389 or 800-252-0310, www.cedarcrestinn.com;* **B&B, Moderate to Expensive**
One of the longest-established B&Bs in the area, Cedar Crest is located a few blocks north of the Biltmore Estate entrance and Biltmore Village, and about a mile south of Downtown. There are 10 rooms in the main house, an 1891 Queen Anne painted pink with some stunning wood paneling in the public space, plus six rooms and suites in a nearby cottages and a carriage house. Some rooms have gas fireplaces and whirlpool tubs. The grounds of this romantic inn are large, about 4 acres. Your stay at Cedar Crest includes free Wi-Fi, tea, coffee and pastries, wine and a three-course breakfast.

Corner Oak Manor B&B *53 Saint Dunstans Rd., South Asheville, 828-253-3525 or 888-633-3525, www.corneroakmanor.com;* **B&B, Moderate**
In a 1920s-era Tudor-style house, this three-room B&B in a quiet residential area between McDowell and Biltmore avenues is a short drive to the Biltmore Estate. Even in-season, rates are lower than at many other B&Bs in Asheville. A delicious breakfast is included.

Festiva Biltmore *8 Village Lane, Biltmore Village, 828-337-3140, www.festiva-biltmorevillage.com;* **Vacation Rental/Timeshare, Expensive to Very Expensive**
Eight one- and two-bedroom condos are available for vacation rental. Decorated in an upscale style with granite counters and plush bedding, most have fireplaces, kitchens, washer-dryers and other modcons, but some units do not have telephones. They are ideally located at the edge of Biltmore Village, in part of what was the old Biltmore Hospital (where the author of this guide was born). It's an easy walk to all parts of the Village and to the Biltmore Estate entrance.

Doubletree by Hilton Hotel Asheville-Biltmore *115 Hendersonville Rd., Biltmore Village, 828-274-1800, http://doubletree3.hilton.com;* ***Hotel, Expensive***

Just south of the entrance to the Biltmore Estate is this Hilton property, owned by Biltmore Farms. It's not one of the newer properties in the Doubletree chain, but it's well maintained and very convenient to Biltmore Village and to the Biltmore Estate. Generally solid service and good hotel breakfasts (extra charge except for elite Hilton Honors members). Indoor saline pool. A **TGIFriday's** restaurant is attached to the hotel. In the same area and operated by the same management company -- Biltmore Farms, owned by a branch of Biltmore's Cecil family -- is the more economical **Biltmore Village Lodge** *(117 Hendersonville Rd., Biltmore Village, 828-399-2254, www.biltmorefarmshotels.com;* ***Motel, Moderate***. A continental breakfast is included, and guests may use the pool at the Doubletree.

Grand Bohemian Hotel *11 Boston Way, Biltmore Village, 828-505-2949 or 866-599-6674, www.bohemianhotelasheville.com;* ***Hotel, Expensive to Very Expensive***

Part of a small chain of upscale hotels, the Grand Bohemian, which opened in late 2009, is the closest lodging to the Biltmore Estate. In fact, the "Tudor-inspired" hotel is directly across the street from the entrance. Note that while the location is convenient to the Estate and to Biltmore Village (and to a McDonald's across the street, itself designed to blend into Biltmore Village architecture), is it at the heart of a very busy intersection. Most of the rooms and suites -- some are in an annex -- are spacious, with plush bedding and tufted velvet headboards. Vegetarians beware: The hotel's lobby, with a central four-sided fireplace, and the restaurant, the Red Stag Grill, go for a hunting lodge decor with chandeliers of antlers and stuffed animal heads on the walls. Heavy on the dark crimson, the bar evokes more of a New Orleans bordello ambiance. You book the hotel through Marriott. It is listed as part of the Marriott Autograph group.

The Inn on Biltmore Estate *1 Antler Hill Rd., Biltmore Estate, 828-225-1600 or 866-336-1245, www.biltmore.com;* ***Hotel, Very Expensive***

The Inn on Biltmore Estate enjoys a stunning hilltop setting in a private area of the 8,000-acre grounds. The architectural design echoes (but does not attempt to duplicate) the chateau style of the main Biltmore House.

Rooms are impressively decorated but, except for the suites, are on the small side. Many guests say it's worth a little extra to get a room on a higher floor with a better view. On a chilly day, it's pleasant to sit in the lobby and enjoy a drink by the large stone fireplace. Staff and service are excellent. Surprisingly, although there's a large outdoor pool open seasonally the hotel has no indoor pool. Packages are available, especially in the off-season and for 12-month passholders that bring the normally Very Expensive rates ($500 or more on in-season weekends) down to near $200 in the dead of winter. Some rate packages include admission to Biltmore House, spa treatments and some meals. Note that holders of Biltmore's 12-Month annual pass can often get some very good deals during the off-season. The inn's restaurant, available only to hotel guests and to those with paid admission to the Estate, is one of the best in Asheville for dinner. Breakfast is expensive and not particularly exceptional. However, there are several other good dining options on the Estate, and of course you can leave the estate to sample Asheville's great restaurants. For guests, there is a free shuttle van to take you anywhere you wish to go on the Estate. Note that a second hotel, a 209-unit, four-story inn called the **Village Hotel** is opening on the Biltmore Estate in late 2015. It will be somewhat less expensive than the Inn

North Lodge on Oakland *84 Oakland Rd., South Asheville, 828-252-6433, www.northlodge.com;* **B&B, Moderate**

Originally built in 1904 as a three-story shingle-style cottage, a first floor stone exterior and stone porte-cochere were added in the late 1940s. The house, which had deteriorated over the years, was extensively renovated and expanded by new owners in the 1990s. The present owner, Greg Adkins, bought the property in 2008 and turned it into a B&B. The inn is located in a quiet residential area off Victoria Drive near the A-B Tech campus a short drive from Mission Hospital, Biltmore Village, Biltmore Estate, River Arts District and Downtown Asheville. The six rooms and suites in North Lodge are moderately priced, around $120 to $160, with discounts off-season and on weekdays.

Oakland Cottage B&B *74 Oakland Rd., South Asheville, 828-994-2627, www.vacationinasheville.com;* **B&B, Moderate**

A fairly modest, value-priced B&B in a residential area near the A-B Tech campus and a short drive to Biltmore Estate and most points of interest in Asheville. The Arts & Crafts-style house dates to 1910. There are two suites and four rooms, with prices from around $110 to $160. Discounts available weekdays.

Residence Inn Asheville Biltmore *701 Biltmore Ave., South Asheville, 828-281-3361, www.marriott.com;* **Motel, Moderate to Expensive**

Due to its proximity to Mission Hospital, this extended stay Marriott brand and other lodging properties along Biltmore Avenue north of Biltmore Village get a good deal of business from the families of patients at Mission. It also gets guests wanting to be within a short drive of the Biltmore Estate and of Downtown. Rooms and suites have kitchenettes, and there's a complimentary breakfast daily, with a free manager's afternoon reception with snacks and light drinks Monday-Wednesday. The motel has been renovated recently.

Sweet Biscuit Inn *77 Kenilworth Rd., East Asheville, 828-250-0170, www.sweetbiscuitinn.com;* **B&B, Moderate to Expensive**

This seven-room B&B in a 1915 brick Colonial Revival house in the Kenilworth section is about one-half mile from the Biltmore Estate entrance. It has been a B&B since 1999, and Claudia and Christian Hickl took over as innkeepers in 2012. Rates are $139 to $199, with the carriage house going for $209 without breakfast (breakfast is an additional $15 per person.) The carriage house accepts pets. There's a two-day minimum for all rooms on most weekends.

The Residences at Biltmore *700 Biltmore Ave., South Asheville, 828-350-8000 or 866-433-5594, www.residencesatbiltmore.com;* **Suites Motel, Moderate to Expensive**

Don't confuse this with either the Marriott's Residence Inn or with the Inn at Biltmore. Instead, it is an all-suites property just off Biltmore Avenue a little north of Biltmore Village. A total of 55 studio, one-, two- and three-bedrooms units are offered. Attractively decorated suites feature kitchens, washers and dryers, stacked stone fireplaces and hardwood floors. Most have whirlpool tubs.

Montford

The Montford area just north of Downtown Asheville is Asheville's unofficial bed and breakfast district, with nearly 20 B&Bs in the area. You can walk to Downtown from anywhere in Montford, although B&Bs at the north end of the district require a hike of six to ten blocks to the edge of Downtown.

Most B&Bs are in late 19th or early 20th century large homes. Nearly all of the B&Bs in this area offer the expected modcons, including air-conditioning, free Wi-Fi, cable TV (some only in a common room). Many are truly luxurious, with rates to match, but more modest and more affordable B&Bs are also in Montford. Breakfast is included, except where noted. Rates are higher on weekends, with discounts often available on weekdays and from January to March. Rates in most cases are for either one or two persons, and additional persons usually incur an extra charge. As noted, rates listed do not include sales and accommodation tax or service charge, if any (it's rare).

Free parking is offered at all B&Bs, though in some cases it is on the street. The B&Bs here are gay-friendly, and some are gay-owned, specifically targeting LGBT guests as a significant part of their market.

If you have any mobility issues, keep in mind that most of the B&Bs in Montford and elsewhere in Asheville are in older homes, most of two or three stories with flights of stairs and no elevators. When booking, mention any issues you have and ask for an accessible, first-floor room.

1900 Inn on Montford *296 Montford Ave., Montford, 828-254-9569 or 800-254-9569, www.innonmontford.com;* **B&B, Expensive to Very Expensive**

A 1900 Arts & Crafts-style house designed by Richard Sharp Smith has been turned into a luxury B&B furnished with antiques by owners Ron and Lynn Carlson. There are four rooms and a suite in the main house, and three large suites (all pet-friendly) in a modern cottage out back.

All the suites and rooms have gas fireplaces, flat-screen TVs and deluxe furnishings. The Cloisters mega-suite in the cottage is 1,300 square feet with a two-person whirlpool and two-person shower, 50-inch and 40-inch TVs and kitchenette; it goes for $325 to $625 depending on time of year. The Fitzgerald room in the main house has a king bed, bathroom with two-person tub, walk-in shower and fiber optic lighting on the floor and ceiling, a 47-inch TV, and brick fireplace; rate ranges from $215 to $325 depending on the season. A three-course breakfast is served. The same owners have a cabin for rent in a rural area north of Asheville.

A Bed of Roses B&B *145 Cumberland Ave., Montford, 828-258-8700 or 888-290-2770, www.abedofroses.com;* **B&B, Moderate to Expensive**

This 1897 Victorian gem is located less than six blocks from downtown.

The B&B has four lovingly decorated rooms plus one suite, from around $119 to $209, plus tax The owners serve a two-course included breakfast.

Abbington Green B&B *46 and 48 Cumberland Circle, Montford, 828-251-2454 or 800-251-2454,* www.abbingtongreen.com*;* ***B&B, Moderate to Very Expensive***

One of Asheville's top-rated B&Bs, Abbington Green is known for its beautiful, award-winning gardens and English-style main house by architect Richard Sharp Smith, built in 1907. The same owner has run this B&B for more than 20 years. Abbington Green has four rooms and a suite in the main house and three suites in the carriage house. All have fireplaces, along with flat-screen TVs and Wi-Fi. Organic, mostly locally sourced breakfasts are included in the rates, which range from around $160 (two rooms off-season in the main house) to $425 (two-bedroom suite in the carriage house, peak season). Abbington Green is located a bit farther from Downtown than some of the other B&Bs in Montford, but it's still walkable to Downtown restaurants and attractions. Parking is available on the grounds.

At Cumberland Falls B&B Inn 254 Cumberland Ave., Montford, 828-253-4085 or 888-743-2557, www.cumberlandfalls.com; B&B, **B&B, Moderate to Expensive**

Nearly everyone who stays at this B&B loves it. They like the location, within walking distance of Downtown; they like the gourmet breakfasts; they like the gardens; they like the owners, Gary and Patti; and, most of all, they like the Victorian house with six comfy rooms. There are some discounts off-season and mid-week, and two-day minimum stay is required on some weekends. Rooms have whirlpool tubs and some have a fireplace or wood stove.

Applewood Manor Inn B&B *62 Cumberland Circle, Montford, 828-254-2244 or 800-442-2197,* www.applewoodmanor.com*;* ***B&B, Expensive***

Applewood is one of Asheville's most popular B&Bs. The inn is a wood-shingled Colonial Revival house on about an acre and a half. The accommodations – four rooms and a suite in the main house, plus a separate cottage -- are named after varieties of apples, Winesap, Macintosh, etc. Amenities include individually controlled heating and air-conditioning, a social hour with complimentary drinks, a turndown service with chocolates and Wi-Fi throughout. It's about a 25 to 30 minute walk to Downtown.

Asheville Seasons B&B *43 Watauga St., Montford, 828-263-9494, www.ashevilleseasons.com;* **B&B, Moderate**

Although in the Montford Historic District, this B&B is something of a hike – about a mile --to Downtown Asheville. Most of the five rooms in this three-story early 20th century house have gas fireplaces, and the inn has central air and heat.

Black Walnut B&B Inn *288 Montford Ave., Montford, 800-381-3878, www.blackwalnut.com;* **B&B, Expensive to Very Expensive**

Originally built in 1899 and designed by Richard Sharp Smith in the English vernacular style for which he was known, with half-timbered pebbledash exterior. It also has Queen Anne elements. Beautifully restored, the Black Walnut is now a luxury B&B ideally located on three-quarter-acre grounds and gardens on the main street through Montford, within a few blocks of Downtown. There are six rooms in the main house and two in the carriage house, usually with a two-night minimum. The owners formerly operated bakeries in Martha's Vineyard and Palm Beach, so you can expect delicious pastries and breads in the included breakfast. Hors d'oeuvres and wine served each afternoon.

Carolina B&B *177 Cumberland Ave., Montford, 828-254-3608, www.carolinabb.com; B&B, Moderate to Expensive*

Completed in 1902, this is an unpretentious but pleasant pebbledash stucco house by Richard Sharp Smith, done in his English vernacular style, with an Arts and Crafts front porch. Rooms have heart pine floors. There are six rooms and one cottage, with rates from $180 to $230. There is a two-night minimum on most weekends.

Lion and Rose B&B *276 Montford Ave., Montford, 828-255-7673 or 800-546-6988, www.lion-rose.com;* **B&B, Moderate to Expensive**

Adjacent to the Black Walnut B&B just a few blocks from Downtown is this elegant rose-colored B&B, beautifully restored and maintained and with extensive landscaping. Completed in 1896, the house combines Colonial Revival, Neoclassical and Queen Anne elements. A special detail is the large stained glass Palladian window at the top of the oak stairs. Tommy French, one of the characters in Thomas Wolfe's novel, *Look Homeward, Angel*, was said to live in this house. Rates in the five rooms for weekend nights in-season are $140 to $230.

Pinecrest B&B *249 Cumberland Ave., Montford, 828-281-4275 or 888-811-3053, www.pinecrestbb.com;* **B&B, Moderate to Expensive**

Pinecrest Bed and Breakfast is in a 1905 Tudor Revival home, with walking distance of Downtown. It is another popular Montford lodging spot that gets high ratings on TripAdvisor and other crowd-sourcing hospitality sites. The owners and their daughter serve a delicious full breakfast, included. Complimentary wine and sweets are offered in the afternoons.

1899 Wright Inn and Carriage House *235 Pearson Dr., Montford, 828-251-0789, www.wrightinn.com;* **B&B, Moderate to Expensive**

The Wright Inn is one of Asheville's largest B&Bs, with 10 rooms plus a three-bedroom cottage. Originally built for local businessperson Osella B. Wright and wife Leva D. Wright, the Queen Anne-style house was from a design by George Franklin Barber, a Knoxville architect who marketed his home plans across the United States by mail order. Eventually Barber sold more than 20,000 house plans, and homes from his designs were built in all states in the U.S. and in several other countries. The Wright house was renovated in the 1980s for use as a B&B and has been operated by several different owners since then. The current innkeepers are Barbara and Bob Gilmore.

North Asheville

1889 White Gate Inn 173 E. Chestnut St., North Asheville, 828-253-2553 or 800-485-3045, www.whitegate.net; **B&B, Expensive to Very Expensive**

Romantic inn with lovely grounds and gardens, within walking distance of Downtown, the White Gate Inn has eight suites, two rooms and one cottage, with rates from $179 to $389, plus tax, with the highest rates on weekends and in October. Several of the suites have fireplaces and whirlpool baths, and two have kitchens. A three-course breakfast with custom-blended coffee is included.

Albemarle Inn *86 Edgemont Rd., North Asheville, 828-255-0027 or 800-621-7435, www.albemarleinn.com;* **B&B, Expensive to Very Expensive**

This upscale B&B in a stunning 1907 Neoclassical Revival mansion in the lovely North Asheville residential Grove Park neighborhood was for a short time home to Hungarian composer Béla Bartók. He lived here in the early 1940s, working on his "Asheville Concerto," the Third Concerto for Piano.

You can stay in his room, now called Bartók's Retreat, on the third floor though some of the other 10 suites and rooms are more deluxe.

Some rooms have working fireplaces and canopied beds. Gourmet breakfasts are included. The inn is just a bit too far from Downtown for an easy stroll, but if you enjoy a little exercise it's certainly walkable. Originally the home of Dr. Carl Von Reynolds, a noted Asheville physician who helped found the University of North Carolina at Chapel Hill School of Public Health, the home was later a school for girls. It was turned into a B&B in the 1990s by a Connecticut couple, both lawyers; the new innkeepers are Fabrizio and Rosemary Chiariello.

Beaufort House Inn *61 N Liberty St., North Asheville, 828-254-8334 or 800-261-2221, www.beauforthouse.com;* ***B&B, Expensive***

This B&B in the Chestnut Hill Historic District about a one-half mile from Downtown is one of Asheville's most popular inns. The rambling Queen Anne-style Victorian house was built in 1894 for North Carolina Attorney General and Asheville Mayor Theodore Davidson. For a short time in the 1940s it was the home of actor and National Rifle Association enthusiast Charlton Heston. The architect was Allen L. Melton, who also designed the Drhumor Building Downtown. There are eight rooms in the main house and attached terrace, plus three cottages in the carriage house. Beaufort, by the way, is pronounced BO-fort, as with the North Carolina coastal town, not pronounced like the South Carolina town, BEW-fort.

Chestnut Street Inn *176 E. Chestnut, North Asheville, 828-285-0705 or 800-894-2955, www.chestnutstreeinn.com;* ***B&B, Moderate to Expensive***

This B&B in a 1905 Colonial Revival house has eight rooms, with rates from $169 to $249 plus tax (lower rates mid-week). It's a fairly short walk to Downtown.

Crooked Oak Mountain Inn *217 Patton Mountain Rd., North Asheville, 828-252-9219 or 877-252-9219, www.crookedoakmountaininn.com;* ***B&B, Moderate***

This six-room B&B in a rustic octagonal house on three acres is on a mountainside above the Grove Park Inn, about 3 miles from Downtown. There's a stone fireplace in the common room and wrap-around decks. Rates are $145 to $185 per night, plus tax, with a two-night minimum.

Grove Park Inn, An Omni Resort *290 Macon Ave., North Asheville, 828-252-2711 or 800-438-5800, www.groveparkinn.com;* **Resort Hotel, Expensive to Very Expensive**

The grande dame of Asheville hotels celebrated its 100th anniversary in 2013. Its first century has seen many high points and some low ones, as the original six-story, 150-room hotel, inspired by the New Canyon Lodge in Yellowstone National Park and by other national park hotels in the West, evolved into the present-day 551-room resort and convention hotel with its own Donald Ross-designed golf course, award-winning spa and full resort and meeting facilities. Ten U.S. presidents (Taft, Wilson, Coolidge, Hoover, Roosevelt, Eisenhower, Nixon, Bush, Clinton and Obama) have stayed at the inn, along with many famous movie stars, celebrities and writers.

The Grove Park was the idea of Edwin Wiley Grove, a Tennessee patent medicine multi-millionaire who also built Asheville's Grove Arcade and the second Battery Park Hotel. Grove and his son-in-law, Fred Seely, a developer, designed the inn, with some consultation with New York architect Henry Ives Cobb, but it is fair to say that the massive hotel was built without the benefit of an on-site architect.

The inn was constructed of huge granite boulders, some weighing as much as five tons, mined nearby on Sunset Mountain. It also used local chestnut, oak, pine and other woods for the rooms and the nearly 10,000 square foot lobby, which is bookended by two huge stone fireplaces, all crowned by a striking red tile roof. Four hundred men worked 10-hour shifts six days a week, using mules and hand tools, and completed the hotel in just a year.

The Grove Park has gone through a series of owners since E. W. Grove's day. The longest-tenured owner was Charles Sammon, an insurance magnate, who bought the inn in 1955 and whose company owned it until 2012. Sammons added the 202-room Sammons Wing in 1984 and the 166-room Vanderbilt Wing in 1988. The additions, along with the purchase of the Asheville Country Club golf course in 1976 and the opening of a large spa in 2001, has made the resort much more viable as a business, but the new wings are architecturally inferior to the original section, cheap imitations of the classic original construction.

In 2012, the Grove Park Inn was sold by the Sammons company to KSL Capital Partners, a private equity firm in Denver and then in mid-2013 it was re-sold by KSL to Omni Hotels. Omni operates a number of resorts including Omni Amelia Island Plantation Resort, Omni Cancun and Omni Hilton Head.

The inn offers grand views of Downtown Asheville and the golf course from the Sunset Terrace off the main lobby.

The furnishings in the lobby and in the rooms of the original section are by Roycrofters, the famous Arts and Crafts collective in East Aurora, N.Y., near Buffalo. The lobby has paddle arm sofas and chairs of wormy chestnut. The Grove Park Inn has the largest collection of Arts and Crafts furniture in the world.

The hotel has several restaurants, including the long-established Sunset Terrace with its wonderful views and the new Edison featuring Southern comfort food, and Vue 1913, a brasserie with Art Deco decor.

If you can overlook the occasional physical, staff, food and service shortcomings that come with being a large meeting and convention property, the inn remains a stunning statement of the glory of the Golden Age of hospitality. The inn's location and atmosphere are unmatched, and the grounds and resort facilities are superb. To stay here, when things go right, can be a magical experience. Just to have a cocktail by the fire in the lobby on a glorious autumn evening is something you will never forget.

Hill House B&B *120 Hillside St., North Asheville, 828-232-0345 or 855-447-0002, www.hillhousebb.com;* **B&B, Moderate to Expensive**

This B&B is in a Craftsman style home constructed in 1885 for local furniture manufacturer James Hill. For most of the 20th century it was an apartment building. In the mid-1990s it was turned into a B&B. There are eight rooms in the main house and two additional rooms in cottages. Hill House is in North Asheville, about midway between Merrimon Avenue and Broadway Street, within a (longish) walk to Downtown. It has a casual, down-to-earth atmosphere, rather than a formal one. Rates are around $100 to $240, with discounts for mid-week stays, for business travelers and for visitors under 30. David Raphael Smith is the current owner.

Princess Anne Hotel *301 E. Chestnut, North Asheville, 828-258-0986 or 866-552-0986, www.princessannehotel.com;* **Inn, Moderate to Expensive**

Completed in 1924, the Princess Anne opened as a hotel for the families of tuberculosis patients but went through several owners and uses. Among the owners were the father of songwriter Johnny Mercer and Maharishi Ayurveda University, for a time spiritual advisors to the Beatles. The three-story, flat iron-shaped Shingle-style building was renovated in 2003-2005 by local preservationist Howard Stafford who returned it to its original use. It has 16 rooms and suites. Rates in-season start at around $150. The location is a bit of a walk to the heart of Downtown.

Reynolds Mansion *100 Reynolds Heights, North Asheville, 828-258-1111 or 888-611-1156,* www.thereynoldsmansion.com; **B&B, Expensive**

Located in an historic Colonial Revival brick mansion built in 1847, this B&B on 4 acres on Reynolds Mountain scores among the top B&Bs in the U.S. on TripAdvisor and often is ranked number one in Asheville. The location is a bit unexpected, in a mixed-used residential and retail development, Reynolds Village, about 4 miles north of the heart of Downtown. The mansion has been a B&B since 1970. The current Reynolds Mansion owners, Billy Sanders and Michael Griffith, purchased it in 2009 and after restoration re-opened it in 2010. They must be doing a lot of things right. Unusual for a B&B, there's a swimming pool, open Memorial Day to Labor Day. There are 12 fireplaces in the inn, and reportedly 3,000 square feet of porches. The mansion, which was built by Daniel Reynolds and 15 slaves over a period of three and a half years, was constructed of bricks made from clay mined from the bottom of nearby Beaver Lake.

In the 20th century it was the home of the colorful and controversial Senator Robert "Bob" Rice Reynolds, who served North Carolina in the U.S. Senate from 1932 to 1945. Some historians say that Reynolds, even during World War II, was a Nazi and Fascist apologist. President Franklin Roosevelt attempted to get the isolationist Reynolds defeated, but he failed. Reynolds was married five times. His fifth wife, Evalyn Washington McLean, was a daughter of *Washington Post* publisher Edward Beale McLean, the last private owner of the Hope Diamond. Bob Reynolds married Evalyn in 1941 when he was 57 and she was 19. Evalyn died of a sleeping pill overdose age five years later. Some attribute the death to the curse of the Hope Diamond. The national Democratic Party finally succeeded in getting Reynolds out of the Senate, and he lived in Asheville until his death in 1963, practicing law.

Sourwood Inn *810 Elk Mountain Scenic Hwy., North Asheville, 828-255-0690, www.sourwoodinn.com;* **Inn, Moderate**

The Sourwood Inn, built in the 1990s, is constructed of stone and cedar. It sits on about 100 acres off Elk Mountain Scenic Highway near the Blue Ridge Parkway in North Asheville. The twelve rooms in the main house are casually chic, each with wood-burning fireplace and a bathtub with views of the woods. There's also a cabin.

Rooms start at $155 to $175 a night, plus tax. Initially, the inn didn't have air-conditioning, with the owners claiming that at 3,200 feet it was cool enough even in July. Not all guests bought that, given the warming climate, so finally the inn broke down and added A/C, a good move.

Breakfast and afternoon refreshments are included in the reasonable rates, and the inn serves dinner (advance reservations required) for $30 per person. It's BYOB, as alcohol isn't sold at the inn. Sourwood, by the way, is a small native tree that blooms in July, and honeybees make a delicious, very light-colored honey from the nectar.

East Asheville/Tunnel Road

The Tunnel Road area east of Downtown is home to the Asheville Mall, by far the largest mall in the region, and most fast food and casual chain restaurants known to humankind. Save for the heavy traffic, often bumper-to-bumper, staying here offers fairly convenient access to Downtown and to the Biltmore Village area.

Country Inn & Suites *199 Tunnel Rd., East Asheville, 828-254-4311 or 800-830-5222, www.countryinn.com;* **Motel, Moderate**

This 77-unit motel is about typical of the chain, with free Wi-Fi, included continental breakfast and coin laundry, although it also has a heated indoor pool.

Hampton Inn Tunnel Road, *204 Tunnel Rd., East Asheville, 828-255-922 or 800-426-7866, www.hampton.com;* **Motel, Moderate**

This Hampton Inn is a little larger than average, with five floors and 119 rooms. As usual, you get complimentary breakfast and free Wi-Fi and local calls. Recently renovated. Heated indoor pool. It's near busy Tunnel Road and the Asheville Mall, but it sits a bit away from the heavy traffic.

Holiday Inn & Suites *42 Tunnel Rd., East Asheville, 828-225-5550 or 800-439-4745, www.holidayinn.com;* **Motel, Moderate**

This six-story, 111-unit motel with heated indoor pool is one of the best Holiday Inn chain properties in the Asheville area. Note, however, that the company lists this as being in Downtown Asheville, which it is not.

Homewood Suites by Hilton *88 Tunnel Rd., East Asheville, 828-252-5400 or 800-225-4664, www.homewoodsuites.com;* **Motel, Moderate to Expensive**

This extended stay motel has 94 suites with kitchenettes on six floors. Breakfast and free Wi-Fi included in the moderate rates (expensive on certain fall or event weekends). There's a manager's reception weekdays with free drinks and virtually a complete dinner.

West Asheville/Asheville West Area

There are two main conglomerations of accommodations, mostly chain motels, in the West Asheville and Asheville West areas. One area is off Exit 33 of I-26 at Asheville Outlets (formerly Biltmore Square Mall.) The general location offers easy access to Asheville via I-26 and also I-240 and I-40, along with shopping bargains at the new outlet mall, and there are several good, inexpensive restaurants nearby, including Papas and Beer (Mexican), Moose Café (country), Stone Ridge Tavern (burgers and casual food) and Harbor Inn (seafood, no alcohol). Among the motels here are Country Inn & Suites, Hampton Inn, Holiday Inn Express and Comfort Suites. The other is off Exit 44 of I-40 at U.S. Highway 19-23/Smoky Park Highway. This is a major interstate exit and has plenty of gas stations, fast food places and casual chain restaurants including IHOP, Applebee's, FATZ and Cracker Barrel. Motels here include Holiday Inn, Country Inn & Suites, Red Roof Inn, Ramada Inn and others. It offers good access to Asheville via I-40 and I-240.

Country Inn & Suites Asheville West *1914 Old Haywood Rd., West Asheville, 828- 665-9556 or 800-830-5222, www.countryinns.com;* **Motel, Moderate**

Newer, well-run Country Inn & Suites at the Exit 44 interchange of I-40 near Smoky Park Highway. Don't confuse this with the Biltmore Square location of the same chain. It's near a plethora of fast food and casual chain restaurants.

Country Inn & Suites Biltmore Square *845 Brevard Rd., West Asheville, 828-670-9000 or 800-830-5222, www.countryinns.com;* **Motel, Moderate**

Slightly above-average Country Inn & Suites with reasonable prices. It is directly across from the Biltmore Square Museum ... er, Mall. Outdoor pool, continental breakfast included.

Crowne Plaza Resort *One Resort Drive, West Asheville, 828-254-3211 or 800-733-3211, www.ashevillecp.com;* **Hotel, Moderate to Expensive**

This resort hotel opened as a Hilton in the 1960s and has gone through a number of changes since, not all of them positive. On about 125 acres it has a 9-hole golf course, 20 tennis courts (10 indoor), three pools, a large fitness center, and, believe it or not, a zipline.

The location is a little odd, just on the west side of the Capt. Jeff Bowen Bridge, formerly the Smoky Park Bridge, behind Asheville's first shopping center, Westgate. The Crowne Plaza makes a valiant attempt to provide first-class accommodations and resort services, and occasionally succeeds.

Fox & Fiddle *31 Toms Rd., Candler (Asheville West), 828-665-9830, www.foxandfiddle.net;* ***B&B/Inn, Inexpensive***

This little B&B (well, they don't serve breakfast Monday-Friday) is in an old farmhouse in the Candler area. It has only four rooms, some with shared bath. The appeal is the downhome atmosphere and the low prices, $50 to $60 a night, plus $15 if you want breakfast (Saturday and Sunday only). The owners are bluegrass musicians. No air-conditioning. Make of it what you will.

Hampton Inn Biltmore Square, *1 Rocky Ridge Rd., off Brevard Rd. at I-26 (Asheville West) 828-667-2022, 800-426-7866, www.hampton.com;* ***Motel, Moderate***

Typical Hampton Inn, with indoor pool, decent included breakfast and free Wi-Fi. As with other motels in this area, there's easy access to Asheville via I-26, I-240 and I-40.

Holiday Inn Biltmore West *435 Smoky Park Hwy. at Exit 44 of I-40 (Asheville West), 828-665-2161 or 888-465-4329, www.ihg.com;* ***Motel, Moderate***

Formerly a Ramada Inn, this property right at Exit 44 of I-40 was substantially upgraded a few years ago when it was reflagged as a Holiday Inn. The swimming pool is in the lobby, a remnant of the old Ramada design. The name, apparently designed to take advantage of the Biltmore Estate draw, is confusing because it's at least a 10-minute drive via I-40 to the Biltmore Estate entrance, longer in traffic. The motel is near plenty of fast food spots and casual chain restaurants.

Holiday Inn Express *1 Wedgefield Dr. off Brevard Rd. at I-26 (Asheville West), 828-665-6519 or 888-465-4329, www.ihg.com;* ***Motel, Moderate***

About average Holiday Inn Express, with easy access to Asheville via I-26, I-240 and I-40. Reasonable rates for Asheville.

Honey Hill Asheville Inn and Cabins *2630 Smoky Park Hwy, Candler, (Asheville West), 828-633-1110, www.honeyhillasheville.com;* **B&B and Cabins, Moderate to Expensive**

About 15 minutes west of Downtown Asheville, Honey Hill has four rooms and a suite in an 1885 Queen Anne-style home, plus six cabins on 12 acres. Rooms, with air-conditioning, ceiling fans, four-poster beds and Wi-Fi and some with fireplaces and claw foot tubs, are $169 to $229 in-season on weekends, and higher in October. Cabins are $179 to $279, with higher rates in October. Some weekday and other specials are available. Three of the cabins accept pets. There's a two-night minimum on both rooms and cabins.

South Asheville Area/Airport

This area has mostly chain motels serving Asheville Regional Airport overnighters and passers-through on Interstate 26, along with some guests doing business with manufacturing plants and other businesses in the fast-growing South Asheville area. In addition to the airport area motels listed below (the best of the bunch), there also are units of the Clarion Inn, Econo-Lodge and Comfort Inn chains near the airport. Note that the Hilton is not at the airport but at Biltmore Park, about 5 miles north of the airport via I-26.

Fairfield Inn Airport *31 Airport Park Rd., Fletcher (South Asheville), 828-684-1144 or 888-236-2427; www.marriott.com;* **Motel, Moderate**

Standard Marriott Fairfield Inn set up, with comfortable, affordable rooms, included continental breakfast and free Wi-Fi.

Hampton Inn & Suites *18 Rockwood Rd., Fletcher (South Asheville), 828-687-0806, 800-426-7866, www.hampton.com;* **Motel, Moderate**

Convenient to the Asheville Regional Airport and WNC Ag Center, this 96-unit Hampton Inn & Suites offers the usual Hampton quality, but prices are a little above what you'd expect. Included breakfast and free Wi-Fi.

Hilton Asheville Biltmore Park *43 Town Square Blvd., Biltmore Park Town Square, Off I-26, South Asheville, 828-209-2700 or 800-445-8667, www.hilton.com;* **Hotel, Expensive**

Located in the Biltmore Park multi-use planned community just off I-26 in South Asheville, the Hilton offers the expected Hilton amenities, including spa, restaurant and bar.

Within walking distance are a number of mostly chain restaurants, such as P.F. Chang's, a large multiplex cinema and a number of boutiques, galleries and stores, including an R.E.I. and a Barnes & Noble.

Mountain Laurel B&B *139 Lee Dotson Rd., Fairview (South Asheville), 828-712-6289; www.mountainlaurelbnb.com;* **B&B,** *Inexpensive/Moderate*

This gay- and lesbian-friendly three-room B&B in a rustically modern house is set on a hilltop south of Asheville in Fairview. The deck and common areas have great views of the surrounding mountains. Rates for any of the three rooms are around $100. Mountain Laurel B&B has an extensive library of library of GLBT books and films.

Mountain Cabins

Many visitors to the Asheville area would rather stay in a little log cabin or cottage rather than in a hotel, motel, inn or B&B. Since these are spread out all over the area, and often are owned by someone with just one cabin or at most a few, it's difficult to cover these cabins adequately in a guidebook. Our suggestion is to go to a website such as **Vacation Rentals By Owner** *(www.vrbo.com)* or **Air BnB** *(www.airbnb.com)* and search for the type of property and price that best suits you. You'll find hundreds of cottages and cabins in the mountains. However, here are a few we're familiar with in the immediate Asheville area.

Asheville Cabins of Willow Winds *39 Stockwood Rd. Ext., East Asheville, 828-277-3948 or 800-235-2474, www.ashevillecabins.com;* *Cabins, Expensive*

This cabin colony in East Asheville, on 39 acres adjoining the Blue Ridge Parkway, has more than two dozen one-, two- and three-bedroom cottages. Cabins are air-conditioned, with decks or porches, hot tubs, Wi-Fi and fireplaces (usable from mid-October to mid-May). On the grounds are a trout pond and outdoor games including bocce and horseshoes. Rates for weekend nights in-season are around $190 to $275, with a two-night minimum. No pets permitted. There is no cleaning fee.

Asheville Cottages *29 Asheville Cottage Lane, West Asheville, 828-712-1789, www.ashevillecottages.com;* **Cabins and Other Rentals, Expensive**

This management company has about a dozen cabins, houses and other vacation rentals in the Asheville area, ranging in price from around $170 to $330 on in-season weekend nights. There's a cleaning fee of around $60 to $100 per stay.

Asheville Swiss Chalets *5 Delano Rd., East Asheville, 828-776-0509, www.ashevilleswisschalets.com;* **Cabins, Moderate to Expensive**

Asheville Swiss Chalets has 11 rental cottages off Tunnel Road in East Asheville. The management stresses that the rental chalets accept dogs. Rates for one- to three-bedroom cottages range from $145 to $350, with a three- to seven-night minimum, depending on the time of year. Weekly rates are $910 to $1,900. The premier units, such as the Matterhorn ($225 per night on weekends in-season, sleeps four) two-bedroom, two-bath units have gas fireplaces, decks, large, flat-screen TVs and other amenities.

Log Cabin Motor Court *330 Weaverville Hwy. (U.S. Hwy. 25 North), North Asheville, 828-645-6546 or 800-295-3392, www.theashevillecabins.com;* **Cabins, Inexpensive to Moderate**

This collection of 20 vintage log cabins about six miles north of Downtown Asheville dates from the 1930s and the early days of mass auto travel. Rates are $85 to $145 weekends in-season, and $10 less mid-week. These are the kind of roadside cabins, with white daubed clay and red window shutters, you see in old movies. In fact, some scenes from the 1958 classic, *Thunder Road,* starring Robert Mitchum were shot in one of the cabins, now called Goldview. It rents for $140 double on weekends, plus tax. All cabins have air-conditioning, cable TV and Wi-Fi, and some have kitchens, fireplaces or gas stoves.

Mountain Springs Cabins *27 Emma's Cove Rd., Off Pisgah Hwy. (NC Hwy. 151), Candler (Asheville West), 828-665-1004, www.rvcoutdoors.com/mountain-springs;* **Cabins, Moderate**

Mountain Springs Cabins, about 14 miles southwest of Downtown Asheville off the Pisgah Highway, has 13 rustic mountain log and wood cabins. Rates from $110 to $170 per night, double, with a three- or four-night minimum. Extra adults are $20 each, children $10 each. Most cabins have kitchens, gas fireplaces and air-conditioning. Pets accepted in most cabins. Mountain Springs Cabins is now owned by RVC, an eight-unit group of cottages colonies and campgrounds in the Southeast.

Pisgah View Ranch *70 Pisgah View Ranch Rd., Candler, (Asheville West), 828-667-9100,* www.pisgahviewranch.net; **Cabins, Moderate**

On a 2,000-acre piece of mountain land about 16 miles southwest of Asheville that has been in the same family since 1790, Pisgah View Ranch is a collection of around 30 mountain cottages with a dude ranch atmosphere, where families come to enjoy horse-back riding, home cooking and outdoor activities. Rates for lodging, all meals, horseback riding and most other activities are $150 per person per day for adults, and $135 for children 5-14. With lodging and meals but not horseback riding, rates are $115 for adults and $110 for children. Cabins can be rented without meals for $125 double per night. Pisgah View Ranch also has an RV and tent campground with rates from $15 to $25 per site. For those not staying at the ranch, horseback rides are $40 to $50 an hour. The ranch is open April-November.

Other Lodging Options

In addition to hotels, motels, B&Bs, inns and resorts, you also have other options for booking lodging, often direct with the owner of a house, condos or apartment. These include **Airbnb** *(www.airbnb.com),* which has more than 500 short-term rentals in the Asheville area, and **VRBO** *(www.vrbo.com),* which has more than 450 short-term rentals in the Asheville area. Also there's **Couchsurfing** (www.couchsurfing.org), where members stay for free at the homes or apartments of hosts, sometimes in their own rooms and sometimes literally on a couch, and **Wwoofing** (www.wwoof.net), with members typically trading work on a natural or organic farm for room and board.

BEST RESTAURANTS IN ASHEVILLE AREA

DOWNTOWN ASHEVILLE

Restaurants are listed alphabetically. Price categories are per person for dinner with appetizer or salad, entree, vegetable or other side, glass of wine or a cocktail, tax and tip. If the restaurant doesn't serve dinner, then the price category is for a full meal at breakfast or lunch without alcohol but with tax and tip.

Price Categories
Very Expensive $65+ per person
Expensive $35-$64 per person
Moderate $20-$34 per person
Inexpensive $10-$19 per person
Very Inexpensive Under $10 per person

The opinions on dining, and everything thing, in this book are our own. We do NOT accept comped meals, free lodging or other gratuities, so that even if you don't agree with us you can be sure it's our honest opinion, unswayed by any monetary consideration.

Ben's Tune Up *195 Hilliard Avenue, Downtown, 828-424-7580; www.benstuneup.com;* ***Japanese-Chinese-Southern Fusion*** *with sake brewery, dinner Mon.-Fri., brunch and dinner Sat.-Sun.,* ***Moderate to Expensive***

The opening of Ben's Tune Up in June 2013 was one of the most highly anticipated food events of the year in Asheville, but it turned out that the owners and cooks, from the highly touted The Admiral in West Asheville and other eateries, apparently didn't know quite as much about running a restaurant as they thought they did. Early reviews from bloggers and diners were pretty negative, and the original chef/co-owner from The Admiral left after only about a month.

The menu was a little bizarre, even for Asheville. Fortunately, the original menu has been considerably changed. The changes in the menu under the new kitchen regime -- basically going from Japanese-Southern-eclectic to Chinese-Southern-eclectic -- were a big improvement. One visitor called the food an *homage* to Trader Vic's but prepared by hip chefs. Well, maybe.

On one visit we had the Pu Pu Platter appetizer ($26 for two, but plenty for the four of us), which was full of tasty treats. My General Ben's Chicken -- seared chicken with sesame seeds in an orange sauce with rice -- was fabulous, and a filling deal at $12. The only complaint is that it was a little too heavy on the salt. The Dan Dan Noodle bowl ($10) was good. We have to admit the outdoor dining area is charming, although it's nothing but concrete block walls with a few plant containers, picnic tables (which often are shared by two or three parties) and assorted used furniture. Since 80% of the seating is open air -- and there's no roof on this section -- Ben's Tune Up isn't the same place on a cold winter's eve. Overall, though, the atmosphere is appealing, especially on a nice clear night. The restaurant stays open late ('til 2 pm), and most nights as the evening wears on Ben's Tune-Up becomes more of a bar, with dancing, though you can get food service right up until closing. Some nights there's a DJ.

Blackbird *47 Biltmore Ave., 828-254-2502,*
www.theblackbirdrestaurant.com; **Steaks and Seafood**, *New Southern, dinner daily and brunch Sun.* **Expensive**

This restaurant moved in late 2012 from Black Mountain, where it was very popular, to ground level retail space at the new Aloft Hotel, where it has also been popular. Blackbird did a great job with the design of the restaurant, with its glass front on Biltmore Avenue, high ceilings, flying blackbird accents all around and the imaginatively named "Crowbar" in the center. If full, a it can be a little noisy. Since opening, the Blackbird menu has evolved in several different directions and nixed lunch.

As of this writing the restaurant is now emphasizing its steaks and seafood ($25 to $42 with two sides), though it still gives a nod to some Southern appetizers and main dishes. For this and all the other restaurants on or near Biltmore Avenue just south of Pack Square, including Cúrate, Limones, Wicked Weed, Chestnut, Seven Sows, Doc Chey's and others, the public garage under the Aloft Hotel is an easy place to park. Normally you'll pay just $1.50 or so for parking at dinner, unless there's a big event at the nearby Orange Peel nightclub, when the flat rate goes to $7.

Bouchon *62 N. Lexington, 828-350-1140,*
www.ashevillebouchon.com; **Bistro French,** *daily for dinner, no*
reservations **Moderate to Expensive**

Bouchon ("Cork") advertises French comfort food. It has a great location on North Lexington Avenue. There's dining in the little brick alley courtyard in the back, pleasant on a nice evening but perhaps a bit warm in the summer, as well as dining inside. Monday, Tuesday and Wednesday are "all you can eat" mussels nights – unlimited mussels prepared five different ways and an order of herbed French fries for $18. If you're not doing the mussels, for appetizers consider the escargot ($9, the standard preparation in garlic butter sauce, served really, really, really hot) or onion soup ($6). Both are good if not exceptional. The steak au poivre ($24) in a cognac sauce with sautéed vegetables and pommes frites, is a solid choice. Bouchon offers a house "private label" wine. We tried the red, a French Syrah and Grenache mix -- not bad and $20 a bottle.

For lighter dining, try **Crepêrie Bouchon** in the patio next door, under the same management. Street parking on Lexington Avenue is free after 6 p.m. and there's a small "honor" lot next to Downtown Books and News across the street from Bouchon. The Rankin public garage is one block to the west.

Chai Pani *22 Battery Park Ave., 828-254-4003, www.chaipani.net;*
Indian, *open daily for lunch and dinner* **Inexpensive**

Chai Pani bills itself as serving "Indian street food," snacks that you might find street vendors in Mumbai serving. However, you don't have to buy from a street stall here. The space is pleasant, comfortable and Asheville funky. Service is friendly and prompt. We're partial to the pakoras, chicken nuggets fried in a curried chickpea batter. The matchstick okra fries are delicious, too, though a tad greasy. The coconut uttapam (savory crepes) are very tasty. Indian beer is available, along with a few cocktails and wines. No reservations.

The **MG Road Bar,** operated by the Chai Pani owners, around the corner at 19 Wall Street, serving some food plus cocktails flavored with Indian spices. The Wall Street public garage is nearby, and street parking often is available on Battery Park or around the Grove Arcade.

Chestnut *48 Biltmore Ave., 828-575-2667,*
www.chestnutasheville.com; **New Southern,** *lunch and dinner Mon.-Sat.,*
brunch and dinner Sun. **Moderate to Expensive**

Opened in late 2012 by the owners of the Corner Kitchen in Biltmore, Chestnut is in a 1920s building at 48 Biltmore Avenue – at one time this building was a plumbing supply store, which shows how much Downtown has changed -- across from the Aloft Hotel and next door to Barley's Tap Room. The space, designed by Samsel Architects, is pleasant, with a high ceiling made to look like pressed tin, with the usual exposed ducting and refinished wood floors. There are tables with bar stool chairs by the windows, a bar on the right with a lot of wood and some beautiful pottery on loan from Blue Spiral Gallery, rows of booths down the main room, and a fairly large open room at the back, with art on the brick walls and a light-filled back wall. Chestnut is popular at lunch and dinner and is often fully booked at peak times.

The menu is fairly limited but changes frequently. There's a selection of "medium plates" that double as appetizers, priced at $9-$14, a few salads and soups and some "large plates" that range from $16 to $28. We like the calamari, perfectly fried, on kale, ($11) as a medium plate appetizer, and the 3 oz. petite filet with mashed potatoes and green beans is surprisingly filling for $14. In large plates, you'll have choices such as a strip steak ($30), apple-glazed Sunburst trout ($24). You do pay for the bread here -- $4 for a basket of three kinds of house-made breads. Wash it down with one of about 18 beers, mostly local craft brews, on tap. Plus, there's an eclectic wine list with most wines from $30 to $50 a bottle and $6 to $11 a glass, plus a full bar with drinks that are mostly reasonably priced. The whiskey sour is a good buy at $7.

Cucina 24 *24 Wall St., Downtown Asheville, 828-254-6170, www.cucina24restaurant.com;* **Italian,** *dinner Tue.-Sun., closed Mon.* **Expensive**

Cucina 24 delivers a sophisticated take on classic Italian food, using locally sourced ingredients from area farms and other fresh ingredients The menu changes seasonally, but you can't go wrong with the mountain trout, scallops and, in-season, the oysters on the half shell. The pasta is perfect, and even the beef steaks are good. Most dinner entrees are $16 to $26. Wood-fired pizzas, with unusual toppings such as bacon, grapes, radicchio and smoked fontina, are $16-$17. The atmosphere is pleasantly upscale, with low lighting and an open kitchen.

Cúrate *11 Biltmore Ave., 828-239-2946, www.curatetapasbar.com;* **Spanish Tapas,** *open for lunch and dinner Mon.-Sat.* **Expensive**

Eat here just once and you'll find out what the buzz on Cúrate is all about. You'll have to go back and try more, more, more of the authentic Spanish tapas. Unless you are unlucky enough to hit a bad night or an out-of-sorts waiter, which did happen to us once, what a delightful experience it is to have dinner here. There are about three dozen small plates on the menu, not including desserts. About 80% of the menu stays the same every day, though seasonal and special dishes are added.

Most everything is worth trying, but look especially at the gazpacho ($5), the Iberian ham ($11), the eggplant with honey ($6), the fried calamari on bread ($6) and the chocolate mousse with raspberry sorbet and hazelnut praline ($6), among others. Even the home-cured olives (three or four different kinds, $4) are special. We have been less enthralled with the *croquetas de pollo* (chicken fritters) and *patatas bravas*. There's an interesting list of Spanish wines and ports, most moderately priced, and a nice selection of cocktails. We like the Cuba Libre ($9) with Mount Gay rum and fresh lemon, served with an individual Coca-Cola in a little 8 oz. bottle.

The restaurant is long and narrow, with high ceilings and exposed ducting. If you want a quieter experience, try to get seated in the small roomette at the back. Some say they like sitting at the bar, to watch the chefs cook and be at the heart of the action, but note that the bar stools don't have backs. One street over is **Nightbell** *(32 S. Lexington Ave., Downtown Asheville, 828-575-0375, www.thenightbell.com)*, a bar and restaurant, under the same ownership. It's so hip it doesn't serve Jack Daniels.

Doc Chey's Noodle House *37 Biltmore Ave., 828-252-8220, www.doccheys.com;* **Asian Noodles,** *lunch and dinner daily* **Very Inexpensive to Inexpensive**

"Peace, love, noodles" is the theme of this outpost of an Atlanta noodle house. Located in one of the oldest buildings in Downtown Asheville, Doc Chey's serves Vietnamese, Thai, Japanese and Chinese noodle bowls and rice plates fast, cheap and tasty. Noodle and stir fry dishes are mostly under $10, and most dim sum items are around $5. It's always packed. No reservations.

Early Girl Eatery *8 Wall St., 828-259-9292, www.earlygirleatery.com;* **Casual Southern,** *breakfast, lunch and dinner Tue.-Sun, breakfast and lunch only Mon., reservations for dinner only* **Inexpensive to Moderate**

Named after an early-maturing tomato variety, Early Girl Eatery is casually Southern with a farm-to-table approach.

At breakfast, choose big stacks of whole grain pancakes ($8), a full Southern breakfast with eggs, grits, sausage, bacon, ham or tempeh and biscuits ($8) or shrimp and grits ($10). The breakfast menu is served all day. The lunch and dinner menus include dishes such as fried chicken and bacon salad ($9), tempeh Reuben ($9), sautéed mountain trout with collard greens and gingered cole slaw ($16) or meatloaf with hormone-free beef, mashed potatoes and honeyed beets ($15). Early Girl is often very busy, especially at breakfast and lunch. The same owners have opened King Daddy's, a fried chicken/Southern spot in West Asheville. See below.

Farm Burger *10 Patton Ave., Downtown Asheville, 828-348-8540, www.farmerburger.net;* **Burgers,** *open daily for lunch and dinner, open late* **Inexpensive**

Atlanta's popular Farm Burger opened an outpost in Asheville in spring 2013. It specializes in grassfed burgers ($6.75 for the basic burger with lettuce, tomato, red onions, Duke's mayo, jalapeños and such, plus $1 to $2 for more exotic extras like red bean chili, fried egg, pork belly or oxtail marmalade). Handcut fries are an extra $1.50-$2.50 with the burger. Vegan and chicken burgers are also available, along with a few other dishes. There's a popular $8.50 lunch special every day that includes cheeseburger, fries and a soft drink.

Located next door to Salsa's, Farm Burger sources most of its dishes from Hickory Nut and other farms in the Southeast. A few wines, local drafts and other beers are offered. Order at the counter and take out, or eat in of the tables inside the restaurant – the restaurant has a rustic farm decor with many photos of cattle -- or on the open-air patio out front. The burgers are cooked medium unless you prefer otherwise. While we like the idea of grassfed beef, as apparently do a lot of diners in Asheville, to our taste a little corn-fed fat goes a long way in making burgers tasty.

Food Truck Lots *51 Coxe Ave., Downtown Asheville, and Masonic Temple lot, 80 Broadway St., www.thelotasheville.com;* **Various Cuisines,** *lunch Mon.-Fri. and sometimes other times* **Very Inexpensive to Inexpensive**

After a long debate, Asheville City Council finally allowed a dedicated food truck lot to open in March 2012. The lot, next to Wells Fargo Bank on Coxe, has been successful, with sometimes six or eight trucks trying to squeeze into space for just four trucks, despite prices at some trucks that are no cheaper than eating at a restaurant.

There's a second, smaller food lot at the Asheville Masonic Temple on Broadway Street. This lot opened in the fall of 2013, but at present can only handle a couple of trucks at a time. Food trucks also often set up at different locations around town, including at the Wedge Brewery, Bywater Bar and elsewhere. Among the food trucks are ones selling Korean, Lebanese, Mexican, Venezuelan, Vietnamese, pizza, vegetarian, specialty coffee, burgers and other items. Trucks vary day to day, and they have to meet the same cleanliness and quality standards as regular restaurants.

Karen Donatelli Cake Designs *57 Haywood St., Downtown Asheville, 828-225-5751, www.donatellicakedesigns.com;* **Bakery,** *closed Mon.* **Very Inexpensive to Inexpensive**

This is like a small pastry shop in Europe. You can buy brioche, tarts and other pastries and eat them at one of the handful of tables in the bakery, or order and pick up beautifully designed cakes and pastries.

Isa's Bistro Haywood Park Hotel *1 Battery Park Ave., 828-575- .9636, www.isasbistro.com;* **New American,** *lunch and dinner daily* **Expensive**

For dinner at Isa's Bistro in the Haywood Park Hotel on Battery Park, we used the hotel's complimentary valet, which is a nice touch, and our first impression of the restaurant entering from the hotel lobby side was very positive. The atmosphere and design of the restaurant are supercalifragilisticexpialidocious -- an open layout with tables around the windows and walls, facing a bar, with tasteful touches of food-related photos and architectural pieces. We had a seat at a window looking out over Battery Park, and service from the very first was first rate.

We started with drinks at very reasonable prices. We then tried the Bang Bang Cauliflower ($7), as an appetizer, which was interesting but not something I would order regularly. My companion had the "Three for Thirty" special, an appetizer (in our case, mussels), main (trout and rice) and dessert for $30. The mussels were fine, but the trout entree was probably the smallest serving of trout ever seen in a restaurant. It might have been 2 ounces, to be generous, on a big bed of rice. If it were called Rice with a Trace of Trout it would be more honest. Dessert was, of all things, parsnip cake, again interesting but not something you'd come back for.

Your stodgy old author ordered the Black Angus Filet with whipped potatoes and broccoli ($32). The potatoes were perhaps the most interesting part of the meal, mashed/whipped potatoes fried in a stiff Phoenician boat-shaped batter. The 6-oz filet was quite good, and prepared exactly to my medium-rare order. I had a VERY generous serving of Mendoza Malbec ($10) with the meal. I was tempted by the double burger with fingerling fries, which has good word of mouth, but I wasn't really up for a burger that night.

With a total of four drinks, one glass of wine, one appetizer, two entree courses and sides and an espresso, plus tax, our usual generous gratuity plus a tip to the valet, the total for two came to about $155, reasonable for an Asheville upscale dinner. The renovated Haywood Park Hotel is charming, with a player piano in the lobby greeting the few guests who brave January in Asheville, and the elevators still charmingly bark out "Fourth Floor, Women's Wear" or whatever, just as in the days when my Aunt Dean worked at Ivey's.

Jerusalem Garden Cafe *78 Patton Ave., Downtown Asheville, 828-254-0255, www.jerusalemgardencafe.com,* **Middle Eastern,** *lunch and dinner daily, brunch Sat.-Sun.* **Inexpensive to Moderate**

Owner Farouk Badr has been serving tasty Mediterranean and Middle Eastern food in Asheville for more than 20 years. You'll find a fairly standard repertoire of lamb, chicken, chick pea and other dishes, plus falafel, sandwiches and wraps, at very reasonable prices. There's belly dancing on Friday and Saturday nights.

Kathmandu *90 Patton Ave., Downtown Asheville, 828-252-1080, www.cafekathmanduasheville.com;* **Indian/Nepalese,** *lunch and dinner daily* **Inexpensive to Moderate**

While billed as Nepalese/Tibetan/Himalayan, the food at this small spot on Patton Avenue is more or less what you'd get in a Northern Indian restaurant. There's a lunch buffet, and service is usually friendly. Wine and beer only.

Laughing Seed Café *40 Wall St., Downtown Asheville, 828-252-3445, www.laughingseed.jackofthewood.com;* **Vegetarian,** *lunch and dinner, Mon. and Wed.-Sat., brunch and dinner Sun., closed Tue.* **Inexpensive to Moderate**

Laughing Seed is one of longest established and best vegetarian restaurants in town. You'll get more than brown rice and beans here.

The café bills itself as being a "global fusion" restaurant, with flavors and dishes influenced by the cuisines of Korea, India, Thailand, Mexico, the Caribbean, Mediterranean and elsewhere. Many dishes are vegan or gluten-free or vegan. Fruits and vegetables are sourced from local organic farms. Breads are baked daily on premises. In good weather, there's outdoor dining on Wall Street. Most lunch and dinner entrees are $8 to $14. Laughing Seed has a full bar with many interesting cocktails, wines and local beers.

Laurey's Catering *67 Biltmore Ave., Downtown Asheville, 828-252-1500, www.laureysyum.com;* **Catering and Takeout***, breakfast, lunch and dinner Mon.-Fri. 8-8, breakfast and lunch, Sat. 9-4, closed Sun.* **Very Inexpensive to Moderate**

This is a good place to get take-out sandwiches for lunch, full meals for dinner at home or items for a picnic. There also are some tables for eat-in dining. Sandwiches (try the Reuben or the roast beef) are mostly $8 to $9 for a full sandwich and $4-$5 for a half. Soup and salad options change daily. Laurey's is very green and locally sources most of its ingredients.

Sadly, owner Laurey Masterton, who operated Laurey's for many years, died in February 2014 at age 59 after a long battle with cancer. Besides running a popular café and catering business for more than 20 years, Masterton was the author or co-author of several cookbooks. She was an avid bicyclist and beekeeper and had been an activist against cancer. Masterton was first diagnosed with uterine cancer when she was 25 and had since had other types of cancer. To raise awareness for ovarian cancer, she once rode her bicycle 3,100 miles across the country. Masterton, whose Asheville catering business began in 1987 and her café in 1990, was a spokesperson for the National Honey Board and most recently in 2013 had published *The Fresh Honey Cookbook: 84 Recipes from a Beekeeper's Kitchen*. She also was an outspoken supporter of diversity and the LGBT community in Asheville and an advocate for sustainable, local agriculture.

Lexington Avenue Brewery (LAB) *39 N. Lexington Ave., Downtown Asheville, 828- 252-0212, www.lexavebrew.com;* **Brewpub***, lunch and dinner daily, open late* **Moderate**

The owners did this place right. The shiny brass brewpub equipment and 92-feet-long curved bar alone must have cost a fortune. The menu goes beyond the usual bar snacks, with items such as blackened salmon, a12-ounce strip steak and eggplant lasagna. However, you can also order more typical brewpub food, such as beef sliders.

The house-brewed beer selection is sizeable, and new brewmasters arrived in 2013. There's also wine and a full bar. Unless the weather's really bad you can sit in a covered open-air patio area at the front. A soundproofed music stage area is at the back. If it's late and you're having too much fun, the same owners have the **Sweet Peas** upscale hostel upstairs, with access from Rankin Avenue. Parking is available in a private lot across the street from LAB at the intersection of Walnut and N. Lexington, and the Rankin Avenue public garage is about a block behind LAB.

Limones *13 Eagle St., Downtown Asheville, 828-252-2327, www.limonesrestaurant.com;* **Mexican-California**, *dinner Mon.-Sat., brunch and dinner Sun.* **Expensive**

This little narrow restaurant just half block off Biltmore Avenue is charmingly decorated, with the atmosphere of a San Francisco bistro. Dining here is always a pleasure, and we'd put in the same top category as spots like Fig, Zambra and Cúrate. The dining room has pressed tin ceiling and exposed ducts, and the service level is just right, not too little, not too much. It can be a bit noisy, so you might want to come early and try to get a table by the windows at the entrance.

Start with one of the appetizers, such as ceviche or fried calamari (both $9). The calamari is brilliant, maybe the best we've had in Asheville. There's a nice selection of cocktails and wines. Don't miss the blood orange margarita ($11) with fresh ingredients and good quality tequila. Entrees change regularly, but you can't go wrong with the Angus beef tenderloin ($29), served on a bed of organic kale, with a lot of vinegar -- unexpected but a nice contrast to the beef – and the truffle macaroni and cheese. Seared sea scallops ($25) are huge, tender and delicious. Surprisingly, Limones doesn't offer espresso, but the Dynamite coffee from Black Mountain is fine.

No, it's not inexpensive. A meal for two, with a total of two drinks, one glass of wine, two appetizers, two entrees, one dessert and one coffee, was $120, before our usual generous tip. But definitely worth it.

Loretta's Cafe *114. N. Lexington Ave., Downtown Asheville, 828-253-3747, www.lorettascafe.com;* **Sandwiches, Louisiana Dishes**, *open Mon.-Sat. 11 to 5* **Very Inexpensive to Inexpensive**

Loretta's, which moved to a new location at the foot of Lexington, is now a little off the beaten path for the lunch crowd, but it has good sandwiches and soups. On Fridays you can get an authentic New Orleans muffaletta and gumbo. In 2013 Loretta's opened a downstairs area with espresso bar.

If you can't find a muffaletta at Loretta's, try **Mayfel's** *(22 College St., Downtown Asheville, 828-252-8840, www.mayfels.org)* at Prichard Park, which is under the same ownership and has the Louisiana muffalettas daily, along with Mountain City Coffee.

Mela *70 N. Lexington Ave., 828-225-8880, www.melaasheville.com;* **Indian,** *open for lunch and dinner daily* **Moderate**

When it comes to Indian food, whether you're a fairly conservative diner, tending to order tried-and-true dishes like Tandoori chicken, or whether you're more venturesome, you'll be well served at Mela. The Tandoori dishes, especially chicken and lamb, are very good, prepared in an authentic tandoor oven, and for those who like them there are spicy curries and vindaloo dishes. The lunch buffet ($11) is very popular with the Downtown crowd. The restaurant space is a delight, with high ceiling and brick walls, though it can be a little noisy and some seats are close together. Service is friendly and spot on. Drinks tend to be hit or miss, depending on the bartender, but the Indian beers are always a good choice. Tip: If you pay cash rather than use a credit card, you'll get a small discount.

The Market Place *20 Wall St., 828-252-4162, www.marketplace-restaurant.com;* **New American,** *open for dinner Mon.-Sat.* **Expensive**

Under founder Mark Rosenstein, The Market Place, which opened on Market Street in 1979, was a pioneer in creative, farm-to-table cuisine in Asheville. It moved to Wall Street a couple of years later. Under new owner-chef William Dissen, it has continued to live up to its reputation.

Pack's Tavern *20 S Spruce St., Downtown Asheville, 828-225-6944, www.packstavern.com;* **American/Pub Food,** *open daily for lunch and dinner* **Moderate**

Location, location, location. That's a big part of what Pack's Tavern has going for it, as it's located next to the Pack Square Park, the Asheville City Building and the Buncombe County Courthouse, plus it's an easy walk from the heart of Downtown, an ideal spot for government and office workers to have lunch or a lunch meeting. After office hours, easy free parking is available behind the restaurant in a city government lot.

The restaurant and bar are in an historic 1907 building that once housed a lumber company and auto parts store. The original burnished wood floors have been retained.

However, beneath a building is a basement and passageways used in the early part of the 20th century as a storage and distribution system for bootleg liquor. Often parked at the entrance to Pack's Tavern is a 1930s vintage yellow pickup truck with a beer keg in the back. In good weather, there's outdoor dining overlooking Pack Square Park and the remarkable Art Deco Asheville City Building.

Selection here is another plus, with pub food such as wings, fish and chips and sandwiches, plus a variety of burgers (beef, bison, chicken and turkey) and a number of more expensive entrees including salmon, crab cakes and baby back ribs. For those with big burger appetites, there's the half-pound Mt. Mitchell burger with bacon, cheddar and Swiss cheese, fried green tomato, fried egg and jalapeño peppers. We like the fish 'n chips, too, one of the most popular items on the menu. More than two dozen craft beers are on draft, plus a small selection of wines and a full bar. Live music on weekends.

Posana Cafe *1 Biltmore Ave., Downtown Asheville, 828-505-3969, www.posanacafe.com;* **New American***, dinner Tue.-Sun., brunch Sat. and Sun., hours may expand in-season* **Moderate to Expensive**

Posana Cafe has a prime location on Pack Square, serving what Chef Peter Pollay calls Contemporary American cuisine, with mostly locally sourced ingredients. Your meal might start with hemp salad ($8), with hemp seeds and hemp oil on local greens. Your entree could be pecan-crusted local farm-raised trout ($21) or organic flank steak with pommes frites ($18) and end butterscotch cheesecake ($7). At dinner, small plates are $12 to $15 and entrees $17 to $23. Full bar. When Posana was open for lunch, we heard some complaints about the tiny portions.

Rhubarb *7 Southwest Pack Square, Downtown Asheville, 828-785-1503, www.rhubarbasheville.com;* **Eclectic,** *lunch and dinner daily except Tue.* **Expensive**

New, very hip, very different and very well located, Rhubarb and its chef, John Fleer, are getting regional and national press. Many start with the rabbit-leek rillette ($12) or lobster corndog ($9) before hitting the full plates such as wood-roasted Sunburst trout with potato-turnip latke ($27) or goat-cheese gnudi ($21).

Roman's *75 Haywood St., Downtown Asheville, 828-505-1552, www.romanstakeout.com;* **Deli,** *lunch Mon.-Sat., closed Sun.* **Very Inexpensive to Inexpensive**

———

Popular Downtown deli and lunch restaurant offers deli items plus sandwiches, paninis, veggie burgers, soups and more. Most ingredients are local. The beef burger uses Hickory Nut Gap meat and is terrific. Service can sometimes be a little slow, and sandwich prices are higher than at most delis. Roman's is next door to U.S. Cellular Center.

Salsa's *6 Patton Ave., Downtown Asheville, 828-252-9805, www.salsas-asheville.com;* **Caribbean/Latin***, lunch and dinner daily* **Moderate**

Salsa's is the flagship restaurant of Asheville food entrepreneur Hector Diaz. Diaz, originally from Puerto Rico, also operates **Chorizo** and **Modesto** at the Grove Arcade (neither of which we are very hot about, though many people like them, and they can be good choices for lunch). Salsa's, in an expanded space near the head of Patton Avenue at Pack Square, is still going great guns. It offers new takes on traditional enchiladas, tacos and fajitas, adding lots of vegetables and fruits and combining flavors in creative ways. Something called Pom Pom Pom comes in various versions – the tofu version has blackened crumbled goat cheese with pineapple, avocado slices, plantains and steamed vegetables. Even the drinks are different – try the spicy margarita. While prices are a little higher than you might expect, portions are large and many take home part of their meal for later. There are only about 30 seats in the restaurant itself, and they're packed close together. (In good weather you can get a seat in the small alleyway next to the restaurant.) Expect a wait at peak times. No reservations accepted. **Bomba's,** also run by Hector Diaz at the corner of Patton and Pack Square, is a sandwich and coffee shop.

Best Bets for Breakfast

Sunny Point, West Asheville – best spot in town for breakfast, and it's served all day

Tastee Diner, West Asheville – world-class country ham biscuits in a friendly, blue-collar atmosphere, just $2.50 (closed weekends)

Early Girl, Downtown Asheville – farm-to-table breakfasts

Biscuit Head, West Asheville and on Biltmore Avenue near Mission – often a line of biscuit-hungry customers

Homegrown, North Asheville – natural, local and Southern

Seven Sows Bourbon & Larder *77 Biltmore Ave., Downtown Asheville, 828-255-2592, www.sevensows.com;* **New Southern,** *dinner daily plus brunch Sat.-Sun.* **Expensive**

This spot on Biltmore Avenue's restaurant row opened in 2013. It started as over-the-top Southern, with a website that leaned heavily toward farm images and decor that uses farm stand signs and flooring planks from a family barn of one of the owners, but has since toned down the down-home Southern stuff. However, the ingredients are sourced from farms in the Asheville area and elsewhere in the region. The website for Seven Sows is so slick that we were surprised at how the restaurant actually looks. It's a bit like a combination of the Downtown Tupelo Honey and The Admiral in West Asheville. It's a modestly sized rectangular space, with booths along one side and part of the other, with rustic "shed roofs" with shingles over them, and then the rest of the seating is small tables in the middle of the room. At the far end is a small bar. While there's a striking, large painting of a young woman holding a large ham as the centerpiece on one wall, most of the rest of the paintings are of vegetables and other food, okra and such. Start with chicken livers sliders ($14) or buttermilk hushpuppies ($5). Large plates feature a Cheshire pork chop ($27), a hanger steak with collards ($31) and buttermilk fried chicken ($19).

Suwana's Thai Orchid *11 Broadway St., Downtown Asheville, 828-281-8151, www.suwanathaiorchid.com;* **Thai**, *lunch and dinner daily* **Inexpensive to Moderate**

Thai Orchid, in the heart of Downtown, serves fairly standard Thai food – we enjoy the Phad Thai and drunken noodles, usually for takeout. Most dinner dishes are around $9 to $14, with some of the dinner specials in the $20-range. Prices are better at lunch, and often portions are not much smaller. The owner, Suwana Cry, is from Bangkok.

Table *48 College St., Downtown Asheville, 828-254-8980, www.tableasheville.com;* **New American,** *dinner daily, lunch Wed.-Sat, brunch Sun.* **Expensive to Very Expensive**

Table is an intimate restaurant, serving New American cuisine, with a strict farm-to-table philosophy. You enter and wait for your table right beside the open kitchen, and the main dining room is surprisingly small, with a high noise level. Table has been open Downtown since 2005. In 2012, it debuted a swank new "grown up" bar on the second floor. The **Imperial Life Bar** serves craft cocktails, small batch spirits and a small plate menu.

The main restaurant menu is a fairly short one, but it changes frequently and on any given evening there's enough choice to please most everyone in your party – for example, from lamb chop and sausages ($30) to scallops with carrots ($28) to an excellent Brasstown beef burger with fries ($18). With appetizers, drinks or wine, entrees and desserts, plus tax and tip, you're going to spend close to $100 per person. Lunch is more affordable, with sandwiches and entrees from around $10 to $14. In 2013, on a visit to Asheville the cast of the "Wait Wait ... Don't Tell Me" NPR show had dinner here, trying the rabbit meatloaf.

Tupelo Honey *12 College St., Downtown Asheville, 828-255-4863, www.tupelohoneycafe.com;* **New Southern,** *breakfast, lunch and dinner daily* **Inexpensive to Moderate**

Tupelo Honey thrives on its consistency, the varied menu, the farm-to-table focus, the central location across from Prichard Park and the reasonable prices (though these days you can pay well over $20 for an entree at dinner). Always busy and bustling, the restaurant recently renovated its Downtown location. It's hard to get a bad meal here, although on a recent visit here our shrimp and grits, usually a fave, was gummy. A second, suburban Asheville location is in South Asheville *(1829 Hendersonville Rd., South Asheville, 828-505-7676)*. Tupelo Honey marketing isn't anything to scoff at either – it has a popular new cookbook and was named in a group of the first 16 "Green Restaurants" in America. The growing little Asheville-based chain has 10 locations outside Asheville, in Knoxville, Chattanooga, Myrtle Beach, Charlotte, Atlanta and elsewhere.

Wicked Weed Brewing *91 Biltmore Ave., Downtown Asheville, 828-575-9599, www.wickedweedbrewing.com;* **Brewpub**, *lunch and dinner daily, tasting room downstairs opens mid-afternoon, earlier on weekends* **Inexpensive to Moderate**

Wicked Weed opened in late 2012 on a high-test section of Biltmore Avenue in a former auto repair shop next door to the Orange Peel nightclub. Our first reaction was, "Wow, they've done a great job with the space!" High ceilings, lot of raw brick walls, glassed-in open kitchen on the main floor, with the tasting room and brewery downstairs. The exterior looks great, too.

The upstairs restaurant serves mostly pub food with a twist, deals like a fried chicken sandwich with kimchi and a bison burger, at reasonable lunch prices, but after 4 pm the Weed has more real restaurant stuff, such as Sunburst trout and Carolina bison meatloaf.

Wicked Weed Brewing and restaurant in Downtown Asheville

Full meals at dinner are under $20. On a recent visit, our calamari appetizer with romesco and coriander was a clue that this place has its act together – the squid was nicely fried, not heavy or greasy. The Wicked Weed's classic cheeseburger (single or double) with lettuce, tomato, onions, pickles and mayo on a toasted bun is one of the better ones in town, with loads of shoestring fries. With a flight of six Wicked Weed beers and two 16-ounce pours, a porter and an ale, our bill came to around $45 before our usual generous tip. Sure can't complain about the prices! Service was very good, friendly and prompt. Wicked Weed tends to stay busy, even at off-peak times. The noise level is energetic but not painful. Wicked Weed also operates the **Funkatorium,** a music venue at 147 Coxe Avenue.

Zambra *85 W. Walnut St., 828-232-1060, www.zambratapas.com;* ***Spanish Tapas,*** *dinner daily* ***Moderate to Expensive***

After a lapse of a couple of years, recent revisits to Zambra exceeded our expectations. Everything we tried was interesting, with some creative taste combinations, with the basis in Spanish tapas but with Southern influences. Prices are reasonable, and servings are surprisingly large for a tapas restaurant.

The atmosphere hasn't changed -- still dark and cave-like but not uninviting – but the food is better than ever. One evening we started with cocktails, and we love that Old Overholt rye was just $5, at least that night.

It's tough to decide what are the best tapas -- possibly the braised pork spring rolls ($7.50), the trout ($10.50), sesame scallops ($11) or the beef heart ($7.50). The patatas bravas (crispy potatoes with a tomato sauce, $3.50) are wonderful.

Zambra is another of the many Asheville restaurants that for some reason don't serve espresso. The restaurant has good Counter Culture coffee, but we don't understand why a local restaurant serves out-of-town coffee (from Durham, 225 miles away). Dinner for two with drinks and a gaggle of tapas came to around $85 before our usual generous tip. A fair price. Easy parking is available at the nearby Rankin public garage. Don't park in the private lot behind the restaurant, because you may be towed.

Best Restaurants Outside Downtown Asheville
Biltmore Village • West Asheville • River Arts District • North Asheville

Price Categories
Very Expensive $65+ per person
Expensive $35-$64 per person
Moderate $20-$34 per person
Inexpensive $10-$19 per person
Very Inexpensive Under $10 per person

BILTMORE VILLAGE

Corner Kitchen *3 Boston Way, Biltmore Village, 828- 274-2439, www.thecornerkitchen.com;* **New Southern**, *breakfast, lunch and dinner Mon.-Fri., extended brunch Sat. and Sun.* **Expensive**

The Corner Kitchen is one of Asheville's most popular restaurants. Even President Barack Obama dined here, in 2010. The menu changes regularly, and many dishes are locally sourced. At dinner, entrees are around $19 to $30. Try the chargrilled New York Strip with gas station fries ($30) or the pecan-crusted mountain trout with sweet potatoes ($24).

The restaurant is in a Victorian cottage in Biltmore Village, with plaster walls painted in serene colors and a fireplace in one dining room. Corner Kitchen did a full interior renovation in early 2015. The restaurant is known for its breakfast (try the homemade corned-beef hash with poached eggs and toast, $11), lunch and dinner, and the Sunday brunch is always busy.

Fig Bistro *18 Brook St., Biltmore Village, 828-277-0889, www.figbistro.com;* **Bistro French***, lunch and dinner, Mon.-Sat., brunch Sun.* **Expensive**

Stuck in a nondescript modern building across the street from the main part of Biltmore Village is one of our favorite restaurants in Asheville. We could eat the steak frites here three times a week at Fig, if our cardiologist permitted it. The hanger steak with Bordelaise sauce and pommes frites is fantastic. Fig's hand-cut fries are perfect.

Fig is small, only around 36 seats inside, with some extra seating in a courtyard (if the weather cooperates). The decor is modern minimalist, with a few French posters for atmosphere and a bar at one end, but you don't come here for the decor, or for the view, which is of the less appealing side of Biltmore Village. What you come here for is the food – like a real French bistro, it's low key, unpretentious and just plain delicious. Beside steak frites, consider the salmon, duck, the wonderful macaroni and cheese and the mussels appetizer (the broths vary from day to day). The espresso, with coffee from Bean Werks, is good.

Dinner for two, with an appetizer, salad, entrees, a cocktails or a couple of glasses of house wine, plus the espresso, runs around $130 with tax and a generous tip, a fair price for a superb bistro meal.

The Dining Room at Inn at Biltmore Estate *1 Antler Hill Rd. Biltmore Estate, Asheville, 828-225-1699, www.biltmore.com;* **Regional American,** *breakfast and dinner daily;* **Expensive to Very Expensive**

This is arguably Asheville's most elegant dining room, though coats and ties for men are not required, just collared shirts and slacks, and suggested attire for women is dresses, skirts or dress pants. It serves what the chef calls regional American dishes such as duck breast, king salmon, roasted sea scallops and Angus filet. Most beef, lamb and many vegetables served at the restaurant are raised on the estate.

Dinner entrees are around $28 to $40, and fixed price five-course dinners are $58 to $85, with a seven-course degustation dinner for $135. With drinks or wine, appetizers, entrees, perhaps a dessert or two, a couple can easily spend $150 to $200 or more. But this is a beautiful room, especially with a fire going in the fireplace. To dine at the inn's restaurant, you must be an inn guest, have a day admission ticket or be a twelve-month season pass holder.

We were overnighting at the Inn at Biltmore Estate (at the low 12-month passholder January-February weekday rate, about one-fourth the high-season price) and decided to spend our savings at the Inn's Dining Room. We started with drinks at the bar in the lobby. There's a small bar, an outdoor open air hall with tables and chairs (and heaters for cold weather). You can also have your drinks in the Library area of the lobby, which also serves a limited menu of food and usually has live music. This is what we did -- we sat by the big fireplace (gas, however) and enjoyed a glass of Biltmore Merlot ($8) and a cocktail ($13), plus tips.

After drinks, we went downstairs to the Dining Room (you can either walk down a flight of stairs or take the elevator). The Dining Room itself is very attractive, done with understated elegance. It has a large fireplace on the wall in the center of the room, and the room is lit by a number of chandeliers. It's all very tasteful and romantic. We were seated somewhat away from the fireplace but at a window table. It was a table for two, but unlike so many such tables, this was large enough so that you didn't feel crowded. Service was excellent. Our waiter was obviously quite experienced and provided just the right amount of contact, not too little, not too much.

My companion had a frisee and endive salad ($13), very good, and I started with split pea soup ($12), which was nicely presented, with the cream soup poured at the table over small pieces of ham. For an entree, I had a 6 oz. beef filet, with whipped Yukon Gold potatoes, caramelized brussels sprouts and a brown sauce ($39). The filet was excellent, tender with good flavor, but the servings of brussels sprouts and potatoes were very small. My companion had the short rib ($30). With Biltmore wine (Merlot and Syrah, each $8 and a nice large pour), and an after-dinner espresso (which came with complimentary cookies, as we didn't order desserts), the meal came to a little over $130, including taxes and my usual general tip. That price included a 15% discount for 12-month passholders, which our waiter kindly reminded us that we were entitled to.

Rezaz 28 *Hendersonville Rd. Biltmore Village, 828-277-1510,* www.rezaz.com; **Mediterranean,** *open for lunch and dinner Mon.-Sat.* ***Expensive***

Rezaz is in a former hardware store on Biltmore Avenue near Biltmore Village.

The dinner menu is divided into four sections -- labeled one, two, three and four. One and two are appetizers or small plates and three and four are large plates or entrees. We love the atmosphere at Rezaz, which is owned by Iranian-born Reza Setayesh. The dining room walls are a deep red, with abstract art, the layout is perfect, with tables not too close yet set up so that the restaurant has a buzz, and the lighting is just right. It's romantic without overdoing it.

The calamari appetizer we used to always order has been replaced by a calamari and shrimp appetizer, with a sweet and sour glaze, cabbage, scallions and sesame seeds ($9) – we like it, but it's not an improvement over the former one. We also had deep-fried okra appetizer. It's breaded and fried long-wise and served with what is billed as remoulade sauce ($6).

We wanted beef and unfortunately took the well-meaning advice of our waiter and ordered the braised beef brisket, essentially roast beef, with arrancini (sort of a fried risotto ball with mozzarella and shredded ox tail) and broccolini ($22). However, we probably would have been a happier with the grilled filet mignon or the ribeye ($25 and $26, respectively). Expect to pay around $120 to $130 for two with starter, drinks, entrees, dessert and tip. Lunch is a better bargain.

Under the same ownership is **Piazza** *(4 Eastwood Village, East Asheville, 828-298-7224, www.piazzaeast.com; lunch and dinner Tue.-Sun., Pizza, Inexpensive)* serving wood-fired pizza, spaghetti bowls, subs and wraps.

Ruth's Chris Steak House *26 All Souls Crescent, Biltmore Village, www.ruths-chris.com/asheville;* **Steak House,** *open daily for dinner* **Very Expensive (Moderate to Expensive for Happy Hour Bar Menu)**

We've dined at 50 or 60 Ruth's Chris different restaurants over the years (there are more than 130 around the world), and it's great to now have a location in Asheville. It's my all-time favorite of the premium steak house companies, such as Morton's, Del Frisco's, Fleming's and The Palm. You just can't go wrong with the "aged U.S. Prime beef, the top 2% of beef sold in America, cut by hand, broiled at 1800 degrees and served sizzling so it stays hot and juicy to the last delicious bite." For the sake of full disclosure: When we lived in New Orleans, the author of this book was a long-time consultant to the founder of the chain, Ruth Fertel, and to Lana Duke, the marketing guru for the steak house.

Among other things I wrote many of the ads for the restaurant group, including the above copy, and came up with the "Home of Serious Steaks" slogan that was used for many years.

The Asheville restaurant, with which I have no business relationship, is a franchise by the same folks that operate Ruth's Chris in Savannah, Charlotte and Charleston.

The restaurant design and exterior fit well in Biltmore Village near the Biltmore Estate entrance. However, the parking is very limited so most guests will use the complimentary (except tip) valet parking, which is well handled. Inside, the ambiance is upscale and sophisticated, and the main entrance hallway is lined with glass-fronted wine displays. There's a center fireplace, a little outside seating beside the bar and live jazz a couple of nights a week.

Although the filet mignon ($43 a la carte) is the best seller at Ruth's Chris, my favorite has always been the New York Strip ($45). I'm a traditionalist at Ruth's Chris. I usually go with the lettuce wedge with bacon and the amazing, thick Ruth's Chris blue cheese dressing ($9), the creamed spinach (founder Ruth Fertel's favorite side, $9) and the one-pound baked potato with the works ($9). We used to love the big, thick steak fries, but this location doesn't serve them, instead offering fried shoestring potatoes.

At the main restaurant with appetizers, a drink and a bottle of wine, U.S. Prime steaks and sides, and maybe a few extras and tip, a couple is likely to spend $200, or more. You can spend less, but when we go to Ruth's Chris we don't scrimp. When you want the best steak in town, period, you have to pay for it.

On most occasions we'd rather do the whole Ruth's Chris Steak House dinner thing, but recently we enjoyed the happy hour and bar menu ... and especially the jazz entertainment in the bar by up-and-coming Asheville and New York jazz singer and pianist Rockell Scott. The Papa We had the sliced filet steak sandwiches with béarnaise sauce and fries (a bargain at $8) and a couple of appetizers -- fair calamari and crab stuffed mushrooms. There's a small selection of $8 cocktails. The happy hour deals are offered Monday through Friday from 4:30 to 6:30 pm.

SOUTH ASHEVILLE

Asiana Grand Buffet *1968 Hendersonville Rd., South Asheville, 828-654-6879, www.asianagb.com;* **Chinese Buffet***, lunch and dinner daily* ***Inexpensive***

Okay, this is buffet, but it's a giant one, and if you're really hungry and want a huge selection of Chinese standards, plus sushi, this is where to go. Two people can eat 'til they bust for $25, less at lunch.

Just don't expect gourmet food. You can also order from a menu, but few do. Free lunch buffet on your birthday (you have to prove it's really your birthday.)

Sierra Nevada Brewing Co. Restaurant and Taproom *100 Sierra Nevada Way, Fletcher, 828-681-5300, www.sierranevada.com;* **Brewpub**, *lunch and dinner daily,* **Moderate**

This national craft brewer opened a 400-seat restaurant and taproom near the Asheville Regional Airport in spring 2015. The decor features giant copper vats and rich woods, some harvested from the brewery's 190-acre site. The food is mostly bar food – wings, duck-fat fries, a burger with gouda cheese, wood-fired mushrooms and the like. Appetizers are $3 to $14, and medium plate entrees are $10 to $13, with vegetable side dishes $8 to $9. There are more than 20 beers on tap, from $4 to $7, some produced at the brewery here and others from Sierra Nevada's original Chico, Calif., brewery. We didn't try the fried chicken sandwich on a doughnut or the cutesy grilled PBJ with ice cream. On our visit, dinner for two with two beer flights (2 oz. glasses of four beers), two regular pours, two appetizers and two entrees came to a little over $75 including tax and tip. By the way, the access road and the main brewery buildings are beautiful. Sierra Nevada has done a wonderful job with this facility.

Stone Bowl *1987 Hendersonville Rd., South Asheville, 828-676-2172, www.stonebowlkorean.com;* **Korean**, *lunch and dinner daily* **Moderate**

We enjoy the Stone Bowl, though nothing we've had has really left us thinking, "Can't wait to go back tomorrow." The best dish we've tried is the deep fried calamari ($6) -- basically a tempura-style appetizer. It is excellent. The lunch boxes are a good value -- a main dish such as marinated beef or chicken or deep fried shrimp, with a couple of side dishes, kim chi, dumplings, white or brown rice and soup, a lot of food for $9.

We take points off because the restaurant doesn't have any Korean beer, just three Japanese beers, a few local brews and some regular mass beers. Though the Stone Bowl is in a little strip center on Hendersonville Road, the atmosphere and decor are pleasant, low-key and tasteful. There is limited outside seating on a side patio. Lunch is around $30 before tip, dinner about $60 or $70. Asheville needs all the Asian restaurants it can get, so we're doing our little part to support the Stone Bowl and its new sister place.

For other Korean food, there's **Korean House** *(122 College St., Downtown Asheville, 828-785-1500, www.koreanhousenc.com)* and **Koreana** *(221 Airport Rd., Arden, South Asheville, 828-676-2844, www.koreanaasheville.com)*.

WEST ASHEVILLE

The Admiral *400 Haywood Rd. West Asheville, 828-252-2541, www.theadmiralnc.com;* **Eclectic,** *dinner daily* **Expensive**

In a one-story cinderblock building in a fairly downscale part of West Asheville, The Admiral is one of Asheville's top restaurants cleverly disguised as a dive bar for bikers. Small and dark, The Admiral is frequently fully booked days in advance. The menu changes daily, but medium plates such as swordfish, sweetbreads or mussels are $11 to $15, and large plates such as seared scallops with potato and beet hash or a ribeye steak with roasted sweet potatoes are $16 to $32. On Fridays and Saturdays, there's a late night dance party. Several Admiral veterans have opened new restaurants around the city.

Biscuit Head *733 Haywood Rd., West Asheville, 828-333-5145, www.biscuitheads.com;* **Southern**, *breakfast and lunch Tue.-Sun.* **Inexpensive**

This new breakfast spot serves cat's head biscuits (the size of your cat's head) and other tasty Southern fare at breakfast and lunch. Good selection of gravies and jams. A second location of Biscuit Head opened in mid-2014 *(417 Biltmore Ave., South Asheville, 828-505-3449, open daily for breakfast and lunch)* near Mission Hospital in the old Tomato Jam site. Both locations are very popular, and at times you may face a wait in line to order.

Buffalo Nickel *747 Haywood Rd., West Asheville, 828-575-2844, www.buffalonickelavl.com,* **New American,** *dinner daily except Mon.,* **Moderate to Expensive**

On a cold January Friday, Buffalo Nickel was hopping, with a nice West Asheville buzz. The owner has done a good job of renovation, refinishing the original wood floors and adding wood wainscoting from another old building. The downstairs room is a long rectangle, with a single row of tables along each side.

Upstairs, up some rather steep stairs, is a large bar area as you enter the room and then beyond that a game room with pool tables and other games. I noticed that, for a bar, the upstairs gets quite a few families with small kids. Maybe they like the games. Also, a lot of regulars seem to head directly upstairs for a drink or maybe a bar snack.

Of course, we started with drinks. My vodka martini ($8 with well vodka) was as ordered, up, dry and cold and with both olives and an onion. It was a little smaller than the typical martini, but it was good. My companion had the Vieux Carré, at $12 the most expensive cocktail on the menu, and also the Buffalo Nickel specialty drink, $9. I switched to a draft stout ($4.75) from Maine. Buffalo Nickel has about 18 craft beers on draft, some local and some from around the country.

I'm a Southern guy, so I had the deviled egg appetizer ($4) with four half eggs, very tasty. Wish I had had the oysters, though. For mains, I had the burger with fries ($12) -- an unscientific sampling suggests about one-half the customers get the burger, which indeed was very good, filling and one of the cheapest items on the menu. My companion's short ribs ($19) were okay. The menu is rather short and perhaps could do with some expansion or at least a regular rotation. Service was excellent. We parked in the Grace church lot, two short blocks away.

Harbor Inn Seafood *800 Brevard Rd., West Asheville, 828-665-9940, www.harborinnseafood.com;* **Seafood,** *lunch and dinner Tue.-Sun., closed Mon.* **Very Inexpensive to Inexpensive**

The focus at Harbor Inn is on fried seafood, although most items can be ordered broiled. Don't expect gourmet, but this outpost of a small, eight-location Southern regional chain has its act together, and the fried shrimp, fish, clams and other basics are done right. Prices are very modest – for dinner the fried catfish platter with cole slaw, fried or baked potato and hush puppies is around $8 and the broiled jumbo shrimp platter with salad, potato and hushpuppies is around $11. Reservations aren't accepted, and there's often a line at peak times. No alcohol served.

Isis Restaurant & Music Hall *743 Haywood Rd., West Asheville, 828-575-2737, www.isisasheville.com;* **New Southern,** *dinner daily with late night snacks and music, brunch Sat. & Sun.* **Moderate to Expensive**

The owners of Isis Restaurant & Music Hall have done a wonderful job renovating what was a restaurant called Pastabilities and at one point was the old Isis movie theater, which opened in 1937 and closed in 1957.

As small children my brother and I occasionally would walk from nearby St. Joan of Arc school to take in shows at this theater. I remember that we saw *Forbidden Planet* there one time. The exterior front of the restaurant has a marquee that looks like the old movie theater.

On the ground level, there's a mid-size dining area in the front of the restaurant -- with the requisite exposed ducting -- and the main music stage at the back (where the theater's movie screen was), with a bar and hallway connecting the two areas. On the second level (you can enter via either of two stairs) there's a more intimate bar/lounge, with a piano and small stage, ideal for a lounge lizard or jazz trio. Overlooking the main music stage is a standing area for drinkers.

This is exactly the kind of place West Asheville needs. It's the most upscale spot in Westville, yet reasonably priced. It's a classy joint, with many locally sourced items, and we'll definitely be going back for the food, drink and music. Isis has around two dozen local and regional beers on tap, a decent wine list and a full bar. The entree sirloin steak with braised fingerling potatoes and tomato comfit is $22, and the grilled pork chop stuffed with Gouda, chorizo and spinach is $18. Starters and snacks are $6 to $12, and entrees from $14 to $22. On a recent visit, dinner for two, with a total of two cocktails, one glass of wine, one shared appetizer, two entrees and one coffee came to around $75 with tax but before our usual generous tip.

King Daddy's Chicken and Waffles *444 Haywood Rd. , West Asheville, 828-785-1690, www.ashevillekingdaddy.com,* **Southern/Soul Food,** *lunch and dinner daily.* ***Inexpensive to Moderate***

Owned by the same folks who operate Early Girl in Downtown Asheville, King Daddy's is a new eatery on Haywood Road in West Asheville. It's about a block east of I-240, next door to Second Gear outdoor shop. There's street parking, plus at least at night you can probably park in the adjoining lot at Book Works. (On a personal note, it's just a couple of doors away from the Universal building that housed a Willys Americar dealership, co-owned by my father in the late 1940s.) We visited shortly after King Daddy's opened, and in fact there was no sign for the restaurant yet.

Basically the restaurant is just a rectangular storefront, with a small bar area and the kitchen in a separate area at the back.

The decor is pretty minimalist, a bit like a diner or even a fast food place. Blue colors dominate, on the walls and in seats and booths on the right side as you enter. Tables and chairs are inexpensive, like 1950s style breakfast furniture.

Now, to the food and drink. King Daddy's is billed as soul food, but to call it that is a bit of a stretch. For appetizers, the three of us shared seasoned pork cracklins, served in a waffle cone ($4), and chicken livers with andouille sausage and mushrooms, also served in a waffle cone ($8). We enjoyed these, though I wouldn't come back just for these dishes. However, the main course -- fried chicken -- was first-rate. I had the regular white meat fried chicken (a breast and a wing) for $7. Our friend had the same, except with dark meat. My spouse had the Korean fried chicken ($7). Two of us had mashed potatoes ($3) on the side, and we shared a couple of waffles -- I think one was with cracklins ($4) and the other a Belgian waffle ($3.50).

Most of the mixed drinks are $7 or $8, with the most expensive being $10. Beers range from PBR at $2.50 to a modest selection of craft beers, mostly around $3.50 to $5. There are also a few wines by the glass. Dinner for three, including two cocktails, two glasses of wine and one beer, plus two appetizers and three main dishes with sides, came to $85 before my usual generous tip. This was a little more than expected at a casual spot like this, but it was a lot of food.

Nona Mia Ritrovo *1050 Haywood Rd., West Asheville, 828-505-2028, www.nonamiaasheville.com;* **Italian/Pizza,** *dinner Tue.-Fri., lunch and dinner Sat.-Sun., closed Mon.* **Inexpensive to Moderate**

The wood-fired pizza is the thing here, and when it's good (most of the time) it's really, really good. Nona Mia ("my old Granny") serves a thick-crust Sicilian-style and a thin-crust Neapolitan-style. Most pizzas easily serve two, perhaps with leftovers to take home. The base prices -- $9 to $18 -- make the pizzas a good value, but the toppings, mostly $3 each, can boost the final price considerably. I recommend the Bronx pizza, just $9. Service is very friendly and welcoming, although some of the waitstaff (turnover seems high) are inexperienced and forget things like bringing a wine list or offering to grind pepper on your salad or grated cheese on your pizza. Salads are big and nicely done. The small Caesar ($4.50) with anchovies and house-made croutons is tasty and a bargain. Nona Mia is often very busy, and if you arrive at prime times you may have to wait.

When dining inside the noise level can be VERY high -- the restaurant is in a steel-side building, with one largish dining space and an open kitchen, with nothing to dampen the sound. Sometimes there's live music, which makes it even louder. There are quieter tables on a deck out back and near the parking lot in the front, open in good weather. Nona Mia has a friendly neighborhood vibe and overall a nice if noisy atmosphere.

Papas and Beer *1000 Brevard Rd., West Asheville 828-665-9070;* **Mexican,** *daily for lunch and dinner* **Inexpensive**

These guys know how to run a Mexican restaurant. The food isn't going to win any gourmet magazine awards, but service is friendly, food is tasty and you get your order pronto. The restaurant, despite having expanded into space next door in the little strip center, is often full, and you'll likely have a short wait unless you come a little before or after peak times. We've eaten here frequently and keep going back because most of the flavors work, especially on dishes like the *carne asada* platter, the combination dishes such as cheese enchilada and tamale platter (all served on heated plates), the steak or chicken fajitas (served on a sizzling cast iron plate), the Top Shelf margarita with a shot of Grand Marnier on the side (terrific and only $6.95) and the Mexican beer on draft. Chips and a salsa bar with some interesting salsas come free with your meal, which will only set you back around $7 to $14 plus drinks and tip. Papas and Beer (sometimes spelled Papa's and Beer) has two other locations in Asheville, one on Tunnel Road -- not nearly as good as the Brevard Road location -- and one in South Asheville on Hendersonville Road, as well as a location in Hendersonville.

Rocky's Hot Chicken Shack *1445 Patton Ave., West Asheville, 828-575-2260,* www.rockyshotchickenshack.com*;* **Fried Chicken***, daily for lunch and dinner* **Inexpensive**

Rocky's gets local hype for its spicy fried chicken. The actual fried chicken we rate as very good, but not everyone cares for the hot dry rub used on the chicken. The heat level varies from plain to XX Hot. For us the rubs are too thick and dark and overwhelm the flavor of the chicken, and we don't really find even the hottest levels all that hot. If we eat again at Rocky's, we'll just have the plain fried chicken. The fried okra and corn pudding are very good, fries are just okay, about what you'd expect from crinkle-cut frozen fries, and the fried pickle appetizer is way too heavily breaded. Rocky's has announced plans for a second location in South Asheville.

Sunny Point *626 Haywood Rd., West Asheville, 828-252-0055,* www.sunnypointcafe.com*;* **New Southern/Breakfast***, Tue.-Sat. breakfast, lunch and dinner, Sun.-Mon. breakfast and lunch Inexpensive to Moderate*

Sunny Point is famous for its breakfasts (most $7-$11), which are served all day, but you won't be disappointed in lunch or dinner either. The restaurant has a small, usually crowded inside seating, plus a covered patio, recently redone, all with a nice West Asheville vibe. Service is always friendly and engaging.

On a recent dinner visit we had a daily special, a risotto and chanterelle mushroom dish, which was one of the best vegetarians dishes we've had recently. The meatloaf with mashed potatoes and sautéed greens ($14.50) had a bit too much sage and pork and not enough ground beef for our taste, but it was still good, and the potatoes and greens were excellent. The shrimp and grits ($14) -- chipotle cheese grits topped with blackened shrimp, roasted tomatoes, white wine Dijon sauce, garnished with bacon -- are top-notch. Dinner entrees are $14-$17, but you can order from the breakfast or lunch menu, too. Sandwiches at lunch or dinner are mostly $9-$12. Beer, wine and cocktails.

Tacos Jalisco *1328 Patton Ave., West Asheville, 828-225-3889,* **Mexican***, open daily for lunch and dinner Very Inexpensive to Inexpensive*

Tacos Jalisco is a little taqueria in West Asheville, off Patton Avenue near the West Asheville post office. We like the atmosphere -- no frills but pleasant, clean, well lit, and the owners are friendly and welcoming. Big serving of chips with a freshly made salsa comes out right away -- included with the meal. The food? It probably depends on what you order. The tacos, one fish and one steak ($2.25 each) were tasty and well priced, but the cheese enchilada plate ($8) wasn't hot enough (either in actual heat or spiciness). You may need to come back several times and explore the menu until you find something you like. Tacos Jalisco does have some unusual and authentic items such as taco de lingua (tongue taco) and tripe, and many customers favor the pastor (pork) tacos, though the tortillas are not hand-made. The draft Dos Equis is cheap at $2.50 for a 16-oz in a nicely frosted mug. Service is friendly and very prompt. The horchata (a popular Mexican rice drink) is authentic. Value is the deal here. With a total of three drafts and two entrees plus sides, the total came to about $21 before tip -- very reasonably priced.

Tastee Diner *575 Haywood Rd., West Asheville, 828-252-9644;* **Southern Diner,** *breakfast and lunch Mon.-Fri.* **Inexpensive**

Dirt cheap, authentic traditional diner-style Southern food, friendly waitresses, NASCAR-themed decor, lot of regulars from West Asheville. What else can you ask for? The daily special of a meat such as beef stew or country-style steak, three vegetables and cornbread or biscuits is under $6. Great country ham biscuits ($2.50). No alcohol. Almost always full. There's extra parking around back, in addition to spaces in front and along Haywood Road.

Universal Joint *784 Haywood Rd., West Asheville, 828-505-7262, https://sites.google.com/site/universaljointasheville;* **Burgers and Pub Food**, *daily for lunch and dinner* **Inexpensive**

Universal Joint, in what used to be a Pure gas station at the corner of Haywood Road and Sand Hill Road in West Asheville, is popular for its burgers. The burgers aren't bad, among the better efforts we've had in Asheville. The Steinbeck burger has pimento cheese, bacon and jalapenos, with okay fries (around $10). The Joint also serves some basic Mexican items and other pub food. Under the same ownership are about a dozen other similar restaurants around the South. Up close the Universal Joint isn't quite as appealing as the charming renovation of the white Pure building with blue roof would suggest, and the waitstaff (mostly heavily tattooed young women) can come across with an air of bored nonchalance. With two draft microbeers, tax and tip, our meal for two came to a little over $30. We'd go back for a cheeseburger and hope the manager spiffs up a little and that the waitstaff takes some happy pills. After banking hours and on weekends, handy free parking is available in the Wells Fargo lot across the street; at other times, you may have to scout for a nearby street space.

WALK *401 Haywood Rd., West Asheville, 828-505-7929, www.walkavl.com;* **Pub Food,** *daily for lunch and dinner (brunch on Sun.)* **Inexpensive**

We love the way the owners of the West Asheville Lounge and Kitchen or WALK have done the renovation of the old Rocket Club location across from The Admiral -- brick walls, high ceilings, garage-type doors on two sides that open to let in the mountain air. We found the service excellent -- friendly and prompt. And we enjoy the West Asheville vibe.

The food? It's a step up from the usual bar snacks. The 6 oz. Hickory Nut Gap Big Burger (well priced at $8 with a side of fries) wasn't the best cheeseburger in Asheville that we've been searching for in vain, but the fries were excellent. Don't get the 2 oz. Little Burger with fries despite the $4 price tag – it's too easy to overcook the little piece of hamburger. The shrimp po-boy ($9.50 with a side of tater tots) was just okay.

With the juke box blaring, two pool tables going, the place full and a ballgame on the giant screen, it is LOUD. Definitely not a place for a quiet tête-à-tête. With a beer or two, a couple can eat here for around $40.

Zia Taqueria *521 Haywood Rd., West Asheville, 828-575-9393, www.ziataco.com;* **Mexican**, *daily for lunch and dinner, open late Thu.-Sat.* **Inexpensive to Moderate**

Zia is in the old Delores & Jose's Mexican Restaurant location on Haywood Road in West Asheville, where we were regulars for more than 20 years -- in the old location and then in the new one -- so naturally we had mixed feelings about Zia when this new Mexican restaurant opened in early 2013. Delores & Jose's was an institution in West Asheville, especially in the 1980s and early 1990s when it was in a former drugstore building at the corner of Haywood Road and the I-240 ramp. D&J's kept the drugstore's locally famous hot dogs and served them until the bitter end, along with the Mexican dishes. In its later years D&J's had some issues, was sold and then reopened and never fully recovered, and José passed on, but on good days it had some great Mexican dishes -- plain working class food but authentic and inexpensive. In the early days it was run by Delores, José and Mena, who had come to Asheville from Mexico City, and then after Jose's passing by Delores and Mena.

Zia's Asheville location is the restaurant's second. The first location is in Charleston, S.C. Zia's calls its food Southwest or New Mexico style, but, frankly, there aren't many true Southwestern dishes on the menu.

You can order at the counter, pay and get your drinks and then go to your table, to wait for the food to be prepared and delivered to your table, or you can sit at one of the tables that offer table service.

To the food: On our first visit we ordered guacamole that, oddly, is "market price." The cheese enchilada platter with two sides, and the carne asada plate, again with a choice of two sides, such as pinto beans, black beans or Spanish rice. The tacos are mostly around $4, and platters are in the $9-$13 range. The total for the two of us came to about $45 for the appetizer, two entrees and two margaritas, a little steep for a neighborhood taqueria.

On a revisit we're glad to report that the food was much improved. I was with a group of 11, and I heard no complaints about the food. Service was excellent and well organized. My *taza de sopa de tortilla* ($3.95) was *muy buena* -- lots of interesting flavors and full of chicken and tortilla strips. For an entree I had the Chicken Yucatán (just grilled chicken) with black beans, yellow rice and a large serving of mixed vegetables, plus corn tortillas ($12). I also had a house Zia Rita (margarita) and a Dos Equis draft. The total came to around $27 with tax, before my usual generous tip.

RIVER ARTS DISTRICT

All Souls Pizza *175 Clingman Ave., River Arts District, 828-254-0169, www.allsoulspizza.com;* **Pizza,** *open Tue.-Sun. for lunch and dinner*
Inexpensive to Moderate

At the site of the old Silver Dollar diner, and more recently the short-lived Asheville Public, All Souls does really good wood-fired pizzas from organic flours ($10 to $15, with toppings $1 to $3), along with a few salads and sandwiches.

The Bull and Beggar *37 Paynes Way, River Arts District, 828-575-9443, www.the-bull-and-beggar.com;* **Eclectic, Seafood;** *open Tue.-Sun. for dinner, Sat.-Sun. for brunch* **Expensive** *to* **Very Expensive**

The instant you see the Bull and Beggar you know you're going to a hip, eccentric, creative restaurant. First, there's barely a sign for the restaurant. It's in the River Arts District at the end of an unpaved drive in the old industrial building that houses the ever-popular Wedge Brewery, a hair salon and Wedge Studios and Gallery (guarded by a giant metal dinosaur). To get to the restaurant you have to wind your way around the Wedge Brewery and its food trucks, and the casual visitor might give up before finding it. Inside, the high-ceiling space retains a lot of its industrial/warehouse feel, with mostly unadorned brick walls, concrete floors and the obligatory HVAC ducting on the ceiling. To the right is a large bar, and a mirror on the far wall gives the illusion that the space is even larger than it is. There is seating at the bar, at tables on the first level and also on a loft level (unused at times).

But the menu is where it really gets creative. And eccentric. If there's a unifying theme to the menu, it's hard to figure. Southern? French? Seafood? What? If there's a pricing strategy, we couldn't see it. Some dishes and drinks are real bargains, while others verge on the outrageous. There are small plates, snacks, a big selection of cheeses, a good bit of seafood -- from mussels and french fries (a bargain at $13) to charred octopus ($12), and a variety of oysters on the half shell for $3 each, or clams at $2 each.

A few large plates or entrees (trout, filet mignon, sheepshead porgy, venison) cost from $23 to $37. I had the filet ($30), nicely done but overwhelmed by the Madeira sauce. What stands out is the mostly raw and steamed two-tier seafood platter for $85, easily enough for three or four, and a smaller one for $65, and caviar for $80 to $100. On recent visits, the raw bar and even the seafood platters were half price from opening at 5 to 6:30.

There's a small and, yes, eccentric, wine list -- I couldn't find a cab on it to go with the filet mignon and settled for a Merlot blend -- some local craft beers and a nice selection of premium liquors and intriguing drinks at mostly reasonable prices. Maybe it sounds like we didn't like the place, but in fact we did. We love the space and the atmosphere, and the service was friendly and peppy.

Several of the dishes were wonderful, though in other cases the chef's reach far exceeded his grasp. Our tab for two cocktails, two glasses of wine, two entrees and one snack, with tax and our usual generous tip, came to around $165. But we saw couples come in and probably drop less than $50, as they stuck to the snacks and small plates.

Gallery Mugen and Yuzu Patisserie *Cotton Mill Studios, 122 Riverside Dr., River Arts District,* **Bakery,** *open Mon.-Sat. 11-4* **Inexpensive**

This is a combination pottery studio, gallery and patisserie. While craft artists Akira Satake and Barbara Zaretsky work in ceramics, Cynthia Pierce's medium is sweet and savory pastries. Pierce, formerly a pastry chef at a local restaurant, sold her pastries under the Sweet Life Bakeshop name at the Asheville City Market. Most of the baked goods are in the French or German tradition, but some have a Japanese influence. For example, galettes and tarts might have green tea flavors.

The Junction *348 Depot St. # 190, River Arts District, 828-225-3497, www.thejunctionasheville.com;* **New Southern,** *open for dinner Tue.-Fri., brunch and dinner on Sat., brunch only Sun., closed Mon.* **Expensive**

We are knocked out ... by the hip River Arts District atmosphere at The Junction (everybody seems cooler, thinner and better looking than we), the friendly and professional service, the interesting drinks selection and the food, which we'd describe as eclectic contemporary Southern/New American. Most ingredients here are locally sourced, and all meats are antibiotic and hormone-free. The menu changes seasonally or more frequently. You'll pay about $6 to $16 for appetizers (most appetizers serve two or more), $6 to $15 for small plates and $17 to $24 for large plate entrees.

Among the highlights: pork rind appetizer with Crystal hot sauce ($7), meat and cheese board with a half-dozen smoked meats and artisanal cheeses ($16), tea-brined fried chicken ($19) and smoke lamb and pork crepinette with popcorn grits and snow peas ($23).

The author is more of a vodka martini or Jack on the rocks type, but many seem impressed with the innovative cocktail menu (mostly $9 to $12). The PBR, however, was only $2. If there's a downside, it is that the noise level can be high. The brick walls and concrete floors send sound ricocheting, and even sound-deadening panels on the ceiling don't help much. On one visit, with tip and tax, our meal ran a little over $80, a fair price for a nice evening. On another visit with a party of five, we spent about $200.

---

12 Bones Smokehouse *5 Riverside Dr., River Arts District, 828-253-4499, www.12bones.com;* **Ribs & BBQ**, *lunch only 11-4 Mon.-Fri.* **Inexpensive to Moderate**

Only open weekdays from 11 to 4, 12 Bones in the River Arts District draws a crowd, and the wait to place your order can be long. Even President Barack Obama had to wait during his three visits here ... well, at least for a little while. As with any top barbecue house, 12 Bones has little atmosphere. What it does have is delicious baby back ribs, flavored with a variety of fresh-made sauces such as blueberry chipotle or brown sugar. A half rack of six bones is $12 with two sides and cornbread, and a full 12-bone rack is $20.50 with sides. Sides include collard greens, corn pudding, mac and cheese, buttered green beans and mashed sweet potatoes. Also served are pork, chicken, turkey and beef brisket BBQ sandwiches and plates ($6-$9). There's limited inside and covered outdoor seating, though many order for takeout. The crowd ranges from hippie potters from nearby art studios to downtown business people to construction workers. Service is friendly if harried. A second location in South Asheville *(3578 Sweeten Creek Rd., Arden, 828-687-1395)* is open 11-6 Tuesday-Saturday, but after 4 pm it's only open for takeout. 12 Bones was sold to some long-time employees in mid-2013 but appears to be continuing its winning ways. In 2015, there was talk that the RAD location would have to move, due to local government exercising its right of eminent domain.

White Duck Taco Shop *1 Roberts St. #1, River Arts District, 828-258-1660, www.whiteducktacoshop.com;* **Fusion Tacos,** *lunch and dinner Mon.-Sat., closed Sun. Very* **Inexpensive to Inexpensive**

White Duck Taco is a neighborhood joint for the River Arts District, serving a limited menu of interesting a la carte "fusion tacos" such as Banh Mi Tofu, Black Bean, Bangkok Shrimp and Lamb Gyro.

All are moderately priced -- most under $4 or $5-- and two tacos make a filling meal. The atmosphere is funky but structured, if that's possible. You line up to place your food and drink order-- the menu is hand written on a large board above the counter -- pay for it, then find a table inside (fans but no A/C) or in good weather at picnic tables outside. Waitstaffers bring your order, and it's all quickly and efficiently prepared and delivered.

You're warned, though, that waitstaff don't take drink orders. The website specifically says "We are a restaurant, not a bar. With this in mind please understand our view of alcohol is as an accompaniment to food. ... Our food runners and bussers will not take drink orders (or any orders) from you after you are seated."

In short, if you need a second beer to wash down your tacos, you'll have to get back in line and wait. Our bill for four tacos, chips and two margaritas came to $33 with tip.

The restaurant is Living Wage Certified. A first-time visitor might have a little trouble finding the restaurant. Look for the bright orange building on Roberts Street toward the north end of the River Arts District, with picnic tables out first and below that a parking lot. There's a small sign for White Duck below a much larger sign for The Hatchery, a group of galleries and studios.

White Duck Taco has a second location at 12 Biltmore Avenue in Downtown Asheville. The owners, Ben and Laura Mixson, also have to James Island near Charleston, S.C.

NORTH ASHEVILLE

Asheville Pizza and Brewing *675 Merrimon Ave., North Asheville, 828-254-1281, www.ashevillebrewing.com; **Pizza**, lunch and dinner daily* ***Inexpensive***

A combination restaurant, brewpub and movie house, Asheville Pizza and Brewing is a popular family spot in a former movie theater on Merrimon Avenue. Order a burger, pizza or vegan sandwich, along with a fresh-brewed beer, and you can enjoy your meal in the restaurant area or grab a sofa or comfy chair in the theater and dine while you watch a second-run movie. Movie tickets are $3 and often sell out. The company also operates a pizza restaurant in South Asheville (carry out and delivery only) and its main brewery on Coxe Avenue Downtown (see Beer City section). This is arguably the most kid-friendly of Asheville brewpubs.

Avenue M *791 Merrimon Ave., North Asheville, 828-350-8181, www.avenuemavl.com; **American,** dinner Tue.-Sat., brunch and dinner Sun., closed Mon.* ***Moderate to Expensive***

In the site of a former paint store and then a bar, Avenue M is a neighborhood restaurant with a good following in North Asheville. Dinner entrees, mostly $11 to $18, range from hanger steak to salmon to a vegetable tangine. The grass-fed burger is one of Asheville's better burgers, and a bargain at $12 with fries. Service is friendly, the atmosphere pleasant and the food is consistent and reasonably priced. The bar has a good selection of local and other craft beers, plus wine and a number of unusual cocktails. There are half-priced martinis on Thursday – well-brand martinis are normally $8, going for $4 on Thursdays. Bring a DD.

Dough *372 Merrimon Ave, North Asheville, 828-575-9444, www.doughasheville.com;* **Bakery and Prepared Foods,** *Mon. 8-5, Tue.-Sat. 8-8:30, Sun. 9-3* **Inexpensive to Moderate**

You'd think by the name, Dough, that this spot is mainly a bakery, but it's not. While it does have a variety of breads -- though not always a huge selection -- by the time we got there at lunch there were few if any pastries or other bakery treats left, except for several appealing-looking cakes by the slice and some cookies. If anything, the emphasis here seems to be on the prepared foods in the cooler, everything from chicken pot pie to veggie lasagna and other pasta dishes to tamales, soups, wraps and sandwiches. Plus there are several different pizzas, calzones and strombolis and a variety of salads and prepared vegetables for take-out or to eat-in at picnic tables. (There also are several picnic tables outside.) Dough has a few market items -- spices, olive oils, wines, etc. -- in its market section. Our muffaletta (around $9) was an excellent sandwich, with enough ham, salami and cheeses for two sandwiches. The bread was freshly baked and delicious, though it bore little relationship with the muffalettas you get in New Orleans, such as at Central Grocery. The main difference is in the olive salad and the bread -- New Orleans muffalettas use a large Sicilian-style bun, fairly dense bread, and they load on the olive salad. The restaurant/bakery has a nice open, well-lighted atmosphere. Staff seem friendly, and there's a good amount of parking beside and the behind the building on busy Merrimon. Dough also offers cooking classes. The bakery/restaurant is open daily, though hours vary day by day – don't you hate that?

Gan Shan Station *143 Charlotte St., North Asheville, 828-774-5280, www.ganshanstation.com,* **Contemporary Asian,** *lunch Mon. and Wed.-Fri., dinner daily except Tue.* **Expensive**

Gan Shan Station, which opened in late 2014, may deserve four stars on the basis of its kitchen's creativity, the excellent service, the delightfully original renovation of an old service station space and the nice selection of Asian beers in bottles from Vietnam, Laos, Thailand, Sri Lanka and China, though there are few local beers. There's also sake and a full bar for cocktails.

But like the sticky rice used in several of the dishes, the sticky question is whether we will become regulars here. Gan Shan, which means Sunset Mountain in Mandarin, is in a former Gulf service station, and the owners have done a stunning job converting the space, leaving the shell of the old building and some of its original elements, while bringing energy through the open kitchen.

There's plenty of parking, except possibly on the busiest of nights, and in good weather there is outdoor seating. We arrived at a little after 6 pm on a Thursday and were immediately seated at one of the last remaining tables. The restaurant was full while we were there, but there were people waiting only during one short period. It's walk-in only here, no reservations accepted.

As for the food: We stayed with the starters ($6 to $8) and small plates ($9 to $14), although there are several mains ($14 to $19) and family plates ($25 to $40). On this night the special family plate was a deep-fried whole flounder, fresh from Charleston, at $40. The Szechuan Pig Ears appetizer ($7) was interesting, with crispy strips of fried hog ears mixed with tree ears, lime, cilantro and garlic, but, unexpectedly, it was served cold, and is not something we would try again. The Thai fermented sausage ($8) with sticky rice, a cabbage leaf and peanuts, was much better. Then, with our Hue and Lao beers ($4 a bottle), we enjoyed the Glazed Pork Ribs ($14) with a honey, lime, chili and scallion sauce. These seem to be a favorite among customers, and they were good, falling-off-the-bone tender. We also ordered the spicy pork meat dumplings ($9 for 5). To offset the heartier meat dishes, we had the heart of palm salad (a steep $9), with a little bit of green mango, carrot, grapefruit and quite a bit of shaved fennel bulb – not bad, but again, nothing that would draw us back and overpriced.

For Gan Shan Station to make us regulars, they'll need to expand their menu or at least rotate a larger variety of dishes and specials. We wish the owners and staff well, as Asheville is still lacking in first-rate Asian spots, but we think they have some tuning up to do. With three beers, two starters, three small plates and a side of sticky rice ($3), our meal including taxes and our usual generous tip came to $80 for two, a not unreasonable price though hardly a bargain.

Geraldine's Bakery *(840 Merrimon Ave., North Asheville, 828-252-9300, www.geraldinesbakeryavl.com)* serves some of the area's best pastries, pies, cakes, donuts and bagels. It's run by a second-generation baker who ran a baker on Long Island for 25 years.

Homegrown *371 Merrimon Ave., North Asheville, 828-232-4340, www.slowfoodrightquick.com;* **Southern,** *breakfast, lunch and dinner daily* ***Very Inexpensive to Inexpensive***

Homegrown is serious about locally grown, farm-to-table food. It sources virtually all its ingredients from around 10 area farms.

While the atmosphere isn't exactly white tablecloth, service is friendly and you can eat here for a song (well, for around $10 for lunch with tx and tip). You order at the counter and your food is brought to your table. The menu, mostly soups, sandwiches and basic Southern cooking, changes fairly frequently, depending on what's locally available.

For breakfast, try the sweet potato hash and a free-range egg for under $8, or a fried chicken biscuit for $3.50. For lunch or dinner, meatloaf with gravy, roasted parsnips and collard greens is under $10, as is buttermilk fried chicken with two large sides. The restaurant's power is partly solar, and Homegrown provides compostable takeout boxes and recycles wherever possible. Beer and wine only, no cocktails. Homegrown has a fairly low visual profile on busy Merrimon Avenue – look for Blackbird Frame & Art, which is next door. It's across from Dough.

King James Public House *94 Charlotte St., North Asheville, 828-252-2412, www.kingjamespublichouse.com,* **New American,** *lunch and dinner daily,* **Moderate to Expensive**

This small, intimate bistro, which opened in 2014, sounds as if it should be a British pub, but while it has a few pub-style items, it follows the Asheville plow-to-table ethos, and the chef –owner and co-owner are well established in the local restaurant scene. Lunch features mostly sandwiches with an edge (the burger has Spam and Velveeta, for example, and the Rueben uses beef tongue) at $10 to $12. At dinner, the small plates are mostly $9 to $14, with large plates such as buttermilk fried chicken and Sunburst trout at $16 to $18. Cocktails, creative combos with names like Jesus Built My Hotrod and Where is My Mind, are $8 to $10, and there's a decent selection of artisan beers on draft and in the bottle or can.

Nine Mile *233 Montford Ave., North Asheville, 828-505-3121, www.ninemileasheville.com;* **Jamaican/Caribbean***, daily for lunch and dinner Inexpensive to* **Moderate**

This is another of those restaurants whose popularity and high rankings on social media sites we are at a loss to explain. It's a perfectly good small neighborhood restaurant, with amiable staff, affordable prices and a comfortable setting in the heart of the Montford Historic District, but why do so many consider it one of Asheville's best restaurants? It's a mystery to us.

At dinner, you might start with hummus and natty bread (about $6). For a main course, you can have jerk trout with cauliflower, carrots and rasta peppers, sautéed in a white wine and coconut ginger curry sauce and tossed with linguine or served over basmati rice. Or try the signature dish, grilled jerk chicken with peppers, tomatoes and squash, served over pasta, quinoa or rice. Dinner entrees are $9 to $18. Lunch entrees are around $7 to $10. Beer and wine only.

Plant *165 Merrimon Ave., North Asheville, 828-258-7500, www.plantisfood.com;* **Vegan/Vegetarian**, *daily for dinner, brunch Sat.-Sun.* **Expensive**

This is not your Aunt Jane's veggie place. Plant, in a former TransSouth loan office and coffee shop, a little away from churning downtown crowds, has become what most everybody says is Asheville's best vegan and best vegetarian restaurant. Plant serves sophisticated dishes like Applewood Smoked Porto-House (no, not that porterhouse) with polenta and chard for $18 and Pecan-Crusted Seitan ($20) with "enlightened cauliflower" and broccolini. Appetizers such as Caramelized Jerusalem Artichokes are $5 to $8. For dessert, freshmade ice cream (with coconut milk) is fantastic. We had the banana ice cream with macadamia nut topping and caramel sauce ($2.50 for a single scoop). Fabulous, especially with a shot of espresso.

Plant's decor is minimalist, with just one piece of art and a window overlooking the Harris-Teeter supermarket across Merrimon. There's outside seating on the south end of the building, though it's not exactly a sidewalk-in-Paris setting. The staff is amiable. Plant now offers cocktails along with local beers and organic wines. Dinner for two with drinks or wine is likely to be $80 to $100.

Stoney Knob *337 Merrimon Ave., Weaverville, 828-645-3309, www.stoneyknobcafe.com;* **Greek-American**, *lunch and dinner Mon.-Sat., brunch Sun.* **Moderate**

Stony Knob is one of the long-time favorite neighborhood restaurants for those in Weaverville and far North Asheville. The menu is extensive and varied, the servings are large, prices are moderate to high-moderate, and service is friendly and prompt.

Words fail us in trying to describe the decor. The booths near the open kitchen remind us of a diner, while the two end dining rooms are on the funky side of interesting, with Greek busts mixing with religious sculpture and icons, all with a 1960s psychedelic twist.

On one visit, we had a selection of appetizers rather than main courses. The Greek sampler with hummus, falafel, spanakopita, pita bread, olives and cheese was huge, more than enough for an entree. The fried calamari, "Southern oysters" and fried green tomatoes were far from delicate, with heavy breading. The small Greek salad was ordinary. With one draft microbeer, a glass of wine and a Jack on the rocks, and with tip and tax, the total came to about $75, reasonable for the amount of food. Bottom line: worth considering if you're in the neighborhood, but not worth a special trip. We do admit on a recent revisit for lunch, our falafel pita sandwich (about $9) was quite good.

Vinnie's Neighborhood Italian *641 Merrimon Ave., North Asheville, www.vinniesitalian.com;* **Italian,** *open daily for dinner* **Moderate to Expensive**

Vinnie's claims to feature "old school" neighborhood Italian food reminiscent of Brooklyn, the Bronx and the North End of Boston. True, portions are large, staff is very friendly and overall the place has a nice North Asheville feel, but in our opinion the food lacks nuance and delicacy, and prices are a little high for a neighborhood eatery. On a recent revisit, our appetizer calamari ($8) was well prepared, but the blushing pink marinara dipping sauce was heavy. The veal parmigiana ($18) was a sizable hunk of veal, a little overcooked, on a huge bed of spaghetti with that pink marinara sauce. The Wednesday-special all-you-can-eat steamed mussels in a white sauce were pretty good. Pizzas (16-inch, enough to serve two) are popular here and are only $11 to $16, plus $1.75 per extra topping.

The Cream of the Crop
(In alphabetical order)
The Admiral, West Asheville
Chestnut, Downtown
Corner Kitchen, Biltmore Village
Cúrate, Downtown
Fig Bistro, Biltmore Village
The Inn on Biltmore Estate Dining Room, South Asheville
The Junction, River Arts District
Limones, Downtown
Plant, North Asheville
Rezaz, Biltmore Village

Ruth's Chris Steak House, Biltmore Village
Table, Downtown
Zambra, Downtown

Places to Eat Well at Very Affordable Prices
(In alphabetical order)
Chai Pani, Downtown
Doc Chey's Noodle House, Downtown
Food Truck Lots, Downtown
Homegrown, North Asheville
Nona Mia Ritrovo, West Asheville
Papas and Beer, West Asheville
Roman's Deli, Downtown
Sunny Point, West Asheville
12 Bones Smokehouse, River Arts District and Arden
White Duck Taco Shop, River Arts District and Downtown

Asheville's Best Pizza
(In alphabetical order)
Acropolis, South Asheville
All Souls Pizza, River Arts District
Asheville Pizza & Brewing, North Asheville
Barley's Taproom & Pizzeria, Downtown
Black Bear Pizza, South Asheville
Grand Central Pizza, North Asheville
Marco's Pizzeria, North Asheville
Mellow Mushroom, Downtown
Nona Mia Ritrovo, West Asheville
Vinnie's Neighborhood Italian, North Asheville

BEER CITY USA

"Work is the curse of the drinking classes."
--Oscar Wilde

With 20 microbreweries and brewpubs in Asheville and a total of about 40 in the Western North Carolina area, plus two large national craft breweries (Sierra Nevada and New Belgium) opening their East Coast headquarters here, Asheville has won national online polls as "Beer City USA." Beer tourism is big in Asheville, and many locals take their beers very seriously. You can expect that better local restaurants will have a large selection of artisan beers on tap.

A 2014 National Public Radio story said that Asheville has more breweries per capita than any other U.S. city and has become "a sort of Napa Valley of beer."

The new **Sierra Nevada Brewing Co.** *(100 Sierra Nevada Way, Fletcher, 828-681-5300, www.sierranevada.com)* is open at a 190-acre site in Mills River about 20 minutes south of Asheville, near the Asheville Regional Airport. The California-based craft brewery is already turning out some of the well-known Sierra Nevada beers and ales at its North Carolina brewery and is adding other specialty brews for sale in the Eastern U.S. and in Europe. Sierra Nevada opened its 400-seat restaurant and taproom in spring 2015, with 18 brews on tap. Brewery tours are offered, but these must be reserved in advance, and there can be a one-month wait for weekend tours. At opening the brewery and restaurant employed about 225, with additional staff expected to be added.

New Belgium Brewing *(Craven St., West Asheville, site update 888-598-9552, www.newbelgium.com)* broke ground in 2014 on its $175 million East Coast brewery along the French Broad River in West Asheville and the River Arts District. When completed in late 2015, it will be Asheville's largest brewery, a capacity of a half million barrels annually, including such products as Fat Tire amber ale.

There also are about a half dozen microbreweries in Upstate South Carolina, less than an hour and a half from Asheville. If you're absolutely beer-crazy, you could visit nearly 50 breweries within about a two-hour driving radius of Asheville, one of the largest concentrations of craft beer making in the entire United States.

Altamont Brewing Company *(1042 Haywood Rd., West Asheville, 828-575-2400, www.altamontbrewingcompany.com)* is a brewpub that opened on St. Patrick's Day in 2012. The funky, brick-walled taproom (under NC law it operates as a private club) has live music some evenings.

Andrews Brewing Company *(565 Aquone Rd., Andrews, 828-321-2006, www.andrewsbrewing.com)* is a small brewer in the small town of Andrews. The store is open from noon to 5 pm Mon.-Tue. and Thu.-Sat. We love the 1950s-style logo.

Appalachian Mountain Brewery *(163 Boone Creek Dr, Boone, 828-263-1111, www.appalachianmountainbrewery.com) is a prolific brewery in Boone that has produced some 50 different beers, ales and ciders.* The tasting room has a 120-foot bar and outdoor seating (with heaters) overlooking two creeks.

Asheville Brewing Co. *(77 Coxe Ave., Downtown Asheville, 828-255-4077; www.ashevillebrewing.com)* makes beer at its downtown microbrewery and pub, and also sells its suds in a converted movie theater in North Asheville, **Asheville Pizza & Brewing** (675 Merrimon Ave., 828-254-1281). Here you can enjoy a second-run movie ($3, and often sold out), a pizza or burger and a freshly brewed beer, seated on sofas and reclining chairs. An expansion in 2014 increased the brewery's capacity to 13,000 barrels a year.

Bearwaters Brewery *(130 Frazier St., #7, Waynesville, 828-246-0602),* formerly Headwaters Brewing, usually has around 10 craft beers on tap in its tasting room.

Biltmore Brewing Company *(1 Approach Rd., Biltmore Estate, 828-225-1333, www.biltmore.com)* sells a small line of Biltmore Estate beers called Cedric, supposedly named after one of the Vanderbilt family dogs. However, the beer is not brewed by Biltmore locally but by another company for Biltmore.

Blind Squirrel Brewery *(4716 South Hwy. 19E, Plumtree, 828-765-2739, www.blindsquirrelbrewery.com)* is an Avery County brewer in the High Country associated with Toe River Lodge. It also has a small winery. Blind Squirrel – don't ask us where the name came from -- has done about 15 different beers. The restaurant and lodge are open Mother's Day through October.

Blowing Rock Brewing *(152 Sunset Dr., Blowing Rock, 828-414-9600, www.blowingrockbrewing.com),* associated with Blowing Rock Ale House and Inn, specializes in ales. The restaurant serves a mean bison burger. The same company brews beer in Hickory.

Blue Mountain Pizza and Brewpub *(55 N. Main St., Weaverville, 828-658-8778, www.bluemountainpizza.com)*, a Weaverville bar and pizza place that added brewing, specializes in Belgian and American ales. The bar has live music many nights.

Boojum Brewing Company *(50 N. Main St., Waynesville, 828-944-0888, www.boojumbrewing.com)* is a taproom and microbrewer in downtown Waynesville. It opened in late 2014.

Brevard Brewing Company *(63 East Main St., Brevard, 828-885-2101, www.brevard-brewing.com)* says it is the only brewery in the area to specialize in producing lagers. It does German-style lagers but also brews some American ales. Brevard Brewing expanded its capacity in 2014.

Burial Beer Co. *(40 Collier Ave., South Slope, Downtown Asheville, www.burialbeer.com)*, owned by folks who moved here from Seattle, opened in Asheville in mid-2013. Most nights its South Slope taproom will have about a dozen Burial Beer brews.

Catawba Valley Brewing Company *(212 S. Green St., Morganton, 828-430-6883, www.catawbavalleybrewingcompany.com)*, formerly in Glen Alpine, brews a selection of ales year-round, along with several seasonal beers. It also has a tasting room in Asheville at *(63 Brook St., 828-424-7290)* and is opening a boutique brewery in Asheville at 32 Banks Avenue in 2015.

Dry County Brewing Company *(585 Oak Ave., Spruce Pine, 828-765-4583, www.drycountybrewing.com)* is a small brewpub/pizzeria in downtown Spruce Pine.

Flat Top Brewing Company *(567 Main St. East, Banner Elk, 828-898-8677, www.flattopbrewing)* is a nice place to sit in front of the fireplace and enjoy an IPA after hiking or skiing.

French Broad Brewing Company *(101-D Fairview Rd., South Asheville, 828-277-0222 www.frenchbroadbrewery.com)* brews lagers and specialty ales. Wee-Heavy-Er, Scottish ale, is a best seller. The tasting room near Biltmore Village has live music some nights, usually on weekends.

Frog Level Brewing Company *(56 Commerce St., Waynesville, 828-254-5664, www.froglevelbrewing.com)* is a new brewer in the up-and-coming Frog Level section below downtown Waynesville. One of its beers is named Lily's Cream Boy, after the owner's sphinx cat, and another beer from rye is called, uh, Catcher in the Rye.

Funkatorium *(145 Coxe Ave, South Slope, Downtown Asheville, 828-552-3203, www.wickedweedbrewing.com)* opened in late 2014 as the latest addition to the Wicked Weed operation. It specializes in barrel and sour beers. There's a tasting room with indoor and outdoor seating for more than 150. The Funkatorium is expected to have about 1,000 barrels of sour beer aging in the back room.

Green Man Brewery *(23 Buxton Ave., Downtown Asheville, 828-252-5502, www.greenmanbrewery.com)* is one of North Carolina's oldest microbreweries, having opened in 1997 as a brewpub (part of Jack of the Wood bar). In 2010 new owners turned Green Man into an independent brewer specializing in ales. Green Man expanded in 2012 with a 30-barrel system and in 2013 began bottling its beers in 12-ounce bottles. The company is in its third expansion, this one costing $4 million. It will include a new 18,000-square-foot building with a packaging facility, retail store and ale garden. Its best-known product is the very hoppy Green Man IPA. The expanded facility on Buxton Avenue is expected to be completed in late 2015. The Green Man historically is a representation of a man's face made of leaves and vines, often seen in churches in Europe. It is a popular name for pubs in England; there's a Green Man Pub in the basement of Harrods in London.

Heinzelmännchen Brewery *(545 Mill St., Sylva, 828-631-4466; www.yourgnometownbrewery.com)*, run by German-born *brewmeister* Dieter Kuhn, concentrates entirely on ales in two-liter glass growlers or in 5- or 15-gallon kegs for carry-out. The ales must be kept refrigerated.

Highland Brewing Company *(12 Old Charlotte Hwy., Suite H, South Asheville, 828-299-3370, www.highlandbrewing.com)* is Asheville's first (1994) and largest microbrewer. Highland's year-round brews including Oatmeal Porter, Gaelic Ale and Black Mocha Stout and its seasonal beers are available in many restaurants and in supermarkets around the Southeast. The latest expansion boosted capacity to around 50,000 barrels a year. Brewery tours, which take about 30 minutes, are offered several times daily. The Highland tasting room also is open daily, generally from 4 pm, earlier on weekends. There's no charge for tours, but a donation to MAANA Food Bank is requested.

Hi-Wire Brewery *(197 Hilliard Ave., Downtown Asheville, www.hiwirebrewing.com)* in mid-2013 took over the site of the late, lamented **Craggie Brewing,** which closed in late 2012. It offers four year-round brews -- Prime Time Pale, Hi-Pitch IPA, Bed of Nails Brown and Hi-Wire Lager – plus seasonal beers in its tasting room and other outlets.

Lexington Avenue Brewery *(39 N. Lexington Ave., Downtown Asheville, 828-252-0212, www.lexavebrew.com)*, locally known as LAB, is a popular brewpub and restaurant. LAB produced more than 25 regular and seasonal brew, including several Belgian-style wheat ales, hoppy IPAs and rich stouts. Open daily with live music many nights.

Lookout Brewing Company *(103 S. Ridgeway Ave. #1, Black Mountain, 828-357-5169, www.lookoutbrewing.com)* uses mostly locally grown malted grain and hops, and Mozart's music is played during the fermentation process.

Lost Province Brewing Co. *(130 N. Depot St., Boone, 828-265-3506, www.lostprovince.com)* is a microbrewer and wood-fired pizza restaurant in downtown Boone, just behind Mast General Store. It's popular with App State students.

Nantahala Brewing Company *(61 Depot St., Bryson City, 828-488-2337, http://nantahalabrewing.wordpress.com)* opened in 2010 near Great Smoky Mountains Railroad depot in Bryson City. Its inaugural and flagship beer is Noon Day IPA, and it also offers the easy-drinking Bryson City Brown. Its tasting room is open daily (hours vary) March-October, with reduced hours the rest of the year. Tours and tastings, which cost $15 and include a flight of six beers and a mug, are held on weekends.

One World Brewery *(10 Patton Ave., Downtown Asheville, 828-785-5580, www.oneworldbrewing.com)* is located between Farm Burger and Salsa's in Downtown Asheville. It has a small 1½ barrel system and 10 taps.

Oskar Blues Brewery *(Railroad Ave., Brevard, www.oskarblues.com)* is a Longmont, Colo., Top 50 craft brewer that in late 2012 opened a new 30,000 sq. ft. brewery and a separate restaurant in Brevard. Oskar Blues founder Dale Katechis chose Brevard in part because he has long mountain biked in the area. In 2014, the company bought 145 acres near the brewery for use as a bicycle park.

Oyster House Brewing Company *(625 Haywood Rd., West Asheville, www.oysterhousebeers.com)* is associated with the Lobster Trap restaurant. It moved to a location across from Sunny Point restaurant in West Asheville in mid-2013, where it brews around 10 varieties of beer, ale and stout. Its Moonstone Stout is brewed with oysters.

Pisgah Brewing Company *(150 Eastside Dr., Black Mountain, 828-669-0190, www.pisgahbrewing.com)* just east of Black Mountain is a certified organic brewer that puts out around five year-round beers, ales and stouts, not including about 30 seasonal and specialty brews. Its best-known product is probably Pisgah Pale Ale, available in half-gallon growlers. Free brewery tours are offered at 3:15 pm on Saturdays.

Satulah Mountain Brewing Company *(454 Carolina Way, Highlands, 828-482-9794, www.satulahmountainbrewing.com)* is a bar and brewpub at an elevation of 4,118 feet. It has about a dozen of its own and other microbrews on tap, with live music on some Fridays.

Southern Appalachian Craft Brewery *(822 Locust St., Hendersonville, 828-684-1235; www.sabrewery.com)*, formerly Appalachian Brewery in Fletcher, has a dog-friendly tasting room in downtown Hendersonville serving their pilsner, blonde and amber ales, IPA and stout beers on draft, along with pretzels.

Thirsty Monk Open Brewing *(Gerber Village, 1836 Hendersonville Rd., South Asheville, 828-505-4564, www.monkpub.com)* in Gerber Village bills itself as the first commercial brewpub for homebrewers. Under the same ownership are the Thirsty Monk craft beer bars, with its main location Downtown sporting 60 tap lines, plus two other locations. It also has a craft cocktails bar, the Top of the Monk.

Tipping Point Tavern *(190 N. Main St., Waynesville, 828-246-9230, www.tippingpointtavern.com)* is a bar and brewpub in downtown Waynesville.

Twin Leaf Brewery *(144 Coxe Ave., Downtown Asheville, www.twinleafbrewery.com)* is a new brewpub in the South Slope brews about a half-dozen beers.

Urban Orchard Cider Co. and Bar *(210 Haywood Rd., West Asheville, 828-774-5151, www.urbanorchardcider.com)* specializes in making its own hard cider, not beer, but we've included it here. It does have some local beers on tap and also serves beer in its tasting room. Urban Orchard gets all its apples from Hendersonville and makes a variety of delicious ciders.

Wedge Brewing Co. *(125B Roberts St., River Arts District, 828-279-6393; www.wedgebrewing.com)* brews artisan beers in the River Arts District. In good weather, you can join the crowds in a picnic area outside, where there are also food trucks. Movies are sometimes shown outside under the stars.

Wicked Weed Brewing *(91 Biltmore Ave., Downtown Asheville, 828-575-9599; www.wickedweedbrewing.com).* opened in late 2012 near the Orange Peel and instantly became one of Asheville's most popular brewpubs. There's a good restaurant upstairs, serving pub food and a little more, including steaks and trout, in a beautifully built out space with raw brick and a glassed-in open kitchen. Prices are a good value. The tasting room and brewery are downstairs. The **Funkatorium** at 145 Coxe Avenue in the South Slope area is Wicked Weed's brewery on the South Slope, specializing in barrel and sour beers. Wicked Week also is building a large production brewery in Enka-Candler, in the new Ingles center on Sand Hill Road.

Brews Cruises

Amazing Pubcycle *(828-214-5010, www.amazingpubcycle.com)* is the people-powered way to see some of Asheville. The custom-made Pubcycle seats 13 –10 pedalers and three non-pedalers -- who bike their way around town (the Pubcycle has a motor to assist on hills). Tours, which generally start at the Aloft Hotel on Biltmore Avenue, take 40 minutes to 1½ hours and cost from $13 to $23. The longer tours make one or two stops, usually at Ben's Tune-Up and at Pack's Tavern. You can BYOB (beer and wine only) and sip while you tour.

Asheville Brewery Tours *(101 N. Lexington Ave., 828-233-5006, www.ashevillebrewerytours.com)* offers a variety of van and walking tours. The walking tours usually visit about four microbreweries in Downtown Asheville, and the van tours about the same number. There also are tours that visit breweries in Black Mountain and elsewhere. Most tours cost $59 for drinkers, $29 for non-drinkers. The tour guides seem to know their beer.

Asheville Brews Cruise *(*828-545-5181*; www.brewscruise.com)* takes beer fans on tours of three or four local breweries for $55-$57 per person. Van tours last about three hours and visit three or four breweries. Offered some days are walking tours, also $55 per person. This was Asheville's first beer tour company, founded in 2008, and has since expanded to Charleston, S.C., Denver, Atlanta and elsewhere.

BREW-ed (828-278-9255, www.brew-ed.com) offers tours of about three breweries and brewpubs in Downtown Asheville. Tours, which must be booked 72 hours in advance, start at 2 pm on Fridays, Saturdays and Sundays, leaving from Asheville Brewing Company at 77 Coxe Avenue. Cost is $50 per person, and all participants must be at least 21 years old.

Beer Festivals

The city has several beer festivals. **Beer City Fest** *(www.ashevillebeerweek.com)* is a part of Asheville Beer Week, sponsored by the Asheville Brewers Alliance and held in late May and early June at Roger McGuire Green at Pack Square Park in Downtown Asheville. **Brewgrass Festival** *(www.brewgrassfestival.com)* on a Saturday in mid-September showcases more than 40 microbrewers in Martin Luther King Park just east of downtown Asheville, along with a line-up of bluegrass and country musicians. Asheville's own little **Oktoberfest** *(www.ashevilledowntown.org)* is a one-day happening in mid-October on cobblestoned Wall Street Downtown. It's sponsored by the Downtown Asheville Association.

Winter Warmer Beer Festival *(www.ashevillebeerfest.com)* is held in late January in the US Cellular Center in downtown Asheville, with around two dozen local and regional brewers participating.

For news and information on the beer scene in Asheville, read Tony Kiss ("the Beer Guy") in the *Asheville Citizen-Times* or check the frequent brewing updates in *Mountain Xpress*. The **Asheville Ale Trail** website *(www.ashevillealetrail.com)* features news on breweries and beers in the Asheville area.

Taverns with Big Beer Selections

Though they don't brew beer onsite, these Asheville bars and taverns are known for their large selection of craft beers. Most also offer wines and liquors in addition to beers. Also, see the chapter on restaurants for information on other dining spots with good beer selections.

Barley's Taproom & Pizzeria *(42 Biltmore Ave., Downtown Asheville, 828-255-0504, www.barleystaproom.com)* has more than 40 draft beers on tap. The restaurant, main bar and stage for live music are on the first floor. On the second level is the Billiard Room with four regulation billiard tables and five darts lanes.

Bier Garden *(46 Haywood St., Downtown Asheville, 828-285-0002, www.ashevillebiergarden.com)* offers about 200 different beers, including around 30 on draft, most priced at $4 to $5 for a pint. It also serves wine and has a full liquor bar.

Bruisin' Ales *(66 Broadway St., Downtown Asheville, 828-252-8999, www.bruisin-ales.com)* is a package store, not a bar. It claims to sell 1,000 different beers. Closed Monday.

Bywater *(796 Riverside Dr., North Asheville, 828-232-6967, www.bywaterbar.com)*, a unique combination of picnic grounds and bar near the French Broad River, has 18 mostly local beers on tap, served in 20-ounce portions. Bring your own food and cook it on one of the charcoal grills beside the bar, or buy from a rotating food truck. Bywater is set up as a private club, due to licensing laws, which essentially means one member of your party must pay a $5 membership fee. Live music most nights.

Jack of the Wood *(95 Patton Ave., Downtown Asheville, 828-252-5445, www.jackofthewood.com)* is a Celtic-style bar that features English ales from Green Man Brewery along with many other microbrews.

Pack's Tavern *(20 S. Spruce St., Downtown Asheville, 828-225-6944, www.packstavern.com)*, in a historic building facing Pack Square Park, offers more than 30 local and other microbrew beers on draft, along with a full menu.

Tasty Beverage Co. *(162 Coxe Ave., South Slope, Downtown Asheville, www.tastybeverageco.com)*, long known for its Raleigh store with a huge selection of beers, has a new 4,500 sq. ft. store in the South Slope area of Asheville.

Thirsty Monk *(92 Patton Ave., Downtown Asheville, 828-254-5470, www.monkpub.com)* has around 60 tap lines with a rotating list of draft beers. It claims that over the course of a year the bar serves more than 1,200 different beers. **Top of the Monk**, a cocktail bar, is in the same building. Thirsty Monk has two other bar locations in Buncombe County. Its **Open Brewing** brewpub in Gerber Village in South Asheville focuses on home brewers.

Westville Pub *(777 Haywood Rd., West Asheville, 828-225-9782, www.westvillepub.com)* has food and a decent selection of local craft beers.

CLUBS AND NIGHTLIFE

"The problem with the world is that everyone is a few drinks behind."

--Humphrey Bogart

Drinkers and clubbers are fickle, so music clubs, watering holes and dive bars tend to change frequently. For the latest hotspots and openings and closings, see Asheville's *Mountain Xpress* newspaper (a free tabloid-size paper published every Wednesday) or check review sites such as Yelp and TripAdvisor on the internet.

Note that a number of the clubs and bars in Asheville are "membership clubs," which basically means that under rather ridiculous North Carolina beverage control laws the bars don't serve enough food to qualify for a restaurant liquor license (to do so food sales must total at least 30% of revenue), so they are licensed as private clubs. This doesn't mean you can't go in and drink, but you'll have to pay a small fee (sometimes as little as $1), separate from any cover or admission charge, to join the private club, or often you can be signed in as a guest of a member.

Here are some of the Asheville nightspots popular at the time of this writing in 2015. *For more options see also the Beer City USA and Dining sections.*

Music Clubs and Listening Rooms

Barley's Tap Room *(42 Biltmore Ave., Downtown Asheville, 828-255-0504, www.barleystaproom.com)* has live bluegrass and other music three or four nights a week, with no cover charge. The bar and restaurant (serving pizza, wraps and burgers) on the first level offers about two dozen microbrews on draft, and a second bar upstairs has a pool table, darts and more taps. Despite the fact that this is a bar, Barley's is family friendly.

Broadway's *(113 Broadway, Downtown Asheville, 828-285-0400)* is a dive bar with a good jukebox and a pool table and cheap PBR on the first floor. Live music, mostly garage rock, happens on the second floor. The popular 80s night is on Wednesday and attracts a local crowd. This is a private club, so you have to join or sign in as a guest.

Bywater *(796 Riverside Dr., North Asheville, 828-232-6967,* www.bywaterbar.com*)* is a unique combination of picnic grounds, bar and music club near the French Broad River. Bring your own food and cook it on one of the charcoal grills beside the bar, or buy from a rotating food truck. Bywater is set up as a private club, with a $5 membership fee. Live music most nights.

Grey Eagle *(185 Clingman Ave., River Arts District, 828-232-5800,* www.thegreyeagle.com*)* in the River Arts District is a popular listening room with live music most nights. Mostly this is a rock venue, with national and local bands. Some name artists like Loudon Wainwright III, Chris Smither and Arlo Guthrie have played here. Ticket prices vary but range from around $10 to $25 and usually with no age limitation. There's contra dancing on Mondays and occasional open mic nights. By day, Grey Eagle is a taco restaurant.

Isis Restaurant & Music Hall *(743 Haywood Rd., West Asheville, 828-575-2737,* www.isisasheville.com*),* in a full-tilt renovation of the old Isis Theater, most recently Pastabilities restaurant, comes alive with music after 10 pm. On the ground level, after you enter under a faux movie theater marquee, there's a dining area in the front of the restaurant and the main music stage at the back (where the movie screen was), with a bar connecting the two areas. On the second level, a more intimate bar/lounge, with a piano and small stage, is ideal for a lounge lizard or jazz trio. Overlooking the main music stage is a standing area for drinkers and music listeners. Music is an eclectic mix of bluegrass, rock and reggae, with jazz or a lounge singer upstairs. Drinks at Isis are moderately priced, with cocktails mostly $6 to $10, wine around $7 or $8 a glass and draft micro-brew beers mostly $4.

Jack of the Wood *(95 Patton Ave., Downtown Asheville, 828-252-5445,* www.jackofthewood.com*)* is a comfortable, friendly Celtic-style bar Downtown featuring English ales from Green Man Brewery. The music is mostly acoustic, with bluegrass picking and Irish tunes.

Lexington Avenue Brewery *(39 N. Lexington Ave., Downtown Asheville, 828-252-0212,* www.lexavebrew.com*),* known as LAB, is a popular brewpub and restaurant. Open daily with live music many nights in a recently renovated music room. If you don't want to go home, there's a hostel, Sweet Peas, above LAB.

The Mothlight at Mr. Fred's *(701 Haywood Rd., West Asheville,* www.themothlight.com*),* new in the fall of 2013 at the location of Mr. Fred's Beds, is open daily except Sundays from 5 pm to 2 am.

There's live music most nights, mainly by local and regional bands, and you can dance. Tickets are usually $10 to $15. The Mothlight space has brick walls and a West Asheville feel. Street parking is available along Haywood Road; avoid parking in areas marked for local residents only.

The Odditorium *(1045 Haywood Rd., West Asheville, 828-575-9299, www.ashevilleodditorium.com)* is a funky bar and music room, featuring punk, indie garage rock and metal bands. Currently, Tuesday night is the open mic Comedy Freak Show.

Orange Peel Social Aid and Pleasure Club *(101 Biltmore Ave., Downtown Asheville, 828-225-5851, www.theorangepeel.net)* is Asheville's top mid-size venue for live music. In the 1950s the building that now houses the Orange Peel was a skating rink, and then it became a series of R&B clubs. It opened as the Orange Peel in 2002. In 2007, the Smashing Pumpkins played a nine-night gig at the Orange Peel, drawing national attention since this was the group's first performance in the U.S. in six years. The next year, *Rolling Stone* named it one of the top five rock clubs in the country.

Although it features many local and regional bands, it has hosted a number of big names, including Bob Dylan, Joan Jett, Blondie, Beastie Boys and Modest Mouse. After an expansion in 2009, the club now can handle up to 1,100 standing. And we do mean standing – there's limited seating at the Orange Peel so be prepared to stay on your feet. The dance floor has springy wood slats. The PULP is a private club below the main level, seating up to 150 and serving drinks. The Orange Peel doesn't have a parking lot, so you'll need to park on the street or in nearby lots such as the City of Asheville garage under the Aloft Hotel. (When popular groups are at the Orange Peel, you'll pay event parking rates at the Aloft garage, generally $7.) If you don't have a car or don't feel you should drive, when you're ready to leave the club will call a taxi for you. Ticket prices at the Orange Peel vary from around $5 to $35, and more for a few acts.

Tressa's Jazz and Blues Club *(28 Broadway, Downtown Asheville, 828-254-7072, www.tressas.com; closed Sun.-Tues.)* at one time was a lesbian club, but Tressa's is now more focused on a broader audience and on its jazzy, bluesy music (think New Orleans) though it still gets a significant LGBT crowd. Tressa's has a full bar. It operates as a private membership club, usually has a cover ($5 or so) and attracts an older crowd than some of the other clubs.

Bars and Taverns

The Admiral *(400 Haywood Rd., West Asheville, 828-252-2541, www.theadmiralnc.com)* you probably would consider more of a dive restaurant (but an excellent one) than a dive bar, but some people consider it both. It does have a divey bar feeling, dark, with low ceilings, and it's in a concrete block building in a downscale section of West Asheville's Haywood Road. It's usually packed, though, so it's not a place you can just drop in for a beer. On weekends, after dinner they stack up the tables and chairs and people dance.

Asheville Yacht Club *(98 Patton Ave., Downtown Asheville, 828-255-8454, www.ashevilleyachtclub.com)* is a take off on a 1950s tiki bar with strong drinks (most $9) and bar food. Open daily from 4.

Battery Park Book Exchange & Champagne Bar *(Grove Arcade, 1 Page Ave., Downtown Asheville, 828-252-0200, www.batteryparkbookexchange.com),* relocated to the Grove Arcade from the Battery Park Senior Apartments, is a combination used book store (with some 22,000 titles) and a wine and champagne bar (you also can get beer). Books and wine – what a great concept! This is one of Asheville's jewels.

Ben's Tune Up *(195 Hilliard Ave., South Slope, Downtown Asheville, 828-424-7580, www.benstuneup.com)* is a restaurant and sake brewery, but after dinner hours, as the night wears on, it turns into a bar with dancing. Sometimes there's a DJ.

Bier Garden *(46 Haywood St., Downtown Asheville, 828-285-0002, www.ashevillebiergarden.com)* offers about 200 different beers, including around 30 on draft, most priced at under $5 a pint.

Red Stag Bar at Bohemian Hotel *(11 Boston Way, Biltmore Village, 828-505-2949, www.bohemianhotelasheville.com)* with its garish decor, heavy on the reds, may put you mind of an old New Orleans bordello, but if you're in Biltmore Village it's a convenient place to get an after-dinner drink.

DeSoto Lounge *(504 Haywood Rd., West Asheville, 828-255-1109, www.desotolounge.com)* was voted Asheville's best dive bar by *Mountain Xpress* readers. Limited bar food, mostly small plates and sandwiches. There's Ethiopian food on Tuesdays. Jukebox with a lot of indie music, pinball and foosball. Very loud.

Double Crown *(375 Haywood Rd., West Asheville, 828-575-9060, www.thedoublecrown.com)* is a hipster bar in a house in West Asheville with a good jukebox and reasonably priced drinks, kitschy art and photos on the walls and bar and a big sofa. There's a DJ several nights a week.

5 Walnut Wine Bar *(5 W. Walnut, Downtown Asheville, 828-253-2593, www.5walnut.com)* has added more jazz and other music, so now it's a place to hear music, not just to have a quiet glass of wine. Lots of brick and wood, and the wines are affordable, most $7 or $8 a glass.

Great Hall Bar at Omni Grove Park Inn *(290 Macon Ave., North Asheville, 828-252-2711, www.groveparkinn.com)* in the bar in the lobby of the century-old resort, but what a lobby this is! Two 14-foot wide stone fireplaces bookend the historic room, and you can wander out to the Sunset Terrace dining room and take in the views of Asheville. Drinks are fairly expensive -- signature cocktails are $12 to $16 and aren't big pours, beers are around $5 and wine by the glass averages $10 – but you're paying for the ambiance and part of the hotel overhead.

The Imperial Life *(48 College St., Downtown Asheville, 828-254-8980, www.imperialbarasheville.com)* above Table restaurant and under the same ownership, is a cozy, sophisticated craft cocktail bar. There's limited food service – think cheese and charcuterie plates – and creative cocktails by experienced mixologists. Some customers dance.

The Junction *(348 Depot St., River Arts District, 828-225-3497, www.thejunctionasheville.com)* is primarily a restaurant with a hip River Arts District atmosphere, but it has an interesting drinks selection. The cocktails menu (mostly $9 to $12) is one of the most creative in town. In good weather there's outside seating.

Lex 18 *(18 N. Lexington Ave., Downtown Asheville, 828-620-5404, www.lex18avl.com)* is a supper club, an "Appalachian restaurant" with a speakeasy atmosphere, a dinner theater and a moonshine bar. Put all that in your pipe and smoke it. Most of the talk seems to be about the moonshine bar, which serves about 20 kinds of (legally distilled) moonshine from distilleries in North Carolina, Tennessee, Georgia and Kentucky.

MG Road *(19 Wall St., Downtown Asheville, 828-254-4363, www.mgroadlounge.com)* is a cocktail bar by the owners of, and round the corner from, Chai Pani. It also serves food currently sourced from Chef Elliott Moss at Thunderbird restaurant.

Nightbell Restaurant and *Lounge (32 S. Lexington Ave., Downtown Asheville, 828-575-0375, www.thenightbell.com)* began as a cocktail bar by the chef-owner of Cúrate around the corner but quickly evolved into a restaurant-cum-bar with innovative small plates and a creative cocktail list. Some cocktails use nitrogen. The bar and restaurant are on the second floor.

The Prospect *(11 Buxton Ave., South Slope, Downtown Asheville, 828-505-0766)*. This is a no-frills old-school bar with a jukebox and a pool table.

Rankin Vault Cocktail Lounge *(7 Rankin Ave., Downtown Asheville, 828-254-4993, www.rankinvault.com)* is dark, popular and mostly local, with cocktails moderately priced at around $7 to $9 for most. It does have an actual room-sized bank vault. Parking is handy across the street at the City of Asheville's Rankin garage.

Santé Wine Bar & Tap Room *(Grove Arcade, Suite 152, 1 Page Ave., Downtown Asheville, 828-254-8188)* serves both wine and beer out of kegs. There's also wine in bottles. In good weather there's outdoor seating.

Social Lounge and Tapas, formerly Sazarac *(29 Broadway St., Downtown Asheville, 828-575-9005, www.socialloungeasheville.com)* is Asheville's take on an adult cocktail bar. There's bar (and limited table) seating on the main level, and an appealing rooftop bar upstairs.

Sovereign Remedies *(29 Market St., Downtown Asheville, www.sovereignremedies.com,* new in late 2014, serves coffee, teas, lunch and dinner, but its main focus is on craft cocktails. The setting is appealing, with high ceilings, lots of plants and wood.

Sky Bar *(18 Battery Park Ave., Downtown Asheville, 828-225-6998)* in the historic Flat Iron Building is Asheville's bar with a view. The bar literally is on the fire escapes of the sixth, seventh and eighth floors, with nice views to the west especially at sunset. To get there, believe it or not, you take an elevator with a real live attendant. There's no cover charge but there is a one-drink minimum, and the drinks are a little on the pricey side ($10 or so).

Storm Rhum Bar and Bistro *(125 S. Lexington, Downtown Asheville, 828-505-8560, www.stormrhumbar.com)* is more of a restaurant than a bar, but you can get cocktails ($8 to $12) and a good burger with fresh-ground meat. Fairly dark, and it can be a bit noisy.

Thirsty Monk *(92 Patton Ave., Downtown Asheville, 828-254-5470, www.monkpub.com)* has around 60 tap lines with a rotating list of draft beers. Over the course of a year the bar says it serves more than 1,000 different beers. Some complain about the relatively high cost of brews here. In the same building is the **Top of the Monk** cocktail bar, with drinks mostly $9 to $13.

Timo's House *(5 Biltmore Ave., Downtown Asheville, 828-575-2886, www.timos-house.com),* near Pack Square, with a DJ and dancing most nights, bills itself as "Asheville's underground party house."

Tiger Mountain Thirst Parlour *(103 Broadway St., Downtown Asheville, 828-407-0666)* opened in mid-2012 on the lower end of Broadway near the expressway and was an instant hit. (It was voted "Best Scenester Bar" in one *Mountain Xpress* poll.) Kitschy atmosphere with red lights and velvet paintings. Some consider it a singles spot.

Wedge Brewing Company *(125B Roberts St., River Arts District, 828-505-2792, www.wedgebrewing.com)* in the old Farmer's Federation Building in the River Arts District is one of Asheville's most popular brewpubs. A kid's playground and picnic/seating area is outside. The bar doesn't serve food, except free peanuts, but you can buy Korean BBQ or tacos from food trucks that set up here. In summer, the Wedge shows movies outdoors. The bar is very dog friendly.

Westville Pub *(777 Haywood Rd., West Asheville, 828-225-9782, www.westvillepub.com)* is a popular West Asheville bar with live music many nights. Food is so-so.

Wicked Weed Brewing *(91 Biltmore Ave., Downtown Asheville, 828-575-9599; www.wickedweedbrewing.com)*, next to the Orange Peel, opened in late 2012 and instantly became one of Asheville's most popular brewpubs. There's a good restaurant upstairs, serving pub food and more, including steaks, mussels and trout, in a beautifully built out space with raw brick and a glassed-in open kitchen. Prices are a good value. The tasting room and brewery are downstairs, and Wicked Weed's new **Funkatorium** featuring barrel and sour beer is on Coxe Avenue in the South Slope.

W xyz Bar at Aloft Hotel *(51 Biltmore Ave., Downtown Asheville, 828-232-2838, www.aloftashevilledowntown.com)* is on the second floor of the hotel. You can sit at stools at the bar, in chairs in eye-popping colors or sip your drink on an outdoor ledge patio overlooking Biltmore Avenue. **Re:mix** lounge, connected to W xyz bar, has free Wi-Fi and a pool table.

LGBT Bars and Clubs

O. Henry's *(237 Haywood St., Downtown Asheville, 828-254-1891, www.ohenrysofasheville.com)* is one of the oldest gay bars in North Carolina, usually attracting an older, quieter male gay crowd. The Underground at O. Henry's is a second bar and dance space at the club.

Scandals Nightclub *(11 Grove St., Downtown Asheville, 828-252-2838, www.scandalsnightclub.com)*, around for more than 30 years, is usually considered Asheville's top gay bar, though many patrons are not LGBT. It's actually three venues in one, part of a complex of clubs and bars at historic 11 Grove Street, at one time Asheville's YMCA, the others being Boiler Room (a live music space) and Club Eleven on Grove (a somewhat quieter lounge). The main Scandals Nightclub has a lot of room for dancing, drag shows and live music.

Smokey's After Dark *(18 Broadway, Downtown Asheville, 828-253-2155)* is a small, long-established gay bar with a jukebox and a couple of pool tables in the back.

WINERIES AND DISTILLERIES

"I cook with wine. Sometimes I even add it to the food."
-- W.C. Fields

Asheville is known as for its beer microbreweries, but the area is also home to a number of thriving wineries, including the most visited winery in the country, Biltmore, and now to three small liquor distilleries.

Wineries and Vineyards

North Carolina has more than 400 vineyards and 100 wineries. About 20 of the wineries are in Western North Carolina.

The Piedmont of North Carolina, immediately east of the mountains, with its milder winters and longer growing season, has the most vineyards and wineries in the state. The biggest cluster of wineries and vineyards is in the Yadkin Valley northwest and southwest of Winston-Salem, home to some three dozen wine operations.

The Carolina mountains, with winter temperatures sometimes dropping below zero, and killing frosts possible in some mountains areas from October to May, are not easy places to grow wine grapes. However, some enterprising mountain vintners have succeeded in creating very drinkable chardonnay, riesling, sauvignon blanc, merlot, syrah and cabernet sauvignon wines.

Here are some selected winery operations in the mountains. Hours for vineyards and wineries vary seasonally. Call or email in advance to see if the places you want to visit are open and accepting visitors. Most tours and wine-tastings are free, except where noted otherwise, though you likely will be encouraged to buy a bottle or two of wine.

Don't expect the Napa Valley.

Note that you must be at least 21 to participate in a wine, beer or distilled liquor tasting.

Addison Farms Vineyards *(NC Hwy. 63, Leicester, www.addisonfarms.net),* a 55-acre family farm, has around 4 acres in mostly French-American hybrid wine grapes, with plans to expand to around 10 acres. It produces cabernet sauvignon, cabernet franc, sangiovese, montepulciano, petit verdot and petit manseng. A tasting room opened in late 2012.

Banner Elk Winery *(60 Deer Run Lane, Banner Elk, 828-260-1790, www.bannerelkwinery.com)* produces about a half dozen wines from its own French-American hybrid grapes and from grapes from other local producers. Its cabernet sauvignon, seyval blanc and marechal foch wines have won medals at the North Carolina State Fair in Raleigh. Tastings and tours are scheduled year-round, with varying hours. The winery also offers a villa for overnight stays.

Biltmore Winery *(Antler Hill Village, Asheville, 800-411-3812 or 828-225-1333, www.biltmore.com)* with more than 700,000 visitors a year, is America's most-visited winery, mostly because a visit to the winery (the modern fermentation room and a rather unimpressive wine cellar) and tasting room is included in estate admission, and the estate gets more than a million visitors a year. There's often a long line for the tasting, especially in the late afternoon. Tasting of Biltmore's standard reds, whites and rosés, a total of about 20 kinds, is complimentary, but there's an up charge of $3 for each premium wine. Biltmore first planted wine grapes in 1971, and now there are more than 94 acres in vineyard, producing some 250 tons of grapes. Biltmore makes chardonnay, riesling, viognier, cabernet franc, cabernet sauvignon and merlot, some from grapes grown on the estate but most, about 80%, from grapes purchased from other vineyards, mainly in California and Washington State. (The North Carolina mountain climate is not always friendly for growing French and hybrid French-American wine grapes; in the winter of 1995 the estate lost 100 acres of vines to three days of extreme cold.) The first Biltmore wines, especially the reds, were barely drinkable, but thanks to Biltmore winemasters Philippe Jourdain and later Bernard Delille and winemaker Sharon Fenchak the reputation of the winery has greatly improved in recent years, and the estate's wines have won many awards in national and international competitions. The wine is bottled under three labels: Biltmore, Century and Biltmore Estate. The Biltmore Estate labeled wines are made only from North Carolina grapes. Biltmore wines are sold at the winery shop and in stores in more than 20 states. The winery is open 365 days a year.

Burnshirt Vineyards *(2695 Sugarloaf Rd., Hendersonville, 828-685-2402, www.burntshirtvineyards.com)* has 25 acres of grapes in production in Henderson County. Its gruner veltliner and merlot wines have won awards. Tours are offered at 2 pm Wednesday to Sunday, or by reservation.

Calaboose Cellars *(565 Aquona Rd., Andrews, 828-321-2006, www.calaboosecellars.com)* claims to be the smallest freestanding complete winemaking operation in the country. The 300 square foot winery is located in the former jail in the little town of Andrews. Calaboose grows some of its grapes on its own and leased land near Andrews. It has seyval, chambourcin, chancellor and catawba grapes.

Grandfather Vineyard & Winery *(225 Vineyard Lane, Banner Elk, 828-963-2400, www.grandfathervineyard.com)* produces a dozen or so wines, mostly from purchased grapes. Wine tasting are $8, afternoons Wednesday-Sunday April to October, reduced hours rest of year.

Lake James Cellars Winery *(204 East Main St./Hwy. 70, Glen Alpine, 828-584-4551, www.lakejamescellars.com)* produces about 20 varieties of red, white and sweet wines in a winery in an old textile mill.

New River Vinery *(165 Piney Creek Rd., Lansing, 336-384-1213, www.newriverwinery.com)* is community-owned by around 80 local Ashe County shareholders, who each invested a relatively small amount of money. In the library of an old school building in Lansing, owned by one of the shareholders, New River produces seyval, baco noir, noiret and several fruit wines including blackberry peach and blueberry, from local growers. Wine tastings are usually held on Friday and Saturday afternoons April-October. Check the website for current schedules.

Overmountain Vineyards *(2012 Sandy Plains Rd., Tryon, 828-863-0523, www.overmountainvineyards.com)* has five varieties of grapes planted -- cabernet sauvignon, cabernet franc, merlot, petit merdot and petit mansing – on 12 acres. The tasting room is open year-round Thursday-Sunday from 1-6. There are about 18 vineyards in the Tryon area in the foothills of the mountains. Before Prohibition, Tryon was one of the major grape growing areas of North Carolina.

Saint Paul Mountain Vineyards *(588 Chestnut Gap Rd., Hendersonville, 828-685-4002, www.saintpaulmountainvineyards.com)* is Henderson County's newest vineyard and tasting room. The vineyard, on a 10-acre tract of land off U.S. Highway 64 northeast of Hendersonville, with another 10 acres in nearby Ednyville, produces 14 varieties of wine grapes and so far sells about a half dozen different reds and whites. It is open to visitors daily, usually from 11 a.m., for tours and wine tastings. Tastings are $7 and include a souvenir glass. Call ahead to confirm times.

South Creek Vineyards & Winery *(2240 South Creek Rd., Nebo, 828-652-5729, www.southcreekwinery.com)* produces mostly Bordeaux-style wines in a farmhouse in Nebo near Lake James. The winery's cabs, merlots and chardonnay have won several awards.

Thistle Meadow Winery *(102 Thistle Meadow, Laurel Springs, 800-233-1505, www.thistlemeadowwinery.com)*, a small winery and tasting room off Blue Ridge Parkway Milepost 246, is open afternoons daily April-October and daily except Sunday the rest of the year. It produces around 2,000 cases of red, white, blush and sweet wines a year.

Valley River Vineyards *(4689 Martins Creek Rd., Murphy, 828-837-0691, www.valleyrivervineyards.com)* currently produces about eight wines, including two reds, two whites and four sweet. You can pick your own grapes for winemaking, and the company sells winemaking supplies. There are tastings on Friday and Saturday afternoons from 1-6 and tours by reservation.

Distilleries

Some North Carolinians like to drink. Others would like it if nobody drank.

Prohibition began in North Carolina in 1909, a decade before the 18th Amendment to the U.S. Constitution prohibiting the sale and distribution of alcoholic beverages was ratified. National Prohibition began in January 1920 and ended in 1933 with the repeal of the 18th Amendment. Of course, many Tar Heels didn't abstain, and in the 1920s North Carolina reportedly had the largest number of illegal distilleries of any state in the country. Now there are fewer than a dozen legally licensed distilleries in the Tar Heel State. Two of these are in the Asheville area.

Nationally, there are more than 400 licensed micro-distilleries.

Piedmont Distillers in Madison – yes, in the Piedmont -- which opened in 2005, was the first micro-distillery in the U.S. to offer legal moonshine. It now offers several moonshine brands including Junior Johnson Moonshine, along with Cardinal gin.

Now there are three or four legal moonshine distilleries in the Asheville area, and yes, there still are a few illegal ones.

Asheville Distilling Co. (Troy & Sons) *(12 Old Charlotte Hwy., 828-575-2000, www.ashevilledistilling.com)* distills and sells legal moonshine under the Troy & Sons brand, made from locally grown heirloom white corn. Located in a former Southern Railway Wheelhouse, in space in the same building as Highland Brewery, Asheville Distilling has a German-made 5,000-liter copper still.

Currently run by Troy Ball and her husband, Charlie Ball, the distillery has several products including T&S Platinum Moonshine, T&S Oak Reserve and Blonde Whiskey. The Platinum Moonshine is classically clear, but the Oak Reserve is aged in bourbon barrels and has a rich bourbon color. Both go for around $30 a fifth and are sold at many North Carolina ABC stores and online (it can't be purchased at the distillery). Distillery tours are offered at 5 and 6 pm Fridays and Saturdays, with samplings of several batches of moonshine.

Howling Moon Distillery *(Woodfin, www.howlingmoonshine.com)* makes legal 100-proof moonshine from what it says is a 150-year-old recipe from bluegrass musician Raymond Fairchild. The distillery uses a primitive, old-school still. It also makes flavored liquors including Apple Pie and Strawberry Pie. The distillery in Woodfin currently is not open to the public and tours aren't offered, but its moonshine is sold at some North Carolina ABC stores for around $25 a bottle.

Petzold Distilleries LLC (*6461 Highway 212, Marshall, 828-656-2863, www.petzolddistilleries.com*) makes Carl's Carolina Applejack Moonshine and Spiced Sorghum Rum.

Liquor and Wine Stores

ABC Stores *(828-251-6192, www.ashevilleabcboard.com, all stores open 9-9 Mon.-Sat.)* In North Carolina, liquor by the bottle (as opposed to wine and beer, or liquor by the drink) is sold only in state-owned Alcoholic Beverage Control (ABC) stores. After Prohibition ended in 1933, ABC stores were established in the state beginning in 1937, and the first ABC store in Asheville opened in 1947. A few other municipalities in Buncombe County, including Woodfin and Black Mountain, have since voted for ABC stores. Only three counties in the state do not have ABC stores: Madison, Graham (both in Western North Carolina) and Yadkin. Although ABC stores carry many of the same brands, some stores are larger than others and have a wider selection. The stores in **North Asheville** *(807 Merrimon Ave.)* and **East Asheville** *(145 Tunnel Rd.)* are the largest in Asheville. Henderson County's **Fletcher** ABC store *(37 Rockwood Road)* near the Asheville Regional Airport is one of the friendliest and best-stocked stores in the region.

Until about 35 years ago, to get a drink here in a restaurant you had to "brown bag" your bottle, and the restaurant sold set-ups. In 1979, local citizens voted to permit liquor by the drink in restaurants and private clubs within the Asheville city limits.

There are about 250 establishments in Asheville and some other municipalities in Buncombe County that have permits to sell liquor by the drink. Beer and wine are sold in grocery supermarkets, convenience stores and package stores.

Appalachian Vintner *(745 Biltmore Ave., 828-505-7500, www.appalachianvitner.com)* is a newer store with an interesting selection of organic wines. About 90% of the wines in stock are organic. A lounge serves draft beer and wines. The AV has regular wine tastings. Closed Sunday.

Asheville Wine Market *(65 Biltmore Ave., 828-253-0060, www.ashevillewine.com)* is Asheville's largest freestanding wine store. The Wine Market has an automated "tasting station" where you can buy a 1-ounce tasting of one of about 20 wines for around $1 to $3. Closed Sunday.

Earth Fare *(66 Westgate Parkway, 828-253-7656, and 1856 Hendersonville Rd., 828-210-0100, www.earthfare.com)* has a reasonable selection of wines at both Asheville locations. Earth Fare's house brand of wines, Ambler's, was created by the Biltmore Estate winery.

Fresh Market *(944 Merrimon Ave., 828-252-9098, www.thefreshmarket.com)*, the Asheville outpost of this growing upscale grocery chain, has a decent selection of reds and whites but a terrible selection of champagnes. Don't expect a lot of wine help from employees.

Greenlife Grocery *(70 Merrimon Ave., 828-254-5440, www.wholefoodsmarket.com/stores/asheville)*, now owned by Whole Foods, which has another outlet on Tunnel Road under the Whole Foods name, has a good selection of wines, including organic wines, and attentive staffers.

Hops & Vines *(797 Haywood Rd., West Asheville, www.hopsandvines.net)* has a friendly, knowledgeable staff. Under new ownerships, it's also Asheville's best source for wine and beer making supplies.

Table Wine *(1550 Hendersonville Rd., 828-505-8588, www.tablewineasheville.com)* carries some 500 wines, most from small artisanal wineries, and many are organics. Closed Sunday.

Weinhaus *(86 Patton Ave., 828-254-6453, www.weinhaus.com)* is Asheville's oldest operating wine store. It has a good selection of beers, too.

The Wine Guy *(555 Merrimon Ave., 828-254-6500, www.theashevillewineguy.com)* has free wine tastings on Saturday afternoons 2-5. The store changed owners in 2013. The new "wine guy" is Richard Dorsey.

Wine Tunnel *(148 Tunnel Rd., 828-254-0504, www.winetunnelashevillenc-com.webs.com)* opened in late 2012.

SERIOUS ABOUT COFFEE?

Downtown Asheville has more than dozen local coffeehouses, with others nearby. In addition there are several Starbucks outlets in the area.

Allgood Coffee (*10-B S. Main St., Weaverville, 828-484-866, www.allgoodcoffee-nc.com*), new in early 2013, has a lodge-like atmosphere. It sells coffee roasted by Mountain Air Roasting in Asheville and 1000 Faces Coffee in Athens, Ga.

Asheville Coffee Roasters (*85 Weaverville Hwy., North Asheville, 828-253-5282, www.ashevillecoffeeroasters.com*) roasts and sells the egregiously named "Pitbull on Crack" French roast and other coffees.

Battle Cat Coffee Bar (*373 Haywood Rd., West Asheville, 828-713-3885*), in an old house with a front porch in West Asheville, formerly was the West Asheville location of Izzy's. Fans say it's a laidback, funky place to hang out and have a cup. Cheap beer, too.

Bean Werks Coffee & Tea (*753 Haywood Rd., West Asheville, 828-254-7766, www.beanwerkscoffeecompany.com*) roasts its own coffee in small batches in an old Diedrich roaster.

Bee Hive Coffee Bar (*3732 Sweeten Creek Rd., Arden, 828-676-3188*) is a new spot in Royal Pines, serving Dynamite Roasting's organic coffees, plus pastries. The owner, from Colorado, seems serious about her espresso, with single-cup pour-overs for drip.

Biltmore Coffee Traders (*518 Hendersonville Rd., South Asheville, 828-277-9227, www.biltmorecoffeetraders.com*) roasts its own and sells beans by the bag as well as coffees by the cup.

Bomba (*1 Pack Square, Corner of Patton Ave. and Biltmore Ave., Downtown, 828-254-0209, www.bombanc.com*) is a coffee house and bistro that opened in late 2012 by Hector Diaz, on Pack Square next to his Salsa's restaurant. It serves espresso from 1,000 Faces in Athens, Ga., along with homemade donuts, sandwiches and tapas. Because of seating size, it currently doesn't serve alcohol.

Clingman Café (*242 Clingman Ave., River Arts District, 828-253–2177, www.clingmancafe.com*), near studios and galleries in the River Arts District, attracts an arts crowd for its fair trade organic coffees and light meals. The café has rotating shows of paintings, photography, pottery and sculpture.

Dobrá Tea *(78 N Lexington Ave., Downtown Asheville, 828-575-2424, www.dobrateanc.com)*, while not a coffee place, is a fine alternative for tea, familiar and exotic, and sweet and savory snacks. The Moroccan-inspired decor of the Lexington location attracts a crowd who seem to know and relish their teas – green, white, black, yellow, Ooh-long, pu-er and others. Dobrá's owner, Andrew Snavely, formerly operated Dobrá Tea Room in Burlington, Vt., an offshoot of Dobrá Cajovna, a teahouse opened in Prague after the fall of communism. (*Dobrá* means "good" in Czech.) Snavely now travels the world looking for the best teas, and the Lexington shop features tea-related accessories brought back from his travels. In 2013, Dobrá opened a second area location in Black Mountain *(120 Broadway St.)*, with Lindsay Thomas. There also are Dobrá locations in Burlington, Portland, Me., Madison, Wis., and Pittsburgh, loosely affiliated with the local teashops but under different ownerships.

Double D's Coffee in Downtown Asheville – photo by Rose Lambert-Sluder

Double D's Coffees & Desserts *(41 Biltmore Ave., Downtown Asheville, 828-505-2439, www.doubledscoffee.com)* is hard to miss, as it's located in an old red double decker British bus. You order on the first level and can sip your latte on the second.

    Dripolator *(221 W. State St., Black Mountain, 828-669-0999, www.dripolator.com)* is the original Dripolator location. There was a spinoff in Asheville, what is now High Five.

Dynamite Roasting Co. *(3198 U.S. Hwy. 70 West, Black Mountain, 828-357-8555, www.dynamiteroasting.com)* is the only certified organic roaster-retailer in the area. You can sip a cup on the deck or by the fireplace at their coffee bar. Dynamite is served by quite a few restaurants in the Asheville area.

Eagle Street Coffee Emporium *(39B Market St., corner of Eagle and Market Sts., Downtown Asheville, 828-708-7534, Facebook page only)*, formerly Wall Street Coffee House and Emporium, welcomes dogs, hipsters, gamers, thinkers and socialists. Some evenings are devoted to games, comedy, poetry and music. The emporium aspect means that art, furniture, knick-knacks and other items are for sale in the coffee shop.

Edna's of Asheville *(870 Merrimon Ave., North Asheville, 828-255-3881, www.ednasofasheville.com)*, formerly Port City Java and then Mountain Java, is named for a pug dog that is said to make occasional appearances at the shop in North Asheville. Coffees, teas, sandwiches and other light meals.

Emerson's *(Asheville Mall, 3 S. Tunnel Rd., East Asheville, 828-298-0202, www.emersons.com)*, though in a big mall, isn't a national chain – it started at a location in the Biltmore Square Mall and later opened a location in Hickory. Along with coffee and tea, it has bagels, croissants, cookies and other pastries.

Filo *(1155 Tunnel Rd., East Asheville, 828-298-9777, www.filopastries.com)* is a European-style coffee house in a light and airy space, serving pastries, cakes and chocolates.

Firestorm Café & Books *(www.firestormcafe.com)* is a worker-owned cooperative café and bookstore selling organic coffees and light meals. As of this writing, its Commerce Street location Downtown has closed, and reportedly it will reopen in West Asheville across from Sunny Point in 2015.

Green Sage Coffee House & Café *(*5 Broadway St., Downtown Asheville, 828-252-4450, www.thegreensage.net) near Pack Square gets the morning crowds for organic coffees and natural foods. Green Sage also has a location at 1800 Hendersonville Rd. in South Asheville.

High Five Coffee Bar *(190 Broadway St. #2., North Asheville, 828-398-0209, www.highfivecoffee.com,* formerly the Dripolator in Asheville, has opened in the Five Points area behind Greenlife. It serves Counter Culture coffee.

Izzy's Coffee Den *(74 N. Lexington Ave., Downtown Asheville, 828-258-2004, www.izzyscoffeeden.com)* is an alternative, slightly hipster spot on a funky park of Lexington. It serves Counter Culture coffee, of course.

Karen Donatelli's *(57 Haywood St., Downtown Asheville, 828-225-5751, www.donatellicakedesigns.com)* creates beautiful and delicious pastries and cakes, but there are a few tables where you can enjoy coffee and a sweet. It's like a European pastry shop.

Mountain Air Roasting *(828-423-0321, Asheville, www.mtnairroasting.com)* says its roasts to order "in the Nordic style."

Mountain City Coffee Roasters *(828-667-0869, www.mountaincity.com)* is Asheville's premier roaster of high-grade specialty coffee. Each bag has the roast date on it, so you know how fresh it is. Some interesting information and photos on the history of coffee roasting in Asheville are on the website.

Odd's Cafe *(800 Haywood Rd., West Asheville, 828-505-7776, www.oddscafe.com)* debuted in spring 2014, purveying Counter Culture coffee, baked goods and teas and displaying the work of local artists. It opens early and stays open fairly late every day.

Old Europe *(*13 Broadway *St., Downtown Asheville, 828-255-5999, www.oldeuropepastries.com)* remains popular for its locally roasted Mountain City coffees and freshly made Hungarian pastries.

Panacea Coffee Company (66 Commerce St., Waynesville, 828-452-6200, www.panaceacoffee.com) is a rustic coffee house and café in Frog Level in Waynesville. You can sit out back by the creek and sip coffees roasted in-house.

Rejavanation Cafe *(909 Smoky Park Hwy., Enka-Candler, 828-670-5595, www.rejavanationcafe.com)* has coffee, sandwiches and beer and wine. Formerly Mountain Java.

True Confections *(East Arcade, Grove Arcade, 1 Page Ave., Downtown Asheville, 828-350-9480, www.trueconfections.net)* focuses more on its cakes, pies and other baked goods than on coffee and teas, but it's a good spot for a fresh-made cookie and cup of Mountain City coffee.

Ursa Minor *(51 Coxe Ave., Downtown Asheville, 828-308-3610)* is a mobile coffee truck based on Coxe Avenue, but sometimes it's in the River Arts District or elsewhere. It serves Dynamite coffees.

Vortex Doughnuts *(32 Banks Ave., South Slope, Downtown Asheville, 828-552-3010, www.vortexdoughnuts.com)* serves drip, espresso and cold-brew coffee from 1000 Faces, along with freshmade donuts.

Waking Life *(976 Haywood Rd., West Asheville, 828-505-3240 www.wakinglifeespresso.com)* arguably has the best espresso in town. Currently, it is rated the #1 coffee house in Asheville on TripAdvisor. It's closest thing in Asheville to a pure "third-wave shop." For drip, Waking Life uses just single cup pour-overs (except when it's really busy when they use an airpot brewer).

For espresso, they use only lightly roasted single-origin coffees, and only from East Africa or Central America. No Sumatra or other Indonesian or Pacific Rim coffees -- and no dark roasts -- allowed for either drip or espresso.

World Coffee Café *(18 Battery Park Ave., Downtown Asheville, 828-258-3999, www.worldcoffeecafe.com)* has a terrific location on the first level of the Flatiron Building. Old Europe was originally here, but World Coffee doesn't live up to its heritage. Under the same ownership is the more interesting Sky Bar, accessible by one of the few remaining elevators in Asheville with an attendant. Sky Bar occupies three levels of a fire escape – yes, a fire escape -- with great views of Asheville.

MMM...CHOCOLATE ASHEVILLE

Downtown Asheville has several chocolate shops and bistros. (A chocolate bistro, now that's a great concept!) Most aren't touristy candy shoppes such as you find in Gatlinburg but serious chocolatiers that make sophisticated chocolates and other confections from imported cacao and other high-quality ingredients.

Chocolate Fetish (*36 Haywood St., 828-258-2353, www.chocolatefetish.com), the original European-style chocolate store in Asheville, is famous for its truffles, with more than 30 dozen different varieties. In season there are chocolate-dipped local fruits such as blackberries, raspberries and strawberries. Also you can buy novelties such as chocolate cowboy boots or high-heeled shoes.

Chocolate Gems (*25 Broadway St., 828-505-8596, www.chocgems.com) has chocolates and gelato, too.*

French Broad Chocolate Lounge (*828-252–4181, 10 South Pack Square, www.frenchbroadchocolates.com*) has a moved to a larger, higher profile location on Pack Square, where you can sit, sip a glass of pinot noir or a cup of coffee or tea and sample the handmade chocolates and liquid sipping truffles. It's open daily from morning to early evening. Or you can just buy chocolates to go. At prime times, there's often a line out the door. French Broad Chocolate also has a factory (*21 Buxton Ave., tel. 828-505-4996*) where it has a tasting room open noon-6 daily, with a guided factory tour at 11 am Saturdays for a $10 fee. Call ahead for reservations. Self-guided tours are available Saturdays from 2 to 5:30 pm.

Kilwins (26 Battery Park Ave., 828-252-2639, www.kilwins.com) is a chain candy store that sells fudge, chocolates, ice cream and other sweets. There also are Kilwins shops in Black Mountain and Hendersonville.

In early December, Asheville hosts a **Chocolate and Arts Festival** at the US Cellular Center with crafts, world music and, of course, lots of chocolate.

FESTIVALS, FAIRS AND CONCERTS

Here are some of the annual festivals, fairs, and music concerts in and around Asheville. Many of the events have free admission. Note that **Bele Chere,** at one time billed as the largest free street festival in the South, was discontinued by the City of Asheville after 2013, based on an analysis that the high costs to put on festival and the disruptions to business owners Downtown outweighed the advantages. The strategy seems to be to replace Bele Chere by supporting a number of smaller and more targeted festivals.

Asheville Cinema Festival *(www.ashevillecinemafestival)* **in early November** presents around 40 indie and student films, with personal appearances by around 20 filmmakers. Films are shown downtown at Asheville Community Theater and Mt. Hermon Masonic Lodge and at Regal Biltmore Grande in Biltmore Park.

Asheville Fringe Arts Festival *(www.ashevillefringe.org)* **in mid-January** at several venues in downtown Asheville including the BeBe Theater on Commerce Street and the Black Mountain College Museum + Arts Center, focuses on unusual and alternative expressions of dance, performing arts, puppetry and music.

Asheville Herb Festival *(www.ashevilleherbfestival.com)*, a three-day sale held the **first weekend in May** at the WNC Farmers Market, attracts about 60 herb growers, many organic, and makers of herbal products. Free.

Big Crafty *(www.thebigcrafty.com)* is a twice-yearly bazaar and sale for independent craftspeople, with music and beer, usually held in **early July and early December** at Pack Place. Free.

Brevard Music Festival *(www.brevardmusic.org)* is a nationally known classical music festival held at the Brevard Music Center in Brevard from **mid-June to early August.** The Brevard Music Center Orchestra and guest musicians present symphony concerts, chamber music and operas.

Brewgrass Festival *(www.brewgrassfestival.com)* on a Saturday in **mid-September** showcases more than 40 microbrewers with around 120 beers in Martin Luther King Park just east of downtown Asheville, along with a line-up of bluegrass and country musicians. Tickets must be purchased in advance, and they usually sell out weeks in advance.

Concerts on the Quad at UNC-Asheville *(828-251-6674)* after a hiatus of four years due to a lack of funding resumed in 2015. The free concerts, featuring pop, country and other genres of music, at UNC-Asheville's main quad are held on five Monday evenings in June and July from 7 to 8:30 pm. They are family affairs, and many bring picnics.

Coon Dog Day in Saluda in **July** attracts some 10,000 attendees to celebrate the coon dog, with a parade, food and crafts booths and dog shows. Free admission, but there's a $10 parking fee that includes transportation to the festivities.

Craft Fair of the Southern Highlands

(www.southernhighlandguilde.org) fills the US Cellular Center (formerly Asheville Civic Center) with more than 200 of the South's most talented craftspeople, members of the Southern Highland Crafts Guild. It has been held twice yearly, in **mid-July and mid-October**, since 1948.

Downtown After Five *(www.ashevilledowntown.org),* 5-9 pm the **third Friday of the month from May to September** at the foot of North Lexington Avenue near the I-240 Overpass in downtown Asheville, Downtown After Five draws a big crowd for free local music. Food and beverages available.

Downtown Asheville Art District

(www.ashevilledowntowngalleries.org) holds Art Walks **from 5 to 8 pm the first Friday of the month from April through December.** You can visit more than two dozen Downtown galleries. Get a Downtown Art Gallery map at any participating gallery, the Asheville Chamber of Commerce or Pack Place.

Drumming Circle *(www.ashevilledowntown.org)*, every **Friday night 7-10 pm May-October** (weather permitting) at Prichard Park downtown on Patton Avenue, is an authentic Asheville experience, with drumming and dancing. Bring a drum, tambourine, or cowbell and join in. Dreadlocks not required. Free.

Farm Tour sponsored by ASAP, the Appalachian Sustainable Agriculture Project *(www.asapconnections.org)* in **September** spotlights more than 40 area sustainable farms. You tour the ones you choose by car or bike. Fee is $25.

Festival of Flowers at Biltmore Estate *(www.biltmore.com)*, **late March to mid-May,** showcases tulips, azaleas and other flowers in the Biltmore Estate formal gardens and on the grounds. Regular admission rates apply.

Fiesta Latina showcases Mexican and other Latina food, music and dance. It's held on a Saturday in early to mid-October at Pack Square Park. Free.

Folkmoot USA *(www.folkmootusa.org)* brings dance and folk music groups from several countries to downtown Waynesville. It is held during the **last two weeks of July**.

Goombay! Festival *(www.packplace.org)*, a street festival in **mid- to late August**, celebrates the region's African-Caribbean heritage with Caribbean food, African dancing, and reggae, gospel, funk, and soul music. The weekend festival is on South Market and Eagle streets in downtown Asheville just south of Pack Square, near the YMI Cultural Center. Free.

Greek Festival *(www.holytrinityasheville.com)*, on the grounds of the Holy Trinity Greek Orthodox Church on Cumberland Avenue in the Montford section, usually the **last weekend in September**, celebrates Greek culture, music and food.

HardLox *(www.hardloxjewishfestival.org)*, a one-day festival held annually in **mid-October** in Pack Square Park in downtown Asheville, focuses on Jewish culture and food.

LAAFF (Lexington Avenue Arts and Fun Festival) is on the Sunday of Labor Day in September, featuring two stages and three other areas for music, food and stall shops on three blocks of Asheville's Lexington Avenue.

Laugh Your Asheville Off *(www.laughyourashevilleoff.com)* is billed as the largest stand-up comedy festival in the Southeast. It's held annually over four nights in **August**, with 60 comedians.

Lake Eden Arts Festival (LEAF) *(www.theleaf.org)*, which happens twice a year, in **mid-May and mid-October**, on 600 acres at the former site of Black Mountain College near Black Mountain, features more than 50 musicians and musical groups, plus arts, crafts and poetry. LEAF admission is limited to around 5,500 and always sells out. You must buy tickets in advance, as tickets aren't sold at the gate. Full weekend adult tickets including camping start at around $125 if you buy several months in advance. In the Woodstock tradition, many attendees camp on the grounds. Accommodations in cabins, lodges and dorms also are available, starting at $50 per person. RV permits are available for an extra charge.

Montford Park Players Shakespeare Festival

(*www.montfordparkplayers.org*) has been producing the Bard's dramas in Montford Park in North Asheville for more than 40 summers. The Players usually do six or seven plays from **April to September**. Bring a picnic. Admission free but donation requested.

MoogFest (*www.moogfest.com*) for three years was held in October, but in 2014 it switched it to an **April** date. It is held at various venues in downtown Asheville. MoogFest honors Robert Moog, a pioneer in electronic and synthesized music who spent the last 30 years of his life in Asheville. Around two dozen music groups participate in the multi-day event.

Mountain Dance and Folk Festival (*www.folkheritage.org*) is the longest-running folk festival in America, having begun in 1928. The three-day event featuring Appalachian ballad singers, string bands and square dance teams is held "along about sundown" (or 7 pm) the **first weekend in August** at the Diane Wortham Theater in Pack Place.

Mountain Sports Festival (*www.mountainsportsfestival.com*) combines sports and music. Usually held on a weekend in **late May**, this family-oriented event has martial arts, disk golf, Frisbee, motocross, triathlon, kayaking, bike racing, and 5K and other runs.

NC Mineral and Gem Festival (*www.ncgemfest.com*) attracts sizeable crowds to Spruce Pine in **late July/early August** to shop for jewelry, gemstones, minerals, beads, crystals and fossils.

NC Mountain State Fair (*www.mountainfair.org*) runs for 10 days in **early September** at the WNC Agricultural Center in Fletcher off I-26 near the Asheville Regional Airport. It has the usual midway rides and bad carnival food, but the livestock shows, antique tractor displays and competitions for flower arranging, canned foods, baked goods, crafts and local art and photography are the real fun.

North Carolina Apple Festival (*www.ncapplefestival.org*) celebrates Henderson County's position as the leading apple producing area in the state. Held for more than 60 years on **Labor Day weekend** in early September, the Apple Festival occupies most of Main Street in downtown Hendersonville, with music, craft booths, freshly picked apples, and cooked products like cider and apple pies. No pets allowed. Free.

North Carolina Arboretum Festivals

(www.ncarboreturm.org) over the year has weekend shows on orchids **(late March)**, roses **(May)**, day lilies **(June)**, bamboo **(mid-July)**, bonsai **(mid-October)** and chrysanthemums **(late October)**. Most shows have free admission, but parking fees of $12 per car apply, unless you are a member.

———

Organicfest *(www.organicfest.org)* **on a Saturday in early September** in Pack Square Park celebrates everything organic, with gardening workshops, organic living demos, music and food (organically grown, of course). Free.

Ramp Festival celebrates the odiferous mountain wild onion, with food, live bluegrass and mountain music and clog dancing. It is one of the oldest festivals in Western North Carolina -- the 2013 festival was the 79th annual event. Usually it is held the **first Saturday afternoon in May** at American Legion Field, 171 Legion Drive, near downtown Waynesville.

River Arts District Studio Stroll *(www.riverartsdistrict.com)*, the largest studio tour in the region, is held the **weekends of the second Saturday in June and November** when some 200 artists and craftspeople at dozens of studios and galleries in Asheville's River Arts District demonstrate and sell their work. Free.

Riverfest *(www.riverlink.org)* celebrates the revitalization of the French Broad River with local music, river rafting, an "anything-that-floats" parade on the river, and activities for kids. The festival is held in **early August** on Riverside Drive in Asheville. Free.

Shindig on the Green *(www.folkheritage.org)* brings traditional mountain music and dancing to Pack Square Park in downtown Asheville most **Saturdays in June, July and August.** The free fun starts at 7 pm, weather permitting. Bring a lawn chair or blanket and stake out your place on the green.

Sourwood Festival in Black Mountain in **August** celebrates the famed, light-colored honey of the mountains, with some 200 vendors.

Village Art & Craft Fair *(www.biltmorevillage.com)* features more than 100 artists in ceramics, fiber, wood, metal, jewelry, and other media. The fair is held the **first weekend in August** on the grounds of Cathedral of All Souls in Biltmore Village. Free.

White Squirrel Festival *(www.whitesquirrelfestival.com),* held **Memorial Day weekend** in Brevard, celebrates the town's population of white squirrels, has live music and a soap box derby. Free.

Winter Warmer Beer Festival *(www.ashevillebeerfest.com),* unrelated to the Brewgrass Festival, is held in **late January** in the US Cellular Center in downtown Asheville, with around two dozen local and regional brewers participating

ASHEVILLE TOURS

Grayline offers tours and hop-on, hop-off travel around Asheville

Asheville offers enough tours to keep you occupied for weeks. Here are some of the most notable tour offerings in Asheville. A few are free, but most have a fee. Some offer discounts for seniors, military personnel and AAA and AARP members, along with discounts or special offers for local residents. Some of the tours operate with a cell phone and a website and without an office address. Most operators must now add 7% sales tax on tickets.

Amazing Pubcycle *(828-214-5010, www.amazingpubcycle.com)* is the people-powered way to see some of Asheville. The custom-made Pubcycle seats 13 –10 pedalers and three non-pedalers -- who bike their way around town (the Pubcycle has a motor to assist on hills). Tours, which generally start at the Aloft Hotel on Biltmore Avenue, take 40 minutes to 1½ hours and cost from $13 to $23. The longer tours make one or two stops, usually at Ben's Tune-Up and at Pack's Tavern. You can BYOB (beer and wine only) and sip while you tour.

Asheville by Foot *(www.ashevillebyfoottours.com)* offers 90-minute walking tours of Asheville from for $20 (youth under 18 are free with paying adult.) You meet at the Vance Monument on Pack Square and walk about 1.9 miles. Tours are offered spring through fall on Saturdays, currently at 10, 2 and 4.

Asheville Brewery Tours *(101 N. Lexington Ave., 828-233-5006, www.ashevillebrewerytours.com)* offers a variety of van and walking tours. The walking tours usually visit about four microbreweries in Downtown Asheville, and the van tours about the same number. There also are tours that visit breweries in Black Mountain and elsewhere. Most tours cost $59 for drinkers, $29 for non-drinkers.

Asheville Architectural Tours (*email AvlArchTours@gmail.com)*, established in summer 2012, offers a walking tour of significant architectural examples in and around downtown Asheville. Tours start at $15.

Asheville Brews Cruise *(828-545-5181, www.brewscruise.com)* takes beer lovers on tours of three or four local breweries for $55-$57 per person. Van tours, daily except Monday (less frequently in winter), last about three hours and include samples of around a dozen beers and ales. Walking tours are offered at $55 per person. The same company, which started in Asheville, now offers brews cruises in Atlanta, Denver, Charleston, Nashville and elsewhere.

Asheville Food Tours *(828-243-7401, www.ashevillefoodtours.com)* offers tasting tours of Downtown Asheville. Typically, in the 2 1/2-hour walking tour you'll visit seven to 10 food shops and restaurants, taste some items and perhaps meet the chef. Tours are Tuesday-Friday at 2 pm March-November. Downtown tours meet at 1:40 at the elevators in Grove Arcade at 1 Page Avenue. Downtown tours are $44.

Asheville Free Walking Tours *(828-210-8185, www.ashevillefreewalkingtour.com)*, run by a local travel agency, Wilcox Travel in the BB&T Building on West Pack Square, is a free daily tour of Downtown that began in mid-2013. The tour starts at 11 am Fridays. It lasts about an hour, ending at a local restaurant where you are encouraged, but not required, to have lunch. Meet up is at the Vance Monument on Pack Square. The tour is a way for Wilcox to promote its paid tours, but it's a nice service for visitors. Free tours operate April-October with a fee ($50 for up to five persons) charged for private tours in winter and other times.

Asheville Hot Air Balloons *(909 Smoky Park Hwy., Candler, 828-667-9943, www.ashevillehotairballoons.com)* lets you get a mile high and experience Asheville and the nearby mountains from the sky. Sunrise balloon flights (winds are usually calmer at daybreak than at other times) last about an hour, and the whole process takes about 2 ½ hours. Cost for a shared flight is $235 per person. A private flight is $600 per couple and includes complimentary Biltmore champagne. The company flies daily, mostly over the Hominy Valley southwest of Asheville, as long as weather conditions permit – a minimum of 3 miles visibility, wind less than 8 mph and no thunderstorms. Asheville Hot Air Balloons has a staff of three experienced pilots (one is also qualified on 747s) and about 11 "chasers" who follow the balloon to its landing site.

Asheville Running Tours *(828-280-1867, www.ashevillerunningtours.com)* allows you to experience Asheville on the run. ART's jogging tours of downtown Asheville are available for runners of any level, and there are even "waddle wine tours" for those who don't or can't run. Rates vary, but the original "beer run" is $30 and the wine waddle is $45. See website or call for dates and times.

Asheville Urban Trail *(Asheville Parks & Recreation Department, 70 Court Plaza, 4th Floor, 828-259-5800, www.ashevillenc.gov/parks)* is an excellent self-guided, free walking tour that takes you to 30 of Asheville's most important historic, literary and architectural sites, on a 1.7-mile route. It takes about 2 hours to complete the tour. The Urban Trail was established by the City of Asheville. Free Urban Trail maps are available at the Asheville Visitor Center at 36 Montford Avenue or its satellite kiosk on Pack Square and at businesses in Asheville. Download a free map, brochure and audio mp3 files from the City of Asheville website.

Balloons Over Asheville *(Grove Arcade, 1 Page Ave., #322, Downtown Asheville, 828-545-2329, www.balloonsoverasheville.com)* offers group rides from $99 per person and private rides for $599. The balloons generally leave from the Candler area – you'll be notified by email of the time and place to meet.

BREW-ed *(828-278-9255, www.brew-ed.com)* offers tours of about three breweries and brewpubs in Downtown Asheville. Tours, which must be booked 72 hours in advance, start at 2 pm on Fridays, Saturdays and Sundays, leaving from Asheville Brewing Company at 77 Coxe Avenue. Cost is $50 per person, and all participants must be at least 21 years old.

Eating Asheville Walking Food Tours (*828-489-3266,*
www.eatingasheville.com) has regular and premium food tours of Downtown
Asheville. The 2 ½-hour regular food tours operate Sun.-Wed at 2 pm.
Guided tours visit six local restaurants that offer samples of their food and
drink. Cost is $49. The "High Roller" premium tour visits seven or eight
restaurants and offers food and drink pairings at six of them for $59.
Currently, these tours are at 2 pm Thursdays and Fridays and at 1 and 2 pm
on Saturdays. Check the Eating Asheville's website calendar page for
information. You meet at Battery Park Champagne Bar in the Grove Arcade
at 1 Page Avenue.

Electro Bike Tours (*24 College St., 828-513-3960,*
www.electrobiketours.com) offers the chance to bike Asheville with a little
help from electricity. Electro Bike Tours offers pedal-assisted biking tours
and rentals. Electro uses Ketler Twin electric bikes, which are similar to a
Moped – you pedal but the power assist helps you get up hills or move more
smartly in the flats. A two-hour guided tour at 10 am daily ($55 including the
bike) takes you to the highlights of Asheville. You meet at Weaver Park in
North Asheville. Rental bikes also are available.

Ghost Hunters of Asheville (*828-779-4868,*
www.ghosthuntersofasheville.com), billed as "Asheville's only interactive
ghost tour" with "free access to ghost-hunting equipment," Ghost Hunters
offers downtown and Montford walking ghost tours. Hours and dates offer
vary seasonally but most leave after dark from the Grove Arcade at 1 Page
Avenue. Adults $18, children 8-14 $10, children 7 and under free. There's a
Ghost and Grapes tour, adults only, for $65. Tours not offered in winter.

Grayline Trolley Tour (*828-251-8687 or 866-592-8687,*
www.graylineasheville.com, closed Jan.-Feb.) offers narrated historic and
ghost tours of Asheville on a fleet of trolleys. The company says that in
season (March to December) its tours leave every half hour from the
Asheville Visitor Center at 36 Montford Ave., with around 10 stops on a 1
½-hour circuit. Historic tickets provide hop-on/hop-off privileges for two
consecutive days. Ghost tours (about 75 minutes in length) are offered at 7
pm Thursday-Saturday April-October, leaving from Pack's Tavern on 20 S.
Spruce Street. Historic tour tickets are $24 for adults, children 5-11 are $12,
children under 5 free; ghost tour tickets are $21 for adults, $10 children 5-11.

Haunted Asheville Tours (*www.hauntedasheville.com, times
and days vary, fees $20 adults, $15 for youth 9-14, under 9 free*) started by
local writer Joshua Warren have several guided ghost tours of Asheville,
including the Classic Walking Tour, Haunted Pub Crawl, Haunted Biltmore
Village Mystery Tour and the new Vampire & Occult tour.

Most tours last about 2 hours and usually conclude with a visit to the Warren's Asheville Mystery Museum in the basement of the Masonic Temple Building.

Herstory Tours (*828-423-3819, www.herstoryasheville.com*) is a tour of Asheville focusing on the stories of women in Asheville's history and in Asheville today. Call or email for information on tours, times, dates and costs.

History@Hand Tours (*828-777-1014, www.history-at-hand.com*) owner Sharon Fahrer of has been collecting oral histories and researching local history for several years. History@Hand offers guided tours of Downtown Asheville, Montford, Riverside Cemetery, Biltmore Village and Jewish Asheville. All tours are $20 adults, $12 students 7-15. Tours must be booked in advance.

LaZoom Tours (*Ticket office 1 ½ Battery Park Ave., 828-225-6932, www.lazoomtours.com*) is a popular tour where you ride a big purple open-air bus and listen to comedy skits and over-the-top jokes. Does that sound like fun? Well, it is (usually), and quite a few LaZoom tours sell out. If you're 21 or over, you can bring your own wine or beer, in unopened containers, (no hard booze) on the bus and really live it up. Pace yourself, though, as there is no restroom on the bus. In peak periods such as October weekends, LaZoom has three or four tours a day, including City Comedy Tours ($24 adults) and one-hour Haunted Comedy Tours ($21). In slower period tours such as winter are not be offered every day. Check the LaZoom website for schedules. Due to adult-oriented comedy routines, riders must be at least 17 on the Haunted Comedy Tours and at least 13 on the City Comedy Tours. Haunted Comedy Tours leave from the Thirsty Monk at 92 Patton Avenue. City Comedy Tours leave from the French Broad Co-Op at 90 Biltmore Avenue.

Moving Sidewalk Tours (*Asheville Visitor Center, 36 Montford Ave., 828-776-8687, www.movingsidewalktours.com*) lets you tour Downtown by Segway personal transporter. Moving Sidewalk Tours offers 2- to 2½-hour guided tours (including 20 to 45 minutes of training) on Segway i2s for $55 weekdays, $65 weekends. Tours are daily at 10 am and 1 pm. Riders must be at least 14 years old, must weigh between 100 and 260 pounds and must be fit enough to stand for up to three hours.

BEST FREEBIES IN ASHEVILLE AND WNC

Here are some of the best free activities, sites and tours in Asheville and nearby. *See details in the pertinent sections of this book. Some sights and activities are seasonal.*

Blue Ridge Parkway (free admission daily)

Great Smoky Mountains National Park (free admission daily – the only major national park that is free to all; charges apply for camping and a few other activities)

Asheville Urban Trail walking tour, Downtown (free, with free map and guide)

Folk Art Center, Milepost 382, Blue Ridge Parkway (free admission daily)

North Carolina Homespun Museum, grounds of Grove Park Inn (free admission daily when open, parking fee may apply)

Estes-Winn Antique Automobile Museum, grounds of Grove Park Inn (free admission daily when open, parking fee may apply)

Shindig on the Green music concerts at Pack Square Park Downtown (free admission most Saturday evenings June-August)

Carl Sandburg Home grounds and farm, Flat Rock (admission charged only for tour of house)

Biltmore Estate, South Asheville (unlimited free day-time admissions with 12-Month Pass, which is often available for $89 a year)

Zebulon Vance Birthplace, near Weaverville (free admission)

North Carolina Arboretum, off Brevard Road at Blue Ridge Parkway Milepost 393 (free admission daily, free parking first Tuesday of month, free parking daily for members)

Asheville Botanical Gardens, near UNC-A (free admission daily)

Asheville Art Museum (free admission first Wednesday afternoon of month from 3-5, members free daily)

Cradle of Forestry in America near Brevard (free admission on Tuesdays, free admission daily for Senior Passholders)

Pisgah Center for Wildlife Education, trout hatchery and wildlife education center in Pisgah Forest near Brevard (free admission daily)

St. Lawrence Basilica, Haywood St., Downtown (free self-guided and group tours)

Big Crafty crafts show, Pack Square Park Downtown (early July and early December weekends, free admission)

Highland Brewing Company, East Asheville, free brewery tours and beer tastings (you must be 21 for beer tastings) on afternoons Monday-Saturdays (donation to MANNA Food Bank requested but not required)

Downtown After Five music concerts, Lexington Avenue near I-240 (third Friday of month May-September, free admission)

Drumming Circle, Pritchard Park Downtown (Friday evenings May-October, free admission)

Downtown Asheville Parking (free on-street parking after 6 pm and on Sundays)

Montford Park Players Shakespeare Festival, Montford Park (selected dates April-September, donation requested but not required)

Wolfe Ridge Ski Resort (free snow skiing for seniors 65+ anytime November-March, weather permitting)

Beech Mountain (free snow skiing for seniors 70+ anytime November-March, weather permitting)

Pisgah National Forest (free admission daily to most areas)

Nantahala National Forest (free admission daily to most areas)

Mt. Mitchell State Park (free admission daily, weather permitting)

River Arts District (free admission to most open studios and galleries, also during RAD Studio Stroll weekends in early June and early November)

Colburn Mineral Museum, Pack Place (free admission first Wednesday of month from 3-5 pm, members free daily)

Apple Festival, Hendersonville Labor Day weekend (free admission)

Museum of North Carolina Minerals, on Blue Ridge Parkway near Spruce Pine (free admission)

DuPont State Park, near Brevard (free admission)

RESOURCES:

Asheville and Western North Carolina
Books, Movies and Internet Sites

This is a necessarily selective bibliography, filmography and listing of websites about Asheville and Western North Carolina.

BOOKS
Architecture

Bisher, Catherine W.; Southern, Michael T.; and Martin, Jennifer F., *A Guide to the Historic Architecture of Western North Carolina,* University of North Carolina Press, Chapel Hill, 1999, 471 pp. Part of a three-book series on architecture in North Carolina (the other volumes are on Eastern and Piedmont North Carolina), this volume ranges wide but not always as deep on individual buildings as one might hope.

Hansley, Richard, *Asheville's Historic Architecture,* The History Press, Charleston, S.C., 2011, 173 pp. Written by a former Asheville High School teacher, this guide highlights individual buildings of note in Asheville and provides considerable information on each, typically with a photography.

McAlester, Virginia and McAlester, Lee, *A Field Guide to American Houses,* Alfred A. Knopf, New York, 2011, 525 pp. While not specifically about Asheville, this in-depth guide helps you identify the various architectural styles of American houses.

Neufeld, Rob and Neufeld, Henry, *Asheville's River Arts District,* Arcadia Publishing, Charleston, S.C., 2008, 127 pp. Excellent collection of photographs along with some history of the RAD. This one of the Images of America series that has also published photo books of Asheville, Hendersonville, Biltmore Estate, Biltmore Village and elsewhere.

Arts and Literature

Eubanks, Georgann, *Literary Trails of the North Carolina Mountains,* University of North Carolina Press, Chapel Hill, 2007, 426 pp. This is another wonderful title from the UNC Press. It goes beyond just a listing of WNC authors, providing a guidebook to literary journeys in the mountains.

Kirk, Stephen, Scribblers, *Stalking the Authors of Appalachia,* John F. Blair, Winston-Salem, 2004, 248 pp. Kirk recounts the history of some of the major literary figures of Asheville and interviews writers with connections to the area.

Neufeld, Rob (Introduction), *27 Views of Asheville, A Southern Mountain Town in Prose & Poetry,* Eno Publishers, 2012, 204 pp. An eclectic collection of pieces on Asheville by many writers with Asheville connections, including Gail Godwin, Charles Frazier, Wayne Caldwell, Dale Neal, Nan K. Chase, Rick McDaniel, Robert Morgan and others.

Baseball

Ballew, Bill, *A History of Professional Baseball in Asheville,* Hickory Press, Charleston, S.C., 2007, 128 pp. Well-researched history of the Tourists and other pro baseball teams in Asheville.

Terrell, Bob, *The Old Ball Yard: McCormick Field, Home of Memories,* Worldcomm, Alexander, N.C., 1997, 96 pp. Long-time *Asheville Citizen-Times* columnist and sports editor Bob Terrell's recollections of McCormick Field.

Biltmore Estate

Bryan, John M., *G.W. Vanderbilt's Biltmore Estate, The Most Distinguished Private Place,* Rizzoli International, New York, 1994, 157 pp. This coffee-table format book chronicles the construction of Biltmore House, with extensive architectural drawings and sketches. It also presents stunning new full-color photographs of the house and grounds.

Covington, Jr., Howard E., *Lady on the Hill, How Biltmore Estate Became an American Icon,* John Wiley & Sons, Hoboken, N.J., 2006, 331 pp. Although this book was underwritten by Biltmore, its author is a Publisher Prize-winning journalist who paints a fair and balanced picture of Biltmore in the 20th century, and especially of the important role William A.V. Cecil played in making Biltmore House a tourism success.

Black Mountain College

Duberman, Martin, *Black Mountain College, an Exploration in Community,* Northwestern University Press, Chicago, 2009, 616 pp. First published in 1972 by Dutton, Duberman's book remains by far the best and most complete overview and history of this important and radical institution, despite, and perhaps partly because of, the author's self-revelatory style.

Rumaker, Michael, *Black Mountain Days,* Black Mountain Press, Asheville, 2003, 542 pp. Readable memoir of the college in its end days in the early to mid-1950s.

Blue Ridge Parkway

Johnson, Randall, *Hiking the Blue Ridge Parkway,* 2nd ed., FalconGuides, 2010, 352 pp. Exhaustive guide to the long and short of parkway hikes.

Logue, Victoria; Logue, Frank; and Blouin, Nichole, *Guide to the Blue Ridge Parkway,* 3rd ed., Menasha Ridge Press, 2010, 160 pp. It is what it is.

Whisnant, Anne Mitchell, *Super-Scenic Motorway, A Blue Ridge Parkway History,* University of North Carolina Press, Chapel Hill, 2006, 464 pp. Originally done as a Ph.D. dissertation, this is a well-researched, detailed yet readable history of the building of the parkway.

Crafts

Eaton, Allen H., *Handicrafts of the Southern Highlands,* Russell Sage Foundation, New York, 1937, republished by Dover Books, New York, 1973, 373 pp. This pioneering survey of the crafts of the Southern Appalachians was inspired by the work of Olive Dame Campbell of the John C. Campbell Folk School in Murphy. Eaton played a key role in the establishment of the Southern Highland Handicraft Guild.

Fields, Jay and Hurst, Betty, *The Craft Heritage Trails of Western North Carolina,* 3rd Ed., Handmade in America, Asheville, 2003, 237 pp. This popular guide lists many of the craft studios and galleries in the region, along with suggested driving routes. However, it needs updating.

Food and Cooking

Daniel, Diane, *Farm Fresh North Carolina,* University of North Carolina Press, Chapel Hill, 2011, 283 pp. A guide to farmers' markets, wineries, U-pick spots and farms in WNC and elsewhere in the state.

Parris, John, *Mountain Cooking,* Citizen-Times Publishing Co., Asheville, 1978, 372 pp. The best collection of articles on mountain cooking and mountain recipes by the long-time *Asheville Citizen* columnist.

Fiction

Caldwell, Wayne, *Cataloochee,* Random House, New York, 2008, 368 pp. Asheville native's first novel follows three generations of 19th century families living in the Cataloochee Valley in what is now the Great Smoky Mountains National Park.

--- *Requiem by Fire,* Random House, New York, 2010, 335 pp.
Caldwell's second novel takes place mostly in the Cataloochee Valley in the 1920s, just before the coming of the Great Smokies park.

Ehle, John, *The Journey of August King,* Harpercollins, New York, 1971, 218 pp. This is one of 11 novels by Haywood County-born novelist Ehle, most set in Canton or elsewhere in Western North Carolina. August King explores a white pioneer's involvement with a runaway slave.

Frazier, Charles, *Cold Mountain,* Atlantic Monthly Press, New York, 1997, 356 pp. This National Book Award winner and best seller tells the story of a wounded Civil War deserter who walks for months to return to the love of his life on a mountain farm in Western North Carolina.

Godwin, Gail, *Unfinished Desires,* Random House, New York, 2010, 416 pp. Godwin grew up in Asheville and has set a number of her 14 novels here. Some, including *Unfinished Desires,* take place at a Catholic girls' school that resembles Asheville's St. Genevieve's, now closed.

Morgan, Robert, *Gap Creek,* Algonquin Books, Chapel Hill, 2000, 324 pp. Born in Hendersonville, Morgan has written several books of poetry and novels. He has taught at Davidson and now teaches at Cornell. *Gap Creek* is set in Western North Carolina.

Percy, Walker, *The Second Coming,* Farrar, Straus, Giroux, New York, 1980, 368 pp. Dr. Walker's fifth novel takes place in Western North Carolina.

Wolfe, Thomas, *Look Homeward, Angel,* Scribner, New York, 1929, 554 pp. Wolfe's first novel was highly biographical, focusing on his youth in Asheville (called Altamont in the novel) and on its citizens. Its reception in Asheville at first was hostile, though as the years passed local residents began to admire Wolfe and his books.

--- *Of Time and the River,* Scribner, New York, 1935, 896 pp.

--- *The Web and the Rock,* Scribner, New York, 1939, 712 pp.

--- *You Can't Go Home Again,* Scribner, New York, 1940, 656 pp.

Great Smoky Mountains National Park

Hiking Trails of the Smokies, DeFoe, Don; Giddens, Beth; and Kemp, Steve (eds.), Great Smoky Mountains Natural History Association, 1994, 575 pp. By far the most comprehensive guide to hiking in the Smokies, though now somewhat dated.

Frome, Michael, *Strangers in High Places, The Story of the Great Smoky Mountains,* University of Tennessee Press, Knoxville, 1966, 391 pp. A 20th century classic in the field of environmental journalism.

Johnson, Randall, *Best Easy Day Hikes Great Smoky Mountains National Park,* FalconGuides, 2010, 128 pp. Has brief descriptions and maps for 22 day hikes in the park.

Kemp, Steve, *Trees of the Smokies,* Great Smoky Mountains Association, Gatlinburg, 1993, 128 pp. Features 80 color photos and 100 drawings of trees found in the Smokies.

Lawrence, H. Lea, *The Fly Fisherman's Guide to the Great Smoky Mountains National Park,* Cumberland House Publishing, Nashville, 1998, 183 pp. Good guide to trout fishing in the park, by a Tennessee writer.

Manning, Russ, *100 Hikes in the Great Smoky Mountains National Park,* 2nd. Ed. The Mountaineers, Seattle, 1999, 286 pp. Comprehensive guide to most of the main hiking trails in the Smokies.

Minetor, Randi and Minetor, Nic, *Great Smoky Mountains National Park Pocket Guide,* FalconGuides, 2008, 96 pp. Short and sweet guide to the highlights of the park.

Sluder, Lan, *Fodor's InFocus: Great Smoky Mountains National Park,* Fodor's, New York, 2009, 221 pp. Pocket-sized guide to the park; includes a chapter on Gatlinburg by Michael Ream.

Strutin, Michal, *History Hikes of the Smokies,* Great Smoky Mountains Association, Gatlinburg, 2003, 352 pp. This guide focuses on hikes to historic places in the Smokies and provides detailed information on the history of the hiking destinations.

History

Arthur, John Preston, *Western North Carolina History (From 1730-1913),* The Edward Buncombe Chapter of the Daughters of the American Revolution, Asheville, 1914, 710 pp. An early history of the region that just goes on and on.

Blackmun, Ora, *Western North Carolina and Its People to 1880,* 2nd ed., Appalachian Consortium Press, 1980, 458 pp. Born in Minnesota, Ora Blackmun moved to North Carolina in 1944. She became intensely interested in the history of the western part of the state and wrote and lectured extensively on it. The first edition of this history was published in 1977.

McDaniel, Douglas Stuart, *Asheville,* Arcadia Publishing, 2004, 128 pp. Part of the Images of America series, it sketches the history of Asheville through old photographs with captions.

Sondley, Forster Alexander, *Asheville and Buncombe County,* The Citizen Company, Asheville, 1922, 200 pp. Sketches of the history of Asheville-Buncombe, published as a small book by the *Asheville Citizen* newspaper, along with an article on Buncombe County by Theodore F. Davidson. Sondley's personal library became the nucleus of Pack Memorial Library's North Carolina collection.

Tessier, Mitzi Schaden, *Asheville, A Pictorial History,* Donning Company, Norfolk, 1982, 232 pp. The history of the Asheville area is told in wonderful old photographs with informative captions.

Mountain Culture

Ager, John Curtis, *We Plow God's Fields, The Life of James G. K. McClure,* Appalachian Consortium Press, 1991, 477 pp. Ager tells you more than perhaps you'd ever want to know about Jim McClure, a prominent Asheville area farm owner and founder of the Farmers Federation.

Kephart, Horace, *Our Southern Highlanders,* Outing Publishing Co., New York, 1913, 548 pp., Macmillan, rev. ed. 1923, republished in various editions and by different publishers since. This is the groundbreaking work on life in the Appalachian mountains by a man who played an important role in establishment of the Great Smoky Mountains National Park.

Parris, John, *Roaming the Mountains,* Citizen-Times Publishing Co., Asheville, 1955, 246 pp. The first in a wonderful series of collections of prose poems to the mountains of Western North Carolina and its people. The pieces were originally published as daily columns in the *Asheville Citizen* newspaper.

--- *My Mountains, My People,* Citizen-Times Publishing Co., Asheville, 1957, 257 pp.

--- *Mountain Bred,* Citizen-Times Publishing Co., Asheville, 1967, 372 pp.

--- *These Storied Mountains,* Citizen-Times Publishing Co., Asheville, 1972, 372 pp.

Music

Fussell, Fred C. with Kruger, Steve, *Blue Ridge Music Trails of North Carolina: A Guide to Music Sites, Artists, and Traditions of the Mountains and Foothills,* University of North Carolina Press, Chapel Hill, 2013, 281 pp. This well-researched guide, which includes a CD of mountain music, points readers to sites in WNC where authentic bluegrass, old-time, gospel and string band music can be experienced.

Sharp, Cecil, and Karpeles, Maud. (ed.) *English Folk-Songs from the Southern Appalachians,* Oxford University Press, Oxford, 1932, republished in two volumes, by Loomis House Press, 2012. Sharp made three visits to the United States between 1916 and 1918, recording and collecting hundreds of songs. He originally came to the Southern mountains because of Olive Dame Campbell of the John C. Campbell Folk School in Murphy.

Outdoors

Bost, Toby, *North Carolina Gardener's Guide,* rev. ed., Good Springs Press, Nashville, 2002, 272 pp. Helpful guide to flower gardening in North Carolina and also has useful color photographs of flowers and trees commonly seen in North Carolina.

Davis, Jennifer Pharr, *Five-Star Trails: Asheville: Your Guide to the Area's Most Beautiful Hikes,* Menasha Ridge Press, 2011, 240 pp. Pocket-sized guide provides maps, directions and highlights of the best hiking trails in the Asheville area.

Davis, Ricky; Potter, Eloise F.; Parnell, James F.; and Teulings, Robert P., *Birds of the Carolinas,* 2nd Ed., University of North Carolina Press, Chapel Hill, 2006, 399 pp. A standard reference for Carolina birders, although the photos are not nearly as useful for identification as those in, say, *The Stokes Field Guide to the Birds of North America.*

Dykeman, Wilma, *The French Broad,* Holt Rinehart, New York, 1955, republished by Wakestone Press, 1992, 371 pp. Asheville native Wilma's Dykeman's "poem" to the French Broad River.

North Carolina Birding Trail, Mountain Trail Guide, distributed by University of North Carolina Press, 2009, 190 pp. Handy guide to the best birding sites in Western North Carolina, put together by six North Carolina organizations: Audubon North Carolina, North Carolina Cooperative Extension, North Carolina Sea Grant, North Carolina State Parks, North Carolina Wildlife Resources Commission and the U.S. Fish and Wildlife Service. Ring-bound format.

Travel

Bothwell, Cecil, *Finding Your Way in Asheville,* CreateSpace, Asheville, 5th ed., 2013, 164 pp. The author is an Asheville City Council member and former alternative journalist. What's good about the self-published guide is that it provides a nice sense of Asheville. Also, it does an excellent job leading you on a tour of the various areas of Asheville.

Jacobs, Fred L. and Davis, Roger (illustrator), *Standard Guide to Asheville and Western North Carolina,* Fred L. Jacobs, Asheville, 1887, 55 pp. Possibly the earliest published guidebook to the Asheville area.

Lindsey, *T. H., Lindsey's Guide Book to Western North Carolina,* The Randolph-Kerr Printing Co., Asheville, 1890, 92 pp. One of the earliest travel guides to the WNC mountains.

Pantas, Lee, *The Ultimate Guide to Asheville & The Western North Carolina Mountains,* 4th Ed., R. Brent & Co., Asheville, 2011, 485 pp. As much a collection of lists as a guidebook, it covers a lot of ground. There are striking pen-and-ink sketches by the author.

Richards, Constance E. and Richards, Kenneth L., *Insiders' Guide to North Carolina Mountains,* 10th Ed., Globe Pequot Press, Guilford, CT, 2010, 387 pp. Part of the series of Insiders' Guides, this one is comprehensive and easy-to-use, if slightly dated.

Sakaowski, Carolyn, *Touring the Western North Carolina Backroads,* 3rd ed., John F. Blair, Winston-Salem, 2011, 316 pp. Superb guide to the by-ways of WNC.

MOVIES

The Biltmore Estate takes the prize for being the locale of the most movies shot in the Asheville area. At least 15 movies have been filmed at least partly at Biltmore House or elsewhere on Biltmore Estate, including *Being There, The Swan, Richie Rich, The Last of the Mohicans* and *Patch Adams.*

A Breed Apart is a 1984 movie starring Rutger Hauer, Kathleen Turner and Donald Pleasance, much of which was filmed in Asheville. It was not a success.

All the Real Girls, featuring Zooey Deschanel and Paul Schneider, about a stud who falls in love with a small town girl, was filmed in Asheville and released in 2004. The film bombed at the box office.

American Masters: The Day Carl Sandburg Died is a documentary partly filmed at the Carl Sandburg house in Flat Rock, was released in 2012 on PBS.

Being There was filmed on the Biltmore Estate. Starring Peter Sellers stars as a half-witted gardener whose simplistic comments are considered profound. Shirley MacLaine and Melvyn Douglas also appear in film based on a novel by Jerzy Kosinski, who also wrote the screenplay. Released in 1979, it was a critical and box office hit.

Bull Durham, the popular 1988 movie about baseball, had a small segment filmed at McCormick Field in Asheville, before the minor league stadium was renovated. It stars Kevin Costner, Susan Sarandon and Tim Robbins.

The Clearing, despite its big-name cast that included Robert Redford, Daniel Defoe and Helen Mirren, did a modest box office when it was released in 2004. It had something to do with a kidnapped executive. Most of the movie was filmed in Georgia, but some segments were filmed in and near Asheville.

Conquest of Canaan, a silent movie released in 1921, was probably the first movie filmed in Asheville. It was considered lost until a print was found in a Russian archive in 2010.

Dirty Dancing (1987), with Patrick Swayze, Jennifer Grey and Roy Orbach, was shot around Lake Lure. On a summer camp holiday, Grey's character falls in love with a dance instructor played by Swayze. *Dirty Dancing* grossed around $60 million in its first release but has become a cult film, and the movie's locations have become minor tourist attractions.

A segment of 1994's *Forrest Gump,* starring Tom Hanks, was filmed at the Biltmore Estate. The movie was a huge hit, grossing almost $700 million worldwide.

A number of scenes of the 1993 movie version of the hit 1960s TV show, *The Fugitive,* were shot in Western North Carolina. See the stars Harrison Ford and Tommy Lee Jones in Dillsboro and Bryson City and on the Blue Ridge Parkway, Great Smoky Mountains Railroad and Cheoah Dam.

The Green Mile (1999) starring Tom Hanks, about a prisoner on death row, was filmed in Blowing Rock, on the Blue Ridge Parkway and elsewhere in the mountains.

Hannibal the cannibal, played by Anthony Hopkins, was creepily shot at the Biltmore House. The 2001 movie wasn't as well received as 1991's *Silence of the Lambs* featuring Jodie Foster and Hopkins.

The Hunger Games (2012), the first film not released by one of the Big Six studios to gross over $400 million, was primarily filmed in Central and Western North Carolina, including Charlotte, Shelby, Black Mountain and Asheville. One of the author's nephews was an extra in it.

The Journey of August King (1995), based on the novel by Canton native John Ehle, was filmed in the North Carolina mountains.

The Last of the Mohicans (1992), starring Daniel Day-Lewis, was filmed entirely at various locations in Western North Carolina, including the Biltmore Estate, Chimney Rock Park, the Manor Inn in Asheville, the Blue Ridge Parkway, Weaverville, the Pisgah National Forest and other spots.

Mr. Destiny (1990), starring James Belushi and Michael Caine, was filmed on the Biltmore Estate.

My Fellow Americans (1996), featuring Jack Lemmon and James Garner playing two former U.S. presidents, and Dan Akroyd, was mostly filmed in Western North Carolina, with locations at the Black Mountain train station, Biltmore Estate, Marshall and Waynesville.

Nell (1994) stars Jodie Foster as a hermit discovered in the forest. It was filmed around Robbinsville, in Franklin and at Fontana Lake.

The Odd Life of Timothy Green (2012) had segments filmed at the Biltmore Estate.

Patch Adams, starring Robin Williams and Philip Seymour Hoffman, was filmed at the Biltmore Estate and at the University of North Carolina at Chapel Hill and in California. It was released in 1998 to moderate success.

Private Eyes was an awful 1980 Sherlock Holmes spoof and a terrible vehicle for Don Knotts and Tim Conway. It was redeemed only by Biltmore House as a haunted mansion.

Richie Rich (1994) was another bomb shot at Biltmore House (and at a mansion in Beverly Hills). It stars a 13-year-old Macaulay Culkin as one of the richest kids in the world, who just wants other kids to play with.

Songcatcher (2000), directed by Maggie Greenwald, stars Janet McTeer, a brilliant musicologist who is based on the real-life Olive Dame Campbell, co-founder of the John C. Campbell Folk School in Brasstown near Murphy. The film was shot in the Asheville area.

The incredibly beautiful Grace Kelly graces the Biltmore House in 1956's *The Swan,* which also starred Louis Jourdan and Alec Guinness. This was the film that helped give a boost to Biltmore attendance.

28 Days (2000), starring Sandra Bullock in rehab. Among other locations, it was shot at the Blue Ridge Assembly in Black Mountain and in Asheville.

Tap Roots is a 1948 Western with Van Heflin, Susan Hayward, Julie London and Boris Karloff as the horse – just kidding. It was filmed in the Great Smokies Park.

Thunder Road (1958), a B-movie about moonshine runners in the mountains, originally a mainstay on the drive-in circuit, has become a cult classic. Starring Robert Mitchum, with a small role as his son by his real-life son James Mitchum, was filmed in and around Asheville. Some scenes were shot in what is now the River Arts District and also in the Downtown area. In some of the most famous scenes Robert Mitchum drives a souped-up 1951 Ford. Russ Offhaus, a popular Asheville and Boston radio personality known as Farmer Russ, appears as a drunk in a scene filmed at the original Sky Club, a well-known nightclub on Town Mountain.

Winter People (1989), filmed in Asheville, featured Kurt Russell, Lloyd Bridges and Kelly McGillis, later of *Top Gun* fame. The film is set in the 1930s and involves feuding mountain clans. McGillis eventually made the Asheville area her home.

INTERNET SITES

Here are some of the best and most useful websites on Asheville and Western North Carolina:

Attractions, Destination, Media and Guidebooks

Amazing Asheville Guide (www.amazingasheville.net) is the website of the *Amazing Asheville* guidebook by Lan Sluder.

Asheville Citizen-Times (www.citizen-times.com) has current and archived articles from the region's leading daily newspaper, but most are behind a pay wall.

Asheville.com (www.asheville.com) is a commercial site, recently redesigned, with some good information, but you always wonder which recommendations are based on advertising.

Biltmore House and Estate (www.biltmore.com) covers everything Biltmore.

Blue Ridge Parkway (www.nps.gov/blri/) is the National Park Service site on the parkway.

Blue Ridge Parkway Association (www.blueridgeparkway.org) has been the official marketing partner of the parkway for more than 60 years. While it does present commercial information on hotels, restaurants and other businesses near the parkway, it also offers a lot of valuable assistance to parkway visitors.

Buncombe County (www.buncombecounty.org) is the official site of Buncombe County, with information on county services, real estate, the Asheville-Buncombe Library and more.

City of Asheville (www.ashevillenc.gov) is the official cite of Asheville city government. It has tons of information on city services, parks and recreation, parking, public transit and other useful facts.

Great Smoky Mountains Association (www.smokiesinformation.org) helps raise money for the Great Smoky Mountains National Park, through the store on its website and by running shops in visitor centers at the park, but it also has valuable park information for visitors.

Great Smoky Mountains National Park (www.nps.gov/grsm/)is the official site of the National Park Service. It is a superb site that will help you get the most out of the park.

Mountain Xpress (www.mountainx.com) is the online edition of the Asheville alternative weekly, with especially good information on entertainment and dining.

Romantic Asheville (www.romanticasheville.com), while a commercial site, has a tremendous amount of visitor information presented in an easily accessible, appealing way.

Real Estate Websites

Trulia (www.trulia.com) provides extensive home value, listing averages and home sale prices averages, plus some community data, on most communities in the U.S. It includes many specific listing for homes for sale. Most information is free.

North Carolina Mountains Multiple Listing Service (www.ncmmls.com) is a multiple listing service that covers homes and other property for sale and for rent listing in 15 counties in Western North Carolina, including the Asheville MSA (Buncombe, Henderson, Haywood and Madison). In most cases it provides detailed information properties actively for sale or rent. As of this writing, it has about 19,000 listings. It is co-owned MLS services in Asheville, Brevard, Henderson County and Haywood County. About 2,500 REALTORS® subscribe to the service. Members of the public can use most of the site for free but must register.

Zillow (www.zillow.com), like Trulia, provides extensive home value, listing averages and home sale prices averages, plus some community data, on most communities in the U.S. It includes many specific listing for homes for sale. Most information is free.

Visitor and Relocation Websites

Asheville Area Chamber of Commerce (www.ashevillechamber.org) focuses on business and business development.

Black Mountain-Swannanoa Chamber of Commerce (www.blackmountain.org) provides information on the Black Mountain area.

Blowing Rock Chamber of Commerce (www.blowingrock.com) provides visitor and relocation information on Blowing Rock and the High Country.

Boone Area Chamber of Commerce (www.boonechamber.com) and **High Country Host** (www.highcountryhost.com) offer visitor and relocation information on Boone and the rest of the High Country.

Brevard-Transylvania County Chamber of Commerce
(www.brevardncchamber.org) proves relocation and visitor information on
Brevard and Transylvania County.

**Bryson City-Swain County Chamber of Commerce & Visitor
Center** (www.greatsmokies.com) provides visitor and relocation
information for Bryson City, Swain County and the Great Smoky Mountains
National Park.

Discover Franklin (www.discoverfranklinnc.com) provides visitor
and relocation information on Franklin and Macon County.

Explore Asheville (www.exploreasheville.com) is the official
tourism website of the Asheville Convention and Tourism Bureau and is
affiliated with the Asheville Area Chamber of Commerce. It offers a wealth
of information on the Asheville area. It also sells a relocation kit.

Graham County Travel and Tourism
(www.grahamcountrytravel.com) provides visitor and relocation
information on Robbinsville and Graham County.

Jackson County Chamber of Commerce
(www.mountainlovers.com) offers visitor and relocation information on
Sylva and elsewhere on Jackson County.

Haywood County Chamber of Commerce
(www.visitncsmokies.com) provides travel and relocation information on
Waynesville and elsewhere in Haywood County.

Highlands Chamber of Commerce (www.highlandschamber.org)
has visitor and relocation on Highlands, along with some on neighboring
Cashiers.

Historic Hendersonville (www.historichendersonville.org) has
information on Hendersonville and Henderson County. It sells a relocation
package.

Hot Springs (www.hotspringsnc.org) has some information on Hot
Springs.

Mitchell County Chamber of Commerce (www.mitchell-
county.com) offers visitor and relocation information on Spruce Pine and
Mitchell County.

Visit Cherokee (www.visitcherokeenc.com) has information on
Cherokee and the Qualla Boundary Reservations.

Visit Dillsboro (www.visitdillsboro.org) has information on
Dillsboro and Jackson County.

Visit North Carolina (www.visitnc.org) is the official tourism site
of the state of North Carolina, with loads of information on attractions,
lodging, trip itineraries and more.

Yancey County Chamber of Commerce
(www.yanceychamber.com) provides visitor and relocation information on Burnsville and Yancey County.

ABOUT THE AUTHOR

LAN SLUDER is the author of more than a dozen books on travel and retirement in the United States and Central America including *Fodor's Belize, Amazing Asheville, Living Abroad in Belize, Frommer's Beach Vacations The Carolinas and Georgia* and others. He also has published books on classic cars and the game of bridge, authoring *Buy a Classic Rolls-Royce or Bentley* and *Play Bridge Today*. Sluder has contributed to many newspapers, magazines and online media around the world including the TravelChannel.com, *Chicago Tribune, The New York Times, Where to Retire, Charlotte Observer, Bangkok Post, New Orleans Business, Belize First, Caribbean Travel & Life* and *Globe & Mail.*

A former newspaper editor in New Orleans, magazine editor and publisher and marketing executive, Lan lives on a mountain farm near Asheville with his wife, Sheila M. Lambert, an attorney. They have two children, Brooks Lambert-Sluder, a program manager at Harvard, and Rose Lambert-Sluder, a graduate student at the University of Oregon.

For questions, comments and criticisms email Lan Sluder at lansluder@gmail.com.

Made in the USA
Lexington, KY
06 July 2017